Magnetic Mountain

Stalinism as a Civilization

STEPHEN KOTKIN

T0315013

University of California Press

BERKELEY   LOS ANGELES   LONDON

The publisher gratefully acknowledges the contribution
provided by the General Endowment Fund of the
Associates of the University of California Press.

University of California Press
Berkeley and Los Angeles, California

University of California Press, Ltd.
London, England

First Paperback Printing 1997

Kotkin, Stephen.
   Magnetic mountain : Stalinism as a civilization / Stephen Kotkin.
      p.   cm.
   Includes bibliographical references (p.   ) and index.
   ISBN 978-0-520-20823-0 (pbk.: alk. paper)
   1. Magnitogorsk (Russia)—History.   2. Soviet Union—Politics and
government.   3. Communism—Soviet Union—Case studies.
I. Title.
DK651.m159K675   1995
947'.87—dc20   94-11839
                                                        CIP

Printed in the United States of America

10   09   08
12   11   10   9

The paper used in this publication meets the minimum requirements of
ANSI/NISO Z39.48-1992 (R 1997) (Permanence of Paper). ∞

A version of chapter 2 was first published in William Rosenberg and
Lewis Siegelbaum, eds., Social Dimensions of Soviet Industrialization
(Bloomington: Indiana University Press, 1993); of chapter 4 in William
Brumfield and Blair Ruble, eds., Russian Housing in the Modern Age:
Design and Social History (New York: Cambridge University Press,
1993); and of chapter 5 in Lewis Siegelbaum and Ronald Suny, eds.,
Making Workers Soviet: Power, Class, and Identities (Ithaca: Cornell
University Press, 1994).

Magnetic Mountain

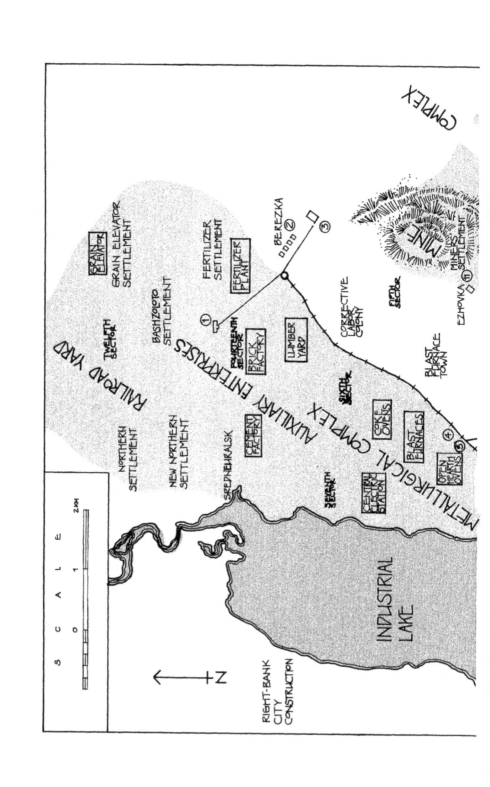

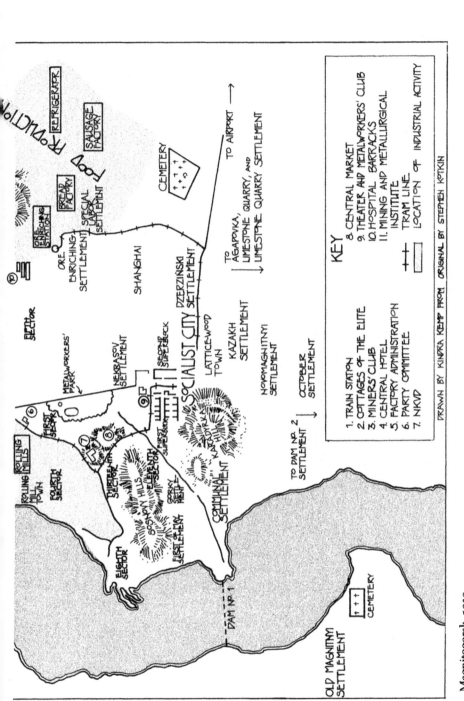

Magnitogorsk, 1939

To M. F.

I propose a toast to simple, ordinary, modest people, to the "little cogs" who keep our great state machine in motion. . . . No one writes about them, they have no high titles and few offices, but they are the people who maintain us. . . . I drink to the health of these people.

Joseph Stalin

Contents

Illustrations and Tables

Photographs follow pages 145 and 354

Acknowledgments

This project began as a Ph.D. dissertation at the University of California, Berkeley, where I had the great fortune of being trained in history by an extraordinary group of scholars, including Lynn Hunt, Susanna Barrows, Martin Jay, Jan de Vries, and many others. Had I not met Reginald Zelnik, my thesis advisor, I might never have moved from the study of Western and Central Europe to that of Russia. Reggie's scholarship and professional behavior have been an inspiration, and his guidance outstanding. My interest in the Soviet period was aroused and nurtured by Martin Malia, my other thesis advisor, whose thinking has left a deep impression.

At Berkeley, my conceptual tools were sharpened by contact with many people outside the history department, particularly Leo Lowenthal, Gregory Grossman, Victoria Bonnell, David Hooson, and Paul Rabinow. Much stimulation was provided by fellow graduate students in various fields, including David Horn, Jonathan Simon, Scott Busby, Alex Levine, and, above all, Keith Gandal.

At Princeton, where I have taught since 1989, I have benefited from the exceptional breadth of learning and warm-hearted support of my colleagues. Special mention goes to Gyan Prakash, who read and commented on some of the chapters and has always been ready to engage in illuminating discussions on a broad range of subjects; Phil Nord, who offered penetrating comments on my introduction and introduced me to his views on nineteenth-century Europe in a seminar we co-taught; Arno Mayer, who challenged me with his interpretations of Europe in the twentieth century; and Mark Mazower, who has left Princeton for Sussex but still suffered through more versions of more chapters of this book than anyone else, and yet through it all never tired of sharing ideas and offering much-needed companionship.

Princeton's Carl Schorske, now retired, may not know it, but reading his magnificent book on Vienna as an undergraduate at the University of Rochester (in a course taught by his former student, William McGrath) inspired me to go on to graduate school not in my first major, English literature, but in European history.

Being able to spend parts of two academic years at Columbia University's Harriman Institute, first as a student, then as a fellow and adjunct assistant professor, brought me into contact with Richard Wortman, Rick Ericson, and Mark von Hagen, who has generously guided and encouraged my work from the beginning. Mark's comments on various versions of this book and his insights into the history of the USSR have proved invaluable, as has his friendship.

I owe a large debt to the University of California Press, its editorial director, Sheila Levine, and its general director, Jim Clark, who have shown exceptional interest in my work and made available the resources of their fine publishing house. Dore Brown was a superb project editor. Three readers engaged by the press, R. W. Davies, John Barber, and Lewis Siegelbaum, made important suggestions on shaping the book and have commented on my work or helped me in other forums.

My thanks also to Blair Ruble for his support over the years; to Sheila Fitzpatrick, who despite my obvious attempts to revise her views has always been helpful and encouraging; and to Moshe Lewin, whose work I have also been wrestling with for years and who welcomed me during a pilgrimage I made to him while still an impressionable graduate student.

Many of my ideas were refined in conversation with graduate students in seminars at Princeton and Columbia. I thank them for their remarks, questions, and insights.

The manuscript was completed during a sabbatical at the University of Tokyo's Institute of Social Science, for which I am most grateful to Wada Haruki, who introduced me to the Japanese community of scholars on Russia. The opportunity to present my ideas to Tokyo's Russian Research Society, the European history seminar at Waseda University, and the Slavic Center of Hokkaido University in Sapporo enabled me to think through many problems of interpretation. Thanks to Kazuhiko Takahashi, Ishii Norie, Takao Chizuko, Nakai Kazuo, Minagawa Shugo, and Matsuzato Kimitaka.

Several chapters of this book were also presented at conferences in Ann Arbor and East Lansing, Michigan, and at the University of Birmingham, England. For their invitations, criticisms, and suggestions I am grateful to the organizers and participants of these sessions, especially William Rosenberg, Ron Suny, Lewis Siegelbaum, Robert Johnson, Laura Engelstein, Michael Burawoy, Sonya Rose, Bob Davies, and John Barber.

This study was made possible by the opportunity to conduct archival research and fieldwork in the former USSR during the opening up after 1985. In the spring of 1987, while on a ten-month research trip, I had the chance to spend six weeks in Magnitogorsk. I returned in 1989 and again in 1991. The opportunity to walk the streets and talk with surviving residents from the 1930s, local archivists, and many others influenced my views significantly. To see the city struggling with the legacy of the 1930s some fifty years later put the events of the past into very sharp focus.

In Magnitogorsk, the number of people who assisted my research was legion. I will never forget Valerii Kucher, Volodia Mozgovoi, Nina Kondratkovskaia, Galina Osolodkova, Vilii Bogun, Mikhail Lysenko, and, above all, Zhena and Tamara Vernikov. The photographer Anatolii Kniazev made available to me the vast collection of old photographs owned and preserved by the steel plant. The team of archivists in Magnitogorsk really looked after me, despite the restrictions that were placed over them by superiors in Moscow. Having finished this book, I remain overwhelmed by the warmth and generosity extended to me, even as I relentlessly investigated a painful decade of another country's history.

My visits to Magnitogorsk for fieldwork were part of extended research trips throughout the former USSR, two of which were sponsored by the International Research and Exchanges Board (IREX). In Moscow I enjoyed the support and stimulation of my companions on the academic exchange, especially Elizabeth Wood, Ken and Libby Straus, Steve and Stella Kimball, Bruce Allyn, and David Hoffman. While writing my dissertation I had several discussions with Michael Gelb, who also directed me to source materials. Kindra Kemp compiled the index and expertly redrew the maps and diagrams. Ann Chun retyped on short notice a chapter erroneously erased from the computer memory, and put up with me for a long time.

Funding for this project was provided by the University of California at Berkeley Center for Slavic Studies, Institute of International Relations, and Graduate Division; the Kennan Institute for Advanced Russian Studies of the Woodrow Wilson Center in Washington, D.C.; the International Research and Exchanges Board; the Harriman Institute of Columbia University; Princeton University's history department and University Committee on Research; and most of all, the Social Science Research Council.

Grateful acknowledgment is made to the above institutions and to the Library of Congress; the New York Public Library; the libraries of the University of California at Berkeley, the University of Illinois at Champaign-

Urbana, and Columbia University; the former Lenin Library in Moscow; the Public Library and the Library of the Academy of Sciences in St. Petersburg; the National Archives in Washington, D.C.; the Hoover Institution; the State Historical Archives of Wisconsin in Madison; the Case Western Historical Reserve in Cleveland; the Press and Cultural Section of the U.S. Embassy in Moscow; the Russian State Archives in Moscow and the State Archives Affiliate in Magnitogorsk; the Magnitogorsk City Museum; the American Section of the former Soviet Ministry of Higher Education; the Foreign Department of Moscow State University; the Magnitogorsk Mining and Metallurgical Institute; and the editorial board of the Magnitogorsk daily newspaper.

The idea of pursuing a study of power at the micro-level on the subject of Stalinism crystallized in conversations with the late Michel Foucault, whom I met at Berkeley while he taught there in 1982 and 1983. No doubt the final product would have been far better had he not died in 1984. But what did result, I dedicate to his memory.

USSR Organizational Structure, 1930s

In the absence of private property, all institutions in the USSR were technically part of the state. A key exception was the Communist party, which officially was a voluntary public (*obshchestvennaia*) organization. The party maintained a "cell" in every institution, and party administrations at all levels had departments paralleling those of the state. The USSR was thus a dualist party-state.

At the same time, the state structure was multiple. As a result, although all lower-level organizations were subordinated to upper ones in a pyramid, the parallelism of the party-state pyramids and the multiplicity of the state itself created overlapping jurisidictions. It also needs to be borne in mind that the Soviet Union was nominally a federation, with Magnitogorsk located in the Russian republic (RSFSR). Only all-union bodies bore the designation "USSR."

PARTY PYRAMID

ALL-UNION COMMUNIST PARTY (BOLSHEVIKS)

All-Union Party Congress. Irregularly convened. Formally the highest
   body of the party. Served between sessions by a Central Committee.
USSR Central Committee (CC). Dominated by its nominally subordinate
   political bureau (politbureau) and administrative secretariat. Headed in
   the 1930s by General Secretary Joseph Stalin.
Urals provincial party committee (*obkom*). Divided in three in 1934.
Cheliabinsk provincial party committee (*obkom*). Formed out of the Urals
   oblast in 1934. Headed by the obkom bureau.

Magnitogorsk city party committee (*gorkom*). Headed by the gorkom bureau.

Urban-district party committees (*raikom*).

Primary party organizations (PPOs). The lowest level of party organization. Called "cells" before 1934.

Communist party youth league (Komsomol). The apprentice organization for the party.

The RSFSR did not have its own Communist party structure; obkoms in the RSFSR were subordinated directly to the USSR Central Committee.

STATE PYRAMID

LEGISLATIVE AND EXECUTIVE

All-Union Congress of Soviets. Biannual congress of representatives of local soviets. Replaced in 1936 by the Supreme Soviet.

USSR Supreme Soviet. Permanent body of elected representatives.

All-Union Congress of Soviets/USSR Supreme Soviet Central Executive Committee (TsIK).

RSFSR All-Union Congress of Soviets/Supreme Soviet and Central Executive Committee.

Cheliabinsk provincial soviet and soviet executive committee.

Magnitogorsk city soviet and soviet executive committee.

Urban-district soviets.

Soviet sections (volunteers).

City-soviet planning commission.

At all levels, the full soviet, consisting of popularly elected representatives, was nominally charged with policy formation; executive committees, elected by the soviets, were responsible for implementation. Thus, soviets technically had both legislative and executive power. The head of the USSR Supreme Soviet was the head of state.

GOVERNMENT AND BUREAUCRACY

USSR Council of People's Commissars (Sovnarkom). Coordinating body of the bureaucracy, made up of the heads of each commissariat. Essentially the Soviet government. The chairman of Sovnarkom held a rank equivalent to prime minister.

Council of Labor and Defense (STO). High-level special government commission, technically subordinate to Sovnarkom but in practice above it. Temporarily abolished in 1937.

RSFSR Sovnarkom. Because the Magnitogorsk factory had all-union status, it was subordinated directly to the USSR, not the Russian republic.

People's Commissariat of Heavy Industry (NKTP). One of the commissariats represented on the USSR Sovnarkom. It owned and supervised most of the economy. Replaced the Supreme Council of the National Economy (Vesenkha) in 1932.

Main Administration of the Metallurgical Industry (GUMP). A subdivision of the Commissariat of Heavy Industry. Converted to the Commissariat of Ferrous Metallurgy (NKChM) when NKTP was divided into several commissariats in 1939.

Magnitogorsk Metallurgical Complex (MMK). Factory and mine. Under the Main Administration of Metal Industry.

Everyday-Life Administration (KBU). A division of the Magnitogorsk Metallurgical Complex. Renamed Municipal Economy Administration (UKKh) in 1938.

People's Commissariat of Internal Affairs (NKVD). Security police. Represented on the USSR Sovnarkom; in practice subordinated directly to the Communist party secretariat. For most of the 1930s, the regular police, called the militia, were attached to the NKVD. Prior to 1934, the security police was organized as an independent commission called the Main Political Administration (GPU). Both the NKVD and the GPU were colloquially referred to by the acronym for their predecessor organization, the "Cheka."

Provincial NKVD.

Magnitogorsk NKVD. Controlled the administrations of the Magnitogorsk Corrective Labor Colony (ITK) and Special Labor Settlement (Spetstrudposelok).

NKVD boards and *troika*. Summary sentencing bodies for crimes deemed to involve counterrevolution.

People's Commissariat of Justice (Narkomiust). Headed by USSR general procurator.

Provincial procurator.

Magnitogorsk procurator.

USSR Supreme Court.

Provincial court.
Magnitogorsk people's courts.
Comrade courts.

Narkomiust had jurisdiction only over non-counterrevolutionary crimes. The procurator technically had supervisory power over the NKVD, but the NKVD effectively resisted outside supervision of its operation. Railroads and waterways had a separate procurator and court system.

People's Commissariat of Municipal Economy (Narkomkhoz). Represented on USSR Sovnarkom. Completely eclipsed in Magnitogorsk by NKTP.

People's Commissariat of Trade (Narkomtorg). Represented on USSR Sovnarkom. Responsible for urban supply.
Provincial trade (Obltorg).
Magnitgorsk trade (Magnittorg).
Central Workers' Cooperative (TsRK). Reorganized and renamed the Department of Workers' Supply (ORS) in 1933.
City dining trust (Narpit).
City food processing complex.
Cooperatives.

State Planning Commission (Gosplan). Important for industrial operation and supply, parallel to NKTP.
State Institute for the Design of Metallurgical Factories (Gipromez), in Leningrad. Small role in the design of the Magnitogorsk factory.
Urals branch of Gipromez. Renamed Magnitostroi in 1927.
Magnitostroi. Design and construction trust (also the name for the construction site). Subordinated to GUMP. Merged with MMK in 1934; reinstituted as a separate trust in 1936.
Koksostroi. Coke plant construction, merged with Magnitostroi in 1933.
Mining Administration (GRU). Merged with Magnitostroi in 1933.
"Subcontracting" trusts (Stalstroi, etc.). Abolished in 1932 with the formation of GUMP.

State Institute for the Planning of Cities (Giprogor). Organization that employed the German architect Ernst May.
Oblast urban planning (Oblproekt).
City urban planning (Gorproekt).

SOCIAL WELFARE

All-Union Central Council of Trade Unions (VTsSPS). Trade unions were responsible for access to recreation facilities, accident insurance, pensions and other benefits.
USSR Metal Workers Union.
Provincial branch of the Metal Workers Union.
Magnitogorsk branch of the Metal Workers Union.

COMBINED PARTY AND STATE AGENCY

Central Control Commission and Workers' and Peasants' Inspectorate (TsKK-RKI). Combined party control commission and state commissariat (Rabkrin) with wide investigatory powers. Parallel to the GPU. Abolished in 1934 when the GPU was reorganized into the NKVD. In 1935 separate party and state control commissions were created.
Oblast control commission (OblKK). Abolished in 1934.
City control commission (GorKK). Abolished in 1934.

Note on Translation

All translations are the author's, unless otherwise indicated. For Russian words and names, the Library of Congress transliteration system has been used, with the exception that diacritical marks for soft signs have been suppressed.

Introduction:
Understanding the Russian Revolution

To *remake* everything: to organize things so that everything should
be new, so that our false, filthy, boring, hideous life should become a
just, pure, merry, and beautiful life.
   Aleksandr Blok, on the meaning of the Russian revolution[1]

About forty miles east of the southern tip of the Ural mountains lies a
semicircular group of five low hills, two of which contained some of the
richest and most accessible iron ore in the world. The existence of the ore
had been known since at least the middle of the eighteenth century, when
the area was settled with a small Cossack fort, or *stanitsa*, and the settlers
noticed that their compasses behaved strangely. No doubt for this reason
the outcrop came to be called *Magnitnaia gora*, or Magnetic Mountain.[2]

For centuries the sparsely populated area surrounding Magnetic Mountain led a tranquil existence. True, in the late eighteenth century the leader
of a peasant-Cossack rebellion, Yemilian Pugachev, while gathering his
forces, bathed near the mountain in the Iaik River, thereby marking it as a
symbol of defiance. But the rebellion that had momentarily paused to draw
its forces near the iron-ore deposits was put down, and the Empress Cath-
erine renamed the river the Ural, so as to dissociate the site from the deeds
of Pugachev. From that point, aside from the small quantities of ore that
were carted by horse to a tiny factory in nearby Beloretsk in the late nineteenth century, the iron-ore mountain, touched only by the icy arctic
winds sweeping down across the steppe, stood majestically undisturbed—
until 1929, when the Bolshevik leadership decided to initiate an assault.

Nowhere was it inscribed in stone that the Bolsheviks had to turn this
bump in the earth into a gigantic steel plant with a sprawling settlement of
200,000 people. Nor was it preordained that they would build everything
the way they did. The Bolsheviks brought along their banners and slogans,
their agitprop newspapers and circles for the liquidation of illiteracy, their
bread factories and mass dining rooms. They brought along the Communist party and the portraits of the Father of All Peoples, bourgeois specialists and young Red engineers, peasant prisoners and peasants turned shock

1

workers. And they brought along foreign designs and equipment for state-of-the-art blast furnaces, open-hearth ovens, and rolling mills. In short, to that group of semicircular hills the Bolsheviks brought "the revolution." This book attempts to tell the story of how the revolution came to Magnetic Mountain, and how the inhabitants of the resultant urban center—"Magnetic Mountain City," or Magnitogorsk—took part in the creation of what would come to be known as Stalinism.

Among the most widely observed phenomena in history, Stalinism is rightly infamous as a despotic political system. A close look at Magnitogorsk in the 1930s, however, will demonstrate that the distinctiveness of Stalinism lay not in the formation of a mammoth state by means of the destruction of society but in the creation, along with such a state, of a new society—manifest in property relations, social structure, the organization of the economy, political practice, and language. Stalinism signified the advent of a specifically socialist civilization based on the rejection of capitalism, the appreciation of which is perhaps best approached through a sharply focused case study.[3]

APPROACHES TO THE STUDY OF STALINISM

Whereas the early public debate in the United States on Stalinism was dominated by informative journalistic treatments and less informative travelers' accounts (along the lines of either "the country with a plan" or "how I escaped the Soviets"), the first professional research agenda for the study of the Stalin era developed in the aftermath of World War II around the so-called totalitarian model. This approach focused on the issue of state control and its extension over more and more areas of thought and action—as exemplified by Merle Fainsod's estimable case study of Smolensk province, which was based on documents captured during the war.[4] In what amounted to a replication of Stalinism's self-presentation (with the values inverted), political structure and ideology loomed large in the totalitarian model, while power was conceived in terms of the pronouncement and implementation of an organized political will. As far as Soviet society was concerned, in the absence of "independent institutions" or "autonomous actors" it seemed unclear *what* to investigate, or even whether there *was* a society per se. When it came to interpreting popular attitudes, great skepticism was shown toward published Soviet sources. Instead, disaffected émigrés were interviewed in depth for clues to the suppressed feelings assumed to lie behind propaganda and censorship.[5]

At the same time, however, Fainsod and others could not deny that the

USSR had managed to beat back the Nazi onslaught in a total war requiring enormous sacrifices by nearly the whole population, and that both before and after the war there was surprisingly little evidence of organized opposition to what was thought to be a sinister and illegitimate regime comparable only to that of the Nazis. Struggling to account for these ostensible anomalies, as well as for the Soviet Union's evident stability, these scholars predictably pointed to the state's use of mass repression. But on this crucial point, they became increasingly vulnerable, for not only did overt repression abate after Stalin's death, instability did not follow. Thus, despite the prolific and high-quality research they carried out, the result of these scholars' work was something of an analytical cul-de-sac.[6]

With good reason, the early analysts of Stalinism came under attack from a subsequent generation of self-proclaimed revisionists, who were led by an outsider, the transplanted Australian Sheila Fitzpatrick.[7] The scholars who rallied around Fitzpatrick came of age during the Vietnam War and the domestic convulsions that shook America's postwar sense of complacency and superiority. More inclined to the methods of social history, and using a far wider range of Soviet sources, including some archival materials, this group asserted plausibly that Stalinism could not be explained by coercion alone and set out to demonstrate that many people had accepted the values and ideals of the Stalin revolution.[8] Fitzpatrick in particular singled out the sizable stratum of educated, upwardly mobile managers/engineers, who, she argued, supported the Stalinist regime precisely because the regime had created them.[9]

The new elite, which lasted into the 1980s, began its trajectory to the top in 1929 during what Fitzpatrick called the "Cultural Revolution," by which she meant the mobilization of class-based radicalism when higher education was thrown open to the children of workers and peasants. This electrifying episode ended abruptly, however, in 1932, the point at which Fitzpatrick claimed that the momentum of the revolution was checked.[10] What followed as the upwardly mobile cadres were graduated and promoted to high positions, she argued, was a version of what Nicholas Timasheff had called the "Great Retreat" (a variant of Trotsky's thesis on the revolution's "betrayal"). Born of Stalin's revolution from above, the new elite supposedly turned around and repudiated further revolutionary mobilization in favor of stability and the revival of familiar patterns.[11]

Fitzpatrick traced the humble origins and rapid rise of the new elite, or what she alternately called the new "middle class," in terms of culture, purporting to explain its philistine tastes, puritanism, acceptance of pervasive state intervention, and loyalty to the system. She also noted, however, that its main education was in technical subjects, making it well suited to the demands of managing an industrial society. By characterizing the new Soviet elite as culturally conservative yet technically literate, she sought, in effect, to make Trotsky's assertion that Stalinism had a "social basis" in the bureaucracy less conspiratorial and pejorative. Exploring Trotsky's insights on the revolution far more deeply than he himself had, Fitzpatrick shared little of his disapproval with the revolution's outcome.[12]

Yet whereas even in his most condemnatory outbursts Trotsky had refused to disavow the socialist nature of the USSR, Fitzpatrick never seemed to decide whether her explorations into the social history of the Soviet elite revealed a socialist society or a traditionally Russian one, with a socialist veneer. She claimed that the Civil War mentality of the 1920s, although temporarily revived during the first Five-Year Plan, was eventually supplanted in the second half of the 1930s by a conservative, antimodern "Soviet" mentality. But she appears to have left intentionally unresolved the key issue of whether the resultant Soviet society was socialist, advocating more research.[13]

Meanwhile, a parallel drive for a revisionist understanding of Stalinism in the American academy was carried out by another outsider, Moshe Lewin.[14] Also taking up the Trotskyite framework, Lewin focused on the formation and character of the Soviet bureaucracy as a key to explaining the revolution's supposed demise under Stalin. In a series of highly influential books and essays, he argued that the predominantly peasant nature of Russia ended up overwhelming the process of modernization embarked on by the socialist regime, particularly because the regime had difficulty understanding its options vis-à-vis the peasantry and also because the peasantry supposedly underwent a process of "archaization" in the prolonged dislocation following the downfall of the old regime.[15]

In Lewin's view, a delicate situation calling for forbearance and farsightedness was whimsically destabilized in 1929 with the drive to coerce the peasantry into "collectivization." That such a decision could be taken at all, Lewin argued, was a consequence of the "degeneration" of the Bolshevik party into a bureaucratic, hierarchical administrative body to which such a strong-armed developmental policy held a certain appeal. Predictably, the more the Stalinist clique insisted that the country rush to overcome its agrarian nature, the greater the chaos that resulted—and the more the regime felt a need to resort to coercion. The "backwardness" of the rural social structure, in the hands of a group of poorly comprehending and impetuous leaders, culminated ironically in the establishment of a "backward" and "demonized" authoritarian political system.[16]

Elaborating the "social background" to the formation of the Stalinist political order, Lewin in turn underscored society's penetration by the state. During what he called the descent into a "quicksand society" and the "ruralization of the cities" that supposedly occurred during the initial stages of the Stalin revolution, he wrote that "the whole social structure" was "sucked into the state mechanism, as if entirely assimilated by it."[17] Highlighting this process of statization, however, he continued to lay great emphasis on societal influences, offering the maxim, "the quicker you break and change, the more of the old you recreate."[18] He employed the term "the Soviet system" to describe the outcome whereby the state bureaucratized the society and yet the social patterns of the village reasserted themselves within this enormous statism.[19] What the Soviet system amounted to, he argued, was a paradoxical, backward form of modernization, with peculiarly jerky rhythms, a tendency toward frenzied immoderation, and an in-built sense of permanent crisis. A self-proclaimed socialist, Lewin vehemently denied that such a "system" could in any way be equated with socialism, in effect scorning the self-perception not only of the Soviet regime but of millions of Soviet inhabitants.[20]

Both Fitzpatrick and Lewin directed their explorations in social history at the totalitarian paradigm's premise that the Stalinist state could do whatever it wanted. Whereas Fitzpatrick and her followers have attempted to analyze the supposed role social groups played in the state's policy decisions and ethos, Lewin has treated society more or less as an aggregate "force," akin to gravity, that exerted an almost invisible pull on the course of events. Ultimately, however, these varying approaches converged on the bottom-line proposition that the Stalinist state was permeated throughout by social influences, a notable modification of the then prevailing one-sided view on state-society relations in the Stalin era.

Lewin and Fitzpatrick have rarely admitted the existence of common ground between them, yet it is striking that in carrying out their respective projects of revisionism, both have tended to view Stalinism as an end to the revolution and something of a return, under conditions of great stress, to nonrevolutionary traditions. To be sure, Lewin's abandoned revolution was the compromise known as the New Economic Policy, or NEP, while Fitzpatrick's was the so-called Cultural Revolution, a revival of the Civil War's anticompromise spirit. She has emphasized, furthermore, this reversal's apparently logical development, essentially benign nature, and long-term stability, while he has argued, by contrast, that the Stalinist modernization was far from inevitable,[21] highly "pathological," and yet in dialectical fashion contained the means for its own "cure" (in the long-term process of urbanization, whereby an urban social structure replaced the rural one).[22] Despite these differences, however, in terms of what each has determined "the revolution" to be, Lewin and Fitzpatrick have both argued that Stalinism constituted a reversal. In the end, it is difficult to avoid the conclusion that the turn to social history has led to the replacement of the manifestly flawed totalitarian thesis by the basic perspective laid down by Leon Trotsky, the revolution's greatest loser.[23]

Such a perspective ignores the fact that at no time did the Soviet regime declare or seek to effect a counterrevolution—a turn of affairs that would not, in any case, have been tolerated by the Soviet population. To the vast majority of those who lived it, and even to most of its enemies, Stalinism, far from being a partial retreat let alone a throwback to the Russian past, remained forward-looking and progressive throughout. This was particularly so in light of the Great Depression that overtook the leading capitalist countries, and the commensurate rise and spread of fascism, whose overt militarism cast a pall over Europe. By virtue of its rejection of capitalism and its dramatic internal development, the USSR assumed the role of antifascist bulwark during a time when elsewhere reaction or indecisiveness appeared to be the order of the day.[24] More than that, Stalinism exerted a powerful influence over the entire world because what happened in the USSR during the 1930s seemed to be an implausible achievement in the forward march of European (universal) history.[25]

SCIENCE, UTOPIA, AND REVOLUTIONARY POLITICS

It is impossible to comprehend Stalinism without reference to the eighteenth-century European Enlightenment, an outpouring of impassioned public discussion that took as its point of departure the seventeenth-century innovation of modern "science." Applying the new models of nature to the political world, many thinkers during the Enlightenment embarked on a quest for an explicitly "rational social order," a well-regulated organization of human beings independent of the "arbitrary" authority of a sovereign. Arguably it was the French *philosophe* Condorcet—the first to give wide currency to the expression "science of society"—who conferred the prestige of Newtonian science on the search for a rational social order. For Condorcet, among others, science offered "the means to transform the social world" at the same time as it "suggested the model of the rational social organization to be implemented." Above all, science promised not simply the possibility of immediate improvement but "a vision of constant progress."[26]

What gave this worldview tremendous force was, of course, the French revolution, which appeared to offer a mechanism for realizing the vision of a rational social order. To be sure, the revolution brought forth a variety of applications, including the ideas and practices of liberalism, a "radical" strand of republicanism rooted in notions of equality, and Bonapartist dictatorship. But each of these different traditions emerged from the common source of what came to be called "revolutionary politics." This innovation signaled a simple yet profound discovery: that politics could be used to direct and possibly even remake society.[27]

Many of the Russian revolutionaries were guided by a highly developed awareness of the bewitching French experience and conceived of their own actions as an elaboration of that great chain of events, in the direction of what they imagined to be a more genuine version of radical democracy. Rather than a democratic order in the name of the nation, which allegedly concealed the class rule of the bourgeoisie, the Russian revolutionaries envisioned what was supposed to be a more inclusive order founded on the putative universality of the proletariat. Paradoxically, the goal of greater inclusiveness was to be reached by means of fierce class warfare and exclusion. Nonetheless, in the reinvention of revolutionary politics on the basis of class, the Russian revolutionaries were still following the central vision of the Enlightenment. The Russian revolution, too, was about using politics as a means for creating a rational, and therefore just, social order.

Not only did the revolution in the Russian empire partake of the most highly valued traditions in European history, but even the revolution's ostensibly exotic class character was quintessentially European, an effect of the nineteenth-century fossil-fuel industrialization that had swept England and the continent and rendered problematic the universalism of the Enlightenment's vision. Indeed, far from beginning with the Russian revolution, the task of reconstituting "the nation" by alleviating, or somehow overcoming, deep class divisions had been a central preoccupation throughout Europe for nearly a century—especially in the great "kingdom of the ideal," German-speaking Central Europe, where the inspiration for a specifically proletarian revolution originated.

It was, of course, Karl Marx who combined the Enlightenment's application of scientific rationality to society with the French revolution's discovery of the magic of politics and proclaimed the definitive science of society aimed at bringing about the ultimate political revolution that would eliminate the class divisions wrought by industrialization. Profoundly influenced by the great elaborator of the French revolution, Georg W. F. Hegel, who had articulated a dynamic vision of the progressive movement of history, Marx named his design for a future, classless society "socialism"—a term already in wide use that signified either the amelioration or, more often, the complete transcendence of what were the truly appalling living conditions of Europe's working majority.[28]

Emphasizing transcendence, Marx and his followers believed his conception of socialism to be new. In a famous essay entitled "Socialism: Utopian and Scientific" (1880), Friedrich Engels argued that if with Hegel the world began to be viewed as a developmental process, with the onset of industrialization and the rise of the working class in the 1830s socialism had ceased to be "an accidental discovery of this or that ingenious brain" and had become instead "the necessary outcome" of a larger historical struggle governed by scientific laws. Accordingly, the task for critical analysis was no longer to imagine a society as perfect as possible but to lay bare the present pattern of socioeconomic relations in which the next "stage" of historical development was already nascent. Marx, according to Engels, had done just that for the "capitalist mode of production," and thus with Marx "socialism had become scientific."[29]

Engels's distinction between utopian and scientific socialism, which was embraced by the Soviet state, has been dismissed by philosophers who argue that Marxian socialism was in fact no less utopian than the unattainable visions of Fourier or Owen. Far from having been "science," the argument goes, Marxism was nothing more than a bogus religion claiming falsely to be science.[30] But the historian should not so quickly dismiss Marxism's claim to be scientific. This claim inspired millions of people, both inside and outside the Soviet Union, and informed the thinking of much of what went on under Stalin (and after), from the establishment of economic planning and school curricula to the capacity for opposition to the regime.

If the scientificity of Marxian socialism needs to be taken seriously, however, so does its utopian aspect. Like the Enlightenment mentality out of which it grew, Marxian socialism was an attractive schema for realizing the kingdom of heaven on earth. Of course, as a supreme rationalist of the nineteenth-century type, Marx himself never wrote a utopia. But he asserted that a utopian society would—indeed must—come about for the sake of humankind, and his voluminous, often esoteric writings inspired the most extensive effort ever to realize just such an outcome in the eastern fringes of Europe. That the scientific utopianism of Marx found an appreciative audience in the Russian empire was due to the specificities of Russian history, especially to certain intensely felt aspirations that predated the 1917 revolution and found expression in the revolutionary process.

REVOLUTION IN THE RUSSIAN EMPIRE

If in hindsight the French revolution appeared as "so inevitable yet completely unforeseen,"[31] the double revolution in the Russian empire was by contrast long foreseen yet hardly inevitable. Decades before the upheaval in 1905 that accompanied a humiliating defeat by Japan, there was widespread talk of the coming revolution. Various groups devoted themselves to its realization, while successive government ministers undertook large-scale reforms of the sociopolitical order, in large part to prevent just such a contingency. All of this might make revolution in Russia seem a foregone conclusion. But had it not been for the severe strain brought by the folly of the Great War, which triggered the autocracy's sudden, total collapse, increased the politicization of the populace geometrically, and rendered impossible the situation of the short-lived Provisional Government, the improbable seizure of power by conspiratorial revolutionaries would scarcely have been possible.[32]

The debacle of the Great War and the ensuing changes in power of February and October 1917 stemmed from the great-power pursuits of the Russian state. Russia's need to adapt to changing circumstances could scarcely be denied. Yet the stakes of internal reform were fatefully increased, in part by the autocracy's resistance over many decades to any moves to limit its power, but even more so by the grandiosity of the autocracy's ambitions regarding the preeminent place Russia ought to occupy in the international state system—in the context of the empire's enormous size, primarily agricultural population, and multinational character.[33] That the autocracy proved inept in meeting its self-assigned task of leading a robust Russia became a source of general disillusionment, as well as a clarion call to action for others who imagined they could do better.[34]

A sense of the despised autocracy's abject failure, a desire to stave off further disintegration, and a belief that they could take matters into their own hands were among the chief motivations behind the upper class's critical abandonment of the autocracy, the soldiers' mutiny against the war, the peasants' expropriation of the land, the workers' assumption of control over the factories, and the series of national uprisings against the politically centralized empire. These far-reaching actions reinforced the prevailing sense of fantastic possibility that accompanied the abdication of the tsar, but they also contributed to a rising trepidation and calls to avoid further breakdown and potential chaos. It was as a result of a search for a new order that the disparate events of the revolution came to be united into a vehicle for the elite aspiration to see the country become supremely powerful while at the same time remaining true to itself and the higher ideals it supposedly represented. This was the task that the phenomenon of Bolshevism came to embody.[35]

Bolshevism arose in the repressive conditions of tsarist Russia not as a political party in the parliamentary sense but as a conspiracy within a diverse revolutionary underground dedicated to the overthrow of the autocracy. Comparable Carbonarist conspiracies, also penetrated by police agents and informants, had existed elsewhere in Europe, presenting no more plausible alternative to the existing order than did the Bolsheviks, the most energetic of whom spent extended periods in Siberian or foreign exile.[36] In February 1917, however, when the tsarist regime gave way under the pressure of mounting military fiascos, the so-called Provisional Government had little choice but to sanction the release of persons imprisoned or exiled for political reasons by the now fallen autocracy. Bolshevik leaders began making their way to the capital. These included Vladimir Lenin, who was able to reach Petrograd from the unofficial Bolshevik headquarters in Zurich, Switzerland, only through the mal-intentioned assistance of Russia's wartime enemy, Germany.

Suddenly and unexpectedly, when the Russian empire became in effect the freest country in the world, Bolshevism was transformed into an above-ground and essentially unobstructed conspiracy.[37] Finding themselves in a position to fill the political and symbolic vacuum occasioned by the autocracy's absolute collapse and the Provisional Government's uncertain legitimacy, the Bolsheviks put forth an engaging long-term vision of Russia's future in the form of a supremely confident narrative of the laws of history and all-purpose explanation of the present—a vision that was calculatingly enhanced by expedient borrowings from the programs of other political parties. Dynamic leadership, not just a Marxist revolutionary worldview, helped make possible such a turn of events and proved to be one of the Bolsheviks principal assets.[38]

Divided and quarrelsome, the Bolsheviks suffered from a series of bungled efforts to take charge of events, such as the embarrassing confusion of July 1917 when they vacillated over whether to stage an uprising that occurred without them and failed.[39] But following the attempt in August 1917 by the commander of the army to organize an immediate march on Petrograd to oust the leftist revolutionaries, which also failed, the Bolsheviks managed spectacularly to ride the waves of popular upheaval.[40] They came to power during mass seizures of land by the peasantry, a revolution in its own right (without parallel in the French revolution) and one that liberal political groups believing in private property could not readily sanction but that the Bolsheviks supported perhaps even more vocally than the great peasant party, the Socialist Revolutionaries.[41] And the Bolsheviks took charge while the country was at war—another revolutionizing process to which they gave the utmost attention, sanctioning an immediate end to hostilities, without explaining how the Germans were to be stopped.[42]

What strikes one about the Bolshevik triumph in 1917, however, is less their opportunism than their reckless sense of a world-historical mission, which made possible such opportunism amid the mind-boggling swirl of events. As products of the nineteenth-century intelligentsia, the Bolsheviks were inclined to that tradition's obdurate sense of righteousness and paternalism. They claimed to be able to speak and act for the people with tyrannical assurance, yet they saw no contradiction in staunchly championing the use of centralized authority to achieve their aims. In fact, it was this amalgam of raw *raison d'état* and beneficent devotion to the commonweal that characterized the Bolsheviks and became the main dynamic of the revolutionary process following the October coup.

The importance of the revolutionary process, particularly of the year 1918, needs to be emphasized.[43] No account of the revolution that stops in 1917 can explain the triumph of Bolshevism, an outcome for which the Civil War, not the October seizure of power in the capital, proved decisive.[44] Indeed, rather than the "spread of the October revolution,"[45] we should think in terms of the transmutation of the October coup into both a social and supranational cause during the Civil War.[46] This transpired under the banner of class war, which permitted; indeed necessitated, territorial reconquest in areas controlled by "bourgeois nationalists," as well as the merciless application of terror against the "bourgeoisie" and their apparent accomplices, who could include unwittingly or even consciously "traitorous" socialists.[47]

The desperate need to mobilize for the Civil War provided the Bolsheviks with a vehicle for rescuing the Russian empire from oblivion and themselves from the virtual collapse that seemed to have overcome them by the summer of 1918, when, among other developments, the leader of the Bolshevik security police, Feliks Dzierżyński, was captured and Lenin wondered whether the new regime would survive until the morning.[48] Not long after this episode, the "October revolution" began in earnest, as chaotic institutions, such as the Red Guards, the Military Revolution Committee, and the Communist party, began to be transformed into regularized components of a new central administration.[49]

The Bolsheviks' desire to build a mighty state was fueled not only by the pressures of the moment but also by the longer-term urge to match the achievements of the European powers and the United States, and this made their efforts widely appreciated, even among many military officers and functionaries of the old regime. Although the Bolsheviks' methods and much of their rhetoric may have seemed bizarre or extreme, many declared enemies of socialism still came to recognize that the country's new rulers, notwithstanding their complete repudiation of the past, were *implicitly* building on Russia's state-led, survival-oriented social engineering tradition. That tradition had been inaugurated by Peter the Great and resorted to most recently by Sergei Witte and Petr Stolypin in what seemed to be a never-ending cycle of perceived external challenge and wrenching internal response.[50]

Russia's obsession with socialism can also be understood in this light, for along with the desire for a strong country there existed—well before the Bolsheviks came to power—a widespread feeling that Russia had, or ought to have, a special mission. Within educated society, people disagreed on how closely Russia, in achieving its "rightful place," ought to imitate the so-called advanced countries, a concern that gave rise to the schism between Slavophiles and Westernizers. But even the strongest advocates of Westernization felt that, while modernizing, Russia must somehow maintain its distinctiveness. Socialism promised to allow just that. Through socialism, Russia would industrialize, matching and eventually superseding the great powers economically and militarily while retaining a supposed moral superiority. Moreover, by so doing Russia would give Europe and the United States a taste of their own medicine, confronting *them* with something of a challenge.[51]

For achieving these formidable aims the Bolsheviks and their supporters imagined Marxist class analysis to be an almost supernatural device, but it was the depth of Russian ambitions that gave Marxist developmentalism its importance and made it appear to be a trump-card method for reaching the coveted goal of modernity. In the end, the remarkable fact about the Russian revolution was that although the desire to exalt the might and standing of Russia had proved a heavy burden and brought down the old regime, far from being shunned, this aspiration was embraced by the country's new rulers. More than that, it turned out to hold the key to their longevity and became the source of their identity. The Bolsheviks were not simply makers but also instruments of history.[52]

Just by their survival, let alone their remarkable recovery of most of the empire, the Bolsheviks shocked the world, and no doubt each other. Having imperiously placed themselves at the forefront of the politicized masses and at Lenin's urging adopted a seemingly dubious revolutionary scenario, this fractious caste of self-styled professional insurrectionists managed to capture and *hold* the reins of an imperial state. Notwithstanding the image of iron resoluteness which the Bolsheviks zealously sought to project (and which their enemies readily accepted), they were not sorcerers who could turn over all of Russia with a few decrees.[53] Rather, their success in wielding the powerful lever of the state depended on an impressive ability to create effective new institutions, such as the Red Army (successor to the Red Guards) and the Cheka (successor to the Military Revolutionary Committee). That ability, in turn, derived from their assiduous assertion of dominance over the ensemble of concepts and practices that together made up the experience of the revolution.

In the months leading up to the February 1917 assumption of power by a Provisional Government there had been mass demonstrations and strikes, but "the revolution" did not so much bring down the tsar as the fall of the tsar opened up "the revolution," a participatory and millenarian cause for which millions of people were ready to give up their lives. This multifaceted revolution, which was molded into an elite-sponsored dream of a mighty Russia, was propelled by notions of popular sovereignty, or "all power to the soviets," and the feeling that the needs of "the people," from housing to wages to schooling to medical care, should be attended to. It was this sensibility that gave such force to the slogan "peace, land, and bread" (and the less frequently cited "national self-determination") and with which the Bolsheviks' class language and view of the world remained in partial overlap even after their almost immediate betrayal of the 1917 slogans in the all-out struggles for political supremacy.

To be sure, the Bolsheviks' apparent betrayal of one of the revolution's core principles—popular sovereignty—induced various groups of revolutionaries to take up arms against them in defense of the revolution. But the efforts by White armies to restore landowner rights, and the misguided intervention and half-hearted support for the Whites by the "imperialist powers" (ostensibly to force Russia back into the war), pushed much of the mass of everyday revolutionaries into the Bolshevik camp. The place to look for the "social support" of the "October revolution" is less in the radicalization of 1917 and the supposed feelings of the workers toward the seizure of power than in the formation and operation (in 1918 and after) of the Red Army,[54] and even more so, in the staffing of the rapidly expanding, new state institutions by tens of thousands of white-collar functionaries.[55]

In sum, the Civil War not only gave the daring, opportunistic Bolsheviks a modus operandi and helped solidify their still amorphous identity as the consummate builders of a socially oriented, powerful state; it also furthered the process whereby the Bolsheviks' being in power came to be identified with the cause of "the revolution." In elections immediately following the seizure of power, the Bolsheviks garnered little support among the peasantry (the overwhelming bulk of the population) and failed to win the allegiance of many workers—the groups in whose name they had seized power.[56] But whatever their difficulties in these and subsequent elections—which could be and were dismissed as a bourgeois institution—the Bolsheviks did assert an effective claim, backed by a willingness and a *capacity* to use force, to protect "the revolution" against the threat of "counterrevolution."[57] Although the struggle over who had the right to define "the revolution" continued for several years (in Kronstadt and elsewhere[58]), the Bolsheviks, by leading the defense of "the revolution," were able to take advantage of the emotions and hopes unleashed by the overthrow of the old regime and consolidate their precarious rule.

More than simply a battle for political power culminating in the Bolshevik dictatorship, however, the revolution constantly announced itself as being about values, behavior, and beliefs. This cultural dimension is critical. Our understanding of the revolution must not be reduced to the onset of the Bolshevik political monopoly and its internal debates, even though almost all expression of revolutionary values and beliefs was eventually forced within the confines of Bolshevism. Put another way, any explanation for the establishment of the Bolshevik monopoly requires a cultural dimension. Bolshevism itself, including its evolution, must be seen not merely as a set of institutions, a group of personalities, or an ideology but as a cluster of powerful symbols and attitudes, a language and new forms of speech, new ways of behaving in public and private, even new styles of dress—in short, as an ongoing experience through which it was possible to imagine and strive to bring about a new civilization called socialism.[59]

THE STALIN REVOLUTION

To its legions of proponents, the revolution in the Russian empire marked the dawn of a new era. In the first history of the Russian utopian novel—published, appropriately enough, in 1922—the author, Vladimir Sviatlovskii, enthusiastically acclaimed the revolution itself as "the first great utopia in modern history."[60] Such testimony to the revolution's millenarian character later acquired a host of dubious associations, as people warned about the supposed perils of allowing "utopianism" to influence politics. Mention of utopianism in the Russian context became a way to assail the revolution, socialism, and political nonconformism more generally.[61] In 1989, however, an American historian of the revolution, Richard Stites, sought to revive Sviatlovskii's apt characterization—not to malign the revolution, but again to celebrate it.

Stites argued that in Russia utopianism was not some peculiar and supposedly dangerous proclivity of the revolutionary intelligentsia, but a widely shared and legitimate aspiration with a long history that was finally given free reign in 1917. For Stites, the multifarious attempts following October to "live the revolution" in daily life, from revolutionary festivals and "Communist" birth and death rituals to housing communes and science fiction writing, demonstrated "that almost the entire culture of the revolution in the early years was 'utopian'." By unashamedly adopting such an idealistic approach, Stites was able to reclaim much of the revolution's captivating power.

Stites's panoply of everyday revolutionaries recalled that of the gifted eyewitness, René Fülöp-Miller, a Hungarian philosopher whose unorthodox record of "the mind and face of Bolshevism" appeared in 1926.[62] Like Fülöp-Miller, Stites highlighted the supposed variety, spontaneity, and autonomy of this early experimentalism and evoked a broad-based revolutionary celebration involving "not a handful of cranks, but whole communities of intellectuals, political figures, economic planners, architects, musicians, . . . workers and peasants." Going further than even the enthusiastic Fülöp-Miller had, Stites granted the experimenters the status of a "movement," and moreover one that was uniformly predicated on egalitarianism. In a range of disparate and often unfocused activities he saw the noble dream of a just community founded on equality, sharing, and fairness.[63]

In contrast to this image of early revolutionary utopias as inherently broad-minded, tolerant, and egalitarian—and thus "true" utopias—Stites presented the Stalin revolution as "a rejection of 'revolutionary' utopianism in favor of a single utopian vision and plan, drawn up at the pinnacle of power and imposed on an entire society without allowance for autonomous life experiments." Stites obviously sought to distance what he regarded as the laudatory utopian impulse from any complicity in Stalinist authoritarianism. But even as he denied the Stalin revolution a "genuine" utopian quality, Stites conceded that Stalin's "administrative utopia" was radical and dynamic, although he stopped short of acknowledging that genuine enthusiasm and widespread coercion coexisted.[64]

Stalinism in fact revived the revolutionary utopianism that had been so encouraged during the Civil War but that had suffered a blow in 1921 when the "Peasant Brest-Litovsk" policy of replacing grain requisitioning by a tax-in-kind was extended beyond Tambov province.[65] The extension of the tax-in-kind was followed by other measures that together coalesced into what was dubbed the New Economic Policy (NEP), which partially legalized the anathema of private trade and the market, reversed much of the holy-grail policy of nationalization of urban property and industry, yet failed to generate convincing signs of the anticipated new world associated with socialism.[66] During the NEP, the dictatorship of the proletariat was beset by high unemployment, rising prostitution, millions of orphaned children (many of whom roamed the country engaging in criminal activities and forming gangs), and an explosion of private trade. The authorities were largely at a loss as to what to do about these ills and the disappointment they fostered.[67]

Back at the Tenth Party Congress in March 1921, when the hesitant steps that led to the NEP were taken over strenuous objections, Lenin had asked apologetically, "How could one start a socialist revolution in a country like ours without dreamers?"[68] As the 1920s wore on, many people had begun to wonder just what had happened to the great dream of a new Russia and to the powerful class rhetoric of haves versus have-nots, oppressors versus oppressed, for not only had industrial production barely managed to climb back to 1914 levels, but the most striking results of the revolution seemed to be the formation of a new urban bourgeoisie, the Nepmen, and an incipient alliance (*smychka!*) between what few party officials there were in the countryside and a new rural bourgeoisie, the kulaks.[69]

To be sure, the NEP had a constituency, which stretched beyond the so-called Nepmen and kulaks to embrace elements of the expanding state bureaucracy (largely the Commissariats of Finance and Agriculture) and certain sections of the Communist party.[70] The country had recovered. But even to many of those who supported the NEP, the socialist revolution seemed to have lost much of its momentum. Proposals for putting the revolution back on track, either largely within or even outside the NEP framework, were hotly debated throughout the decade,[71] but it was unclear what, if anything, might come of them—until 1929, when the country was suddenly launched on what was called the Great Break (*velikii perelom*).

The precipitating factor behind this colossal improvisation may have been the grain crises of the late 1920s. But the Great Break's significance

extended well beyond the regime's self-inflicted showdown with the peasantry, a confrontation that, it needs to be recalled, took place against the
background of deep-seated anxieties about capitalist encirclement and the
Red Army's inability to fight a war against the advanced European countries. In the context of this perceived vulnerability, the Great Break promised not only to secure the regime's political control over the countryside
but also to bring about in the shortest possible time what Russia had not
been able to achieve in several centuries: to become an undisputed great
power and, what was more, an example for the rest of the world to admire
and emulate, by building socialism.[72]

That the initial launching of this remarkable turn of events could have
been determined essentially by one man turned out to be another of the
unforeseen yet central developments of the revolution during the 1920s.
Lenin, the socialist revolution's undisputed moral and political leader and
the symbol of the new Russia, fell ill and died (exerting virtually no influence on policy matters during the last two years of his life). After a nasty
struggle, Stalin emerged as Lenin's successor, filling a role already created
by his predecessor but then remaking it into a personal despotism.[73] This
Stalin achieved not only by his oft-remarked dominance of the bureaucracy, but also by his careful attention to questions of ideology and their
relation to political power.[74] Not Bukharin, the party's "theorist," nor Trotsky (by far the most original mind among the Bolsheviks) but Stalin first
systematized the "foundations of Leninism"—and through constant maneuvering made sure he was recognized as Leninism's main arbiter.[75]

Whatever concessions or apologies Stalin continued to make at meetings of the politburo or Central Committee, as soon as the meetings ad-
journed he retreated to his office atop the apparat and acted virtually as he
saw fit. Yet he always made sure that everything he did was explained and
justified within what he effectively characterized as the Leninist legacy.
When Stalin mobilized the powerful class-war rhetoric of the revolution's
"heroic age"—kept alive after 1921 in patterns of dress, images, songs, festivals, names, storytelling, a new pantheon of heroes—and launched a vicious campaign against the kulaks, he had no conceptual difficulty in presenting this, or the concurrent decisions to push forward with the forcible
collectivization of agriculture and accelerate the pace of industrialization,
as a continuation of the work begun by Lenin and October.[76] He went further, however, and, in re-revolutioning the revolution, skillfully invoked
scattered remarks by Lenin on the importance of national strength and *explicitly* tied the building of socialism to imperial Russian history.[77]

As masterful a political infighter as Stalin proved to be, he could scarcely have succeeded in garnering the required support for such an immense mobilization without the vision of building socialism he was able to articulate, and the genuine passions that such a bold plan for a bountiful world, remade along class lines, evoked among many people. As the decade of the 1930s began, the great eastern country's time in the sun seemed to have truly arrived. The terrible ordeals of the "imperialist war," Civil War, epidemics and famine had not, after all, been in vain. The Stalin revolution seemed like the second, and potentially more lasting, dawn of a just, pure, merry, and beautiful Russia, where he who was nothing would become everything.

THE CITY AND THE WELFARE STATE

Nowhere was the euphoric sense of the revolution's renewed possibilities in the 1930s more in evidence than at Magnetic Mountain. Numerous other instant cities were also created, such as Komsomolsk-na Amure, Novokuznetsk (Stalinsk), and Karaganda, while virtually all established urban centers underwent such dramatic expansion and transformation that they became in effect new cities.[78] (Indeed, according to the January 1939 census, in the twelve years since the December 1926 census the registered urban population of the Soviet Union jumped from 26.3 to 55.9 million.)[79] But Magnitogorsk remained the quintessential emblem of the grand transformation whereby the Enlightenment goal of using science to perfect society, having been bonded to the French revolution's discovery of political mobilization and filtered through industrialization and the attendant rise of the working class, had become a reality one could participate in firsthand. This prospect transfixed large numbers of foreign observers, as well as many of the inhabitants of the USSR.

That Magnitogorsk, as the encapsulation of the building of socialism, appeared to embody the Enlightenment dream, once improved, would have been reason enough for the world attention it received. At the same time, Magnitogorsk also appeared to exemplify the unique benefits supposedly derived from the advance of urbanism. Before the revolution in Russia, cities were feared as anomalies of development and dangerous threats to the sociopolitical order, but after 1917 they came to be viewed as the epitomes of progress and therefore the prime bulwarks for the existing order. More than that, cities were welcomed as the training grounds for producing the armies of model citizens whose collective activities would increase the Soviet state's great-power potential. Even though on the eve of the war in

1941, still only one-third of the population lived in cities, the revolution in Russia was a decidedly urban-centered one.

Revolutionary Russia's embrace of the city could claim an extended genealogy in the experience of Europe, where cities had long been celebrated as the principal agents of civilization.[80] Before the Enlightenment gave birth to the notion of a science of society, a tradition of trying to imagine the ideal city arose whereby cities served as the settings for, and the objects of, analyses of how best to organize human affairs, a goal that presupposed continual regulation by centralized authority.[81] It was this legacy that helped make possible, and in turn came to be elaborated by, the Enlightenment (which took place more or less simultaneously throughout the great urban centers of Europe).[82] This legacy also made feasible the programs for the state regulation of society in the name of the commonweal, beginning in the nineteenth century with efforts to confront the special problems of urban life and urban populations and continuing into the twentieth.

In the grand narratives of European history, the nineteenth century most often appears as the period when the twin challenges of the French and Industrial revolutions transformed the various old regimes into modern polities with parliaments, political parties, and universal male suffrage—in short, into what today we recognize as "democracy." Such a narrative of the birth of "the bourgeois world," which triumphed in the Great War when all remaining old regimes collapsed, has been given substantial support by the fact that European states, their elites, and opposition groups were themselves preoccupied with the problem of how to respond politically to the new conditions brought about by the French and Industrial revolutions.[83]

There is, however, another story, one that begins before 1789 and continues well after 1914: the formation of the welfare state. This other, parallel development is largely one of social regulation—procedures, rules, categories, and social practices, almost all of which arose outside the state but came to be taken over by it—as well as self-imposed normalization and micro-level resistance. A far less visible historical drama, not of political parties and parliamentary clashes but of identities and the clever tactics used in the invention of daily life, the formation of the welfare state was linked to the efforts at pacification in Europe's colonies, a process that took place simultaneously and exerted a reciprocal influence on the articulation of social-control and welfare-related programs "at home."[84]

In part a conservative response to the rise of the working class and the "dangers" it supposedly represented, especially those of contagious disease and political militancy, the welfare state also emerged from the variety of concerns articulated by experts pursuing such varied goals as workplace efficiency, psychological normalization, and healthy populations.[85] Industrialists, concerned about obtaining a reliable, docile supply of labor, and social reformers, crusading for what they took to be the best way to minimize social costs and maximize social benefits, shared a logic, even if their aims often appeared divergent. And because the welfare state rested on a certain social logic and a number of transferable social practices, it was viable in a variety of political settings, including Stalin's Russia.[86]

Rather than being viewed as a pathological case (deviating from the European norm because of the country's backwardness or agrarian social structure, the long history of Russian authoritarianism, the experience of the Civil War, Marxist ideology, the single-mindedness of Lenin, or the evilness of Stalin), the USSR in a narrative of the welfare state might appear as the standard whose uncanny success challenged the rest of the world to respond. More than in any other country, Stalinism seemed to bring together the elements of what was then the prevalent conception and experience of "progressive modernity": on the one hand, the deployment of a coordinated, purposeful economy, within which small, supposedly inefficient producers were replaced by larger and therefore mightier ones; and, on the other, the formation of a government of national unity that was above the seeming paralysis of parliamentary rule *and* unequivocally dedicated to the advancement of the commonweal.[87]

Despite administrative and financial limitations, the Soviet social insurance system that came into being following the revolution specified benefits (in many cases equal to total earnings) in the event of death, disability, sickness, old age, pregnancy and childbirth, or unemployment, for working people and family members. In 1930, temporary unemployment benefits were abolished, but this was because, incredibly, unemployment itself was eliminated. By this time, moreover, the Soviet understanding of welfare had come to include not only a guarantee of a job for everyone, but the payment of pensions upon retirement (a system that was made universal in 1937). The amount of benefits, particularly pensions, remained small, but there was no denying that the Soviet state had embraced a broad conception of social welfare—extending from employment and income to affordable housing, health care, and organized leisure—and had done so without prodding.

Not only could the USSR under Stalin plausibly assert that it had developed the programs and practices of state-guaranteed social welfare to a greater extent than had previously been the case anywhere, but it could do so in a way that contrasted with the fascist reaction: by embracing fully the illustrious European heritage known as the Enlightenment. For all these reasons, the Soviet example, as showcased at Magnitogorsk, could be said to have exerted a direct and profound influence on the rest of the world's industrialized countries. In a word, the USSR decisively shaped part of the bedrock of the world in which we live, a bedrock that today is coming apart everywhere.[88]

THE POLITICS OF EVERYDAY LIFE

The Bolshevik leadership, with its grand designs for building socialism—along with the will and wherewithal to try to realize such a goal—set what might be called the broad agenda for what was meant to happen at Magnetic Mountain. Important as these intentions were, they constitute only the beginning of the story. For one thing, the policies and programs enacted contained irreconcilable aspects that surfaced during the attempts to implement them; indeed, the methods of implementation themselves were often at odds with the stated goals of programs and policies. For another, these policies and programs formed part of the lives of people, ordinary and higher-ups alike, and their actions and reactions, initiatives and responses, in significant ways influenced how those programs were carried out, circumvented, and changed in unforeseen ways.

When we look closely at the USSR in the 1930s we see that the results of building socialism were not entirely what the Bolsheviks intended (that is, what the central party decrees said should happen). This does not mean, however, that the intentions can therefore be ignored or discounted. Although it is necessary to look beyond them, such intentions, programs, and policies were responsible for the fields of action within which the behavior of individuals took place. It is within these fields of action that we must look to see how the intentions were played, how the programs were implemented and what their consequences were—to see, in short, what kinds of lives people were able to lead, and how they understood their lives. To this end, there is no substitute for letting people speak as much as possible in their own words.[89]

As we shall see, the kinds of lives that the urban inhabitants came to lead and the identities they formed involved eager participation in, frequent circumvention of, and resourceful, albeit localized, resistance to the terms of daily life that developed within the crusade of building socialism. One resists, without necessarily rejecting, by assessing, making tolerable, and, in some cases, even turning to one's advantage the situation one is confronted with. An appropriate analogy is to the Japanese martial art of judo. Even when the weight of the force against one is seemingly overwhelming, as was the case with the Soviet state, the possibility remains to sidestep and thereby use that heavy force against itself.

Rather than the extension of Communist party control over more and more areas of life, therefore, it is possible to see—without denying the heavy coercive force of the Communist project—a two-way struggle, however unequal the terms, over the drawing of lines of authority, a struggle that involved continuous, if usually indirect, challenges to the perceived rules. It is not necessary to romanticize "the people" to argue that simply by living life, the urban inhabitants discovered that power was pliable. At the same time, their actions also demonstrated that power was productive: power relations created effects—of experience, identity, resistances. Concentrating on the rule articulation process in the encounters of daily life involves shifting the focus from what the party and its programs *prevented* to what they *made possible*, intentionally and unintentionally.

In sum, the analysis employed here begins with the party's noncapitalist agenda, follows the attempts to implement that agenda, recognizes ad hoc modifications in the agenda, particularly those occasioned by the actions of the citizenry (letting those citizens speak as much as possible in their own words), regards as resistances many actions normally seen as passive or "deviant," thereby adopting a widened view of the political, and is ultimately guided by the belief that the subject of inquiry should include not only what was repressed or prohibited but what was made possible or produced. Put another way, this study seeks to establish the varied and often unexpected effects of the identification of certain issues as problems, the attempts to introduce programs and practices to address these problems, and the struggles that ensued, especially the terms on which they were fought.

Such a methodology for doing social history is derived from the writings of Michel Foucault, who focused on what he called the problem of subjectivity, or the processes by which individuals are made, and also make themselves, into subjects under the aegis of the state.[90] Foucault singled out resistances as perhaps the most important element in the formation of modern subjectivity, yet he never gave resistances the empirical attention they deserved; nor did he spell out the kinds of compromises resistances forced on would-be social engineers at the top. By contrast, in this monograph the empirical investigation of resistances will occupy a central place, widening the analysis of subjectivity to include not only what Foucault designated as disciplinary techniques but also the politics of daily life.[91]

As Foucault has argued, studying power relations at the micro-level hardly means ignoring the state. At the same time, however, he has repeatedly demonstrated that power is not localized in the central state apparatus.[92] This holds true even when there is thought to be no separation between the spheres "state" and "society," as was the case in the USSR, where everything was formally part of the state.[93] In the chapters ahead, mechanisms of power—such as mutual surveillance and self-identification—will be shown to exist alongside the state machinery, on a much more ordinary level, yet to sustain the state just as effectively as its primary institutions, including the police. In the USSR under Stalin, no less than in modern France, the state understood that its power rested on the characteristics and behavior of the people.

Applying Foucault's work to the USSR underscores yet again the contention made by the revolutionaries themselves that the enduring drama of the Russian revolution must not be sought in the supposed black-magic qualities of Marxism, the cunning opportunism and pitiless determination of the Bolshevik state-builders, or the evolution of the countryside in the 1920s, but in the historically conditioned merger of long-held geopolitical objectives with potent social concerns. National power and social welfare drove the revolutionary process and culminated in the formation of an industrially based welfare state with an attendant consciousness. Stalinism was not just a political system, let alone the rule of an individual. It was a set of values, a social identity, a way of life.

When it comes to Stalinism, what needs to be explained and subjected to detailed scrutiny are the mechanisms by which the dreams of ordinary people and those of the individuals directing the state found common ground in this Soviet version of the welfare state. The aim of this book is to convey the nature of these partially intersecting dreams and to investigate at the level of the habitat the intricate encounters, conflicts, and negotiations that took place in and around the strategy of state-centered social welfare in its extreme, or socialist, incarnation. What follows, then, is an inquiry into the minutiae of urban life and how certain ways of thinking and accompanying social practices fit into the grand strategies of Soviet state building during the formative period of the 1930s, when the revolution came to Magnetic Mountain. The emphasis throughout is on experimentation and discovery.

A LOOK AHEAD

Reflecting the approach outlined above, this book has two parts (to orient the reader, both parts are provided with their own brief introductions). Part 1 covers what is conventionally called Soviet industrialization and urbanization but which contemporaries called "the building of socialism." It addresses the grand strategies pursued by the state, placing particular emphasis on the process of implementation, as seen from the perspective of the locality.

Specifically, chapter 1 treats the establishment of the planned economy, endeavoring to recapture some of the surprise, even wonder, that participants felt as they created such an unprecedented form of economic organization. Chapter 2 takes up the massive movement and resettling of population, showing the existence of many sometimes underappreciated patterns within the oft-remarked flux and foreshadowing the main theme of the struggle over daily life treated in part 2. Chapter 3 deals with the attempts to plan and build a recognizably socialist city from scratch, as well as with the resultant urban geography, including the dynamic role played by the urban inhabitants in the city's formation.

Part 2 offers a description and analysis of the new society that was formed as a result of the macro-processes described in part 1, a society that contemporaries called socialism. Chapter 4, which takes up the question of housing under socialism, represents a preliminary effort to treat the largely unexamined problem of domesticity in the Stalin years. Chapter 5 engages the difficult and infrequently tackled questions of social identity and personal belief under socialism, in the context of the defining role attributed to labor. Chapter 6 addresses the formation of a socialist municipal economy, that is, one without private property and legal private trade, treating the commensurate advent of the shadow economy not in economic or moral terms but as a question of social organization and individual initiative. Chapter 7 examines the terror as a process, describing the mechanisms by which the terror was made possible and individuals came to participate in their own destruction. In this closing chapter, I also put forward a revisionist characterization of the Soviet political system as a theocracy, a view that has sometimes been suggested but never systematically laid down.

Part 2 ought to have had a separate chapter on culture under socialism (in the sense of popular entertainment as well as highbrow pursuits), to be placed between chapters 4 and 5. But during the course of my writing, I discovered that there was only enough material for twenty pages. The result, a kind of mini-chapter, was placed inside chapter 4. In the broad sense of socialist culture (meaning values and ideals), however, all of part 2 can be said to be devoted to the problem of the culture of socialism. In this regard, it should be noted that every chapter pays close attention to the categories of thinking employed by contemporaries.

Because a study of Magnitogorsk offers a microcosm of the USSR, it could not be limited to economics, politics, culture, or society but unavoidably encompasses all these dimensions. This circumstance enlarged not only the size of the manuscript but also my burden in confronting the existing literature on the USSR under Stalin. In order not to interrupt the narrative, only the most immediate historiographical controversies impinged upon in each chapter are referred to directly in the text. The bulk of the discussion of historiography is contained in the notes.

Finally, this book is based on primary sources, both published and unpublished, a discussion of which appears in the Note on Sources.

I

BUILDING SOCIALISM

The Grand Strategies of the State

To transform our country from an agrarian one into an industrial one capable with its own powers of producing essential machinery—that is the essence, the basis of our general line.

Stalin, 23 December 1925[1]

Stretching from the Urals to the Pacific Ocean, Russia's steppe frontier through the centuries beckoned the afflicted and the adventurous alike.[2] For some a land of last resort, for others one of promise, the steppe was above all a symbol of the seemingly boundless space of the country and a persistent reminder of the impotence of human beings in the face of the power of nature. But for the Bolsheviks, supreme champions of humankind's ability to bend nature to its will, the steppe was a fortress to be taken. And take it they did.

On the twelfth anniversary of the October revolution, Stalin, speaking for the leadership, served notice to the country and the rest of the world that after more than a decade of recovery (*vosstanovlenie*), the Bolsheviks were going on the offensive. "We are advancing full steam ahead along the path of industrialization—to socialism, leaving behind the age-old 'Russian' backwardness," Stalin declared. "We are becoming a country of metal, an automobilized country, a tractorized country. And when we have put the USSR on an automobile, and the *muzhik* on a tractor, let the esteemed capitalists, who boast of their 'civilization,' try to overtake us. We shall see which countries may then be 'classified' as backward and which as advanced." It was 1929, the "Year of the Great Break"—the year the party leadership turned the entire country into an internal frontier to be mastered through what was called "the building of socialism."[3]

By socialism was meant the party's monopoly on power combined with the headlong expansion of heavy industry—carried out in a determinedly noncapitalist way. Capitalism, notwithstanding its historically "progressive role," was said to have become a "fetter" to further development. Because socialism entailed the replacement of the "chaos" of markets with the assurance of planning, it would supposedly do a more effective job of industrializing Russia than capitalism (and foreign ownership) had or could.[4] In short, socialism was a "higher" or "more advanced" stage of development, and one that promised to vault Russia into the first rank of nations.

By industrializing in a socialist way, moreover, the USSR would not only "catch up" with Europe and the United States but at the same time retain its supposed moral superiority. With the replacement of private property by state ownership, the Bolsheviks claimed to be eliminating the exploitation by the bourgeoisie in favor of the free and creative toil of workers working for themselves, as well as the contradictions that had led to the frequent outbreak of war. Socialism represented nothing less than the full transcendence of capitalism. There was no more potent symbol of this exalted vision than the conquest of the steppe, and no greater device for its realization than planning. Through the magic of planning the Bolsheviks promoted what they thought was a superior archetype for a modern society.[5]

The Soviet blueprint for this new society, "the Five-Year Plan for the Development of the National Economy," may have been a calculated piece of propaganda, but much of its propaganda appeal derived from a corresponding commitment to development, the acclaimed universal goal of civilization, and a grounding in science, the supreme language of modernity. The published three-volume text of the Plan, with its numerous charts and graphs,[6] proclaimed on every page the reliability of scientific planning and the seemingly limitless possibilities afforded by modern technology, when combined with the ultimate science of society, Marxism. Soviet industrialization could be "utopian," in other words, precisely because it was "scientific." This was one reason why the Plan riveted the world's attention; another was the possibility of a shift in the world strategic balance.

Strategic concerns played a crucial role in the decision by the Soviet leadership to commence a wholesale social transformation of a new and putatively superior kind. Socialist revolution had occurred only in the USSR and—what was further contrary to expectations—by the mid-1920s capitalism seemed to have stabilized. Consequently, as Stalin explained to the Fourteenth Party Congress in December 1925, the world had been divided into two camps: the imperialist, led by America and England; and the anti-imperialist, led by the USSR, which was encircled by the other camp. If the socialist motherland was to avoid becoming an "appendage of the capitalist system," or worse, it had no choice except to change itself from an agrarian country that exported agricultural products and imported machines to an industrial one that made the machines needed to make machines. This was the central idea that Stalin articulated in the late 1920s and early 1930s, and to which he gave the appellation "the general line."[7]

Making concrete these considerations, the year 1927 had brought a war scare (as well as internal discussions on the unreadiness of the Red Army to fight such a war with European powers).[8] The threat of imminent war passed, but as Stalin pointed out, even if the capitalist powers had decided not to "intervene" militarily in the USSR, their interests and those of the Soviet state remained inimical. "It would be stupid to think that international capital will leave us in peace," he explained in April 1928. "Classes exist, international capital exists, and it cannot look calmly on the development of a country building socialism." This formulation became the immutable premise guiding Soviet internal developments. Building socialism seemed to be both a grand historical undertaking and a life-or-death necessity.[9]

In such a context, it was more than a little paradoxical that for the initial technology and expertise to jump start the socialist offensive, the Soviet Union had no choice but to rely on the very advanced capitalist countries whose supposed objective hostility made the USSR's position so vulnerable. But the acquisition of the modern technology from the capitalists was promoted as temporary and, moreover, undertaken on terms that assured the country's sovereignty. What was therefore a compulsory arrangement could be interpreted with a certain hopefulness as a clever ploy to have the capitalists' participate in the sowing of their own demise. Still, that capitalist firms showed great eagerness to do business in the land of socialism could not help but arouse enormous distrust within the USSR, given the prevalent understanding of the international situation.[10] Deep-seated suspicions were built into the logic of Soviet industrialization.

THE TECHNIQUE OF TOTAL MOBILIZATION

Socialism was the goal, planning the method. In theory planning embodied the scientific transcendence of the contradictions of capitalism, but in practice it resembled a sustained, albeit improvised, crash mobilization characteristic of an economy at war.[11] Such a mode of operation was conceived in largely defensive terms, to be sure, but what stands out is less the absence of an intention to make or foment war abroad than the adoption of a military model for industrialization at home.

That the Plan took on the tone and style of a military campaign derived in part from the country's centuries-long history as a self-consciously militarized society, but also from the fact that Bolshevik notions of planning were essentially appropriated from Germany's wartime experience. Notwithstanding all that had been written about socialism during the nineteenth century, this brief interlude when the German government, in its eagerness to prosecute the war, had sought to expand state ownership of industry and control over private production constituted the only concrete instance when something thought to approximate socialism had been tried.[12] During the Civil War and again during the Five-Year Plan, Soviet Russia self-consciously followed Germany's lead, but there were crucial differences in how and why the technique of war mobilization was adopted in the two countries.

Whereas the German policy of "war socialism" was based on a vision of class collaboration in the public interest, for the Bolsheviks such an "accommodation" between labor and management (the state) was dictated not by expediency but by the fact that the country had a proletarian state. Furthermore, in the USSR the pact between labor and management involved not reconciliation but "class struggle" against the bourgeoisie—an antagonism that persisted even after the domestic exploiting class was liquidated, for class struggle was also international. If Soviet industrialization was not simply "development" but war, it was not just any kind of war but class war, against real and imputed enemies, requiring every possible method, including organized violence. [13]

No doubt some policy of overhauling industry and the armed forces was required to bolster the country's security in the interwar period. But by no means does this "justify" either the frenzied Stalinist bacchanalia, or even what Moshe Lewin and others regard as the more "moderate" Leninist-Bukharinist alternative, for in any guise Bolshevik conceptions of the options before the country were narrowed considerably by their anticapitalist mission. No international threat could be said to have necessitated the near exclusive reliance on heavy industry, let alone the abolition of private property. [14] Moreover, the sense of urgency evoked by perceived strategic concerns was magnified beyond all measure, becoming the rationale for the breathless tempo adopted in the defiant schemes chosen to meet the strategic challenge. Gripped by insecurity, this was a party in a self-defeating hurry, mesmerized by the elixir of heavy industry. [15]

Of course, an intoxication with the power of heavy industry—especially as manifested in large, automated plants that pumped out mass quantities of standardized goods with semi-skilled workers—was by no means limited to the Soviet Union. Just as Soviet images of the miraculous future based on industrialism borrowed freely from an international vocabulary, so the message of the Five-Year Plan resonated around the world. But in the USSR the obsession with big steel and the dawn of a "machine age" was taken much further. It became not merely a rallying point for a technologically perfected future that inspired several decades of design and social organization but the almost exclusive basis of the country's economy. [16] The dizzying upheaval that was Soviet industrialization was reduced to the proposition: build as many factories as possible, as quickly as possible, all exclusively under state control. That was planning; that was socialism. That was the way to bring modernity to Russia—a new Russia, a country of metal. Mobilization, the essential method of the Bolshevik strategy of forced-pace "modernization," served as a fitting counterpart to militant noncapitalism, the guiding principle.

INTERNAL COLONIZATION: POPULATION AND TERRITORY

The Soviet plan, with its proposals for astronomically large increases in industrial capacity, can be read as both an enraptured paean to industrialism and a terrified acknowledgment of industrial inferiority. At the heart of this industry-envy cum industry-worship stood iron and steel. Iron and steel became the venerated symbols of the Bolsheviks' determination and the distinctive industrial age they were determined to bring to the USSR.[17] For this reason, the most celebrated showcase of the new, superior industrial age being realized in Soviet Russia became the Magnitogorsk Metallurgical Complex.[18]

The building of the Magnitogorsk factory was the epitome of the Bolsheviks' commitment to massive social transformation, their martial style of economic mobilization called planning, their understanding of industrialization as class war, their yearning to overcome Russia's historic "backwardness" and to master the country's expanse, their obsession with outracing time, and, above all, their infatuation with heavy industry.[19] "Near Magnetic Mountain," beamed one Magnitogorsk pamphleteer, "the steppe has been turned into a battlefield, the steppe is retreating. The steppe is already no more."[20] In its place was arising a gigantic steel plant—a plant intended to be the equal of the best of the capitalist world, a plant directed against the capitalist world, a plant erected by and for the working class in the international class struggle. At Magnetic Mountain the Bolsheviks were on the march for metal.

Alongside the steel plant at Magnetic Mountain a new city was to be built that, no less than the factory, was understood as a symbol of the new civilization. But whereas the basic design of the factory seemed obvious enough—one as good as what the capitalists had—the design of the accompanying "socialist" city appeared far less certain, as was evident from the wide-ranging debate toward the end of the 1920s and into the 1930s on the nature of the "socialist city" and the "socialist form of population settlement."[21] Magnitogorsk was to be the quintessential example of the "socialist city of the future," but what was Magnitogorsk to look like?[22]

Several of the Soviet Union's internationally renowned architects submitted proposals for the future city, but the Bolshevik leadership looked on the proposals of the eminent architects with incomprehension and dismay.[23] For the leadership, that is, the patrons, the issue of the socialist city was only partly one of form or layout. True, the Bolsheviks no less than the German National Socialists, the Italian fascists, or the New Deal Americans expected architecture to play an important role in glorifying their regime. But more fundamentally, the Bolshevik leadership felt that the design of the socialist city needed to address the question of how to realize a specifically Soviet way of life: a new economy, society, politics—in short, a new culture, broadly conceived.

Whatever form it eventually took, Magnitogorsk would house an urban population, but it would not do so "passively." Just as the physical environment could be remade, it was thought that the social and political milieu of the city could remake people.[24] The socialist city, therefore, was not simply a place where an urban population was located, but a device for inculcating a new set of attitudes as well as new kinds of behavior in its urbanized inhabitants—in a word, an instrument for creating socialist people. As one propagandist proclaimed, Magnitogorsk "is a future center of the Sovietization of the southern Urals, Sovietization not formally or administratively, but deep inculcation of the new socialist way of life."[25]

In this sense, building socialism entailed not merely an accumulation of "wealth" but also of people. As the Magnitogorsk newspaper explained in a discussion of the 1937 census, "the socialist state considers people its most valuable asset."[26] To be sure, the 1937 census was annulled, apparently because it enumerated an insufficiently large total population, but a new one was taken in 1939, with the same goals: to measure the population and thereby establish bureaucratic influence over what the state considered to be a vital phenomenon. In the words of the Magnitogorsk newspaper, "the population is a matter of the utmost political importance" and "the all-union population census, a matter of huge significance for the state."[27] And censuses were only the most conspicuous instances of a policy directed at reconstituting the demographic makeup of the country, person by person.[28]

In addition to their roles as instruments of demographic transformation, industrial cities such as Magnitogorsk served as the leading edge in an ambitious strategy of mastering territory.[29] The most striking feature of Russia's geographical position had always been its "continentality." Rather than follow the tsarist pattern of risking all for outlets to the sea, the Soviet Union tried to adapt itself to this continentality, seeking economic self-sufficiency through the development of formidable industrial complexes in the interior.[30] Geographically speaking twentieth-century Russia "found itself," much like another large continental power, the United States, had done in the nineteenth century.[31] In contrast to the relative youth of the U.S. transcontinental drive, however, the Bolshevik-led industrialization in the form of an internal colonization followed a centuries-long process.[32] Nonetheless, as one contemporary Soviet geographer enthused, "the transformation of old Russia into the USSR" was viewed as tantamount to "the discovery of a new continent."[33]

In sum, city building played a crucial role in the geopolitical processes of internal territorial colonization, demographic transformation, and the expansion of industrial and military capacity. But the city served also as a strategic device in the micropolitical processes of creating new urban inhabitants. It was, after all, those new urban inhabitants who would operate those machines, produce that steel, administer those factories, in short populate the cities. This circumstance was well understood by contemporaries, who were engaged in minute but nonetheless momentous struggles in neighborhoods and homes over how to define and organize urban life and who would make such determinations. These confrontations, which arose out of resolute efforts to create a new civilization called socialism, formed part of what might be called "the little tactics of the habitat." Although more properly the subject of part 2, they will of necessity crop up in part 1.

1 On the March for Metal

Metal is not produced simply for its own usage. . . . Metal draws all
industry along with it, all spheres of human life, beginning with the
production of turbines, tractors, harvester combines, textiles, food,
and ending with books. Metal is the basis of modern civilization.

Magnitogorsk pamphleteer[1]

Following a resolution calling for industrialization issued by the Fourteenth Party Congress in December 1925, work on the design of the Magnitogorsk Works commenced with the formation in February 1926 of the
State Institute for the Design of Metallurgical Factories (Gipromez). Gipromez managed to assemble a large staff, yet it had trouble finding qualified technical personnel, in part because some of the country's engineers
had emigrated during the October revolution and Civil War. Those engineers who had not fled, however, were overmatched by the challenges of
modern industrialization. "Although practically all known experts in contemporary technology were in Gipromez," the official history of the organization noted, "neither in Gipromez nor in any other design or research
bureau of the USSR was it possible to find experienced specialists for a
whole range of new technical production processes."[2] To fill this vital gap,
a new generation of "red" engineers was to be trained—somehow.

In the meantime, on 19 May 1927 the Supreme Council of the National
Economy (Vesenkha) engaged the services of the accomplished Chicago engineering firm, Henry Freyn and Co. By 1928, a group of Freyn engineers
had taken up residence at Gipromez headquarters in Leningrad, turning
the Soviet agency into an overseas branch of the American firm.[3] The arrival of the Americans, who were given the task of reconstructing the Soviet Union's strategic steel industry, was later recalled by the leading Soviet
specialist on metallurgy as a watershed.[4] As for the American view, in the
enthusiastic words of the company's president, Freyn's assignment was
"extraordinarily interesting" and "entailed great responsibility."[5]

Magnitogorsk loomed as a major test of Freyn's abilities, but before the
American company had been brought in, Gipromez demonstrated its own
initiative by opening a number of "branch" offices, including one in the

Urals.[6] Vitalii Gasselblat, chief engineer of the Urals branch and a graduate of the Petersburg Mining Academy, together with a small team of "bourgeois specialists" wasted no time in suggesting a site for the proposed Magnitogorsk factory, alongside the famous iron-ore outcrop.[7] In 1926, construction even began on the rail line connecting Magnetic Mountain with the rest of the Union through the junction of Kartaly, 145 kilometers to the east. The crudeness of the preliminary drawings for the steel plant, however, demonstrated that the problem of design was not so easily solved.[8]

Even as the Urals branch of Gipromez struggled with the formidable problem of designing the Magnitogorsk Works, yet another kind of struggle was underway throughout 1927 inside the State Planning Commission (Gosplan) over the determination of priorities in the pending Five-Year Plan. A group of Ukrainian economists centered in Gosplan's Ukrainian branch argued that whereas the high quality of the ore, its location at or near the surface, and the proximity of various other important deposits necessary for steelmaking (such as limestone and fire-brick clay) made Magnetic Mountain a particularly attractive site for a steel plant, the lack of coking coal—the key energy source for the metallurgical process—raised doubts about the suitability of the location. Pointing especially to the anticipated high cost of transporting coal long distances to the Urals, the Ukrainian economists called for abandoning the new plant in the Urals in favor of greater investment in the Ukraine.[9]

At a joint meeting of the Gosplan and Vesenkha Presidiums on 16 June 1927, Valerii Mezhlauk, Vesenkha's chairman and a candidate member of the party's Central Committee, made it clear that cost was not the most important consideration. Just as crucial were strategic concerns: the location of the Magnitogorsk Works would make the plant impregnable to attack and serve as a base for developing the eastern regions of the country and spreading industry more evenly throughout the Union. No less important was the considerable propaganda value to be derived from building a colossal industrial plant in the middle of the empty steppe.[10] Indeed, the Magnitogorsk project's principal weakness—the need to import coking coal almost two thousand kilometers from the Kuznetsk basin of western Siberia—was soon repackaged as the mainstay of a gigantic development scheme encompassing all industry in the Urals and Siberia and billed as the Ural-Kuznetsk Combine.[11] By uniting a coal-producing area with an iron-ore one and thus creating a "second metallurgical base" (on the model of the Ukraine's Donetsk basin), this scheme promised to transform the liability of territorial expanse into an apparent economic asset.[12]

Initially, however, these grandiose visions were not matched by com-

parable actions: the Magnitogorsk project, to say nothing of some transcontinental program, quickly became bogged down. Although the bureaucratic tug-of-war over regional investment contributed to the delay, the
problem was really the inability of the Urals branch staff to design a modern iron and steel plant. After only forty kilometers of track were put in
place, work on the rail link to the site ceased. For the rest of 1926 and all
of 1927, nothing at all happened at the site. It was at this point that the
small group of Freyn employees arrived in Leningrad with a mandate to
overhaul the USSR's entire ferrous metallurgy sector.

After Freyn's arrival, the Urals branch, now renamed Magnitostroi, did
not cease activities. In February 1928, fully two years after being given the
assignment, the Urals specialists finally submitted a "project" that called
for construction of Magnitogorsk to begin later that year.[13] This design
came in for immediate and severe criticism by the Leningrad office, and
even the project's authors had to concede that it had a number of "weak
points."[14] Throughout 1928 the Urals project was purportedly being "reworked" by the foreign experts in Leningrad, but as the year drew to a
close, no revised proposal materialized. In the words of one Soviet historian of Magnitogorsk, "1928 was a lost year."[15]

Some sense of the unreality of the situation can be gleaned from the fact
that although there was little sense of how to design such a steel plant, a
conference was convened on the time frame for completion of the factory's
construction. The debate proceeded over two alternatives, five years or
seven years. Gasselblat felt that building the factory within five years
would constitute a miracle, but an official informed him that three and a
half years was "all the party could afford." This pronouncement was followed by a temporary suspension of discussion. When discussion resumed,
the options had been reduced to either six years or three. In arguing for the
six-year time frame, one participant in the debate, Professor Pavlov, reasoned that "even if we were Americans, we could not build the factory in
four years." On this ambiguous note the discussion of "tempos" ended as
it had begun: still without a viable design almost three years after Gipromez had been formed.[16]

The fourth year of the Magnitogorsk project, 1929, seemed to mark a
turning point, for the Leningrad office finally published its own project for
the steel plant.[17] More than seven hundred pages, the weighty volume contained an impressive apparatus of charts, graphs, and tables. Yet like the
text of its Urals branch office, this volume appears to have been published
less as a guide to building the plant than as reassurance against the mounting doubts that a plant would in fact be built.[18] The publication was, in any

case, a long way from the thousands of blueprints necessary to guide actual construction.[19]

Whatever the technical insufficiencies of the Leningrad project, it instantly became obsolete when developments outside Gipromez radically changed the scope of the industrialization effort. Just months after the optimistic Five-Year Plan was belatedly adopted at the Sixteenth Party Conference in April 1929, even its "optimal" variant proved to be too modest for the country's impatient political leadership. In 1930, the annual "target" for pig iron, which had been set at an ambitious 10 million tons in the Five-Year Plan, was raised to 15 to 17 million tons. This jump required drastic revisions in pending steel plant designs, including the industry's future flagship, Magnitogorsk.[20]

This was not the first time the proposed capacity for the Magnitogorsk Works had undergone upward adjustment. The original 1928 project for the plant envisioned an annual capacity of 656,000 tons (40 million poods) of pig iron. By the summer of 1929 the capacity was raised on paper to 850,000 tons. Almost immediately, it was raised again, to 1.1 million tons; and then again, to 1.6 million—a result in part of fierce lobbying by the Urals oblast authorities in the scramble for investment. When the new national plan targets for steel were disclosed in early 1930, Magnitogorsk's capacity was raised once more, this time to 2.5 million tons.[21]

Over the course of one year, in other words, the capacity of the future factory quadrupled, making a mockery of the project published in 1929 by Leningrad Gipromez, to say nothing of the lesser efforts by the Urals branch (or of the now obsolete text of the Five-Year Plan).[22] The most recent conception of the Magnitogorsk plant's design, moreover, called for the largest possible capacity and also, as Bolshevik leaders were fond of saying, "the latest word in technology." In the thinking of the time, the two—size and sophistication—went hand in hand. The desire to have such a plant, however, was not easily converted into the capacity to erect one. To build a Magnitogorsk, it appeared that something extraordinary needed to be done.

■   ■   ■

The story of the metamorphosis of the December 1925 summons to begin industrialization into the launching by 1930 of a delirious superindustrial drive—a tale of political struggle at the top of the party over competing policies in which Stalin won out—remains a matter of dispute.[23] Access to Kremlin and KGB archives may well provoke some genuine rethinking on how policy-making was conducted within the inner circle, including the relative influence of various individuals and the extent and nature of behind-the-scenes maneuvering. What is not going to change, however, is the basic picture of a very small group deliberating momentous decisions about complicated questions with very little public input, no public scrutiny, an array of scapegoats at the ready, and a revolutionary rhetoric and élan that closed off certain options while continually making possible great leaps of faith despite a multitude of dubious episodes. The aim of this chapter is not to reanalyze the decisions rendered in Moscow, however, but to examine their long-term reverberations.

When the Fourteenth Party Congress issued the resolution on industrialization in late 1925, neither the country's administrative apparat nor its technical experts—to say nothing of the psychology of the general population—were prepared or even aware of what was involved. Even as late as 1929, when the Plan was formally adopted and the country stood on the threshold of an explosion of planning and management agencies paralleling the vertiginous expansion of industrial capacity, there was scarcely more comprehension of the undertaking.[24] Industrializing on a massive scale at breakneck speed was one means of sending a powerful signal that the situation was serious and that whoever was not prepared better somehow become so posthaste. It was almost as if the country's apparent unreadiness to carry out a precipitous industrial transformation propelled the political leadership to become more, rather than less, ambitious in forcing the country to do so. The consequences of pursuing this desire for a revolutionary break (*perelom*) were far-reaching.

"Gigantism, immoderation, refusal of realism, *la démesure* as policy"—the rupture purposefully instigated in 1929–30 resulted, as Moshe Lewin has argued, in a state of profound disequilibrium, a circumstance that strongly colored the emerging authoritarian apparatus, which struggled with limited success to manage the flux it itself had created.[25] But struggle the state economic apparatus did, pursuing a seemingly endless search for workable administrative structures through endless decrees and multiple splits, mergers, and reorganizations of the massive bureaucracy. At the same time, party leaders fought an equally monumental battle to assert control over the operation of the gigantic industrial-administrative complex.[26]

By the middle of the 1930s, what has come to be known as the "planned economy" was taking shape—a form of economic organization that resembled the allocation and mobilization processes of the military, characterized by hypercentralization, extreme rigidity, and colossal waste and inefficiency, but also by the knowing violation or circumvention of rules and procedures in the interest of "getting the job done."[27] This outcome was less an orderly implementation of a preordained program than an effect of the plunge into breakneck anticapitalist industrialization and of the exigencies that followed. Planning, as R. W. Davies has emphasized, was a world to be discovered.[28]

The paradoxical character and consequences of the USSR's vast, noncapitalist industrial improvisation were nowhere more evident than in the construction of the Magnitogorsk Metallurgical Complex, the incarnation of the hoped-for revolutionary breakthrough in industry.[29] From the regime's manic obsession with speed and craving for legitimacy to the often self-defeating operation of the ponderous bureaucratic apparatus and the ineradicable inefficiencies of a nonmarket economy, Magnitogorsk encapsulated the novelty of socialist industrialization.

CATCH AND OVERTAKE

In the early twentieth century rapid advances in steelmaking technology had been made and incorporated in what was then the largest integrated iron and steel plant in the world: the U.S. Steel plant in Gary, Indiana, the construction of which had begun in 1906, according to a design by Freyn.[30] Alluding to the Magnitogorsk plant, Grigorii "Sergo" Ordzhonikidze, politburo member and people's commissar for heavy industry, indicated that no sooner had Stalin found out about the Gary Works than he ordered that just such a factory be built in the Soviet Union.[31] Notwithstanding the tendency in the 1930s to attribute all acceptable ideas to Stalin, it is plausible that Stalin promoted the idea of a Soviet Gary: if the capitalists had such a steel plant, surely the workers and peasants should have one too. In any case, the Soviet leadership was acutely aware of capitalist experience and measured Soviet industry against it.[32]

"Catch and overtake" (*dognat i peregnat*), that was the party's slogan, that was the way to handle the capitalists. "But," Ordzhonikidze conceded, "we are . . . a peasant country, a country of the wooden plough. You'll never catch the capitalists that way. They have tractors and caterpillars, millions of cars, and world-class technology. How in the world could we catch them from such a position?" Although he did not say, there was a way: if the capitalists would sell the Soviet Union their technology and help to install it.[33] Despite deep mutual suspicions between the governments, such business-based cooperation seemed entirely possible.

After the 1929 American stock market crash was followed by a world economic bust, the prospects for expanding domestic industrial capacity, in steel or any other industry, vanished. But even had there been no Great Depression, the USSR's ambitious plans to remake itself industrially would no doubt have attracted solicitations from foreign firms. The Soviet Union was, as any capitalist could have pointed out, a huge new market waiting to be captured. Freyn, for one, had managed to translate this potential into a hefty contract in the strategic ferrous metallurgy sector.

For reasons that remain unclear, however, it was decided that Freyn was not to design Magnitogorsk.[34] In 1929, the Soviet government instead advertised a Magnitogorsk "concession," a form of cooperation that promised part ownership. One of the early responses came from the German firm Siemens-Bauunion, which had built the Berlin metro, along with various power stations, and had worked on Dneprostroi. "[Siemens] had no experience in steelmaking factories," wrote one Soviet official familiar with the negotiations, "but they boldly offered their services."[35] By contrast, the other principal foreign bidder, Arthur McKee and Co. of Cleveland, Ohio, was famous for the most advanced and largest blast furnace design to be found in the pages of the leading "capitalist" technical journals. In the competition, McKee had the obvious edge, and on 14 March 1930, after several months of negotiations, representatives of the Soviet government ceremoniously signed a "technical assistance" contract with the American firm at a meeting in New York City.[36]

Specialists in the construction of blast furnaces and oil refineries, McKee undertook to design the entire steel plant, including all auxiliary shops and the iron-ore mine. The firm was also responsible for directing work on the site until the factory and mine were put into operation, for consulting on equipment orders, for building an electric power station and a dam, and for training Soviet engineers both at the site and in the United States.[37] The Soviet government agreed to pay McKee 2.5 million gold rubles, of which 40 percent were to be delivered the first year, 30 percent the second, 15 percent the third, and the final 15 percent after the factory was put into operation. Responsibility for the wages of the McKee staff at the site, who were to be paid partly in rubles and partly in convertible currency, fell to the Soviet side.[38]

The agreement further specified, according to William Haven, then a company vice president, that McKee was to design everything to be as large as possible, allow for future expansion, economize on the use of materials and on fuel, avoid unnecessary complications or specifications for unusual equipment, keep in mind the availability of construction materials in the USSR, follow Soviet standards and norms, and prepare all designs in both

English and Russian, using the metric system. It was a tall order. To top it off, after four *years* of having accomplished virtually nothing on their own, the Soviet authorities gave McKee two *months* to submit complete designs for the largest and most advanced iron and steel plant outside the United States. Such were the imperatives of the policy of catch and over-take.[39]

To the Soviet authorities, even two months must have seemed like a long time to wait, for without plans or a design, the Council of People's Commissars (Sovnarkom) and the Council of Labor and Defense (STO)—the two highest government agencies—had already given the go-ahead for preliminary work at the construction site to begin more than a year before, on 17 January 1929.[40] Acting on this directive from above, the Urals oblast party committee (*obkom*) had dispatched an urgent telegram to the lower-level Troitsk *okrug* party committee (into whose jurisdiction Magnetic Mountain fell), instructing it to send a commission in February to prepare the remote site for the upcoming spring construction season.[41] "The time for talk had passed," one Soviet commentator explained. "The country needed metal."[42]

In May 1929, work began on a local brick factory and on the foundations for the various shops of the as yet undesigned steel plant. Strings were stretched across the thawing earth where the shops were supposed to rise, and the ground was cleared for foundation work to start. Construction of the rail connection from Kartaly was renewed and, with the help of the Red Army, the final stretch of a hundred kilometers was finished by late June. More had been accomplished in a few months than in the previous several years.[43]

But serious problems soon surfaced, on-site leadership being among the first to arise. The initial director of Magnitostroi, Sergei Zelentsov, had gone blind and had to be replaced. His successors, E. I. Martynov and Gri-gorii Bessonov, turned out to be technically incompetent and were also re-moved. Their successor, Vadim Smolianinov (who had worked in Sovnar-kom with Lenin), was sent to the United States as part of the Soviet delegation in Cleveland and was replaced by his deputy, Chingiz Ildrym, a Kurd who took part in the storming of the Winter Palace and had been the first commissar of the Navy in Azerbaijan, but who knew absolutely nothing about metallurgy. Yet another new director, Iakov Shmidt, was dispatched to the site in June 1930, but after a few months he too was sent to Cleveland. And so the Caucasus revolutionary Ildrym served as de facto on-site chief.[44]

Ildrym had his hands full. In early 1930 a scandal broke out over the lack of any progress at the brick factory, and several people were arrested for sabotage. Almost the entire site was beset by fires and other manmade catastrophes. The continental summer heat and the fierce steppe winds (with their dust storms) proved too much for many of the first workers and officials, a large number of whom simply fled.[45] There were, in any case, no blueprints to guide the work of those who remained.[46] Nineteen thirty was threatening to become another "lost year," the fifth in a row.[47]

A deal for technical assistance had been struck with the highly touted Americans, however, and the first group of McKee personnel dispatched to the USSR left the United States in May 1930, arriving in Moscow several weeks later. Bemused by the Soviet insistence on the breathless time frames for a completed design of so complex an undertaking, the Americans were then treated to a week-long train ride from Moscow to the site.[48] Just the last 145 kilometers from Kartaly took almost a full day, as the track had been put down without ballast and, after repeated accidents, a speed limit of ten kilometers per hour had been imposed. "From Kartaly to Magnitogorsk," one passenger recalled, "we played soccer along the tracks, then we ran to catch up with the train, which had gone only a little way."[49]

Finally, the American team arrived at the site in early summer, only to disembark in the virtually empty steppe and discover, in the words of one Soviet eyewitness, that "there was not a single well-built settlement [and] no roads." Indeed, there was little of anything, including food or potable water.[50] As for the status of the future factory, a Russian engineer recalled that the Americans "couldn't fathom how it was going to be possible to work without skilled workers, without complete sets of tools, without machines or construction materials."[51]

This state of affairs was exacerbated by the primitiveness of the rail connections, upon which the improbably isolated site was wholly dependent. The first freight shipments from Moscow were said to have taken seventy days to arrive.[52] There were moderately successful efforts to speed up the movement of sorely needed supplies and equipment en route. But the weak capacity of the trunk line connecting Magnitogorsk with the rest of the country continued to choke the site for years (all freight was, of course, unloaded by hand).[53] In any case, no improvement in transport, however dramatic, could overcome the woeful state of scarcity.[54]

Inadequate transport and chronic shortages of vital materials compounded an already difficult construction task, but even more disorganizing was the Soviet approach to management. Much time and energy were spent on long-winded speeches to the effect that "only we Bolsheviks could undertake such tasks," although the many bold-sounding directives were often no more than desperate reactions to unexpected turns of events and had little chance of being carried out. There was, in addition, considerable intrigue, including the spreading of (false) rumors that the iron-ore deposits, contrary to initial reports, were not substantial enough to justify the plant's construction.[55]

The chaotic results of such activities were predictable. Far from being able to "lead" operations, the leadership at Magnitogorsk had its hands full just responding to each new crisis. Iakov Shmidt described the state of continual tensions with which he and the rest of the local leadership and work force had to contend:

> As soon as the phone rang, you knew it was a breakdown somewhere. The switchboard operator notified me immediately of all emergencies. Simultaneously, on the site, in the event of a fire, warning signals on all train engines were sounded, along with the siren on the electrical station. This unusual "symphony" made disturbing impressions on all those living in Magnitka.[56]

All the while, the number of administrative personnel mushroomed.[57]

If the state of "permanent crisis" induced by the difficult circumstances was compounded by intrigue and bluster, a confused organizational structure did not help matters. Magnitostroi was at first subordinated to a new agency, Novostal, whose name was soon changed to Vostokostal, but the coke plant came under a separate administration, first called Soiuzkoks, then Vostokokoks. Many of the smaller organizations operating on the site were subordinated to still other central trusts. The mine, furthermore, was a separate entity, and all railroad transportation came under its own administration. Not surprisingly, this multiplicity of responsible organizations led to a vacuum of responsibility.[58]

To streamline operations, the many trusts on the site were organized on the American model into subcontractors with which the parent company, Magnitostroi, contracted to perform various tasks. This arrangement, however, was undermined by Magnitostroi's lack of experience with subcontracting and by the subcontractors' inexperience in constructing steel plants. To take one example, one of the largest trusts assigned to build the steel plant in Magnitogorsk was Tekstilstroi, a firm that specialized in building textile mills; upon reassignment to Magnitogorsk, it was simply renamed Stalstroi.[59] "The fundamental thing that sharply struck us," wrote the chief of open-hearth construction, "was that among those who were at the site, there was no clue as to what a steel plant was."[60] Of course, this was precisely the goal: in building a steel plant, everyone would learn—

and quickly. But it would be a while before a workable management system was in place.[61]

At the time, a steel plant with a working capacity of 2.5 million tons of pig iron (expandable to 4 million) constituted a formidable industrial venture, even for experienced foreign engineering firms. Upon completion, the Magnitogorsk Metallurgical Complex was supposed to be able to produce almost as much steel as the entire Russian empire had done in 1913 (and as the Soviet Union did in 1927–28).[62] Moreover, Magnitogorsk was to be distinguished not only by its huge scale but by its integrated design, which was to be as automated as possible and based on the linear flow from raw materials to finished products in which even by-products were to be fully utilized. This had been the key to the design of the Gary Works.[63]

Magnitogorsk was also to contain an army of auxiliary enterprises, as well as its own power station, and to be serviced by its own maintenance and repair shops, many of which were to be as large as whole factories. "On account of the isolated location of the plant and mines of Magnitogorsk, repair shops of unusually large capacity and completeness as to equipment have been provided," wrote Haven, who added that "it is safe to say that no other steel plant in the world will be more self-contained with regard to making repairs and replacements."[64] Magnitogorsk was not simply a steel plant but a huge mining-energy-chemical-metallurgical complex, and one in which housing and schools, no less than the production of rails and girders, were the responsibility of the plant's administration.[65]

The unusual audacity of the venture did not fail to make its impression on the Americans.[66] But under pressure to produce a basic design for the mammoth steel plant within a mere thirty days and still scrambling to assemble a staff, McKee managed only a highly schematic "report," accompanied by a similar document for the mine prepared by the firm of Ogleby Norton, with which McKee had contracted. Soviet officials claimed to be upset by what they regarded as the flimsiness of the McKee report and, above all, surprised that McKee had had a different firm prepare the proposal for the mine.[67]

McKee's next suggestion, that the highly respected firm of Koppers and Co. handle the coke plant, was taken as yet another sign that McKee was not able by itself to handle the design of the whole factory. For McKee this was obvious enough, but the American company's intention to subcontract the work it could not itself complete was rejected by its increasingly sophisticated customer, which began to approach the proposed foreign subcontractors directly—a decision fraught with commercial significance for McKee.[68] A trip to the USSR by Arthur McKee to reassert the firm's hold over the entire undertaking had the opposite effect. On 24 December 1930 a revision of the contract was drawn up circumscribing the firm's responsibilities (and hence its compensation),[69] ostensibly because the firm had chronically failed to meet the impractical deadlines specified in the contract for the delivery of drawings.[70]

Despite a strong mutual interest, the partnership from the start was marred by suspicion and misunderstandings, which only worsened as time wore on.[71] From the American point of view, the Soviets were constantly making a difficult situation more so. The chief means for Soviet engineers to demonstrate their capabilities and political allegiance, for example, was to criticize American designs and alter them, with utter disregard for the often catastrophic consequences. Another problem was that installations and materials sent to Magnitostroi by Soviet factories were often received in disrepair or were not at all what had been ordered.[72] Even equipment purchased abroad did not always correspond to specifications.[73] Under such conditions the Americans were charged with supervising the construction of a huge dam and power station, state-of-the-art coke batteries, and unprecedentedly large and complicated blast furnaces, two of which were supposed to be put into operation within fifteen months, by 1 October 1931.[74]

If the Americans seemed to have had grounds for their reservations, Soviet personnel also had reasons to worry. Evidently, the original McKee personnel sent to the site turned out to be less than stellar.[75] And when the Americans found themselves de facto, fully empowered chiefs on the site and soon insisted—in an obvious effort to reduce their formal responsibility for a feared fiasco—that they were only consultants, Soviet officials took this as a sign of cowardice and ill will. In addition, the Americans objected principally and repeatedly to one of the main Soviet goals: the speediest possible tempo. The Americans always cited technical justifications, but for the Soviets, it was almost as if the Americans were trying to hold the USSR back, afraid of allowing a socialist country to advance too far too rapidly.[76]

Pressure to hurry came from Moscow and was strongly felt at the site itself. On 1 July 1930, the first brick of the blast furnace foundation was laid in front of an estimated fourteen thousand people, including the McKee group. To shouts of "hurrah" and the singing of the "Internationale," Iakov Shmidt gave what two eyewitnesses deemed an inspired speech, "pointing out that, in the event of an enemy attack on the USSR, the foreign bourgeoisie could not shell the factory." Such a precipitous action may have seemed reckless, but local officials no doubt hoped that by laying the foundation stone they could force the issue of the long-awaited design.[77]

Despite this rousing send-off complete with a nose-thumbing of the "bourgeoisie" in its very presence (represented by McKee personnel), the construction of the Magnitogorsk furnaces begin inauspiciously. According to Konstantin Valerius, then deputy chief of Magnitostroi, the coordinates for the location of the blast furnaces had been received by telegram from the Soviet delegation visiting McKee headquarters in Cleveland. It was on this basis that the foundation stone had been laid. But when the Americans finally arrived with the blueprints, it was discovered that the telegrammed coordinates were off by thirteen meters.[78] What is more, McKee had turned the factory ninety degrees, so that the blast furnace shop was perpendicular to the river, and had enlarged the factory area by 3.6 square kilometers, in accordance with the Soviet insistence on allowing for future expansion. It became necessary to undo most of the preliminary work.[79]

More problems followed, coming to the attention in January 1931 of the Central Committee, which replaced Shmidt with Iakov Gugel.[80] A decorated Civil War veteran, Gugel set about making sure that everything would be ready by the party's 1 October 1931 deadline, putting his revered "mobilization" skills to work, with some effect. Midway through the year, the ore-crushing equipment had been installed and iron ore was being mined, a dam was more or less finished, and the electric station and first coke batteries were put into operation. But the priority job remained the blast furnaces—symbol of the whole project—and in late August 1931 a forty-day "storm" to complete them began.[81]

Under Gugel's direction the full panoply of Bolshevik organizers campaigned furiously to "mobilize" the work force for the task. As one participant recalled a few years later,

> At that time the slogan was: "Blast Furnace By the Deadline!" You would see this slogan literally everywhere. . . . You'd go to the toilet, to take care of your natural needs, and even there you'd see it: "The Blast Furnace By the Deadline!" . . . The only thing they didn't do was to write it in the heavens.[82]

Virtually every worker on the site was "thrown over" to blast furnace construction, and many people never left the structure day or night.[83] But despite the Herculean efforts, the blast furnace was not ready by 1 October. Nor was it ready by the 7 November holiday.[84]

Rumors circulated in Moscow that the entire construction was a hopeless mess and that nothing at all might come of it, yet work proceeded at fever pitch through the winter.[85] With the Seventeenth Party Conference scheduled for February 1932, the leaders of the construction had a new deadline to aim for. That would mean, of course, that the furnace would be started up under the extremely difficult conditions of the Urals winter, a decision the Americans vigorously protested. But Magnitostroi officials appealed directly to Ordzhonikidze, and although, in general, Moscow backed the foreign specialists in disputes with local authorities, deadlines were another matter. Ordzhonikidze telegrammed permission.[86] Furious about the winter start-up (and Soviet tardiness in its payments), McKee sent a cable to Haven forbidding him to provide any more assistance and ordering everyone to return home immediately. But the cable was read by the Soviet authorities, who urged Haven at least to see the first furnace into operation. Having so much at stake in the work thus far, Haven agreed.[87] As the day for the start-up of the blast furnace neared, a feeling of being involved in world-historical events pervaded the site at Magnetic Mountain.

By late January the temperature had dropped to − 30°C, but the frozen air was buzzing with excitement and suspense as the final preparations for the start-up were being made. On 29 January, blast furnace no. 1 began to blow, but immediately, problems with the water supply necessitated a shutdown. For forty hours the workers frantically tried to correct the problem. "Everybody felt like he was at the front," recalled Iakov Gugel. On 31 January 1932 at 10 A.M. the workers again tried to blow in the furnace. This time it worked. "At Magnitostroi, to which the attention of the whole country, of the whole world, was riveted," Gugel wrote, "life was given to blast furnace No. 1."[88]

On the next day, the first pig iron was produced. Jubilant people gathered pieces as souvenirs; busts of Lenin and Stalin were made from it. Telegrams went off to Communist parties around the world and to the Seventeenth Party Conference.[89] In the name of the Soviet state, Mikhail Kalinin read the triumphant message to the assembled delegates: "On 1 February [1932] at 9:30 P.M. the first pig iron of Magnitogorsk blast furnace No. 1 was produced. The furnace is functioning normally." The delegates rose to their feet and erupted into an ovation.[90]

No more than a month after this triumph, in March 1932, exactly two years after it had been signed, the contract between McKee and the Soviet government was officially "annulled" in what appears to have been a belated recognition of a fait accompli.[91] Before departing the USSR, William Haven graciously offered his congratulations. "Considering the inexperience of the Russians in construction work of this type," he told an American correspondent sympathetic to the Soviet cause, "the magnitude of the work accomplished at Magnitogorsk is astonishing, if the isolated location and the extreme climatic conditions are kept in mind."[92] In truth, the construction was years behind schedule, but this hardly seemed to matter.

What did matter was that the construction was happening at all. After several years of innumerable delays and difficulties, the "battle" seemed to have been "won": Magnitogorsk pig iron existed. All the foolhardy deadlines, all the pain and suffering now seemed fully justified. On a visit to the site back in May 1931, Valerii Mezhlauk had told an assembly of the Magnitogorsk faithful that the construction carried

> enormous political and economic significance. Political because the construction of the Magnitogorsk factory has become a standard by which the capitalist world, on the one hand, and the workers located abroad, on the other, evaluate the success of socialist construction in our country. Economic because the country is suffocating from the lack of metal.

It was this attitude that undergirded the authentic sense of triumph on 1 February 1932.[93]

On the very day of triumph, however, disaster struck. No sooner had the telegrams gone off to Moscow than an accident occurred, requiring that the Magnitogorsk blast furnace be shut down. And no sooner had that problem been corrected than an even more serious one occurred: a chunk of the upper conal construction collapsed, injuring several workers. The cave-in, which took more than 60 hours to fix, was followed by a 12-hour shutdown on 21 February and another one of 115 hours that began on 3 March. Altogether, there were no fewer than 550 stoppages of the furnace in the first year alone. (In November 1933, after only twenty-one months of operation, Magnitogorsk blast furnace no. 1 would be shut down and completely rebuilt.)[94]

The sad results were foreseeable: when the furnace was blown in, not only had many makeshift hookups been used, but many key components were still not installed.[95] Yet, celebrating as the first pig iron was produced, the Magnitogorsk leadership smugly chided the Americans for suggesting that longer time frames and American operating personnel were necessary for success and for opposing the winter start-up. "Mister Haven was unquestionably a capable and knowledgeable specialist," Iakov Gugel wrote. "But he did not understand why it was necessary to hurry. He did not understand why it was necessary to put the blast furnace into operation in winter, when it would have been so much easier to do it in summer." True enough.[96]

Notwithstanding the many self-inflicted setbacks, however, construction of Magnitogorsk pressed forward in 1932. On 7 June, blast furnace no. 2 was blown in, and before the year was over, a second coke battery and the ore-crushing plant were completed. Although by this time the entire complex was supposed to have been finished, these were definite achievements. Moreover, their import was greatly magnified by the capitalist depression. In the United States, the world's symbol of industrial prowess, the production of raw steel had fallen from more than 60 million tons in 1929 to around 15 million in 1932. Steel production in the U.S. would not climb above its 1929 level until 1940.[97]

The social consequences of the decline in American steel output were far-reaching. As of 1931, the famed Gary Works was operating at less than 20 percent of capacity. Unemployment in the "city of the century" was sky-high. Housing foreclosures on the properties of the city's small middle class became epidemic, and financial panic set in. After more than a dozen banks in Gary folded, one prominent banker committed suicide, precipitating a further bank run. To top it off, the belated efforts to confront this litany of deep social and economic problems—what would be known as the New Deal—met with suspicion and visceral opposition. William Wirt, a pupil and disciple of John Dewey and a man who had become the acclaimed architect of the renowned Gary public school system, wrote a pamphlet in which he asserted that Communists had infiltrated the U.S. government and were busy making President Roosevelt into a Kerensky.[98]

With much of the capitalist world's industrial capacity idle and its societies torn by social dislocation, the Soviet government declared the "early fulfillment" of the goals of the Five-Year Plan toward the close of 1932. Not only had the Bolsheviks built factories while the capitalist world was mired in depression; not only had the Bolsheviks developed industry at a rate unseen ever before in world history, they had even bested themselves and completed the brazen Five-Year Plan in four years and three months: "Five in Four"—this was the banner of socialist construction, the magic of "Bolshevik tempo." It was a seductive message and one that the construction of Magnitogorsk seemed to confirm.[99]

Even as celebrations of the fulfillment of the Plan were underway,[100] another large-scale disaster occurred at the Magnitogorsk blast furnaces. On 28 December 1932, the city was hit by a severe blizzard. So strong were the winds and so heavy the snowfall that several installations, including parts of the blast furnaces, collapsed. At first the workers tried to patch the furnaces, but soon they had to shut them down. It took two months before both furnaces were back to normal.[101] An immediate investigation began, as a result of which Gugel was removed in January 1933 and replaced by P. G. Myshkin.[102]

Under Magnitostroi's new director (at least the eighth since 1929), a major cleanup of the blast furnace shop was carried out, and in a short time 564 platform cars and dump-truck loads of refuse were hauled away.[103] But at this time, serious problems with the supply of iron ore began to threaten the operation of the repaired blast furnaces.[104] And while the two blast furnaces in operation worked very poorly, producing only a small amount of low-quality pig iron, construction of the open-hearth steelmaking shop had barely even begun.[105] The question of design work loomed ever larger.

After McKee's departure, it had been announced that all design work would be given over to Soviet agencies.[106] Since the inability of these agencies to perform such work was the very reason that the Soviet government had initially gone to McKee with billions of gold rubles in hand, the announcement was baffling.[107] But Soviet agencies already had a large supply of McKee drawings, including most everything needed for the mine and blast furnace shop. German firms continued to design and supervise construction of the rolling shop. And foreign designs from rolling shops built in the Ukraine were copied and sent to Magnitogorsk for some of the mills.[108]

Although foreign drawings, equipment, and expertise continued to be available,[109] the circumstances under which the entire project was being conducted made design work extremely difficult. A multitude of agencies were involved in design, creating much confusion. More important, in the best case design and construction went on simultaneously. Not infrequently, construction not only preceded design but was almost always pushed forward without regard to preparation or logistics.[110] But in the minds of officials, this was just the way things had to be done, and anyone who raised questions simply did not understand—or what was far worse—perhaps secretly wished that the party's industrial program not be carried out.[111] "Couldn't we somehow go a bit slower?" Ordzhonikidze asked, mimicking the critics of the breathless pace adopted by the party as he dismissed them. "That was the whole question. The whole question was: What tempo was to be adopted."[112]

The leadership's braggadocio, however, was giving way to more sober reflection.[113] In January 1933, amid the whispers that the first Five-Year Plan had been a debacle, the second Five-Year Plan, far more "realistic" in its targets, officially began.[114] But if the pace of expansion was somewhat slowed, the basic impulse of catch and overtake was nonetheless retained: there was no retreat from the goal of creating a self-sufficient, fully state-owned and state-managed industrial economy that could match in size and performance what the capitalists had.[115] The battle to erect Magnitogorsk and the new kind of industrial economy it embodied had been joined, and it would be waged to the end. There was, in any case, no going back.

PLANNED ECONOMY

In 1933, construction at Magnitogorsk continued apace. The third coke battery and third blast furnace were completed.[116] And even more important, on 8 July the first open-hearth oven began operation. Magnitogorsk finally began producing steel.[117] Three weeks later, in the presence of Ordzhonikidze himself the first blooming mill was launched, and the metallurgical cycle—from raw material to specialized steel—was pronounced "complete." Prizes were awarded and speeches made.[118] Before the year was out, three more open-hearth furnaces, the fourth blast furnace, and sorting mill 630 were put into operation. A steel plant was beginning to emerge.[119]

Ordzhonikidze visited Magnitogorsk in 1933 not just to celebrate the start-up of the blooming mill but also, like other members of the leadership who had visited the site earlier (Molotov, Voroshilov, Mezhlauk, and others), to discover what was going on.[120] As the first Five-Year Plan yielded to the second, the task at Magnitogorsk mirrored that for the whole country: not simply to slow things down a bit but to bring some order to what had irreversibly been set in motion by the blitz to industrialize in a socialist, that is, noncapitalist, manner.[121]

Thousands of enterprises were either being constructed from scratch or undergoing such dramatic enlargement that they could be considered essentially new factories—and they were all under the direct supervision of the rapidly burgeoning state. The staggering expansion posed enormous challenges of operational management, which had not been imagined during the initial plunge into superindustrialization. Soon enough, however, the burden of assuming responsibility for the thousands upon thousands of decisions that under capitalism were handled by entrepreneurs and the market hit home.[122]

What Ordzhonikidze found at Magnitogorsk became clear in a blistering directive he issued on 29 July 1933.[123] Along with frequent breakdowns that he said "threatened to destroy various installations and even the entire factory," the industry commissar cited a lack of responsibility for imported equipment, a low level of productivity, excessive requests for materials and supplies, and knowing violations of the managerial chain of command. He called for a reorganization of industrial management to prevent the issuing of contradictory orders and for the subordination of all organizations on the site, including those carrying out design work, to the director. He further warned that future evaluations of management's performance would be made not simply on the basis of the materials successfully consumed (*osvoeno*), the number of installations brought to completion, or the quantity of output, but on the quality of that output and its costs. It was a devastatingly frank analysis and a spirited call to resolute action.[124]

In the aftermath of Ordzhonikidze's trip, Magnitogorsk's director, Myshkin, was accused of keeping a double set of books: a realistic one, which he used to manage the factory, and a "cooked" one, which he had sent to Moscow in April 1933 to cast the factory in a highly favorable light. This was an old problem in Russia, but it was given vastly new significance by the increasingly higher stake "the center" now had in outlying regions. Just as it set the level of investment in the Magnitogorsk factory and thus the rate at which the plant grew, Moscow arrogated to itself the right to control the allocation of the factory's entire output. Simply put, Moscow "owned" Magnitogorsk and everything produced in that location, and it exercised that proprietary interest by appointing or removing Magnitogorsk's directors at will.[125]

In what became the fourth time since 1930 that a Magnitogorsk director was dismissed in disgrace, Myshkin was removed in 1933 and replaced by Avraamii Zaveniagin, who had been part of Ordzhonikidze's delegation.[126] A former chief of Gipromez and most recently the director of a steel plant in the Ukraine, Zaveniagin was a protégé of Ordzhonikidze, to whom he professed absolute loyalty. As a 1930 graduate of the Moscow Mining Academy (later nicknamed the "nursery of scientists and ministers"), Zaveniagin was also the first Magnitogorsk chief who had any training in metallurgy.[127] "In those years, the names of the leaders of metallurgical factories were known not simply to a narrow circle of economic officials, but to broad sections of the Soviet public," one Soviet journalist recalled. "The country followed their work and their successes as in the days of war it had followed the successes of the most visible military leaders."[128] Zaveniagin may have been the country's most famous "metallurgist." This gave him enormous authority and clout.[129]

To take charge of the various shops, the fast-track Zaveniagin was supplied with a contingent of rising specialists, such as E. Ia. Bekker and Fedor Golubitskii, who arrived in January 1935. Most of these executives were as young, or even younger, than the thirty-two-year-old new director. All had a measure of technical education and some practical experience.[130] "Essentially our entire management staff consists of young engineers," commented Leonid Vaisberg, chief of the medium sorting mill who was mobilized from the Donbas to Magnitogorsk in April 1935. "These were people, as they say, of the revolutionary epoch."[131]

That Magnitogorsk's new director was the son of a humble railroad depot worker was in itself remarkable, but even more noteworthy was that a proletarian child born to poor and virtually uneducated parents had been graduated from the prestigious Moscow Mining Academy—and had been appointed head of Gipromez only two days later.[132] Such a life history conditioned Zaveniagin to embrace the "civilizing mission" of inculcating "industrial culture." He extolled what was championed as the second Five-Year Plan's more "considered" approach to management, a style of industrial leadership that was better informed and outwardly more genteel but also far more exacting and, if necessary, downright ruthless.[133] Prior to Zaveniagin's arrival, informal channels of administration were often more important than formal ones.[134] Now, just as he would be answerable to those above him, Zaveniagin would be expected to subordinate all those below him in the "chain of command."[135]

Zaveniagin personified the watchword "one-man rule" (edinonachalie), which had been proclaimed in September 1929 as a way to improve managerial coordination and affix responsibility, but which at Magnitogorsk had never been realized—as Ordzhonikidze made clear in his July 1933 directive. In appointing Zaveniagin, the industry commissar's objective was not simply to cultivate and assign the right "commanders" to the localities but also to establish a more or less functional command structure. Accordingly, Zaveniagin's posting to Magnitogorsk coincided with a further consolidation of the economic administration.

Back in September 1931, on the model of such giant American corporations as U.S. Steel—which in 1901 had become the largest company relative to the size of the economy in American history—the USSR formed the Main Administration of the Metallurgical Industry (GUMP).[136] As one of its first moves, GUMP abolished the contracting system and most of the trusts at Magnitogorsk, leaving only three organizations on the site: Magnitostroi, Koksostroi, and the Mining Administration (GRU). Not long thereafter, Koksostroi and the GRU were absorbed by Magnitostroi, which was divided into two departments: construction and production. Magnitostroi was subsumed under the People's Commissariat of Heavy Industry (NKTP), which had absorbed GUMP and superseded Vesenkha in January 1932 as the agency responsible for all industry. When Zaveniagin arrived in 1933, the departments of Magnitostroi were united in a single entity, the

Magnitogorsk Metallurgical Complex (MMK). The vertical hierarchy was thus complete.

The establishment of a hierarchical command structure with authoritative commanders in the field did not, of course, mean that all bureaucratic conflict had been eliminated. Quite the opposite: "turf battles" only intensified, especially those between the industrial bureaucracy and the police and between the party and the economic administration;[137] but also those among the numerous agencies of the sprawling central economic administration, between central agencies and the enterprises they supervised, and within the enterprises themselves. When administrative jurisdictions did not nominally overlap, rivalries and jealousies made sure that they did. The number of bureaus and departments made it hard to sort out who was responsible for what, and, more importantly, who was *not* responsible for certain matters. Appeals to settle the smallest disputes were not infrequently made to the people's commissar.[138]

In a further complication to the tensions and rivalries fostered by the multicentered yet hierarchical command structure, Vissarion "Beso" Lominadze, who had been the party chief for Georgia and worked high up in the Comintern before being demoted as an "oppositionist," was sent to Magnitogorsk as city party secretary at the same time as Zaveniagin was appointed director. Lominadze's organizational skills were vastly superior to those of his predecessors, and his arrival opened a new era in the local political leadership. But he clashed with Zaveniagin, and the goal of one-man rule did not fully obtain in Magnitogorsk as long as the two men were on the scene.[139]

Even without these added complications, Soviet enterprises had trouble fully coordinating operations and disciplining their own people, notwithstanding the beneficial effects of the administrative reorganizations of 1931–33. The Magnitogorsk plant issued an avalanche of internal directives admonishing personnel to follow established regulations, which were themselves frequently rewritten. Top management at the steel plant, for example, tried to control the internal distribution of raw materials and supplies, just as Moscow did for the whole country. One stern internal factory decree expressly prohibited shop chiefs from sending "people to various cities of the Union in connection with supply and equipment questions without receiving the permission of the respective departments of the complex administration."[140] But it was precisely management's failure to provide each shop with adequate basic materials through regular channels that motivated the practice of foraging, and would continue to do so.

Indeed, one of the most surprising phenomena of the emerging planned economy was the rise of an unlimited demand for raw materials and inputs. Never sure how much they would be allocated but pressured to meet plan targets, large firms routinely requested far more than they thought would be necessary. Central planners were aware of this practice but still had a difficult time judging how much was "actually" needed. In addition, what were called "interruptions" (*pereboi*) in the delivery of supplies became so regular that firms guarded against them by stocking up, concealing their industrial "bread crusts" from the central authorities. Busy bombarding the economic bureaucracy with requests for more of everything, enterprises were engaged in hoarding. The paradoxical result was that increases in industrial capacity, far from satiating the hunger for metal, resulted in perpetual shortages. Comprehensive central planning, it turned out, produced its own forms of "anarchy" to rival the market's.[141]

Within the tentacular apparatus that was taking shape to oversee everything from the wording of inscriptions to be printed on note pads to the precise amounts of dozens of grades and hundreds of shapes of all the structural steel to be produced by the country in the foreseeable future, the relations between the MMK and NKTP were prototypical. Reflecting the pressures on Moscow, Ordzhonikidze registered strong dissatisfaction with what he called the "aggrandizing" attitudes on the part of Magnitogorsk management, which was allegedly putting in requests for construction materials well beyond what was "truly" needed. But the steel complex, facing the center's tyrannical production targets, often found itself without materials essential to meeting those marching orders.[142]

To be sure, state ownership of industry did not *necessarily* mean centralized micromanagement, and in late 1932 a short-lived debate took place in the pages of the Industry Commissariat's newspaper over the introduction of a kind of "socialist market." One economist proposed that prices for industrial goods should reflect supply and demand, and that firms should deal directly with each other, rather than place orders for equipment and supplies through the central bureaucracy. To everyone's shock, in November 1932 Ordzhonikidze abruptly introduced just such procedures for the iron and steel industry. As R. W. Davies has argued, this impulsive move, which was to begin on 1 January 1933, showed just how unsettled the emerging planned economy still was.[143]

Did such "market relations" between state firms undermine the supposed superiority of planning: the determination of priorities by science, rather than by what enterprises found it advantageous to produce? What if suppliers decided to refuse orders for much-needed goods, preferring to produce what *they* decided was more expedient? Were planning and the market at some level compatible? In the event, no answers to these complex questions were forthcoming. The experiment, launched precipitously and conducted amid great flux, was called off, much to the relief of the central economic apparatus. There would be no legal "market" in industry, although one did arise anyway.

The allotments of coking coal arriving at Magnitogorsk in 1938, to take one vivid example, weighed on average 30 percent less than when they were shipped from Kuzbas mines. Some coal was simply lost in transit, while much was pilfered en route by "agents" of other enterprises less favored in the supply network, or by "freelancers."[144] The Magnitogorsk factory had no choice but to recoup this shortfall, yet further requests through the central supply network would take months and in any case were not likely to yield any more coal. The lesson for the plant was clearly to request more coal than would be necessary and to cultivate alternative sources outside the central allocation network. Here was the "socialist market" in action, despite the abrupt cancellation of Ordzhonikidze's experiment with firm-to-firm ties. It is even possible that the Magnitogorsk steel complex wound up buying back, at black market rates, some of the "lost" coal that it had been allocated. Such were the unavoidable realities of the emerging "planned economy": plans were many, as were the efforts to "correct" them.[145]

Meanwhile, the inefficiency of the centralized allocation system threatened to overwhelm the apparatus itself. With all transactions among enterprises administered by Moscow, unremitting telegrams begging for raw materials or equipment, along with detailed reports answering suspicious queries, competed with industrial goods as a given factory's chief "output." As early as 18 January 1930, Ordzhonikidze lamented at a meeting of the Central Control Commission that "if we don't put a stop to the paper flow it will drown us. We defeated Denikin and Iudenich, Wrangel and every other counterrevolutionary scum, but paper of all things will smother us."[146] But as Moshe Lewin has pointed out, the efforts to combat the "flood of paper" with decrees and investigations led only to the further proliferation of officials, and thus to more paper.[147]

Perpetual shortages, torrents of disabling paperwork, internecine battles over, and even pilfering of, raw materials were by no means the only unanticipated yet intractable problems of the planned economy. In a long speech given in early 1934—its publication occupied almost the entire local newspaper for three full days—Beso Lominadze delivered a stinging critique of the state of affairs in Magnitogorsk's construction. At the time of the speech, the steel plant was officially considered 30 percent complete,[148] but looking over the whole site, Lominadze claimed to have found "not a single fully completed shop or objective." The open-hearth shops and rolling mills were well behind schedule, while the coke plant was still without its by-products division: valuable chemicals were being released into the air. Some shops put into operation were so incomplete that snow fell freely into them. Even the blast furnace department, the most advanced objective, was "still far from completion." Lominadze concluded that "not a single construction objective was without serious design defects," and that "not a single day goes by without some kind of breakdown in the factory or transport."[149]

Little that was built at Magnitogorsk proved reliable. In 1934, no sooner had blast furnace no. 4 been finished than the construction team returned to no. 1, which was utterly rebuilt, after less than two years of operation. The blooming mill required shutdown for capital repairs in 1935, after less than two years of use (rather than the customary ten), and a special representative from the German firm Demag had to be called in to oversee the delicate work.[150] Mill 500, planned to operate without extensive repairs for a minimum of ten years, was shut down for total overhaul in 1938, after less than three years.[151]

Nor were projects started up anywhere near on time. In 1936 the newspaper issued harangues to "mobilize" all forces to put mill 300 no. 3, which was well behind schedule, into operation. What "forces" were to be mobilized remained unclear, but the newspaper revealed that the factory had not yet received crane-support girders ordered from a Donbas factory. Without the girders the mill could not be assembled.[152] Two years later, when the mill had finally been assembled and was being tested prior to being put into operation, a 6,300 volt charge was emitted. An investigation revealed numerous examples of egregious assembly work, including bolts that were so short they had no hope of holding the structures together and electrical work so shoddy cables frequently gave off sparks.[153] To anyone familiar with the day-to-day details, the construction of the Magnitogorsk Works must have seemed constantly in doubt, even as it was slowly and painfully being achieved.[154]

The secret of "success" was the all-purpose practice of "making-do." The near total absence of spare parts, for example, frequently led to the cannibalizing of unassembled equipment so that equipment that had already been installed could be put back in operation.[155] This might seem short-sighted, but much of the unassembled equipment just sat around deteriorating in what was called the "Zero Storehouse," a graveyard of imported and domestic equipment that had been misplaced.[156] ("Storehouse" was just a euphemism, of course, for until much later there were few actual storage structures and equipment more often than not was camped out under the open sky, gathering dust until it was "washed by the rain.") The newspaper reported that on the site there were 1,300 unopened crates of freight, and nobody could say what was in them.[157]

Of course, some of the difficulties at Magnitogorsk were less the result of the planned economy than inexperience and the general low level of development.[158] Konstantin Valerius, the chief of the resurrected independent construction trust Magnitostroi,[159] revealed that as late as 1936 two-thirds of all earth-moving work was still being done without mechanization.[160] And the chief bookkeeper lamented that "practically all designs issued by the design bureau of the complex suffer from one deficiency or another, including mistakes in dimensions and incorrect or even missing sections."[161] But many of the intractable problems of construction, particularly those involving supply, were largely the result of the *normal* functioning of the planned economy, which ensured that the rhythm of work remained very irregular.[162]

Just as construction was subject to fits and starts, so production was very uneven, one day over plan, the next well under. The pace picked up considerably as each quarter, especially the fourth, drew to a close with the newspaper reminding workers that "every day decides the success of the struggle to fulfill the Plan."[163] But the plant was never able to sustain the frenzies. In June 1936, Ordzhonikidze sent a forceful telegram "categorically forbidding the stoppage of any equipment for repairs without the express permission of GUMP." He also ordered that the plant telegraph him personally with a report "on what measures were being taken in order that, finally, the production plan was fulfilled." Echoing the commissar's words, the city newspaper railed that not a single shop was meeting its targets, and that idle time was extraordinarily high. Less than two weeks later, the newspaper reported that blast furnace no. 1 was being shut down two days for repairs, "with GUMP's permission."[164]

Faulty construction and terrible maltreatment of equipment were major problems in the shops. Another was that construction was not yet finished and some equipment had yet to be installed.[165] A further encumbrance derived from persistently severe transport bottlenecks. A report in the oblast newspaper in 1935 painted a bleak picture of irregular and unpredictable freight transfer in Magnitogorsk. "During twenty days of February, only 229 wagons of coking coal were unloaded, against a plan of 700," the correspondent wrote, adding that "for coke you need Hoppers and open

Table 1. Metal Production at Magnitogorsk, 1931–1940
(in tons)

	Iron Ore	Coke	Pig Iron	Steel	Rolled Steel
1931	117,800	—	—	—	—
1932	1,343,100	437,600	361,500	—	—
1933	2,039,600	801,700	570,400	85,200	57,700
1934	3,707,800	1,590,000	1,224,100	436,200	288,200
1935	5,399,800	1,733,900	1,286,200	815,500	607,600
1936	5,414,200	1,977,300	1,582,200	1,164,700	959,500
1937	6,574,700	1,937,400	1,592,700	1,402,700	1,116,700
1938	5,832,000	1,620,100	1,582,800	1,490,100	1,180,300
1939	5,119,300	1,615,600	1,697,300	1,453,400	1,127,000
1940	5,606,400	1,838,700	1,756,100	1,654,700	1,213,200

SOURCE: PAChO, f. 288, op. 19, d. 14, ll. 127-29, reprinted in Eliseeva, ed., *Iz istorii*, p. 215.

cars but instead they get closed or platform cars. Clearly, it's impossible to load coke in them."[166]

Deficiencies in construction, poor maintenance, and faulty transport, along with the same endemic supply shortages which plagued construction, had even greater effects on production because of the interconnectedness of the steel plant's operation. A lack of coking coal limited blast furnace operation and hence pig iron production, which then hindered raw steel production, which reduced rolled steel production, and so on. In this regard, the open-hearth shop was notorious.[167] But there were near constant shortfalls all along the metallurgical cycle, and their effects were invariably multiplied.

Perhaps the greatest factor inhibiting improved performance was that in the planned economy all production was "planned," that is, regulated by quantitative output plans, or targets, assigned by Moscow. The evaluation of a factory's performance, and thus the degree of remuneration of its employees, were determined by the percentage "fulfillment" of these quotas. Each edition of the Magnitogorsk newspaper displayed on its front page the previous day's output in all shops. Aggregate output totals were also displayed and celebrated by the week, month, quarter, and year.

Magnitogorsk's official output totals seemed impressive, constituting roughly 10 percent of all-Union output (see table 1).[168] What these figures measure, however, is difficult to say, aside from the weight of the pressures on plant management to secure people's bonuses (and perhaps their lives) by claiming production figures that were as close as possible to the assigned plan targets, and the pressures on the regime to live up to its boasts.[169] Anyway, even by the official reports, plant performance was not especially good. Actual production achieved only 92 percent of the pig iron, 97 percent of the steel, and 99 percent of the rolled steel called for in the production targets of the 1937 plan for the Magnitogorsk factory—and the 1937 targets had been adjusted downward.[170] More important, it was not clear how much of this metal actually existed. Measurements of daily production were so "inaccurate," according to the newspaper, that warehouse and storage inventories had to be redone every month. What this probably means is that various oversight agencies, including no doubt the security police, disputed the daily counts and sought to compare them with stock on hand.[171]

Gross output totals presented one story. "If one instead looks at plan fulfillment in terms of customers' orders," the newspaper wrote, "then a different picture emerges." For the quarter January–March 1937, the paper reported that the factory fulfilled its plan for pig iron at 91.4 percent, but the target for the highest quality grade, 0, was fulfilled at only 26.1 percent, and that for the next best, grade 1, at just 27.1 percent. Conversely, grade 2 pig iron accounted for 16.3 percent of the total produced, against a plan that foresaw 11.4 percent. Grade 3 pig iron accounted for 13.4 percent of total production, against a planned quantity of 1.8 percent, and grade 4, which was not anticipated by the plan, nevertheless accounted for 4.4 percent of all pig iron produced. Taken together, the two lowest quality categories and an even lower subcategory accounted for more than a third of all pig iron produced. At the same time, millions of rubles' worth of fuel above-plan was consumed by the blast furnaces.[172]

A similar state of affairs obtained in the open-hearth shop, where a spot check in 1936 of one smelting revealed that 60 percent of the steel had cracks. When the smelting was repeated, near identical results were observed and, according to the newspaper report, such mishaps transpired every day. Between January and June 1936, 31,130 tons of steel, valued at more than 6 million rubles, were found to be defective. Most of this was high-quality, specialized steel, the chemical content of which was not always subjected to laboratory analysis during smelting, as required.[173] Meanwhile, in the rolling shop, the acknowledged factory leader, production in tonnage reached almost 100 percent of plan in 1936 but in customers' orders was 83.4 percent. Most important, only a third of the orders for rolled steel of the highest quality were delivered.[174]

Plan fulfillment in the linchpin internal factory transport department for the first nine months of 1936 was reported at 101.6 percent, but shop chief Leontii Metelskii revealed that this figure included "unplanned transfers." Metelskii added that a great many train cars were not in working condition, that there was a severe shortage of rails and ties, and that recently repaired locomotives required repairs again.[175] Another newspaper article reported that it could take as long as two weeks for freight to pass from one shop to the next. Destinations were written in chalk on the freight cars, and when they became wet the chalk washed off. All the same, reported plan fulfillment stood at 101.6 percent, and everyone got their bonuses.[176] The rail transport shop, like the rest of Magnitogorsk's shops and, for that matter, those at enterprises around the country, worked feverishly toward the same goal: strive for and claim high quantity, whatever the quality. Quantity exercised a tyranny over the economy, resulting in the indiscriminate consumption of inputs and the production of enormous wastage, called *brak*.

It is instructive to put evaluations of the steel plant's performance in the context of its development. In 1938 one of the country's leading experts in metallurgy, Academic I. P. Bardin, spent twenty days in Magnitogorsk four years after he was last there. The difference enabled him to draw comparisons. In an overview of the plant's operation published in the oblast newspaper, Bardin wrote that "production is conducted in a far more cultured manner than in 1934." He suggested that the efficiency of coal and iron-ore consumption was improved, that the equipment of the coke shop looked better, that there were no longer constant breakdowns in the blast furnace shop, and that the rolling mills were fulfilling their plans. At the same time, he pointed out that the coke plant was still not finished, that the blast furnace shop still suffered from a lack of raw materials, and that the equipment in the rolling mills was not in very good shape. But the biggest problems, in his opinion, were to be found in the open-hearth shop, which he wrote looked "not four years old but twenty-four." Bardin claimed that the open-hearth design had been seriously flawed, and that the "barbaric treatment" of the ovens exacerbated matters. In conclusion, he singled out raising quality and lowering costs as the steel plant's main goals.[177]

Bardin's reminder of the improvements made between 1934 and 1938 needs to be kept in mind, but in the oblast newspaper version of his assessment he omitted any consideration of the staggering amount of defective metal produced by the plant. The city newspaper reported in another context, however, that as of early 1937, the Magnitogorsk Works had accumulated 6.5 million rubles' worth of unusable pig iron and 9.7 million rubles' worth of rejected rolled steel—all useless, except for when it came time to count and report total output.[178] In addition, John Scott noted that by 1940 about eleven million tons of inferior quality iron ore had accumulated at Magnitogorsk and was hampering the operation of mine transport.[179]

These totals might well have been far higher except that much of the output determined to be defective by state inspectors was shipped anyway. And despite their protests metal-starved firms had little choice but to accept it, pressured as they were to fulfill their own production plans.[180] So desperate were other enterprises for metal—and anything else—that they stationed "expediters" (*tolkachi*) in Magnitogorsk to facilitate the shipment of their orders, even though back in January 1933, the Commissariat of Heavy Industry had (again) expressly forbidden this practice. The Magnitogorsk Central Hotel housed no fewer than fifty expediters who traveled, lodged, and dined at the state's expense. In 1936 the city newspaper reported that one of them had lost the hotel bed linen for his room in a game of cards, and that all of them looked for chances to purchase equipment "on the left," as the saying went, offering high prices for scarce items such as railroad cars.[181] Such finagling aside, the bottom line was that the often poor quality steel whose shipment the expediters were supposed to facilitate meant defective inputs throughout the industrial economy.[182]

Manifest poor quality and vast waste argue for a skeptical approach to the assessment of Soviet "growth" rates, a subject that has received more attention than any other from scholars of the Soviet economy.[183] Even that portion of Magnitogorsk's steel output deemed acceptable does not lend itself to ready evaluation. What, for example, is the value of thick structural shapes that must be machined by customers to thin strips before they can be used? Do we also, as the planners did, count the sheared-off metal that ends up on a customer factory's floor as "output"? And what value does one attach to the machines made from such metal that function poorly but are the only ones available to Soviet industrial customers in an autarchic economy? Surely measurements of "growth rates," even nuanced ones, cannot be used to make ready international comparisons.

And yet, it would be equally misguided to dismiss all Soviet output as worthless, even if assessing the value of that output remains highly problematic. Soviet machines may have performed less well than equivalent foreign ones, but there were far more Soviet machines than before. Even if the Soviet economy did not treble in size, as was claimed by the regime and confirmed by some non-Soviet scholars, in a single decade the country's industrial base was visibly transformed.[184] Magnitogorsk steel, for example, had not existed before the industrialization drive. By the second half of the 1930s, the new plant helped supply what had become a substantial if wasteful heavy-industrial economy serving the Red Army, whose fighting capacity had been decisively upgraded.

The orientation toward the military, a strategy pursued by the country's leadership as early as 1926, could not but affect the Soviet economy. Julian Cooper has argued that "while the pursuit of rapid industrialization necessarily required that priority be granted to heavy industry, the extent of this bias was in practice accentuated by defense production considerations."[185] Calling this a "diversion of resources," Cooper suggests that "given a more favorable international environment the Soviet path of industrialization could have been modified in a number of important respects," by which he means in directions more beneficial to the people.[186] Although this argument is on the mark about the social "costs" of emphasizing defense-related industry, its assumption that such an approach was dictated exclusively, or even primarily, by the nature of the external threat, rather than internal preferences and aims, appears questionable.

Heavy industry, especially steel and machine building, was pursued zealously by the Soviet leadership as the key to modern civilization. The concomitant disregard, even scorn, for consumer industry, services, and other vital spheres of economic activity—some of which were labeled "nonproductive" in official statistical compilations—cannot be laid at the door of foreign hostility; rather, it derived from an anticapitalist view of economics. In a way, it could be argued that the orientation toward the military "saved" production at Magnitogorsk and elsewhere from becoming production chiefly for production's sake: making steel to make machines to make more steel to make more machines, regardless of whether anyone was in a position to use them or to use them effectively.[187]

If the planned economy found in its all-encompassing military mission both its administrative model and its rationale, all of this could just as readily be seen as production for employment's sake. The Magnitogorsk plant provided a source of employment for tens of thousands of people, and the guaranteed job security instituted by the regime made that livelihood virtually permanent. Job rights were taken seriously. In the first half of 1937, the Magnitogorsk court tried 120 "labor cases," mostly involving alleged improper firing. In 91 of the firings the complaint was found justified, and the dismissals were reversed.[188] In the planned economy there were neither booms nor busts, and although production rhythms fluctuated, employment remained full year-round. This was revolutionary.

Without undermining everyone's right to work, central planners expressed a desire to use the work force more "rationally." In 1938, the Magnitogorsk Works was cited for being 2,055 people "over plan" (the previous years' wage fund was said to have been exceeded by 15.5 percent). Altogether at this time the complex employed more than 27,000 people, including a bit more than 4,000 in the key shops (blast furnace, open-hearth, rolling), another 4,000 in transport, and 4,000 more in the Everyday-Life Administration, or KBU. (By comparison, Bardin wrote that "an American factory equipped roughly the same as Magnitka has 9,000 to 10,000 workers.")[189] In addition, a great deal of other personnel, in places such as the mechanical workshops, were said to be underused or not used at all.[190] But if "overstaffing" did periodically attract official condemnation, it was ultimately considered unavoidable, given the dearth of mechanization and the inexperience of personnel.[191] Only the growth of "bureaucracy" provoked concrete measures, but here the recurring calls for reductions seemed to have little long-term impact.[192]

Maintaining as large a permanent work force as Magnitogorsk did was possible only because considerations of cost, and hence profit, were not overriding. Yet costs were not ignored altogether. Magnitogorsk was isolated and thus was far from the regions where its products were used, a situation that should have added considerably to the cost of the metal it produced (keep in mind the near indiscriminate consumption of inputs and fuel). Only 11 percent of Magnitogorsk's beams and channels, for example, were consumed in Cheliabinsk oblast, combined with another 10 percent in Sverdlovsk oblast. Another 8 percent went to distant Siberia and the Far East. The rest, more than 70 percent, had to be shipped to the European part of the country, especially the central and southern industrial regions—a costly prospect.[193] But as with the prices of fuel and raw materials, so with freight: the planners simply lowered the rates, and so the "cost" of Magnitogorsk steel was nominally not high.[194]

The elevation of quantity over cost considerations did not preclude concerted efforts to determine each firm's "profits" (or at least the difference between its revenues and expenditures) and to hold down expenditures through what was called *khozraschet* (short for *khoziastvennyi raschet*: literally, "economic calculation").[195] Revenues for the Magnitogorsk Works in 1938, for example, were said to be 46.5 million rubles, against a "plan" of 83.4 million (revenues for 1937, upon which the plan for 1938 was presumably based, had been 59 million). During the same year, costs rose, although a decline had been planned—a development that further magnified the import of the shortfall in "planned" revenue. The factory, in other words, was having financial trouble even with the advantageous pricing and transport policies. How the instability of prices, which were rising, affected these and other calculations was not addressed.[196]

If production at Magnitogorsk was financially behind, construction was in far worse shape. A confidential financial report prepared by the chief bookkeeper of the Magnitogorsk complex for the Commissariat of Heavy Industry (dated 16 March 1935) painted a picture of a financial morass: missing funds, missing supplies, missing equipment, unrecorded expenditures, plus mistakes from previous years yet to be cleared up.[197] In later years, "budgets" were still mostly drawn up after the fact, if at all, yet cost overruns became routine.[198] In 1936, the newspaper carried reassuring reports of how construction costs were, as per plan, continually being lowered—until a bitter feud broke out between bank officials and the management of the construction trust.[199]

"The glowing results heralded in the year-end report of [the construction trust] conceal the realities of cost overruns and overstocking," wrote an angry Aleksandr Lopaev, the director of the Magnitogorsk Branch of the Industrial Bank. To fulfill the plan for equipment acquisition, he disclosed, the construction trust simply ordered any equipment it could get its hands on, regardless of its use value. Even so, the equipment acquisition plan was not fulfilled.[200] And despite mandated staff cuts and strict marching orders to improve bookkeeping, the Magnitogorsk construction trust remained a financial black hole, devouring state credits. In 1935, Lopaev revealed, the construction department of the MMK, which owed its suppliers more than 20 million rubles, was given a special 15 million rubles state "loan." But six months later, he reported that it owed another 20 million.[201] And a newspaper article reported the next day that the construction organization had just received 30 million rubles to pay its suppliers, but that it still owed 3 million more.[202]

Given this dismal picture of financial irresponsibility as outlined publicly by Lopaev and others in the Magnitogorsk newspaper, it should come as no surprise that determining how much the steel plant cost to build is impossible. In one official publication, a figure of 1.4 billion rubles was given for all expenditures as of late 1939.[203] By contrast, John Scott, who had access to the factory archive (such as it was), wrote that more than 2.5 billion rubles had been spent by the early 1940s. But Scott appears to have simply reproduced the official cost estimates as of 1934.[204] In fact, despite

the insistence of GUMP, there were no meaningful construction cost profiles for the entire period 1934–38.[205]

Although it is not possible to know how much the plant cost, one thing
is sure: the Magnitogorsk Metallurgical Complex cost a fortune.[206] But the
regime had its own calculus. By the end of 1938, the Magnitogorsk Works
had already produced more than 7.5 million tons of pig iron, 5 million tons
of steel, and 3 million tons of rolling stock. This was considerably less than
the plan targets, much of this total did not reflect usable steel, and the costs
of production were far higher than anticipated. In the program of "building
socialism" the results were wasteful, to put it mildly. But all the same,
there *were* results—and a sprawling contingent of officials, as well as an
even larger army of workers, to perpetuate, record, and try to live off these
results, without the threat of unemployment.

IRON, STEEL, AND BOLSHEVISM

The Soviet superindustrialization drive was suffused with a radical ethos,
a repudiation of the conciliation with "capitalist elements" embodied in the
New Economic Policy of the 1920s and a revival of the "heroism" of what
in retrospect had come to be known as "war communism."[207] The Five-Year
Plan went forward with "Bolshevik tempo" as the principal watchword,
and a pervading sense that time was a dangerous enemy. In *Vremia,
Vpered!* (*Time, Forward!*), Valentin Kataev's 1932 novel based on his experiences at Magnitogorsk, a brigade of shock workers struggles to break
the "work record" for pouring concrete in one eight-hour shift. The attempt for the world record—which takes place during a violent storm, the
storm of the Five-Year Plan—is an assault on time: "Time did not wait. It
raced. It had to be outdistanced." Centuries of "backwardness" were going
to be made up in a decade.[208]

The industrialization held out the promise of a bold leap forward, and
the realization of this promise was demonstrated by the construction of
Magnitogorsk. To begin with, there was the scale of the construction: millions upon millions of cubic meters of earth moved, hundreds of thousands
of cubic meters of concrete poured, tens of thousands of tons of structural
steel assembled. "It was impossible to imagine the future plant," confessed
one eyewitness, who added that "even though I saw the blueprints and
some sketches, I never really understood what it was going to be like. I only
knew it was going to be something colossal."[209] Even after the plant was
erected and people finally began to get a sense of what they were building,
they continued to gape in disbelief and awe. "No one could have imagined

the scale of production in mill 500," wrote the chief of the mill. "Even rolling mill operators from other parts of the USSR could not fathom the colossal scale."[210]

Not just the scale but the power of the new technology bowled people over. Magnitogorsk contained the largest and (on paper) most sophisticated blast furnaces in the world, the largest mechanized mining enterprise in the USSR, a coke plant that stood on the same level with the best of Germany and the United States, one of the first large blooming mills ever in the USSR, a whole series of technologically advanced rolling mills that stretched for miles, "auxiliary" shops that were as large as whole factories—the complex was a revolution in Soviet industry that could be seen and admired. When Ordzhonikidze bragged in 1935 that "our factories, our mines, our mills are now equipped with . . . the latest word in world technology," everyone in Magnitogorsk possessed a concrete picture of what his words meant, even if not all the technology at the plant was brand new.[211]

Along with its massive scale and power, the undertaking was further distinguished by the speed of its construction under nearly impossible conditions. As the Magnitogorsk plant rapidly began to take shape, Ordzhonikidze remarked dismissively that "even among us there were people, nonparty and party alike, who didn't believe, who said it was an adventure."[212] What else to call it! What was the whole Five-Year Plan! Bolshevism itself! A gigantic steel plant in the empty steppe in a few years—how was it possible? It was not possible, but there it was.

As of 1 January 1937 the Magnitogorsk Works had a total of seventy-two shops, with more to come.[213] Even if the plant's actual capacities were closer to half those set by Gipromez in 1933, Magnitogorsk was still a very large steel plant.[214] A new vocabulary—*gigant, kombinat*—was used to set off the undertaking and underscore the point that this was no ordinary factory. Around the country and internationally, Magnitogorsk stood as a symbol of achievement and of the newfound power of the Soviet Union, bringing legitimacy to the regime. "The Magnitogorsk Works," gloated the propagandists, "is living proof of what Bolsheviks are able to achieve."[215]

To be sure, the plant that arose at Magnitogorsk reflected the circumstances of its rushed construction (for which, ironically, the Soviet leadership would later be credited with prophetic foresight.)[216] What is more, the plant operated within an economic order in which it was extremely difficult to ensure quality, control expenditures, or match output to precise needs. But even though the country's novel planning and economic management system was found by its operatives to be cumbersome and inefficient, Magnitogorsk produced steel, and that fact could not be gainsaid. "The unprejudiced visitor," one foreign convert wrote, "may be struck by the waste, the perpetual outbreaks of anarchy; but he is still bound to recognize that the Soviets have raised a regular industrial town here out of the ground within two years. After that, their boasts do not seem quite so ridiculous."[217]

By 1929 the October revolution had come to mean "building socialism," and building socialism had come to mean not only the party's monopoly on power but the deployment of Soviet blast furnaces and rolling mills. With the industrialization drive, a typical speech about "the revolution" was taken up with the class war (both internally as expressed in intraparty struggles and externally as expressed in German and Japanese military postures) and with tables of data on gross pig iron output and rolled steel production. Steel, as the basis of the state's power and identity, held a kind of magic aura, a glow nowhere more in evidence than at the gigantic Magnitogorsk Metallurgical Complex. At once perhaps the most visible blow against the international bourgeoisie and the party's internal enemies *and* the proudest trophy of the international working class and of the toiling Soviet people, Magnitogorsk was no mere business for generating profits; it was a device for transforming the country: its geography, its industry, and above all its people.[218] Magnitogorsk was the October revolution itself, the socialist revolution, Stalin's revolution.

In 1934 the steel plant at Magnetic Mountain became the Stalin Magnitogorsk Metallurgical Complex. Stalin's very name—Man of Steel—embodied both the iron rule of the Bolshevik party and the production of steel. A volume put out in 1937 to commemorate the five-year anniversary of the Magnitogorsk plant contained little else besides statistics on production and homages to Stalin: Stal i Stalin, Steel and Stalin.[219] An oversized likeness of Stalin presided on the wide square in front of the factory gates, greeting everyone who came and went. Long after that statue would be torn down and Stalin's name removed from the steel plant, the Magnitogorsk Metallurgical Complex, and the civilization that arose with it, would remain an eloquent monument to Stalin and the epoch of his rule.

2 Peopling a Shock Construction Site

What is Magnitostroi? It is a grandiose factory for remaking people.
Yesterday's peasant . . . becomes a genuine proletarian . . . fighting
for the quickest possible completion of the laying of socialism's
foundation. You are an unfortunate person, my dear reader, if you
have not been to Magnitostroi. I feel sorry for you.

R. Roman, a visiting Moscow correspondent[1]

In March 1929 the first party of settlers arrived on horseback at Magnetic
Mountain to prepare the snow-covered site for the upcoming construction
season. Their immediate task was to build some barracks and a small bakery, organize a workers' cooperative, and recruit more people.[2] By the middle of the summer the rail link was completed, and on 30 June the first train
arrived at the site decorated with banners: "The Steel Horse Breathes Life
into the Magnitogorsk Giant"; "Long live the Bolshevik party!" If many
of the several thousand people present had never before seen a train, the
train had perhaps never before seen such a wild and isolated place.[3]

Whereas the site had obvious advantages for operating a steel plant, the
hinterland surrounding the site designated as Magnitostroi lacked any of
the elements necessary to sustain a large construction. There were almost
no trees and neither coal nor any other source of energy. There were few
established agricultural centers; indeed, there was virtually no good pastureland. The severe continental climate with long and bitterly cold winters exacerbated by brisk winds from the Arctic, followed by unbearably
hot and dry summers, rendered the steppe even more inhospitable. Meanwhile, there were no nearby population clusters from which the construction site could draw its inhabitants.[4] The nearest large urban center, Cheliabinsk, was several hundred kilometers away, and primitive connections
made it seem much farther.[5]

Without sustenance from its own hinterland and far from a larger urban
center that might have served as a logistical support base, Magnitostroi was
utterly dependent on long-distance rail. Everything had to be brought in:
supplies, machines, and especially people. Perhaps as few as twenty-five
people were in the original party that arrived in March 1929. But by the
fall of 1932 *Pravda* announced that the population on the site had reached

250,000.[6] From twenty-five people to a quarter million in three and a half years: who were these people, where did they come from, how did they get there, and what became of them? The short-term answer is that they came and went, largely as they pleased. The long-term one is that notwithstanding the considerable flux, they soon formed a permanent urban population.

·   ■   ·

In a memorable phrase, Moshe Lewin christened the social upheaval brought on by the first Five-Year Plan as "a quicksand society."[7] Conversely, Sheila Fitzpatrick wrote of the same period as a time of "terror, progress, and upward mobility."[8] These broad characterizations convey a sense of what the far-reaching social changes effected by the superindustrialization drive looked like from on high. Both characterizations, however, fail to capture something of the view from the ground, where neither quicksand nor terror and progress quite had the same meaning. The goal of this chapter is to offer just such a ground-level perspective.

In analyzing the story of the peopling of Magnitostroi, it must be kept in mind that it was more than a construction site for a colossal and technologically advanced steel plant: it was also a political device. At Magnitostroi, as the busy pamphleteers tirelessly pointed out, "it is not only the mountain and the steppe that are being rebuilt. Man himself is being rebuilt."[9] Accordingly, an analysis of this process must treat both the importation of a large population to a previously almost-uninhabited location and the ultimately even more challenging task of transforming each incoming individual into a specific kind of urbanite.

In their attempts not merely to populate Magnitostroi but to populate it with people who lived and thought in new ways, the authorities were confronted with subtle and not-so-subtle forms of resistance and with unforeseen contingencies that necessitated reformulations in their strategies. As the new population programs unfolded, the leadership's resolve showed itself to be greater than its abilities to control the course of events it had set in motion. The methods to which the central authorities resorted for realizing their ambitious transformational goals remained predictable even as the results of their policies continued to surprise.

SQUEEZING THE VILLAGE INTO THE CITY

People came to the site Magnitostroi by one of several methods: first of all, in keeping with Bolshevik practice, people were "mobilized," that is, ordered to the site by party, government, or trade union organizations. In mid-1930 the office of the Magnitostroi trust, housed in the cozy quarters of the grandest building in Sverdlovsk, was suddenly mobilized to the site.[10] According to one contemporary, "many specialists did not feel like moving from the oblast center, where there were theaters, cinemas, and other cultural activities, to the bare, wild steppe."[11] Another member from the original group recalled that "many greeted the [relocation] notice as a personal tragedy. It was very difficult, even pitiful, to forsake the comfort of one's own apartment in the busy and well-known city. And for what? To settle God knows where, in the middle of some deserted mountain of the steppe."[12]

Back in Moscow, the reaction was just as severe, if not worse. One mobilized employee from the eastern-branch steel trust recalled seeing what he called "an interesting picture in the offices of Vostokostal." The mobilized, he explained, "were mostly old specialists, whose wives sometimes begged tearfully not to be sent to Magnitostroi or Kuznetskstroi, and produced hundreds of slips of paper, claiming objective reasons. Many even got away with it, but with a reluctant heart and tearful farewells the majority . . . went into 'political exile' [*ssylka*], as they said back then."[13]

Vesenkha, the agency overseeing the country's economy, sent many "specialists" from the capital to Magnitostroi on temporary assignment (*komandirovka*). Although these consultants were housed in the comparatively comfortable quarters of the Central Hotel, they did not relish the duty. "In the hotel," recalled one contemporary, "the majority of residents were employees from the administration who would gather at night to discuss whose assignment ended when." A favorite trick of these people was to put in for a short "vacation" and not return.[14] "Everyone had the same thought," recalled local party official Mordukh Dmitrii Gleizer: "what was the quickest way out of Magnitka, at any price."[15]

Graduates of higher education institutions were looked upon as prime material for mobilizations. Vesenkha sometimes dispatched entire classes (up to 200 people or more) of a technical or trade school immediately upon graduation.[16] In a similar vein, some of those sent to Magnitostroi had just been "graduated" from the Red Army. When construction resumed on the rail link in spring 1929, an entire army regiment was sent, and in 1930, almost a thousand demobilized soldiers were dispatched to Magnitostroi.[17] Magnitostroi sent representatives as far as the Belorussian military district to gather in demobilized soldiers before they could disperse.[18]

In the directives for mobilization, the authorities paid particular attention to party members and skilled workers. In May 1930, for example, the

Central Committee ordered "Communists" and "skilled" workers to be sent to Magnitostroi from Dneprostroi, Turksib, and other construction sites.[19] Such mobilizations were numerous and usually effected with great commotion and fanfare. One party official sent to the site in 1931 as part of a special mobilization of twenty "leading" party activists recalled how a deputy in the Central Committee Organization Department broke the news about their mobilization:

> "Comrades, you're going to Magnitka. And do you know what Magnitka is?"
> "No, we haven't a clue."
> "Unfortunately, neither do we, but you're going to Magnitka all the same."[20]

The party's whim—more precisely, the whim of functionaries within the layers of the apparat—was a force which could strike at any moment.

Most of those mobilized, although rarely pleased with being ordered to Magnitostroi, expected upon arrival to see large blast furnaces, steel mills, and the socialist city. Instead, what greeted them were the empty expanses of the steppe and the primitive conditions of their new life, which could turn their trepidation into outright panic, not to say despair. "They told us, 'Well, here's Magnitogorsk,' and we began to look around," one astonished contemporary recalled. "But there was nothing, just a few barracks. So we began to press them, 'Where's the city?' but they answered: 'Here's the city, what else can we do for you?'"[21] The lamentations over having to undergo exile contained an element of truth.

For some people the notion of exile was more than an analogy. In 1932, a skilled worker named Tomilov sent to Magnitostroi with a group from Mariupol was accompanied by his wife, who, upon seeing the famous "world giant," screamed: "Where have we come, like exiles,"[22] referring to "political" exiles of the tsarist days.[23] In fact, among those "mobilized," but not including the Tomilovs, there were a few dozen so-called prisoner specialists, older engineers victimized in the fabricated 1930 Industrial Party trial and sentenced to banishment.[24] It was one of the many paradoxes of the times that Magnitogorsk, the most potent symbol of the heroic building of socialism, could also be a place of exile—and not just for "bourgeois engineers," as we shall see.

All local party officials were of course assigned to their posts, but given the demand everywhere for party workers, such political mobilizations never involved large numbers. Moreover, not all of those lower-level party members and their counterparts in the larger ranks of the Communist

Youth League (Komsomol) who were sent actually made it to the site. Despite the fact, for example, that the Moscow Komsomol continually mobilized hundreds of Komsomols for Magnitostroi in 1930, all told only twenty or so individuals arrived on the site, including five young girls not allowed by law to work eight hours; some of the others in the group of twenty were called up for military service immediately after arrival. The Urals oblast Komsomol sent more than one hundred Komsomol activists, but only fifteen made it to the site.[25] Notwithstanding the mixed and often meager results, mobilizations of political workers continued (a bit later, a handful of party members who had belonged to the various "oppositions" were exiled to Magnitostroi).[26]

Mobilizations were often connected with the transfer of an important official, who would bring along associates. For example, when Iakov Gugel from the Mariupol factory arrived to head Magnitostroi in January 1931, wrote one eyewitness, "behind him stretched a string of hundreds of people."[27] But the people Gugel attempted to bring with him to Magnitostroi had a hard time leaving Mariupol. "For a long time they didn't want to let us go," recalled the man who became the head of open-hearth construction under Gugel. "Then came an order directly from Ordzhonikidze," which was heeded.[28] In other cases, however, even phone calls from the offices of the People's Commissariat of Heavy Industry could not "liberate" mobilized workers and specialists from their factories.[29]

A small but vital contingent of people "mobilized" to the site by Soviet authorities were foreigners, of which there were essentially three groups. One consisted of political refugees from Europe who had fled east and who, upon crossing the Soviet border, had promptly been arrested. During 1932 and 1933, some of these freedom-seekers were shipped to Magnitostroi, which by then was being called Magnitogorsk, and placed under the surveillance of the security police (GPU). During the latter part of the 1930s virtually all of these people were deported to camps further east.[30]

A second group of foreigners consisted of hired technical personnel. Most of the highly qualified specialists went to Magnitogorsk on individual contracts with Amtorg or were sent by the Western firms that had contracted to design, equip, and supervise the construction. By late 1930 Magnitogorsk contained eighty-six American engineers representing various European and American firms.[31] Beginning already in 1931 and continuing for the next two years, however, foreign specialists were recalled by their companies when disagreements arose between the companies and Soviet authorities, and by 1933 the number of *valiuta* (foreign currency) Americans had shrunk to seven.[32]

The third group of foreigners consisted of those who had come to the USSR on tourist visas but were looking for work. Upon arrival they usually went to the offices of some construction trust or industrial enterprise, where they were gladly enlisted and sent to sites such as Magnitogorsk. In the mid-1930s there were some two hundred skilled German workers working for rubles in Magnitogorsk (among them the future East German party chief, Erich Honecker), a good number of them members of communist or socialist parties who had their own understanding of socialism.[33] Similarly, as of 1933 there were around seventy American workers, including thirty who were members of the Soviet Communist party (one of whom was John Scott). Many of the American workers were returning emigrants.[34]

Altogether, despite discrepancies in the sources, it seems that the number of foreign specialists and workers in Magnitogorsk, excluding refugees, probably did not exceed one thousand, with fewer than that at any one time.[35] In this way, the number of foreign workers and specialists at Magnitogorsk probably matched that of the Soviet specialists and officials who were mobilized to the site—a very small number of the total who came.

Still, mobilizations never ceased. Both the Central Committee and the People's Commissariat of Heavy Industry considered commanding people to go wherever these authorities felt they were needed an indispensable method of administration. The Bolshevik leadership would have decreed the whole country mobilized, if it had thought it could succeed. In a way, it did just that, as mobilizations by command gave way to mobilizations by exhortation, or "recruitment."

Recruitment (*orgnabor*) was the sole way that ordinary Soviet citizens—those who were neither foreigners, demobilized Red Army soldiers, party officials, nor specialists—were supposed to reach the construction site. Accordingly, industrial trusts and construction sites were empowered to negotiate with collective farms, offering raw materials and machines in exchange for labor power. The authorities also called for greater efforts to recruit members of workers' and white-collar employees' families, members of artisanal cooperatives, laborers, and noncollectivized "poor" peasants. At the same time, the People's Commissariat of Labor had local labor bureaus in each oblast and, according to a Soviet scholar, in the second half of 1931 the People's Commissariat of Labor for the Russian Federation (RSFSR) recruited 12,655 workers from the Central Black Earth Region, including 7,205 for Magnitostroi. The next year 22,520 people were recruited from the same region, 2,250 of whom were slated for Magnitostroi.[36]

Despite these impressive numbers, however, I. A. Kraval of the People's Commissariat of Labor reported on 25 January 1931 that his commissariat was not up to the task of supplying Magnitostroi and other large projects even farther east with the mandated labor power. In response, on 27 March 1931 an important meeting was called with representatives of the All-Union Council of Trade Unions (VTsSPS), Gosplan, the Labor Commissariat, and Vesenkha, and various measures were suggested for redoubling recruiting efforts. Vesenkha, for example, was finally allowed to recruit labor power for its industrial and construction centers on its own (a serious encroachment on the Labor Commissariat's turf). But the real consequences of these reports and meetings would become apparent only later that spring.[37]

Like all large construction concerns, Magnitostroi had its own recruitment apparatus that sent representatives into officially designated areas of the country.[38] *Verbovshchiki*, or recruiters, went to villages and told of the wonders of the world-historical giant being built at the foot of the iron-ore deposits, offering free rail transportation to the site and the promise of workclothes and a bread card upon arrival. After July 1930 they could also offer an extra month's pay to those who put in five months on the site, and they often gave recruits "advances" to see them to the site.

Such recruitment efforts were supported by a national press campaign. Every major newspaper carried exhortations to work on the new construction sites, Magnitostroi especially: "Tebia zovet Magnitostroi!" [Magnitostroi is calling you!]. Documentary films and newsreel footage about the great construction were shown in factories and movie houses.[39] Sometimes worker-correspondents would visit factories and construction sites to stump for recruits, handing out train tickets right there. "Evenings," or nighttime discussions, on Magnitostroi were conducted in factories and other institutions.[40] One former Red Army soldier and tractor driver, F. Kadochnikov, recalled how such recruitment pitches were made:

> I first heard about Magnitka in my political training classes at the Frunze Artillery School, in Odessa. The commissar explained that, near the Ural River, they were going to build a gigantic metallurgical factory and a large modern city. He asked: "Who wants to go to this shock construction site?" More than ten hands shot up—all were from the Urals.[41]

Some potential recruits were more cautious, sending "scouts" to the site to investigate the promises of adventure and good pay and report back to the collective on what the actual conditions were.[42]

Other construction sites proved an especially good source for recruitment, particularly when various short-term goals were nearing completion. Viktor Kalmykov, who was featured in a special photographic essay on the newcomers, was one of hundreds who went to Magnitostroi after preliminary foundation work had been finished at the Stalingrad tractor site in 1930.[43] In the enthusiasm of the moment, entire work gangs would sometimes declare their desire to participate in the building of socialism at Magnetic Mountain. Such was the case with Khabibulla Galiullin, a Tatar, who was recruited along with some fifty compatriots from a construction site in Moscow.[44] In such cases the line between recruitment and mobilization became blurred.

The press campaign and other recruitment efforts were supplemented by letter writing to friends and relatives back home, some officially sponsored but much of it spontaneous, by those already living at the site.[45] "At that time there was so much in the papers about the building of the new cities, and about industrialization, and we young people were all enthusiastic about the new cities," explained Mariia (Masha) Scott. "My sister had already gone to Magnitogorsk and she wrote me how interesting it was, how nice, how it was something new." A student in Moscow at the time, Scott boarded a train and upon arrival took up residence with her sister and brother-in-law.[46]

But recruitment in all its forms met many obstacles. Industrial enterprises, compelled to enter into agreements to provide workers for Magnitostroi, sent far fewer people than had been agreed upon, if they sent anyone at all.[47] Magnitostroi signed agreements with dozens of factories to send skilled workers, but these workers were needed where they were, and usually only those few skilled workers without small plots of land (*pashnia*) were even willing to consider the offer.[48] As for the supposed reserves of the collective farms, they supplied no more than 11 percent of all those who came to the site in 1932 and only 6 percent in 1933.[49] Collective farm chairmen reportedly concealed recruitment announcements from members and lied to them about the requests being made to collective farms for supplying construction workers.[50]

The traveling recruiters were apparently not very capable or trustworthy. In the second half of 1930, for example, of the sixty-five recruiters sent out by Magnitostroi, thirty-six returned without having recruited a single person, in the process spending 200 to 2,000 rubles each.[51] And even those few people actually recruited did not always make it all the way to the site. The recruiters "were clever; they promised the moon and brought with them brochures," recalled one recruit, "but many recruits disappeared before reaching Magnitostroi, some even drinking their advances, while many left just after arrival."[52]

Locally known recruiters were often the most successful,[53] but they too faced many obstacles, as the following story about the efforts of a Novostal agent illustrates. "A recruiting [Novostal] agent for Kuznetskstroi came to our village," an eyewitness recalled. "Two thousand people showed up at a meeting. He spoke about the details of the contract and tried to paint a rosy picture. But we were experienced workers, and so we didn't believe him. He flopped and was powerless to recruit even a fraction of our village." But this was not the end of the story. The narrator of this vignette had himself gotten a telegram from an old acquaintance who now worked for Magnitostroi and who had asked him to go to the site, which he did. Not long after arrival, he was sent back to his village to recruit, at which time he discovered the presence of the Novostal agent. "Since I was well known and trusted," the local explained, "already on the second day my neighbors began knocking at my door."

But anyone wanting to sign up with him had somehow to bypass the spurned Novostal agent, who refused to leave the village. A list of around two hundred names was compiled by the local and sent to Novostal headquarters, and a new agent came with 15,000 rubles advance money to pick up the workers for Magnitostroi. Yet even this was still not the end of the story, for most of those on the list belonged to the local trade union, which naturally refused to let its workers go. This meant that they would be without valid travel documents and thus would have difficulty using the advance to buy the train tickets. Recruitment was a tricky business.[54]

In fact, the overwhelming majority of people went to Magnitostroi not through recruitment but haphazardly, by what was called *samotek*. Official statistics, heavily biased to demonstrate the success of recruitment, nevertheless could not conceal its failure. In 1931, 48 percent of all workers who came to the site were supposedly recruited; in 1932, 29 percent, and in 1933, 24 percent. These already meager numbers should be reduced still further because not everyone "recruited" made it to the site, while even those who made it often did not stay. Even top officials recognized that the policy of organized recruitment never amounted to much more than whistling in the dark. To central authorities doggedly committed to supervision of the country's labor supply, a change in strategy was called for. As it happened, a solution of sorts presented itself in the form of new village policies that accompanied the industrialization drive.

After a series of increasingly burdensome taxes and other means of harassment, on 30 January 1930 the Central Committee adopted a resolution formally calling for the "liquidation of the kulaks as a class."[55] "Dekulak-ization" had already been taking place in some areas, but now it became an officially declared policy, and persons accused of being "kulaks," kulak "henchmen," or "ideological" kulaks had their property confiscated and were forbidden "to join" the collective farms. Many were shot or sent to camps; the rest were "sentenced" to exile with forced labor and deported to the North, Siberia, the Urals, Kazakhstan, or remote areas of their own regions.[56]

A second and far larger wave of "kulak" deportations occurred following a formal decision by the leadership in February 1931—that is, right in the midst of the nervous top-level discussions on labor shortages at all the major construction sites of the Five-Year Plan, including Magnitostroi.[57] The aforementioned 27 March 1931 panicky meeting on the shortfall in the labor supply for Magnitostroi and other large construction sites found its resolution. The scientific authority of class analysis and the pliability of class categories, when combined with the Bolshevik leadership's eagerness to resort to state-organized violence, helped to make possible the deportations, which in turn facilitated the authorities' ambitious plans for the new construction sites.

Tightly packed boxcars carrying dekulakized peasants began to arrive at Magnitostroi in May 1931 and continued to do so throughout 1931 and 1932.[58] (In the month of June 1931 alone, the population at Magnetic Mountain jumped some 50,000.)[59] One Soviet eyewitness to their arrival recalled when

> they began to drive the special resettlers to Magnitogorsk. An extraordi-nary plenipotentiary arrived. They called for me. A car came at 1 A.M., and I rode to them. Comrade Gugel Iakov Semenovich, the chief of the con-struction, was there. The plenipotentiary turned to me and asked my name. Then he asked: "Do you [ty] know who you're speaking with?" I said, "I don't know you [vy]." He answered: "Here's how you can help me. In three days there will be no fewer than 25,000 people. You served in the army? We need barracks built by that time." . . . They herded in not 25,000, but 40,000. It was raining, children were crying, as you walked by, you didn't want to look.[60]

Of course, the barracks were not built in three days or even three months. Instead, the peasant exiles, who numbered upwards of 40,000 men, women, and children, lived initially in tents. Thousands died during the winter.[61]

Concerned about the political loyalties of these people and the threat they supposedly posed, the authorities attempted to gauge their mood by monitoring conversations. One was overheard to say: "Why did they send us here to work, I'm a peasant. I don't know industry, teaching me, an old man, 49 years old, is useless. It would be better to have stuck me in an isolation prison than to force me to work barefoot in industrial construction." In the same conversation, someone characterized as a "kulak" reportedly remarked, "with Soviet power there is no unemployment and no labor power, and here they need many workers. And so the best and cheapest labor power are colonists, special resettlers. With us the Bolsheviks have less expense and trouble."[62]

This was not far off the mark. It is as hard to imagine the construction of the Magnitogorsk Works in the empty steppe without the abundant reserve of penal labor as it would be to conceive the construction of the Gary Works in the marshes south of Chicago without the ready supply of cheap immigrant labor from southeast Europe. But, whereas Gary drew its initial work force after 1906 largely from the generous ranks of the urban unemployed or semiemployed,[63] the deportations from Soviet villages to Magnitogorsk were part of a general rise in demand for labor at remote construction sites that Soviet urban populations—recruited voraciously for construction work in established cities—could not satisfy.

During the first Five-Year Plan, urban unemployment in the Soviet Union was "liquidated."[64] Yet while the construction sites helped to eliminate registered unemployment, the unemployed could not have provided the number of people needed for the construction projects: those officially counted as unemployed disappeared like a pitcher of water poured into the sea. Rather, the new construction sites were largely peopled by peasants driven from their villages, sometimes at gunpoint, sometimes out of hunger and desperation, or, in many cases, leaving out of genuine enthusiasm to see the cities.

Significant movement from countryside to city had been occurring ever since the emancipation of peasants in 1861. Within the Urals, *otkhodniki*, or peasant seasonal workers, traditionally left the villages for temporary work in timber, mining, or construction. This movement, which had essentially ceased during the Civil War but was renewed during the NEP, increased considerably during the first Five-Year Plan, when the number of *otkhodniki* in the Urals region was estimated to be 148,000 on 1 January 1931, 205,000 on 1 June 1931, 301,000 on 1 August 1931, and 424,800 on 1 January 1932.[65] N. Efremov, the Soviet historian who provided these numbers, claimed that the 1932 total for *otkhodniki* represented more than 25 percent of all people of working age living in the Urals at the time.

That Magnitostroi, a place to which obviously no *otkhodnik* had ever traveled before (because it did not exist), was now receiving an influx of something resembling *otkhodniki* in tremendous numbers shows that with collectivization *otkhod* was undergoing transformation. This is not the place to examine the complicated *otkhod* issue in depth.[66] Although statistics on *otkhod* per se are inconclusive, reflecting the confusion which prevailed at the time and continues to baffle scholars to this day, there can be no doubt that the number of those traveling from villages to cities and construction sites was increasing dramatically.[67]

For the Bolshevik leadership, however, the point was not to increase *otkhod* but to render it unnecessary by the permanent transfer of peasants to the cities. Accordingly, one of the main tasks at the new construction sites was to transform the construction industry into a year-round activity, eliminating its seasonal character, which was determined by weather and the rhythms of agriculture. This effort was particularly evident at Magnitostroi, where, among other things, winter concrete work was done outdoors in bitterly cold weather. There was even a special decree (*prikaz*) on work in cold weather: below $-20°C$, frequent breaks and more frequent shift changes were called for, while no work was supposed to be done when the temperature reached $-41°C$.[68] These guidelines, even if not always followed, indicate that construction work was indeed being conducted in winter and that the seasonal character of construction, one of the basic structures of the *otkhod* system, had at least been partially undermined. Efremov claims that of the 424,000 *otkhodniki* tabulated by January 1932, more than 250,000 stayed on in the cities permanently,[69] meaning that despite his use of the contemporary designation attached to these people, technically they were no longer *otkhodniki*.

Whether as temporary, seasonal workers or as one-way out-migrants, then, it was those lumped into the category of *otkhodniki* who were helping to people the new construction sites most extensively. During the first Five-Year Plan the urban population of the Urals climbed 1,172,000, from 1,635,000 (1928–29) to 2,807,000 (1932). During the same period, the village population declined by more than 600,000.[70] Clearly, the countryside was populating the cities of the Urals, but which countryside?

According to one Soviet scholar, 70 percent of the new urban population in the Urals came from within the region.[71] That may have been so for the Urals as a whole, but the one year for which detailed data were available to me on the region of origin for the population coming into Magnitostroi, 1931, shows a different picture (see table 2). As is evident from the table,

Table 2. Origin of Incoming Population, Magnitostroi, 1931

	Plan	Recruited	Samotek	Total
Urals	12,930	13,022	5,156	18,178
Tatar ASSR	10,795	9,019	1,649	10,668
Bashkir ASSR	—	3,646	1,306	4,952
Middle Volga Krai	12,030	5,451	2,142	7,593
Nizhnii Novgorod Krai	7,470	2,989	514	3,503
Western oblast	16,000	7,273	582	7,855
Ivanov oblast	7,680	3,746	186	3,932
Kazakhstan, Kirghizia, Central Asia, and Central Black Earth	—	10,905	6,650	17,555
Region unspecified	—	—	42,471	42,471
Total		56,051	60,656	116,707

SOURCE: The table is adapted (with totals corrected) from a table reproduced, without citation, in Serzhantov, "KPSS—Vdokhnovitel'," p. 183, citing *Magnitostroi*, nos. 1–4, 1932, pp. 85–86. See also RGAE, f. 4086, op. 2, d. 119, l. 22, where a similar table can be found.

the largest single category consisted of people whose region of origin was unspecified. No doubt many of these people came from within the Urals region, but it is impossible to conclude that the majority, let alone 70 percent, of all in-migrants did. In 1931 *at least* 55,000 out of the 116,000 did *not* come from the Urals.[72]

Consider again the dekulakized. One Soviet source asserts that between 1930 and 1932, 15,200 "kulak" families in the Urals were deported (how many more escaped deportation but had to flee?), although it gives no indication of their destination.[73] Some certainly were sent to Magnitostroi. But according to John Scott, the majority of dekulakized at Magnitostroi came from Kazan and its surrounding districts, and according to a Soviet source they came from Kazan and the Ukraine.[74] It seems clear from the example of Magnitostroi that, both through deportations and the transformation of *otkhod*, the Urals region was experiencing an influx of population from outside, particularly from the territories to its immediate west.

That Magnitostroi was primarily peopled from villages outside the Urals, through deportation and the transformation of *otkhod*, can be highlighted by a brief examination of the national composition of the site's population.[75] According to a 1931 pamphlet, Russians made up 83.7 percent of Magnitostroi's population, Ukrainians 6.8 percent (around 8,000 people), White Russians 1.6 percent, Tatars 2.7 percent (around 3,000), Bashkirs 1.4 percent, with no other groups above 1 percent.[76] Kazakhs are not listed, but the local newspaper revealed that some 4,000 Kazakhs "came" to the site at some time.[77] It seems, then, that there were at least 1,000 or so Bashkirs, 3,000 Tatars, 4,000 Kazakhs, and 8,000 Ukrainians, or a total of some 16,000 non-Russians at Magnitostroi in 1931.[78]

Despite the population's largely Russian character, these scattered figures indicating the presence of a sizable number of non-Russians at Magnitostroi are suggestive, for although bordered to the west by Bashkiria and Tataria and to the south by Kazakhstan, the Urals had had a population according to the 1926 census that was 91.21 percent Russian. In the words of one geographer (writing just prior to the founding of Magnitostroi), the Urals region was "a Russian island surrounded by a sea of nationalities."[79] In other words, by 1931 there were significantly higher proportions of non-Russians at Magnitostroi than had been the case previously for the Urals.

The Ukrainians are a good example. Although Ukrainian peasants had been migrating eastward in large numbers since the end of the nineteenth century, it seems that few settled in the Urals.[80] In fact, in 1926 Ukrainians constituted less than 1 percent of the population in the Urals, a figure so small that allowances for the notorious underreporting of Ukrainian nationals outside the Ukraine could not alter it significantly. In contrast, Ukrainians at Magnitostroi in 1931 accounted for almost 7 percent of the total population. Many perhaps had been deported to Magnitostroi, while of those who came "freely" very few would have been *otkhodniki* in the original sense of the term, given the distance involved.

In sum, the (at least) 16,000 Bashkirs, Tatars, Kazakhs, and Ukrainians present at Magnitostroi in 1931 could hardly have been indigenous to the Urals. They came from elsewhere, as seems true of half, at the very least, of Magnitostroi's aggregate population. Villages outside the Urals were "peopling" Magnitostroi. With mobilizations producing no more than a drop in the ocean and recruitment a disappointing failure, central authorities, having created chaos in the countryside with the radical policies of collectivization and dekulakization, were in effect "squeezing" people out of the village—Russians, Ukrainians, Tatars, Kazakhs—and trying to direct them to distant destinations, such as Magnitostroi.

THE STRUGGLE FOR CADRES

The conductor announced that we had arrived in Magnitogorsk. From the train a motley crowd quickly poured out. The clothes of the newly arrived were primarily home-spun. Only a few wore jackboots or shoes. The rest wore bast sandals. Waiting until the flow of new construction workers dispersed, I started along. Along the way horses were carrying bricks, cement, and logs. From the left could be heard incessant hammering, resembling machine-gun fire. I caught up to the horse laden with cement. Behind the horse was walking a tall, lean, unshaven *muzhik*. I asked him, what was that hammering? The *muzhik* answered severely: "You mean you don't know! They are building a blast furnace [*domna*]. It will be bigger than all the others on the earth!" What a blast furnace was, I didn't know, and I didn't ask.[81]

Who were the people congregated at Magnitogorsk? How were they categorized? What was expected of them?

A countrywide sampling of members of the Metal Workers Union in 1932–33 indicated that 57.2 percent of all such workers at Magnitogorsk were "peasants."[82] (And how many of those listed as "workers" had been peasants until rather recently?) Another Soviet source expressed concern that as many as two-thirds of all those on the construction site had no previous industrial experience, and very few had any "skills" beyond wielding an axe.[83] Also, in 1931, when the criteria for literacy were not very stringent, as much as 30 percent of the Magnitogorsk work force was pronounced illiterate or semiliterate.[84] Finally, the population at Magnitogorsk was generally young—as of 1 January 1933, almost half the workers were under twenty-four years of age[85]—and primarily male.[86] Here, then, was the bulk of the new people who would build socialism and populate the new city as they appeared to the agents charged with characterizing them: former villagers, young, male, unskilled, and either illiterate or semiliterate.

Such a profile of the country's new work force—which applied, although to a lesser degree, to other cities and factories throughout the Soviet Union[87]—caused the Bolshevik leadership considerable alarm: a proletarian revolution, it was felt, needed a "real" proletariat, not a peasant work force. In the leadership's thinking, "consciousness" was strongly dependent on social background. The much-feared "peasantization" of the urban work force and city population induced the leadership to commission numerous studies and censuses of the politically vital proletariat and to issue various decrees and instructions, all of which made clear that the authorities were inclined to take special measures to address what they perceived to be a critical problem. That problem was defined in a specific way, the analysis of which requires step-by-step treatment.

In its simplest form, the point was as follows: when completed, the Magnitogorsk Works was going to need a large number of workers— 19,500 workers, according to a 1931 Vesenkha calculation (up from the original projection of 14,610). Of that work force, 7,000 were to be supplied by other factories, 2,000 would come from active recruitment by the factory, another 2,000 from the factory's training programs, and the rest, 8,500, simply from among the workers of the construction site itself.[88] In other words, even with the overly optimistic assessment of how much of the operating personnel would come from other factories, the majority (8,500 plus 2,000) were to come from the population already at the site. Yet how were they going to make skilled workers and urbanites out of the people on hand? Machines and equipment could be imported, but operating personnel could not. As one Soviet historian wrote, "the most important problem in the construction of the factory was supplying it with cadres."[89]

For the authorities, creating a skilled work force for Magnitogorsk was understood as a "struggle for cadres," cadres in the sense of qualified technicians. To begin with, the authorities reasoned that they needed some sort of mass training program for the peasants who lacked industrial skills. To this end, they sent potential workers to nearby Verkhne-Uralsk, fifty kilometers north of the site, where they were enrolled in "courses" that were based on the pedagogical methods of the Central Institute of Labor.[90] In a few weeks, these youngsters would learn, for example, how to lay bricks. But when they returned to the site, there were no bricks to be found, a situation that led to the questioning by local authorities of sending inexperienced workers to training schools. Not surprisingly, such mass training schools away from the site were abandoned and replaced by on-the-job training supplemented by all sorts of makeshift courses, circles, technical hours, night schools, and brigade instruction.[91] To a great extent, the subject of the training did not matter, for trainers discovered that "workers who were in training courses, no matter how brief, mastered the production process faster than those who were not, commanded complicated machines better, and showed higher productivity with less idle time."[92] It was the inculcation of new attitudes, habits, and rhythms of work that was the key, and these could be (indeed, had to be) acquired in the "heat of construction."

Building factory shops and creating personnel to run them went hand in hand, and in the words of the popular contemporary expression, technicians "grew like mushrooms" on the site.[93] As a leading historian of

Magnitogorsk has written, "thousands of workers of the Magnitogorsk complex in a very short time traversed the path of unskilled laborer, *zemlekop*, master, brigadier, foreman, and so on."[94] It should be added that on-the-job training applied to so-called engineers as well as laborers. In 1931 less than two-thirds of the "engineers" on the site had higher or middle-level educations, and certainly only a handful had real engineering experience.[95] As late as 1935, 70 percent of the 1,465 "specialists" at Magnitostroi had no technical training and were qualified as specialists solely "from experience."[96]

But acquiring technical skills formed just one element of the larger goal. "The struggle for cadres in Magnitostroi," a Soviet scholar has written, "was a struggle for the rearing of workers coming from the village in the spirit of socialist relations to labor."[97] The Magnitogorsk factory was not only to supply the country with metal; it would also supply it with a proletariat, and the creation of a proletariat was not simply a question of producing skilled workers, but of skilled workers who were "socialist." The struggle for creating skilled workers was equally a struggle for instilling political allegiance, which in turn was part of the establishment at Magnetic Mountain of "Soviet power." At Magnitogorsk Soviet power did not arise automatically from a decree; nor was it based solely on the party and the police. Soviet power existed through the people's belief and participation in it.

Pamphleteers, whose ranks served as a graphic manifestation of the existence of a battle for the allegiance of the people, were finely attuned to what was at stake in such a battle, as the following conversation, which reportedly took place on the site in the first years, shows:

> "Did you catch that, old woman? A Giant is being built. There's going to be a factory here. It will make iron."
> "Why are you bothering me? You're accursed. They're not going to build anything here. The Bolsheviks are only fantasizing. Agitating the people."

The old woman, who lost two sons in the Civil War and had another leave her, roared that the Bolsheviks "sit on our necks! They suck our blood!"[98] And it was not just old women who spoke thus (although we cannot expect the pamphleteers to give us examples) or whose attitudes and allegiances constituted an arena of contestation. Let us, for example, examine the issue of the associations and groupings of the workers who arrived on the site.

Many of the peasants came to the site in traditional groups of migrant villagers known as artels whose leaders were generally older peasants, men who commanded absolute loyalty from the other members and brooked no incursions into their authority. One enthusiastic party member explained what he thought was at stake here:

> An artel was completely composed of fellow villagers, and people came to the site as artels. In general, we did not have the right to interfere in their affairs. They divided the wages among themselves. Every artel had its own tradition [for dividing wages]. In the artels they had their own "masters of the first hand," "masters of the second hand." To the master of the first hand, they gave more money, to those of the second a little less, and so on. It did not depend on how a person worked, but only on his position. These traditions were strongly maintained. . . . We had to smash the artels.[99]

That artels might somehow coexist with Soviet power seems not to have been considered.

Instinctively suspicious of even a hint of an alternative center of authority, the Bolshevik leadership at Magnitogorsk, following national directives, adopted several strategies for curbing the power of the local artels. First, they introduced piece rates, trying to tie wages to individual job performance. This policy was of course resisted by the artels and by itself would have had no effect.[100] But in addition, the authorities sought volunteers among the artel members to form "brigades," led by "new men," in the hope that they would drown out the artels. This approach seems to have had some effect. True, "there were cases in which old artel leaders somehow became brigade leaders," recalled one participant, "but in the majority of cases brigadiers were 'new' people."[101]

Despite certain surface resemblances between the artel and brigade forms of organization, and despite the periodic continuities in leadership, there could be no doubt that with this tactic the local Bolshevik leadership began to make inroads into the power of the artel leaders.[102] But breaking the authority of the artel leaders was just the beginning. In forming brigades, the local authorities tried not only to undermine the old allegiances but, more importantly, to create new ones. In this critical task they were aided by the trade union organization and especially the Komsomol, which, along with the brigade, served as a Bolshevik wedge between the powerful artel leaders and the artel members.

It was at Magnitostroi and other large construction sites that, beginning in 1930, the Komsomol became a mass organization.[103] Entrance into the Komsomol occurred in waves. Membership in Magnitogorsk's Komsomol rose from just over 3,000 as of 1 January 1931 to 14,241 by 1 January 1932. Virtually all the new members had joined during 1931.[104] In 1930 Magnitostroi was declared the first all-union Komsomol construction site,[105] and a traveling brigade from the newspaper *Komsomolskaia pravda* set up an office there in a railroad car and in September 1930 began issuing *Komsomolskaia pravda na Magnitostroe*. By October the paper became *Magnitogorskii komsomolets*, purportedly the first localized regular Komsomol newspaper in the USSR.[106]

As the Bolshevik authorities at Magnitogorsk discovered, the Komsomol could be used for everything from night watches protecting the site to making the rounds in the barracks to fight carousing. Komsomols were particularly active in the campaigns for the liquidation of illiteracy (and not just their own), and they also played a key role in construction work: blast furnace no. 2 was christened "Komsomolka," as virtually everyone working on it joined the Komsomol. "The Magnitogorsk Komsomol," wrote one of the first directors of the site, Iakov Gugel, "was the most reliable and powerful organizing force of the construction."[107]

The effectiveness of the new organizational strategy centered on the Komsomol and the brigade was developed through socialist competition and shock work. It is not possible here to examine these devices in detail. For the moment, it will suffice to illustrate how they were used in the programs for "peopling" Magnitostroi through an example: the construction in 1930 of a dam on the Ural River to supply the steel factory with water, celebrated as the first great event in the history of Magnitogorsk. Such a construction would seem a simple and straightforward matter, yet it turned out to be anything but that.[108]

Excavation work for the dam began on 26 July 1930. At first, the work went poorly. There was virtually no mechanization, not enough laborers to make up the difference, and in any case no one seemed to know what to do.[109] In August representatives of the Central Control Commission-Workers' and Peasants' Inspectorate (TsKK-RKI) visited the site of the future dam and sounded the alarm: "The dam is in danger!" A new local party organization was formed that, on 21 August, issued a special decree on the dam. Speeches were made, mobilizations were ordered, brigades were organized, shock work began: "Everyone to the dam! Everything for the dam."[110]

In extremely cold temperatures, work continued around the clock (one brigade reportedly remained at its "post" heroically for thirty-six straight hours). Meals were skipped, and workers were often called back to the job for emergencies immediately upon returning home after long shifts.[111] There were not enough heaters to keep the cement from freezing, and sometimes, when the electricity went down, cement was mixed by hand.[112] "The chronicle of these days," wrote a journalist, "is a long list of cubic meters, of cement mixes, of Komsomol mobilizations, of emergency duty, and of storming nights."[113]

In a time-honored tradition, the authorities attempted to compensate for the low skill level among the builders with the greater motivation derived from a sense of higher purpose. Not everyone shared the same level of commitment, however, judging by the posters that were put up: "Entrance for all absentees and shirkers is blocked!"[114] A "black" bulletin board carried the names of everyone who did not show up or "deserted" his or her post and thus "betrayed" the construction, and a "penalty" brigade was formed to combat absenteeism by seeking out the deserters and slackers to embarrass and shame them back to the job.[115]

On 3 September 1930 someone came up with the idea, inspired by the experience of the famed Dneprostroi hydroelectric dam, of having a "socialist competition" between the left and right banks of the river: first side to reach the middle wins.[116] The American consultants in charge of overseeing the dam construction protested vehemently (to no avail) that there would be serious consequences if the two sides did not meet properly. To the Americans, the socialist competition was a technically unsound gimmick.[117] Others protested the socialist competitions for different reasons, as one Soviet partisan recalled:

> We spoke about socialist competition with the leader of an artel—a strong, tough old guy in a red calico peasant shirt, girded with a patterned sash. He listened to us with a reserved expression on his face. It seemed that he understood everything, and was agreed. . . . And then the old carpenter exclaimed: "It's not your business to teach me how to work faster. With my axe I've brought forth dozens of churches and no one hurried me, nor told me that I worked slowly."[118]

And not just old "peasants" but new men in the "brigades" resisted the socialist competitions as well.[119] One journalist revealed that some of the peasants had their own competition: who could eat the most bread.[120] In such an atmosphere, the dam would become, as would the construction as a whole, a highly charged field of political reckoning.

As evidence of the political significance engulfing the construction of the dam, the local leadership decided, against all technical considerations, that it should be finished in time for the 7 November holiday. But even this was not enough, for to this propitious date "counterplans" demonstrating greater ambition (and thus allegiance) were proposed: 1 November, then 15 October. In fact the dam, which was named in honor of the Ninth Komsomol Congress, was reportedly finished in early October—a "record" of just 74 days (as opposed to the 120 supposedly proposed by the Americans). The right bank won (by varying degrees, according to different accounts). Banners were hung, speeches were given, "heroes" were decorated, and busts of Lenin and Stalin were made from the cement. The atmosphere was described as "saturated" with "labor enthusiasm"[121] (although at first, as one Soviet journalist tells it, the workers had not even been able to pronounce the word *entuziast*).[122] Aleksandr Voroshilov (no relation to the marshal) composed a poem, "Pervaia Pobeda" (The First Victory), which is how the story of the dam was still known in Magnitogorsk fifty years later.

Did it matter that it was soon discovered that the dam was not deep enough and the water froze, so that the local authorities had to beg Moscow to send dredging explosives?[123] Or that the water shortage became so acute that the same authorities begged Moscow for a water specialist to be sent immediately and began to build makeshift pipelines to distant streams? That this chronic water shortage persisted for years?[124] And what of the fact that the capacity of the factory in the meantime had been raised considerably, so that the dam was utterly inadequate the moment it was finished, and that a whole new dam, over five times larger, had to be begun almost immediately; that when the second dam was completed (planned for 1932, it was not finished until 1938),[125] the original dam was submerged? This all meant nothing.

What mattered instead was that the dam had been built—not only built but built ahead of schedule—and in the process hundreds of youths had come of age as loyal partisans of the cause. The number of shock workers skyrocketed during the building of the dam from 1,635 to over 6,000 in one month.[126] And their "enthusiasm" soared.[127] "As at a military front, where the will to victory decides the success of battle," wrote Iakov Gugel, "so on the construction front of Magnitka, enthusiasm and labor upsurge became deciding forces."[128] This was not a mere dam but a gigantic crusade in which the lowest individual could become a great hero by straining to pour an extra load of cement. In a way, experiences on the construction site, such as building the dam, cemented Soviet power as much as the production of the steel plant itself would. "The Magnitogorsk dam," wrote one pamphleteer, "was a school at which people began to respect Bolshevik miracles [*chudesa*]"—a telling word meant to be taken literally.[129]

Surrounded by empty steppe as far as the eye could see, hounded by freezing cold and blizzards, with little food or warm clothes, living in a crowded barracks and working sixteen-hour shifts moving earth in horse-drawn carts or pouring concrete in the dead of night—Magnitostroi workers soon divided into those who believed in the dream, in the great future, and those who did not. And allegiance was what Magnitostroi was, in a way, all about.

A group of young enthusiasts, working double shifts, whole days without rest and with little food, met to discuss the work on blast furnace no. 2, "their" furnace, the Komsomolka. One of them opened the meeting by asking, "Does anybody have any suggestions?" Someone else was quoted as saying, "What kind of suggestions could there be—everybody straight to the site for a *subbotnik* [any time extra work was performed without compensation]." If we are to believe the credible account from which this conversation is taken, the youths "worked until dawn."[130] Such pathos was genuine, and it was widespread. "Everyone, even the laborers, felt that Magnitogorsk was making history, and that he, personally, had a considerable part in it," wrote John Scott, himself deeply affected by the enthusiasm of the crusade. "This feeling was shared to some extent even by the exiled kulaks."[131]

But what about those who refused to be caught up in the excitement, who refused to perform all the outrageous requests that were made of them, who voiced an alternative view, even if on a seemingly trivial matter? They were branded "class enemies," regardless to which class they belonged (either by birth or occupation). Here, for example, are the words attributed to Komissarov, a Donbas miner who had come to Magnitostroi: "Why are we working here? There is no bread, they pay us no money, there are no apartments, the chow is lousy, they don't give us any work clothes. Is this living?"[132] From these observations it was concluded that Komissarov, thirty years a miner, was a "class enemy." In the logic of the struggle, anyone who asked for more rations, for better work, for more pay, for anything at all, "threatened" to undermine the *whole* enterprise, to bring the *entire* revolution to a halt. Such people were dubbed "kulaks" or "kulak henchmen," people with a "doubtful past," and were subjected to humiliations, expulsion from the site, and arrest.[133] Even rumors were thought to constitute a threat to Soviet power.[134]

From the very beginning in Magnitogorsk, before the cement foundations were even poured, class enemies, right opportunists, and counterrevolutionaries were being "unmasked."[135] And every such "discovery" brought new exhortations to struggle harder and achieve more.[136] The so-called struggle for cadres at Magnitostroi, where even "neutrality" could seem as suspicious as opposition, was an intricate political encounter. What the Red Army had been for the regime in the 1920s, the new construction sites became in the 1930s: its device for transforming and assimilating the

Table 3. Labor on Hand, 1931

1st of Month	Total Workers	Came	Left
January	18,865	3,597	3,853
February	18,609	4,398	3,402
March	19,605	8,570	5,934
April	22,241	9,391	7,166
May	24,446	17,640	9,826
June	32,280	17,292	10,825
July	38,747	10,983	12,694
August	37,006	8,693	11,447
September	34,252	10,381	9,421
October	35,162	8,003	10,072
November	33,093	10,350	10,797
December	32,666	7,440	7,835

SOURCE: *Magnitostroi v tsifrakh*, pp. 236–37, 242.

peasantry into the collective crusade, the building of socialism, the Five-Year Plan, "the revolution,"—in short, the new civilization.

THE ART OF MANAGING AN ARTFUL RESOURCE

By the end of the first Five-Year Plan, according to one source, there were 305,000 people on construction sites in the Urals, compared with 42,000 at the beginning.[137] More than half of these would have been at Magnitostroi. It was the biggest construction site in the Union. By the end of 1931, when the population of Magnitostroi was closing in on 200,000, the population of Karaganda was 96,000.[138] At Novokuznetsk in 1931 there were said to be exactly 45,903 people, with another 5,862 across the river and six miles away in old Kuznetsk.[139] Magnitostroi dwarfed the largest of the other "shock" (*udarnyi*), meaning priority, construction sites.

But Magnitostroi, the biggest shock construction site in a country that worshiped bigness, did not have enough "labor power," even of the "unskilled" variety. In 1931, when the construction plan called for 47,105 semiskilled workers, the monthly average, no higher than 33,000, left the site some 14,000, or 30 percent, short. In detail, the breakdown for labor on hand by month in 1931 is provided in table 3. The planned targets of labor power were not met even during the peak months. The chief cause of the labor "shortfall" at Magnitostroi was not insufficient arrivals but excessive departures—a problem that attracted considerable attention.

What the authorities called labor fluidity (*tekuchest*, literally "leakage") existed in the Urals before the establishment of Magnitostroi.[140] Indeed, the authorities probably hoped that Magnitostroi would become a magnet that could draw in and retain the large roaming population. And crammed trains did come to Magnitostroi regularly, even if there was as yet no train station there, as expressed in this ditty from the barracks:

Ekh mne Milka napisala—	My arriving Mila wrote to me—
Vstrechai, milii, u vokzala.	Let's meet, honey, at the station.
Telegrammu Milke dal:	I sent Mila a telegram:
Privozi s soboi vokzal.	Bring the station with you.[141]

No matter: an incoming train approaching the site would simply come to a halt where a sign—"Magnitogorskaia"—had been placed on an uncoupled boxcar that sat on a siding, and unload its human cargo, or labor power.

The construction sites themselves had become "recruiters." Arrivals were greeted, asked a series of questions about their point of origin, social status, skill-levels, and so on and signed up for work on the spot. "Thousands would get off," wrote Zinovii Chagan, an essayist for *Rabochaia gazeta* stationed at Magnitostroi. "[They] were carrying homemade knapsacks [and] would ask: 'Are there felt boots? work pants? Is there butter? How is it with eggs? Can one find milk? Are people joining trade unions?'" As an enticement, Chagan claimed that officials dispensed "bread and makhorka, some herring."[142]

But if people were streaming into Magnitostroi, they were also streaming out. Vissarion "Beso" Lominadze, for a while city party secretary, presented figures for the number of those workers who had come and gone from Magnitostroi (see table 4).[143] Since the average number of workers on the site was around thirty thousand, by early 1934 almost ten times as many workers had passed through the site than were at hand. Indeed, who had not been to Magnitostroi!

> You tell someone you're going to Magnitostroi, and everywhere you hear: "Magnitka, I'm going there," or "I just came from there." Somebody says he has a brother there, somebody else is waiting for a letter from his son. You get the impression that the whole country either was there already or is going there.[144]

Many people in fact came and left several times in the course of a single year.[145]

Table 4. Workers Arriving and Departing
Magnitostroi, 1930–1933

	Came	Left
1930	67,000[a]	45,000
1931	111,000	97,000
1932	62,000	70,000
1933	53,000	53,000
Total	293,000	265,000

SOURCE: *Magnitogorskii rabochii*, 15 and 20 January 1934.
[a] It is possible that the figure of 67,000 for 1930 is a typographical error and should have read 57,000.

People were coming and going by the tens of thousands, and in between, they were not staying very long. Of the 116,703 who left during 1931, 30,756 registered their exit, and of those who complied with the mandatory exit registration, fully 27,649 people (90 percent) had been at the site less than six months; 16,031 (over 50 percent) had been there less than three.[146] According to another official source, in 1931 the average length of stay for a worker was 82 calendar days.[147] And it was not only the workers who were leaving. In 1931 almost three thousand white-collar employees (*sluzhashchie*—there were around six thousand on hand in March 1931) left the site. The average length of stay for employees was 186 days; for engineering and technical personnel, 221 days.[148] Only the handful of top-level administrative personnel, the one thousand or so highly skilled workers, and the forty thousand dekulakized exiles behind barbed wire were not fleeing the famed construction site.

Some departures were to be expected. A few hundred youth, for example, were called up for service in the Red Army.[149] Even more workers left after having completed the terms of their contracts. Out of desperation to entice workers to the site, six-month and even three-month contracts were offered to workers, who were then free to leave, as some apparently did.[150] Of the 30,756 who registered their departure in 1931, 6,130 (20 percent) did so after having completed the terms of their contracts.[151] Many young construction workers considered production as a supplementary income to their basic earnings in agriculture.[152] Some were probably returning to the villages to take part in the land redistribution and to look into reports of hard times or trouble. In short, given the high demand for labor and the woeful inadequacy of the recruitment apparatus, Magnitostroi had no choice but to accept all comers, however long or short a time they agreed to stay, and many agreed to stay only briefly.

Others, however, were leaving out of dissatisfaction, for even by the standards of the day, living conditions on the site were harsh. Most workers lived in filthy, overcrowded barracks (see chapter 4). There was a severe shortage of warm work clothes, little to do besides work, and the food and service in the public dining halls was generally despised. Moreover, by the fall of 1931 (well before the onset of the famine), food shortages began, and getting even bread became a problem.[153]

To be sure, some people stayed despite the wretched living conditions. D. D. Lushenko, sent from Moscow in 1931, recalled a few years later that

> there were forty of us sent. All the others have gone back. Back then it's true, living conditions were not so hot. My group tried to get me to leave Magnitka and go back, but I said that there's no defender of Soviet power who is afraid to endure all difficulties. I am going to stay the length of my mobilization period, and then I'll return. I worked my year, and I then stayed on to work. And look, I'm working in Magnitogorsk three years.[154]

But many more fled. Even the vaunted Komsomols were bolting.[155] If as of 1 January 1933 there were 11,000 Komsomols, one year later there were only 5,400. Some 800 had been kicked out, another 1,000 were known to have quit and were taken off the rolls, and the rest just evaporated.[156] Some of those "voting with their feet," as if in confirmation of Lenin's apt phrase, literally left on foot, just setting out for the Ural mountains in the distance.[157]

Magnitostroi became a revolving door, a literal "labor exchange" in the form of a railroad junction. The train, that ally of the Bolshevik leadership and its bureaucrats and planners, was being used against them: construction workers were using the trains to tour the country.[158] As one Soviet historian has written:

> Such workers knew everything: what kind of lunch they served at Stalingrad, what kind of industrial goods they had at the distribution points of Dneprostroi, what kind of wages were paid at Magnitka. In one season they succeeded in visiting all the huge construction sites of the Union—having seen that everywhere there were recruiters who paid for trains without asking you for birthplace or social origin, but only that you take up work.[159]

In 1931 alone, the bacchanalian fluidity was said to have cost the Magnitostroi trust seven million rubles in transportation outlays and another two million in lost work clothes.[160]

At least initially, the creation of new construction sites such as Magni-

tostroi had not resulted in the establishment of stationary working populations but instead further fueled the fluidity. The Bolshevik leadership
concluded not that people were taking advantage of the confused situation
and traveling perhaps in part out of a sense of genuine adventure but that
the harsh living conditions were understandably driving workers from the
new construction sites. This state of affairs was called a "disease" of the
construction sites and a "blight" on the Five-Year Plan.

And how deeply it seemed to be embedded: in a speech delivered before
a select audience in Magnitogorsk in 1933, for example, Sergo Ordzhonikidze went so far as to decry the "suitcase mood" (*chemodannye nostro-
eniia*) among even the comparatively privileged leading personnel. If in
Magnitogorsk the stalwart leaders "felt as if on a temporary business trip"
(*komandirovka*), how were the humbler to feel?[161] But little would change,
central authorities reasoned, until concrete steps were taken to improve
living conditions.

In fact, local authorities tried to combat the dread fluidity in several
ways. They declared mandatory registration for anyone leaving the site
and deployed worker watch groups (*zaslony*) to enforce the decree. But
given the conditions at the site, such a policy was unenforceable. Beyond
restrictions, however, there were various incentives for those who agreed
to stay, such as advances for workers to bring their families to Magnitogorsk or preferential supply allotments for those who had stayed at the site
for a certain period: a little extra bread, maybe some more sugar—at least
that was what was stamped on the paper, though the supply depot often
found it impossible to comply.[162] Another popular approach was to allow
the workers to cultivate small plots of land, on which they could grow potatoes and other vegetables. According to one party official, this had the
desired effect.[163]

Beyond the enticement of extra supplies and an allotment of land, considerable moral pressure was brought to bear. The authorities launched
much-publicized campaigns to get the workers to sign contracts to stay until the end of construction, or at least the end of the Five-Year Plan. But
these proved to be no more enforceable than the system of mandatory exit
registration. "Thousands signed up," one Soviet eyewitness remarked of
the solemn pledges, but "then most left anyway."[164]

Ordinary people seemed to be holding all the cards. Here is how one
petty official at Magnitostroi characterized his attempts to battle the labor
fluidity: "They called me on the phone and told me that the *Dneprope-
trovtsy* were leaving. . . . A scandal! I had to go straight to the barrack.
What's the matter? They said they had been cheated, they get sent to work

where they can fall and kill themselves, and so on. I spoke with them for two hours, and they stayed."[165] Not everyone could be talked out of leaving, and in any case a situation which required them to beg workers to stay was one the authorities would tolerate only so long.

It is against this background that we can begin to understand the reintroduction of the tsarist internal passport system, announced by Sovnarkom on 28 December 1932. The immediate cause for the "passportization" of the urban population might well have been the fear that famine conditions in the countryside would drive the peasants en masse into the cities in search of food. But there can be no doubt that the Bolshevik leadership was also trying to bring some order to the construction sites. Seen from the vantage point of the peopling of Magnitostroi, the passport campaign appears not as the culmination of a premeditated policy designed to establish total control over the populace but rather as a typically heavy-handed Bolshevik improvisation to combat a problem their policies had done so much to create. Still, what stands out is the leadership's willingness to employ any means necessary to advance its aims, and to express all such radical measures in the sanctifying language of defending "the revolution."

In Magnitogorsk the passport campaign was announced on 10 February 1933, and individuals were required to present valid documents at their place of work beginning immediately. From 15 February until 25 April, all those in charge of the various construction objectives were to turn in lists of their workers containing name, year of birth, place of origin, current residence, and job title. Beginning 1 March, all hiring was to be done strictly upon the presentation of a valid passport. A brigade was sent from Moscow to ensure that the passport campaign was taken seriously by enterprise bosses (normally more preoccupied with industrial tasks) and that no passports "fell into the hands of the class enemy."[166]

True to the political quality that came to envelop every aspect of human activity, the first internal passports were given out with much fanfare at a meeting in the dining hall of the elite rolling mill construction group. There were speeches on the building of socialism, on the building of new cities, and on cleansing Magnitogorsk of "parasitic" elements. "The class enemy is stretching out its hand to snatch a passport!" the newspaper warned. "We must strike that hand!"[167] By April it was reported that the the passport campaign was practically complete, but unfortunately the number of passports issued was not made public.[168] On the other hand, it seems that some two thousand people had their outstretched hands struck, so to speak, and were banished from the city, while another eighteen thousand did not even try to stretch out their hands but just fled.[169]

But registering the entire population tested the endurance and skills of the local authorities, who, though not afraid to exercise their wide powers, were numerically overmatched.[170] During the passport campaign, on a normal day at a small neighborhood militia station hundreds of people would come to request immediate signatures or documents, to air complaints, or to comply with demands to provide further information.[171] The staff was too small to handle the volume, slip-ups occurred, and some cases deemed suspicious could not be fully investigated, while others escaped investigation altogether.[172] Some people survived for decades under a false identity with bogus documents. Some even survived entirely without documents, hired by enterprises desperate for labor power.[173]

Not surprisingly, documents became particularly valuable objects, among the first things stolen from an apartment by a thief. Escapees from the corrective labor colony mugged the first people they encountered for their documents.[174] And it seems that documents were being "lost" all the time. If the loss of a particular document was duly reported in the newspaper, the person was entitled to obtain a replacement. During 1936, for example, there were many days when there were lists of twenty or more lost and no longer valid documents. Where did those lost documents go? A market in documents arose.

In 1936, during what seems to have been an unannounced campaign to root out bogus documents (for which today's researcher can be grateful), the newspaper reported on what it called the case of the "factory for bogus documents." One Popik decided to change his social position from middle to poor peasant. He made his own official seal to stamp the forged documents. Seeing how easy it was, he evidently decided to make a business of his newly discovered craft. He stole blank trade union booklets and membership cards and was able to write them up as necessary, applying the official seals in his possession. When he was arrested, the authorities found blank forms and seals at his place of residence. For his counterfeiting operation, the extent or duration of which is not recorded, he was given three years' "loss of freedom."[175]

Such activity as practiced by Popik was facilitated by the absence, until 1938, of photographs in passports.[176] People could and sometimes did try to rework some of the details on their passports.[177] But such an approach could be dangerous. It was better to "play it safe," taking advantage of the underground market in the kinds of documents one needed to obtain a passport, making sure that the passport itself would not need homemade "emendations." One case was reported in the local newspaper of a person who for twenty-five rubles bought documents with a new family name to be used in obtaining a passport.[178]

Everyone knew that one could buy or obtain important documents, if only from newspaper accounts intended to expose the practice. One pickpocket, when apprehended, turned out to have four different passports, which he probably would have sold for the right price.[179] Meanwhile, some people simply created their own documents.[180] Particularly popular seems to have been the technique of forging letters from officials, detailing invented positions a person supposedly held to obtain work (and thus new, unimpeachable documents).[181]

Those who plied the documents market evinced an awareness of the importance of having not simply valid documents but ones that described activities that were valued. If one of the effects of the passport campaign was to generate a proliferation of illegal activities involving documents, another was to demonstrate—at the margins of legality, in the forged and phony documents—the outlines of the new boundaries of social and political life, the new rules of the game, of who one should or should not claim to be (a theme explored further in part 2).

Internal passports were but one element of the new approach to population management. Back on 13 October 1932, just prior to the announcement of the passport campaign in Magnitogorsk, there was a city soviet decree, following a directive from central authorities, to establish mandatory registration of local residence (*propiska*) at the militia stations for all Magnitogorsk citizens over sixteen years of age. The registration was to be enforced by the individual in charge of a given residential building (*kommendant, starshii, zavobshchezhitiem*). Foreigners, too, were required to register.

Through the rationing system then in force (see chapter 6), supply officials were instructed to give out products only when shown a receipt proving local registration, and all outstanding wages were to be dispensed only upon registration. Particular attention was to be paid to the fulfillment of military obligations. The documents acceptable for registration included birth or marriage certificates, a note from the place of employment, military service papers, a trade union membership card, or school or student identification. Those without valid documents could obtain a three-month temporary registration. Submission of false documents would be penalized.

The registration system was the necessary complement to passports; within the city, passports meant little without such a system. In turn, registration was predicated on "control" over places of residence. Such a watchdog system was partially undermined by both lack of staff and the nature of the housing and urban geography of Magnitogorsk, which was spread out over twenty kilometers (see chapter 3). Up to a point, the less than strict registration system provided a measure of slack in the operation of the city's passport control. And yet the registration system could be quite troublesome for residents.[182]

Despite the give and take, the document shuffle was a tricky and dangerous game. There were periodic "exchanges" of documents, and not just of party cards but also of Komsomol and trade union cards, even driver's licenses.[183] The newspaper reported that in 1936, 9,390 expired passports were exchanged.[184] Such document exchanges could be harrowing, the least suspicion—not to mention the anonymous affidavits from peers or neighbors—setting off an investigation. Although the militia and other authorities were not very organized or efficient, all the registrations, re-registrations, questionnaires, document exchanges, and anonymous informing and denunciations meant exposure could occur at any time. Many of those arrested for petty criminal activity turned out to have phony passports, or none at all.

The continuous registration of the entire population was a major operation requiring considerable effort and resources that often overtaxed the local officials. Indeed, authorities were still battling the hiring of workers without *propiskas*, with only temporary *propiskas*, or with phony documents as late as 1938.[185] But by this time the document battle was heavily weighted in the authorities' favor. Some people continued to live and work under their adopted identities, and the document market never entirely disappeared. But the penalties became greater and the police net wider, as trains into and out of the city began to be patrolled systematically and local cinemas and other public places were subjected to spot document inspections.

Migration into and out of Magnitogorsk continued after the passport system went into effect.[186] But as Raphael Khitarov, Lominadze's successor as city party secretary, proclaimed on New Year's Day, 1936, "the days when being sent to Magnitogorsk was considered a painful ordeal and when the majority of workers felt like temporary visitors are over. Gone are the days when the construction site resembled a revolving door."[187] By this time, managing the movement of the population had become "regularized," and Magnitogorsk's population movement came to resemble what were deemed "normal" migration patterns for established cities.[188]

The resolute actions undertaken to manage the labor supply, important as an indication of the authorities' worldview and of what some forms of state coercion amounted to in everyday terms, no doubt had some effect in slowing down people's movements. In the end, however, it was less the deployment of restrictive measures that "settled" the population at Magnitostroi than the fact that a viable urban settlement, the city of Magnitogorsk, and new way of life had arisen there. Far more than a process of "upward mobility," this entailed the creation of a new society. What began at the Magnitogorsk dam and was known initially as "the struggle for cadres" became much more involved, as we shall see.

THE POLITICS OF DEMOGRAPHY

Soviet authorities understood the notion of "population" as a problem of the supply of labor and, ultimately, of the strength of the state. Of course, securing and managing a sufficient supply of "labor power" are critical goals in any industrial undertaking. Such, for example, has always been the explicit purpose of the so-called company town, a nineteenth-century response to labor unions and worker unrest that was intended to "attract, hold, and control labor."[189] But according to a survey by the U.S. National Resources Committee, in 1938 only about 2 million people (out of a population of 130 million) lived in what could be classified as company towns.[190] In the USSR, virtually all towns had become company towns.

In the USSR, moreover, beyond the unstated goal of containing possible worker unrest, there was the additional consideration that a "free" labor market on which individuals sold their labor power to the highest bidder was thought to be characteristic of capitalism and thus inimical to socialism. The central allocation of labor power—meaning, the regulation of population movement—was viewed as an integral part of central planning. In the event, "planning" labor allocation over so large a country proved to be a formidable task but one that the Bolshevik leadership did not shrink from even after the enormity of this proposition began to sink in. Nowhere were these ambitions and their repercussions more in evidence than at Magnetic Mountain.

The peopling of Magnitostroi can be read as a case study in the Bolshevik leadership's crude methods of administrative rule, and in the resourcefulness of individuals when confronted with difficult choices. Much of the country's peasantry was confined to the new collective and state farms, but millions of rural inhabitants were offered a chance to out-migrate permanently. For some this "offer" came in the form of deportation, while others could and often did turn the enormous demand for labor to their own advantage, touring the country. When during the famine these mobile peasants were joined by those desperately in search of food, the regime adopted strong measures to deter the whirlwind "labor fluidity" and settle the peasants-cum-construction workers at the new construction sites permanently with the passport and *propiska* systems.

Such draconian measures proved easier to declare than to enforce. Neither the size and efficiency of the regular police nor the level of document technique permitted the full realization of the passport system. And these built-in limitations, in the face of the uncompromising inflexibility of the system's goals and rules, made likely the adoption of tactics for the circumvention of the new restrictions. Several methods for falsifying documents or for getting by without them—even a market in illegal documents— arose. It was a game of unequal risk for the two sides; nevertheless, it was a two-sided game. Many people were forced to play the dangerous game, yet the authorities were compelled to expend considerable efforts putting it into play.

At the same time, the goal of populating the construction site at Magnetic Mountain had been reached, albeit at greater cost than had been anticipated. The authorities' unwavering insistence on the right to command individuals' relocation and, above all, their readiness to use force against "class aliens" certainly made the daunting task less difficult. In a word, the horrendous situation created in the village contributed mightily to the Bolshevik leadership's efforts to create a large permanent population at Magnitostroi. The people streaming into Magnitostroi resembled refugees, and their large numbers and the circumstances that impelled them on their journeys gave the impression that war was raging outside the territory of Magnitostroi, as, in a sense, it was.

Still, from the authorities' point of view, populating Magnitostroi, along with the many other large new construction sites, was a remarkable achievement. In the chaos and dislocation of the 1930s—admittedly engendered by their own policies of compulsory collectivization and forced-pace industrialization—the authorities nevertheless managed to "bring in" and maintain some 200,000 people at an isolated location under harsh and difficult conditions. No amount of coercion by itself is sufficient to achieve such an outcome, except at an exclusively Gulag-controlled site. Although Magnitogorsk did have its share of people transported and held there against their will, the majority of people were not prisoners but the inhabitants of what they rightly viewed as a new society coming into being, and one where they were able to find a niche for themselves: a job, a place to live, perhaps a family and some sense of self-worth.

Had the daunting feat of gathering an urban population been all the authorities sought to accomplish, the story of peopling Magnitostroi would have been dramatic enough. But in addition to settling a very large contingent of people at an isolated site in a brief period, the authorities endeavored to re-create these people. The goal was to teach them to work and think of themselves in specific ways, to imbue the new urbanites with a sense of historical mission: the building of a socialist world. The effects of these efforts, in the context of the new society that emerged, have only been touched upon here. This story will be taken up in part 2. Before that, however, we must examine the patterns of Magnitogorsk's urban geography for what they tell us about the nature and parameters of the new world being built.

3   The Idiocy of Urban Life

> But what was this? A village? Of course not. A small town? No. An
> encampment? A workers' settlement? A burg? No, officially this huge
> populated place was called a city. But was it a city?
>
> Valentin Kataev, *Vremia, Vpered!* (Time, Forward!)[1]

What was this place, Magnitogorsk? In truth, it was not easy to say, even
if, like the novelist Valentin Kataev, you had visited it. And it was no easier
for the permanent urban inhabitants, or the city's leaders. Simply locating
Magnitogorsk presented difficulties, since it did not yet appear on any map.
But you could buy a train ticket to Magnitogorsk or, more precisely, to a
destination of that name. In the first years, a train ride to Magnitogorsk
from Moscow required five changes and routinely lasted more than a week,
even when everything went smoothly, which it rarely did. After one eight-
day ride from Moscow in 1930, the train came to its usual abrupt halt in
the middle of the open steppe. Passengers looked out the window and,
seeing nothing, assumed there had been yet another breakdown. But then
the conductor bellowed, "Magnitogorsk!" Could this barren, windswept
wasteland be the famous World Giant? The colorful journalist Semen Nariniani disembarked from the train, looked around, turned to the station
man, and asked, "Is it far to the city?" "Two years," the man answered.[2]

As it happened, the station man was doubly wrong. It would be far more
than two years to the completion of the fabled "socialist city of the future."
But it would be far less than two before the emergence of the actual city,
which was growing that very minute in front of the station man's eyes.
The train station, or rather the site of the future train station (it too was a
few years away), formed the gates to the emerging urban territory:

> Every day when the train arrived a panic broke out. Another four hundred
> workers! It was of course known beforehand that workers were coming,
> that they would come every day. But all the same, every day their arrival
> posed an unpleasant dilemma. . . . In a forty-person barracks up to one
> hundred fifty people would be squeezed. Of course they figured it was only

for a day or two, but on the very next day, a new trainload arrived and they forgot about those from yesterday.[3]

In such apparently haphazard fashion did Magnitogorsk come into being.

Of course, Magnitogorsk was supposed to be the modern world's first completely planned city, the real-life laboratory that planners worldwide believed would demonstrate for all time the advantages of urban planning.[4] In a sense, Magnitogorsk was "planned." Various sketches were made of the future city, and some of these schemas did guide part of the city's construction. Soviet town planning, however, turned out to resemble after-the-fact "bootstrapping" as much as the coordinated realization of a prior vision of the eventual form and function of a city—even in the case of Magnitogorsk, where there at least were some preliminary conceptions for a modern industrial city.[5] Paradoxical as it sounds, then, Magnitogorsk was a planned city that arose largely in spite of the plans.

And yet, despite the generally chaotic conditions under which the city's main residential sections took shape and the corresponding emergency nature of Soviet town planning, Magnitogorsk's urban geography coalesced into a distinct, if not immediately obvious, pattern. In its own way, Magnitogorsk ended up faithfully reflecting the circumstances of its conception and construction as the urban form for a new world founded on heavy industry. For this reason, the maligned planners, however much they may have been offended by the outcome, could not completely disown the urban milieu they had a part in creating. Their designs and the apparently spontaneous urban configurations that resulted turned out to have much in common.[6]

*   *   *

Urbanization in the early Stalin period has been discussed largely in general terms, without reference to the experience of actual cities, and almost always only in the context of industrialization. Moshe Lewin, for example, has written of the large-scale "ruralization" (*okrestianivanie*) of Soviet cities during the industrialization drive, arguing that the movement of millions of "backward" peasants into urban areas transformed Soviet urban society for the worse, ultimately paving the way, in combination with the characteristics of the growing bureaucracy, for the deepening of political authoritarianism. Between Bolshevik modernizers and the great mass of peasant *muzhiks* Lewin sees a clash "of almost two nations or two civilizations" whose outcome turned out to be tragic for both.[7]

In Magnitogorsk, however, such "ruralization"—if that is the appropriate term—appears to have been largely beneficial, both materially and in terms of social cohesion, given that the "peasant" urbanites helped prevent the rest of the town from starving and showed remarkable abilities to cope in what proved to be a difficult, even dangerous, urban environment. In this chapter, though, we are less concerned with the supposed consequences of the movement of peasants to cities than with the particular vision of urban modernity that guided the rebuilding of existing cities and the construction of new ones.

As in the formation of an industrial economy so in town planning, the transcendence of capitalism was the vague but grand goal. And once again, something less than transcendence became the unexpected result, although in the case of the city, the failure to meet what were towering expectations proved far more disappointing. Yet no less than with the construction of the modern factory, the uncommon opportunity to participate in and witness the building of what was supposed to be a new kind of urban formation inspired extraordinary efforts and emotions.

SOCIALIST CITY OF THE FUTURE

As a socialist city, Magnitogorsk was to be the very opposite of a capitalist city—more accurately, the opposite of the capitalist city as vilified by contemporaries. Rather than narrow, dark alleys and desolate slums, Magnitogorsk would be composed of wide, bright streets, where the workers would live in shiny superblocks. A socialist city would not be founded on ignorance or superstition but on education and science. And it would not be rampant with alcoholism but overflowing with "culture." In short, Magnitogorsk was to be a place of hope and progress.[8] But who knew how to design such a city, or what form it should take?

In January 1930 the government of the Russian republic, Sovnarkom RSFSR, announced a contest for the design of Magnitogorsk, with a projected population of forty thousand.[9] A bit earlier (December 1929), a parallel competition was announced for a new kind of domicile.[10] The deadline for receipt of proposals for the contests was March 1930. "To create a city and new type of domicile, different from all existing ones that had been built thus far, in three months—as the conditions of the competition demanded—was truly quite difficult," wrote Ignatiem Vernshtein, in an unpublished essay on the history of the design of Magnitogorsk which he signed I. Ivich.[11] But during the Five-Year Plan time was considered of the essence—in this specific case even more so, for there were already more than the projected forty thousand people at work building the factory on the cityless site.

Of the at least nineteen projects submitted in the 1930 city-design competition, the one submitted by Professor Chernyshev was declared the winner.[12] In keeping with the limits imposed by economy and a preference for a vaguely defined "socialized" organization of city life, Chernyshev's plan called for public dining halls, baths, and reading rooms. But according to Ivich,

> there were no great innovations in it: symmetrical superblocks [*kvartaly*] of apartment buildings distributed along a central axis of the city from north to south. On the main street were the public buildings. Every apartment building would contain . . . 1,500 people and would be square with an inner courtyard.

Perhaps because it was altogether a less frightening and more conventional project than what some of the famous architects were proposing in the country's leading architectural journals, Chernyshev's conception met favor with the State Institute for the Planning of Cities (Giprogor), the agency initially charged with designing the new city.[13] Be that as it may, Giprogor decided, in Ivich's words, to add a few details of "socialist settlement patterns."[14] These, however, were still to be worked out. All anyone knew was that socialist settlements patterns were to be different from capitalist ones, whatever those were.

Simultaneously, an agency of the Soviet government other than Giprogor sought to import the services of Ernst May from capitalist Germany to design the vaguely understood noncapitalist city. May had won international acclaim at the International Congress of Modern Architecture in 1929 for his workers housing settlements in Frankfurt.[15] There, he created a series of semi-independent, compact, but not densely populated, settlements (*Siedlungen*) equipped with extensive public facilities, such as day-care centers, common washing areas, playgrounds, schools, and theaters. As for the housing itself, May—a functionalist who paid due attention to sanitary and health considerations and an egalitarian who planned for equal access of all to sunlight, air, and municipal services—used standardized, prefabricated housing, right down to the kitchens and furniture, to minimize costs and construction time. In the first year, against a plan for 1,200, 2,200 new dwelling units had been built. In the second year, 3,000 more were built.[16] Intrigued, the Soviet government sent a commission to Frankfurt in 1929 and invited May to come to the USSR to plan not just large housing developments but whole cities.[17]

For his part, May was very enthusiastic about the possibilities of urban planning in the Soviet context. In his position as chief architect of Frankfurt, he had enjoyed wide powers in zoning, financing, and building instruction. Now, it seemed he would have even greater powers. Accompanied by virtually his entire Frankfurt staff and a few non-German architects,[18] May arrived in the Soviet Union in 1930 with, in his words, a "free hand to solve the problems of the contemporary city."[19] "No one can predict whether, what is the greatest national experiment of all times, is going to succeed," he wrote, "but it is infinitely more important for me to take part in this immense task than to worry about the security of my private existence."[20] It was a promising collaboration.[21]

Even before May had set foot in the USSR, however, "from Magnitogorsk came telegram after telegram: it's time to build!" Although under severe pressure to work quickly, May, when asked to critique Chernyshev's existing plan, decided instead to offer his own alternative.[22] Patterned after one of his settlements in Frankfurt, May's proposal for Magnitogorsk was billed as a "linear city." First developed by Arturo Soria y Mata in the nineteenth century, the "linear city" held sway over the imaginations of many celebrated architects. It called for an elongated stretch of uniform rows of superblock neighborhood units running parallel to the industrial zone (minimizing transportation to and from work) that was protected by a green belt wedged between the living and production zones. According to his biographer, May worked on the Magnitogorsk linear city sketch for an entire year.[23]

But after being whisked to the site in late October 1930 as part of an unwieldy commission made up of representatives from Tsekombank, Giprogor, and several other organizations, May discovered that a linear city alongside the steel plant could not be accommodated to the local topography.[24] Much the same had happened several months earlier to the less elaborate plan of Chernyshev, who "looking over the future site of Magnitogorsk" was said to have "rejected his own project" as unsuitable.[25] May had not been forewarned.

Even more surprising, when he arrived at the site May found that the city he had been asked to design was already under construction. On 5 July 1930, three months ahead of the German architect's arrival but just in time for the opening of the Sixteenth Party Congress, the local authorities in Magnitogorsk organized a ceremonial laying of the foundation stone for the first apartment building on what was named Pioneer street. This was done even though Chernyshev had just repudiated his own design, and a proposal from May had not yet been received. The ceremony, conducted with the usual fanfare and in the presence of fourteen thousand people, marked the commencement of work on the first part of the city, whose configuration and positioning were still unresolved.[26]

For the city's location there were two very different choices: build either on the left bank, or eastern side, of the Ural River, where the factory and mine were situated and where temporary settlements had sprung up; or on the right bank, that is, on the other side of the industrial lake, at a distance of several kilometers from the industrial zone and the existing settlements (see maps 1 and 2). Given the necessity, with the right-bank variant, of building what loomed as a costly and logistically complicated bridge and mass transit system across the lake—to say nothing of difficulties of carrying out construction work on the right bank, far away from the economic base provided by the factory—the left-bank option seemed the more feasible. Above all, the left-bank variant promised far more finished housing by the time the steel plant was to be put into operation, supposedly in 1932.[27]

When the left-bank site was indeed chosen by government authorities in 1930, assurances were made that the prevailing wind direction would carry the smoke and harmful emissions from the future factory to the southwest and not toward the southeastern city. But on the site, it was immediately discovered during construction that all of the harmful smoke and fumes blew directly southeast.[28] Instead of shifting to the right bank, however, the solution adopted was to move the proposed left-bank city a distance of at least two kilometers from the factory. (Remarkably, Chernyshev's proposal for the left-bank city had called for building the city directly adjacent to the factory gates, and construction of the city center was well underway, despite his repudiation.)[29] It was at this point, after the city had been placed on the left bank but shoved back a bit, that May had arrived at Magnetic Mountain to discover that he had been betrayed by the undulating terrain on the eastern side of the river and by the premature start of construction.[30]

Ultimately, it was not the lay of the land that hemmed May in but the siting of the factory, which meant that the only area remaining on the left bank within reasonable proximity of the factory turned out to be hilly. Obviously, the mountain containing the iron ore could not be moved, but because it was out in the middle of the wide open steppe, there was plenty of space. Yet once the site was chosen for the factory (adjacent to the mine, east of the river), and once the first dam on the Ural River was completed and the plain flooded (producing a huge artificial lake some fourteen kilometers long and more than one kilometer wide), the territory around the

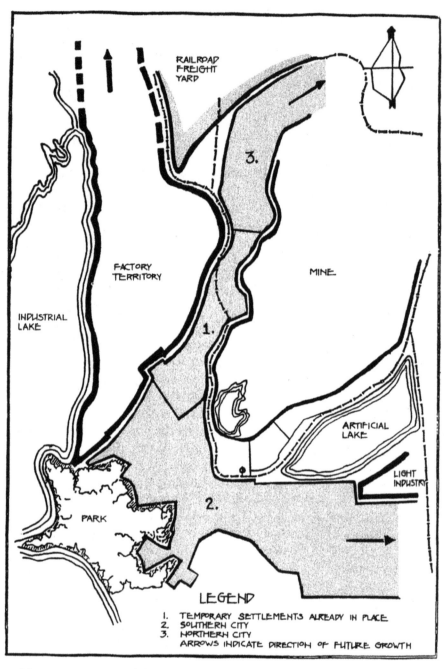

Map 1. Ernst May, Left-bank variant for Magnitogorsk, 1933. Adapted from *Sovetskaia arkhitektura*, 1933, no. 3.

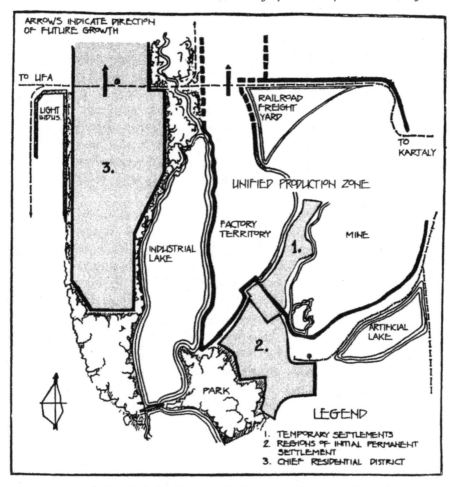

Map 2. Ernst May, Right-bank variant for Magnitogorsk, 1933. Adapted from *Sovetskaia arkhitektura*, 1933, no. 3.

iron-ore deposits was all of a sudden sharply redefined. Well before Ernst May, or anyone else, was invited to design the new city, the left-bank siting of the factory had been settled, and, although virtually none of the actual drawings and blueprints for the factory was at hand, construction on the plant had begun, making the decision as immutable as the iron-ore mountain itself.

May returned to the site in February 1931, along with the on-site operational team director, the Dutchman Mart Stam, and the rest of his "German" brigade.[31] Parallel development of the production and living spheres, May's quintessential idea, had been summarily rendered out of the question, but the need to minimize the distance between home and workplace persisted. This would of necessity involve coming up with some kind of plan for the territory east of the factory and south of the mine. In this space, the presence of three smaller hills—which did not contain iron ore—meant that almost all the remaining flat territory on the left bank that was not as far away from the factory as the right bank had already been accounted for—except for a small triangle stretching from the factory gates to a knoll called Karadyrka (black hill, in Kazakh). In what became willy-nilly a modification of Chernyshev's design radiating out of the factory, May adapted himself as best as he could to this geography, shoehorning a "socialist city" into the triangle.

The hilly and difficult terrain in this area limited the size of the city that the triangular site could accommodate. Moreover, the projected dimensions for the factory had been vastly increased, taking into account probable future expansion. And the apparently unavoidable relocation of the left-bank city into that triangle placed it very close to the mine and the cleansing lakes of the ore-enriching plant. Not only would the space required for these lakes further diminish the land available for the city, the lakes' release of sulphurous gases posed a potential health hazard. With the location of the factory and its water supply (the industrial lake) shoving him into an ever-smaller triangle harassed by the poisonous gases of the mine and the noxious fumes from the steel plant, May could very well have felt that he and his left-bank city were characters in a Greek tragedy: doomed by the contrivance of circumstances to fail, yet destined to struggle to the end.

It was impossible not to see the advantage, even the necessity, of building the city on the right bank. But indecision, rather than forceful measures to address the problems, characterized the government's response. With debate over the location of the city taking place at various levels of the Soviet bureaucracy and different decisions being taken by different authorities, the proposed location of Magnitogorsk flopped back and forth between the left bank and the right.[32] In the words of one popular ditty,

Nalevo li? Napravo li?	To the left? To the right?
Sotsgorod, budesh gde ty?	Socialist City, where will you be?
Tvoi proekty plavali	Your designs have been drifting
Dva goda bez otveta.	Two years without an answer.[33]

So it would be until after the war.

Given the conflicting instructions he received, May was compelled to draw up plans for both a left-bank and a right-bank city. For the former, he modified his already once-revised plan to include a northern satellite city above the factory, located some distance from the southeastern triangle. As could have been expected from May, the northern satellite was to be built as an independent city, with its own city center, cultural facilities—in short with everything the southeastern city would have. Thus, despite the undesirable separation of its two parts, May's modified left-bank city with a northern satellite seemed sensible because the factory could be expected to expand in precisely a northerly direction. In any case, short of moving the city farther from the factory, beyond Karadyrka, thereby defeating the purpose of a left-bank city (proximity to work), it is difficult to see what else May could have suggested for the left bank.

By contrast, the right bank offered May the freedom in design that he had originally counted on. In May's project, the right bank formed a single residential zone, while the left bank, with the factory and mine, formed a unified production zone. Only the distance between the residential and industrial zones could evoke criticism, but this also had its positive aspect, for the industrial lake could serve as a "green belt" neatly separating the two zones and shielding the city from the harmful emissions of the steel plant. Upon completion of the right-bank city, all residential sections on the left bank were to be removed. In short, with the right bank variant the "linear city" was revived.

In early 1932, May's two proposals were under consideration by the scientific and technical council of the People's Commissariat of Municipal Economy (Narkomkhoz), which seems to have reendorsed the left-bank variant.[34] Despite the obvious superiority of a right-bank city from so many points of view, it is not difficult to comprehend the council's decision, for at the time there were more than 100,000 people living on the construction site in temporary installations that were *all* on the left bank. Furthermore, construction of the permanent city on the left bank was already underway. In effect, a decision for the left bank was not necessary, while one for the right bank did not seem practical. Yet the very same council that ruled for the left bank ordered that investigatory work on the suitability of the right bank *begin*. This could inspire little confidence in the long-delayed and evidently reluctant decision in favor of the left bank.

At the site, construction on the left-bank city (without the northern satellite) continued, independently of all decision-making bodies, according to May's drawings.[35] For the triangular Magnitogorsk tract, May designed parallel rows of five-story equidistant apartment buildings positioned to allow each inhabitant generous access to light and air. The buildings were divided into single-room sleeping "cells" joined by a corridor. They had no kitchens, not even communal ones, as the city plan called for an extensive network of public dining halls. Buildings were grouped into superblocks, which contained housing and public facilities for eight thousand to ten thousand people. May's egalitarian plan of identical, equidistant structures also called for highly simplified design and construction work, so that the settlement could be put up in something approaching assembly-line fashion.[36]

Such a "communalist" design followed the mandate issued by Sovnarkom RSFSR in its 11 November 1929 decree calling for the construction of a "socialist" city with "maximum socialization of everyday life."[37] Uniformity was also an explicit objective. In the words of one governmental report issued in the early 1930s, "life in every superblock will be the same. . . . There will be no reason to go to a different one." For solving the problem of how a resident could tell in which identical superblock he or she actually lived, the author of this official report hit upon the obvious solution: "paint each superblock a different color."[38]

On the site, meanwhile, when it became clear what kind of buildings were being built, a protest meeting was called to voice concern. "Engineer [Mart] Stam proved that he was building exactly what had been designed by the architect May," Ivich wrote. "With this no one could argue, but people pleaded that what was being designed by May was not at all what a Soviet worker needed." Instead of having the communalist design altered, however, the stormy meeting ended with "its initiators being booted from the trade union" for "'engaging in the discrediting of German specialists.'" "The criticism," Ivich concluded, "was smothered," at least for the time being.[39]

In truth, what May sketched on paper was often altered during construction through no fault of his "brigade." Two German engineers who went to check on the woodworking factory, for example, reported being horrified at the quality of work being done.[40] Similarly, although May's design specified a central heating system for the buildings, allowance for which had duly been made, there were no radiators (and no kitchen stoves to compensate for the absence of central heating). Likewise, his design called for indoor toilets and space had been set aside for them, but there was no equipment to install and, in any case, no sewage system in the city to hook the pipes up to.

Of all the deficiencies, the sewage problem was perhaps the most regrettable. "When the buildings were about to be occupied, work on the sewage system had only gone so far as to dig a dozen trenches in different places," Ivich wrote. "At night, in the dark, passersby would fall into them.

The trenches were not filled in, and neither were pipes laid in them." He added that "along the street across from the buildings they built a number of outhouse-like temporary toilets. In the wintertime at 40° below, people had to climb down from the fourth floor and dash across the street in order to go to the toilet." More than inconvenience was at issue, however, for the outhouses proved to be highly unsanitary.[41]

Many of the problems plaguing May's left-bank city, and residential construction generally, stemmed from local officials' fixation on industrial construction, an obsession that can be illustrated by the story of the building of the movie theater, Magnit. According to Ivich:

> At the beginning of 1932 the equipment for a sound cinema was sent to the construction site. Funds for the construction of a building were appropriated. Comrade Molotov sent a telegram, inquiring how the construction was proceeding. The city party bureau gathered, summoning the chief of industrial construction for a report on the construction of the cinema. There wasn't much to report. The cinema was not being built. Ten days later came a telegram from Comrade Postyshev: "How is the cinema construction?" Again the city party bureau; again a report. But they began to see that this was a serious matter. They couldn't escape with words alone. So they had some construction materials brought in, sent over a few dozen workers, and began to build a bit. Ten days later—another telegram from Molotov: "How's the cinema?" City party bureau; report. Some more materials were brought in, the number of workers was doubled. A few more telegrams and the cinema was completed.[42]

This did not, of course, prevent propagandists from enveloping the opening of the cinema in the usual avalanche of sloganeering. A newspaper article, neglecting to mention any problems with the cinema's construction, called the opening an event of "enormous political significance" and "a great achievement in the struggle for the creation of a socialist culture."[43]

In fairness to local authorities, not only were their necks on the line for the pace of factory construction, which was constantly lagging, but every amendment to the city design, no matter how apparently trivial, required approval from Moscow.[44] Although local leaders did fail to take the initiative on certain projects, after which they invariably scrambled to cover their tracks, it is clear that Moscow did not trust its representatives on the spot to make even elementary decisions. Be that as it may, the larger point remains: construction of the steel plant, at the same time as it haunted the location of the city, gutted residential construction.

"The construction of the city," Ivich wrote, "was a sort of reserve storehouse for the construction of the factory."[45] Lazarev, the on-site representative of Giprogor, reported that of the 8 million rubles allocated for housing construction in 1931, only 1.5 million were actually spent on housing, the rest having been diverted to the factory and related enterprises. As a result, Lazarev pointed out in the spring of 1931, "right now on the left bank, aside from two unfinished apartment buildings, there is nothing built." Of course, the higher authorities were still deliberating upon which bank of the Ural River to place the city. In the opinion of Lazarev, the right bank was clearly superior, but he was overseeing left-bank construction, admittedly without great success.[46]

More than a year later, little improvement had been made. During an era in which anything less than 100 percent fulfillment of targets was potential cause for a criminal investigation, the 1932 plan for housing construction was being fulfilled at 10 percent.[47] Recall that one of the chief reasons for locating the city on the left bank had been that housing for steel workers would be ready when the plant began operation. This illusion was shattered. Moscow, in the words of Ivich, "was shocked by this incomprehensible situation," which reached the agenda of the country's highest governmental commission, the Council of Labor and Defense (STO).

In August 1932, STO ordered the formation in Magnitogorsk of a separate residential construction agency, with its own money, materials, and workers. Furthermore, STO decreed that all the unfinished buildings (forty-six of them) be brought to completion, and that a definitive city plan, which had yet to materialize in one and a half years, be ready in four months.[48] It was quite a mystery, however, from which hat local officials would pull a residential construction agency, complete with building materials, tools, and skilled workers.[49] A "new" detailed city plan did not materialize until March 1933, when the government newspaper simply republished May's left-bank design with the northern satellite, even though this idea had been rejected.[50] From the point of view of Magnitogorsk officials, meeting STO's strictures may have seemed desirable yet scarcely feasible. In the event, the directives of the country's highest government commission were destined to be unheeded.

Painfully aware that the construction of brick apartment buildings was not keeping pace with factory construction, local authorities obtained permission to build 225 two-story shchitovye, or lattice-wood, buildings with twelve apartments each.[51] But even these easy-to-build structures, which outnumbered brick apartment buildings until well after the war, were put together shabbily.[52] Residential construction was one of the Soviet Union's most backward industries, and in Magnitogorsk, where most energies, materials, personnel, and money were riding on industrial construction, residential construction lagged, swallowing up not a few people in those years, including the internationally acclaimed German architect, Ernst May.[53]

Removed from the Magnitogorsk job in November 1932, May departed the USSR in 1933 a frustrated, bitter, and disappointed man.[54] That year public criticism of his Magnitogorsk superblock was renewed and shifted from the remote site to the central press. In a leading Soviet architectural journal, May was taken to task for failing to adopt a sufficiently "Leninist" approach in his design work. No mention was made of the string of obstacles to a viable design he had encountered, or even what was meant by the formulaic condemnation of his work.[55] Ivich, writing some two years later, however, was more specific. Describing May's buildings as "box-like structures without the least attempt to embellish their military barracks [*kazarmennyi*] facade," he concluded that they "could elicit enthusiasm only among lovers of prison architecture."[56]

Yet were not May's buildings merely the expression in stone of the standardized communal life that Soviet pamphleteers had championed? Should not radical communalization itself have been on trial? That is, in effect, what was happening, although May was absorbing all the blame. To be sure, May was a supreme champion of communalization, but this was one of the reasons he had been hired. Another important factor, however, was at work here. For May, there was no need to adorn a building with flourishes that could not be justified functionally. But for the Soviet authorities, no less than many ordinary people, their buildings had to "look like something," had to make one feel proud, make one see that the proletariat (not literally) would have *its* attractive buildings. May chose neither to conceal the disciplinary quality of modern living nor to stylize it with the socialist-realist aesthetic.

What further bothered the Soviets about May's design was that the buildings were not arranged so as to form inner courtyards. Given that his project provided for communal facilities to be evenly distributed throughout the city, May had reasoned that a physical sense of community would arise naturally and need not be planned into the orientation of the apartment buildings. Moreover, optimal accessibility for each and everyone to sun and light was by definition impossible if enclosed inner courtyards were designed. But in Magnitogorsk, there was a long and severe winter. Rather than sun and air, it was for the snow and wind that an architect should have oriented the buildings, shielding the people as much as possible. What in theory looked like equality, and might have been in a different climate, in the USSR turned out to be exposure. May's superblock resembled a wide open "passageway" (*prokhodnoi dvor*). Failing to take into account the conditions in which his egalitarian planning ideas would be given expression, the great German architect had blundered.[57]

May's failures, only partly his fault, were shocking, for when he first arrived in the USSR everything had pointed toward success. The architect himself had spoken wide-eyed of the "free hand" he would have in the Soviet Union for planning cities, given the absence of private property. But as it turned out, May had to contend with constraints far more powerful than private ownership, including working without a real building industry and within the Soviet bureaucracy. It was, however, something more fundamental that had cornered May right from the start, and from which he could never escape. One of his earliest articles in a local Magnitogorsk publication explaining the socialist city was accompanied by a single illustration. It was not of a residence, a boulevard, a park, a school house, or a laundry but a blast furnace.[58]

By the time of May's departure, construction on only one of his proposed superblocks had been started. When Sergo Ordzhonikidze visited Magnitogorsk in July 1933 to inquire about the steel plant, he also hoped to take stock of this "socialist city." He was evidently shocked. In a speech delivered locally on 27 July 1933, a furious Ordzhonikidze fumed that in general local officials only knew how to beg central authorities for help, instead of tackling matters on their own, and that the chief of city construction, Khrashchevskii, at first had not wanted to show him anything. No wonder. Upon approaching the single superblock, "the scent of the outhouses whacked him in the nose," Ivich wrote, adding that "those who knew comrade Ordzhonikidze well remarked that he rarely was in such a foul mood."[59]

Ordzhonikidze issued an avalanche of impatient decrees calling for improvements in living conditions. Instead of the lofty designation "socialist city" he ordered the use of the mundane "urban *raion*," or district (later named the Kirov district in honor of Sergei Kirov, the Leningrad party secretary assassinated in December 1934). "When referring to your socialist city it is wrong to speak about a 'socialist city,'" the industry commissar remarked during his speech. "This is a direct insult to socialism. One ought not to use the word *socialist* when it is inappropriate to do so. You have named some manure a socialist city. A 'socialist city'—and it's impossible to live in it."[60] On the spot, Ordzhonikidze scrapped the idea of a left-bank city altogether, ruling that after the completion of the work underway, further construction of permanent housing on the left bank was to stop. Back in Moscow, a 23 November 1933 decree of STO once again shifted the socialist city to the right bank.[61]

Maybe they could get it right the second time: a fresh start, a totally new socialist city, just like that, by decree! Construction was to commence right away, since not a few years had already been wasted with what was now viewed as the escapade on the left bank. But a detailed plan was still years off.[62] Meanwhile, a preliminary conception of the new right-bank city was severely criticized in January 1934 by Magnitogorsk party secretary Beso Lominadze, who revealed that of the eight thousand workers engaged in residential construction, *all* were busy repairing what had been done so far. Lominadze warned that on the right bank, "we are in for the exact same mess [*kasha*] that we currently have on the left bank."[63]

When the year 1934 brought no progress toward a right-bank city, the date for "beginning" construction was moved to 1935 (another fresh start). That year the city launched an experiment which had been inspired by May to build prefabricated housing made of large concrete panels. A visiting correspondent for the oblast newspaper, who called these buildings "the most interesting part of the construction," said they "resembled the little houses that children build out of blocks." "This is the future," he wrote with clairvoyance. But in 1935 that future was some time away. Only two such panel buildings were completed, both near the Magnit cinema.[64]

After the new start for the right-bank socialist city had been declared in 1935, not a word was heard until 1937. That year, the newspaper reported the following grim news:

> The construction was begun in 1935. Last year [1936], the walls of four buildings were erected. Now the only thing they are doing is building a single school. There is a night watchman on the site, but in the daytime, construction materials are carried off by whoever bothers to take the trouble.

When pressed in May 1937 to explain the unpromising situation, Vikentii Zverev, the new chief of residential construction, promised that "we'll be conducting the work when it gets warmer." He admitted, however, that "for us, it is still unclear what we are to build there."[65]

In 1938, Aleksandr Semenov, Magnitogorsk's new city party secretary (the third in the brief four-year history of the right-bank city), reported that as of the first of the year, there should have been 150,000 square meters of living space in well-built, permanent buildings on the right bank sufficient for 30,000 people. As of late 1938, however, there was not a single square meter of space in a completed permanent building. On the right bank, in place of Magnitogorsk's (second) fabled socialist city, there were just a few lattice-wood "carcass" buildings, some primitive makeshift shelters, and a labor colony (whose existence was omitted from the subsequently published version of Semenov's report).[66]

Back on the woebegone left bank, with May's departure Soviet architects had taken over the design of what was designated the second superblock, where by 1936 two outwardly impressive apartment houses with spacious apartments arranged around an inner courtyard were completed. Also, May's first superblock was redone: communal kitchens were installed inside the buildings and many of the one-room apartments were consolidated, forming larger spaces. In size, appearance, and interior design, the second superblock buildings were far more generous than May's, even in the latter's redesigned form. But the Soviet-designed buildings suffered from almost as many problems connected with faulty construction, ranging from profusely leaking faucets and toilets that did not flush to windows that for want of glass had to be covered with boards and stuffed with rags.

There had been so much trouble that when another large apartment building, the third of superblock number two, was finished in the spring of 1937, no one was allowed to move in: heaters were leaking, bathtubs had yet to be installed, and there were no wall sockets. Such *nedodelki* ("things not completed") were the bane of Soviet construction. Just as frustrating was the fact that so much of what was built had to be redone. "The residential construction trust builds badly and expensively," the newspaper wrote in 1937. "The same work is done and redone several times."[67] The dream socialist city was built on both banks, but really on neither.[68]

From the start there had been little comprehension of the task of building a complete new city, of whatever design.[69] In the original competition guidelines, for example, the projected size of the future city had been estimated at only forty thousand people. This measly figure was arrived at by taking the number of workers necessary to operate the metallurgical plant (estimated at twenty thousand) and then multiplying it by the average number of people per family (four), giving a result of eighty thousand. This number was reduced by half because it was assumed that women were to be "released" from the drudgery of housework and cooking, thanks to the proposed system of communal dining halls and laundries, and thus made available for "productive" work. There would be no "waste" of unproductive labor, that hallmark of the antiquated bourgeois family, but instead, a superior economy of people.[70]

In the event, however, not many women were "released" for "productive" work, and the projected number of a mere 40,000 inhabitants had to be raised. And what about the people who would not be employed in metallurgy, such as barbers, launderers, teachers, shoemakers, dining hall servers and cooks, members of the city soviet and the party apparat? None of them, indeed no one not directly employed in ferrous metallurgy, had been included in the calculations, for socialist cites were devoted to industrial production, not to "non-productive" services. When this "oversight" finally forced its way into the planners' heads, it became necessary to forego the anticipated "economy of people." By an August 1932 STO decree, the target urban population of Magnitogorsk became 200,000, which was nothing but a guess as to how many inhabitants were already there.

How was it possible to plan for a city without planning for the people necessary to make it function? At bottom the Bolsheviks understood the city as a place to settle their factory and that factory's skilled workers. In all the dozens of pamphlets written about Magnitogorsk during the 1930s, there was never one issued that was devoted exclusively to the city. Discussion of the city, if it was included at all, came as the last chapter, after each of the industrial shops had been enumerated. In the apt words of the ubiquitous journalist Semen Nariniani, the city was the factory's "everyday-life shop" (*kulturno-bytovoi tsekh*).[71] Originally, such an everyday-life shop was to be no more than a simple "workers' settlement." Only when the proposed dimensions of the factory grew did the idea of a socialist city displace that of a factory settlement.[72] But the two were really one and the same.

Before Ernst May had been called in, before the first competition for the new city had been announced, Gipromez published an artist's conception of the future city in its 1929 volume on the design of the factory (see map 3). As can be seen from the drawing, the city emerges wholly out of the factory, with the streets emanating radially out of the factory gates.[73] This pictorial fantasy starkly revealed the nature of the Bolshevik conception of the world. The Bolsheviks thought that once the steel plant had been established, everything else would flow naturally: build a steel plant and civilization will follow; more exactly, build a steel plant, and that *is* civilization. In a way, this is precisely how things turned out.

DOMAINS OF THE PRIVILEGED

The 1932 plan fulfillment rate for residential construction of 10 percent was a lowpoint, but in subsequent years results remained well below 50 percent.[74] Yet even these lowly figures indicate that if not a radiant city, at least *something* was built. That something was the Kirov district, still known colloquially as Socialist City, which in 1938 John Scott, like most

Map 3. Artist's rendering of the factory and city, 1929. From Pavel Egorov, *The Magnitogorsky (Magnetic Mountain) Metallurgical Works* (Moscow, 1929).

people who remembered it in worse days, thought was "something to be seen."[75]

Providing a clue to the identity of the Kirov district's inhabitants, Scott related that "it was 1933 before the first buildings in the Socialist City were occupied" and that "some 200 non-valiuta foreigners were the first to occupy these apartment buildings. Most were German-speaking skilled workers." Scott and his family also lived there, as did many other people of relative advantage. Simply put, the Kirov district was not a place in which one obtained living quarters without having earned the favor of the authorities.[76]

In praising Socialist City, Scott seems to have had in mind only the first superblock, which by 1938 boasted a pedestrian mall graced with fountains and tenderly nurtured saplings, as well as most of the city's decent stores. By contrast, the second superblock—whose three main buildings and many other carcass buildings housed more than three thousand people—still had no streets, sidewalks, or shops, and no one could say when they would have them.[77] But the coveted second superblock's generous-sized apartments were perhaps even more exclusive than the first's, judging by a quasi-sociological survey of the inhabitants of one building in the second superblock published in the city newspaper.

What was known as building no. 11 in the second superblock was said to consist of fifty apartments in which one hundred wage-earners lived, along with their dependents. The tenants' average monthly earnings were given as 554 rubles (the city average was approximately 300). Thirty of the inhabitants of building no. 11 were said to have a higher education and thirty-eight more to have completed middle school (impressive by Soviet standards). A remarkable fifty-seven had been to a resort that year. Fuller responses, including photographs, were published for fourteen people, among whom were a senior economist, the head of the factory's auxiliary smithing shop, five distinguished skilled workers, a shift foreman, a high-level bureaucrat, a school director, a professor, an employee of the chemical laboratory, and a youth official (the latter two being women). The happy message—deserved success—was exhibited for all to see.[78]

Taken together, the handful of brick and numerous carcass buildings of the Kirov district's two superblocks housed approximately 15 percent of Magnitogorsk's population, along with the city's best schools, children's nurseries, and other facilities. This made them a place for the relatively better off, professionals and skilled workers—what might loosely be called the Soviet equivalent of middle and lower-middle classes, as long as we bear in mind their extraordinary degree of dependency on the authorities.[79] Privileged as it was, however, the Kirov district was not the domain of the most privileged. That distinction was reserved for another part of town, whose formation spoke volumes about the emerging society.

In 1930, the top leadership on the site was suddenly informed by the authorities in Moscow that American specialists were coming and that suitable housing for them should be completed before they arrived. The order stipulated that the foreigners were to be afforded living conditions approximating those to which they were accustomed—this at a remote, virtually barren construction site. Despite the constraints, Moscow's order was carried out to the letter.

For the new "American town" (Amerikanka), the local leadership chose the only wooded area anywhere near the site: a small birch grove to the north of the factory and across the far side of the hills from the mine.[80] Here they built some individual homes and a few larger multi-occupancy, two-story stucco bungalows with separate sleeping quarters, a common living room, a kitchen with a wood-burning stove, indoor toilets, and bathrooms with water heaters. One structure functioned as a communal dining facility, which provided waitress service and where, as one Magnitogorsk inhabitant tellingly remembered, the Americans were supplied with "their own silverware."[81] On the grounds the authorities also installed volleyball and tennis courts for summer recreation.[82] One Soviet official recalled that the Americans, who were said to be no strangers to Russian vodka, "managed to dance the foxtrot to the accompaniment of a balalaika."[83]

At first, the on-site director, Iakov Shmidt, stipulated that only foreigners were to be quartered in Amerikanka, but with the arrival in January 1931 of Iakov Gugel, Shmidt's edict restricting the enclave to foreigners was forgotten. "The local secretary of the party was the first to get in, as did the chief of the GPU," wrote Raymond Stuck, one of the American specialists stationed at Magnitogorsk. "From then on it was a stampede." The free-for-all, which included incidents of squatting in partially completed structures and forced evictions, continued until Gugel proclaimed that as far as Soviet citizens were concerned, only higher-ups were to be permitted. Gugel "promptly installed himself in the best house in the American village and completely refurnished it with fine furnishings," wrote Stuck, who added that the Soviet Civil War veteran maintained a retinue of servants, two cars, the finest local team of horses, and the best carriage and sleigh.[84]

By the time the last Americans and other foreign specialists sent by the big firms had left in 1932, only Soviet officials remained. To reflect the new situation, the name of the enclave was changed from Amerikanka to Berezka (birch tree). Viktor Kizenko, Gugel's chief of blast furnace construction who moved into the renamed Berezka in February 1931, later remembered it as "something of an oasis."[85] At the time, Kizenko and the other chiefs of construction for each future shop under Gugel appear to have been known as the "appanage princes."[86]

With the arrival of Magnitogorsk Director Avraamii Zaveniagin in mid-1933, Berezka really came into its own. Zaveniagin had a dozen large individual houses built for himself and his closest associates that according to John Scott were "copied almost exactly from American architectural catalogues" with a result "very much approaching Mount Vernon."[87] Along with the factory director on the new street lived the city party secretary, the chief of the Magnitogorsk security police (as of 1934, the NKVD), the factory's chief engineer (Zaveniagin's deputy), the chiefs of various shops, the chief engineer of the mine, and the factory's chief electrician (the latter two were valued "prisoner" specialists in exile).

Predictably, Zaveniagin's own house was the largest: a three-story, fourteen-room stuccoed brick structure that contained individual bedrooms and a playroom for his two children, a music room, a large study, and a billiard room. This mini-estate, enclosed by a high brick wall complete with steel gates and an armed guard, boasted a luxurious garden. "My garden at Magnitka," Zaveniagin proudly recalled many years later, "was, if not the first and only, surely one of the very, very few gardens in the Urals."[88] John Scott, who had access to the Magnitogorsk archives, wrote that Zaveniagin's house cost a quarter of a million rubles. All expenses, from the construction materials to the labor to the ongoing maintenance, were ascribed to the factory budget.[89]

Other "cottages," as they were called, may have been less impressive than the big boss's—altogether in Berezka there were about 150 buildings, not all of them single-family—but each far exceeded in comfort any accommodations outside this walled community. Moreover, along with relatively luxurious accommodations in a garden setting, the inhabitants of Magnitogorsk's elite enclave also enjoyed the services of well-stocked, restricted-access stores, chauffeur-driven Ford automobiles, expense accounts, and the steel plant's lakeside resort, built about forty kilometers away in the Ural mountains at Bannoe ozero. Here they and their families could swim, fish, and hunt in the mountainous outdoors, staying over, if they wished, in a cabin.[90]

As could have been expected, the local elite's takeover and transformation of Amerikanka was not publicly chronicled, but rather remarkably, the emergence of a kind of "high society" centered in Berezka was. Toward the latter part of the decade, for example, the newspaper was filled with stories of a new specialty perfume shop, Téjé, which was a smashing success, its sales being "way above plan" according to gushing reports accompanied by photographs of women in fashionable attire.[91] Besides the eau de cologne "Carmen," Téjé had its customers wild over the latest scent, "Caucasus Riviera."[92]

The city newspaper also noted that on May Day in 1936, Magnitogorsk began a tradition of masquerade balls. Held in the Engineers' and Technicians' Club (DITR), the first ball was organized by the so-called Council of Engineers' Wives—in effect, the successor to the Zhenotdel or women's department of the party, and the clientele who picked the shelves bare in Téjé (no less a personage than Mariia Zaveniagin, the wife of the steel plant director, was elected council president).[93] The ball, like the perfume shop, was by invitation only. As it happened, however, the organizers had to issue a second set of tickets, canceling the first (apparently, "undesirable elements" had managed to get hold of some tickets, threatening to undermine the event's exclusivity). According to the city newspaper, the revelers danced until 3 A.M.—the factory worked around the clock—but the costume contest was a major disappointment. No first prize was awarded. "The majority of costumes did not shine with special creativity and originality," sniffed the newspaper, which bore the name "The Magnitogorsk Worker."[94]

To be sure, privilege had from the beginning been an integral part of life in Magnitogorsk. The authorities made conspicuous efforts to reward the loyal and the industrious. There were special dining halls for "shock workers," engineers and technical personnel, as well as special housing.[95] The "survey" of the inhabitants of building no. 11 in Socialist City deliberately conveyed as much. But the privileges of party and other officials—whose principal ethic was supposed to be one of sacrifice and service to the people—were for the most part strenuously concealed, with the striking exception of the newspaper accounts of the shopping and after-hours exploits of Berezka society.[96]

Magnitogorsk's "high society" did not compare with Moscow's, where the party, police, and military elite lived in far greater luxury than had the well-off nobles before the revolution, but the inhabitants of Berezka aspired to an upper-class lifestyle in what was supposed to be a proletarian town. Echoing the writings of Vera Dunham, Sheila Fitzpatrick has argued that the *embourgeoisement* of the Soviet political elite—much denounced at the time by some diehard revolutionaries—was nothing more than the "natural consequence" of the rise of people with working-class backgrounds.[97] Whatever the origins of the elite's predilection for a glamorous lifestyle, its appearance could not help but jar public sensitivities.

John Scott, who wrote that "Berezka was a little world in itself," believed that "most of the Magnitogorsk workers had no idea who lived there or how."[98] The writer Nina Kondratkovskaia who lived in Magnitogorsk during the same period as Scott took a different view. "In the early 1930s everybody lived essentially the same," she recalled in an interview in 1987. "There were differences at the extremes, but for everyone tough conditions were the rule. By the second half of the 1930s, however, there appeared a conspicuous group who lived better and enjoyed definite privileges." She added that "they were an elite, considered themselves such, and were viewed by the people as such. And they lived in Berezka." Indeed, despite the enclave's exclusivity, word-of-mouth reports from cleaning and other service personnel helped spread stories of high living throughout the rest of town.[99]

In 1937 the Magnitogorsk elite again greeted the New Year with a masquerade ball, along with the outpourings of gratitude to the "most humble Leader of All Peoples" for all the joy he had brought them that year and would presumably bring in the new one. But this turned out to be the year Stalin began his own special masquerade for the members of high society. In Magnitogorsk, the NKVD's Black Marias, on their nightly rounds to collect "enemies of the people," headed to Berezka and the Kirov district. Even the terror had its specific—although by no means exclusive—urban geography, a subject addressed in detail in chapter 7. Here we can note that the celebrated birch trees of Berezka began to disappear mysteriously not long after the assassination of Sergei Kirov in December 1934: by 1938, 60 percent of the grove had dried up and died, and local specialists were at a loss to forestall the disaster.[100] That year the tradition of New Year's Eve masked balls accompanied by jazz concerts was temporarily interrupted, but it resumed in 1939.[101]

TEMPORARY CITY OF THE PRESENT

Without the option of apartment buildings in the Kirov district or cottages in Berezka, the overwhelming majority of Magnitogorsk's inhabitants took up residence in tents and waited their turn to move into one of the hundreds of barracks being built according to the short-term settlement strategy. Such stopgap lodgings were supposed to be replaced after two or three years by permanent structures. But given the numerous setbacks in building the socialist city of the future, the planned "temporary" barracks became the dominant form of shelter in the greater urban agglomeration.

Logically, the first barracks were located around the initial priority construction objects: to the north, where the brick factory was being built; in the central area, at the iron-ore mine and the factory administration building; and to the south, at the limestone quarry near the village of Agapovka.[102] The perhaps not completely foreseen result of this seemingly sensible location policy, however, was that less than two years after the first settlers arrived, the embryonic urban territory stretched for more than twenty kilometers from north to south. These far reaches became the boundaries of Magnitogorsk, so that in 1938 the newspaper could write that "the first impression of the city one gets upon arrival is its spread out quality [*razbrosannost*]."[103]

What spread the city out, of course, was the layout of the steel plant and its many attendant enterprises. As the newspaper aptly stated, "Magnitogorsk grows very fast," springing up "wherever shops and enterprises are located."[104] So strongly did industry define the urban territory that most of

Table 5. Population by Selected Area, 1939

Fifth Sector	20,925
Ezhovka	3,017
Sredne-Uralsk	6,995
Fourteenth Sector	4,817
Blast Furnace Town	4,532
Fertilizer Settlement	4,072
Berezka	1,868
RIS	838
Miners' Settlement	1,911
Twelfth Sector	2,229
Socialist City	
First superblock	8,447
Second superblock	3,053
Lattice-Wood Town	7,282
Right Bank	541
Total	70,527

SOURCE: MFGAChO, f. 16, op. 1, d. 104, l. 40.
NOTE: Total population in 1939 for the city proper, not including the surrounding raion, was officially given as 145,900.

the earliest settlements were named for factory shops, such as Rolling Mill Town, Blast Furnace Town, Miners' Settlement. The rest were simply called by numbers assigned to the various industrial construction sectors (*uchastki*), such as the Seventh Sector (the central electric station), or the Sixth Sector (the coke and chemical plant).

Sometimes the settlements were named for auxiliary shops or enterprises, such as the settlement Ore-Enriching Station (RIS) to the east or the Fertilizer Settlement in the north. Many of these "auxiliary" settlements were small—at the RIS there were fewer than a thousand people—but others contained several thousand people (see table 5). Whatever their size, these parts of the city owed their origin to an industrial installation, on whose territory they arose and whose soot and gas fumes they received in generous doses.

Having divided the urban territory into sectors by shop or enterprise, the local authorities, unencumbered by considerations of private ownership, sought to house each sector's work force in the sector's barracks.[105] But given the sheer number of arrivals and departures, as well as the myriad number of organizations, such coordination proved impossible. Even when, in 1931, the construction of "temporary" housing was made the responsibility of the heads of each industrial sector, the disorganized patterns continued to dominate. "No matter how many times the city party committee tried to carry out a population transfer," grieved one low-level official, "it never worked."[106]

Because of the size of the factory and the dispersal of its many auxiliary shops and enterprises, and because of the difficulties in coordinating residences with workplaces, distances between work and home for many people reached eight or ten kilometers.[107] This was the very dreaded "irrationality" that urban planning had been expected to overcome. To be sure, distance is a relative concept, dependent on the modes of transport. Such was the nature of transport in Magnitogorsk, however, that the connections between various parts of the city could seem very great indeed.

The impediments to efficient movement began with the local road system, or rather with the lack of one. Magnitogorsk's only paved thoroughfare was the Central Chaussée, which wound for over fifteen kilometers from the train station, along the front of the factory, down to and around the NKVD building, and up toward the Kirov district, beyond which it changed its name to Club Prospect, finally becoming a dirt path called Karadyr Prospect on its way another five kilometers to the aerodrome.[108] Aside from this artery there was a proto-road system on the factory grounds and a few paved roads connecting the factory and the mine.[109] But the rest of the city "streets," despite such imposing names as Soviet Power, Radiant Future, Red Partisans, Ordzhonikidze, Ernst Thälman, and Sacco and Vanzetti, were just downtrodden paths largely incapable of carrying vehicular traffic.[110]

But much of road system's inadequacy was beside the point, for on the whole site there were only about five hundred vehicles. Almost a tenth of these were regularly out of service, and all but a handful were the exclusive property of the factory and used for industrial purposes. The most important shops and enterprises acquired buses to circle the city and round up or drop off their workers, regardless of where they lived. But these nonmunicipal buses had small capacities and were subject to frequent breakdowns. The lack of spare parts, not to mention gasoline, often kept them from running.[111]

As for the city, in 1933 it was served by only three buses, which were slow and almost always late, when they ran at all.[112] True, by the end of the decade the number of city buses had increased to eight, but only three of them worked regularly, and their hours were limited.[113] Service between the Kirov district and the settlements of the north, for example, stopped at ten in the evening. This mattered little for the nearly four thousand inhabitants of the Twelfth Sector, also known as the Settlement of Railroad Workers, whose community lay more than two kilometers beyond the last bus stop, which was located at the Grain Elevator Settlement.[114]

For certain areas of the city the transportation situation improved dramatically in January 1935, when the first streetcar was ceremoniously put into operation, bearing a portrait of Stalin. With its speed limit set at ten kilometers per hour, the heavy single-car tram rumbled from the top of the Kirov district past the central market to the main factory gates (and then slightly beyond to a secondary entrance), carrying the denizens of the first and second superblocks to and from work and many others on shopping expeditions for only 20 kopecks per ride.[115] Unequivocal testimony to the tram's utility was provided by the fact that it was almost always packed full, making it difficult for the passengers to close the hand-operated wooden doors.[116]

In what was a further demonstration of the authorities' salutary commitment to public transportation, the tram line was extended northwards by 1938 to the Thirteenth Sector. But problems with a poorly built bridge (over the piping from the mine to the steel works) necessitated closing the extension for what turned out to be a lengthy period.[117] In any case, most ordinary people still lived far from the tram route. The streetcar was a welcome addition to life in the city, but with the exception of the handful of vehicles and a sizable number of horses (plus a few camels) intended for official purposes, getting about Magnitogorsk in the 1930s more often than not meant going on foot.[118]

The streetcar received considerable publicity as an emblem of the city's "modernity."[119] Beyond symbolism, however, the need for adequate public transportation remained a crucial issue in Magnitogorsk, given the city's sprawl. The Kirov district was situated as if it were a satellite of the steel plant, and the streetcar link solidified that relationship. But the rest of the residential sections, outside the tram network and poorly served by buses, took on the character of "outskirts" (*okrainy*)—isolated from the city's center of gravity and in most cases, from each other. It was this situation that imparted to Magnitogorsk its peculiar physiognomy, making it seem something other than a city.

In what was taken as a further sign of the lack of Magnitogorsk's true "urban" character, the isolation of the "outskirts" was matched by their comparative underdevelopment. Fertilizer Settlement, which consisted mostly of makeshift housing along a single dirt road, was covered by huge puddles of filthy water, piles of garbage, and numerous open outdoor toilets. The situation was the same if not worse in the Communal and First of May Settlements to the southeast, and even in Lattice-Wood Town, which was just behind the Kirov district and often included in statistical surveys of it. At least Lattice-Wood Town was not physically isolated from the rest of the town, however.[120]

But isolation came in various forms. The smallest settlements, such as the Third Sector, were known dismissively as bears' lairs (*medvezhki ugolki*), since they contained no mailboxes or other means of communication with the outside world. Such small settlements of the outskirts also often housed groups of national minorities. One outlying region, a gold prospecting settlement at the northern end of the city, consisted of about one thousand Bashkirs and was known as Bashkir Town. There was also a so-called Kazakh Settlement, near Lattice-Wood Town, where both Kazakhs and Tatars lived. In these cases, "isolation" stemmed less from distance than language and custom.[121]

Only a few of the settlements in Magnitogorsk's outskirts were large, but one was very large indeed: that of the so-called special resettlers, or dekulakized peasants, who in 1931 were placed in an area behind the iron-ore mine that was christened the *spetstrudposelok*, or Special Labor Settlement, and enclosed by barbed wire.[122] Within two years, four other divisions of the Special Labor Settlement were founded: at the New Fertilizer Settlement, the Northern Settlement, the Limestone Quarry Settlement, and the village of Agapovka. But the barbed wire came down, and the original encampment was renamed the Central Settlement, even though it was situated in the eastern fringes of town.[123] With more than thirty thousand inhabitants, these "cities" within the city were largely self-contained.[124] Some peasant exiles were apparently granted permission to live outside the five divisions of the settlement with relatives,[125] but most continued to live within its boundaries even after their "rights" as citizens were officially restored in 1936 (in connection with the new constitution of that year).[126]

These inhabitants of Magnitogorsk's "islands" in the "Gulag Archipelago" had been brutally brought there against their will, many dying along the way or not long after arrival. But the subsequent experience of the dekulakized peasants who managed to survive differed significantly from that of the "zeks" dispatched to the infamous camps of the Far North.[127] Within their enclaves, the peasant exiles, despite an initial period of severe hardship that bordered on famine, came to have some of the best household plots in the city. They also raised a significant number of livestock. In his July 1933 speech Ordzhonikidze had joked that the Special Labor Settlement was better maintained and far more orderly than Socialist City. It is likely that this was true.[128]

The other large settlement of Magnitogorsk's outskirts, in addition to the misnamed Central Settlement for peasant exiles, was a so-called *Ispravitelno-trudovaia koloniia* (ITK), or Corrective Labor Colony, for criminal offenders. The Magnitogorsk colony was established in July 1932, according to the camp's main newspaper, *Borba za metall*, whose first issue appeared on 7 November 1932. It received convicts from around the country; many also came from within the city. In the official language, convicts were known as "citizens temporarily deprived of freedom" (*grazhdane vremenno lishennye svobody*, l/sv), or sometimes as "those serving measures of social defense" (*otbyvaiushchii mery sotsialnoi zashchity*, OMSZ). In everyday parlance, they were known as *itekovtsy*.[129]

Although not permitted to leave Magnitogorsk and subject to a nighttime curfew, the *itekovtsy* were initially unconfined since according to Soviet penal science they were "class allies" and "socially friendly" elements who, in contrast to the "class alien" kulaks, could be "reforged."[130] After a rush of "escapes" and much mayhem, however, the authorities evidently decided that these "class allies" were more dangerous than the supposed class aliens. In late 1932 the ITK was enclosed in barbed wire and divided into sectors, with punishment or isolation areas, as well as "special regime" barracks.[131]

Once the barbed wire went up (and convicts were expressly forbidden from going to work sites with their belongings), escapes from the colony declined in frequency, although they did not cease.[132] Through 1933, the total number of convicts sent to the colony was officially given as 26,786, of whom 8,122 had escaped (1,905 were recaptured). Over the years many more convicts arrived, and thousands were released. Throughout the decade, an untold number died in captivity.[133] The colony "regime" appears to have been further strengthened in 1936, when according to John Scott armed guards were used to escort convicts to and from labor sites.[134] By this time escapes became rarer; convicts became easily identifiable by their clothes and, even if they managed to change clothing, by their haircuts, while control through documents became stricter. But even after the barbed wire was installed, convicts continued to escape from work sites.

This large pool of "socially friendly" criminals provided a ready supply of bandits and contributed to the pervasive lawlessness in Magnitogorsk. Magnitogorsk was literally situated on the frontier. There was nothing as far as the eye could see, and even beyond, save a few railroad stations and an isolated town or two. Carousing, fist fights, knife fights, and murder seem to have been common, perhaps more so than in established cities.[135] Because of widespread "hooliganism," many inhabitants, especially women, reported that venturing outside at night was dangerous.[136] With time, as more permanent buildings went up, Magnitogorsk lost some of its "wild east" character. But throughout the second half of the 1930s the newspaper carried daily reports of what were called "incidents" (*proishetviia*), mostly petty heists and break-ins, but also ax murders and occasional shootings.[137] Many of the culprits came from the labor colony.[138]

Taking account of the deaths and escapes, the colony's population seems to have remained at about ten thousand inmates. These convicts were distributed among five separate installations, which included a compound for orphaned children and adolescent offenders.[139] The largest colony compounds were located on the right-bank construction site across the industrial lake, in the Eleventh Sector above the blast furnaces, and near the giant lumberyard and woodworking plant (DOK) due north of the factory gates.[140] All these areas were in the outskirts.

From the labor colony to the Special Labor Settlement, from the northern reaches to the southeastern communities, Magnitogorsk was a whole city of outskirts. Even Magnitogorsk's immense Fifth Sector—the city's most heavily populated region and the one that came to shape its image in the popular imagination—was considered part of the outskirts.[141] Moreover, most people in Magnitogorsk discovered that they lived not only in the city's outskirts but in the country's "outskirts"—doubly isolated. The Ural River alongside the city was not navigable (before the dam was built the river was so shallow that people walked across it). Important officials often traveled by air from the aerodrome—located in the opposite direction from the train station, out in the plain beyond Karadyrka hill—which they reached by car. For most people the primary way into and out of the city was by train, and although passenger trains left the city reasonably often, Magnitogorsk, far from being on the main trunk line, was twice removed from it.[142] Difficulties with the rail connections were matched by deficiencies in other means of communication. The newspaper complained about the erratic mail delivery, in part a consequence of the city's notorious indeterminacy,[143] and the frequent tie-ups of the overburdened telephone and telegraph networks.[144]

Relative isolation was the main but not the only consequence of the city's internal disconnectedness. The paradigmatic Fifth Sector, which also included the settlement of Ezhovka (named for an eighteenth-century miner, not the NKVD chief), consisted of nothing but barracks. The barracks were wooden, stucco-coated, whitewashed, one-story structures that stretched in rows as far as the eye could see and had no individual or distinguishing features. "You'd come home, searching and searching," explained one bemused barracks resident, "but all the barracks were identical and you couldn't find yours."[145]

Such indistinctness went beyond the barracks in the Fifth Sector. In the Seventh, Eleventh, and Fourteenth Sectors no street names were created until the census of 1937. And many sectors were without building numbers even after street names had finally been affixed. The city soviet began numbering buildings only in 1935, but it was a long time before it got around to many areas of the city. Often, numbering buildings did not help much, as numerous neighboring barracks were found to have the same number.[146] Buildings in some sectors were never assigned numbers, while those that had been outfitted more than once had a mixture of old and new numbers that did not mesh.[147] Rather than giving an address when summoning an ambulance, the newspaper advised, it was better to describe the location with landmarks, depending on the season, such as "the big puddle" or "the tall mound of snow."[148]

Magnitogorsk's geography, characterized by deliberate social differentiation, unwitting internal remoteness and disassociation, and a kind of generalized anonymity, was also to a large extent conspicuously agrarian. The city's "rural quality" derived partly from the kind of shelter many people had. Faced with the prospect of living in a tent, a barracks, or nowhere at all, many new urbanites built their own housing out of whatever materials they could find, mostly sod, thatch, and scraps of metal. These structures, built over a dugout in the ground, were called mud huts (*zemlianki*), a form of housing common throughout the Soviet Union. In Magnitogorsk, mud huts, like barracks, were grouped in clusters resembling villages.

Beyond the appearance of the mud huts, echoes of village life were evoked by the agricultural practices of the population. In one mud-hut settlement, Miners' Settlement, which was adjacent to the largest mechanized mine in the country, city authorities counted 352 households, and some 300 cows. Household size at the Miners' Settlement was also "rural," averaging almost five members.[149] It is likely that those families without a cow simply could not afford one, but this did not mean they lacked other livestock. Of the mud huts John Scott wrote that "the same house was inhabited by the family, the chickens, the pigs, and the cow, if there was one."[150]

Some of the mud-hut settlements were actual villages absorbed by the city. This was the case with Sredne-Uralsk, which was founded some ten years before construction of the steel plant began and whose population by the mid-1930s was nearly seven thousand. Here, as on many such settlements of the outskirts, there were neither kiosks with newspapers on sale nor regular mail deliveries for subscribers. Indeed, without as much as a single makeshift club, this agrarian community had few of the markings of a Bolshevik presence. "If Christmas is still celebrated anywhere in Magnitogorsk," the city newspaper wrote, "it is in Sredne-Uralsk," hinting without saying so directly that the settlement had a church.[151]

But everywhere one looked in Magnitogorsk, not just in the village-like settlements, there were plots and livestock. By 1938, the city claimed more than ten thousand cows, goats, and pigs, whose presence was much appreciated if sometimes sorely felt.[152] Attempts to construct cement sidewalks in Lattice-Wood Town, for example, proved unsuccessful because grazing animals destroyed them before the cement could harden. Meanwhile, on one side of Lattice-Wood Town stood a Cossack-style farmstead (*khutor*) and on the other side, the original Socialist City, which itself was dotted with fruit and vegetable plots.[153] Much of Magnitogorsk's population pressed the local leadership for land.[154] And partly to keep people in the city and partly to help alleviate food shortages, the leadership acceded to these requests even though it was bent on eradicating the country's despised "backwardness"—of which such plots were thought to be an unpleasant reminder.

Agricultural plots and livestock could seem out of place because of the vision of urban modernity that inspired the construction of Magnitogorsk; indeed, when Soviet power came to Magnetic Mountain, along with it came the great "modernizing" force, electrification. By the end of the 1930s about four-fifths of the city was "electrified."[155] Except for the Central Chaussée and parts of Berezka and the Kirov district, however, streets were unlit, and at nightfall whole areas of the city became enveloped by almost total darkness.[156] With time, more street lights were installed outdoors.[157] But interruptions in the power supply were a continual problem, initially because of breakdowns in the system and later owing to enforced conservation.[158]

Even more important, for many people nighttime darkness could become the general rule indoors as well. The newspaper complained, for example, that the barracks of the Sixth Sector, were more often than not without electricity during the winter months, when night came early.[159] Some areas of the city avoided the regular electrical breakdowns or enforced blackouts of the city's electricity network in that they were served by generators, but these devices could be just as unreliable. And several communities had no electricity whatsoever. Such was the unhappy predicament of the Kazakh Settlement.[160] Although it was possible to use kerosene lamps, the sale of kerosene was introduced only in the spring of 1936, and then in limited quantities. In any case, you also needed the lamp.[161]

Magnitogorsk, coated by ice for months on end, also rarely had adequate warmth. True, in the Kirov district the residents had central heating. But even that system suffered from many problems. During the 1932–33 winter, for example, blizzards knocked out the heating system, leading to subzero temperatures inside offices and residences. Investigations uncovered shoddy workmanship in the laying of pipes and the installation of boiler plates. In the summer of 1934, massive repair work was done on the central heating system, yet the winter of 1934–35 witnessed a repetition of the breakdowns.[162]

Meanwhile, the rest of the city—the barracks and mud huts—was heated by small stoves, in the venerable peasant tradition. In certain barracks, however, not all stoves worked, and even if the stoves were in good working order, there were often shortages of fuel.[163] Though millions of tons of high-quality coal arrived in Magnitogorsk every year, virtually all of it went to the factory, forcing people to scramble to find substitute fuels, especially wood, to keep warm.[164] Every winter complaints were heard at high-level meetings that temperatures inside the barracks "competed" with those outside.[165] Many people slept in their clothes, complete with overcoats and fur hats.[166] (Summer offered no respite, for with the warm weather came the bed bugs, and people slept outside on planks in order to escape the insects.)[167]

Problems with light and heat were matched by those with sanitation. The People's Commissariat of Labor finally allocated the funds for a sewage system for the Kirov district, but aside from seemingly endless discussions, little was accomplished for several years. According to the newspaper, the problem was that management could not decide whether the Trust Soiuzvodstroi or the steel plant itself should do the work. The "solution" was to form a new organization, Stroikanalizatsiia, which maintained a work force of twenty-four people (for a task that required thousands). Besides an adequate contingent of workers, the organization lacked equipment (excavators), materials (pipes, pumps), and elementary blueprints.[168] Later, after sections of the planned sewage system were somehow completed, the newspaper complained that people did not know how to treat pipes and caused frequent stoppages. When the clogged pipes were examined, rags, paper, and even tin cans were discovered.[169]

Some buildings near the sewage system could not be included in it, apparently owing to difficulties with running pipes underground.[170] Instead, residents of these buildings, like most of the city, were served by outdoor cesspits (*iamy*), whose contents were emptied into cisterns hauled away by trucks—provided, that is, there were enough trucks in functioning condition. Otherwise, as frequently happened, the cesspits became overfull and the water there had to be turned off.[171] The problem of overfull cesspits became especially acute with the arrival of the spring thaw, when odors were no longer frozen in their place.[172] Almost all outdoor toilets were uncovered. Even the "permanent" sewage system consisted of many open trenches, since there were often no pipes.[173]

Just as the city lacked an adequate sewage system, it also lacked a clean water supply. For the factory a large artificial lake had been created on the dammed Ural River, but it had trouble meeting the steel plant's enormous appetite for water, let alone the added demands of the city. A second dam to enlarge the lake, due before the 1932 spring flood, was completed only in 1938. In the meantime, the steel plant spewed the thoroughly contaminated lake water back into its source, having added hot slag to it. "Six times every 24 hours water runs from the lake to the factory and from the factory to the lake," the newspaper reported. "Right now, all life in the lake is dead—the fish perished and the underwater plants died."[174]

In the absence of an alternative, however, the lake continued to be used as the principal water source for the city. Eventually the authorities did obtain water processing equipment, although it is unclear how much that helped.[175] In any case, throughout the decade, entire settlements, such as Bashkir Town, remained completely without water, while others, such as the Railroad Settlement, had only temporary water systems that drew untreated water directly from the Ural River long after filters had been installed elsewhere.[176]

Fortunately, boiled water for tea, often the only way to thaw oneself and also by custom the chief beverage, was available from large water heaters called *titany*, which were supplied to most barracks. When these were not functioning, however, life in the barracks became much less tolerable—and more dangerous. Indeed, the consequences of the absence of light or the presence of cesspits, troubling as they were, paled in comparison with those deriving from the lack of clean water. Fires, the perennial urban nightmare, were only part of the problem.

In the summer of 1931, a typhus epidemic descended upon the city, after which the newspaper sadly admitted (by the fall of 1932) that Magnitogorsk, with a large mass lumped together in unsanitary conditions, was a hothouse for the spread of infectious diseases.[177] A frightening report on the city's catastrophic health situation in 1932 singled out the Special Labor Settlement, which was said to account for "up to 70 percent of the typhus cases." In the various parts of the settlement, there was no soap for months, and not nearly enough doctors, in part because they too were getting sick. The report warned that the epidemic had spread to the nearby populous Fifth Sector.[178]

Typhus was but one of the diseases that plagued Magnitogorsk. Malaria was especially virulent in 1932 and still being fought years later.[179] In 1935 almost nine thousand cases of malaria were recorded. That same year there was an epidemic of scarlet fever, which continued to affect more than one thousand people yearly, until 1939.[180] In battling these epidemics, the authorities repeatedly conducted sanitation inspections, tried to issue fines, and organized mass clean-ups, called subbotniki, which produced immediate but often ephemeral results. In the Fifth Sector, which had 1,500 toilets open to the sky, one mass clean-up in 1936 organized under the threat of spreading disease managed to attract one thousand people.[181] The newspaper conceded, however, that the filth piled up again just as high.[182]

Magnitogorsk's first medical facility, a forty-five-bed infection "hospital" opened in 1929 in the Fourth Sector, was housed in a small barracks and staffed by a single doctor who saw ninety-eight people a day.[183] This facility continued to expand until, by the end of 1931, something of a hospital system had formed. In February 1932 the whole operation was moved to a specially built complex in the Fifth Sector.[184] By 1937 there were almost 1,400 beds. Many parts of the complex, however, were without running water, steam heat, or sewage facilities. And the facility was usually overcrowded (especially surgery) and understaffed. It must be said, though, that Magnitogorsk's doctors and nurses often lacked experience, but not dedication.[185] Much attention was focused on people's health.

By design, the hospital complex comprised around twenty wooden barracks rather than permanent brick buildings. After ten long years, the city's chief doctor fumed in the newspaper that "management made a colossal mistake not building a real hospital for such a gigantic construction site."[186] The decision to use barracks had been justified by the hospital's location on what was originally intended as an impermanent sector of the city. As it turned out, however, the "temporary" Fifth Sector, like the rest of the "outskirts," was forced to take the place of the scaled down Socialist City. In the meantime, a city of nearly 200,000 people had no "permanent" hospital, despite the commitment to providing universal health care.

Nor were permanent buildings for schools built in the "outskirts" or "temporary" sections of the city, since these areas were to be torn down and the population moved to the right bank.[187] In the optimistic forecasts of planners, however, that transfer was at least fifteen years away. "Should the [temporary] sectors go without decent schools until then?" asked one indignant school administrator. The answer, unfortunately, was yes. Of the twenty-one schools outside the Kirov district, only five were in brick buildings; sixteen were in barracks, most of which had been scheduled to be torn down after only two or three years but were forced to last decades.

In the "outskirts" most children had to travel long distances to get to school, and although these schools operated on double shifts, they were overcrowded. By contrast, in the Kirov district all schools were located in permanent structures and operated on a single shift. In 1937, against a local recommendation to build a new brick school on the populous but "temporary" Fourteenth Sector, one was built instead on the right bank. With a capacity of 400, the school had only 120 to 130 pupils. Following Moscow's orders, the oblast soviet expressly forbid the construction of new permanent schools on the left bank outside the Kirov district. All three schools planned for 1938 were to be built in or near the Kirov district, the "permanent" city.[188]

What held true for schools and the hospital also held for the water system, sewage, street lights, and roads: why make the effort and expenditure if those parts of the city were only "temporary"? "In city organizations and in the leadership of the factory there is the opinion that everything built around the factory is not yet the city," commented one journalist. "The real city supposedly will be built on the right bank."[189] Meanwhile, the entire population lived on the left bank, and would do so for quite some time, in the temporary city of the present.

A LINEAR CITY AFTER ALL

Magnitogorsk was a colossal industrial territory of one hundred square kilometers. Paradoxically, the highly industrial landscape was composed to a great extent of rural-like settlements of mud huts, while private plots and livestock were spread all over the urban landscape. The mud huts were matched in number only by barracks, layed out in endless rows in all directions, giving the place the look of some kind of mobile military installation. To be sure, there were some brick and stone apartment buildings, a paved boulevard, and even a streetcar. One was more likely to notice, however, the sizable areas with tents and barracks enclosed in barbed wire. No less striking was the secluded suburb of architecture-magazine cottages surrounded by bountiful gardens. It was no wonder that people puzzled over the question: what kind of place was this?

Although different residential regions of the city took on individual identities—Blast Furnace Town, the Fifth Sector, and so on—with the exceptions of the Kirov district and Berezka, most neighborhoods lacked coherence amid the deadening anonymity of forlorn barracks and the incapacity of the local authorities to demarcate the monotonous territory. What is more, residential sections had little connection to one another or to the city as a whole. Magnitogorsk was a city of fragments, and these fragments were widely dispersed.

Because of the dispersion of Magnitogorsk's various parts, combined with the limited coverage of its urban transport network, the overwhelming majority of inhabitants found themselves living in isolation from "the city." "It was a queer city, running for more than ten miles along the valley," wrote John Scott. "The city planners did a bad job."[190] For their part, the city planners freely conceded that Magnitogorsk was built largely without a plan and that the result was near chaos.[191] But from the air one could begin to make at least some sense of Magnitogorsk.[192]

Beneath the billowing clouds of multi-colored smoke, one saw a huge industrial lake, a gigantic tract of land neatly traversed by hundreds of kilometers of railroad track and dominated by the imposing structures and smokestacks of the metallurgical works, and a big open mine smartly sectioned into layers carved out like steps, around which rolled the dumpcars carrying iron ore to the crushing and enriching plants and then on to the steel plant. Following the layout of the industrial geography, the outlines of the city could be discerned, wrapped around the factory like an outer layer of human insulation. A remarkable parallelism of living and production zones ironically made Magnitogorsk seem like the sort of linear city—only without the green belt—that had been the darling of the modernist architects and had inspired the original design by Ernst May.

The city was less a line and more a slightly curved rope, with the population lashed to industry (see map 4). In writing of the planned socialist city (which was not built) that "the population will be distributed so that housing is as close as possible to production," one city planner accurately if unwittingly described the city that was built.[193] Just as there was no green belt, however, neither was there coordination of residence with workplace. The only benefit to be gained by the proximity of residential and productive zones was thereby lost, while the corresponding health disadvantages were exacerbated by endemic problems with the urban water supply.

It all might have turned out differently. The socialist city of the future—

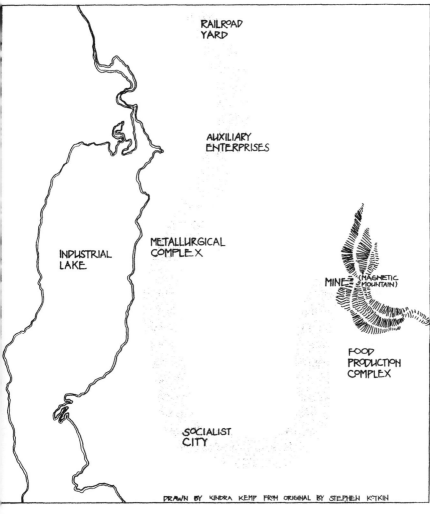

RAILROAD
YARD

AUXILIARY
ENTERPRISES

METALLURGICAL
COMPLEX

INDUSTRIAL
LAKE

MINE (MAGNETIC
MOUNTAIN)

FOOD
PRODUCTION
COMPLEX

SOCIALIST
CITY

DRAWN BY KINDRA KEMP FROM ORIGINAL BY STEPHEN KOTKIN

Map 4. Axis of settlement.

in both versions, left and right bank—was intended to bring a new people victoriously into a new era. But it fell victim to vagueness in its conception, to the terrain, to Bolshevik tempo, to disagreements between the Soviet authorities and their hired capitalist architect, to blunders by that architect under admittedly impossible conditions, to large-scale incompetence, and to the force which not only lorded over the socialist city, but which conquered the terrain and the population: the factory. In retrospect, the nineteenth-century "garden city" ideal, which arose as a reaction to the horrors of industrialization, can be seen to have fit badly with an unapologetic Prometheanism.

Until the latter part of the 1930s, the probable failure of building such a socialist city was not generally accepted. The creeping reliance on the "temporary" city of the present, although unavoidable, naturally brought disappointment. Whereas the magnificence of the Magnitogorsk Metallurgical Complex, that "industrial ballet in four blast furnaces," was never disputed, there was still argument as late as 1937 in the pages of the local newspaper about whether the urban agglomeration of Magnitogorsk was really a city. Some evidently claimed it was not, for the author of a newspaper piece insisted that it was. After attempting to accentuate the attractive aspects of the new city, she broke off and exclaimed: "That is it, our young and wonderful city, a city of pig iron and steel."[194] True enough. However incomprehensible or irrational it seemed, Magnitogorsk was a city—but a city attached to a factory, from which it derived its purpose and form.

Magnitogorsk was not just any steel town, though. Part barracks settlement, part village, part labor camp and place of exile, part elite enclave, and part new city, the hybrid urban form of Magnitogorsk was a microcosm of the Soviet Union during the building of socialism. And what a peculiar mix it was! Long distances and no effective transport system; numerous fires yet not much of a water system; open sewage trenches, overflowing cesspits, and periodic outbreaks of disease but few qualified medical personnel and no permanent hospital; millions of tons of coal but shortages of home-heating fuel; electricity but nighttime darkness and daytime blackouts; and of course, the enormous volumes of smoke, deafening noise, pig iron and steel and slag and coke and iron ore piled up everywhere and to dizzying heights, all enveloped in a thick smog accompanied by the smell of burning chemicals—such was what might be called the idiocy of urban life in Magnitogorsk.

The Bolshevik leadership decreed that a factory and city be built at Magnetic Mountain. From this decision, however, the form of the urban environment did not inevitably follow. The urban geography of Magnitogorsk was defined by the priorities of the socialist revolution, which placed heavy industry above all else, and by the geography of the industrial layout; but it was also defined by the incompetence of the planners and local officials, the actions and preferences of the inhabitants, and even by notions of temporariness. In Magnitogorsk, furthermore, the urban space was not simply defined; it was also made useful, or "productive." Rendering the urban space productive entailed more than simply building a factory; it involved "tying" people to production. The city was attached to the factory, and so were the urban inhabitants in a productive if inefficient way. The mechanisms of this attachment—some overtly, others subtly coercive, but many eagerly self-imposed—are the subject of part 2.

In part 2, the focus narrows somewhat, shifting from the urban space as a whole to its various components: the housing space and the tactics for coping with its characteristics, especially the overcrowding and lack of privacy; the work space and the articulation of a social identity in terms of labor; the market space and the artful stratagems and two-sidedness of the urban supply and trade networks; and the political or administrative space and the bizarre rituals and uncanny twists and turns of the party's rule. If the city began to reveal its secrets from the air, from the perspective of discrete spaces, particular practices, and individual experiences, it revealed even more.

1. Tent city, with Magnetic Mountain in the background, winter 1930.

2. Original Magnitogorsk railway "station," 1930.

3. Arrivals to the site, signing up for work upon disembarking.

4. Two brigades of construction workers.

5. Digging the foundations for the shops.

6. Journalists from *Komsomolskaia Pravda*. Semen Nariniani is at the far left.

7. Contract signing ceremony between the USSR and McKee Co., 1930. Seated, left to right: Vitalii Gasselblat, leading metallurgy specialist in the Urals design bureau; Arthur McKee, president of the U.S. firm; Petr Bogdanov, chief of Amtorg, the Soviet trading company in New York; Vadim Smolianinov, Soviet director of the Magnitogorsk project. Standing, left to right: A. S. Mamaev, of Amtorg; Robert Baker, treasurer of McKee Co.

8. Industrial construction, with residential barracks and Industrial Lake in the background.

9. Blast furnace no. 2, nicknamed Komsomolskaia.

10. The open-hearth shop.

11. Assembly of mill 500.

12. Open air "storage" of finished steel and assembly equipment, with blast furnaces in the background.

13. Ernst May, 1920s.

14. Aerial view of Socialist City, first superblock, mid-1930s.

15. Close-up of one of the apartment buildings.

16. Ernst May's Westhausen settlement, Frankfurt, Germany, 1920s.

17. Aerial view of Berezka, the elite enclave at Magnitogorsk.

18. Close-up of Berezka cottages.

19. Mud hut.

20. Residential barracks, Fifth Sector.

21. Painting the windows of barracks that have been covered with stucco.

22. Interior of communal barracks.

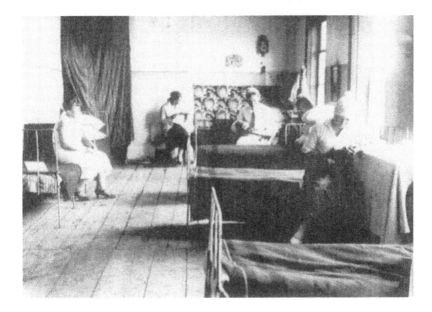

23. Workers eating at a public canteen.

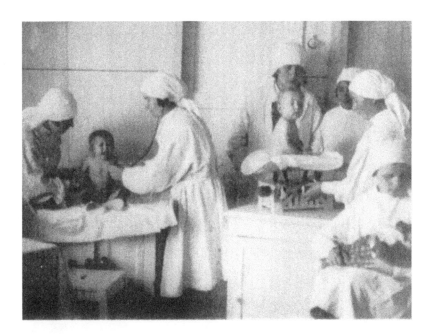

24. Caring for infants.

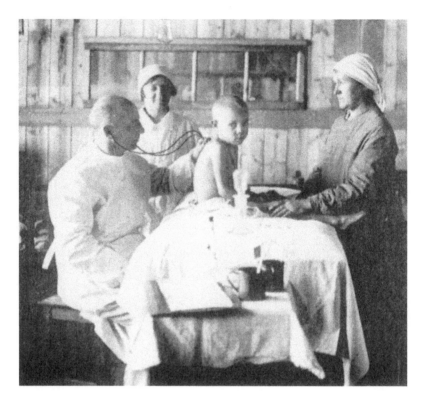

25. Inside one of the barracks of the city hospital.

26. Buses owned and operated by the steel plant.

27. Fleet of cars, with drivers, for the use of high officials.

28. Advertisements in the city newspaper for food products sold in Magnitogorsk stores.

29. The Engineers' and Technicians' Club, or DITR.

30. The sound cinema, Magnit, showing the 1936 musical comedy *Circus*.

31. Newspaper advertisement for Chaplin's *Modern Times*, showing at the Magnit.

32. Newspaper caricature of a day off spent at the nearby lake, Bannoe ozero.

II

LIVING SOCIALISM

The Little Tactics of the Habitat

We lived, ah we knew
Both joy and misfortune,
Having taken, like a fortress,
Magnetic Mountain . . .
        Boris Ruchev,
        "Ode to the Tarpaulin
        Tents" (1933)[1]

The center of the city of the future, one Soviet propagandist accurately predicted, "will be not a castle, or a market, but a factory."[2] In Magnitogorsk
that factory, the metallurgical complex, was owned and managed by the
Main Administration of Metallurgical Industry (GUMP), a division of the
mammoth People's Commissariat of Heavy Industry (NKTP). Through
NKTP, Moscow established a kind of colonial domination over the various
regions of the country, ruthlessly extracting resources and arrogating to itself the exclusive right to allocate the fruits of local economic activity. This
conspicuously exploitative relationship between the center, as Moscow was
called, and the localities continued after NKTP was subdivided by industrial branch in 1939, when GUMP in effect became the new Commissariat
of Ferrous Metallurgy (NKChM).[3] Under NKTP and then NKChM, Magnitogorsk was a loyal soldier in the planned economy, serving the ambitious strategies of the Soviet state.[4]

Magnitogorsk's industrial servitude determined the city's basic structure, which was oriented entirely around the shops of the steel plant and
attendant enterprises—making it at first glance less than the most hospitable place in which to live. Dirty, grimy, full of soot and smoke, and without a clean water supply or an effective system for waste disposal, Magnitogorsk was prone to outbreaks of disease. At the same time, blanketed
by snow and subzero temperatures for long periods but without sufficient
supplies of heating fuel and electricity, the city was often cold and dark.
Most people lived far from work, and transport left a lot to be desired.
Housing, meanwhile, was mostly makeshift. And yet, despite all this, contemporaries insisted that Magnitogorsk retained a special quality.

To be sure, the existence of genuine veneration for Magnitogorsk coincided with a certain disappointment, sharpened by the exceptionally high
expectations that had accompanied the city's construction. One of the early
Magnitogorsk directors, for example, confessed apologetically in 1935, two
years after having been removed (but still another two years before being
summarily shot), that "our mistake was obviously that, [along with] building an industrial enterprise, we should have simultaneously built the ev-

eryday life of Magnitogorsk—a city of new culture."[5] Notwithstanding this rare admission of culpability, however, a city of new culture had in fact been built—admittedly not in the sense the director probably meant of cultural refinement, but a new culture it was all the same.

Magnitogorsk's new culture centered on the communal organization of housing, the centrality of labor in personal identity, the criminalization of private trade, and the primacy of revolutionary politics in all matters. It was this set of distinct characteristics, expressing a dream for a better way of life attendant upon the transcendence of capitalism, that accounted for the admiration Magnitogorsk elicited at home and abroad. Whatever its shortcomings and disappointments, Magnitogorsk stood out as the world's first newly constructed socialist city.

■   ■   ■

At a 1973 conference devoted to the socialist city, several scholars addressed the question of "whether or not the socialist city [wa]s fundamentally different from the city in what may be called, for lack of a better term, capitalist societies." Their answer was a qualified yes, according to one of the organizers, who outlined a number of supposedly distinguishing characteristics. These included the attempts to control urban growth, a generally high population density, an employment structure dominated by heavy industry, the prevalence of public transport, the absence of land values assessed in financial terms, and above all the peculiarity of the decision-making framework. What the relation of these traits was to each other and, most important, where they came from, were questions that remained unresolved.[6]

Other scholars have continued to puzzle over the nature of the socialist city, sometimes also called the Soviet city.[7] One asserted that the Soviet city was indeed different, but not because of the features described for it at the 1973 conference. Rather, he argued that these features were symptoms of a more fundamental cause, "a very distinctive type of socio-economic system," which he called state socialism. This scholar neglected to make fully clear precisely what made state socialism "distinct," and what it was supposed to be distinct from.[8] Such a circular discussion recalled the exasperated words of politburo member Lazar Kaganovich at a June 1931 Central Committee plenum, when he declared an end to the endless debates about the nature of the socialist city, stating that Soviet cities were socialist by virtue of their being located inside the USSR.[9]

Scholars' ambiguity regarding the definition and specificity of the socialist city could be said to reflect the imprecision prevalent at the outset of the 1930s, as exemplified by Kaganovich's uncertain pronouncement. When the Stalin revolution began, contemporaries insisted that there was such a thing as the socialist city, and that Magnitogorsk was its outstanding example, but for some years to come, they could not yet say for sure what a socialist city was. The closest they ever came to a statement about the nature of the socialist city was when excoriating the capitalist city. In fact, this negative image of the capitalist city provided the basis for the solution to the question of the nature of the socialist city that took shape by the middle of the decade. Socialism, which began as a way of looking at the world based on a critique of capitalism, became a concrete form of social organization based on the suppression and ultimate elimination of capitalism.

SOCIALISM BUILT

As is well known, the Bolsheviks were deliberately ideological. By ideological is not meant simply that the Bolsheviks held particular ideas as such, but that they deemed it necessary to possess universal ideas to act at all. In this, of course, they merely reflected a general tendency observable since the French revolution. But the Bolsheviks' adherence to the notion of universal, revealed truth in politics was distinguished by their simultaneous, absolute denial of any possibility of pluralism—an intransigence rooted in a worldview based on class and class struggle, whereby only the interests of the one class, the proletariat, could become universal.

In revolutionary Russia, at any given time there was supposed to be one answer to all questions, a single truth which was held to be the expression of the correct interpretation of the movement of History, as embodied by the Communist party, the vanguard of the universal class. Of course, policies could and did frequently change; indeed, the entire direction of policy, as with family policy in 1936, could be reversed (as we shall see). But throughout, the importance of a "general line" and of the Communist party's infallibility was maintained, while the explanatory emphasis fell not on the fact of apparent change but on the compatibility of the chosen course with Marxism-Leninism and socialism.

It needs to be kept in mind that the management of this official ideology was complex and time-consuming, requiring a considerable commitment of intellectual capital and often embarrassing those responsible for such tasks. But the deployment of ideology was also empowering. Its mastery served as a strategic device in the political alignments among personalities at all levels, including the very top (it played no small role, for example, in Stalin's rise to and maintenance of a position of supremacy). More broadly, ideology was an important instrument in the rule of the regime over the country. For these reasons alone, to dismiss or downplay the significance of ideology in the USSR of the 1930s because the ideological precepts were changed or violated in practice (or because they supposedly represented a degeneration of true Marxism-Leninism) is to render the behavior and thinking of contemporaries incomprehensible.

Just as important, the Soviet regime's official ideology, adaptable as it was, did in fact contain certain fixed ideas that shaped both the course of state action and popular interpretations of state action. Those ideas centered on the proposition, "socialism is the antidote to capitalism." Capitalism had bourgeois parliaments; socialism would have soviets of workers' and peasants' deputies. Capitalism had selfish individualism; socialism would have collectivism. Capitalism had the chaos of markets; socialism would have planning. Capitalism had private property; socialism would have societal property, and so on. In short, whatever socialism was, it was certainly not capitalism. To put it another way, one achieved socialism by eradicating capitalism.[10] It was this understanding that imparted a sense of coherence to the experience of socialism, despite the endless improvisation.

Socialism was a kind of antiworld, but this did not mean that for contemporaries it remained abstract. On the contrary, socialism encompassed a number of tangible precepts bespeaking a staunch commitment to social justice: no one went without food, all children attended school, every sick person received medical care, and there was no unemployment. Beyond the considerable impression made by these concrete circumstances, it was also constantly reiterated that in the USSR, the commitment to social justice was not merely a series of ad hoc policies that could be adopted in various forms even under capitalism. Rather, social justice was said to be a fundamental aspect of a socialist type of society, grounded in putatively nonexploitative property relations.

The elimination of private property, and the exploitation that went with it, was put forward as the distinguishing characteristic of Soviet society and by implication, the socialist city. To be sure, some forms of private property were retained, such as personal and household items, livestock, horses and automobiles, and certain forms of housing. But there was no private holding of land or the means of production. Reflecting the circumstances of expropriation, the original legal designation for socialist property was "state property (nationalized and municipalized)."[11] By the second half of the 1930s, however, the explanatory clause was dropped. Beyond personal effects, private property had become a thing of the past, and socialism could rightly be declared "built in its foundations."

In an interview with a foreign correspondent in 1936, the year of the new constitution and the proclamation that socialism had been built, Stalin explained in plain language that "our Soviet society is socialist because private property in factories, land, banks, and the means of transport has been repealed and replaced by societal [*obshchestvennaia*] property." Stalin defined this term as "state, that is, national [*vsenarodnaia*] property, and collective-farm-cooperative property." To underscore the importance of this point, Stalin added that "neither Italian fascism nor German National 'Socialism' has anything in common with such a society . . . because there, private property . . . has remained untouched."[12]

As contemporaries came to discover, the elimination of private property brought about a process of thoroughgoing statization (*ogosudarstvlenie*), and gave rise to a class of functionaries who exercised a kind of de facto ownership over state-controlled property. To be sure, an extravagantly oversized state administered by an aggrandizing official class was an old story in Russian history. But with the socialist revolution these historical tendencies were greatly magnified and, at the same time, recast as a progressive achievement. Among some long-time participants in the Russian revolutionary movement, and even more so among social democrats abroad, there were those who voiced objections to this largely unanticipated turn of events, decrying it as a defilement of socialism, or even as just another form of capitalism. Yet to the majority of people who participated in building it, socialism in the USSR afforded the means to acquire a niche, as well as a sense of pride, in a society that did seem to be qualitatively different—in comparison with capitalism, which was then synonymous not with wealth and freedom but poverty and exploitation, as well as imperialism and war.

The antagonism between socialism and capitalism, made that much more pronounced by the Great Depression, was central not only to the definition of what socialism turned out to be, but also to the mind-set of the 1930s that accompanied socialism's construction and appreciation. This antagonism helps explain why no matter how substantial the differences between rhetoric and practice or intentions and outcome sometimes became, people could still maintain a fundamental faith in the fact of socialism's existence in the USSR and in that system's inherent superiority. This remained true, moreover, despite the Soviet regime's manifest despotism and frequent resort to coercion and intimidation. Simply put, a rejection of Soviet socialism appeared to imply a return to capitalism, with its many deficiencies and all-encompassing crisis—a turn of events that was then unthinkable.

LEARNING THE RULES OF DAILY LIFE

As we shall see, within a context of the broad acceptance for the goals and results of building socialism, people participated for a variety of reasons—but participate they did. Accordingly, the city of Magnitogorsk must be understood not as a static environment, but as a perpetually shifting, dynamic grid of relations. Evidence of just such a diffuse, relational play of power was presented in part 1—for example, the trade in forged or stolen documents discussed briefly in chapter 2. Such activities, if they have been studied at all, have usually been attributed to the moral bankruptcy of individuals forced to live under an illegitimate regime. But far from showing depravity, the proliferation of illegalities may indicate, if not opposition to Bolshevik rule, creative resistance to a set of written and unwritten rules governing appropriate behavior.

Much about life in the new urban milieu of Magnitogorsk must have appeared incomprehensible, but every urban inhabitant knew, even if only instinctively, what he or she needed to do in order to live.[13] The urban inhabitants knew how to make the best of their lot; they knew what should be avoided and which rules could be bent under what circumstances and which could not. And if they did not know, they learned quickly. The inhabitants of Magnitogorsk were experts in what they perceived to be the rules of the game. That these new rules of urban life were often unspoken did not mean they were less real. Even unspoken rules revealed themselves at their limits, that is, when tested, which they were all the time.

Within the framework provided by the new rules of urban life, the inhabitants of Magnitogorsk were confronted and in turn confronted others with various attitudes, self-understandings, and behavior. These constituted what has already been referred to as the little tactics of the habitat, through which life in Magnitogorsk was lived and made sense. Such petty maneuvers and modest stratagems hold an essential clue, for in them the basic outlines of the new socialist society made themselves manifest. Trite as it sounds, socialism was not only built but lived by people—individuals with hopes, fears, a capacity for survival, and no small amount of inventiveness.

We have seen that in the definition of the urban geography, the inhabitants of Magnitogorsk played an active and, within limits, even a decisive role. This theme will now become our central focus in an analysis of how socialism was lived. Of course, many constraints conditioned the scope for action available to any particular person. Yet in Magnitogorsk there were many creative people, the definition of which might be an individual who manages to discover, even invent, room to maneuver. Beyond individual virtuosity, even ordinary actions undertaken as part of daily life had the effect of realigning, even if only slightly, what might be called the landscape of possibility, opening up some options and closing off others.[14]

In sum, Magnitogorsk, one of the industrial giants born during the first Five-Year Plan, was more than just a colossal steel producer. It was a bulwark in the international class struggle, a powerful lever in the fight to build socialism. Above all, it was a political arena in which relations of power were played out, new experiences were made possible, and new identities were formed. Daily life in Magnitogorsk amounted to a constant negotiation of the political terrain constituted by the totalizing revolutionary crusade. Living socialism was a pioneering adventure.

4   Living Space and the Stranger's Gaze

Future generations will never understand what "living space" means to us. Innumerable crimes have been committed for its sake. . . . It is passed on to one's descendants like a family castle, a villa or an estate. Husbands and wives who loathe the sight of each other, mothers-in-law and sons-in-law who have managed to hang onto a cubby hole next to the kitchen—all are wedded forever to their living space and would never part with it. In marriage and divorce the first thing that arises is the question of living space. I have heard men described as perfect gentlemen for throwing over their wives but leaving them the living space.

Nadezhda Mandelstam[1]

Housing at what would become Magnitogorsk appeared first in the form of large, white tents, each holding about fifteen or twenty people. Inside the tents, recalled one inhabitant, "there were cots [*topchany*]," and "on each cot was a straw mattress—that is, you were given a covering for a mattress and you went out in search of straw."[2] Many of the tents were reinforced with planks and wooden floors, but not all. In winter, blizzards and fierce Arctic winds sometimes ripped open the tarpaulin and carried the unreinforced tents off in a swirl.[3] This was, however, no nomad camp in the steppe but the first housing for a brave new world.

Soon, huge tracts of urban territory were colonized by rows and rows of long, one-story, stuccoed and whitewashed "barracks"—sheds made of boards and clay, with sawdust stuffed inside the walls as insulation. Ivan Kokovikhin, who came to Magnitogorsk in 1929 and lived briefly in a tent, recalled the first barracks as "four walls made out of wood and a big room with lots of beds. It wasn't much, but we were so pleased that we weren't in a tent anymore."[4]

At the booming site, though, there were not even sufficient tents, let alone barracks, to house the influx.[5] Makeshift shelters, especially huts made from thatch and mud, became ubiquitous. People slept wherever they could: in canteens, shops, factory offices, even stationary railroad cars.[6] With the socialist city not yet built, but with a large and still growing population already present, one Magnitogorsk official despaired that "we are building barracks all the time, how many barracks have we built, and all the same we just can't catch up. We have lots of barracks, yet not enough living space [*zhilaia ploshchad*]."[7]

In assessing the size of the urban housing stock this disheartened official did not refer to the number of buildings, apartments, or rooms but to an aggregate amount of floor area, of unspecified configuration, measured in square meters—in short, to living space. The notion of living space as a way to conceptualize housing first arose in tsarist Russia, when the desperate shortage of lodgings in cities meant that finding or affording a separate room was beyond the reach of most people, who instead rented a corner, or simply a cot, in someone else's room.[8] Yet the concept took on a new significance after 1917, for if in tsarist Russia the subdivision of apartments and rooms resulted in the dreaded coming together of strangers and different families, in Soviet Russia this unavoidable situation was heralded as a new model for human relationships that would transcend selfish individualism.[9]

Living space permitted, and indeed came to signify, a reorientation of housing away from the family and toward the collective. "The family, the basic cell of . . . capitalist society . . . loses the economic basis of its existence in the conditions of socialist society," the Magnitogorsk newspaper explained in 1930. "The very word 'family' loses its meaning."[10] Instead, each urban resident, standing in equal relationship to all others, was to occupy a fixed amount of space, determined by scientific norms for health and hygiene. Such an approach meant that a greater number of people could be housed in less space and, furthermore, that in any given structure it would not be necessary to provide for the full range of needs of each discrete household. People would have access to common facilities. In short, under socialism, housing was to be designed so as to encourage an economy of resources and an ethic and practice of cooperation, making possible a new mode of existence called "communal" living. Although in the mid-1930s there would be a partial retreat from the ideal of fully communal living toward promotion of the family, the notion of living space was retained as the basis for the organization of housing in the USSR, a convenient tool in the hands of administrators.

What made this new understanding of housing so important was the Soviet state's commitment to provide low-cost shelter for the entire urban population. In Europe and the United States, the transformation of the concept of housing as a pure commodity to a commodity that was also a social right and state responsibility took place over more than a century, in part as a result of the actions of diverse groups and individuals doggedly pushing what they saw as social reform in the face of ideological prejudices and vested interests.[11] In Soviet Russia, the state did not need to be persuaded to embrace the role of guarantor of societal interests. The Soviet state proclaimed that it existed exclusively for this very purpose, and it pledged to override or otherwise remove any societal or group resistance to its self-proclaimed prerogative to protect and enhance the welfare of the population in all matters, including housing.[12] Equally important, by the time construction of Magnitogorsk began, housing was not only viewed as a state-guaranteed social right but had ceased to be a commodity.

Not long after the October revolution, private property in land was abolished by decree. Although private ownership of buildings and other structures on any given parcel of land was not universally abrogated, "expropriations" of apartments and entire buildings, whether by official proclamation or local initiative, rendered the legal status of dwelling ownership ambiguous.[13] To be sure, expropriations were often little more than loud pronouncements by officials eager to call attention to their new authority. But the number of evictions on the basis of "class background" or "revolutionary need" was considerable, and any reversion back to the prerevolutionary status quo of rentier control over the country's housing was unthinkable.[14]

A retreat of sorts did occur, when the series of concessionary measures that would come to be known as the New Economic Policy also found expression in housing policy,[15] but throughout the 1920s certain imperatives and numerous practices remained as before. First and foremost, the state maintained its duty to provide and oversee housing for the people (not to mention its right to determine who constituted the people).[16] This broad responsibility was thought to include the encouragement of additions to the existing stock and specifications for the types of buildings that could be built, the passage of laws governing the forms of ownership permitted and the conditions for sale or resale of housing units, the regulation of occupancy in private and state-owned dwellings alike, including the articulation and enforcement of minimum health and sanitary standards, and control over rents.[17]

With the onset of the state-led industrialization drive at the end of the 1920s, what private housing remained was again confiscated and redistributed.[18] At the same time, much new housing—including entire new cities—was built by the state in accordance with its celebrated social welfare vision. True, in one sense only the scale had changed, albeit drastically, for the limited residential construction of the 1920s was in large measure carried out by the state. But the virtual abolition of the private dwelling substantially altered not just the parameters but also the basis of the state's activity.[19]

Land owner, developer, builder, manager, rule-maker, and final arbiter all in one, the Soviet state embarked in the 1930s on a housing program that, although inspired by radical ideas from the nineteenth century, took on a qualitatively new dimension owing not just to the magnitude of the undertaking but to the specificity of the new sociopolitical order. Having chosen to pursue the unprecedented task of finding a noncapitalist way of providing housing, however, the Soviet government and its local representatives made numerous concessions and policy reversals—all of which, oddly enough, served to underscore the state's commitment to the radical policies.

.   .   .

From the onset of Soviet power, new housing construction, restricted by a lack of funds, building materials, and effective coordination, fell far short of the state's own assessment of the population's needs. The resulting gap, or "housing shortage," quickly came to define the common understanding of housing in the Soviet Union, overshadowing an unusually rich and provocative set of social and political experiences grouped around shelter and subjectivity. Those experiences are the subject of this chapter.[20]

In housing as in other vital facets of everyday life, complex, overlapping, and contradictory laws and regulations, not systematically codified until the second half of the 1930s, proliferated. These rules, before and after being set down, were inconsistently applied, sometimes circumvented, ignored, or modified, but most of all they were incessantly discussed.[21] In the process, housing emerged as an important arena in which the relationship between individuals and the state was defined and negotiated, and the confines and texture of daily life—the little tactics of the habitat—took shape.

That the configuration of housing was a critical determinant of consciousness and behavior, including a person's political reliability, was a basic premise of the Stalin epoch, when housing became implicated in groping efforts to create a new culture. The authorities were keenly aware of the possibility of ordering and using space to achieve social and political ends, while the inhabitants had ideas of their own. In the end, what stands out in the search for a socialist approach to housing is how the forms of shelter built in Magnitogorsk reflected the currency of certain ideas about collective social organization, and how that shelter served purposes for which it originally may not have been designed but for which it turned out to be unusually well-suited.

TABULATED, DISTRIBUTED, REGISTERED, AND MANAGED

What was termed living space held great appeal for the authorities in large part because it lent itself so readily to manipulation. This circumstance was derived from living space's conceptual detachment from fixed configurations of shelter, such as rooms or apartments. Living space was just space, which could be defined and redefined, and easily measured, wherever walls or doors did, or did not, happen to be located. This facility of measurement, however, although certainly convenient, also proved to be rather awkward for the irrepressibly optimistic authorities.

As of March 1931, for example, when Magnitogorsk's population reached 83,000, there were only about 160,000 square meters of aggregate living space, roughly 1.9 square meters per person.[22] By January 1932, for a population of 196,000 there were 359,000 square meters of living space, or about 1.8 per person.[23] This was not much room, especially considering that at first the central authorities set a "sanitary norm" or minimum of nine square meters per person; this figure was reduced to seven, but even then it went unmet for decades.[24] Moreover, the sanitary norm took for granted that the seven square meters would be in a permanent brick building, the first of which had yet to be completed by the time the city of Magnitogorsk housed those 196,000 people.

With time the situation in Magnitogorsk improved considerably, yet it continued to fall far short of the planners' goals, as demonstrated by their own relentless quantitative measurements. According to an official report, as of January 1935 perhaps as many as 16 percent of the city's population lived in "buildings"—a term subject to expansive application—meaning, of course, that at least 84 percent made their homes in barracks or other "temporary" accommodations.[25] Furthermore, the report gave an average living space in all structures of 3.89 square meters per person. This lowly figure marked a plateau for several decades to come. At no time during the 1930s did the average amount of living space per person in Magnitogorsk exceed 4.0 square meters.[26]

Even with such a modest average, the 1935 report depicted a degree of differentiation. The average space for workers with family members, for example, was 3.20 square meters, whereas for engineers and technical per-

Table 6. Living Space in Magnitogorsk, 1 January 1938

	Living Space (sq. m.)	% of Total
Barracks	271,100	46.9
Permanent buildings (including carcass)	189,200	32.8
Mud huts	101,000	17.5
Individual bungalows	16,300	2.8

SOURCE: PAChO, f. 234, op. 1, d. 594, ll. 1–4, reprinted in Eliseeva, *Iz istorii*, pp. 249–51.

sonnel with family members, it was 6.26, and many of the latter also lived in bona fide buildings.[27]

Such differences, as we shall see, were hardly accidental. But if some people, mostly technical and managerial staff, enjoyed more space, and a very few among the local leadership lived in spaces that could only be described as palatial, for almost everyone in Magnitogorsk living space came in tiny, primitive parcels (see table 6).[28] The reasons for the state's failure to meet its own standards were not difficult to fathom. Across the USSR, overall investment in housing construction during the prewar Five-Year Plans amounted to less than 10 percent of total investment. At the same time, plan fulfillment for housing construction barely exceeded 50 percent for the first Five-Year Plan and fell considerably short of 50 percent for the second. Housing in the USSR may have been a public good, but public goods were considerably lower priorities than state imperatives, such as steelmaking, as the example of Magnitogorsk vividly demonstrated.[29]

How did a Magnitogorsk inhabitant come to occupy a precious parcel of living space? In principle, one could form a cooperative and build one's own housing,[30] but almost everyone was supposed to obtain living space by taking a job with a state enterprise.[31] Newcomers to Magnitogorsk who signed up for work were usually assigned to a barracks, where they went to stake a claim on a bunk or a spot on the floor. The barracks were often already overfull when people arrived, but some room for the newcomers was inevitably found. (Those not fortunate enough to gain a toehold in the barracks, or simply not wanting to live in one, could build a mud hut, a theme to which we shall return.)

With the high rate of mobility and the general chaos that characterized the site in the early years, however, no set of officials could have kept close track of the dispensation of space in all the barracks, which at one point numbered more than one thousand. This meant that living space was allocated, at least for a time, as much by residents as by any official agency. A person departing or knowing of someone else departing could tip off his or her friends or acquaintances (or anyone, for "considerations"). Most people just took up residence anywhere they could, with or without official directives.[32]

Soon enough, however, allocation of even the least desirable space came to be handled through bureaucratic procedures. And, from the beginning, the choicest spaces were very tightly controlled. The authorities were well aware that control over the allocation of living space afforded them considerable power, which they exercised energetically. State policy openly proclaimed that housing be used as one of the most important of a variety of rewards to be granted to the loyal, or withheld from the disloyal.

When limited numbers of one- or two-room lodgings in the more substantial buildings of the Kirov district became available, priority was granted to favored categories of people, such as engineers and highly skilled workers, who often received their dwellings in much-publicized ceremonies. But "deserving" people always far outnumbered vacant spaces, and this scarcity, which undergirded the authorities' power, frequently tied the authorities' hands.

In this regard, the city newspaper highlighted the case of the steel smelter Makarov, who had been living in a mud hut that was torn down, after which he moved with his family into a friend's residence. The two families shared a small two-room dwelling as the Makarovs waited months to get their own lodgings. Finally, he received a voucher granting him the right to occupy a room, but when he went to have a look, he discovered that the allegedly free space had already been occupied. Only after the newspaper chose to become involved—for the reason that Makarov was a well-known Stakhanovite (the top category for workers) in the open-hearth shop—did he finally succeed in obtaining his own separate quarters, although the newspaper neglected to specify exactly how or from whom.[33]

Makarov's relatively benign plight indicated more than a problem of administrative oversight or inefficiency. It suggested that in the provision of housing an intricate allocation process existed that could be pitiless or kind, depending on who you were, whom you knew, and how much cunning, guile, or luck you had. Such a system favored the boisterous, but it encouraged all individuals to become their own advocates or risk being eclipsed by others. Of course, the intervention of the newspaper, or powerful officials, produced the best results, but these were options open only to a select few, many of whom already had sufficient "clout" without such recourse.

Even as it actively intervened in the distribution of precious living space, the newspaper denounced what it viewed as the irregularities of the patronage-like allocation whereby acquaintance (*znakomstvo*) or connections (*sviazi*), rather than merit, proved decisive. The paper never questioned the practice of preferentially awarding living space based on social status and allegiance, or putative importance, to the grand crusade. But in a situation where decisions were rendered entirely beyond the public view, the newspaper did pursue a kind of accountability. All the more curious, then, was the paper's failure to specify to whom it appealed on Makarov's behalf.

This was an important detail, for not only was available space in short supply, it remained far from clear which of the several state agencies at the site held final jurisdiction over any given structure: industrial managers? city authorities? both? In 1933, in an effort to clarify lines of authority and eliminate supposed inequities, local officials divided the urban territory into residential sectors (*zhilraiony*), which were to be responsible for distributing unoccupied living space strictly according to official priorities and procedures. This system was widely criticized, however, and soon changed.[34]

In August 1934, the allocation of all housing was transferred from residential sectors to the steel plant's so-called Everyday-Life Administration (*kulturno-bytovoe upravlenie*), or KBU. Within the factory's KBU a special "apartment" bureau was opened that was to have sole authority to issue vouchers permitting occupancy of free space across the entire urban territory, thereby supposedly ensuring both efficiency and fairness. But the changeover was not smooth: one investigation revealed that residential sectors, far from blithely giving up control over a valuable resource, continued to issue their own vouchers and failed to inform the KBU when lodgings were vacated, with the result that "in the KBU at the current moment [October 1934], there is no free space listed."

Throughout the second half of 1934 the KBU and the residential sectors battled each other to exercise control over the prized resource of living space (between 22 August and 27 September 1934, the KBU allocated 118 spaces, the residential sectors, 260). Such bureaucratic scuffling among rival agencies became routine (and not just in housing questions), often undermining declared policy aims, such as the goal, in this case, of reforming a suspect allocation process. In fact, according to the newspaper account, within the KBU the same patronage system had emerged: allocation there was also done "unsystematically" and *po-semeinomu*—in other words, through connections.[35]

Prospective residents quickly learned from all this that to obtain living space, the key was to establish occupancy, for once ensconced somewhere a person could usually manage to remain. Eviction, limited by law, rarely occurred, even when technically justified. According to the local newspaper, almost no one was thrown out of his or her living space, even for misuse—doubtless a reflection of the desire to avoid creating a homeless population. Instead, the usual approach was to issue warnings or reprimands and impose fines.[36] Although there were periodic evictions for debauchery or criminal activity, when the tenant in question was an important and valuable worker, or had connections, even criminal activities proved insufficient grounds for eviction.

Moreover, even though most people obtained their living space upon having been hired, being fired or even quitting by no means resulted in automatic eviction. In most cases the enterprise was law-bound to find alternative living space for any tenant it wanted to evict—a formidable task. Enterprises could and certainly did try to remove tenants without the offer of an alternative space, but those tenants had recourse to the city soviet, the newspaper, and the courts, not to mention steadfast challenges that they could only be made to leave forcibly. As a result, enterprises found "their" housing occupied by people other than their own workers.

In late 1931, for example, the local Komsomol newspaper divulged that a number of people living in the barracks of the coke and chemical construction trust had no connection to the coke plant, or to the construction site, for that matter.[37] Four years later, a high-level official source reported that more than two thousand people lived in factory-owned housing who had no apparent ties to the factory.[38] The Magnitogorsk steel complex seems to have had less control over the housing it built than private corporations had over "their" housing in American company towns.[39]

A severe-sounding November 1932 decree allowing enterprises to evict employees terminated for absenteeism apparently had less effect than hoped, since an almost identical decree was issued again in December 1938.[40] Data for the first half of 1939 indicate that of the 2,295 firings at the Magnitogorsk factory (1,182 were for absenteeism), only 738 had resulted in successful evictions. In many cases, the living space in question was registered not in the name of the household's main worker employed at the enterprise to whom the space had been allocated, but in the name of a wife or brother or some other relative, so that loss of a job by the chief breadwinner or a severe disciplinary action would not result in the family's loss of housing.[41] People maneuvered as best they could to get living space, and if they got it they clung to it, whatever that required.

As the maneuvers to avoid eviction in the case of firing demonstrated, it was not enough simply to occupy living space; it was also necessary to register (*propisat*) one's occupancy with the local militia, as the regular police were called. The need for a reliable method of residency registration, a task that was begun around the country in systematic fashion only in 1933 (with the reintroduction of the tsarist system of internal passports), was a logical outgrowth of the state's assumption of responsibility for the provision of housing. But because the militia reserved the right to refuse and revoke registration, the *propiska* constituted more than a simple tabulation. To undergo *propiska* meant to receive official permission to live in that particular locality, attested to by a conspicuous stamp in the internal passport, which one was required to carry at all times. This in effect conferred on the state an absolute, legal power to control everyone's movements.[42]

To help enforce the mandatory registration system the local militia relied upon appointed or elected house managers and barracks commandants, who were also responsible for keeping an eye on the property.[43] Nonetheless, it is not clear how efficient the registration system could have been in Magnitogorsk in the 1930s. As discussed in chapter 2, despite the resolve of the authorities to enforce severe restrictions, several factors, including the magnitude of the task, the level of document technique, and the insatiable demands for labor, conspired for several years to impede the realization of the state's ambitious aims to wield control over all population movements. In Magnitogorsk, given that streets were without names and buildings were without numbers for much of the 1930s, it was not always possible to summon people to appear before the court, or to find them at all.[44]

Even for those people unable to obtain permission to reside in the city through proper channels—either because they had no job, had spent time in a labor camp, or were of "doubtful" social origin—there existed a number of alternatives, ranging from the use of false documents to the payment of bribes. These actions, however, carried risks.[45] Far less risk was entailed in the so-called bogus marriage (*fiktivnyi brak*) to someone who had a valid passport and thus could obtain, or already possessed, a local residence permit.[46] Indeed, the dreadful scarcity of living space and the occupancy registration system had a notable impact on personal relationships, inducing some people to marry, inhibiting others, and significantly complicating divorce.[47] Living space was not something to be taken lightly.

Table 7. "Ownership" of Magnitogorsk's
Living Space, 1939

MMK	381,300
Other enterprises	109,400
Individual	94,100
City soviet	14,100
Total sq. meters	598,900

SOURCE: GAChO, f. R-804, op. 11, d. 105, l. 40.

Although everyone had to go through the sometimes cumbersome and time-consuming processes of applying for space, lobbying to see that application fulfilled, and finally bringing all the necessary paperwork to the militia and registering occupancy, which once secured could usually be counted on indefinitely, occupancy did not translate into outright ownership. A percentage of the living space in Magnitogorsk did more or less belong to individuals (as discussed below), but the bulk was "owned" by state enterprises, especially the Magnitogorsk Metallurgical Complex. This meant that occupants were not legally responsible for maintaining what was, because of near permanent occupancy, "their" living space (see table 7).[48] By proscribing legal construction of permanent private housing the state assumed a heavy burden—fiscal as well as managerial.

By dint of its majority ownership, the Magnitogorsk steel plant assumed de facto responsibility (in the form of its KBU) for the maintenance of virtually the entire urban housing stock.[49] Establishing adequate financial and organizational arrangements to handle upkeep, however, proved complicated. The law of 27 January 1921 abolishing rents had been swiftly reversed by a law of 18 July 1921 providing for charging occupants rent to cover the costs of building maintenance and repair.[50] But there persisted both in the popular imagination and in official publications the notion that free accommodations were, if not a fundamental right specified in the constitution, a benefit earned from the victorious revolution.

In such a spirit, for the first few years living space in Magnitogorsk was provided free, which also meant that there was essentially no budget for maintenance. Under budgetary pressure, however, this situation changed. Beginning in 1935 a small rental fee was assessed, calculated on the basis of total living space and the presence of amenities.[51] The next year a more complicated system was introduced. The basic rental rate was set at forty kopecks per square meter; an additional one-ruble fifty-kopeck flat fee was levied for municipal services, such as the emptying of cesspools. In addition, the city was divided into two zones—the immediate city (the southeast), and the north and far west—with a 10 percent reduction in rent for those living far from the city center in zone two. Further discounts were offered for the lack of running water, sewage, or electricity, but a 10 percent surcharge was assessed on those who had hot water and a bath. Finally, there was a small additional charge for each dependent. KBU chief Lukashevich was charged with clarifying the reasons for charging rent and with supervising the operation of the new rent system. Calling for an end to "welfarism" (*sobesovshchina*), he wrote that "those living well should pay," adding that "for the vast majority, there would be no great increase."

To back up these arguments, Lukashevich offered three examples of how the new law had affected people. The metal worker Zakuev, with a family of four, earning 200 rubles per month and possessing 16 square meters was said previously to have paid 4.50 rubles per month; now he would be charged 7.29 rubles. The coke master worker Volotrub, with a family of three, earning 300 rubles and possessing 15 square meters previously paid 5.25 rubles, and now would be charged 11.62. Finally, a foreman of rolling mill construction, Krasnikov, with a family of four, earning 700 rubles and possessing 22 square meters, who previously paid 16.50, now would pay 22.04.[52] After all the calculations were made, in other words, rents turned out to be quite low (usually less than 5 percent of household income), and Lukashevich promised that the KBU would use the new revenues to finance roads, bring electricity to the city's outskirts, and so on.[53]

As the readers of the local newspaper knew from personal experience, the overmatched KBU could not forestall the deterioration of the housing stock, let alone build infrastructure. In 1933, of 1,054 barracks needing repairs, only 190 were worked on.[54] In subsequent years the figures were little better, and in many cases when a barracks was considered repaired, it often still had broken doors, broken or missing windows, and nonfunctioning appliances. In 1935, the oblast newspaper called the situation of the Magnitogorsk barracks "catastrophic," an assessment made every fall on the eve of the beginning of the long winter.[55]

Rather than the steel plant or the local party organization, let alone Moscow or Soviet power, the KBU was always held accountable for these aggravating problems. Naturally, the newspaper led the offensive, reporting that it received ten letters every day on the poor work of the KBU. Some of these venomous diatribes were printed, to which the newspaper appended its own editorial comments. In one typical blast, the paper wrote that "the staff of the Everyday-Life Administration call all these complaints by workers 'everyday trifles.'"[56]

In response, Lukashevich patiently explained that the KBU's 1936 budget for repairs was only 565,000 rubles, and that by midyear, 30 June, 409,000 rubles had already been spent. In July another 130,000 rubles were spent, and the plan for August called for a further allocation of 225,000, provided the steel plant permitted such a budget overrun. Pointing to the lack of adequate building materials, labor power, and finances, Lukashevich said of his forlorn repair policy, "We are doing only what cannot be put off." Meanwhile, he issued a sensible plea for residents to get involved in the improvements and upkeep of "their" housing.[57]

Unable to arrest the disintegration of the housing stock, the local authorities arrested Lukashevich instead (his trial is discussed in chapters 6 and 7). Ananenko, Lukashevich's eventual replacement, took up the unenviable task of explaining the housing calamity to the city's inhabitants but added little to the discussion. "The wooden barracks were built quickly and improperly and do not last very long," he wrote in the newspaper. "Within seven or eight years, most are exhausted and must be taken down."[58] In fact, barracks were constantly being removed, but for reasons other than anticipated decay. Rather, because many of the barracks were built on the factory grounds, their removal was necessitated by completion of industrial construction.[59]

In 1936, the entire Fourth Sector (site of the rolling mill shops) was "reclaimed" when thirteen barracks were torn down to make room for a new mill.[60] That same year, in the old Magnitnyi Settlement, the makeshift homes lying in the flood plain of the second dam were either torn down or moved to another settlement. The newspaper reported in a subsequent article that 407 of 409 buildings (mostly mud huts) were torn down or removed, and that the owners were compensated 341 rubles each and promised new housing, which no doubt meant they would have to rebuild their own mud huts at another spot.[61]

As more and more barracks were torn down, those left standing continued to decay—and the KBU continued to lose ground.[62] In a cost-cutting measure, the already overmatched KBU repair work force was ordered reduced in 1938, from 680 to 450; later that year, after the KBU was reorganized into the Municipal Economy Administration (*upravlenie kommunalnogo khoziaistva*—UKKh), its work force shrank again, this time to 374.[63] "Repairs," warned Ananenko, "are put off, funding and staff are cut—the day of reckoning will come." For Lukashevich, the day of reckoning had already come, vaulting Ananenko into his position. But the state of most of the city's housing remained desperate.

Much of the problem with looking after both temporary and permanent housing stock, and the major reason why the KBU was forced to reduce staff, was financial. In 1937 the KBU ran a deficit of 4.45 million rubles, and the projection for 1938 based on the first half of that year was for a deficit of 6 million.[64] Admittedly, the KBU was not very efficient in its use of those funds at its disposal, but much of the organization's deficit was derived from circumstances beyond its control. The KBU budget came partly from bus and tram receipts, which provided an excellent source of income.[65] But the preponderance of funding came from rent payments, which were deliberately set far below costs. And despite the low rental fees, as of February 1936 the KBU was owed more than half a million rubles in back rent.

In desperation KBU officials began to turn out the lights in the residences of those behind in their rent payments.[66] Some of those who owed back rents, however, had left Magnitogorsk, and of the delinquents who were still living in the city, not all had lights to turn out. Meanwhile, the newspaper, relishing its self-assigned gadfly role, pointed out that many of those owing the nominal payments earned large salaries. The paper took special delight in the discovery that the chief of the KBU's housing department, Efimov, was in arrears.[67]

Besides failing to pay for his own housing, Efimov was accused of keeping a spare housing fund to award to personal favorites. He was also said to have engaged in the sale of choice apartments "for vodka, fabric, and simply for money, to people having nothing to do with the metallurgical complex." For these alleged practices, Efimov, like Lukashevich, was soon fired and arrested. But this, too, did little to increase the amount of available space, or improve the condition of the existing stock.[68]

Mismanagement, an inadequate work force, shortages of the necessary construction materials, malfeasance, and the sorry state of the KBU's financial affairs combined to hinder efforts to maintain the temporary housing. In fairness to the KBU, the organization faced a nearly impossible task in fighting the deterioration of a poorly built housing stock well after the time it was designed to last had expired. And in a situation where the occupants were not owners but where nonetheless the sanction of eviction was undermined by the social goal of ensuring that no one went homeless, few tenants seemed to have recognized a clear incentive to lend a hand in the upkeep of the housing they occupied.[69] In this matter, as in many others, people looked to the state to provide. It was the state after all that built, allocated, registered, and owned the living space.

COMMUNAL BUT NOT EXACTLY COLLECTIVIST

Virtually everyone who lived in Magnitogorsk spent some time, often several years, in a barracks. At first, all barracks were built in the form of dormitories, with large, common areas. "Our barracks was divided into four parts," recalled one worker. "The sections formed one gigantic room, with metal cots."[70] Usually there were separate women's barracks, or, less frequently, a women's section was created by partitioning. True, barracks sometimes contained small separate rooms, often with jerry-built walls. But typically even families lived in one of the large common rooms, hanging a cloth or a sheet for a modicum of privacy.[71]

The first barracks were small, with the largest built for one hundred people, yet they were packed with two hundred people and more. Two workers frequently shared the same cot, one sleeping in it at night, the other during the day. Soon, larger barracks were built, but whatever their capacity, it was always exceeded. In 1931 one barracks was said to house as many as eight hundred people.[72] That same year, one national newspaper said of Magnitogorsk that "inside the barracks it is suffocating, filthy and infested with parasites. People lie on bare boards with their arms under their heads for pillows. There is hardly any space between the beds. Every corner is packed with people."[73]

The extreme lack of privacy in the dormitory barracks was perhaps their most unpopular feature, especially as more and more people married and started families. No doubt partly in response to the inhabitants' demands, beginning in late 1932 dormitory (*obshchie*) barracks were converted into what were called "individual-room" (*komnatnye*) barracks.[74] By 1938 there were only forty dormitory barracks—less than one-tenth of the city total. In most cases, however, the individual rooms were occupied by whole families, and sometimes even more than one.[75]

Whatever the scanty results in terms of added privacy, the reconstruction of the barracks was not intended to alter their basic orientation. The barracks were deliberately built without elementary equipment for personal needs, for the authorities planned a citywide system of service industries—and not just as an expedient to economize resources but as part of a bold vision to create a new type of social organization, a collectivized mode of existence. This remarkable ambition was carried out and maintained even in the face of grave difficulties.

To begin with, Magnitogorsk developed a system of public baths. In 1934, when the local population was between 170,000 and 200,000, the city counted thirty public baths with a total capacity of around 16,000 people a day. Queues were invariably long. Six of the baths were in mud huts, which were described as "dirty, raw, and with absolutely no elementary comforts," raising the question of how clean one could get there.[76] Cleaner than at home, at any rate, where for all but those who lived in Berezka or some buildings of the Kirov district there were no facilities whatsoever.

By 1939, the number of city baths was consolidated into eight, which that year were said to have served 1.36 million people, or roughly every inhabitant a mere seven times.[77] Several were closed for months at a time for repairs.[78] Some indication of the level of personal hygiene can be inferred from the pleas of city doctors who in the pages of the newspaper implored people to bathe. Abandoning the hope of getting them to bathe their whole bodies with some regularity, one doctor wrote that "civilized people" wash at least partially not less than once in four days.[79] If the people wanted to follow the doctors' advice, however, the system of public baths made their task difficult. Only in summer, when people could bathe in the Ural River, was it easy to keep reasonably clean.[80]

A number of public laundries, often attached to the bathhouses, were also opened. The newspaper reported, however, that they were few in number and required leaving the laundry for a few days, something workmen could not afford to do. More modest attempts simply to organize regular changes of bed linen for the barracks—there were also periodic disinfections and haircut visits—proved little more successful. People slept in dirty linen, in their dirty work clothes. Similarly, the interior of the barracks was supposed to be cleaned periodically by maids, but from frequent complaints aired in the local newspaper, maid service appears to have been irregular.

Like washrooms and showers, kitchens were not part of the basic equipment of the barracks. Residents were expected to rely on mass public dining halls, where the meals served were inexpensive. There were, however, frequent complaints that long lines and the lack of eating utensils resulted in annoying delays, that the meals were unappetizing, and that the conditions in the dining halls were generally deplorable, often leading to outbreaks of stomach ailments.[81] A city party committee decree of 5 July 1931 cited bugs and unsanitary conditions in public canteens as the chief causes of near-epidemic stomach problems.[82]

To be sure, with time the public dining system expanded greatly and even improved: by 1939 Magnitogorsk had twenty-five dining halls and another ninety-seven snack bars, and the dining hall trust served more than thirty thousand meals per day, primarily at lunchtime. Despite persistent complaints about poor quality and service, the network of public dining halls provided an indispensable service for the large segments of the population that worked at a considerable distance from home, and for those unable or unwilling to prepare their own food.[83] All the same, many people, especially those not employed in the largest shops of the steel plant, preferred to take meals at home in the barracks when they could, using the heating stoves for cooking.[84]

No doubt the chief virtue of a collectivist way of life was thought to consist in the "liberation" of women from household drudgery, so that they could work in the factories, doing what was called "productive" labor. In Magnitogorsk several nurseries were organized, providing subsidized child care for working mothers. But there were too few nurseries for most working women to be able to take advantage of one. And although the shortfall was to some extent compensated for by people who banded together and formed their own day-care centers in their barracks or building complexes, most households were left to themselves in matters of child care.[85] Even when given the opportunity for child care, some people preferred to avoid the crowded nurseries because of the notorious spread of common children's sicknesses in them.

Thus, although nurseries were to take care of children, public laundries the washing, maids the cleaning, and public kitchens the cooking, the reality in each case fell short of expectations, making the communal nature of barracks existence seem irritatingly out of sync. Too often elemental needs could not be satisfied either at home or in town. Of course, public bathhouses and factory canteen lunches, whatever their deficiencies, were relied upon of necessity (the often legitimate gripes about them being indirect confirmation of their use). But it was an open secret among male workers that whatever the collectivist rhetoric and, to some extent, practice, if they wanted to keep their living areas and clothes clean, and to improve their diet, they needed to get married. Female workers knew this "secret" too, as well as its wider meaning for their lives.[86]

Barracks, of course, were envisioned as merely temporary, and as time passed, some people did relocate to the buildings constructed in the "socialist city." The logic underlying the housing design there, however, exhibited a striking similarity to that of the barracks. Although the collectivized nature of barracks life might be thought to have been largely an expedient, suitable chiefly for unmarried youth, the design of the permanent housing stock, along with the concerted efforts to develop public facilities throughout the urban territory, indicated that collectivism was fundamental to the vision of the new city.

Quite intentionally, the first permanent buildings in Magnitogorsk were made up of single-room "cells" with shared washrooms and toilets in the hall and without kitchens. As with the barracks, the inhabitants were to rely on mass, public dining halls. In the face of strong protests, a kitchen was belatedly installed in each of the first buildings—but only one, regardless of the number of rooms or residents. Thus, even when the residents of a single-room cell managed to expand their territory, laying claim to a vacated adjacent room, these new units were not self-contained apartments. They were variants of what was dubbed the "communal apartment."

After the revolution, most large, single-family apartments were reassigned to several families, who shared the kitchen, toilet, and bathroom. Such lodgings, where there were usually as many families as rooms, gave birth to the expression "communal apartment" (*kommunalka*). Soon this designation came to be applied to the new housing built across the country, such as that of the first superblock at Magnitogorsk. In the new housing, though, far more families shared the common kitchen than was the case in the expropriated and converted private dwellings. There were, in short, degrees of "communality."

Much like barracks, Magnitogorsk's new communal apartments were clusters of rooms, sometimes but not always separated by doors, where complete strangers came together to live. The common washroom, toilet, and kitchen forced inhabitants to devise ways to live with each other; not surprisingly, disputes were common.[87] "In our building there is one common kitchen for eighty apartments, where there are constant scandals: who lives better, who is better at making steel, who lives worse, who makes worse steel," explained one Magnitogorsk resident. "It even happens that food is stolen from pots."[88] Not surprisingly, some people avoided the kitchens altogether.[89]

To handle these everyday conflicts "comrade courts" were organized in each building and in many of the barracks. Attached to the house managements or commandants, these courts could impose sanctions, such as public censure or small fines to be turned over to a fund for the use of the whole building, or they could require the guilty party to perform certain tasks needed by the residents.[90] The efficacy of this judicious approach is hard to gauge. Just as frequently, it seems, the feuding parties sought the intervention of outside authorities, no matter how trivial the alleged offense.[91] Such disputes, moreover, were not always innocent misunderstandings. One way to dislodge someone from his or her living space—perhaps in order to free the space up for oneself, a relative, or a friend—was by denunciation.

No better window onto Soviet domestic life could be had than that provided by a 1935 central decree, "On the Struggle against Hooliganism." The decree stated that hooligan-like behavior on the part of tenants— which it characterized as "the holding of regular drinking bouts in the apartment, accompanied by noise, fights, and abusive language; the inflicting of beatings (especially of women and children), casting insults, threatening revenge by capitalizing on one's work status or party position, perverse conduct, baiting of nationalities, defamation of character, other kinds of mischief (throwing out another person's belongings from the kitchen and other rooms used in common, spoiling food prepared by other tenants, damaging other things and products, etc.)"—was "particularly inadmissible."[92]

If not exactly collectivist, then, life in both the barracks and permanent buildings remained inescapably communal. At the same time, partly because of an absence of services and partly because of strong personal preferences, people struggled to live as separate families. The result of such communalism without collectivism was paradoxical: nominally equivalent and therefore interchangeable inhabitants reconstituted themselves as families. It was something of an inside out world. To the planners and administrators, it could all seem just so much aggregate living space, so many square meters in the various approved types of structures with their various configurations to be tallied, apportioned, and registered. But to the inhabitants, of course, these were their homes.

Nowhere was the persistence of family-centered living patterns, and their collision with a collectivist social vision, more visible than in the mud huts (*zemlianki*), in which about a quarter of the city's population lived, many by choice. The primitive but sturdy structures afforded a degree of family privacy that could not be had in the barracks or even some of the brick buildings. From an official's point of view, mud huts would seem to have offered significant relief from the pressure on the city's insufficient aggregate living space. But the local authorities despised the mud huts and, after a period of grudging toleration, sought to eradicate them.[93]

Beginning in 1935, 376 mud huts were taken down at the authorities' behest.[94] In 1936, a special decree ordered the elimination of all mud huts by the end of the year (recall the case of Makarov), thereby accelerating the removals. The decree also banned the sale of mud huts and instructed the militia to discontinue new residence registration in them.[95] There must have been something of an uproar, however, for the decree was amended three months later: only empty mud huts were to be immediately torn down. The rest would be gradually removed when alternative housing was found for the inhabitants, as prescribed by law. And residence registration was to be prohibited only for those trying to move into an abandoned mud hut.[96]

Desite the partial retreat, these were strong measures with far-reaching consequences. The official reason given for them was that the mud huts were hindering industrial construction. Admittedly, mud huts were often built right on construction territory, so that as construction progressed sometimes they did get in the way. But the motives for the decree and its amendment went beyond those explicitly stated. Mud huts were resented by the authorities as a reminder of the humiliating "backwardness" of Russia. They evoked the country's rural poverty and primitive agricultural ways. In their shabby exteriors, the mud huts created what one correspondent for the oblast newspaper called "a sharp contrast . . . with the wonderful stone buildings" of Socialist City.[97]

Mud huts were strewn all over the city in unsightly clusters, the largest of which, located just to the side of the mine, was popularly known as "Shanghai." The infamous Asian metropolis was synonymous in the early part of the twentieth century with all the evils of a capitalist city: dark, narrow streets littered with trash, drenched in soot, teeming with huddled masses, and generally overcome by squalor and reputed moral decadence. Of course, the new city of Magnitogorsk was intended to leave behind any trace of such Shanghai-like urban life. But here it was, a stain on the new world heroically coming into being.[98]

Beyond their appearance (derived from the agricultural origins and pursuits of their inhabitants), mud huts differed from other kinds of housing in Magnitogorsk in that they were owned by their inhabitants.[99] In a city without private property and predicated on communal living, mud huts were an uncomfortable and ubiquitous anomaly. This was the other side of the charge of "backwardness": mud huts were reviled as a vestige of a "petty-bourgeois" attachment to property incompatible with the new socialist system.

The 1936 mud hut removal decree suggested that mud huts were a convenient hiding place for criminals, a suspicion apparently shared by some city residents. One worker, who recalled that "it's not so bad in the mud huts themselves: warm, dry, and clean," nevertheless insisted that they served as hiding places for runaways and others.[100] For the novelist Valentin Kataev, Magnitogorsk's Shanghai was a place "where, in small sod huts, the refuse of the construction led a dark and isolated existence: bootleggers, sharpers, fugitives, thieves, buyers of stolen goods, prostitutes— all so horrible that they never left their lairs."[101] A 1937 article in the city newspaper devoted to "Greater Shanghai," population five thousand, was less sensational in tone but approached the substance of Kataev's vision of the settlement as a separate world cut off from the rest of the city.

In uncharacteristically poetic language, the newspaper correspondents took the reader to a "mysterious" place where "the lights grow dim, the streets are deserted." They described how "in snow-covered pits, in the pitch dark, the mud huts of Greater Shanghai icily pressed next to each other . . . in crooked, narrow alleys," where "cars did not venture." Shanghai was said to be "cut off from all public life: no school, no library, no pharmacy, no savings bank, not even water (fetched from more than half a kilometer away). There's electric light, but even this is sometimes lacking." In the entire settlement, there was only one public organization: a precinct of the militia, itself housed in a mud hut.[102]

Whatever allowances we may want to make for the "urban" imaginations of the newspaper correspondents, it was clear that Shanghai outlived the 1936 mud hut removal decree. Indeed, finding themselves unable to eradicate the detested mud hut settlements entirely, the authorities tried to will them away by changing the informal designation "Shanghai" to the more comforting "Workers' Settlement." An article appeared in the newspaper in 1938 claiming that the locals had already forgotten the name Shanghai.[103] To root out the mud huts and the "backward" culture they supposedly embodied, however, more serious measures were obviously necessary.

Such measures were already being undertaken. Even before the assault on the mud huts was launched, Magnitogorsk officials, with approval from Moscow, sanctioned what was, from the authorities' point of view, a more acceptable form of "private" housing: so-called individual constructions. These were essentially bungalows, reminiscent of traditional wooden country homes, or dachas. Unlike dachas, however, most individual constructions were intended for year-round use.

Construction of such officially sanctioned bungalows in Magnitogorsk had begun in 1934, but owing to a variety of factors only nineteen had been built by 1936 (forty others were still awaiting completion).[104] To rectify this situation, one of the provisions of the 1936 mud hut removal decree stipulated that credit be extended to the builders for buying bricks, cement, and other construction materials. But anyone granted permission to build a bungalow had to make sure materials were delivered as needed and either undertake the construction or hire others to do so. Permitting an individual to hire labor represented a radical concession on the part of the authorities, and the newspaper complained that this practice created "a bad atmosphere."[105] Even that did not deter the local authorities' enthusiasm for the program, however, for in contrast to the mud huts, individual constructions could be built only with the authorities' approval and assistance. They were, in short, the ultimate reward at the authorities' disposal.

In 1936 a well-publicized campaign touted the various models, all of which were to have separate kitchens and dining rooms. According to Khazanov, deputy chief of the Magnitogorsk complex, there would be four types of individual homes: a single, two-bedroom model costing 5,150 rubles; a single, three-bedroom version costing 5,400; a double apartment, with two bedrooms, for 7,970 rubles; and a double apartment, with three bedrooms, for 9,930. Prospective builders were informed that in addition to providing the necessary materials and technical assistance, the steel plant was to pay 70 percent of all costs.[106] Lists of applicants were compiled in the shops, and demand was enormous. Individual homes cost the factory a small fortune, conceded one official, "but the workers are building them with pleasure."[107]

Inhabitants of the individual houses were invariably singled out as "the best people of Magnitka."[108] Natalia Ogorodnikova, for example, the wife of a well-known Stakhanovite, moved with her husband into such a bungalow in 1936. "It's nice to live in one's own home," the newspaper quoted her as saying. "Having my own home and garden, I can now make my life such that there are no insufficiencies in it."[109] For others beside the fortunate Ogorodnikovs, however, problems with construction materials, transport of materials, credit, and other matters often doomed their efforts. Several hundred bungalows were built, but this was far fewer than the number planned.[110] Individual bungalow homes, with their neat cottage-like appearance, were drowned in a tide of mud huts.

The mud huts' persistence must be seen against the backdrop of the city's housing crunch (and the insufficiencies and unpopularity of communal facilities). These primitive dwellings arose from the earliest days of the construction, not simply a necessity but for many also a preference (as some crusaders for the regime understood) and one that, even in the more "acceptable" form of bungalows, spoke volumes about people's attitudes toward communal living.[111] The regime recognized as much in its promotion of bungalows, and in the new designs for the second superblock in the latter half of the 1930s. This time, not cells or single rooms but apartments were the basic units, each to be occupied by a single family and to have a separate kitchen. Such a family-oriented design was part of a broad policy shift by the regime.

Motivated by a desire to spur population growth and inculcate reverence for hierarchy, and sobered by widespread juvenile delinquency and appalling infant mortality—in Magnitogorsk, the rate was officially 222 per 1,000—the Soviet regime belatedly embraced the family unit.[112] In mid-1935, a campaign to promote motherhood and fertility, conducted with the assistance of the medical establishment, was launched. By the spring of the next year, the Magnitogorsk newspaper was writing of abortion that "the destruction of human life, is unacceptable in our building-socialism state."[113]

In late June 1936 the central authorities issued a decree making divorce complicated and expensive, offering financial and other rewards to multiple-child families, and restricting abortion.[114] In October 1936, another decree was issued making it a crime to refuse to hire or to lower the pay of pregnant women.[115] Abortion constituted the main target. It was pronounced "an evil holdover from the order whereby an individual lived according to narrow, personal interests and not in the interests of the collective." The newspaper added that "in our life there is no such gap between personal and collective life. For us it seems that even such ultimate questions as the family and the birth of children, are transformed from personal to social issues."[116]

This was a long way from the "abolition of the family as the basic cell of society" announced in the Magnitogorsk newspaper back in 1930.[117] But despite the policy reversal and the construction of self-contained apartments in the city's second superblock, the communal apartment remained the basic form of permanent housing in Magnitogorsk. As for the great mass of "temporary" housing, the barracks, communal life also predominated, although well before the regime embarked on its pro-family policy, the inhabitants had introduced their own version of a pro-family orientation. Given the barracks' structure, however, it was a decidedly uphill struggle.

The contrast between the new pro-family policy of the regime and the continued anti-family organization of housing was further brought home by the population's often grudging dependence on the overburdened system of public facilities for meals, bathing and laundry, and child care. The popularity of the individual constructions sponsored by the authorities furnished an eloquent statement of people's preferences. Meanwhile, it was no small irony that the housing most suited to the rehabilitation of the family which was also widely available remained the maligned mud huts. When it came to housing, abolishing capitalism and building socialism had its share of surprises.

BIRTH PANGS OF SOCIALIST CULTURE

Housing in Magnitogorsk was called upon not merely to shelter people but to mold them. For this purpose every barracks had a "red corner" (*krasnyi ugolok*)—an answer to the peasant household's "icon corner"—where the new order was on display. In one typical red corner, according to John Scott, hung "the barrack[s] wallnewspaper, two *udarnik* [shock worker] banners, [and] pictures of Lenin, Stalin, and Voroshilov."[118] Intended as places to read, listen to lectures, watch films, and discuss political issues, the red corners were conceived as not simply showcases but also cultural training grounds for the new civilization of socialism.

What the culture of socialism might be, however, took a while to establish. In the early years at Magnitogorsk, the local Komsomol newspaper persistently hailed the barracks as the "smithy of proletarian culture," by which was meant the places where workers would develop new cultural forms that were recognizably different from the culture produced under capitalism.[119] Such forms largely failed to appear, however, and in the few cases when something resembling proletarian culture did appear (such as worker-written verses about labor), the results failed to inspire a mass following. This led to an approach handed down from on high that in effect recognized cultural output as "socialist" if it was created in the USSR and if it appeared to demonstrate the present (and especially future) superiority of socialism. This new approach was christened "socialist realism."

As a slogan socialist realism may have caught on quickly, but its parameters remained elusive. Broadly speaking the USSR had embarked on an unprecedented search for a socialist—that is, noncapitalist—reality whose representation, no less than its substance, was not known beforehand. Precisely which kinds of images and activities were to be encouraged under the new slogan formed part of the groping process of experimentation that characterized the 1930s in all areas, politics and economics as well as culture. All that was known for sure was that socialist realism as a mirror of the truth would be different from simple or naive realism, which by failing to take into account concealed class "realities" was considered to be anything but realism. In short, however matters eventually played themselves out, the contrast with capitalism would remain paramount.[120]

Indeed, even though the notion of specifically proletarian culture was more or less abandoned after 1932, the category of class did not disappear from the Soviet understanding of culture, for just as the culture of the bourgeoisie was thought to be part of bourgeois class domination, under socialism the culture of the dominant class, the proletariat, was expected to help sustain that class's political and economic "hegemony." Paradoxically, however, actual workers for the most part exhibited what were excoriated as "petty-bourgeois" proclivities, from hard drinking, card playing, and rude speech to wife beating and belief in God. In the case of younger workers, who had recently emerged from the peasantry—viewed as an historically backward and doomed class—this was hardly surprising. But even long-time workers were said to suffer from a similar "absence of culture" [*bezkulture*], which in their case was attributed to the legacy of capitalist exploitation.

Whatever the justifications offered, such manifestations of *bezkulture* among workers remained a source of significant embarrassment and concern to the Bolsheviks. To be sure, well before the revolution, a "cultural gap" between the country's educated minority and its great "unwashed" majority had been a subject of extensive commentary and heart pounding by the intelligentsia. But after October, in the context of the thinking on cultural hegemony, this discrepancy acquired special urgency.

Against the disquieting background of a culturally petty-bourgeois proletariat, and with the content of socialist culture still unsettled, the red corners in the Magnitogorsk barracks became the focus of massive publicity and activity. From this point of entry into the barracks, various cultural and political agencies, such as the trade unions and the Komsomol, joined the battle against the "old" way of life (*byt*) and for the new. Their goal, as they saw it, was "to conquer" (*zavoevat*) the barracks through "cultural work" (*kulturnaia rabota*), meaning not only political lectures and discussions but acceptable forms of leisure and contests for cleanliness.[121] Rather than fostering a distinct proletarian culture, the class struggle on the "cultural front" focused on teaching people to pay homage to the icons and ideas of the revolution *and* on raising the general cultural level (*kulturnost*) of the proletariat, in the hope of forming a culturally worthy Soviet working class.

The depth of the challenge confronting the authorities was highlighted by the case of the mud huts, which in contrast to the barracks afforded no entryway for campaigns to influence people's way of life. There were no red corners in mud huts; there was nothing either "red" or "cultured" about them. It was as if the old peasant hut (*izba*) had reasserted itself—in the socialist city—with all its "backward," "petty-bourgeois" traditions. Moreover, while the mud hut settlements appeared to be impervious to the drive for a new culture, it was not clear how much, if at all, life in the barracks was being affected by the cultural onslaught. All the slogans, rallying cries, and activities organized by the authorities and various enthusiasts did not always amount to much in the face of the severe overcrowding, state of general disrepair, staggering filth, and indifference and even open hostility of many of the barracks inhabitants to the efforts to teach them how to be more exemplary in matters of personal hygiene and recreation.

A typical account of barracks life in the early years painted a picture of anything but cultural refinement:

> In the barracks, mud and ceaseless noise. Not enough light to read. The library is poor, newspapers are few. They are stolen to roll cigarettes. . . . Gossip, obscene anecdotes, and songs emerge from the mud-filled red corners. At night drunks return to the barracks, stupid from boredom. They disturb the sleep of the others. From time to time traveling artists drop in to Magnitogorsk: sword swallowers, jugglers, comedians. The workers laugh, but are sometimes exasperated.[122]

In later years the newspaper continued to carry frequent reports of what it castigated as debauchery. During a 1936 raid of barracks no. 8, for example, once cited for its exemplary condition (see chapter 5), gambling was found to be prominent among the residents. As for the red corner, it had people living in it.[123] To the extent that there was cultural activity in the red corners, informal varieties seem to have predominated. Musical instruments, especially the balalaika and *talianka* (a form of harmonica), were highly valued.[124] A few of the songs sung were political (often relating to the Civil War), but most appear to have been apolitical. A good many were bawdy. Almost all had roots in the genre of village ballads, which covered the gamut of emotions but were especially preoccupied with love—sometimes won, more often lost.[125]

Even if the forms of entertainment predominant in the barracks disappointed the cultural activists, at least a feeling persisted that the barracks were accessible to them. Resolutions adopted at an April 1932 conference on cultural work typically complained that "barracks had ceased to be a center of mass-political work," but the organization of the conference itself testified to the fact that the "battle" was still being waged.[126] Several years later the factory newspaper was still calling the barracks the "homefront of production" (*tyl proizvodstva*).[127]

Cultural and political activists could also reach the urban inhabitants outside the home in workers clubs, the "red corners" of the city. Organized by shops or enterprises, a club was supposed to be equipped with checkers and chess sets, a library, newspapers, billiards, table tennis, movie projectors, "circles" for the study of photography, painting, drama, history (for women it was often crocheting and knitting)—in short, with anything except vodka and playing cards. By the end of the 1930s, Magnitogorsk had twelve such clubs, most of which were situated in large, primitive barracks structures. [128] Sometimes the clubs were without heat and even electric lighting; more often, such elementary services were provided, but this was no guarantee of effective functioning. In one newspaper "raid," or spot investigation, entitled "Dull, Boring, and Disorganized," for example, the Construction Workers' Club came in for heavy criticism: the circles did not function, the chess and checker sets were not loaned out (due to fear that the workers would steal them), and despite the presence of a cleaning lady, the club was filthy inside, while outside there were mounds of garbage. [129]

The same raid, however, found much to praise at the Railroad Workers' Club, and further reports praised other exemplary facilities, such as the NKVD Club (part of the NKVD building in the First Sector), which had its own sports facilities, the Engineers' and Technicians' Club (DITR) opposite the factory gates, and the remodeled Miners' Club above Berezka (on the northern side of the mine). Each of these facilities appear to have been a popular gathering spot, although none came close to matching the grandeur of the most conspicuous and extensively equipped club in the city—the so-called Palace of Metallurgists (*dvorets metallurgov*).

Located at the heart of the Magnitogorsk's "cultural center" on Theater Square (between the first and second superblocks), the Palace's exterior was one of the most architecturally imposing in the city. Inside, its hallways were lined with marble and outfitted with chandeliers, while the walls of its main auditorium were decorated with sculptures. Although repeated complaints were aired in the newspaper that the interior sculptures were generally hackwork and not truly "socialist," the Palace of Metallurgists was nonetheless hailed by the newspaper as a conspicuous monument to the "culture" of the Soviet working class. The implication appeared to be that whatever opinion one had of its architectural style, the Palace was indisputably "socialist" because it celebrated socialism, and also because workers could and did go there, to be "cultured." [130]

Beyond the clubs, which tended to be frequented largely by a particular institution's employees, the city also had a number of "cultural" institutions open to all urban residents, such as the sound cinema Magnit, which opened its doors in 1931 (within a year of the opening of the first sound cinema in Moscow). [131] The Magnit could accommodate several thousand spectators in its big auditorium. A smaller second hall housed a reading room, a book kiosk, an area for playing chess, exhibitions, and a babysitting service for mothers. The foyer, meanwhile, boasted a comparatively well-stocked buffet, as well as busts of Lenin and Stalin. In 1938 Magnit was closed two years for renovations, as a result of which an indoor balcony was added from which an orchestra could be heard before and after screenings.[132]

With more than 600,000 patrons a year, Magnit was easily the most popular form of "cultured" entertainment in the city and a key mechanism for disseminating the values that came to be associated with socialism.[133] True, many of the foreign films shown in the city (accompanied by subtitles and some live translation) had little or no relation to political questions, or to the goal of cultural transformation. (In 1936, for example, the best-liked imported films, judging by newspaper accounts, were *La Cucaracha*, a color production from Hollywood, and *The Last Billionaire*, a French-language farce.) But others, such as Charlie Chaplin's *Modern Times*, were readily assimilated into a "socialist" point of view.

Described as "the tragic story of a little man living in the capitalist jungle," *Modern Times* was hailed by the city newspaper as "a rarity in bourgeois cinema—a great film."[134] Chaplin's classic reinforced with sophistication and persuasiveness the relentless message contained in cruder form in newspapers and radio broadcasts about the capitalist world being one in which the workers had no rights. Moreover, newsreels shown before and after *every* film invariably included clips of goose-stepping German soldiers with Nazi armbands, various Japanese generals bestowing approval on assembled troops, and Italian fascists giving their signature dagger salute.[135] Finally, all of the Soviet-made movies which played in Magnit in the mid- and late 1930s carried forceful political messages—which of course did not preclude them from also being entertaining. In fact, the considerable entertainment value of many Soviet films made their central idea regarding the superiority of socialism over capitalism that much more digestible.

Among the more successful Soviet-made films of the decade were the 1936 thrillers *Party Card* (see chapter 7) and a Mosfilm production called *We're from Kronstadt*. The latter told the uplifting Civil War tale of the 1919 defense of Petrograd against White Guardists and Interventionists by the renowned Baltic Fleet sailors, whose allegiance to the Bolsheviks had been one of the most decisive factors in the party's successful seizure of power in the name of the people. During its first seven days in Magnitogorsk, this historical drama depicting the sailors' milieu, as well as the merciless execution of several of them by their White Russian captors, was said to have been seen by twenty-eight thousand people. The city newspaper reported that the only other domestic film which had been such a sensation was the 1934 production *Chapaev*.[136]

Released in connection with the 7 November holiday (Revolution Day),

Chapaev—adapted for the screen from the novel of the same name by Dmitrii Furmanov, the former political commissar in the division of the real-life Vasilii Chapaev—told the story of a "simple proletarian" who became a national hero during the Civil War. It became one of the most popular films in the history of the Soviet cinema, hailed for its authenticity as much as for its message of the immortality of the people. The music from the film was also a success—although it did not rival the decade's most popular song, "March," which was also from a 1934 hit film, *Happy Guys (Veselie rebiata)*. In that light-hearted musical comedy, the dreams of even the poorest of the poor were shown to come true—in the land of socialism.[137]

The well-received films *Chapaev* and *Happy Guys* formed the two poles of an emerging "socialist" popular culture in its most effective—that is, celluloid—guise. Soviet film studios, although they could not match Hollywood's mythmaking powers, managed to gain large audiences by adapting the proven Hollywood formula: blend escapist fables of a cheerful life with dramatic tales of extraordinary exploits. For Hollywood the most frequent vehicle for portraying daring accomplishments was the Western, whose moral was invariably rugged individualism (often in contravention of the law). For Soviet studios, the preferred vehicle was the Civil War; the basic theme, the ferocity of the class struggle and the great sacrifices it required, sacrifices undertaken by humble representatives of the people for the benefit of the collective.[138]

The efforts to produce a "socialist" culture could also take a self-consciously highbrow turn. Magnitogorsk's elegantly named Pushkin Drama Theater, if not quite as popular as the local sound cinema, managed to maintain a small but loyal following that grew over time. Founded in 1930 by dedicated enthusiasts as the TRAM, or Theater of Young Workers, the local drama group underwent several name changes and for its first seven years floated from one structure to another, often performing in red corners and factory shops. After stints in the NKVD Club and the DITR, in late 1936 the theater finally settled in its own properly outfitted and indeed luxurious building adjacent to the marblesque Palace of Metallurgists on Theater Square. In 1937 it took the name of Aleksandr Pushkin, in connection with the centennial of the great Russian poet's death.

From 1934, when Boris Nikolskii of Moscow's acclaimed Maly Theater was "mobilized" to Magnitogorsk, the professionalism of local productions increased noticeably. Their content also changed.[139] From a concentration on agitprop skits, the players' repertoire shifted to Russian and European classics.[140] Political subjects were not abandoned, however. Instead, they were accorded greater solemnity, appropriate to the theater's growing sense of its own sophistication and to the new international situation. Plays staged in 1936 included the dramas *Enemies* by Maxim Gorky and *The Big Day* by B. Kirshin, a production about how the next world war was going to start suddenly, without a formal declaration.[141]

Critical to the theater's success was the sponsorship, financial and moral, of factory director Avraamii Zaveniagin, who relied on the theater to embellish the image of his reign.[142] Zaveniagin's patronage benefited the artists, too, who, like their counterparts in Moscow, enjoyed elevated status and frequently mingled with the managerial and political elite.[143] A further reflection of this symbiosis was the fact that on the bottom floor of the new theater, the Council of Engineers' Wives organized what was referred to as a "civilized" café. The announcement of the café's opening was accompanied by a flattering photograph of the "high society" women—well-dressed patrons of the arts.[144]

A world away from the Drama Theater, but just around the corner from Magnit, were located the sports stadium and city circus. The stadium hosted matches of the city's football club, Metallurg, first organized in 1936 (a larger second grandstand capable of holding two thousand people was under construction that year).[145] Besides football there were also mini-olympics, called Spartakiads, in which competing teams were organized by shop. The winners moved up to the oblast-level competition, hoping for a shot at the all-Union championships.[146] In conjunction with various holidays, there were also mass demonstrations of "physical culture," and in winter, cross-country ski contests were held, usually paralleling production competitions between Magnitogorsk and other steel factories.[147]

As for the circus, it had a regular troupe and was visited by traveling groups, but performances of so-called French wrestling (scripted wrestling) were more likely to draw large audiences. One newspaper satire published in 1936 ruminated over the question, "Where to go in one's spare time? To a film? A drama? A lecture on Abyssinia?" The answer came quickly: "to the circus to watch French wrestling, and argue if it's real or not."[148] The paper made light of such facts but at the same time implicitly recognized that workers' cooperation in the programs of cultural transformation had a limit. What to the proponents of *kulturnost* no doubt appeared as vulgar entertainment, however, was allowed to flourish.

Such was also to an extent the case with the city's Metallurgists Park, which was carved out of the territory between the factory and the original socialist city, or Kirov district. Opened in June 1936 after a tree-planting "storm,"[149] the park was an immediate success, receiving more than fifteen thousand visitors in its first two days. Anyone could pay the 75-kopeck entrance fee (later lowered to 50) to enter the grounds, which contained a children's train ride, several outdoor snack bars, as well as a band shell and dance floor.[150] In the summer months, the grounds were always crowded, particularly in the evening, when people could swing or tango to the latest dance tunes.[151] Such frolicking took place in the shadow of various life-size statues of Stakhanovite workers, Soviet aviators, and the city's patron saint, Sergo Ordzhonikidze.[152] There were few more vivid expressions of how some nominally "bourgeois" cultural activities were permitted and at the same time enveloped in a "socialist" setting, without undue conflict.

A similar combination that did produce something of a clash was tried at the circus, whose performances could perhaps be made edifying but did not fit very easily into a socialist mold. The craze over French wrestling had been allowed to overshadow the circus's original program—so much so that one correspondent complained in the city newspaper that for the regular act, even on weekends there were no queues to get in.[153] Responding to this and other criticisms leveled in the press, the circus director, K. Chervotkin, advised that for the 1936–37 winter season there would be music during intermissions and a new dance hall, as well as an expanded cloak room, a café, kiosks selling flowers, an area set aside for chess, checkers, and billiards, plus "a really big program."[154] At the same time, there were also attempts to tie the expanded circus program to socialist construction and plan fulfillment. The newspaper remained silent on the results. John Scott wrote, however, that such efforts "tended to be ludicrous."[155] Nor were circus acts considered an entirely appropriate venue for the display of icons of the country's leaders.

Some attempts to forge a "red" popular culture, such as those on view at the sound cinema, were extremely successful; others, such as those on view at the circus, apparently less so. Yet even in the latter case it bears remembering that no recognizably anti-socialist or avowedly pro-capitalist manifestations of popular culture were permitted. The theme of socialism's superiority over capitalism may at times have been ineffectually put across, but it was never allowed to be publicly challenged—a circumstance whose wide-ranging importance will be considered more fully in chapter 5. Suffice it to say here that when evaluating the capacity of individuals living in the USSR to reject the regime and its values, we have to keep in mind the extraordinarily limited opportunities for acquiring and making use of alternative information and analyses of domestic, as well as international, events.

A new, cultured and socialist way of life was to arise not only through the work conducted in the red corners, clubs, and other cultural institutions but from the influence of the totality of the urban environment on the inhabitants. In this vein, marriage, birth, and death rites—even street names (when the authorities finally got around to naming streets)—formed part of the process of building a new culture. So too did the new Soviet holidays, such as 7 November (mentioned above) and 1 May, the day of labor, which involved a highly coordinated procession in which the people of Magnitogorsk marched in hierarchical groupings based on their place of work.

Leading the May Day parade were employees of the largest and most important enterprise, the steel plant, which was further divided into shops, the largest and most prestigious of which—blast furnace, open-hearth, and rolling mills—were accorded the forward positions in the march. Each shop or enterprise delegation, furthermore, was led by representatives from top management and "outstanding" workers, usually the victors in competitions specially organized to award the honor of marching in front and holding the shop's banner.[156] Contributing to the atmosphere of pride and accomplishment, the parade had numerous floats, most of which resembled blast furnaces, and a large quantity of hand-held portraits of the country's wise leaders. In 1936, some sixty thousand people were said to have turned out, either to march or watch. Among the slogans displayed that year were "Thank You Comrade Stalin for a Happy Life" and "Life Has Become Merrier."[157]

By contrast, the newspaper almost never alluded to religious practices and holidays, such as Ramadan and Orthodox Christmas or Easter.[158] In fact, Magnitogorsk may have been the first city built in what had been a predominantly Christian country in which the construction of a church was forbidden.[159] There was, after all, little point in building a new life and then according a place in it to the opiate of the people. Meanwhile, the May Day celebration, which took place during the Easter season, demonstrated that even as they struggled to provide popular distractions whose "red" character was sometimes questionable, the authorities nonetheless had ample opportunities to emphasize that theirs was a "socialist" city—and often with considerable entertainment effect, too.[160]

Entertainment and the struggle for the new way of life (and against survivals [*perezhitki*] of the old) seemed to go hand in hand, as for example when the authorities made use of the circus and the cinema for trials involving "economic crimes" (see chapter 6) and domestic violence. Such "shows," reported in the newspaper under the rubric "Court Chronicle," seem to have been held regularly and enjoyed considerable popularity.[161] One trial of a woman accused of murdering her husband, given extensive coverage in the newspaper, related how, after being subjected to repeated physical abuse, she had attacked and killed him with an ax. Convicted of murder, the woman was sentenced to seven years. The newspaper account made no mention of who made up the trial's audience, or what their views on it were, except to say that the proceedings had to change location three times to accommodate the ever-increasing crowds, finally moving to the stadium where more than one thousand people were said to have been in attendance.[162]

Stories of male abuse of women were frequently published in the newspaper as part of the campaign for raising the general level of culture.[163] Some men were accused of refusing to let their wives work, or even to go out of the house.[164] Other men in positions of authority were reported to have used their power to force female subordinates to have sexual relations. Such was the case, for example, with Ivan Lomakin, deputy manager of store no. 34, who received a three-year sentence for attempted rape. In condemning such actions the newspaper cited article 122 of the 1936 constitution on the equal rights of women and the protection of mother and child. But the paper conceded that many men "continued to live in the old way," treating women as slaves. Spousal abandonment and nonpayment of alimony and child support were perennial targets of the newspaper's indignation.[165]

As a further demonstration of their determination to use the urban environment to impart new values, and of the obstacles they met along the way, the local authorities struggled to implement a "dry law." While it lasted (the first two years of settlement), the sale of beer or vodka was not permitted. According to one journalist, however, vodka (called *monakh* in slang) could be purchased only a few kilometers out of town for the handsome sum of twenty to thirty rubles a bottle.[166] Despite the prohibitions on open sale and the resultant prohibitive prices, many sources agree that during the dry law drunkenness was common.[167] Not only was the ineffective law soon repealed, but by the mid-1930s the city had special stores for the sale of wine, beer, and vodka.[168] The authorities also opened up a few pubs. In April 1936, for example, the newspaper announced that one beer hall (*pivnoi*) called "Amerikanka" served hot and cold snacks along with alcohol and was open until 1 A.M. It was located in the central building of the dining hall trust on the Central Chaussée, almost directly across from the main factory gates.[169]

Discouraging alcohol consumption turned out to be as difficult as persuading men to respect women. One establishment bearing the nonalcoholic designation "café" appeared in building no. 11 on Pioneer Street, in the Kirov district, and was said to "enjoy exceptional popularity."[170] An investigation by the newspaper uncovered why: the "café" served neither coffee, nor tea, nor cocoa, nor soft drinks, but rather beer and wine, as well as vodka with hors d'oeuvres (*zakuski*). Irate residents living above it led a crusade against the nightly drunkenness that spilled onto the street, but their indignation was drowned in the café's popularity.[171] In 1937, meanwhile, the counterpart to this "café"—the city's first sobering-up station [*vytrezvitel*]—was organized.[172]

Tirelessly exposing these foibles of the vaunted hegemonic working class, the city newspaper also publicized the many "cultured" recreational possibilities available to Soviet workers and continuously advanced the claim that the working class's "best representatives" were availing themselves of such opportunities. In August 1936 there appeared a "survey" of the activities of eight workers of the prestigious blooming mill on a day off from work. According to the list, one worker strolled in the park. Another went swimming in the artificial lake and saw a film at night (*The Last Billionaire*). A third played pool in the red corner of the shop and at night took a walk in the park. A fourth read a book, swung by the shop for a few hours, and then returned home to the book. A fifth went to the nearby mountain lake, Bannoe ozero, to swim, sing songs, and play sports. A sixth spent the whole day at home reading newspapers. A seventh went to the mountain lake to gather berries and go dancing. The eighth stopped by the shop in the morning to collect his pay (it turned out that the cashier had no money) and while there, shot some pool, at night going to see *The Last Billionaire*.[173]

To the extent that these skilled workers enjoyed some form of diversion, all claimed to have engaged in a respectable "cultural" activity. Although most, if not all of their reports, may have been made sincerely and reported accurately, none of these workers would have wanted to claim otherwise. Nor would any answer that smacked of "hooliganism" have been printed, for the publication of such a survey in the newspaper was intended to serve a definite purpose: these people were being exhibited as the standard bearers of the "new culture."[174] It was all the more revealing, therefore, that the newspaper account of worker leisure activities unwittingly demonstrated that their lives were centered neither in the home nor in the clubs, but in the shops.[175] Compared with organized leisure inside and outside the barracks, the factory was potentially a more potent device for transforming people's way of life (see chapter 5).

Nonetheless, what stands out in this survey of workers' leisure time, as well as in the many other accounts of cultural activities, is the strong public accent placed on worker *kulturnost*. Taking particular delight in announcing when workers departed for the Black Sea, the newspaper challenged its readers to "try and find a worker of the open-hearth or blast furnace shops these days who doesn't have a nice suit." It added that four high-priced pianos had appeared in the store on one day, and all four were instantly bought up.[176] Neatly dressed as many workers may have been, obviously only very few had pianos at home. Yet the above-mentioned survey and other reports indicated that some people were evidently receptive to the calls for cultural refinement.

Perhaps the best evidence of this receptivity could be found in the population's reading habits. Newspapers, which were saturated with the idealization of socialism and advocacy for the ethos of self-improvement through culture, were the most widespread source for leisure reading, but books also appear to have been popular. As of January 1936, Magnitogorsk stores were said to have received and sold a staggering 40,000 books, identified as "mostly technical literature and fiction." The city also had several public libraries, whose facilities were said to be too small to accommodate readers or new books, but nevertheless ten thousand people held library cards. The books most frequently borrowed were said to be Nikolai Ostrovkii's *How the Steel Was Tempered* (*Kak zakalialas stal*), André Barbusse's biography of Stalin, the classics of Tolstoy and Turgenev, and the works of the great "proletarian writer" Maxim Gorky.[177] In a country that only a generation earlier had suffered widespread illiteracy, the level of reading interest and ability among the population was remarkable—and it had political implications.

Since almost all workers had become literate, even if some drank too much, mistreated their wives, took a far greater interest in "French wrestling" than in proper toothbrushing, and maybe secretly believed in God, it could still seem to be the case that great strides were being made in the direction of cultural enhancement. And whatever their present shortcomings, the workers were expected to make even greater strides in the radiant future—as the doctrine of socialist realism repeatedly emphasized. In the end, although the notion of the cultural hegemony of the working class had implicitly shifted to that class's "best representatives," much reassurance could be derived from the general advance of literacy, which brought with it a heightened capacity to absorb the lessons of a socialist popular culture containing numerous, if far from exclusively, "red" themes.

That the varied activities made possible by the mobilization of substantial resources somehow added up to a "socialist culture"—which the elite's

indulgence of highbrow diversions did not contradict—appears to have
been accepted by contemporaries, if only because it had become axiomatic,
with the elimination of capitalism, that the inhabitants of the USSR lived
under socialism and therefore by definition could not have had a "capitalist" culture. Looking at the question another way, because of socialism's
supposed inherent moral superiority, the development of culture in the
service of socialism rendered culture under socialism, whatever its content,
qualitatively different from culture under capitalism. The concept of
"socialist culture" may have appeared vague and at times self-contradic-
tory, but for contemporaries it formed an important part of their experience.

To be sure, there were many uncertainties and problems attendant upon
the compromise that came to be socialist culture. The simultaneous quest
for recognizably socialist themes and cultural refinement sometimes con-
flicted, as evidenced by the controversy over the sculptures at the osten-
tatious Palace of Metallurgists. From the opposite side, the indulgence of
various "bourgeois" cultural activities, such as jazz, continued to elicit cries
of incomprehension. But whatever the objections to certain artifacts of cultural enhancement or to occasional cultural "excesses," the Magnitogorsk
newspaper had little trouble repeatedly suggesting that by adopting a refined lifestyle, even if only in part, Soviet workers had risen "above" their
rude prerevolutionary incarnations, as well as their counterparts still living
under capitalism, for whom culture was seen, not without reason, as a
means of social control in a society sharply divided by class.[178]

To prove the point that culturally, socialism involved the conscious advancement of workers, the Magnitogorsk newspaper highlighted the case
of blooming mill operator Aleksei Tishchenko, who along with his wife
Zoia had arrived in Magnitogorsk in 1933 with all their possessions in a
single homemade suitcase. By 1936, the couple owned furniture, including
a couch and a wardrobe, as well as dress clothes, including two overcoats,
some women's dresses, men's suits, shoes, and other items indicative of
anything but a downtrodden, uncouth existence. Lest it be thought that
their acquisition of *kulturnost* was limited to matters of consumption and
grooming, the newspaper pointed out that the Tishchenkos went to the
theater and concerts together and borrowed books from the public library.
In short, no evidence of *bezkulture* emanated from this exemplary socialist
couple, who also enjoyed another advantage afforded by socialism: a working class family living in its own neat, orderly cottage.[179] As long as the
image of capitalism remained what it then was, the cultural rise of the
Tishchenkos could be presented as an achievement of socialism.

HOUSING FOR A NEW WORLD

For a while tents, stationary railroad cars, and even offices; later, a few apartment buildings and some cottages; throughout, numerous mud huts and barracks—such was housing in Magnitogorsk. On the surface, it is a rather unexceptional picture for a new industrial town. But despite similarities in the primitiveness of the building materials or in the jerry-built nature of construction, housing in Magnitogorsk differed sharply from working-class housing in capitalist cities of the past (and from shantytown settlements in developing-world cities of the future). Those differences consisted in the ownership, allocation, maintenance, and very definition of the housing stock, as well as in the fact that housing was thought to have a purpose beyond merely providing shelter.

Nothing except prevailing notions of socialist city planning should have compelled the schema of housing that arose in Magnitogorsk, which was, after all, built from scratch by a single landlord. But the pressure to build, and to do so quickly, forced local leaders to rely on expedient accommodations, such as barracks, to house the majority of the population. It also forced some of the inhabitants to construct their own shelters, which the local authorities grudgingly tolerated, even though such shelters violated many of the authorities' highest goals. Those goals, based on a renunciation of capitalist practice, included the prohibition of the private ownership of housing, the provision of cost-free or inexpensive accommodations for all, the upholding of the superiority of collective living, and the use of housing in programs for cultural refinement and inculcation of "socialist" values.

On each of these points the authorities were obliged to compromise. Indeed, in the competition between mud huts and bungalows the regime compromised some of its most cherished values. But this does not mean that the theoretical underpinnings that guided the authorities' actions can be ignored. It was above all the theory on the withering away of the family under socialism that permitted the orientation of all housing to the collective and the division of urban housing not into rooms or apartments but indeterminate parcels of space. These notions contributed, no less than expediency, to the way Magnitogorsk housing was structured.

A preference for communal living may have been encouraged by the severe scarcity of housing, yet the readiness to design the permanent housing in the same way shows that promoting communalism, rather than merely making a virtue of necessity, was based on the desire to encourage a new way of life. This desire expressed itself in other ways, such as the construction of special red corners in the barracks, the organization of mass leisure activities, and the development of communal dining and service facilities. Organized leisure obviously had an impact, yet leaving aside for now the image of socialism put forth in popular culture (see chapter 5), the extent of organized leisure's impact on personal habits and hygiene remains difficult to gauge beyond the fact that an ethic of self-improvement was widely propagated. It is, however, beyond doubt that the provision of communal facilities to pool resources and to encourage collectivism rarely resulted in a collectivist mode of existence and sometimes caused unwanted dependence on inadequate facilities.

When in 1936 the central authorities "rehabilitated" the family, they came up against what the people themselves had been battling for some time: the anti-family organization of the housing stock. Of course, the regime and the people did not necessarily agree on how to promote the family. For the regime, a pro-family policy meant the production of as many children as possible, regardless of the economic consequences for real families, or the effects on women's lives. For most people, family life seems to have meant the chance to enjoy the privacy of a separate home and the freedom to make their own decisions on family matters, including family size. In the event, living space was conducive to neither's understanding of enhanced family life.

Most new permanent housing built after 1934 was reconceptualized to accommodate the family unit, but the notion of living space was retained. Not only were construction targets for housing conceived and expressed in amounts of living space, a number of operations performed on the housing stock were carried out on the basis of it. In place of sequestering whole buildings, for example, as had been done in the period immediately after the revolution, the authorities "penalized" individuals for having "excessive" space: living space above certain arbitrarily determined "norms" was either taken away or subject to significantly higher rent charges. Similarly, a person legally qualified for new housing on the basis of his or her current amount of living space, which had to be below a certain arbitrarily established "norm." As for these norms, not even the authorities' humiliating inability to meet their own hygienic standards reduced the attraction for them of the category of living space: it was easily quantifiable and as such permitted ready manipulation of the urban housing stock, often for political ends.

The concept of living space, which encouraged the subdivision of rooms and facilitated the use of rooms other than bedrooms for sleeping quarters, did not entirely replace the notion of a room (or apartment). But for official purposes, even when his or her housing came in the form of a room or apartment, a resident technically occupied a measurable amount of space. A curtain hung across the corner of a living room, a partition marking off a section in the back of a kitchen, a bunk in a barracks, a mattress in a parked railroad car, a single-room "cell" in the first superblock, or a self-contained apartment in the second superblock—it was all so much living space, registered with the authorities, who issued permits for its occupancy and struggled desperately to avert its deterioration.

Living space formed an arena in which new kinds of behavior arose and the petty struggles of everyday life were fought, challenging the urban inhabitants to show the extent of their resourcefulness. With more than one generation living together and with several people frequently living in the same room, all manner of tricks were required to secure some privacy. Marital and sexual relations could be enormously complicated and required more planning than spontaneity. Bargains permitting exclusive use of the space for certain periods of time had to be struck with other residents.

Communalism was nothing new in Russia, yet what was once excoriated as a breeding ground of crime and immorality was now, for a time, celebrated as the highest form of living. But if in the Soviet Union few could own their own homes, almost no one had to worry about eviction for failure to pay the rent. Not only did the authorities want to avoid creating a floating, homeless population, they also strove to live up to the promise of improved welfare that everyone understood to be one of the central aspects of the revolution. Nowhere was that commitment to social welfare more evident than in the understanding of housing.

The principle of living space operated independently of the communal organization of life, yet it reinforced many of the worst features of communal life, such as the lack of privacy. Indeed, within the already not very private communal structure, living space provided for even greater juxtaposition of strangers. This circumstance took on important significance in the context of the authorities' all-consuming preoccupation with the people's behavior and political attitudes, especially manifestations of their allegiance to the regime.

For the regime, people's homes were within the public realm, for in practice there was no such thing as a private sphere. Although "the inviolability of the homes of citizens" was guaranteed in the 1936 Soviet constitution,[180] the constitutional guarantee was belied by the searches conducted by the security police, or NKVD. Even if the NKVD did follow procedures governing investigations (including calling in neighbors as in-dependent witnesses and writing out receipts for confiscated property), they went by the maxim, "If you have nothing to hide, why protest? If you protest, you have something to hide." Homes were anything but inviola-ble, and attempts to protest were futile.

Of course, even had they wanted to watch over the lives of all 200,000 inhabitants in Magnitogorsk—which, after all, was their mandate—the NKVD alone could not have performed such a task. They were, however, assisted by the barracks commandants and house managers (*upravdomy*), whose job it was to cooperate in providing information about tenants whenever the militia or security police asked.[181] Some adept *upravdomy*, who could only see and hear so much, did not hesitate to call on the tenants to help them keep track of the goings-on under their roof. Nor did the NKVD, who could appeal directly to residents for information on other residents.[182]

The cooperation of tenants in their own mutual surveillance was the ul-timate weapon of the security police. Although that weapon was not in-voked every minute of every day, there was a pervasive feeling that it could be called on whenever deemed necessary, making it that much more effec-tive.[183] In all of this, the organization of housing as living space came to play a crucial if inadvertent role. The unavoidability of the stranger's gaze that resulted from both the crowded living conditions and the intentional accentuation of communal life turned out to be ideal for the goal of con-stant surveillance that the regime encouraged and intently pursued.

Although the interlocking web of state surveillance and tenants' mutual surveillance was facilitated by the sudivision of rooms attendant upon the principle of living space, there was nothing inherent in crowded conditions or the coming together of strangers that necessitated that residents keep tabs on each other. It took the complicity of the residents. In Magnitogorsk (and elsewhere in the Soviet Union) people did watch one another and re-port, some enthusiastically, others only reluctantly, forming the nets in which they themselves could be and sometimes were trapped. The reasons behind such collaboration should become clearer in the next chapter.

Whatever the hopes and exigencies that brought it into widespread use, the concept of living space, which underlay and facilitated the emphasis on communal life, produced a number of surprises for authorities and ordi-nary citizens alike. This study of housing in Magnitogorsk in the early Sta-lin period has proved to be an inquiry into ingenious and devious ways to establish occupancy, into the ordeals of manipulating pitifully small spaces to obtain some privacy, and into the constitution of an environment con-ducive to mutual surveillance. In the end, even though rapid, across-the-board cultural enhancement by means of red corners and organized leisure proved a formidable task, new ways of thinking and behaving flourished, in housing and elsewhere, under the aegis of socialism.

5   Speaking Bolshevik

Magnitka taught us how to work. Magnitka taught us how to live.
Elena Dzhaparidze, Magnitogorsk Komsomol[1]

Weary of the anonymity of barracks life, the residents of barracks no. 8 in Magnitogorsk tacked a sign near the entrance with a list of all those living inside. It gave their name, year of birth, place of origin, class origin, trade, Komsomol and party membership (or lack thereof), and location of employment. As the initiator of the action explained, "When someone saw the list—for example, that Stepanov, a fitter, a Komsomol, a shock worker, fulfills his plan such-and-such percent, works on the construction of the blast furnaces—one immediately understood what kind of people lived here."[2] Such acts of self-identification became routine and enveloped the entire society.

In the study of tsarist Russia's workers, the chief task has been to explain how it came to pass that "within a period of less than sixty years, the workers of the most politically 'backward' European country were transformed from a small segment of a caste of peasant-serfs into Europe's most class-conscious and revolutionary proletariat."[3] Precisely the opposite question might be posed about Soviet workers: how did it come about that within a period of less than twenty years, the revolutionary proletariat of Europe's first self-proclaimed workers and peasants state were turned into Europe's most quiescent working class? A substantial part of the answer to that question, and to the question of Stalinism's character and potency, is contained on that simple shred of paper tacked onto a Magnitogorsk barracks.

.   .   .

Ordinarily, the study of a working-class town would be expected to devote considerable attention to worker self-expression, even if only in extreme situations (such as during strikes and demonstrations), and to explore the causes of worker unrest. But in Magnitogorsk there were neither strikes nor riots, and the only demonstrations were state-organized glorifications of the regime and its leadership. In this sprawling steeltown, organized worker protest was conspicuous by its absence.

For the Soviet regime and its defenders, this was no paradox. The absence of strikes followed logically from the proposition that workers themselves held power and thus by definition welcomed the policy of industrialization, "their" policy, with enthusiasm. That there *was* mass enthusiasm lends an ostensible plausibility to this Soviet view. Indeed, although there is scattered evidence of worker discontent in the contemporary Soviet press, manifestations of worker consciousness in official sources were overwhelmingly supportive of the status quo.[4]

Rejecting state-censored expressions of worker consciousness, non-Soviet commentators at first adopted two sets of explanations for the apparent "quietism" of the Soviet working class under Stalin. One view held that the regime's mono-organizational structure and repressiveness precluded any possibility of worker autonomy and collective action, an argument bolstered by the testimony of many former Soviet citizens.[5] Another view, not incompatible with the first, saw the lack of worker political activism in the disintegration of the working class as a result of the Civil War and the so-called peasantization of the work force that began in the early 1930s, when the surviving working class was "diluted" by "raw recruits." The new proletarians were characterized by a cultural backwardness that made them desirous of strong rule by a tsar-father and disinclined to pursue their "proper" working-class interests.[6] Against the Soviet assertion of harmony between worker and regime, these scholars assumed the existence of an objective antagonism, even when an overwhelming preponderance of the available sources indicated support.

In reaction to the assumption that the regime and the people had no common interests, a wave of "revisionist" scholarship arose. Agreeing with certain of their predecessors on the existence of widespread support for Stalin and his programs, revisionists regarded such support not as the "false consciousness" of a "backward" proletariat but as an expression of genuine self-interest linked to worker advancement or social mobility. Such a view tended not only to accept at face value the absence of visible social discontent but even to suggest the presence of genuine social cohesion.[7] It would be hard to imagine an interpretive controversy with the opposing sides farther apart: either disgruntled workers who despised the regime, or contented workers who applauded it (whether "falsely" or "correctly"). Perhaps the time has come to approach the issues from a different angle.

There can be no doubt that the regime was repressive, that the influx of millions of peasants changed the composition of the labor force, and that many thousands of workers "moved up" to become administrators and party officials. But the usefulness of all these conceptions for understanding workers' lives and behavior is limited for at least two reasons. First, these categories are trapped within the terms of the phenomena they are trying to analyze. Moving from the primary to the secondary sources, one is struck by the extent to which the categories and debates of contemporaries pervade subsequent "analyses." Historians are able to study the "peasantization" of the work force in the 1930s, to take one example, precisely because the authorities thought in such terms and collected data accordingly. For us the fact that large numbers of peasants entered the working classes ought to be important not because they were "backward" or even peasants but because the regime defined and treated them as such.

Second, these conceptions are limited by their polarization along a single axis of repression and enthusiasm so that one can "demonstrate" worker support by referring to official sources and worker opposition by citing émigré ones. But how, in fact, do we recognize social support? What constitutes evidence of it? Is the absence of organized political protest a sign of atomization or of social cohesion, or of neither? Does it make sense to analyze social support in terms of groups, and if so, by what criteria should such groups be differentiated? By income and social status? Level of education? Membership in the party? Class? Finally, what is the relative usefulness of sources, official versus émigré, that often tell a diametrically opposed story?

Amid such an incongruity of views in the understanding of workers under Stalin, an important advance was made by Donald Filtzer. Taking up where Solomon Schwarz left off (although without saying as much), Filtzer combined a diligent and sophisticated reading of the contemporary Soviet press with an equally exhaustive review of émigré testimony, and displayed a fine appreciation of paradox and contradiction. Characterizing Stalinist industrialization as inherently exploitative in a Marxist sense, he assumed that workers ought to have recognized their "class interests" and resisted the expropriation of their "surplus value" by the emerging elite, or bureaucracy. But workers did not do so.

By way of explanation Filtzer revived the argument that the old working class was crushed by industrialization: depoliticized, it could manage only individualized responses, such as changing jobs and getting drunk. He also argued that although a new "working class" did form, its members were not up to collective action, preoccupied as they were with personal survival in the difficult circumstances of widespread shortages, speed-ups, physical intimidation, and public ridicule. At the same time, Filtzer did show that workers often "resisted" the new terms of work, just not on a collective basis. He recognized the importance of worker self-expression as demonstrated in a variety of behaviors (turnover, soldiering) otherwise dismissed as evidence of disorientation and anomie. Yet he did not treat the remarkable proliferation of statements about workers' identities made by workers and others, including the authorities, with the same seriousness.[8] As a result, his analysis of the terms on which workers became part of the Stalinist enterprise, though the best to date, was unnecessarily incomplete.

The approach adopted here will be to trace the various ways of seeing and conceptualizing work, the work process, and the worker that were prevalent. My point of departure will be the identification of certain problems: productivity, worker discipline and aptitudes, social origin, and political loyalty. My aim will be to show the effects of these conceptualizations on the kinds of lives workers led and on their self-understanding. Such formulations are not reducible to "ideology." They are better thought of as dynamic relations of power. For this reason, the task is to approach them not from the point of view of meaning, or symbolic constructs, but as a question of maneuver and countermaneuver—in short, as part of the little tactics of the habitat.

The far-reaching effects that resulted from understanding work and workers in particular ways were made possible by the links of these formulations with the practices and techniques that were introduced to address the problems identified. Those techniques ranged from questionnaires to the numerical assignment of skill levels, output quotas, and piece rates, to labor books and autobiographical confessions. It is to the techniques themselves and the context into which they were introduced that I turn to analyze the ways that things said about work and the work place became a determinant in how workers were understood by others, and how they understood themselves.

WORK, WORKER, AND WORKPLACE UNDER SOCIALISM

Upon hearing in February 1932 that the first Magnitogorsk blast furnace was blown in, a telegram was dispatched in the name of the party and the state and signed by Stalin. "I congratulate the workers and the administrative and technical personnel of the Magnitogorsk Metallurgical Complex on their successful fulfillment of the first order of the construction program," Stalin said, adding: "I have no doubt that the Magnitogorsk workers will likewise successfully fulfill the main part of the 1932 program, will build three more blast furnaces, open-hearth furnaces, and rolling mills, and will thus fulfill with honor their duty to their country."[9]

As Stalin's telegram, among many other documents, shows, in the Soviet context work was not simply a material necessity but also a civic obligation. Everyone had the right to work; no one had the right not to work.[10] Failure to work, or to work in a "socially useful" manner, was a punishable offense, and the chief punishment was forced labor (*prinuditelnaia rabota*). Convicts were required to work not merely to make good their "debt" to society but above all to be able to rejoin that society as transformed individuals. Work served as both the instrument and measure of normality.[11]

In addition, anyone who belonged to the social group "workers" shouldered the historical responsibilities that, according to the regime's ideology, fell to this special class. As is well known, Marxism-Leninism conceptualized social structure in class terms.[12] Class analysis, which provided a coherent and simplified worldview and thus a ready-made interpretation of any event or situation, explained and justified numerous state policies, including the liquidation of the "kulaks" as a class and their deportation to places such as Magnitogorsk. Class analysis also helped make possible numerous campaigns and mobilizations for increased vigilance or greater industrial output that were predicated on emotional appeals against class enemies, both inside and outside the country. And it allowed mere individuals to become a part of the movement of history.

Whereas under "capitalism" work was thought to consist of the appropriation of "surplus value" by a small number of individuals for their own benefit, under socialism such exploitation by definition did not exist: there were no "capitalists." Instead, people worked for themselves and by doing so were building a better world. Not all work sites were equally "strategic," but through class analysis the output of an individual miner or steel smelter acquired international significance as a blow against capitalism and a contribution to the furthering of socialism. In other words, the exertions of every worker at the bench were inscribed in an international struggle.

Class analysis served as a sophisticated technique of rule, and armed with this class-based view of the world, the Soviet leadership pursued as one of its chief goals the creation of a specifically Soviet working class.[13] Although the country had supposedly experienced a proletarian revolution in 1917, twelve years later the leadership still worried about what it considered to be an embarrassingly small proletariat. With the crash industrialization program, however, the ranks of the proletariat expanded greatly, indeed even more than the planners had originally foreseen.

Total employment was about the only target of the first Five-Year Plan that was surpassed, and the bulge in the country's work force was even greater during the second Five-Year Plan.[14] Magnitogorsk was a case in point. By 1938, less than ten years after the arrival of the first group of settlers, the Magnitogorsk Metallurgical Complex employed almost twenty thousand people in its various shops, from the blast furnaces to the state farms.[15] Several thousand more people were employed by the construction trust Magnitostroi, the coke plant, and the railroad.[16] As of 1940, the city's total work force numbered approximately 51,100 people.[17]

This new work force created virtually ex nihilo had to be trained, and that training was conceived in specific terms.[18] For new workers, learning how to work became more than a question of exchanging agricultural time and the agricultural calendar for the eight-hour shift, the five-day work week and the Five-Year Plan.[19] Anxious to create a Soviet working class, the leadership was no less concerned about workers' political attitudes and allegiance. New workers had to be taught how to work, and all workers had to be taught how properly to understand the political significance of their work. Soviet-style proletarianization meant acquiring industrial *and* political literacy, understood as the complete acceptance of the party's rule and willing participation in the grand crusade of "building socialism."[20]

To attain such goals much faith was placed in the transformative powers of the factory system. With the "Socialist revolution," the factory, far from being a place of exploitation and of shame—as it was reputed to have been under capitalism—was to become a palace of labor manned by politically conscious, literate, and skilled workers filled with pride in their work.[21] In the event, most new workers, even those who eventually staffed the factories, began as construction workers, and it was in construction that they first confronted the problem of what were called "socialist attitudes [otnosheniia] to labor."[22]

Construction work during the Five-Year Plan was performed in rushes, or "storms," a style that, although it has been likened to "the very old, rural, rhythm-setting work cry (*vziali*),"[23] was christened with a new term, shock work (*udarnyi trud*).[24] Predicated on the belief that vastly higher productivity could be achieved through a combination of labor exploits and better work organization, shock work was facilitated by the generally low level of mechanization and was carried out in gangs or brigades. Although the obsession with dramatically raising productivity was sometimes associated with the introduction of new technology, in construction, where shock work was most widely developed, given the level of technology, extra effort became the main method of "rationalization."[25]

The authorities sought to extend the shock brigades into a mass movement (*udarnichestvo*) through a series of campaigns and mobilizations, the most important of which, "socialist competition," began in 1929. Socialist competition took the form of a challenge, often in writing, of one factory, shop, brigade, or individual by another. Challenges were also made of the plan in the form of a counterplan (*vstrechnyi*), or a proposal to accomplish more in less time. In practice, this meant that singular feats of daring and overexertion compelled almost everyone else to do likewise or risk ridicule, suspicion, and, in some cases, arrest.

Theoretically, socialist competition differed from competition under capitalism in that the aim was not supposed to be the triumph of a victor but the raising of everyone up to the level of the most advanced (*peredovik*). Such terms as tugboating (*buksirovat*) and sponsorship (*shefstvo*) were used to express the goal of lifting up the less advanced. Yet although intended as a socially cohesive device to raise productivity, socialist competition more often served as a means of dividing enthusiastic militants willing to attempt extraordinary feats of labor exertion (shock work) from more established workers and workers who generally tried to avoid political effusions.

The effects of the productivity campaigns involving shock work were reinforced by the new wage policy introduced in 1931, when "equalization" was condemned and replaced by differentiation. Wages were individualized and, through the device of piece rates, geared to each unit of output. Each worker was assigned an output quota, or norm, and outstanding work performance, defined as production above the norm, was to be rewarded.[26] In theory, as more and more of the work force moved over to piece rates, wages could become a powerful lever for raising productivity. In practice, managers and especially foremen, desperate to hold onto "scarce" labor power, readily credited workers for fictitious work and, in any case, could award supplementary payments and bonuses to workers to make up for deductions that resulted from the failure to fulfill norms.[27]

Not surprisingly, there were fierce struggles over the calculation and assignment of norms, and considerable invention was displayed in the measurement and recording of output—so much invention that although a large majority of workers in Magnitogorsk theoretically worked above their norms, production at the plant continually fell below plan targets.[28]

(Meanwhile, the number of norm-setters and piece-rate calculators proliferated.)[29] Yet although the impact of the differentiated wage policy on productivity may have been questionable, its effect on the understanding of workers was plain. Workers were individualized and their performance measured on a percentage basis, allowing for ready comparisons.[30]

Shock work, combined with socialist competition, became a means of differentiating individuals as well as a technique of political recruitment within the working class. As such, its effectiveness was augmented by the calculated use of publicity. Mobile displays of honor and shame, colored red and black respectively, carried lists of workers' names. Airplanes were used to adorn those racing forward, crocodiles those lagging behind. "Lightning sheets" were issued in which the best workers and "slackers" were named, and banners were awarded to the victors of competitions. With the banners circulating as the fortunes of brigades rose and fell, sometimes from shift to shift, work could become a sort of sport.[31] Before long permanent honor rolls for recognizing a shop's "best workers" were posted, adding to the pressure on workers.[32]

This extensive politicization of work was facilitated by the presence in and around the work place of agencies other than management. Each construction area and factory shop, for example, had its own primary party organization, which maintained a strong party presence through membership and meetings.[33] The party also sought to reach out to the nonparty mass in the factory, a task for which each shop employed "agitators," that is, people whose job it was to discuss political issues and present interpretations of domestic and international events.[34]

One agitator in Magnitogorsk's mill 300, Z. S. Grishchenko, delivered twelve reports on domestic and international affairs and conducted six readings of newspapers during the course of a single month in 1936. To be able to lead discussions and steer them in the desired direction, Grishchenko prepared by scrutinizing as many Soviet newspapers as possible, paying particular attention to the speeches and directives of Stalin and the party leadership. He could also rely on agitation manuals published by the party's agitprop department. Grishchenko was said to take extra time to tutor those workers who appeared unable to grasp the issues, or who had somehow fallen behind.[35]

Not all of the 214 agitators at the steel plant as of 1936 were as motivated or thorough as Grishchenko appears to have been, and the effects of such agitation varied. When queried as to why he failed to conduct agitation, one organizer in the coke shop remarked, "What will I babble [to them]?" He added ominously, "and what happens if I confuse something, make a mistake, then I will be charged!"[36] Such hesitancy could draw backing from reports in the central press, which ridiculed the way agitators visited a shop and interrupted production to harangue workers about the problems of lost work time.[37]

But shops continued to be visited by agitators, whose work was considered integral to promoting production even though their agitation sometimes subverted it. A speech by Stalin at an All-Union Gathering of Stakhanovites in November 1935, for example, was printed, distributed, and discussed throughout the Magnitogorsk steel plant in a massive effort to induce entire shops into accepting "obligations" for increased output.[38] Typically, such exhortations for increased output—indeed, all discussion of domestic events—were placed against the international background, which was made to seem anything but remote yet could be extremely complex. Only one month into his new job as agitator for mill 500, the activist Sazhko reported that workers asked a great many questions about foreign news, especially after his presentations on the Italian-Abyssinian War and the 1936 Soviet-French Diplomatic Agreement.[39]

If the presence of the party in the factory was the most visible, that of the security police, or NKVD, was no less consequential. In the Magnitogorsk complex, just as in every Soviet industrial undertaking, government bureau, or higher educational institution, there was a so-called special department connected with the NKVD. The special departments, whose work was secret and separate from the factory administration, employed networks of informants, operated without limits, either from law or custom, and generally made sure that everyone, manager and worker, assisted them in their undertakings.[40] For NKVD officials, the discovery of security problems served as a surefire means to advance their careers (see chapter 7).

Trade unions, too, were prominent in the workplace, even though they could not perform their traditional role, as under capitalism, of defending worker interests against owners since in a workers' state the workers were technically the owners. Instead, unions in the USSR were enlisted in the regime's efforts to achieve higher productivity, with the unsurprising result that they commanded little respect from the workers. This situation, known to the Soviet leadership, soon changed, however.[41] According to John Scott, workers' assessments of trade unions were altered in 1934 and 1935, when the unions reorganized their work and assumed responsibility for the wide range of social welfare activities sponsored by the regime.[42]

In 1937 alone, the Magnitogorsk branch of the Metal Workers' Union had a budget of 2.7 million rubles, plus a social insurance fund of 8.8 million rubles (financed by pay deductions). That year, more than 3 million rubles of social insurance funds were distributed for pregnancy leave and temporary or permanent incapacity. Trade union funds were also used to buy cows, pigs, sewing machines, and motorcycles for workers; send workers' children to summer camp; and pay for sport clubs. Trade unions had become central to Soviet workers' lives.[43]

Soviet production space was a focal point for the intersection of a variety of agencies: party, NKVD, trade unions, as well as safety inspectors and health experts. Their many concerns ranged from increased steel production and proper ventilation of the shops to political education, police intrigue, and aiding injured workers or their families. That some of these aims were contradictory and that some organizations worked at cross-purposes only underscored the workplace's designation as an arena of singular importance requiring the utmost attention. Yet although management, the party, the NKVD, the trade unions, and technical experts were all present in the factory, they wielded varying degrees of influence. Some concerns obviously enjoyed a higher priority, none more so than the broadly defined notion of state security (*gosudarstvennaia bezopasnost*), a reflection in part of the international "class struggle."

In the Soviet workplace the terms at issue were neither workers' ownership nor control; both already existed by virtue of the regime's self-definition as a workers' state. What mattered were the performance of the workers and all actions and attitudes related to their work performance, including actual or suspected political loyalties. Within such parameters, the relentless campaigns to boost productivity and political awareness through enhanced individual performance were logically promoted as expressions of advanced worker consciousness and as the distinctive character of labor in a socialist society. No doubt the quintessential campaign in this regard was Stakhanovism, a movement sponsored by the regime following the coal-hewing feats of a Donbas miner, Aleksei Stakhanov, achieved one day in August 1935.[44]

After Stakhanov's "record" shift, attempts were organized to achieve analogous breakthroughs in other industries, and then to convert these record-setting shifts into longer mobilizations. Across the country, 11 January 1936 was declared a Stakhanovite Twenty-Four Hours (*sutki*), which was followed by a Stakhanovite Five-Day (*piatidnevka*) between 21 and 25 January, a Stakhanovite Ten-Day (*dekada*), then a Stakhanovite Month, and so on, until 1936 was christened the Stakhanovite Year.[45] Some Stakhanovites do seem to have become obsessed with making records, coming to the shop early, checking over the work space, keeping it clean, and inspecting the machinery.[46] Other workers, however, were said to have "incorrectly" understood the Stakhanovite Ten-Day: when the rush period ended, they drew the conclusion that "we worked for ten days, now we can relax."[47]

But relaxation was not part of the official program. In early 1936, newspaper headlines proclaimed the advent of "new norms for the new times."[48] Nikolai Zaitsev, chief of Magnitogorsk open-hearth shop no. 2, admitted in unpublished remarks that although Stakhanovism in his shop began only in January 1936, already by February the norms were raised, from 297 to 350 tons of steel per shift. Zaitsev added that no one was meeting the new norms.[49] In this vein, one worker in the coke shop was reported to have told the factory newspaper, "With the norms now in existence I can't work as a Stakhanovite. If the norms are lowered, then I can call myself a Stakhanovite." Another reportedly said to the same source that "in winter I can work as a Stakhanovite, but in summer it is so hot by the ovens, I can't stand it."[50]

The center of the Stakhanovite movement in Magnitogorsk was the blooming mill, where behind the celebrated records lay much sweat and blood.[51] "Nowadays work in the blooming mill has become very difficult physically," the Stakhanovite operator V. P. Ogorodnikov remarked, also in an unpublished discussion. "Earlier it was easy, because we handled 100 to 120 ingots, and for two to three hours of each shift we rested. Now we work practically the full eight hours, and it is very difficult."[52] The increased burden on the blooming's management, moreover, was no less great.

Fedor Golubitskii, who took over as chief of the blooming mill in 1936, expressed what must have been a prevalent view of labor relations, that it was the manager's task to "study people." He suggested that a manager had to get to know subordinates, how to interact with them, what their needs and moods were. Above all, he said, it was necessary not to lose contact with the masses. But Golubitskii conceded that during the periods of heightened activity associated with Stakhanovism, the shops were "working as if at war," and his job had become "a serious strain."[53]

Apart from the pressures, Stakhanovism involved what appears to have been a genuine record-mania that transformed the task of rolling or smelting steel into sport. Under the heading "A Remarkable Year," an article commemorating the first anniversary of Stakhanov's record shift appeared under the name of Dmitrii Bogatyrenko, a worker in the blooming mill. In looking back over the year, Bogatyrenko divided it up by the number of ingots cut in "record-breaking" shifts:

12 September 1935	Ogorodnikov	211
22 September	Tishchenko	214
25 September	Bogatyrenko	219
9 October	Ogorodnikov	230
[?] October	Bogatyrenko	239
29 October	Ogorodnikov	243
11 January 1936	Ogorodnikov	251
(same day, next shift)	Chernysh	264

He concluded succinctly: "This is what enthusiasm could accomplish."[54]

Such gamesmanship, which was lavishly reported in the newspaper (often with accompanying photographs), seems to have captured the imagination of an emergent Soviet working class. In unpublished remarks, Ogorodnikov explained that

> My wife asks, "Why don't you go anywhere, or do anything?" Why? Because I have to leave for work early, prepare everything, check things over, make sure everything's right. Work in the blooming mill is a contagious disease, [and] once you catch it, it sticks.[55]

After their back-to-back records on 11 January 1936, both he and Chernysh received brand new motorcycles.[56] For helping to organize record shifts, shop bosses were also given various awards, including large money bonuses, sometimes as high as 10,000 rubles. In March 1936, just before taking over as chief of the blooming mill, Golubitskii became one of four people in Magnitogorsk to be awarded a motorcar.[57]

The Stakhanovite movement was noteworthy for opening broad new vistas for Soviet workers, whose meteoric rise was something to behold. Aleksei Tishchenko (mentioned in chapter 4), who by the age of seventeen was a stevedore at a Donbas mine, came to Magnitogorsk in the fall of 1933 and was immediately made an apprentice bridge crane operator in the blooming mill. By May 1935, the twenty-five-year-old Tishchenko was a full-fledged scissors operator, and over the next few months he competed with other Young Turks for the record of most ingots cut in a single shift.[58]

The advance on the job of young workers like Tishchenko was usually guided by one of the few established workers on hand. Mikhail Zuev, head foreman (*obermaster*) in mill 300, a veteran worker with fifty years' experience, asserted that whereas in the past, master artisans concealed the secrets of their skills, in the socialist society of 1936 they willingly imparted their skills to the new generation. The sixty-one-year-old Zuev, who had been "mobilized" to Magnitogorsk from Mariupol in March 1935, was frequently called upon to make speeches, usually with the title "All

Roads Are Open to Us," in which he would relate to the younger generation how for more than thirty years he worked for "exploiters," but since
the October revolution he worked "only for the people."[59]

Pay increases for some Stakhanovites, predicated on the bonus system,
were purposefully dramatic. The Zuev family—father Mikhail and three
sons (Fedor, Vasilii, and Arsenii) whom he had trained—together earned
almost 54,000 rubles in 1936, when Mikhail Zuev topped all workers in
Magnitogorsk with an annual salary of 18,524 rubles.[60] In December 1935,
Zuev had become one of the first Magnitogorsk workers to receive the second highest state medal, the Order of the Red Banner.[61] The following
summer, he received a subsidized trip (*putevka*) for his entire family to
Sochi.[62]

Second to Zuev in earnings was Ogorodnikov. The blooming operator
earned 17,774 rubles in 1936, part of which he spent on the construction
of an individual house (discussed in chapter 4). "My house cost 17,000 rubles," Ogorodnikov related in an unpublished interview. "I paid 2,000 rubles [down] of my own money, and will pay another 7,800 in installments
over twenty years. The rest the factory is paying." Before the revolution,
perhaps only a factory's owner and top technical staff could put together
that much money and buy a private home.[63]

Probably no Magnitogorsk Stakhanovite did better than Vladimir Shevchuk. A foreman (*master*) in the medium sorting mill (mill 500), Shevchuk
was said to have averaged 935 rubles per month in the second half of 1935,
and 1,169 in the first half of 1936. When asked what he did with all his
money, he explained that he spent much of it on clothes. "My wife has
three overcoats, a good fur coat, and I have two suits," Shevchuk reported.
"Plus, I deposit money in the savings bank." He also had a rare three-room
apartment and that summer had taken his family to the Crimea on vacation. Along with a bicycle, gramophone, and hunting gun, he was awarded
the Order of the Red Banner. The bargain was completed when, according
to the newspaper, Shevchuk "greeted" the death sentence handed out to
the Trotskyites in 1936 "with a feeling of deep satisfaction."[64]

Shevchuk, Zuev, Ogorodnikov, Tishchenko, Bogatyrenko, Chernysh,
and several others became household names. An August 1936 photographic display in the city newspaper commemorating the first anniversary
of Aleksei Stakhanov's record included a list of twenty Magnitogorsk Stakhanovites: four from the rolling mill, one from the blast furnace shop,
one from the open-hearth shop, and the rest from around the factory. They
were identified as the workers who had been placed on the plant's honor
roll (*pochetnaia doska*) and "earned the right to make a report to Stalin and

Ordzhonikidze."[65] One scholar has suggested distinguishing between "ordinary" and "outstanding" Stakhanovites, limiting the latter designation to perhaps a hundred or so for the entire country. Rather than outstanding, it makes sense to call them "high-profile," for that is how we know of them.[66]

Such publicity surrounding "high-profile" workers was of course part of a calculated strategy. "To bathe individuals [*liudi*] from the people [*narod*] in glory is of enormous significance," Ordzhonikidze had said in *Pravda*. "In capitalist countries, nothing can compare with the popularity of gangsters like Al Capone. In our country, under socialism, heroes of labor must become the most famous."[67] Not long after Ordzhonikidze's remarks were published, Rafael Khitarov, Magnitogorsk party secretary during the heyday of the Stakhanovite movement, declared that Stakhanovites were "revolutionaries" in production.[68]

Khitarov compared the Stakhanovite campaign with party activism, blending Stakhanovism into the political discourse on raised vigilance and equating the "discoveries" in the workplace supposedly made possible by Stakhanovism with those in the party organization supposedly made possible by the exchange and verification of party cards (see chapter 7).[69] Not all Stakhanovites were party members, however. Ogorodnikov, who was apparently prevented from joining the party owing to his class background, wrote that "when I'm rolling steel and I overtake [Dmitrii] Bogatyrenko (a party member), no one notices. But when Bogatyrenko overtakes me, then that's good. I was like a partisan."[70]

Whether such intense competition between Ogorodnikov and Bogatyrenko was healthy became one of the principal themes of an unpublished manuscript about Stakhanovism in Magnitogorsk, written during the course of events. The author remarked on the pressures felt in each shop by each shift and shop boss to produce records, pointing out that one by one the machines broke down and that one worker in the record-breaking blooming shop lost his leg. He also wrote of the "unhealthy atmosphere" that had arisen in the shops where anointed workers went around "thinking they were Gods."[71]

Tensions stemming from Stakhanovism were high. Ogorodnikov, who claimed that he was discriminated against in the shop and called "a self-seeker and a man only after money, an un-Soviet element with a kulak heritage," bolted from the mill on 30 March 1936, relocating to Makeevka and in the process causing a national scandal. It required the intervention of NKTP to return him to Magnitogorsk.[72] A related case involved the forced return of Andrei Diundikov, a distinguished worker with four years' experience in the blast furnace shop, who had departed in a huff because "he couldn't understand why some people were awarded automobiles and he wasn't."[73]

Resentment arose not only among high-profile Stakhanovites but between them and the rest of the workers, as well as management. One Magnitogorsk shop chief, Leonid Vaisberg, after pointing out that "we frequently create conditions, let's say, a bit better than usual, for the establishment of a record," privately expressed dismay that individual workers "failed to recognize that without such assistance they would not be heroes."[74] Without stating his own view, Zaitsev of the open-hearth shop commented that engineers resented Stakhanovites, who were made into heroes at the expense of equipment.[75]

Zaitsev added that some workers held the view that Stakhanovite methods were dangerous for the equipment—not surprising, since during the first attempts to introduce "Stakhanovite methods" in the open-hearth shop, the furnaces were burnt out. Meanwhile, the newspaper reported that one of the scholars at the Mining and Metallurgical Institute lectured that Stakhanovite practices of speeding up the steelmaking process had adverse effects on machinery. "Overloading ovens," the professor warned, "was technologically absurd." The newspaper countered that the factory's shops were proving the opposite.[76]

As the newspaper emphasized, Stakhanovism made possible "assaults" on the technical "capacity" of machines and equipment, much of which had been imported from capitalist countries. Questioning capacities was said to be a way of discovering and unleashing supposed "hidden reserves," thereby proving the superiority of Soviet workers and work methods, asserting Soviet independence from foreigners and foreign technology, and impugning the motives of foreign suppliers—all of which served to heighten the political awareness of the populace. After each new record, Soviet managers would announce that projected capacities set by foreign engineers were being "reexamined" and "revised" by "Soviet specialists."[77] These supposed leaps in productivity acquired further political significance in the context of the international "class struggle." "The Stakhanovite movement," the Magnitogorsk newspaper instructed, was "a blow to fascism."[78]

As managers, engineers, and workers came to learn, however, "revising" capacities upward could backfire; when serious, sometimes fatal, accidents resulted, production had to be halted or curtailed, and arrests were made. In August 1936, the newspaper reported that the chief of the pressing (*obzhimnyi*) shop of the blooming mill, Vasilev, was fired (and replaced by Golubitskii) when the shop had to operate at half-capacity for three days. Vasilev was then turned over to the courts, for "exceeding what was permissible" and allowing the machinery to be "injured." In norm-busting, who decided what was permissible, and how a decision was arrived at, remained unclear.[79] What was clear was that both excessive zeal in promoting Stakhanovism and the failure to do so could be dangerous.[80] One nonparty engineer who apparently did oppose Stakhanovism was criminally charged amid a shower of adverse publicity.[81]

Workers, for their part, could scarcely fail to see that Stakhanovism resembled a sweating campaign, placing inordinate strain on managers and creating much friction between managers and workers, as well as between foremen and workers—with often questionable results in production.[82] But the costs of open opposition for workers were also high. One steel smelter's helper, said to have remarked that Stakhanovism was an attempt to enslave the working class, was arrested in November 1935 and sentenced to forced labor.[83] No less significant, however, were the benefits of acceptance. Stakhanovism meant that the most difficult jobs in the "hot shops" were invested with the greatest prestige, affording anyone who would take them up high status and pay.[84]

Stakhanovism reinforced tendencies already present in the ongoing articulation of industrial activity as a problem of labor productivity, which in turn was understood as a question of "rationalization," that is, inordinate individual exertion, reflecting the attainment of advanced consciousness. The "Stakhanovite" was soon hailed as a new type of worker, and Stakhanovism came to eclipse (without entirely replacing) shock work as the archetypal form of "socialist labor." Throughout 1936, the number of Stakhanovites in Magnitogorsk grew daily, until by December more than half the steel plant had earned either that classification, or the one "shock worker." The dramatic increase in the number of workers so designated was eloquent testimony to the workers' and managements' embracing of such classifications, and the new relations that arose out of them.[85]

With material incentives reinforced by moral ones, workers of all ages, not just younger ones, struggled to "overfulfill" their norms and earn credentials as 150- or 200-percenters—identifications that were duly recorded in a worker's personnel profile and pay schedule, and with luck, reported in the city newspaper for all to read. A certain amount of stratification among workers obviously took place, yet its significance has perhaps been somewhat exaggerated (bosses remained bosses, after all). The more important development was that in the general hubbub, all workers, not just

Stakhanovites, were enveloped in extensive publicity about their importance and membership in a distinct social group.[86]

The constant references to workers as members of a new Soviet working class retained a large audience. Vasilii Radziukevich, who came to Magnitogorsk in 1931 from Minsk (via Leningrad), recalled five years later that when he first arrived the blooming mill was still in crates. He helped build it. When in 1936 the mill celebrated its third anniversary, Radziukevich was a skilled worker in one of the even newer sorting mills.[87] The Rubicon for such people was the acquisition of a trade. P. E. Velizhanin, after arriving in Magnitogorsk on 29 December 1930, was randomly included in a brigade of assembly workers to work on boilers, which he had never before seen. "At that time," he recalled four years later, "I had no conception of what a boiler assembly worker [*nagrevalshchik*] was or what he did." But by 1934 he had mastered his new profession.[88]

Radziukevich's and Velizhanin's fate was that of tens of thousands.[89] They obtained a set of work clothes (*spetsovka*) and real boots (*sapogi*) in place of bast sandals (*lapti*), which marked their arrival as a skilled worker with a trade. Moreover, their ascent in the work world was often paralleled by their movement from tents to dormitory barracks to individual-room barracks to perhaps their own room in a brick building. True, the work was often backbreaking.[90] And it remains questionable whether in private workers felt that they had traversed a notable trajectory from victims of exploitation to masters of production; from forlorn, illiterate, uncouth slaves to builders of a new world and a new culture. But even if workers knew they were not bosses (the rhetoric of the regime notwithstanding), they also knew that they were part of a Soviet working class, and that whatever its shortcomings, such a status was different from being a worker under capitalism. These axioms appeared to be confirmed by their own rise.

Behind the exhortations to self-improvement lay a concrete process of continuous education centered on the labor process. Filatov, who came to Magnitogorsk in January 1931, gave the following response to a question about his work history: "I began as an unskilled laborer, then I went into a brigade and strove to raise my pay category [*razriad*] and to improve my skills. Had I been literate, I would have attended courses, but as an illiterate I only went to the literacy circle [*likbez*]." But Filatov was soon "graduated" from his literacy course and then moved on to production-related matters. "Now I read, write, and solve problems," he added. "And I'm learning the ins-and-outs of blueprints."[91] It was from such people that several of the high-profile Stakhanovites had sprung.[92]

If the workplace was like a school, schools became an extension of the workplace, as workers struggled to acquire literacy, master a trade, and continually raise their skills.[93] In the early years, there were many informal courses and study circles, including open-air, on-the-job discussions and "technical hours," introduced in 1931.[94] Later, the authorities encouraged workers' participation in so-called supplemental training (*dopolnitelnoe rabochee obrazovanie*, or DRO) in a variety of ways, the most important of which was the examination for the technical minimum (*gostekhekzamen*), analogous to basic literacy.[95]

In and out of the workplace, virtually everyone in Magnitogorsk, even those who worked full time, attended some form of schooling, which reinforced the socialization and politicization processes visible at work.[96] John Scott attributed the workers' hunger for education to wage differentials and to the assurance of being able to obtain a job in any profession one learned or supplemented.[97] To these reasons must be added a sense of adventure and, above all, accomplishment.[98] Those singled out by the authorities as "precisely the new type of worker" were said to "understand that the success of their work consists in the uninterrupted raising of their skill levels."[99]

Of course, workers could scarcely afford to be complacent. In addition to their potential job advancement, their access to food, clothes, and shelter was preferentially distributed through the centrally managed supply system (see chapter 6). Strong moral pressure was also exerted on individuals to demonstrate evidence of a desire for self-improvement. But many people were only too glad to take up the party's threat-backed summons and continuously struggle to better themselves.

It is within this cursorily sketched context of the special importance attached to labor and to being a worker, the tying of each individual's labor to the international class struggle, the use of output norms and piece rates to individualize and make quantifiable a worker's performance, the obsession with productivity and the organization of the work process as a series of campaigns, the understanding of worker training as political education, the prominence of political agencies in the workplace, and the strong imperative for self-improvement that we can begin to evaluate the significance of the emerging social identity evident in the list posted on the entrance to barracks no. 8.

THE IDENTIFICATION GAME

For a Soviet worker, reporting on one's work history became an important ritual in defining oneself before others, and among the most important details of one's work history was the time and place of one's original work experience. It was not uncommon for workers to trade boasts about who started work at the youngest age: fifteen, twelve, and so on.[100] Extra value was attached to that initial experience if it had been gained in industry, especially in one of the older and well-known industrial enterprises, such as Putilov (renamed Kirov) in Leningrad or Gujon (renamed Serp i molot) in Moscow. The ultimate boast was when one could trace one's lineage back to a family of workers: father, grandfather, great-grandfather. Such was the proud background of Pavel Korobov, a blast furnace apprentice who was descended from a "dynasty of blast furnace operators" and who catapulted to the Magnitogorsk factory directorship during the dizzying social mobility of 1937.[101]

Elements of a worker's identity stressed achievements, but identification could also be "negative." For example, if a worker was "breakdown" prone, he or she would be labeled as such (*avariishchik*), which was cause for dismissal. In 1936 the newspaper carried a list of breakdown-prone individuals and a table of breakdown frequency.[102] With the passage of time, the negative components of a worker's record received greater and greater emphasis. What remained constant, however, was that everyone had to have a work history, and one conceived in politically charged categories.

Materially speaking, a worker's record was made up of various documents, such as the questionnaire (*anketa*), periodic professional evaluations (*kharakteristiki*), and the short-form personnel file (*lichnaia kartochka*), which all workers filled out upon being hired and which were subsequently updated. Later, workers were required to have a "labor book" (*trudovaia knizhka*), without which they were not to be hired.[103] But the technique of defining workers by recording their work histories was in operation well before labor books were introduced.[104]

Because the practice of identifying individuals through their work history was so integral, it could be seen in almost any official document. The reverse side of one archival file consisting of worker memoirs was found to contain a list from either 1933 or 1934 of individuals granted "shock rations." The list specified name, profession, party status, record on absenteeism, appearances at production conferences, study or course attendance, rationalization suggestions, norm fulfillment percentages, and socialist competitions entered. What made such records particularly significant was that they were not simply collected and filed away but used as a basis to distribute material benefits.[105] Work histories were also reported in public, thereby becoming an important ritual for gaining admission to peer and other groups.

Oral presentations were promoted through evenings of remembrances, which in turn formed part of an ambitious project to write the history of the construction of the Magnitogorsk factory. For the history project, which was never published, hundreds of workers were either interviewed or given questionnaires to fill out. Not surprisingly, the questions were formulated so as to elicit discussion of certain topics (and discourage discussion of others). Much of the discussion was directed at the Stakhanovite movement, which is mentioned in a great many of the memoirs (the majority of which were recorded in 1935 and 1936).[106] And since some memoirs are in handwritten form and contain grammatical mistakes, while others are neatly typed without errors, it is clear that the workers' accounts were at least in part rewritten.[107] It would be erroneous, however, to conclude that the workers' memoirs were "biased" and thus of little or no value. That workers were encouraged to write about certain matters while avoiding others is precisely the point. The very fact that workers sometimes "erred" and had to be corrected, both for grammar and content, shows how they were implicated in a process of adopting the official method of speaking about themselves.[108]

It is, of course, highly significant that workers' memoirs would be sought and celebrated at all. In fact, whether or not he or she was being interviewed for the factory history project, a Magnitogorsk worker was frequently called upon to discuss his or her biography. On the day they arrived, dekulakized peasants were interviewed extensively for their biography, which was thought to be an indication of the degree of danger they posed.[109] But noncriminal workers were also prompted into relating their social origin, political past, and work history for security reasons. More often, they were encouraged to "confess" simply as a matter of course, as something one did.

Even when these confessions extended to nonwork activities, they tended to revolve around work. On the seventh anniversary of socialist competition in 1936, some Magnitogorsk workers were "surveyed" on their activities after work. Of the ten answers published in the city newspaper, virtually all began with a discussion of the relation between plan fulfillment and personal satisfaction (given that both wages and esteem were tied to plan fulfillment, such an equation was not as ridiculous as it might sound). Virtually every worker claimed to read in their spare time, not surprisingly, since reading and the desire for self-improvement were considered necessary. Most revealing of all, almost all spent their "time off" from work visiting the shop, in the words of one, "to see how things were doing."[110]

Identification with one's shop was apparently strong. An apprentice, Aleksei Griaznov, who recalled in November 1936 that when he arrived three years earlier there had been only one open-hearth oven (now there were twelve), kept a diary of his becoming a bona fide steel smelter (*stalevar*). Excerpts were published in the factory newspaper telling the tale of his developing relationship with his furnace.[111] The city newspaper, meanwhile, quoted Ogorodnikov to the effect that Magnitogorsk was his "native factory" (*rodnoi zavod*).[112] The expression *rodnoi*, normally applied to one's birthplace, captured the relation these workers had with their factory: it had given birth to them. For these people there was no dichotomy between home and work; no division of their lives into separate spheres, the public and the private: all was "public," and public meant the factory.

Workers' wives were also encouraged to make the shop the basis of their lives. "Here at Magnitka, more than anywhere else," asserted Leonid Vaisberg, "the whole family takes part in and lives the life of our production." He claimed that there were even cases when wives would not allow their husbands to spend the night at home because they had performed poorly in the shop. And such disapproval was not motivated by considerations of money alone. Wives took pride in their husbands' work performance, and many got directly involved. Wives' tribunals were organized to shame men to stop drinking and to work harder, while some wives regularly visited the shop on their own, to inspect, offer encouragement, or scold.[113]

Just how the new terms of social identity were articulated and made effectual, sometimes with wives' participation, can be seen in a long letter preserved in the history project archives from the wife of the best locomotive driver in internal factory transport, Anna Kovaleva, to the wife of the worst, Marfa Gudzia. It is quoted in full:

Dear Marfa!

We are both wives of locomotive drivers of the rail transport of Magnitka. You probably know that the rail transport workers of the MMK [Magnitogorsk Metallurgical Complex] are not fulfilling the plan, that they are disrupting the supply of the blast furnaces, open hearths, and rolling shops. . . . All the workers of Magnitka accuse our husbands, saying that the rail workers hinder the fulfillment of the [overall] industrial plan. It is offensive, painful, and annoying to hear this. And moreover, it is doubly painful, because all of it is the plain truth. Every day there were stoppages and breakdowns in rail transport. Yet our internal factory transport has everything it needs in order to fulfill the plan. For that, it is necessary to work like the best workers of our country work. Among such shock workers is my husband, Aleksandr Panteleevich Kovalev. He always works like a shock worker, exceeding his norms, while economizing on fuel and lubri-

cating oil. His engine is on profit and loss accounting. . . . My husband
trains locomotive drivers' helpers out of unskilled laborers. He takes other
locomotive drivers under his wing. . . . My husband receives prizes virtually every month. . . . And I too have won awards. . . .

My husband's locomotive is always clean and well taken care of. You,
Marfa, are always complaining that it is difficult for your family to live.
And why is that so? Because your husband, Iakov Stepanovich, does not
fulfill the plan. He has frequent breakdowns on his locomotive, his locomotive is dirty, and he always overconsumes fuel. Indeed, all the locomotive drivers laugh at him. *All the rail workers of Magnitka know him—for
the wrong reasons, as the worst driver. By contrast, my husband is known
as a shock worker* [my italics]. He is written up and praised in the newspapers. . . . He and I are honored everywhere as shock workers. At the store
we get everything without having to wait in queues. We moved to the
building for shock workers [*dom udarnika*]. We will get an apartment with
rugs, a gramophone, a radio, and other comforts. Now we are being assigned to a new store for shock workers and will receive double rations.
. . . Soon the Seventeenth Party Congress of our Bolshevik Party will take
place. All rail workers are obliged to work so that Magnitka greets the
Congress of Victors at full production capacity.

Therefore, I ask you, Marfa, to talk to your husband heart to heart,
read him my letter. You, Marfa, explain to Iakov Stepanovich that he just
can't go on working the way he has. Persuade him that he must work honorably, conscientiously, like a shock worker. Teach him to understand the
words of comrade Stalin, that work is a matter of honor, glory, valor, and
heroism.

You tell him that if he does not correct himself and continues to work
poorly, he will be fired and lose his supplies. I will ask my Aleksandr Panteleevich to take your husband in tow, help him improve himself and become a shock worker, earn more. I want you, Marfa, and Iakov Stepanovich to be honored and respected, so that you live as well as we do.

I know that many women, yourself included, will say: "What business
is it of a wife to interfere in her husband's work. You live well, so hold
your tongue." But it is not like that. . . . We all must help our husbands
to fight for the uninterrupted work of transport in the winter. Ok, enough.
You catch my drift. This letter is already long. In conclusion, I'd like to say
one thing. It's pretty good to be a wife of a shock worker. It's within our
power. Let's get down to the task, amicably. I await your answer.

Anna Kovaleva[114]

In Anna Kovaleva's words, Marfa's husband, Iakov Gudzia, was known to
all as the worst locomotive driver, while her husband, Aleksandr Kovalev,
was known as the best. Whether Iakov Gudzia wanted to see himself in
such terms was in a sense irrelevant; that was how he would be seen. For
his own benefit, it was best to play the game according to the rules. Gudzia's locomotive was dirty and overconsumed fuel. What kind of person

could he be? What could his family be like? Indeed, after sending off the letter, Kovaleva discovered that Marfa Gudzia was illiterate. But Marfa was more than simply functionally "illiterate": she did not know, nor apparently did her husband, how to live and "speak Bolshevik," the obligatory language for self-identification and as such, the barometer of one's political allegiance to the cause.[115]

Publicly expressing loyalty by knowing how to "speak Bolshevik" became an overriding concern, but we must be careful in interpreting these acts. Strictly speaking, it was not necessary that Anna Kovaleva herself write the above cited letter, although she may well have. What was necessary was that she recognize, even if only by allowing her name to be attached to the letter, how to think and behave as the wife of a Soviet locomotive driver should. We should not interpret her letter to mean she believed in what she likely wrote and signed. It was not necessary to believe. It was necessary, however, to participate as if one believed—a stricture that appears to have been well understood, since what could be construed as direct, openly disloyal behavior became rare.

Although the process of social identification that demanded mastery of a certain vocabulary, or official language, was formidable, it was not irreversible. For one thing, swearing—what was called *blatnoi iazyk*—could usually serve as a kind of "safety valve." And we know from oral and literary accounts that a person could "speak Bolshevik" one moment, "innocent peasant" the next, begging indulgence for a professed inability to master fully the demanding new language and behavior.[116] Such a dynamic was evident in the interchange between Marfa and Anna.

With wives writing to other wives, husbands were in a way permitted to continue their faulty behavior. Intended to put pressure on another woman's husband, such wives' letters actually may instead have taken much of the pressure off the transgressor: the wife could constantly reiterate the formula while the husband constantly deviated from it. It might even be said that a kind of unacknowledged "private sphere" reemerged, a pocket of structural resistance based on the couple, playing the game according to the rules and yet constantly violating them.[117]

If indirect, or less than fully intentional, contestations were built into the operation of the identification game, however, more direct challenges to the new terms of life and labor were dangerous. Yet even these were not impossible—as long as they were couched within the new language itself, and preferably with references to the teachings of Lenin or Stalin. In at least one case encountered in the city newspaper, people were allowed to use certain of the officially promoted ideals to challenge regime policy through the very public-speaking rituals normally intended as exercises of affirmation.

Women, when they were quoted in the newspaper, rarely spoke as anything other than loyal wives. One exception occurred on International Women's Day, 8 March, when women were spotlighted as workers.[118] Another exception was the shortlived but startling debate in the pages of the newspaper following the introduction of "pro-family" laws in 1936, when women were heard protesting the new policy. One woman assailed the proposed fee of up to 1,000 rubles to register a divorce as far too high. Another pointed out that the prohibitive cost for divorces would have the effect of discouraging the registration of marriages, which she implied would be bad for women. Still a third condemned the restrictions on abortion even more forcefully, writing that "women want to study and to work" and that "having children . . . removes women from public life."[119]

Even as this example shows, however, the state-sponsored game of social identity as the one permissible and necessary mode of participation in the public realm remained all-encompassing. There were sources of identity other than the Bolshevik crusade, some from the past—such as peasant life, folklore, religion, one's native village or place of origin (*rodina*)—and some from the present—such as age, marital status, and parenthood. And people continued to confront understandings of themselves in terms of gender and nationality. But all of these ways of speaking about oneself came to be refracted through the inescapable political lens of Bolshevism.

Take the case of nationality. Gubaiduli, an electrician in the blast furnace shop, purportedly wrote a letter that appeared in the city newspaper.

> I am a Tatar. Before October, in old tsarist Russia, we weren't even considered people. We couldn't even dream about education, or getting a job in a state enterprise. And now I'm a citizen of the USSR. Like all citizens, I have the right to a job, to education, to leisure. I can elect and be elected to the soviet. Is this not an indication of the supreme achievements of our country? . . .
>
> Two years ago I worked as the chairman of a village soviet in the Tatar republic. I was the first person there to enter the kolkhoz and then I led the collectivization campaign. Collective farming is flourishing with each year in the Tatar republic.
>
> In 1931 I came to Magnitogorsk. From a common laborer I have turned into a skilled worker. I was elected a member of the city soviet. As a deputy, every day I receive workers who have questions or need help. I listen to each one like to my own brother, and try to do what is necessary to make each one satisfied.
>
> I live in a country where one feels like living and learning. And if the

enemy should attack this country, I will sacrifice my life in order to destroy the enemy and save my country.[120]

Even if such a clear and unequivocal expression of the official viewpoint was not written entirely by Gubaiduli himself, whose Russian language skills may in fact have been adequate to the task (as was the case with many Tatars),[121] what is important is that Gubaiduli "played the game," whether out of self-interest, or fear, or both. Perhaps he was still learning how to speak Russian; he was certainly learning how to "speak Bolshevik."

As every worker soon learned, just as it was necessary for party members to show vigilance and "activism" in party affairs, it was necessary for workers, whether party members or not, to show activism in politics and production. The range of proliferating activities thought to demonstrate activism included making "voluntary" contributions to the state loan programs (for which shop agitators and trade union organizers conducted harangues); taking part in periodic *subbotniki*; putting forth "worker suggestions" (*predlozheniia*) for improvements (which were quantified to demonstrate compliance and then usually ignored); and holding production conferences (*proizvodstvennye soveshchaniia*).

Regarding the latter, the newspaper inveighed against their tendency to degenerate into "a meeting fetish" (*mitingovshchina*), and one may suppose that tangible results were not always those intended.[122] Much the same could be said about so-called suggestions.[123] But God help the shop that tried to do without these practices, for workers often took them seriously. According to John Scott, at production meetings "workers could and did speak up with the utmost freedom, criticize· the director, complain about the wages, bad living conditions, lack of things to buy in the store—in short, swear about anything, except the general line of the party and a half-dozen of its sacrosanct leaders."[124]

Scott was writing of 1936, a time when the regime encouraged criticism of higher-ups "from below," and such freewheeling populist activism was common. Just as often, however, official gatherings could be characterized by strict formalism, making activism "from below" a charade.[125] And we know from émigré testimony that workers were held back from expressing their grievances by the fear of informants.[126] But when the signals came from above that it was time to open up, workers always seemed to be ready to do so. And woe to the foreman or shop party organizer who failed to canvass and take account of worker moods before introducing a resolution, or a new rule.[127]

Certain workers no doubt looked for every opportunity to ingratiate themselves, while others perhaps tried to steer clear of the highly charged rituals. But there was really nowhere to hide. If before the industrialization drive virtually two-thirds of the population was self-employed, a decade later such a category scarcely existed: virtually everyone was technically an employee of the state. Simply put, almost no legal alternatives to the state existed for earning a livelihood.[128] Here the contrast between Bolshevization and the "Americanization" of immigrants in the United States is instructive.

Americanization—a variety of campaigns for acculturation—could also be extremely coercive.[129] But not every American town was a company town; even in the case of company towns, people could often leave in search of greener pastures elsewhere. And if they stayed, some had the option of achieving a degree of independence by becoming shopkeepers, merchants, or smallholders. As an arena of negotiation, Americanization, however oppressive, afforded more possibilities and thus contained within it far wider latitude than Bolshevization.

Even so, it should not be thought that Soviet workers were passive objects of the state's heavy-handed designs. For one thing, many people gladly embraced the opportunity to become a "Soviet worker," with all that such a designation required, from demonstrations of complete loyalty to feats of extraordinary self-sacrifice. Acquisition of the new social identity conveyed benefits, ranging from the dignity of possessing a trade to paid vacations, free health care, pensions upon retirement, and social insurance funds for pregnancy, temporary incapacity, and death of the family's principal wage earner.[130] The new identity was empowering, if demanding.

Notwithstanding the existence of an imposing repressive apparatus, there were still many stratagems available with which to retain some say over one's life, in and out of the workplace. Workers reacted to the oppressive terms of work, for example, with absenteeism, turnover, slowdowns (*volynka*), and removal of tools and materials in order to work at home for private gain.[131] To be sure, the regime fought back. There was, for example, the law of 15 November 1932 that provided for dismissal, denial of ration cards, and eviction from housing for absenteeism of as little as one hour.[132] Yet the very circumstances that had in a sense called forth this desperate law rendered it extremely difficult to enforce.

The rapid industrial expansion, combined with the inefficiency and uncertainty characteristic of a planned economy, resulted in a perpetual labor shortage. "Throughout the city," wrote the Magnitogorsk newspaper, "hang announcements of the department of cadres of the metallurgical complex explaining to the population that the complex needed workers in unlimited numbers and of various qualifications."[133] Desperate to hold on to and even acquire more laborers, managers would often not heed instructions ordering them to fire workers for violating the stringent rules, or forbidding them to hire workers who had been fired elsewhere. In the battle against absentees, workers "booted out of one place, were taken in at another," as the Magnitogorsk newspaper continually complained.[134]

The state policy of full employment further reinforced workers' leverage.[135] Workers discovered that in the absence of unemployment or a "reserve army," managers and especially foremen under severe pressure to meet obligations could become accommodating. What resulted could be called a kind of unequal but nonetheless real codependency. Workers became dependent on the authorities who, wielding the weapon placed in their hands by a state supply system that created perpetual scarcity, were able to determine the size and location of a worker's apartment, the freshness and variety of his or her food, the length and location of his or her vacation, and the quality of the medical care available to him or her and to additional family members. But the authorities in turn were dependent on the workers to achieve production targets.

None of this is meant to diminish the importance of overt coercion. The workers' state did not shrink from the use of repression against individual workers, especially when the general "class interests" of all workers was alleged to be at stake. We know from émigré sources that the authorities searched for any signs of independent worker initiative and were extremely sensitive to informal gatherings among workers, lest some type of solidarity outside the state develop.[136] But a far more subtle and in the end no less effective method of coercion was at hand: the ability to define who people were.

The argument is not that the new social identity grounded in a kind of official language of public expression was erroneous, or that it was accurate, but that it was unavoidable and, furthermore, gave meaning to people's lives. Even if we find the notions absurd, we must take seriously whether a person was a shock worker or a shirker, an award-winner or breakdown-prone, because Magnitogorsk workers had to. What is more, if the people of Magnitogorsk took pride in themselves for their accomplishments and rewards, or felt disappointment at their failures, we must accept the reality of these feelings, however disagreeable we may find the social and political values that lent these social assessments significance.

Unavoidable as the new terms of social identity were, they must not be thought of as some kind of hegemonic device, which explains everything and therefore nothing.[137] Rather, they should be seen as a "field of play" in which people engaged the "rules of the game" of urban life. The rules were promulgated by the state with the express intention of achieving unquestioned control, but in the process of implementation they were sometimes challenged and often circumvented. Workers did not set the terms of their relation to the regime, but they did, to an extent, negotiate these terms, as they quietly understood.[138] That negotiation, however unequal, arose out of the restrictions, as well as the enabling provisions, of the game of social identification. It was largely through this game that people became members of the public realm, or, if you will, of the "official" society.

REVOLUTIONARY TRUTH

Granted that behind any given person's participation in the Bolshevik crusade (by adopting the new terms of identity) stood naked self-interest and omnipresent coercion, but what of the possibility of sincere belief? No doubt repeatedly mouthing the proper words involved some degree of internalization, but can we go further and speak about authentic, broad support for the regime, its policies, and its visionary teleology beyond an internalization of values through language? This question—with which the chapter began—is not easy to answer, in part because of the high value placed on the public display of allegiance, but mostly because of a lack of source materials. One way out of this dilemma, however, is to begin not with the question of belief but, following Lucien Febvre, with its opposite: namely, radical "unbelief." The task then becomes to analyze the possible support, the sources and grounds, for the wholesale rejection of the regime and its universal precepts.[139]

During the 1930s the USSR became something of a world closed in on itself. Around the middle of the decade, the borders were essentially sealed, making external travel an impossibility for all but a specially chosen few.[140] Furthermore, strict control was exerted over the information the public could receive, and everything the public was permitted to see and hear was filtered through an all-encompassing ideology.

Never a set of policies, Marxism-Leninism, the official ideology of the Soviet state, has always been a powerful dream for salvation on earth, and one that spoke the language of science. This does not mean that the scientifically derived vision was without uncertainties. On the contrary, the ambiguity surrounding the Communist vision, not to say the usage of other mobilizing phrases as synonyms—Soviet, socialism, Bolshevism—proved very useful, conveniently allowing for appeals on various bases with subtle shifts of emphasis when necessary. Together with this ambiguity, the scientific nature of the official ideology remained one of its principal strengths.

Marxism-Leninism posited that history was governed by scientific laws and that the existing regime embodied those laws. Thus, it was irrational—even psychopathic—to oppose the regime. And if Marxism-Leninism essentially criminalized nonconformity, heavy-handed state censorship denied people the very means for opposition. Censors suppressed "negative" information, reworked statistics, and rewrote history to the point of making sensible discussion, let alone informed criticism, virtually impossible.[141]

No less consequential than their "prophylactic" role was the censors' encouragement of an inexhaustible stream of information and analysis designed to teach people what and how to think. Censors were quintessential "social engineers," with the media serving as their instruments—or weapons, as Lenin wrote—in the battle to *construct* a Communist society. The instructional messages emanating from reading matter, radio, and, especially, films were paralleled by training received in schools, including obligatory courses in Marxism-Leninism, beginning at an early age. Such ideological immersion, although perhaps not remarkable by postwar American standards, was extraordinary at the time, especially in its extent and depth.

Enormous energy and resources went into the deployment of the official ideology, which was grounded in the great revolutionary events of 1917, victory in the Civil War, and the canonical texts of Marx, Lenin, and Stalin. Equally important, the general message conveyed was as simple in its basic elements as it was profound in its implications. Marxism-Leninism offered a total system, a complete and apparently consistent worldview based, not on hate or arrogance, but on a sense of social justice and the promise of a better life for all, and with a call for international solidarity against oppressed peoples everywhere. Much like Christianity's message regarding the circumstances of life in the next world, Marxism-Leninism in power appeared to embody the triumph of the underdog, and the historical vanquishing of injustice—but here, in this world.[142]

Replete with religious overtones, grounded in a body of scientific knowledge, promoted by "positive" censorship, the revolutionary truth was also expressed in a language of citizens' rights, including social rights encompassing the right to work, enjoy recreation, send one's children to school, receive medical care, and so on. And the revolutionary truth was spoken by the highest authority, the party. The party was in power; the party was leading the country to great victories; society was being utterly transformed—how could what the party and its lionized leaders said not be true?

In this regard the role of Stalin can scarcely be overemphasized. If Stalin was a master of the techniques of authoritarian rule, one of the main techniques of that rule was the Stalin cult.[143] Statues, portraits, cast metal, arranged flowers, printed fabric, silk-screened china—Stalin's visage was everywhere. Long before Dubček and the Prague Spring, as two émigré historians have remarked, the Soviet Union had socialism with a human face: that wise, reassuring face was Stalin's.[144] Stalin became the personification of the country's vast construction and rise in status, associated with technology and machines.

Stalin's speeches, his catechizing, his reduction of complexities to almost absurd simplicities and slogans, his logical mistakes, are easy to ridicule.[145] But Stalin, who lived relatively modestly and dressed simply, like a "proletarian," employed a direct, accessible style and showed uncanny insight into the beliefs and hopes—the psychology—of his audience. Although initially portrayed as a political type, when the cult became functional in the mid-1930s, Stalin was transformed into a warm and personal figure of father, teacher, and friend.[146] Again, it is easy to make light of the many public effusions of love and gratitude for Stalin as enforced rituals agreed to by cynical people, but these expressions were often deeply laden with affect and revealed a devout quality transcending reasoned argument.[147] Before the television age, the cult brought about a reassuring immediacy between Stalin and ordinary people, testified to by the photographs, clipped from newspapers, magazines, and books, that hung in people's rooms.

Further diminishing the possibility of unbelief was the international context. In the 1930s, the capitalist world was in deep depression, and the USSR was undergoing unprecedented development—a contrast remarked on tirelessly by the Magnitogorsk newspaper, sometimes in articles written by visiting American workers.[148] Capitalism was, furthermore, marked by militarism. When juxtaposed against the peace-loving social and economic construction prevailing inside the USSR, reports of the ever-present threats of "capitalist encirclement," and fascism—seen as a result of the capitalist economic depression—added greatly to the force of the revolutionary vision.[149]

The strengthening of fascism, and the USSR's response to this threat, played an important part in the reinforcement and subtle redefinition of the country's revolutionary mission: from building to defending socialism. This transformation became most visible in the coverage of the Spanish

Civil War, which was portrayed as the "first phase" in the battle to the death between capitalist fascism and socialism. Whereas Hitler's Germany decisively aided the Falangist forces, the USSR under Stalin appeared to be actively supporting the Spanish people's heroic resistance, a circumstance in which the Soviet population seems to have taken considerable pride. Magnitogorsk, too, did its part. In the fall of 1936 the Magnitogorsk newspaper reported that fifty thousand people had gathered the day before on Factory Administration Square at an outdoor "demonstration of solidarity" with Spain's Republican forces.[150]

If there seems to have been little support or grounds for radical unbelief in the Communist cause for those living inside the USSR under Stalin, however, this does not mean that universal, uncritical acceptance was the result. John Barber, citing the 1950s Harvard Interview Project of Soviet émigrés, estimated that one-fifth of all workers enthusiastically supported the regime and its policies, while another minority was opposed, although not overtly. This left the great mass of workers, who according to Barber were neither supporters nor opponents but nonetheless more or less "accepted" the regime for its social welfare policies.[151] This common-sense assessment has much to commend it but requires some clarification.

Elements of "belief" and "disbelief" appear to have coexisted within everyone, along with a certain residual resentment. The same people who in Barber's judgment "rejected" the regime might well have benefited from, and therefore sincerely appreciated, the regime's social welfare policies. Alternatively, even in the case of the category of "true believers" it is necessary to think in terms of a shifting compromise, of rigidity and the search for slack, of daily negotiation and compromise within certain well-defined but not inviolate limits. Those limits were defined by recognition of the basic righteousness of socialism—always as contrasted with capitalism—a proposition that few people did or could have rejected, whatever resentment or ill-will toward the Soviet regime they harbored.[152]

If acceptance of the basic righteousness of socialism, and along with it the legitimacy of the Soviet regime, went hand in hand with an enduring ambivalence, that ambivalence acquired a special quality. Of course, with any belief system, it would be necessary to admit the possibility of half-belief and of simultaneous belief in contradictory things.[153] But the "regime of truth" in the Stalin years *required* of people just such a tactic, although without public acknowledgment, for the scientifically determined picture of reality sometimes clashed with events of daily life.

The discrepancies between lived experience and revolutionary interpretation appears to have given rise to a dual reality: observational truth based on experience, and a higher revolutionary truth based partly on experience but ultimately on theory. If discrepancies were by no means as jarring as it might seem at first glance, especially given the flexibility and adaptability of the theory, life could still resemble a split existence: sometimes in one truth, sometimes in the other.[154] Problems occurred when a person became suspended between the two, and so people developed a sense of the dangerousness of confusing one for the other and a certain facility for switching back and forth.

How much people consciously thought through the inconsistencies they saw and the affronts they suffered is difficult to gauge. It does seem to be the case that many wives and husbands privately discussed strategies for handling conversation with neighbors, friends, and acquaintances, for talking to the children, for behaving in public and at work. Women appear to have played important roles as counselors and as defenders of the safety of the family and home, which may have afforded some sanctity for unguarded discussion.

Even in the absence of documents from the security police archives it is possible to imagine occasional public moments of "catharsis." But to what effect? Suppose that in the factories some did speak out, did curse the "activists" and the ritual incantations of falsehoods on the shop floor. These may not have been the reckless but the most authoritative "core" proletarians, hard-working, self-sacrificing and dedicated men who had sufficient clout to say what others could not and just had had enough. Their brief but blunt words could have momentarily devastated the lingering falseness, but life would have resumed, speeches would have been made, "contributions" to the latest state loan drive collected, the fight to increase production continued, and so on. And anyway, capitalism was worse, wasn't it?

Whether such moments of catharsis took place, it would be a mistake to regard only the truth of lived experience as "true"; even when the theoretical truth was contradicted by observation and common sense, it still formed an important part of people's everyday experience. Without an understanding of revolutionary truth it was impossible to survive, impossible to interpret and understand a great deal of everyday activity, of what was demanded of one, of what one could or could not do. Furthermore, accepting the truthfulness of the revolutionary truth was not simply a necessary part of daily life; it was also a way to transcend the pettiness of daily life, to see the whole picture, to relate mundane events to a larger design; it offered something to strive for.

This sense of purpose, derived from a revolutionary national mission, became infused with a powerful patriotism promoted from above with increasing effort and effect as the 1930s wore on. Some contemporaries were incensed by what they saw as this "retreat" from revolutionary internationalism and communism. Of course, exactly the opposite argument could be made, namely, that the revolution was in fact consolidated by the skillful cultivation of a renewed national identity.[155]

Indeed, what stands out about the surprisingly powerful new national identity developed under Stalin was its Soviet, rather than solely Russian, character and how a sense of belonging to the Soviet *Union* was melded with the *enhancement* of a parallel, but subordinated, ethnic or national character: Soviet citizens, and Russian, Ukrainian, Tatar, or Uzbek nationals. The polemics about the supposed "great retreat" or betrayal perpetrated under Stalin have drawn attention away from the integration of the country during his reign on the basis of a strong sense of *Soviet* nationhood and citizenship. The Magnitogorsk newspaper did its part, inculcating a sense of the "Union" with such rubrics as "A Day of Our Motherland" and "From Around the USSR."[156]

When a compelling revolutionary vision resembling the "higher truth" of a revealed religion is refracted through patriotic concerns and a real rise in international stature, we should not underestimate the popular will to believe or, more accurately, the willing suspension of disbelief. It is not necessary to argue that popular support forced radical policies on the regime to acknowledge that the revolutionary truth was maintained not merely by the power of the security police but by the collective actions of millions of people who participated in it, for a variety of reasons, including the apparent authenticity of the cause—whatever its nagging deficiencies.[157]

HONOR, GLORY, AND HEROISM

In the absence of primary documents directly attesting to the population's mood, this discussion of revolutionary truth admittedly remains somewhat speculative. Further support, however, can be indirectly adduced from the the margins of the grand crusade—that is, the Magnitogorsk Corrective Labor Colony, or ITK. There, the authorities also tried to create a version of the revolutionary crusade and impart its values to the convicts but with what appears to have been far less success.

Magnitogorsk's ITK was formed in July 1932 (as discussed in chapter 3). John Scott, acknowledging the presence among them of a small group of orthodox priests, wrote correctly that colony inmates were by and large "non-political offenders." Because sentences generally ranged from half a year to five years—some were serving "tenners," then the maximum—the majority of these common criminals were expected to return to society.[158] In the interim, they were supposed to have acquired a profession along with useful work experience—in a word, to have been "reforged." This was the "bargain" the authorities offered, and true to the practice among the city's noncriminal population, the authorities placed the greatest hope for acceptance of these terms on the colony's youth, who appear to have constituted the bulk of the inmate population.[159]

"Every person temporarily deprived of freedom," the colony newspaper proudly proclaimed, "is not deprived of the opportunity to take part in the great construction of the USSR."[160] Except for those confined to punishment barracks, convicts were, just like noncriminal workers, organized into brigades. These convict brigades transported coal and iron ore, built the brick buildings of the left-bank socialist city and the right-bank city, helped assemble the open-hearth ovens and rolling mills, worked on the second dam, and cleaned factory territory. As the colony newspaper wrote, "in the construction of the Magnitogorsk Metallurgical Complex no small place belongs to the colony."[161]

Much like regular workers, convicts were evaluated as to "class position," political loyalty, and labor performance by low-level colony officials, who were often convicts themselves.[162] A convict's labor, which was minimally compensated, was measured in work days put in and norm fulfillment percentages.[163] To encourage better performance the authorities offered short "vacations," warm clothing and felt boots, extra rations, and the possibility of being released early. Convicts who attained especially high plan fulfillment percentages, attended meetings, gave speeches, organized others in various assigned tasks, sat on the comrade court, reported conversations and improprieties, and generally made a convincing show of their dedication to the cause were promoted to brigadiers.[164] As such they earned a spot on the "public honor rolls," and enjoyed not only whatever privileges were to be had, mostly in and around the kitchen, but even powers of patronage.[165]

It is doubtful, however, whether the use of incentives and the promotion of supposed loyalists also had the effect of raising productivity above what were minimal levels. According to the colony newspaper, one cultural instructor (*kulturnik*), responsible for lecturing other convicts on food scarcity being insufficient reason for failing to fulfill the industrial plan, was supposedly more interested in using his influence to obtain more than one lunch, after which he was imagined thinking to himself, "in the end an intelligent person can manage to live in the ITK."[166] Similarly, a convict brigadier was allegedly overheard saying to his forces, "Let them storm [work hard], and I'll watch how it goes." The colony newspaper added that "it is not possible to say that [the brigadier also] doesn't feel as if in a storm, for he storms the public kitchen."[167] Not surprisingly, fictitious labor and double counting—what was generally referred to as *tukhta*—predominated even more so than outside the colony, much to the colony newspaper's chagrin.

Beyond the chicanery, accurate record keeping was in any case subverted by frequent transfers, both within the separate divisions of the Magnitogorsk colony and to and from other colonies.[168] In addition, there were simply not enough record and review commissions to keep track of all the convicts of the various divisions of the colony.[169] Yet because the convicts themselves were no less concerned that officials keep regular labor performance reports, without which their petitions for early release could not be considered, some effective "accommodation" was reached.[170] Thousands of convicts were in fact let go before their terms were formally up on the basis of having performed "shock work."[171] Were these people in fact "reforged"?

Invariably, convicts professed that they had turned over a new leaf.[172] Profiles of convicts claiming to have been reformed appeared in almost every issue of the colony newspaper, in language strikingly reminiscent of what could be heard from accomplished workers outside the colony: they were laboring, studying, making sacrifices, and trying to better themselves.[173] But even if, as John Scott believed, a few of the convicts learned to "value human labor,"[174] there were limits to the authorities' ability to elicit more than minimal cooperation from them. With convicts, threats and, above all, shame, only went so far. Among convicts, open expression of antiregime sentiments appears to have been common, as was knowing sabotage of regime mobilizations.

To foster an atmosphere of labor enthusiasm, the colony held several conferences of shock workers, complete with orchestra and singing of the "Internationale," and in November 1935 even had its own Stakhanovite conference, attended by 1,500 of its best workers.[175] But in a sharp piece on a typical brigade, the colony newspaper described how much of their work day was lost owing to disorganization and the fact that among the convicts there were "not a few slackers."[176] One convict had 750 unauthorized absences (*proguly*). Brigadiers were constantly blamed for temporarily losing track of convicts, who ambled off the job and over to the bazaar to engage in "speculation."[177] Some were said to be agitating among the others against working.[178] Exasperated, the colony newspaper complained that "we are located here not in order to get drunk and simulate [sickness], but in order to build Magnitostroi."[179]

Propaganda among the convicts was extensive,[180] but here again, the crusading colony newspaper reluctantly conceded that the myriad activities organized to raise the level of the convicts' culture could do little in the face of the persistent and ubiquitous use of foul language (*mat*) among them.[181] According to a report in the paper of the oblast labor colony administration by the colony chief, Aleksandr Geineman, there were sixteen periodic newspapers for camp convicts in Magnitogorsk besides the main one, *Borba za metall*, plus a twelve-thousand-book library, regular plays, films, political circles, and technical courses. But Geineman conceded that reading was not compulsory and that there were not enough trained leaders for the circles. More serious problems cited included what he called "the struggle with anti-sanitary conditions, and with old prison traditions (swearing, theft, card playing, and drunkenness)."[182]

Nor was it clear who actually "controlled" the colony on a day-to-day basis. Geineman wrote, no doubt in earnest, that administering the colony was no small task. A distance of thirty kilometers separated the colony's five divisions, one of which was located eighteen kilometers from headquarters.[183] As of January 1933 the colony had only 138 operatives, 111 administrative and economic personnel, and a total staff of 287 people (against a "plan" specifying 457). This was when the number of convicts hovered around 10,000.[184]

Of necessity, the convicts played a large role in managing the affairs of the colony, and the threat of violence by some convicts against those who "cooperated" with the authorities was real.[185] The colony newspaper encouraged anonymous letters concerning observed "shortcomings" and shenanigans,[186] but at a conference of its "worker correspondents," the paper claimed to have discovered that many were afraid to write. One such correspondent was quoted as saying, "As soon as someone writes in, the [other convicts] begin to dig: 'Who, how, and why did he write.'"[187]

In sum, the ITK was a colony for criminals and not a socialist city, however flawed. The convicts were probably less intimidated by the prospect of being sent to a harsher labor colony than nonconvicts were of being arrested. Even after being released, convicts carried the stigma of a criminal record in their official documents.[188] True, upon discharge they received papers, provided they returned their mattress, bedspread, pillow case, towel, boots, summer pants, arm protectors, and padded jacket.[189] And those willing to stay in town were offered space in a dormitory and food until the steel plant found them a job and a place to live (the factory was even willing to pay to bring a former inmate's family to Magnitogorsk). But in an appeal to convicts to remain at the construction site, the colony newspaper admitted that "the majority . . . leave Magnitka without knowing where they're going."[190] They were simply not part of the grand crusade.

A stark contrast to the rootlessness of colony convicts was presented by the social rehabilitation achieved by the dekulakized peasants. At first, exactly the opposite was expected. Because the dekulakized peasants were considered "class aliens" and therefore more dangerous, they initially lived behind barbed wire and went to work escorted by convoy. Each day after work, upon arrival back at the settlement, they were checked off at the command post. Considered incorrigible by virtue of their class background, they were subject to far less intensive propaganda.[191] Soon, however, the barbed wire came down around the settlement. With rare exceptions they were not permitted to relocate to another city and were obliged once a month to obtain a stamp on their registration papers (*kontrolnaia kartochka*) at commandant headquarters. But the dekulakized peasant exiles were allowed to sign up for work individually according to their professional abilities.[192]

"Many of these peasants," according to John Scott, "were terribly embittered because they had been deprived of everything and been forced to work under a system which, in many cases, had killed off members of their families." But Scott added that most "worked doggedly." To be sure, they continued to live in wretched and overcrowded barracks, yet in Scott's opinion "many of them lived comparatively well" and "the rise of some of these men was heroic." Even if they themselves sought nothing, their children's futures were at stake. Although stigmatized, the children of the dekulakized were permitted to attend school, where many worked diligently. Mariia Scott taught in one of the three schools for such children and reported that they were widely considered among the best students in the whole city.[193]

Central authorities adopted a policy of trying to integrate the dekulakized into the new society that after a number of years of half-hearted implementation finally began to be taken more seriously and have an effect. In July 1931 the regime issued a decree on the restoration of voting rights for dekulakized peasants after five years if during this time they proved that they had become honest toilers. The efficacy of this first decree was cast in doubt by the fact that in May 1934, another decree allowed them to apply for early restoration if they met the same criterion.[194] Most of the petitions for reinstatement dating from 1934 were refused, but by 1936 a more favorable attitude toward them was taken. If their request was granted, the petitioners were allowed to leave the Special Labor Settlement, attend school, and even (theoretically) join the party.[195]

Furthermore, well before 1936 the children of the dekulakized were given special attention.[196] With a 17 March 1934 decree, these children had their voting rights restored, once they reached legal age (eighteen), provided they attained the status of shock workers in production and became active in public work. As a sign of encouragement, lists of those who had been reinstated began to be published in the Labor Settlement newspaper.[197] Whatever resentment they might have harbored over their family's fate, the youth had little to lose and everything to gain by joining in. As the paper put it, "the growth of our country is proceeding by gigantic strides forward. From this every special resettler should understand that there is and cannot be any return to the past."[198]

Unlike many of the dekulakized peasants and their children, the predominantly male convicts of the labor colony, despite all the surface resemblances of their lives to the lives of the people in the city, were only partially, if at all, integrated into the grand crusade. An ever-present and persuasive backdrop to the regime's practices of intimidation, the existence of the colony underscored both the necessity of participating in the building of socialism and that the complex identification game arising out of such a process was effective because people accepted at some level the larger political mission put forward by the state. Beyond merely calculating what they had to gain or lose, people made their individual compacts with the regime's ambitions, adopting them in whole or, more often, in part, having little else to guide their thoughts and actions and remaining prone to doubts and ambivalence.[199]

"POSITIVE" INTEGRATION

In 1931 the German writer Emil Ludwig was granted a rare interview with Stalin. Ludwig broached a delicate issue: "It seems to me that a significant part of the Soviet population is experiencing a feeling of fear, dread of Soviet power, and that to a certain extent the stability of Soviet power is based on this fear." Stalin responded forcefully: "You are wrong, although your mistake is the mistake of many. Do you really think that it would be possible to retain power for fourteen years and to have the backing of the masses, millions of people, owing to methods of intimidation and fear? This is impossible."[200] Stalin was right, but for the wrong reasons.

Communism inspired people—so much so that even intimate knowledge and genuine abhorrence of repression need not have induced "true believers" to abandon the cause.[201] But equally important, the image of capitalism inside the USSR had little innate appeal. During an era of depression and militarism, capitalism served as a ready-to-hand, all-purpose bogeyman for excusing socialism's shortcomings. Only if the reality and image of capitalism had been considerably different would it have been possible within the USSR to imagine the wholesale rejection of the cause of socialism.

Given the menacing nature of capitalism, the task of drawing a principled distinction between the cause of socialism and the existing Soviet regime, already difficult because of censorship, was made that much more difficult. Such critiques were, of course, made by the "old guard" of revolutionaries, most famously by Trotsky. But what Trotsky had to say was for all intents and purposes unavailable within the USSR. And even if people had been able to make themselves familiar with his books and articles, it is far from clear whether they would have accepted his ambiguous analysis of "the Thermidor." What could Thermidor matter in the face of the fascist threat and the success of socialist construction? For the inhabitants of Magnitogorsk the descent of capitalism into fascism and the ascent of the USSR into socialism appeared inextricably linked and was felt with great immediacy in their own lives.

That immediacy was achieved by means of the game of social identification, exemplified by the practice of speaking Bolshevik. Through this new social identity, the state was able to appropriate much of the basis for social solidarity and to render opposition impossible. Émigré testimony on the pervasiveness of informants and the perception that the regime meant business has lent credence to the notion that the entire society under Stalin was "atomized," leaving people only the privacy of the kitchen table to express their anger and innermost feelings. In that sense, "atomization," if not as total as some commentators have claimed, was considerable. At the same time, however, the terms of the new social identity also forged the people into a larger political community. This "positive" integration of the Soviet working class brought obligations and a general state of dependency but also benefits and, owing to the absence of unemployment, a degree of control over the labor process.

The process of "positive integration" by which people became part of the "official society" involved a subtle, if unequal negotiation, for which it was essential to learn the terms at issue and the techniques of engagement. Workers marched in choreographed holiday festivals and they were often compelled to listen, and sometimes called upon to deliver, oily speeches.

But they also had occasions when they could express frustrations, and even grievances—within unspoken if widely recognized limits. People had no choice but to learn that there was a boundary in public behavior and even private thought between the realistic and the unrealistic. But they also had to see that they could "work the system" to their "minimum disadvantage."[202] These were the lessons that life itself taught them.

Life in Magnitogorsk taught cynicism as well as labor enthusiasm, fear as well as pride. Most of all, life in Magnitogorsk taught one how to identify oneself and speak in the acceptable terms. If ever there was a case where the political significance of things said, or discourse, stood out, it was in the articulation of social identity under Stalin.[203] This subtle mechanism of power, within the circumstances of the revolutionary crusade, accounted for the strength of Stalinism. Fifty years later, surviving workers in Magnitogorsk still spoke the way they and their contemporaries did in the memoirs from the 1930s. By the late 1980s, however, their image of capitalism would radically change, and with it, their understanding of and allegiance to socialism, as represented by the Soviet regime.

6 Bread and a Circus

That sovereign people which once bestowed military commands,
consulships, legions, what it pleased, now narrows its field, and
anxiously longs for two things only—bread and circuses.

Juvenal, *Tenth Satire*[1]

In the new society of Magnitogorsk, the much-discussed state-owned and
state-managed "supply system," whatever else it failed to provide, could
usually be counted on for low-cost bread, obtainable with ration coupons
at fixed low prices. Even after Moscow authorities decreed the end of food
rationing and the opening of "socialist" trading stores in December 1934,
bread was sometimes the only food easily and inexpensively obtained in
Magnitogorsk. Bread came to symbolize the official urban supply network
run not by individuals for private gain but by the state as a service to the
people.[2]

Seemingly far removed from the daily grind of the bread shops, one
could observe the other side of the state supply system—at the local circus.
The jerry-built but attractive structure, "an odd kind of monumental
building in wood, with a very conspicuous little red and white cupola
perched on top of it,"[3] became a favorite spot of the urban inhabitants. The
circus's popularity, however, derived less from its acrobats, dancing bears,
or even beloved clown, who went by the name of Charlie Chaplin, than
from that most popular of all public spectacles, the demonstration (*poka-zatelnyi*) trial. Staged for educational purposes, these productions were
held for the entire range of what were called "economic crimes,"[4] which ac-
counted for 80 percent of Magnitogorsk's criminal proceedings and frequently filled the big top with what was a deadly serious show.[5]

Between the two closely connected spectacles—the official supply network, with its ration cards, forlorn stores, and fixed prices symbolized by
inexpensive bread, and the circus, where unauthorized "entrepreneurs"
unlucky enough to be caught were demonstratively "tried"—there flourished a game of ruse and camouflage, of opportunity and risk. This game
touched the lives of nearly every urban inhabitant, forming an expansive

238

arena of activities and relationships—a form of the market—that proved remarkably resilient and indeed indispensable to the authorities no less than to ordinary people.

Market activities had been one of the primary targets of the revolution. Nineteen seventeen marked a watershed in the economic life of the former Russian empire because Soviet Russia's new rulers assumed power branding "capitalism" as the source of the country's past misery and hailing the suppression of capitalist relations as the key to a brighter future. True, in 1921 the Bolshevik leadership announced a temporary truce, the New Economic Policy. But throughout the 1920s private trade remained a stigmatized, illegitimate endeavor, with questionable longterm prospects, conducted outside the framework of universally accepted laws and at the forbearance of avowedly anticapitalist officials. If the authorities grudgingly accepted certain forms of private activity, they ardently, albeit inconsistently, applied numerous "administrative measures," from "punitive" taxation and price deflations to arrest and outright confiscation of all property, as a way to voice displeasure and assert political control over such activity.[6]

When the Soviet Union entered the 1930s with what was trumpeted as "the socialist offensive on all fronts,"[7] the private hiring of labor was further restricted and then proscribed. In 1932, the private ownership of shops was prohibited, and all "middlemen" were decreed out of legal existence.[8] Private manufacturing too became illegal, and small-scale urban artisan production, although still legal, was sharply curtailed by the withholding of inputs and raw materials, a tactic that forced most independent artisans into joining state-sponsored "cooperatives." In a brief period, virtually the entire national economy became state-owned and state-run, technically a single entity. Soviet propagandists, with an eye on the largest European and American companies, boasted of "our" firm, "the USSR."

But as it turned out, the complete suppression of capitalism proved impossible. Many privateers took their businesses underground, where some flourished, while the state, after considerable soul-searching, felt compelled to make "concessions" to the "market." These included permitting small household plots for collective farmers[9] and urban markets where the collective farmers could sell their personal output and purchase industrial and consumer goods, as well as enticing harassed artisans to resume plying their trades. Even more significant than such "concessions" to the market, however, was the deployment of the planned economy itself, which gave rise to an economic system that could not function without widespread illicit behavior reminiscent of capitalist relations—the so-called "shadow" (*tenavaia*) economy.

As its name makes clear, the "shadow" economy was a silhouette of the planned economy.[10] Significantly, contemporaries at first had no name for this vast "other" domain and set of relations that, by definition, should not have existed. When such activities nonetheless made their insistent appearance, they fell under the time-honored designation of unwholesome operations performed "on the left" (*nalevo*). So stigmatized, these activities became the targets of the doggedly determined authorities, who sought to eradicate them through a combination of the mobilization of public opinion and the development of a new, socialist court system based on the "hegemony" of the proletariat.

Only glimpses into the formation and operation of the Magnitogorsk court system were furnished by the city newspaper and the local affiliate of the state archives.[11] The picture that emerges is of a rudimentary legal system that was profoundly influenced by the political system, to be sure, but that also had some sense of the law and struggled to regularize its procedures.[12] The courts were chronically understaffed, however, and the staff at hand was not especially qualified.[13] In 1935, an official report complained that Magnitogorsk judges "do not have great legal qualifications," which was putting it mildly. In addition, ten judges left the city during 1933 and 1934, so that by 1935 there was not a single judge on the bench who had been working more than a year. The court chambers, moreover, were located in a barracks, which, ironically enough, was said to "present an unsightly spectacle."[14]

Even though they discovered that instituting and managing a workable legal system was far from easy, the local authorities had come to understand this was something they had to do, in part because unexpectedly for all concerned, the establishment of a noncapitalist municipal economy brought forth a proliferation of illegalities. This is not to say, however, that all the business of the shadow economy was, strictly speaking, illegal. Many of the activities nominally outside the planned economy were prohibited but others were actually promoted, while many of the activities formally prohibited were tacitly condoned. That such activities were often tolerated reflected more than the inability of the authorities to suppress them. These activities were extremely "useful," and not merely in permitting a means of survival for people otherwise unable to get by.

In a sense, here was a part of the "society" in the Soviet Union under Stalin whose existence one generation of historians denied, then another asserted but never demonstrated in detail. It was neither the party, the

Komsomol, nor even the trade unions, but the ubiquitous "market" of trade, resale, barter, and domestic manufacture that was the largest "social organization" in Magnitogorsk—a spontaneous complement to the orchestrated rallies, endless mobilizations, and solemn party meetings.

Market activities in Magnitogorsk cannot be mistaken for the workings of something like a "civil society." There was no private property, and much of market-related activity took place secretly, or at least discreetly, without recourse to the legal system. Market society in the Soviet Union remained a shadowy sphere of existence, even when it was more or less open. Nonetheless, against the background of the official socialist ideology and the party's rule, the unforeseen relations that arose within Magnitogorsk's noncapitalist municipal economy constituted not only an alternative form of economic organization but a kind of "countersociety." This world of quasi-contracts and informal "businesses" was brought into being by people who may not have intended "opposition" to the state but whose actions in many cases came to be interpreted as just that. More simply, Magnitogorsk's inhabitants, finding themselves charged with the task of creating and sustaining a noncapitalist municipal economy, could be seen as pioneers making their way in unmapped terrain—and make their way they did, deploying a rich arsenal in the humble encounters encompassing the little tactics of the habitat.

• • •

Whereas the end of the NEP has been perhaps the most analyzed problem in the history of the USSR (from both a political and economic standpoint), there has been little study of the system of socialist trade and supply that replaced NEP.[15] This chapter should be seen as an attempt in that direction. For such a task, some guidance is provided by a comparison with Peru's "informal economy" in the 1980s, as analyzed by Hernando de Soto.

De Soto, who examines an enormous range and depth of productive economic activity that takes place outside sanctioned channels, defines informality as the "refuge of individuals who find that the costs of abiding by existing laws in the pursuit of legitimate economic objectives exceed the benefits." In contrast to the state's elephantine bureaucracies, with their proliferation of nonproductive, parasitic activities, "the people" work hard against great odds to create businesses that serve their own and others' needs. But because legality is a privilege available only to those with political and economic power, such informal businesses, of necessity built on transitory and tactical alliances, cannot grow easily, find investment hazardous, and become vulnerable to theft and extortion. In conclusion, the author argues that whereas the "informal economy," or black market, is usually thought of as the problem, in countries like Peru "the problem is not the black market but the state itself."[16]

In all these matters the parallels with the Soviet shadow economy as it took shape in the Stalin years are striking. There are also differences, however. In the Peruvian case the people's initiative and creativity become perforce enmeshed with shady operations whose stigma furnishes the state with an apparent justification for condemning and attempting to eradicate manifold productive activities, usually allowing state functionaries to exact tribute in the process. But private property is not banned; the vast majority of people are simply forced to operate with only de facto property. Their activities can be against the law but are just as frequently simply outside it. In many cases, if they accumulate enough wealth, they can, if they chose, pay the fee to register their businesses. In the Soviet case, "protection payments" could have been made to forestall punitive measures, but they could never completely guarantee legal status. "Private" businesses were outlawed.

In the USSR, moreover, "the state" was often the most energetic unauthorized "marketeer" of all. Just to perform their regular jobs, everyone from the low-level managers of Magnitogorsk's public canteens to the big "pine cones" (*shishki*) running the great steel plant came to rely not only on the fruits of the official supply network but also on the inputs, goods, and services provided outside or alongside the sanctioned channels of the planned economy. More than that, such people often took an active role as producers of goods and purveyors of services, in direct contravention of the law.

If the everyday behavior of almost the entire Soviet populace, without repudiating the grand crusade, nonetheless interjected a certain slack or flexibility into the unrelenting drive to build socialism, the mentality and methods of the Bolshevik quest for accelerated noncapitalist modernization shaped the range and type of maneuvers that arose within the arena of supply and distribution, stamping them as "counteractivities." The weight of this contradiction fell on ordinary people, to be sure, but also on the zealous authorities.

FROM RATIONING TO SOCIALIST TRADE

At Magnetic Mountain the first settlers arrived not long after "rationing" was introduced around the country, first for bread, then for other food products and manufactured goods. Normally a wartime practice ensuring fair and orderly distribution of limited supplies, rationing appears not to have been implemented at the remote site until late 1931, however, when the local population suddenly jumped to more than 100,000 people and the food situation in the country took a turn for the worse as a result of the disorganization brought on by collectivization.[17] Still, from the beginning at Magnitogorsk it was in the name of the state that a local supply system was organized, as private operators were prohibited.

The state supply network was officially called the Central Workers' Cooperative (*Tsentralnyi rabochii kooperativ*), or TsRK (add an *i* after the *ts* to pronounce the acronym and you get the Russian word for circus, *tsirk*). TsRK was the first organization formed in Magnitogorsk, predating even the local party organization. It was also one of the largest organizations at the site. By November 1932, after rationing was locally in place, TsRK grew to have a staff of more than five thousand.[18]

TsRK oversaw the city's supply system, but the task of issuing workers their rations cards, which entitled them to purchase a maximum amount of certain goods at so-called hard (*tverdye*)—that is, fixed—prices, fell to the various construction objectives, or to already functioning shops and enterprises. Having distributed pieces of paper, these organizations then struggled in cooperation with TsRK to supply the specified items. This was an awesome responsibility, for in 1932 famine was ravaging many parts of the countryside, and despite the decided urban tilt of regime policies, the cities also experienced less than bountiful supplies. Even without these added difficulties, TsRK's assignment was daunting. Singling out shoes, supplies, work clothes, and especially food, one of the site's early directors, Iakov Gugel, admitted that "organizing the lives of 200,000 people was not easy."[19]

Not much can be said with assurance about the agricultural hinterland surrounding Magnitogorsk, except that it was not exceedingly rich.[20] With time the region's agriculture improved, but in the city there remained a widespread feeling, which the authorities were at pains to dispel, that nothing could be made to grow in such an inhospitable region.[21] The factory, which owned most of the state farms in the immediate vicinity, also operated several successful greenhouses, where onions, radishes, cucumbers, and other fruits and vegetables were grown.[22] But throughout the decade vegetables were treated as if they were a strategic resource. The city's large enclosed vegetable warehouse was located under the watchful eye of the factory administrative building.[23]

To increase local production of vegetables the authorities eventually adopted the same approach that the Soviet government adopted vis-à-vis the collective farms: encouraging the cultivation of household plots. Estimates differ on the number of urban cultivators, but whatever the precise totals they certainly ranged in the many thousands.[24] By the late 1930s, household plots produced a significant amount of Magnitogorsk's food, including more than 20 percent of all potatoes consumed in the city.[25] But such supplementary urban "harvests," important as they became, were no substitute for large-scale agriculture, which grew only gradually.[26]

In the early years, when there was not enough food, local authorities were directed to use the shortages to make people take up work: without a job, a person could not get a bread card, and life with a bread card was harsh enough. So great was the demand for labor, however, that each enterprise or organization became desperate to sign up as many workers as possible and thus gave out bread cards liberally. Some people, especially those who signed up for more than one job, managed to obtain an extra bread card—a perquisite that could provoke condemnation when secured "spontaneously," but one that was handed out readily by bosses.

Rations were differentiated on the basis of profession, skill level, and in some cases, perceived loyalty or political importance. With bread cards, to take the most important dietary item, there was a range for nonbosses of 400 to 1,000 grams per day.[27] These were, of course, upper limits, and as with other items, including milk, sugar, and meat, often much less than the specified amount was actually available.[28] Naturally, those in the lower categories endeavored to raise their status, and there was a limited upward movement toward the upper categories, particularly for anyone who answered the summons to greater labor exertion.[29] Food, no less than housing, was an important political device for the authorities, imposing on them extraordinary responsibilities but also affording them significant leverage.

Magnitogorsk's supply system underwent changes in January 1933 that gave an indication of growing size and complexity. Separate ration cards for each item were replaced by monthly ration booklets (*zabornye knizhki*) to be carried by each person (in part to combat the possession or sale of extra coupons). And the swollen TsRK bureaucracy was reorganized and renamed the Department of Workers' Supply (*otdel rabochego snabzheniia*), or ORS. ORS took over the management of TsRK's numerous subdivisions, or distribution outlets, still known individually as "workers' cooperatives."

Neither of these changes was meant to alter the supply network's openly differentiated structure, which was confirmed in a highly revealing list of the population served by each "workers' cooperative" published in the newspaper along with the announcement of the reorganization. According to the list, "workers' cooperative" no. 1 was allotted to the GPU, or security police; no. 2, to the city party committee; no. 3 was set aside for what were called "responsible workers" while no. 4 was for "special workers"—both euphemisms for favored groups not already included in the police or upper ranks of the party; no. 5 was reserved for the chiefs of the labor colony, and so on down the list to the cooperatives for ordinary workers.[30] The stock available at each outlet varied, depending on whom the outlet was designated to serve: the more important the clientele, the more ample the outlet's selection of goods.[31]

The published list was not the whole story, for it omitted reference to *insnab*, an acronym formed from the words "foreigners' supply," described by John Scott as "the famous and fabulous foreigners' store," which as it turned out was not exclusively for foreigners.[32] At the other extreme, the list also failed to mention "special resettlers," that is, exiled peasants, or the inmates of the city's labor colony, who were both attached to a separate supply system.[33] During a time when hardship was the rule for virtually everyone, the exiled peasants and colony inmates suffered additional deprivations.[34]

Alongside the ranked distribution outlets run by ORS where workers could purchase goods in accordance with their ration coupons (but sometimes without), "each industrial organization ran one or more dining-rooms where workers ate, likewise by card, once a day." Scott described dining hall no. 30 (located in a barracks) as "jammed full: the long bare wooden tables were surrounded by workers, and behind almost every client somebody was waiting." He added that "it was cold in the dining-room; one could see one's breath before one's face; but it was so much warmer than outside that everybody unbuttoned his sheepskin and rolled his hat from around his ears."[35] Such "dining halls" were actually an improvement over the ones from the earlier years, which had been nothing more than outdoor gatherings around mobile kitchens.[36]

Like the distribution outlets for goods, the various dining rooms were organized according to rank. Although there were differences between those in the middle and those at the bottom of the dining hall pyramid, the biggest difference was at the top, in the dining rooms that few people saw, where the highest-level police, party, factory officials, and, for a time, foreigners took their meals.[37] But within even the low-level dining halls there was differentiation: some people accumulated extra meal tickets, usually as incentives or rewards, entitling them to more than one meal.[38] In the dining halls no less than in the workers cooperatives, an elaborate system of "privileges" was created.

In addition to controlling access to better food and hard-to-obtain goods, the authorities could grant or withhold the pick of scarce housing, use of an automobile, and preferential access to medical care. According to a leading physician who subsequently wrote an unpublished history of the city's health care system, "employees [*rabotniki*] of the Magnitogorsk Works had a 'closed policlinic,' opened for them by the city health department on 3 October 1934 in the central medical station of the blast furnace shop, on factory territory. In March 1938, they were [also] given a separate wing of the first floor of the city hospital, with thirty rooms." Doctors said to be among the best in the city even made house calls for bosses as well as favored workers and their families.[39]

Throughout the archives one can find mountains of paperwork devoted to the granting of "privileges" to selected individuals. One such record compiled in 1935 by the factory trade union committee listed clothes, shoes, winter coats, radios, trips for children, and apartments for around twenty workers.[40] Even for the relatively less privileged, there were many "privileges" to be gained or lost; there was always something to be had that someone else did not have, if one could gain the favor of the person who controlled it. Intentionally hierarchical and stratified, Magnitogorsk's official supply network looked more like a heavy-handed political club than the public service it was said to be.

Scarcity, far from being the Soviet political system's Achilles heel, was one of the keys to its strength. The tighter the overall balance of services or supplies, the more leverage the authorities could exercise. Even after basic necessities became more plentiful in the latter half of the 1930s, the distribution of "luxury" items—from suits and better quality sausage to vacations and places in day care for one's children—still provided a powerful mechanism of political control.

For obtaining all manner of goods and services, what were called "connections" (*sviazi*) and "pull" (*blat*) came to eclipse money in importance.[41] Money did not, however, lose all value, for in addition to the sale of goods by ration cards at "hard" prices there existed a system of stores derisively known as "Mikoyan shops," after the people's commissar for trade, that sold goods at what were called "commercial prices." These prices were far higher than those charged for goods obtained with ration cards, but in commercial shops one could usually buy as much as one's income allowed. Such an arrangement also prevailed at the city's Central Market, popularly referred to as the bazaar.

At first the new socialist city of Magnitogorsk was not supposed to have a "market" (*rynok*). But by a city party committee decree of 28 July 1932, the periodically held "interregional collective-farmers' fair" was converted into a permanent marketplace for the exchange of goods between Magnitogorsk and the countryside.[42] Of course, the decree did not conjure informal goods exchange into being; it acknowledged the trade already being conducted, while seeking to localize it at a designated area, where the authorities hoped it could be observed and controlled.[43] This hope proved to be in vain, although it was never relinquished.

Controlled or not, trade at the market apparently attained high volume. Official data for 1937 placed the sale of potatoes there at nearly 1 million tons, and that of meat at 640,000 tons. That year 4,460 head of cattle were also traded at the market (supposedly for an average price of only 800 rubles). It is unclear what percentage of total trade the authorities managed to register, or how these figures were derived. Some trade may have escaped the authorities' efforts at measurements. But the reported totals clearly reflected a significant amount of the food consumed in the city.[44] In the mid-1930s, furthermore, the authorities opened a second market near the railroad station, in Fertilizer Settlement, which was more convenient to the large agglomeration of people in the northern end of town—and a further sign of such markets' indispensability.[45]

In Magnitogorsk the two sanctioned market spaces came to occupy a position in the local economy far beyond what the authorities had envisioned. Many goods notoriously difficult to find in state shops remained readily available at the markets throughout the 1930s, admittedly for much higher prices than they would have been sold for in state shops, as the newspaper repeatedly emphasized.[46] Despite the higher prices, these markets served as the urban dwellers' lifeline.[47] As such, they also served as a constant reminder that the state trade network, if not a failure, was certainly inadequate.[48] Moreover, the availability of goods at the markets cut into the authorities' leverage over people's lives. From the regime's point of view, the promotion of the urban markets was something of a devil's bargain.

As if to compete with the activity at the bazaars, the regime decided to phase out comprehensive rationing in favor of what was called trade (*torgovlia*) in the existing network of state shops. Famine had ended in 1933, giving the country a much-needed respite in 1934, and during the second half of that year the Soviet government decreed that rationing of bread would be discontinued as of 1 January 1935. After the central edict to begin trade was announced, the Magnitogorsk newspaper began sounding the alarm, warning that there were neither enough local "trading points" being organized nor enough salespeople being recruited. "Are we ready to end rationing?" asked the newspaper. "No," was the frightened reply.[49]

The depth of the challenge involved in creating trade was revealed by a satire in the factory newspaper on the administrative mentality accumulated from the several years of rationing. The satire took aim at "the bureaucratic language" in which the city's population was referred to as "supply quotas" (*kontigenty snabzheniia*) and its stores as "trading points." "Not shops [*larki*], not booths [*palatki*], not stores [*magaziny*]," the newspaper emphasized, "but precisely 'points.' 'Quotas' go to 'points' and are supplied with goods."[50]

As the satire demonstrated, the changeover from bread rationing was serious business. It was made even more so in September 1935 when a second decree followed, ordering the closing of commercial stores and the end of rationing for meat, fish, sugar, animal fats, and potatoes.[51] For these and other goods, Magnitogorsk would have to set up a trade network—only without private traders and with low, regulated prices, for this was "socialist" trade. Precisely how socialist trade would work in practice, however, was still a mystery.

To bring about and oversee the unprecedented noncapitalist form of trade, the first step taken was the creation of a new bureaucracy, Magnittorg.[52] Placing a premium on image, Magnittorg ostentatiously opened a handful of "model" food emporiums (*gastromy*), as well as a department store, in select neighborhoods and stocked them with all the goods the city could get its hands on. "New stores were built, and supplies of all kinds made their appearance in quantity and at reasonable prices," according to John Scott, who saw the changeover in 1935 as something of a watershed. "Fuel, clothing of all kinds, and other elementary necessities became available."[53] Newspaper reports for 1936, however, were less ebullient than Scott in their characterizations of socialist trade.

Spot investigations of city store inventories were frequently conducted by various Magnitogorsk agencies, and the grim results were always the same.[54] Despite the existence of an electrical store in the Kirov district, for example, the newspaper reported in January 1936 that "no cords, switches, plugs, electric tea kettles, pots, or irons have been for sale in more than half a year."[55] A similar inspection that same month revealed that there was no ink, mustard, eggs, or shoe cleaner for sale anywhere in the city.[56] And after another raid in May, the newspaper reported that "not a single store has meat," and that in general the sale of meat in state stores "was quite rare."[57]

Scott, too, gave information that contradicts, or at least softens, his upbeat presentation of the changeover from rationing to trade. He noted that "the problem of drygoods, which was eclipsed by the food question until there was enough food, became exceedingly acute after 1936." And in a memorable passage, he described the city as "full of potential buyers, with steady incomes, their pockets full of money, who spent their free days every week hunting avidly for suits, furniture, sewing machines, materials, china, cutlery, shoes, radio sets, and the thousand and one other things which are furnished by light industry and distributed in the United States by Sears-Roebuck, Macy's, and Woolworth's."[58]

It was not that the stores had absolutely nothing for sale. According to a newspaper article in 1938, stores and warehouses held more than 1 million rubles' worth of goods—but no one wanted to buy them. There were, for example, large supplies of dried potatoes, holiday tree ornaments (Christmas trees were "rehabilitated" in 1936 as New Year trees), and an estimated three-year supply of dry *kisel*, a kind of starchy jelly. Evidently even under socialism there was such a thing as customer demand. Some of these accumulated products reportedly had been languishing on the shelves since 1932.[59]

By contrast, rumors of the appearance of a desired item were sure to occasion the sudden formation of long queues, which could become unruly. "When scarce items [*defitsity*] go on sale, such as enamelware," the newspaper revealed, "there are crushes" (*davki*) and even instances of "mob violence." Sometimes the militia would be called in. But in the case of the enamelware, instead of restoring order the militiamen were said to have "gone to the front of the line, made a purchase for themselves, and left."[60]

Part of the reason behind the formation of queues derived from the concentration of the city's stores in the Kirov district. According to a report in the oblast newspaper, industrial goods were, "as a rule, thrown only into the stores located in the center of the city. The population living in the outskirts heads for the center, resulting in the creation of queues."[61] The oblast paper's point is well taken, but the underlying cause remained availability. Indeed, all over town, queuing became one of the many unanticipated yet prominent features of socialist trade.

For most people it was impossible to learn beforehand when, in the piquant language of the day, scarce goods were "thrown out" (*tovary vybrasyvali*) to the public, so one had to be ready to queue at any moment. Not everyone had the time to join a suddenly formed queue, however, and some enterprising people managed to turn this situation to their advantage, as the Magnitogorsk newspaper repeatedly protested. Those who did not need to report to a job during the day, such as housewives, nightshift workers, students, and others, were said to be standing in queues many hours each day for scarce items, in most cases hoping to resell these goods for a profit.[62]

Such resale of goods with the intention of making a profit was known as "speculation" and prohibited by law. A series of central decrees culminated in a 1932 addition to the RSFSR Criminal Code in which speculation was defined as "the purchase and resale by private persons, for profit, of agricultural products and other objects of mass consumption," and made punishable by deprivation of liberty for not less than five years with confiscation of all or part of the accused's property.[63] Following this intensification of the law, which was reinforced with sharp public comments by Stalin, the Magnitogorsk newspaper redoubled its efforts in condemning speculation. The newspaper claimed that despite the tough laws, speculation was going on in full view of the militia and trade inspectors at the city market—an obvious call to action.[64]

That many among the huge throng of peddlers of agricultural products at Magnitogorsk's sanctioned markets were not collective farmers was often cited by the newspaper as damning evidence of wrongdoing. "Speculators" who supposedly bought up the state stores' supply of onions at 1.5 rubles per kilo, for example, were excoriated by the newspaper for breaking up the kilo into eight or nine bunches and selling them for fifty kopecks apiece, netting a resale profit of around 3 rubles per kilo. Never mind that apparently there was no shortage of willing customers: this was scandalous and illegal behavior. Even more confusingly, the newspaper often reported favorably on the officially encouraged, and extensive, practice of home vegetable cultivation—meaning that possibly the onions sold at sanctioned markets were not store-bought but homegrown, and thus their sale was technically not speculation. But even this activity would have been viewed as scandalous given the contrast with state-set prices. Such stigmatization tended to enlarge the coverage of the ambiguous speculation law.[65] In practice, the label "speculator" was applied to anyone who sold goods at a price that happened to offend a responsible official or simply attract an official's attention.

Further ambiguity arose because resale trade at the "collective farmers'" bazaar was not limited to food products but also included household goods and clothing.[66] These kinds of items, made in small quantities by the seller, as well as older articles offered secondhand, could be sold within what were ultimately undefined and arbitrarily enforced price limits—provided one could prove the goods were not purchased in state stores or, if they were, that the goods were "used" and that the price being charged was lower than the original purchase price. Here the line between legality and speculation was perhaps most difficult to establish beforehand. What one got away with was, in a sense, what was permissible.[67]

In the name of combating speculation, the authorities struggled to suppress such transactions.[68] People observed waiting in queues to buy up scarce goods that they allegedly resold at the markets were often singled out for condemnation in the newspaper.[69] One "woman" detained for selling "suspicious goods" at the markets turned out to be a man who had recently been released from the corrective labor colony and was trying to conceal his identity.[70] Insinuating that such individuals constituted a kind of criminal class, the newspaper asserted that it was possible to make one's living solely off such speculation.[71] Perhaps, but more often than not, those selling or reselling goods at the markets were ordinary people otherwise without criminal backgrounds. For the vast majority of people this was just much-appreciated supplementary income, or a way to barter for otherwise unobtainable necessities. The director of a school, for example, when admonished by the factory newspaper for neglecting his duties in favor of unspecified activities at the markets, allegedly told the correspondent, "Ah, but my salary is so low."[72]

In the acquisition and resale of scarce items, some people went to great lengths. The newspaper carried a story on Guzeeva, the wife of a worker of the Magnitogorsk railroad depot, who "used her husband's right to free transport and, together with her friend Kozhevnikova, traveled to the Donbas, to Rostov, and to the gold mines of the Kucharskii region. There she purchased fabrics, shoes, winter and semi-seasonal overcoats, and butter," all of which, we are told, she "resold at the market in Magnitogorsk, and at home in the barracks." Guzeeva evidently realized a handsome profit: the overcoats she picked up for 200 rubles during her travels fetched more than 500 rubles in Magnitogorsk. Her traveling came to an end; she was caught and sentenced to five years with confiscation of all property (otherwise we could not have heard her story). Others less brazen, however, might well have read this story with knowing smiles.[73]

Most everyone who traveled outside the city took advantage of the opportunity to purchase whatever they could and bring it back to Magnitogorsk, sometimes for personal use, sometimes for friends, and often for resale, or at least barter.[74] Some were fortunate enough to be sent on state-paid business trips.[75] Others foraged in search of usable and resalable items on their own. One case reported in the newspaper involved some workers from the rolling mill shop who drove out to a nearby agricultural district with a supply of industrial goods and exchanged them for flour and grain, which they brought back to Magnitogorsk and sold, turning a nice profit.[76]

Ironically, the city's official trading organizations were forced to do the same. In 1936 the newspaper revealed that the nearby Kyshtym pasta factory had informed Magnittorg that it was not able to fill its order for macaroni (for reasons not stated). Magnittorg was chastized for being slow to locate a new supplier of the badly needed product, and the city suffered what were called "interruptions" (*pereboi*) in the supply of pasta. Meanwhile, agents of ORS and Magnittorg were dispatched to Moscow, Leningrad, and other large cities to conclude new long-term agreements with more reliable suppliers, and to purchase goods for immediate resale in Magnitogorsk.[77]

Alongside and even within the state supply network, then, other informal distribution networks arose, comprised of private "middlemen" and even state agents performing their regular jobs. Such a state of affairs was even more true of the metallurgical complex, where scarce resources were concentrated. The newspaper accused the coke shop construction agency of bartering scarce construction materials with a nearby state farm for food. The agency's boss, Fomenko, was said to have wide experience in such matters. Previously as head of blast furnace construction, he had allegedly set up his own de facto "department store."[78]

Not all the goods being resold in Magnitogorsk had been purchased; many were stolen. "The single flourishing branch of criminal activity is theft," revealed the newspaper. "People steal fur coats, suits, and shoes from apartments, crawl their way into stores, break into shops. Every day in the city two to three thefts take place."[79] Much of the stolen property made its way to the markets, where the police were of course on the lookout for it.[80] The newspaper alleged once again that escapees from the local corrective labor colony and from other colonies, such as the one in Zlatoust, perpetrated almost all the petty theft.[81] But many more people than a handful of escaped convicts were engaged in stealing.

Theft from individuals was but one form of what appears to have been widespread pilfering in the new society. Far more serious from the regime's standpoint was the theft of what was called "socialist," or state, property from institutions.[82] This species of theft was evidently extensive. According to Moshe Lewin, who lived in the Urals during World War II, the abbreviation ORS, which officially stood for Department of Workers' Supply, colloquially signified either "dress yourself first" (*odevai, ranshe, sebia*), or "what's left over to the working white-collar employees" (*ostalnoe rabochim sluzhashchim*)—that is, to the ORS staff.[83]

Money, too, was stolen from the state, sometimes in hefty quantities. The dining halls, which handled large amounts of cash, were particularly susceptible to theft. Charges were brought against one Khvorostinskii, from dining hall no. 6, who was accused of stealing 10,000 rubles and disappearing. A similar case from dining hall no. 21 netted 6,500 rubles.[84] Back before the October revolution, it had been thought in Russia and elsewhere that theft might well disappear with the advent of socialism. Tony Garnier, a French socialist known for the first comprehensive design for a modern industrial city (exhibited in 1904, published in 1917), deliberately excluded law courts and a police force. When asked why, he is said to have replied that in the new society, "as capitalism would be suppressed, there would be no swindlers, robbers, or murderers."[85] Garnier was proven wrong—as the authorities in Magnitogorsk's real-life laboratory could have told him.

Sometimes the theft of state-owned property was not a means but a cover for profitable resale. State-dispensed linen turned in to be washed at the public bath-laundry of the Kirov district, for example, was said to have been sold and then reported stolen by employees—a roundabout way of certifying that state stores must not have stocked much linen.[86] And that was the point. People stole or resold needed goods that were otherwise unobtainable. Surveys taken decades later would show that most citizens of the USSR made a distinction between stealing from individuals and stealing from the state, regarding only the former as morally wrong.[87] From his time in the Urals Lewin also recalled the proverb, "He who does not steal robs his family."

The "bazaaring" (*razbazarivanie*), as it was known, of state linen and similar items was small change compared with some of the transactions involving industrial supplies, whether removed bit by bit over the long haul, or grabbed in one swoop.[88] Facilitating industrial larceny, there were at first few enclosed storage facilities and no fences around the sprawling industrial territory, which was guarded by armed soldiers and unarmed Komsomol volunteers.[89] Beginning in 1932, passes were required to enter factory areas, but only in 1936 did construction *begin* on a fence around the steel plant.

Taking advantage of this situation, the chairman of a low-priority collective farm in nearby Bashkiriia periodically visited Magnitogorsk in search of scarce equipment, loading up his truck and driving off in broad daylight with whatever equipment he could "find." Back at the collective farm he would then concoct the necessary paperwork to make it seem as if the equipment had been legally obtained through state supply channels. "In two years," the newspaper reported incredulously, "no one from the Magnitogorsk metallurgical complex noticed the missing motors and other equipment." This culprit was caught and sentenced to ten years. But what of others?[90]

To deter such activity, the Soviet government had promulgated the infamous "law on the strengthening of societal (socialist) property," which became known as the law of seven-eighths after the day it was issued (7 August 1932). For the theft of what was interchangeably called societal and socialist property, the law specified "the supreme measure [*vysshaia mera*] of social defense" (execution by shooting—*vysshka*, in slang), with confiscation of all personal property. In extenuating circumstances sentences were to be commuted to five to ten years' deprivation of freedom, with confiscation of all property.[91] Enforcement was highly selective. But the severe law could come down on one's head at any moment.[92]

Draconian as its provisions were, the seven-eighths law was in a certain sense just a concise statement of the new property relations.[93] In the explanatory preamble, it was remarked that "the Central Executive Committee and the Soviet of People's Commissars consider societal [*obshchestvennaia*] property (state, collective farm, and cooperative) to be the foundation of the Soviet system." Societal property, no less than private property under a capitalist system, was deemed "sacred and inviolable," requiring the state's protection. When it came to socialist trade, however, protection of societal property was no mean feat. Even allowing that a good many, perhaps the overwhelming majority, of trade infractions went unnoticed or unreported, the need to investigate constantly and to prosecute those who were caught increased the already formidable administrative burden of feeding and clothing the population.

Socialist trade was a veritable school for insider theft. One of the myriad tricks involved charging customers a bit more for goods than the official price in an effort to increase income surreptitiously or guard against potential losses.[94] The newspaper reported one especially profitable variant of generating extra revenues that involved taking advantage of the bottle-return policy. A local correspondent claimed to have been startled to learn that none other than the famed Georgian Borzhomi-brand mineral water was being sold in Magnitogorsk stores. It was then discovered, however, that the bottles labeled "Borzhomi" were filled with tap water, which the store sold at the nifty price legally established for the fine mineral water.[95]

Sales personnel and store managers could usually pocket the difference between the specified price and the one charged, or take home the "surplus" goods created by the extra revenues.[96] Such added margins, which ranged from a few rubles to a few hundred,[97] were not always easy to spot despite the system of "hard" prices. Prices for many state goods took into account the distance over which they were transported and thus were not the same as in other cities closer to the goods' origin. As explained in the factory newspaper, the USSR was divided into radia (*poiasy*), and Magnitogorsk was in the third radius for bread, meat, sausage, and sugar, but the fourth for fish. A full list of local prices for these items accompanied the explanation, but it was confusing all the same.[98]

Alongside padded price margins, the Magnitogorsk newspaper spotlighted another connivance that seems to have been particularly common. In one version, a customer paid a store cashier three rubles, then proceeded to the salesclerk to exchange the receipt for three rubles' worth of goods. Instead, her friend, working as a salesclerk, handed her 100 to 200 rubles' worth of merchandise.[99] In another variant, a woman simply walked up to the goods counter without having paid even a nominal amount, and picked up 105 rubles' worth of goods from the saleswoman. The two women involved in the exchange were sisters.[100]

Goods pilfered in this manner from stores were almost always intended for resale, and often involved some kind of "partnership." A man who worked in a grocery store and took home candy without paying, for example, enlisted an acquaintance of his to operate a makeshift stall in the northern outskirts of town where the candy was resold for personal profit.[101] It might be thought that few people could have been so brash as to sell stolen goods so openly, but supply personnel often showed exceptional impudence.[102]

Sales personnel soon learned that it was safest to skim off goods before they went on sale, by putting them aside. An inventory of goods found "under the counter" at one store, as reported by the newspaper, included

> two overcoats (a child's and woman's) two pieces of knit fabric, a child's jumper, a man's suit, two pairs of children's underwear, one child's dress, a man's shirt, four pairs of rubber shoes, one pair of tarpaulin boots, two pairs of leather shoes, two pairs of men's shoes, and fifteen pairs of galoshes, including three pairs of the same size.[103]

The purpose behind these stashes was not in doubt. Letters to the newspaper told of many instances when "there was a lengthy queue, and the salesclerk handed bread to friends out the back door." The newspaper printed such letters regularly, heightening the perception that such actions were widespread.[104]

The replacement of the "natural" economy of distribution, or rationing, with a noncapitalist system of trade turned out to be full of surprises, many of them unpleasant. These included exasperating queues, profiteering, and rampant theft. It did not take a person employed in socialist trade very long to decipher the ins and outs of a situation of perpetual scarcity.[105] There were some extremely "enterprising" people in the city's trade network, although their initiative and talent in working the extremely pliable system for personal gain involved a great deal of deception. In such circumstances, how could the state watch over its inventories?

DEMONSTRATION TRIALS, MASS CONTROL, AND SOCIAL JUSTICE

Beginning in 1930, the so-called people's court (narodnyi sud) became the basic element in the Soviet judiciary, handling both criminal and civil cases. At least one people's court was established in every raion of an oblast.[106] Above the people's court stood the oblast court, responsible for appeals from the people's court and cases deemed serious. The oblast court also oversaw the operation of the people's courts. Above the oblast courts stood the republic-level Supreme Court and then the all-union Supreme Court. (Special courts existed for the railways and waterways, while the People's Commissariat of Internal Affairs, or NKVD, charged with investigating and prosecuting state crimes, had its own special judicial board.) The judges of the people's court, who were elected, had complete authority to pass judgment as they saw fit, although technically they were assisted by two so-called people's assessors (temporary, rotating personnel without legal backgrounds on loan from enterprises). In addition to verdicts, judges were responsible for the popular image of the court and the legal edification of the public.[107]

According to the prevailing notions of socialist justice, the entire socialist court system was supposed to serve an educational function, especially trials—and none more so than the so-called demonstration trial.[108] A demonstration trial differed from a regular trial only in that it was organized to allow as many people as possible to attend and therefore took place in a large public hall, such as the city circus, rather than the smaller confines of the court building. A number of demonstration trials were held after the work day had ended. One evening proceeding in 1938 in which the defendant, Cherniovanenko, was an employee of the dining hall trust was heard in that organization's club. It was said to have attracted 400 spectators in a hall with seating for 150.[109]

As this example shows, the circus was not the only site for such proceedings. During the first five months of 1933, for example, seven demonstration trials were held in the various industrial clubs and the city cinema, Magnit. In a report prepared by City Procurator B. Krepyshev for City Party Secretary Spirov, attendance at these hearings was said to vary from 1,000, for a case involving six people accused of embezzling 18,000 rubles' worth of goods from the milk trust, to 2,500 for a case involving nineteen supply employees accused of having caused a shortfall of 82,000 rubles. True to the demonstrative nature of the trials, death sentences were handed out for at least one of the accused in each case.[110] The "moral" of each production, moreover, was almost always reinforced through media publicity.

Coverage in the city newspaper of the problems surrounding supply reflected a legitimate anxiety on the part of the authorities as well as an apparent curiosity of the newspaper correspondents and editors. And no wonder. One cashier for the hairdressers' artel, accused of stealing more than 3,000 rubles from the hair salon's revenues, was said to have remarked at her demonstration trial: "I needed the money to be able to live the beautiful life [*zhit krasivo*]."[111]

Whether it was acceptable under socialism to live the beautiful life constituted a serious question for contemporaries and was certainly part of the fascination with such trials that came through in the newspaper's reporting. Yet although newspaper reports of theft in socialist trade sometimes betrayed a degree of wistful fascination, they were published for didactic purposes. A story of a group of bookkeepers in the open-hearth shop, for example, related that by padding the payroll, the group managed during the course of a year to swindle the state out of 200,000 rubles. Few details were offered about who they were or how they did it. But such insinuations, which were extended to other shops, conveniently served to explain such highly unpopular problems as delays in the payment of wages.[112] Behind "the circus," in other words, stood the newspaper. The spectators were not only those on the wooden benches but the entire literate public.

Within a month of Industry Commissar Ordzhonikidze's 1933 visit to Magnitogorsk, a widely publicized trial presided over by the Magnitogorsk raion people's court took place. Among the defendants were Bondarev, the chief of ORS, his deputy Ershov, and Ershov's deputy, Sikharulidze, said to be notorious for his drinking bouts and debauchery. In all, some twenty supply officials were in the block, including the heads of most of the supply organization's warehouses. The charge was embezzlement. For a period of fifty days, from 1 July through 20 August, Magnitogorsk workers were said to have experienced a shortfall of 700 tons of bread, or about 15,000 kilograms per day. Unspecified "missing" quantities of sugar, meat, and vegetables were also discovered. The city newspaper let it be known that admission to the circus for the trial of these "speculators" and "thieves" was free.[113]

The Magnitogorsk procuracy and control commission (GorKK) were accused of having protected these thieves, so the criminal investigation was taken over by a brigade from the Central Control Commission, which brought along a correspondent for *Pravda* who provided a national spotlight. ORS was said to have suffered a financial loss (*ubytok*) of 903,000 rubles, of which 400,000 was said to represent missing inventory (the latter number was subsequently raised to 550,000). "Not a single trading unit," the correspondent wrote, "has been without an incident of embezzlement, either in the past or present." Of the eighty-seven embezzlers identified up to that point, thirty were said to be party members. In some cases Communists had organized the theft of entire deliveries. "People stole with the certainty that they would not be punished," *Pravda* reported. "They did not even consider it necessary to cover their tracks." Store no. 18 was said to carry the special designation of being the place that dispensed goods to "favored clientele" (*po blatu*). Documents were also found detailing the home delivery of a suckling pig to the wife of ORS's deputy chief.[114]

Bondarev was relieved of his post and expelled from the party, and much of the high-level staff of ORS was decimated.[115] By contrast, Narpit, the city's dining hall trust, although also technically responsible for feeding the population, did not suffer nearly as badly. It was reported that Pastukhov, the chief of Narpit, had pointed out the irregularities and struggled to fight them before the investigation began. Despite his high position in the city supply network, he was not charged. But N. Kirishkova, party secretary of Narpit, was given a "severe party reprimand" for her supposed "Nepman tendency." Narpit had achieved an annual "profit" of 1.8 million rubles, against a "plan" anticipating only 463,000 rubles.[116]

The great ORS trial under the big top lasted more than a month, and at the end Bondarev was sentenced to death. It was further reported that in connection with the supply deficiencies, Myshkin, director of the Magnitogorsk Works, Spirov, secretary of the city party committee, Krepyshev, city procurator, and A. Savelev, chairman of the city party control commission—in a word, the entire local leadership—were also given party reprimands. They were all presently relieved of their duties. None of them had come up in the first newspaper reports of either the investigation or the trial.[117]

Bondarev's expulsion and conviction, along with the reprimands and removal of high officials, coincided with Beso Lominadze's assumption of control over the city party committee and Avraamii Zaveniagin's over the factory. Marking a transition in the local leadership, the trial served as an opportunity to affix blame for the city's lamentable living conditions on the outgoing leaders.[118] Soviet power was implicitly absolved from its investment policies neglecting consumer goods, and the inherent shortcomings in the socialist municipal economy were passed over. As *Pravda* wrote in a simple formula, "thieves, swindlers, embezzlers, and plunders of socialist property had established a comfortable nest in Magnitogorsk's ORS."[119]

But the investigation had uncovered the curious circumstance whereby ORS, despite being responsible for supplying the whole city, had no money. ORS management was reduced to selling some goods at "speculative prices" to assemble working capital. And whatever agency or enterprise could put up the money to pay for a shipment acquired the right to distribute those goods exclusively to its workers.[120] Instead of considering such a situation as mitigating for the ORS management, however, the opposite conclusion was reached. Less than one year after the 1933 ORS trial, little had apparently changed—and the same scapegoat was found: the ORS leadership was once again given reprimands and replaced, along with the director of the local bread factory, and then put under criminal investigation.[121] Each year, in fact, the story was the same.[122] Supply a problem? Arrest some supply officials and organize a resounding demonstration trial, which would invariably be heralded as a "big lesson" for the chiefs of city trade.[123]

Repeatedly, the newspaper suggested that the city's trading apparatus was "polluted" by degenerate elements, former Nepmen and other "parasites," and that these devious individuals were responsible for the constant shortages and other problems. Anonymous denunciations of "embezzling" store managers, signed simply "salesperson," were continually published in the newspaper for all to read.[124] Periodic "purges" of sales personnel lent concrete substance to the accusations.[125] "Let the enemies of the people who stand behind Soviet sales counters know that the proletarian court will be merciless!" the newspaper foamed, demanding the eradication of the "rotten liberal" attitude supposedly prevalent in trade supervisory circles.[126]

Supply issues already occupied a sizable amount of space in the newspaper when in 1936—the year of the great campaigns (including Stakhanovism in industry)—accounts of trade-related improprieties increased markedly. In the first eight months of 1936, thirty cases of insider theft (*raskhishchenie*) in the city's trade organizations were said to have been uncovered, with a total loss of inventory valued at 100,000 rubles. Examples were made of several people. The impression was given that not just publicity but police activity had intensified.[127]

Whatever the relationship between police activity and newspaper reports of police activity, the statistics on insider theft require clarification. When the newspaper wrote of embezzlement it meant all losses, not just those attributable to theft. In the case of one store manager who was tried for four months' worth of missing goods valued at 16,800 rubles, the accused insisted that he stole nothing but admitted that he did not know where the goods and money had gone. During the trial it was revealed that neither inventory nor accounting were practiced in the store, and that spoilage was high, including almost 2,000 rubles' worth of meat. The manager, however, was convicted not of mismanagement but of peculation (*rastrata*).[128]

Anything less than 100 percent accounting of all items—regardless of the circumstances—could be considered embezzlement, meaning that there was a huge number of potential criminals available for "mobilization."[129] There were some feeble attempts to instill in trade personnel a sense of service, such as the campaign to single out exemplary workers (*otlichniki*) who were commended for getting to know the needs of their customers. But customers needed goods that were very scarce, and in this matter sales personnel had little to offer aside from favoritism. As for the image of store managers, they were accused of everything under the sun, including trying to cover up their misdeeds by attributing missing inventory to the theft of the employees who worked under them.[130] Not surprisingly, trade personnel appear to have been highly unpopular.[131]

The year 1936 began what turned out to be three banner years for public trials involving supply officials. In an April 1937 trial that lasted fifteen days, Pestrov, the chief of the fence building trust, was said to have built three fences (for the factory, hospital, and corrective labor colony) at a cost more than twice the budget. The newspaper further reported that the fence building trust was missing 40,000 rubles' worth of materials, and that Pestrov had delivered construction materials to a nearby Machine Tractor Station for which he received an automobile that he later sold to another state agency (for 15,000 rubles), keeping the money for himself. He was also accused of having sold construction materials to people building individual homes, recorded the materials on the books of fence construction, and then pocketed the payments.[132]

Although he refused to admit his guilt, Pestrov was "sentenced to the highest form of punishment, shooting, with confiscation of all property." His several codefendants received lesser, if still severe, sentences, and the newspaper reported that others implicated in the case would be tried in the near future.[133] No public trial of any of these lesser officials was ever reported, however. Instead, seven months later, a trial of the chief of the powerful KBU, Lukashevich, was publicly held after a long press campaign vilified him.

Lukashevich was accused of diverting construction materials to the building of his own house, setting up his own garden at the expense of the factory, and awarding bonuses to himself—all practices that anyone in a management position was likely to have engaged in. John Scott, who appears to have faithfully rendered the state's version of the case, wrote that "not satisfied with his two-room apartment," Lukashevich "built himself a house. . . . When he moved in, he was able to furnish the five large rooms with silk hangings, a grand piano, and other luxuries. Then he began riding around in a motor car, when it was well known that his organization had none." Scott added that Lukashevich paid bribes to subordinates to keep them quiet.[134]

Presided over by the Cheliabinsk oblast court, the trial, at which more than forty witnesses testified and many internal memoranda were introduced as evidence, lasted six days. For those who could not attend, the most important moments were broadcast over the radio. Lukashevich, said to have admitted his guilt only on the last day, was sentenced to eight years' loss of freedom.[135] Whether he really admitted his guilt (perhaps in exchange for a waiver of the death penalty or to protect his family), Lukashevich became a scapegoat offered up for the disaster of individual home construction and workers' housing in general. What effect his sentencing could have had on the problems of the city's economy was hard to say. But one thing was clear: "the circus" played a large role in defining the city's socialist economy and popular attitudes.

Reports of demonstration trials at the circus and elsewhere rarely mentioned the reaction of the audience, but such events would not have been complete without the participation of the masses. In fact, the "activism" of the masses in matters of trade and supply began even before trials, with the promotion of "suggestions" (*predlozheniia*) for improving trade.[136] These formed part of what was called "mass control," the socialist answer to the "control" exercised in capitalist society largely by the market mechanism.

After the demonstration trial perhaps the most widespread method of mass control was the consumer conference, at which irate consumers angrily criticized officials of the city's trade network and demanded that stores adhere to the so-called assortment minimum. The law on the assortment minimum, introduced in 1936, required all stores to maintain in stock at all times the full range of specified products that the store traded in. Heralded as a lever to force trade officials and employees to perform their jobs better, the law was to be enforced by inspections. Managers were not going to be able to withhold goods for themselves, relatives, and friends any longer. Public meetings on the law were given maximum coverage in the newspaper, putting considerable pressure on store managers and trade officials, who tried to fight off the scrutiny and mass pressure.

In response to a stormy meeting in the Fourteenth Sector in March 1936—which attracted almost two hundred angry consumers who complained that stores were violating the assortment minimum—one hundred trade representatives and store managers hurriedly held a countermeeting a few days later.[137] But in a similar lynch-mob atmosphere, trade officials were forced to admit that of the city's thirty-one trading entities, only five had fulfilled their plans, and that none of the larger, more important stores was among the five successes. Stefanovich, the director of Magnittorg, nonetheless tried to defend trade officials.

He explained that after a store manager heard of an impending investigation to check the store's assortment, he or she would scramble to have special goods brought in so the store could pass the test. When consumers spotted these scarce goods they naturally sought to purchase them. But if the manager allowed the goods to be sold, the items would sell out well before the inspector arrived to verify the store's compliance with the assortment minimum. Unfortunately for Stefanovich, this kind of straight talk was easily dismissed as the sophistry of the class enemy.[138] The effect of the assortment minimum law became not the encouragement of managers to stock scarce goods in order that they be sold but the stocking of goods temporarily to satisfy the inspectors. This logical response on the part of managers to the difficult situation they were placed in by the law only increased consumer dissatisfaction.

Perhaps the assortment minimum law, which was accompanied by all the misinformation and hatred that local propagandists could muster, was a cynical ploy designed to deflect blame for supply problems from Bolshevik policies onto expendable trade officials. More likely, it was sincere. Cynical or not, however, deflecting blame and sacrificing managers was precisely what the law achieved, in the process becoming, through the newspaper, an extension of the mass control that periodically had recourse to the circus. The pressure could be stepped up, as it was in 1937, but the underlying approach grew out of the logic and consequences of suppressing capitalism and creating a socialist municipal economy.

The state monopoly that helped perpetuate the scarcity of almost everything meant that consumers could not use their pocketbooks to express satisfaction or dissatisfaction with a particular store. How, then, could "socialism" address, or appear to be addressing, customers' grievances? The consumer conference was one way; the complaint book, another.

Each store had a notebook in which customers could express themselves. The store's management was compelled to respond in writing to any complaints or suggestions raised by customers and to indicate what concrete measures would be taken. This practice was reminiscent of the procedures at the circus trials: accuse and punish targeted individuals. The newspaper published the following excerpts from the complaint book of a store manager named Zhukov:

[Compl.]   I consider it an outrage when the customer wants to buy a box of matches [which cost one kopeck] and the cashier refuses to give change from a ruble, even though she has plenty of change.

[Resp.]   I won't answer the complaint since the complainer does not give an address.

[Compl.]   It is essential to have sausage for sale since it is required by the law on the assortment minimum.

[Resp.]   If sausage is available from the warehouse, we have it; if there is none there, we have none.

[Compl.]   I consider it totally inappropriate that I came to buy butter and they gave it to me with no wrapping or paper.

[Resp.]   I consider the complaint just, but the store has no paper.[139]

Zhukov wrote an answer beside every complaint registered; similar inquiries into other complaint books showed that complaints almost always went unanswered.[140] But instead of applauding Zhukov for responding to complaints and for doing so reasonably and without malice, the newspaper upbraided him for his dismissive attitude toward customers.

The complaint book both testified to and worsened the bitter relations between customers and store managers and sales help, a situation that the newspaper was eager to perpetuate. Indeed, dissatisfied customers were not limited to the complaint books in stores but could also write to the citywide "complaint book," that is, the local newspaper. Letters from dissatisfied shoppers were frequently published in which the letter writers complained that they could not buy what they wanted, that they had been rudely treated by sales personnel, that such and such a store was in violation of the law on the assortment minimum, and so on. Many of the letters, such as one from a certain Kostyrev, ended with the universal suggestion for solving all problems: "the problem will be solved only when the prosecutor intervenes."[141]

In this vein, the newspaper promoted the notion that "the shelves of our stores are frequently empty while the warehouses are full." One of the articles that conveyed this idea also revealed the contradictory information that at the current moment there was no pasta, tea, vegetables, or salt in any city warehouse.[142] In subsequent reports, the newspaper was evidently more careful not to undermine the image of well-stocked warehouses, remaining silent about warehouse inventories. But the numerous stories about the general inability of the city's trade organizations to secure goods by contract with suppliers served as indirect reminders that the store shelves were empty because the warehouses were empty.

Of course, sometimes when shelves were empty there really were goods languishing in the warehouse. For example, fifty-two tons of fish arrived in the city during the summer of 1936, but the fish were already starting to grow moldy when they arrived. A doctor who inspected the moldy fish ordered that they be offered for sale immediately, before they all went bad. The trade organizations, however, decided not to sell the partially rotten fish but instead to seek redress with the supplier. The supplier held firm, claiming that any spoilage was the fault of the addressee. Meanwhile, the fish, 120,000 rubles' worth, were lying on the ground in the warehouse.[143]

With the example of the fish, the newspaper raised the theme of empty shelves in the face of overflowing warehouses to a "higher level," in the popular phrase, by accusing the trade organizations—specifically, the food department of Magnittorg (headed by Shukin) and the ORS (headed by Smirkin)—of sabotage. Furthermore, in addition to "fresh" fish, the warehouses were said to be bursting with sour cream, preserves, and tomato paste, yet "the trading organizations don't want to trade because, in the opinion of their leaders, it is disadvantageous to deal in such products. They don't move well."[144] By this logic, of course, it could not have been advantageous to the trade organizations to trade in rotten fish, which people would not buy but for which officials in the organizations would be held fully accountable.

There *were* numerous items languishing untouched in the city's stores which the trade organizations had been compelled to purchase from suppliers and which were a financial burden on the organizations; sour cream, preserves, and tomato paste, however, were not likely to be among them. What is more, the newspaper was not above reporting that the warehouse contained large quantities of certain items without explaining that this was a consequence of having just received a shipment. All of this could be seen as secondary to the importance of showing "vigilance" when "threatened" by "saboteurs."

The more the newspaper sought to electrify the atmosphere, however, the more information it provided—until it worked itself into such a frenzy that it began to undermine its own mandate to promote an image of the superiority of socialism. "Filth, queues, rude sales help, the absence of window or other displays, scandalous breeches of the assortment minimum," wrote the newspaper, "all these outrages can be found in almost every store in Magnitogorsk."[145] According to the official record, it was a dismal story. But when examining the system of socialist trade in Magnitogorsk, it is important to keep in mind that even well-financed and high-priority enterprises suffered from a lack of adequate transport, while the lowly trade network possessed just a few dozen horses and a handful of vehicles to distribute goods throughout the entire city.[146] High turnover among trade personnel also took its toll.[147]

Underlying these causes were the many unanticipated complexities involved in trade and supply that threw the local authorities for a loss. "About the fact that trade is not handled well in Magnitogorsk we have written more than once," lectured the newspaper. "But even after the signals from the newspaper, no observable changes in the work of the stores has followed."[148] All the while, Magnitogorsk courts were choking with cases involving trade employees.[149]

Prosecutions for speculation, by contrast, do not seem to have been particularly frequent.[150] Around mid-1936, however, a fierce campaign against that vice was also launched (for which the historian must be grateful), showing the familiar patterns, and limitations, of mass control. To kick off the campaign, a special meeting of trade officials and representatives of the militia and procurator's office was held. One official pointed out that the nature of speculation in the city had changed. "Before, people would buy products in other cities and bring them to Magnitogorsk for resale," he was quoted as having remarked. "Now people are buying goods right in Magnitogorsk itself and reselling them at the market."[151] To combat such activities, four recommendations were put forward: requiring sellers at the markets to submit to the management a prior list of items (*sbor*) to be sold and a valid passport with an authorized place of residence; having Magnittorg improve its secondhand retail shop and open up its own buying outlet; forming a permanent staff of market inspectors; and organizing more demonstration trials.

Of the proposed measures, the trials received the most coverage, and the number of arrests for speculation reportedly underwent a dramatic increase.[152] In trials before large audiences, furthermore, almost no one was acquitted. Few sentences were for less than five years, and ten-year sentences, plus another three or five years disfranchisement, were not uncommon for "ringleaders."[153] Despite such stiff sentences and the continued surveillance at the market, however, repeated attempts to curtail speculation met with little success.

Individuals who recognized opportunities to make something extra were able to respond creatively to police interventions, and to turn what looked like initial defeat into new winning strategies. Given the poor selection of clothes available in state stores, for example, fabric with which people could make their own clothes (or pay someone to do so) became exceedingly valuable. Not long after going on sale in state stores, fabric would frequently appear at the markets, where it was resold for very high prices. The city authorities decided to intervene and began regular, surprise raids at the markets in search of store-bought fabric. Much fabric was confiscated. Arrests were made. But the newspaper had to admit that once it became dangerous to trade in fabric, people instead used the fabric to make clothing at home, which could be sold more easily.[154]

The battle to eradicate speculation revealed a clash of worldviews. Characteristically, the announcement in the Magnitogorsk newspaper of the opening of a "collective farmers" market back in 1932 (during rationing) did not refer to the activities expected to take place there as "trade" (*torgovlia*). Engaging in tortuous verbal gyrations to announce the advent of trade without using the word, the newspaper devoted the better part of the announcement to a discussion of "speculation," the need to combat speculative practices, the supposed "Nepman" atmosphere in supply institutions, and the social importance of inspections and raids.[155] Four years later, the newspaper was still continuously reviling the "bazaar" as a source of hooliganism, fighting, unsanitary muck, and speculation.[156]

By contrast, a satire that appeared in the factory newspaper offered a glimpse into the everyday language of slang expressions for the entrenched practices that the authorities condemned as speculation. "There are people about whom others speak with a touch of envy: 'Yeah, he knows how to live,'" wrote the author of the satire, calling such a person Lovkach ("the dodger"), who, it was imagined, did not mind showing off his special knack. When asked, for example, where he procured (*dostal*) his fancy new suit, Lovkach responds, "Me? I got it by using pull [*po blatu*]. If you want, I can let you have it [*mogu tebe ustupit*].'" Of course, Lovkach names a sum "three times what he paid," with the understanding that he could easily and inexpensively obtain another suit for himself, despite their status as extremely scarce items (*ostrodefitsity*). The author went on to name several real-life Lovkaches, the rare goods they somehow managed to obtain for resale, and the profit they realized, even ridiculing those who settled for less than the "market" price. "No one views this kind of thing as speculation!" fumed the satirist. "No, it is as if it were just the normal order of things."[157]

Commensurate with, and an obvious complement to, the city newspaper's thunderous yet impotent anti-speculation campaign, an attempt was made to glamorize the socialist trade network. Advertisements appeared on the back page of the daily newspaper showing highly desirable items for sale in what looked like well-outfitted stores. To render these messages concrete, photographs of happy workers and their wives, dressed in new clothes and loaded down with bundles, were also published. "A worker of the mechanical workshop of the rolling shop, Andreiashin, and his wife, Marusa," read the caption beneath one photograph, "purchased 1,300 rubles' worth of goods in the new department store: an overcoat, a suit, three pairs of shoes, some women's blouses, a few pairs of men's underwear, bed linen, two pairs of gloves, etc."[158] The ability of the "proletariat" to acquire high-fashion goods had become an event to be celebrated.

As with the anti-speculation campaign, however, the message of such representations was not altogether straightforward. The newspaper did not reveal the prices for any of the items, their general availability, or the income of the Andreiashin family and its relation to the norm. The photograph conveyed an image of status and the link between status and patterns of consumption, yet such enhanced status did not derive from, but in fact permitted, conspicuous consumption. Everyone in the city knew that purchases of the most coveted items in the department store were possible only with official authorization. Moreover, as the newspaper reported, many hard-to-obtain goods were sold directly in factory shops.[159] Pushed to its logical conclusion, the photograph of a "proletarian" acquiring scarce goods underscored the exclusion of the majority from what might be called the "dream worlds" of socialism.[160]

Even if their import was perhaps contradictory, however, such photographs testified that "standard of living" notions constituted an important category used by the Soviet regime to demonstrate the supposed material advantages of life under socialism. Socialism was being built, according to the official ideology, precisely to attain the higher level of abundance that capitalism with all its contradictions was said to be incapable of reaching.[161] In making such comparisons the regime was flirting with danger, but the regime shielded itself with censorship. A Soviet worker's lot could be compared only with the gloomy image of the masses living under capitalism, and with that of his or her undeniably downtrodden prerevolutionary counterpart.[162] "Each month I can buy what I need," one Magnitogorsk worker was quoted as saying in response to questions about his family budget. "We are pleased with the wise decisions of the party and government."[163]

But the people of Magnitogorsk observed with their own eyes the jarring discrepancies between the low "fixed" prices at the often pitifully stocked state stores and the high "real" prices at the plentifully supplied open market. Because of a general acceptance of the superiority of socialism to capitalism (see chapter 5), most urban inhabitants no doubt failed to comprehend the eloquent commentary on the city's state-run economy spoken by this state of affairs. But no amount of dialectics could completely wipe away what they knew to be true from their own daily experience: everything was scarce. Throughout the decade, to take only the example of food, except for a brief period every autumn fruit and vegetables were not plentiful.[164] Meat and milk were also periodically difficult to obtain.[165] And even bread became a problematic acquisition after the bad harvest of 1936.[166]

In recognition of these deficiencies and to prevent hoarding, limits were imposed on the amount of certain items that could be purchased at any one time in state stores, a form of rationing without the coupons. According to the factory newspaper, in 1935 the following limits were in force: meat and sausage, two kilos; fish, three kilos; sugar, two kilos; butter, 500 grams. Shoppers could theoretically make a purchase and get back in line, hoping to get a different salesperson. And if they encountered resistance, they could simply repeat their purchase by waiting in the queue at another store. But the limits on quantity lengthened the time goods were on sale, and thus perhaps widened the circle of those able to buy them directly from the state stores.[167]

Because of the chronic scarcity, such purchase limitations and rationing seem to have been widely appreciated, according to people who lived through the 1930s and were interviewed many years later. As they explained it, rationing implied not equal access to goods but access for all nonetheless. And any differentiation was based on ostensibly meritocratic criteria (labor skills and performance). True, some stores carried goods that could not be purchased no matter how much money the client had. But here too the criteria of "reward" were ostensibly labor performance and patriotic dedication to the cause, while everyone was to be taken care of at a basic level. Underlying rationing and purchase limitations, in other words, was a popular expectation of social justice, an expectation that the regime encouraged and in its own way tried to meet, in the state stores with low fixed prices as well as in the campaigns against embezzlement and speculation.[168]

In the society forming in Magnitogorsk, "food conditions were the subject of constant discussion," according to John Scott, whose depiction of "a day in Magnitogorsk" is itself devoted in large part to questions of food and supplies. While generally freewheeling, these heartfelt discussions, Scott attested, were usually resolved in a flurry of reassurances about the country's achievements and its even brighter future. This was understandable enough given the restrictions on travel abroad and the conjunction of the Great Depression with the great socialist construction, of which Magnitogorsk was the quintessential example.[169] More remarkable than the acceptance of sacrifice in these refrains was the assumption that the government had a duty to provide for the people—an assumption that was revealed in the fervor that its violation engendered.

In Magnitogorsk, a belief in social justice, and of the government's duty to ensure it, appear to have been pervasive. It was after all a socialist, not a capitalist, city. Ultimately, that promise of social justice, and not just a desire for momentary diversion, was what brought the inhabitants of Magnitogorsk to the circus for demonstration trials and made them receptive to the calls to exercise mass control. Conniving as many people proved to be, most appear to have made subtle distinctions regarding the morality of various illegal actions. Struggling to get away with whatever they could, they still evidently believed that no one should have an "unfair" advantage.

SOCIALISM AND THE MARKET

Often lamenting the size of the harvests provided by the region's collectivized agriculture, the Magnitogorsk newspaper also justifiably cursed the inept organization of processed food distribution within the city. When it came to bread, for example, the paper pointed out that "the system of payment for distributors is such that the distributor suffers a loss if he supplies stores with small quantities of bread." As a result, distributors "either refuse to supply a given store or require the store manager to take in gigantic quantities, two to three times more than the store could sell." Here was yet another unforeseen complication of socialist trade, with far-ranging consequences. The paper noted that it was nearly impossible for stores or shoppers to predict when deliveries might be made.[170]

Behind the difficulties encountered in mounting a reliable distribution network lay the decision to organize food processing in a so-called food complex (*pishchevoi kombinat*). Rather than opening, say, several small bakeries or butcheries placed throughout the city where people lived—to say nothing of allowing individuals to open up their own establishments[171]—the food complex was modelled after the Metallurgical Works. Its "shops," just like those of the steel complex, were the size of whole factories and referred to as such: the flour mill, the bread factory, the beverage factory, the sausage factory, the milk factory, the factory for canned foods, and the refrigerator factory that made bulk ice and ice cream.[172] Despite the anticipated economies of scale, distribution was problematic and the goal of the food complex, self-sufficiency for the city, was apparently not reached.

A chance statistic published in the newspaper indicated that the sausage factory produced a total of 1,211 tons of sausage in 1935, and 1,635 tons in the first ten months of 1937.[173] The purpose of presenting the data was, of course, to demonstrate that production had increased. But using a lower-end population figure for 1937 of 170,000, and assuming zero spoilage, the 1937 data still translated into about only two pounds of sausage per person per month—a calculation that the newspaper itself stopped short of making, for obvious reasons. Figures for the intervening year, 1936, were skipped, but in articles published early that year the newspaper indicated that spoilage may have been significant. One report claimed that there was no place at the factory to hang sausages, and thus that they were laid on the floor.[174] Another asserted that not only was the factory itself filthy, sausages were delivered in the same trucks used to transport coal and kerosene and packed in crates previously used for tobacco and shoes.[175]

It is unclear whether the city was able to import sausage. But Magnitogorsk's one large meat factory, intended to take care of all the city's sausage needs, was not able to do so—a conclusion that seems to have applied to other "shops" in the food complex, including the all-important bread factory[176] and the milk factory, which produced only 10 to 13 tons of milk products per day in 1938, against a daily demand estimated at 44.5 tons.[177] As for the local production of nonfood necessities, such as clothing, substantial unmet demand also prevailed, according to newspaper reports on the local shoe and sewing factories.[178] The bulk of clothing worn by Magnitogorsk residents either had to be "imported" from other cities or made by hand.

Magnitogorsk did have a number of city-regulated cooperatives, which were nominally worker-owned businesses, intended as the socialist answer to the small privately owned shops and service enterprises of capitalist cit-

ies. As of 1 January 1932, the city counted only one such artisanal cooperative, called Gigant, which contained around fifty artisans, but a year
later, the number of cooperatives had risen to six employing a total of 851
artisans. The increase was no doubt due to the fact that individual artisans
were pressured to join or cease plying their crafts.[179] Even if formed coer-
cively, these cooperatives might have become a powerful force, compen-
sating for the inadequacies of the city's state-owned light industry. But the
newspaper reported that the cooperatives "eke out a miserable existence,"
their constant ruin being an inability to procure raw materials.

One cooperative, Energiia, had a furniture-making workshop but was
not supplied with any wood. Instead, as the newspaper pointed out, the
cooperative had to "find" its own wood—no mean feat. The predictable result, in the newspaper's words, was the paradox of a city with "220,000
people and no place to buy a stick of furniture." The city's one specialized
furniture store, located in the Kirov district, was said to be almost always
empty. "Once in a blue moon, something will miraculously appear in the
stores. It will be total junk," the newspaper wrote, "but even this will sell
out quickly."[180] In a related story, the paper quipped that "it is as easy to
find good furniture in Magnitogorsk, as it is, say, to find hot tea or coffee
in a Magnitogorsk café."[181]

To foster the development of a state-sector consumer woodworking industry in the provinces, a 1936 Soviet law prohibited the transportation of
new furniture over a distance of more than 150 kilometers.[182] This apparently had little effect, for a new law introduced on 22 September 1938 extended the transport limit to 600 kilometers. In response, no consumer
woodworking factory arose in Magnitogorsk. Meanwhile, within 600 kilometers of the city there were only two small furniture factories whose
production was earmarked for residences. So some people began making
their own furniture, a few even using nickel, which for a time was a bit less
scarce than wood.[183]

The metallurgical complex operated a large woodworking factory, or
DOK (*derevo-obrabatyvaiushchii kombinat*), yet according to the newspaper, the DOK, which operated only one shift, produced exclusively for
the steel plant. While adamantly insisting that the DOK also ought to be
producing furniture for the city, the newspaper had to admit that there
were "no nails to be had."[184] But the problem was really one of priorities—
when one of the steel plant's shops needed nails, they could be found. In
the Soviet economy, the overwhelming emphasis placed on heavy industry—in part dictated by military considerations, in part by Bolshevik pre-
conceptions concerning modernity—the questionable heavy-industrial or-

ganization of consumer production, and the ban on legal private initiative combined to create a situation in which Magnitogorsk suffered perpetual shortages of basic goods amid full employment.

In an unpublished analysis of the municipal economy prepared by the city soviet's planning commission in 1939, light industry was said to have "a subordinate and narrow local significance, and in comparison with the size of the Metallurgical complex," to be "literally insignificant."[185] That year, the newspaper launched a vigorous campaign to promote the development of light industry. One article noted that despite the existence in the city of a large economic base with ample raw materials—the list included metal products, coal debris, sand, gypsum, limestone, granite, and wood discards—light industrial production (in value terms) amounted to only 9.7 million rubles (of which 1 million was accounted for by artels). But as it turned out, only 240,000 rubles of the overall sum represented, strictly speaking, consumer goods—in a city employing more than fifty thousand people.

Widening the scope of the debate, the article raised the parallel issue of the general lack of services in the city. Given the impossibility of finding replacement articles, it singled out as particularly inexcusable the city's lack of establishments for the repair of briefcases, shopping sacks, umbrellas, suitcases, suits, and coats. And dry cleaning was so untrustworthy, the author stated, "only a fool would bring in an irreplaceable article of clothing to be cleaned." In conclusion, the author insisted that it was time to get serious about local industry, but, typically, not a single practical measure was proposed.[186] Seven months later, another exasperated city official fumed that "in the stores and at the market, locally produced products for sale can be counted on two hands."[187]

In organizing the production of consumer goods, local representatives of the state found themselves with a burden as great as that of organizing socialist trade. Indeed, the problems in consumer production obviously underlay the deficiencies of trade. Yet the urban inhabitants needed to eat every day and to dress warmly, not to say fashionably. Regrettably for the regime's professed ideals but fortunately for all concerned, as in agriculture, so too in clothing, household goods, and services: the people, acting as private individuals, took matters into their own hands, come what may.

A vivid illustration of this was supplied by a tailor employed at the Magnitogorsk sewing factory who was promoted from stitching work to taking state orders. In taking orders for the factory, he began taking some for himself, and at home he and his wife made clothes to fill these extra orders, no doubt with materials removed from his workplace. The tailor also used his influence to place his own orders at the sewing factory for suits, which he then sold on the market to raise capital. Some of the suits he traded to the director of a nearby Machine Tractor Station for bicycles, which the tailor resold at the Magnitogorsk market. During a search of his place of residence, the militia discovered more than one hundred children's outfits, many of which he and his wife had made.[188] Such inventories were part of the shadow economy, a theme to which we must now return.

Raw materials, supplies, and tools were the basic capital of the shadow economy, and that capital could only come from one source—state-owned enterprises. People made use of anything and everything available at their state jobs, sometimes working after hours at the shop, sometimes turning their homes into small-scale manufacturing sites and creating informal "businesses."[189] Many "deals," however, were one-time affairs, either the fulfillment of word-of-mouth "contracts" or spontaneous efforts to take advantage of chance opportunities, in both cases predicated on the hope that mutual interest would prevent disclosure.

One-time deals were often connected with drivers who operated vehicles for state firms. Efimov, a driver employed by the auto park, was supposed to deliver bricks—an extraordinarily scarce item—to the site of a nursery being built in the Kirov district. Instead, he took a short detour to the nearby Eleventh Sector, the site of individual home construction, where he discovered how easy it was to sell "surplus" bricks to the eager home builders.[190] Efimov was caught—otherwise we could never have become privy to his activities—but how many more Efimovs went about their business unsuspected, or in collusion with the authorities? Such actions as his were demand-created.

In another shadow-economy transport story entitled "Private Excursion," the newspaper reported that two drivers from the auto park administration decided to use one of the state's buses to take a trip with their wives up to the town of Verkhne-Uralsk. Since gasoline allocations were strictly controlled, the two men found it necessary to use drinking alcohol for fuel. At the end of the day, heading back after the trip, the men decided to recoup their "expenses" by offering people rides into Magnitogorsk, at 10 rubles per person. There was no shortage of willing customers: the drivers stopped to pick up people until the bus was full. The newspaper, which somehow caught wind of the "private excursion," appealed to the public to come forward with information about the incident, since the newspaper's source had failed to note the names of the drivers.[191]

No further report about the incident appeared, nor was the question of the effect of the substitute fuel on the operation of the bus addressed. But the newspaper did report that rather than enter Magnitogorsk with such a conspicuous cargo, the operators of the "private" service thought it prudent to unload everyone at the train station, which was quite far from the rest of the city. This meant that the paying passengers had to walk a considerable distance even to get to the tram line. Perhaps one of the passengers, annoyed at being deposited so far from town, informed the authorities of the illegal activity. Or maybe someone at the train station, eager to ingratiate him or herself with the authorities, witnessed the passengers alighting from the vehicle and blew the whistle. The story of the "Private Excursion" highlighted the risks inherent in the shadow economy.[192]

Judging by the spotty accounts published several times each week in the city newspaper, Magnitogorsk's shadow economy appears to have been extensive. How extensive is difficult to say. Its size belongs to that set of questions that would remain unanswered even if all the surviving documents became accessible. Although it is possible that the police, in conjunction with local economic planners, attempted to determine the rough proportion of nonplan economic activity in the city's economy, there is no reason to suppose that their estimates could be credited. Secrecy was often one of the conditions for the operation of the shadow economy, which existed only insofar as it escaped the view of the police, even if this sometimes meant the police averted their eyes.[193] Keep in mind that the shadow economy was not limited to individuals engaged in short-lived "businesses." Managers and officials under pressure to meet plan targets were constantly wheeling and dealing.[194]

If it would be wrong to try to fix the size of the shadow economy, it would be just as wrong to assume that there were two entirely separate economies. The shadow economy was not an independent entity but a corollary to the official economy; it was the shadow economy that permitted the official economy to function, and vice versa. The two economies were mutually dependent and shaded off one into the other; separated, each would have ceased to exist. Put simply, there was really one economy with a dual aspect: some activities were legal, others were not; some illegal activities were condoned, but not all. And the determination more often than not was arbitrary.

Much, though far from all, of the activity that might be placed under the rubric of the shadow economy was centered on the officially sanctioned but stigmatized city markets. When it came to the markets, much was deemed at stake in the most trivial of actions. The resale of store-bought onions or the sale of home-manufactured shoes—activities which helped keep the city afloat economically—had political consequences regardless of whether behind them there was political intent. Such activities, which we might equate with initiative and entrepreneurship, were denounced as corrupt and dangerous, a violation of the principles on which the socialist economy were founded.

John Scott wrote of the two facing hills in the area between the factory and the socialist city proper. "The plain grey NKVD building dominated one of the two little hills, and the bazaar the other. The latter was teeming with buyers and sellers."[195] The former, Scott might have added, was teeming with investigators and informants. It was fitting that the main urban market and the police should both stand above the city and face each other. There could have been no better metaphor for the new system of economic relations that arose in the city of Magnitogorsk than the juxtaposition of these two hills: market relations had to be tolerated; market relations had to be policed.

Market trade took place under the watchful eye of the police, and it was here that the police recruited much of the unlucky "cast" for the public trials. But the rules governing market transactions were blurred. What was considered honest trade could at one moment suddenly become speculation, or the other way around. Often even the authorities themselves did not know what constituted speculation and what permissible exchange. Activities legal and illegal, encouraged and discouraged, open and clandestine could be found side by side at the city's market, as people traded in all manner of goods at whatever prices the "market" would bear—and the capricious authorities would tolerate.

Whenever the authorities attempted to crack down on the markets as the loci of the shadow economy, market activities were naturally and easily "decentered." One of the primary effects of the anti-speculation drives at the markets was to further disperse marketing activities throughout the city. From the beginning, however, the "marketing" of home-manufactured products was never really completely confined to the marketplaces themselves. Often people sold goods "right out of their apartments," or even traveled "door to door."[196] An amorphous "market space" enveloped the entire city, a whole society of petty traders, barterers, household cultivators, domestic manufacturers, queue sitters, and deal-makers—in the land of socialism!

These were people of disparate activities, to be sure, but they were all tarred with a single brush.[197] In the end, there was little to distinguish between siphoning off scarce construction materials to build one's own home at state expense and concluding a private deal with a state farm to obtain foodstuffs to ensure uninterrupted operation of a public dining hall under one's supervision. Both sorts of activities could lead to prosecution, and both were frequently tolerated. Nothing became illegal until the regime so decided, and decisions had less to do with the nature of the specific activities than with shifting political alignments, or individual whim. The only constant in the economy was inconstancy: the police could lower the boom at any time and for any reason, or for no reason at all. There was perpetual tension, but there was also ambition and hustle, much brazen theft, and enterprise too.

ECONOMICS, SPECTACLE, AND SOCIABILITY

In the second century A.D. the great satirist Juvenal mocked what he saw as the downfall of the once proud "sovereign people" of Rome who, he wrote, had been so confident as to take up and pass judgment on issues of the greatest political moment but now "longed for two things only—bread and circuses." Bread—*panis*—meant the system of supplying corn below the market price to the residents of Rome, a program first introduced by Gaius Gracchus in 123 B.C. Later, the corn was supplied free. Circuses—*circenses*—meant the chariot races that, along with other games, were enormously popular spectacles to which the people thronged.

By an irony of history, Juvenal's encapsulation of the Roman empire in decline would ring true for an empire on the rise eighteen centuries later. The citizens of Magnitogorsk—the microcosm of the Soviet Union—were also sovereign in principle, and they seemed to be attracted by the state's program for providing low-cost bread, as well as the new forms of entertainment. Indeed, bread (meaning state supply) and circuses (meaning the entire panoply of political propaganda and organized amusement) could be taken as a metaphor for the official policy used by the Soviet regime to erect Magnitogorsk—along with a healthy dose of nationalism and the insurance provided by the "security" police.[198]

In the Bolshevik version of bread and circuses, sometimes bread was scarce while coercion was widespread. But the Bolshevik leadership could point to the grand designs of the Soviet state: to lift a thoroughly backward society by its bootstraps high enough until it could support the industrial and military needs of a modern power in an uncertain and technically advanced world, and to do this with the utmost haste. What is more, the Bolshevik leadership chose to undertake this daunting task while simultaneously endeavoring to create nothing less than a new form of existence: socialism.

With the building of socialism, the Bolsheviks imparted to the "bread and circuses" expedient a novel twist. On the one hand, the "bread" aspect was taken to an extreme: not simply bread, but almost everything was supposed to be supplied by the state. On the other hand, the circus was not limited to its "displacement" entertainment value but called on to perform the political function of housing demonstration trials for "economic crimes." Because it was precisely the attempt to distribute supplies that encouraged the proliferation of economic crimes, Soviet bread and circuses were integrally linked.

The building of socialism began with the suppression of capitalism, but in suppressing capitalism and attempting to establish a state-owned and state-run economy, the regime took on tasks it did not have the capacity to resolve. In Magnitogorsk the authorities discovered that organizing a municipal economy along noncapitalist lines was no easy matter. It turned out to be far easier to manipulate the myriad riddles of socialist trade for political purposes than to solve them. Meanwhile, nonplan economic activity flourished, especially in and around the metallurgical works, where resources, labor power, and know-how were concentrated. And because of the system of fixed low prices for goods that were in chronically short supply, as well as the absence of effective mechanisms for controlling state-owned inventories, the purchase and theft of scarce goods for resale— "speculation"—became widespread.

In Magnitogorsk two markets were opened by the authorities for the exchange of goods between city inhabitants and collective farmers, a purpose that was not being particularly well served.[199] At the same time, the markets began to be used for other purposes: quickly unloading stolen goods, reselling goods purchased in state stores, hawking merchandise manufactured at home, retailing raw materials and machine parts removed surreptitiously from factory shops and storehouses, and offering a range of indispensable but otherwise unavailable city services. The markets encouraged and focused a number of activities outside the official economy, and thus outside the control of the authorities.

Even if such activity was thought to be for fulfilling the plan rather than for private gain, it still could invite the attention of the investigative authorities. What for individuals was primarily a question of survival or personal gain, for the authorities was often a manifestation of political opposition, of "economic counterrevolution." Because of the expressly noncapitalist nature of the Soviet economy, the markets became spaces of "resistance," and marketing a tactic of "resistance," to the state system of trade and supply.

What bothered the authorities most about the markets as the set of relations they entailed, relations that were not only outside their control but resembled the very system against which the revolution had been directed. The markets represented in concrete form the supreme evil in the Bolshevik imagination: capitalist economic relations. This concern was not merely an abstract hatred for capitalism but also a realistic assessment of the relation between economic power and political power, between the freedom to make decisions and to engage in associations within a political system that arrogated to itself the sole authority to make all decisions and expressly forbid individuals the right to enter nonsanctioned associations. The markets, particularly as "bazaar," implied forms of sociability, interaction, and perhaps political conversation inimical to Communist ideals and the grand crusade of the revolution.

The vast extent of conniving does not mean that the official socialist supply system and its low prices were unappreciated. In fact, the establishment of a nonmarket economy in the USSR brought to the fore manifestations of a popular concern for social justice, just as in eighteenth- and nineteenth-century Europe the spread of a market economy produced a flood of talk about speculators and hoarders derived from an outraged sense of "moral economy" centered not on the rights of individuals but on the community.[200] If in the case of market societies this language was ultimately rendered invisible by the market, in Magnitogorsk the language of social justice was conspicuously stage-managed and appropriated by the state, although perhaps not as fully as it might seem.

To be sure, the various guises of mass participatory action were orchestrated, yet even the most heavy-handed orchestrations retain degrees of unpredictability. It is possible to imagine—if not to prove, given the source limitations—that the tensions revealed in the accounts of the circus dimension of Magnitogorsk's nonmarket economy reflect not just obsessiveness and general apprehension but justified anxiety, on the part of state functionaries, over the spontaneity inherent in demonstration trials, consumer conferences, suggestion solicitations, and complaint books.

In the end, the interlocking set of circumstances formed by the imperative to police extralegal economic relations and the fact that policing could in no way keep pace with the spontaneous generation of illegalities inherent in the official economy proved inimical to correction. And yet, the efforts at reform, far from being abandoned, were redoubled—at what must have been a considerable cost in manpower and energy. Given the enormity of the task and the strains on their resources, perhaps the regular police engaged in a kind of selective enforcement against economic crimes.

But the authorities could never abandon the struggle without also relinquishing their fundamental ideals.

Finally, it is important to remember that the perverse assemblage of unintended consequences that flowed from the implementation of the Bolshevik understanding of economics was kept in motion by the actions of individuals, actions bespeaking ingenuity and undertaken sometimes despite considerable risk. The state's monopoly on the legal production of consumer products meant that Magnitogorsk was a city virtually without a "first floor," or commercial infrastructure, but into this gap rushed an army of private individuals. In that sense, the municipal economy in Magnitogorsk more than any other "organization" showed the potential of the masses for "activism." It was the participation of the masses in the socialist system, on negotiated terms, that helped account for that system's basic stability. Between bread and the circus took root one side—the hidden or "unofficial" side—of the extensive society formed under Stalin.

7   Dizzy with Success

Metal is important, but politics is more important.
Mark Riazanov, a fictional
construction site chief modeled
on Avraamii Zaveniagin[1]

Gradually, yet inexorably, the construction site Magnitostroi was becoming the city Magnitogorsk, challenging local authorities to maintain the housing stock, provide medical care, collect taxes, dispose of waste, and educate the next generation.[2] In late 1936, officials of the city soviet prepared a detailed report on the immense work they had undertaken that year.[3] Around this time the soviet also organized an "extraordinary" plenum to honor the new Stalin constitution, proclaimed "the most democratic in the world" because, unlike bourgeois constitutions, it supposedly did not support the hegemony of a ruling class.

To the strains of an orchestra, the festive gathering of Magnitogorsk bosses and invited guests in December 1936 opened with the collective singing of the proletariat anthem, the "Internationale." When the names of the country's top leaders were put forth as honorary members of the meeting's presidium, all present rose and combined in a thunderous ovation. One speaker after another hailed the new constitution and the advent of a new epoch. The plenum concluded with a tribute dashed off to Stalin in which the participants exclaimed, "we cannot express in words the full force of our love for you," and pledged their readiness to "meet the enemy."[4] The officials who made this vow of absolute loyalty did not know it then, but as it turned out, *they* were the enemy.

In the months that followed this celebratory plenum, "the enemy" came to include not only the city soviet but the local party leadership, the factory administration, the medical and educational establishments, local literary figures, the procuracy, and eventually even the mighty agency charged with ferreting out enemies, the NKVD. As the great showcase of socialism entered the new epoch, it was rocked—along with the rest of the country—by mass arrests for wrecking, spying, and diversion. Almost all the people who had devotedly led the arduous construction at Magnitogorsk were ignominiously chased from the historical stage, accused of vilely betraying the cause.

At one level, for those living in the USSR during the 1930s the ubiquity of enemies was to be expected. Building socialism was an adversarial process from which several immutable consequences seemed to flow. Soviet industrialization, carried out under the banner of social justice, was not simple "development" but class war, and with the destruction of the old property relations through the expropriation of private capital, the elimination of the Nepmen, and the deportation of the kulaks or peasant "bourgeoisie," legions of internal enemies were created. Secondly, because capital and the bourgeoisie were international, socialist construction in the USSR also created battalions of external enemies.

Regardless of what they might say or do at any given time, bourgeois powers were thought to be incapable of accepting socialism, the advent of which was assumed to signal their eventual demise. Had the capitalist powers not intervened in Russia during the Civil War? With the "socialist offensive along the whole front" having been launched, was it not conceivable that the capitalists might recruit agents among the remnants of the USSR's "dying classes" to engage in sabotage and diversion, or even to overthrow socialism and restore capitalism, as various trials in the late 1920s and early 1930s seemed to indicate? Stalin often emphasized, and events repeatedly seemed to confirm, that the "class struggle" became sharper the closer the USSR moved to socialism.

At another level, however, the outbreak of seditious plots and criminal conspiracies was confounding, for with the adoption of the new constitution, socialism was declared built in its foundations, yet the "class struggle," seemingly won, only intensified. Moreover, all of a sudden a colossal number of enemies and wreckers were identified throughout the highest reaches of industry, the state, and the military. Faithful servants of the people metamorphosed into enemies of the people overnight—and after a succession of spectacular achievements. It was just such a stunning turn of events that Stalin addressed in his frightening report to a Central Committee plenum on 3 March 1937.

Precisely the USSR's unprecedented triumphs, Stalin argued, had paradoxically brought about its increased insecurity. Members of the counterrevolutionary "underground," dangerous apostates from the revolutionary movement, were said to have sensed their impending doom and had begun resorting to "the most desperate means." This was supposedly happening at a time when Soviet officials had become complacent owing to the country's economic progress and had forgotten what Stalin called "the basic fact" determining the international position of the USSR, the "real and very unpleasant phenomenon" of capitalist encirclement. The only proper response to such a state of siege, Stalin insisted, was to check each and every official until all internal wreckers were unmasked (*razoblachen*). So that his message would be clear, Stalin recapitulated the possible objections to his analysis of the increased danger that had resulted from the USSR's success, citing such objections as prime evidence of the very lightheartedness (*bespechnost*) that gravely imperiled the encircled country.[5]

Press reports before and after Stalin's speech reinforced his grim assessment, contrasting the ever more daring feats performed by Soviet aviators and the Herculean Stakhanovites with the imperialist war waged and won by the Italian fascist Benito Mussolini in Abyssinia, the threat to Europe posed by a rearmed Germany under Hitler (attested by the Nazis' support for General Franco's Falangist forces in the Spanish Civil War), and Japanese aggression and expansion in the Far East. The depression and militarism of the surrounding capitalist world, with whom Trotsky and his diabolic followers were said to be in league, appeared to necessitate internal unity and constant vigilance inside the USSR. With the revolution itself said to be at stake, it was better to be safe than sorry.[6] As the clouds of war hovered, the inhabitants of Magnitogorsk practiced marching in gas masks while all around them spies and wreckers were unmasked.

．　　．　　．

Few historical problems have been studied more than Soviet politics and administration of the 1930s. To briefly assess this extensive literature, a good point of departure is Merle Fainsod's case study of Smolensk, based on what for a long time remained unique access to party archives.[7] Fainsod chose as his line of inquiry "the organization of authority in the region, the way in which controls operated, and their impact on the people who lived under their sway." Implicit in such a formulation was the presupposition that structures of authority were "controls," rather than a form of legitimate political representation. Fainsod called the Communist party's assumption of such "control" over all areas of life "the process of totalitarianization."[8]

Fainsod appeared to undermine his own interpretive framework, however, when he admitted that "the impression derived from the archive is one of almost chaotic disorganization, with the party itself more a helpless victim than master of the whirlwinds which it had helped unleash." So chaotic was the party's rule in the locality that the wonder became "not merely that the party was victorious, but that it managed to survive at all."[9] Still stressing the totalitarian aspirations of the regime and its local representatives,[10] Fainsod presented a picture that, when reduced to its essentials, amounted to a combination of the regime's monopoly on power and its inefficiency.[11]

Despite this sensible, if incomplete, explanation for the regime's durability, and many insights into its craving for control amid manifest bureaucratic clumsiness, Fainsod's characterization of the Soviet political system remained remarkably vague. He noted, for example, what he called "the deliberate overlap in Soviet methods of rule," but offered no explanation for the origin, continued existence, or significance of duplicate state and party structures. As for his treatment of the "great terror," which he viewed as a continuous process reaching climax in 1937–38, narrative substituted for analysis.[12] In the end, Fainsod seemed not to have made up his mind whether he had discovered an awesome administrative machine, or a congenitally inept one. These are the issues that have engaged a vast scholarly literature still grappling with the question, "What kind of political system was this?"

Of the many students of the Soviet political system, few have made as significant a contribution as T. H. Rigby, best known for his characterization of the USSR as a "mono-organizational society." In an influential article, Rigby argued that since "nearly all social activities were run by hierarchies of appointed officials under the direction of a single chain of command," Soviet society was actually "a single, vast and immensely complex organization" united by the rule of the Communist party.[13] Ironically, the value of such a formulation has been called into question most strongly by Rigby's own work, which has traced the establishment of two separate and parallel ruling bodies, the Communist party and the Sovnarkom (Council of People's Commissars). Rigby shows that the latter came to be dominated by the former, but that both still operated.[14]

Other scholars have noted the party's "domination" over the network of state organs, or soviets, and how nonetheless the soviets also continued to function and maintain their own apparat.[15] As for industry, it was managed both by a self-standing economic bureaucracy—the various "commissariats" whose chiefs sat in the Council of People's Commissars—and parallel departments of the party's Central Committee apparat (after January 1934). Far from being mono-organizational, in other words, the Soviet political system—to say nothing of the "society"—comprised a set of overlapping, parallel governing structures, a fact, to be sure, that Rigby (and Fainsod) pointed out. But obsessed with the party's assertion of "control" over other institutions, these and other commentators have failed to take seriously the persistence of dualism, using the term "party-state" to call attention not to the redundancy of power structures but to party supremacy. The duplication of state and party structures remains a question crying out for historical conceptualization.[16]

Stranger still, what most scholars regard as the defining episode for understanding the Soviet political system, the great terror, seems scarcely better explained today than when it happened.[17] Robert Conquest's study remains the prevailing interpretation. For him the terror, although "rooted in" the nature of the party created by Lenin, was a gratuitous, methodical assault on the country's elites by a dictator. However appropriate the assignment of primary responsibility to Stalin, in Conquest's narrative there is a notable absence of dispute or infighting among leading actors during the vast upheaval. The terror appears to have been carried out as if its scale and the identity of almost all its targets were known in advance. Everyone, executioners and executed, seems to have dutifully assembled for the mass liquidation as if it were a holiday parade.

Conquest reduces the terror to a problem of explaining the motivations of Stalin (a power-hungry and paranoid personality) as well as those of the Old Bolsheviks who "confessed" to imagined crimes at the three great "show trials" (coercion, combined with a tragic belief in the infallibility of the party). His other main task, to catalogue the extent of the suffering, gives his book its enormous length. But notwithstanding such bulk, Conquest's study pays virtually no attention to the language of the accusations and indictments, the international context, the regime's problems of administration, or institutional dynamics. In a word, Conquest's is a terror largely without process.[18] This manifestly problematic work long provoked remarkably little criticism, but there have finally appeared two related challenges.

Where Conquest sees calculation and obedient implementation, J. Arch Getty, relying on the Smolensk archive, sees the confusion, inefficiency, and "chaos" Fainsod noted in his study of the same materials. Getty goes much farther than Fainsod in his emphasis on chaos, however, until it seems almost to become the force driving events. Similarly, in recovering the "discord" within the top leadership (even among Stalin's entourage), Getty omits direct discussion of Stalin's personal despotism.[19] His main goal is to diminish the scope and significance of the terror, which he depicts as neither a continuous nor a premeditated process but, rather, a series of "conflicts" arising out of a "natural" center-periphery "struggle" that somehow got out of hand. He reaches this startling and baffling conclusion on the basis of party, not police, documents received by an agricultural backwater rather than those of the inner workings of the regime in Moscow (which remained inaccessible). Still, in the end Getty's challenge of Conquest succeeds in shifting some of the attention from Stalin to the process, even if his revisionist interpretation of that process is shot through with unsupported assertions and lapses in logic.[20]

Gabor Rittersporn, whose forceful critique of the standard historiography's irreconcilable gaps surpasses Getty's, proposes an equally idiosyncratic alternative. Rittersporn argues that the party-state, having assumed responsibility for managing everything, found itself incapable of doing so; when it tried to correct itself, the terror—a civil war within the apparatus fought against a background of "dangerous social tensions"—was the "inevitable" result.[21] At one point Rittersporn seems to concede that Stalin unleashed the campaigns that began the terror, but he substantially reduces the tyrant's role, insisting that "police violence, rather than proceeding from the realization of a single will and design of an omnipotent center of power by its invincible armed forces, was in fact increasingly chaotic and out of control." In other words, if the terror can be shown to have been chaotic (which it surely was) and rife with contradictions (ad infinitum), then there was *no* central design, just an "uncontrollable process."[22] Rittersporn never explains how an uncontrollable process could have been halted as it was in 1938, or why chaos and powerful elements of design cannot coexist, as appears to have been the case.[23] Ferreting out the least signs of diversity of opinion in the party press, he treats the "apparatus" as an abstract monolith, failing to specify the institutional links of power, especially to the NKVD. In short, although he offers many insights, Rittersporn, like Getty, has an easier time knocking down the standard account than constructing a replacement.[24]

With regard to the terror, we are left, it would seem, with an orthodoxy that cannot stand and alternatives that cannot take its place. The impetus came either from Stalin or from the "system"; the terror was either a gratuitous planned operation or an unplanned yet inevitable descent into chaos; there was either total central control or the virtual absence of control. It is tempting to take the path of least resistance and argue for a "middle ground." But in doing so we overlook another compelling problem. We need to know not just why the terror occurred but *how* it could happen.

Instead of seeking the origins of the terror, a problem that must await detailed study of the NKVD and party secretariat archives, we can ask what made the terror possible, what forms it took, and what its effects were. Answers to these questions require a consideration of the adversarial character of Soviet industrialization (as briefly outlined above), a sense of how the international context appeared in the minds of contemporaries, and an analysis of the institutional dynamics of the party and NKVD, with due attention to political language. It is just such an approach that will be tried here, as we seek to relate the *process* of the terror in Magnitogorsk to an understanding of the dualistic nature of the Soviet party-state.

What became the epic struggle against counterrevolution and sabotage waged at the hour of socialism's "victory" was the culmination of efforts to "reactivate" the Communist party. The mobilization of the party for the sake of mobilizing the country convulsed both party and country and threatened to overwhelm the success of the grand crusade itself. If during the building of socialism the leaders in Magnitogorsk went through a crash course in urban administration, the structures of authority they helped deploy made their experiences that much more dizzying. Life in and around the party was easily the most complex dimension of the little tactics of the habitat.

The terror, which touched a large number of people, involved far more than the use of massive force by the state against the population. Thousands of the country's most loyal cadres were arrested for, and in many cases confessed to, the most improbable crimes in what seemed a grotesque episode almost defying rational understanding. But the terror had a certain rationality, and no matter how apparently bizarre or disgusting, at some level it "made sense" if one accepted the premises and categories of the Communist party's self-understanding and crusade. Showing how the terror made sense, and thus why so many people could and did participate in a process that often led to their own undoing, is the chief goal of this chapter.

DUPLICATE STRUCTURES OF AUTHORITY: THE PARTY-STATE AS THEOCRACY

With the establishment of the settlement at Magnetic Mountain, the area to the immediate east of the proposed main factory entrance was designated the First Sector. Here makeshift wooden buildings for offices sprung up, as well as a path-like street that led from the First Sector to the rising "temple of industrialism." Just before reaching the still unbuilt factory gates, the path opened onto a large, formless space across which caravans of horses, wooden carts, camels, and Fords lugged construction materials from the temporary railroad terminus to the various locations of the future shops. This initially amorphous territory between the nascent steel plant and the First Sector became both the symbolic and functional hub of local authority, which centered on the industrial enterprise (see map 5).

On one flank of the future factory gates appeared the first brick structure in Magnitogorsk, the five-story factory administration building. On the other flank, appeared the Central Hotel, which housed offices that could not be accommodated within the factory administration building, as well as all personnel on temporary assignment—a sort of second factory administration building.[25] Together these two buildings formed the nerve center of the site, housing the telephone and telegraph network, and thus the communications link with Moscow. A visiting journalist, impressed by the contrast between the emptiness and chaos of the site and the physical presence of the administration building, wrote in 1930 that the factory administration "looks like an army headquarters located in the frontline area," which indeed it was, controlling virtually all local resources.[26]

Among the residents of the Central Hotel was a sprawling contingent of journalists and writers assigned to Magnitogorsk to make it an international symbol of the first Five-Year Plan. At first the correspondents lived in the hallways, awaiting completion of the hotel, but very soon they all got rooms, except the representative of the satirical magazine *Krokodil*, who, it was said, lived in the toilet.[27] Locally the press furnished a "Bolshevik" presence, casting the spell of what was called Soviet power (*Sovetskaia vlast*) over a wide-open territory that stretched out in all directions from the emerging central square. The square itself, meanwhile, served as the site for all large outdoor celebrations. In 1936 a large statue of Stalin was placed in front of the factory gates and equipped with a small platform from which the local leadership observed all mass gatherings, waving to the banner-carrying builders of a new world who marched by arranged according to factory shop.

Across from the factory administration and hotel on the central square—in addition to a branch outlet of the state bank, a model school, and the exclusive club for engineers and technical personnel (DITR)—were eventually located the offices of the city soviet and the Communist party city committee, or gorkom. The eight-story gorkom building was the tallest local structure, dwarfing the squat city soviet that stood parallel to it, on the other side of a dirt path. Even though it was the institution from which the country derived its name, no one could have mistaken the soviet for the party, whose physical presence bespoke a greater concentration of energies and higher political stakes. But neither would anyone have

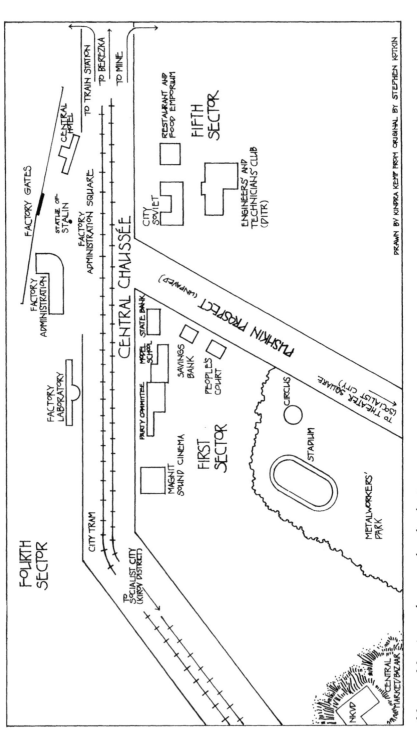

Map 5. Magnitogorsk, geography of authority, 1937.

mistaken the party for the factory headquarters. The central square bore the name Factory Administration Square (*ploshchad zavodupravleniia*).

The layout and architecture of Magnitogorsk's administrative agencies expressed a complicated system of authority: a weighty factory administration, a lofty party committee, and a lowly soviet, situated around a central square that was presided over by Stalin and enveloped in a whirl of talk and ritual. Two different institutions, city soviet and factory administration, represented the state, each with essentially the same unlimited mandate. Moreover, both state agencies contained party committees, which came under the jurisdiction not of those agencies but of the gorkom, whose mandate was equally comprehensive. Given such overlap, it should come as no surprise that all three organizations existed in uneasy relationship with each other, a circumstance that did not cause the terror but was central to the process.

There was, in addition, a fourth political agency in the city whose existence complicated matters even more, and without which there could have been no terror. This was the GPU, which in 1934 became the NKVD, or People's Commissariat of Internal Affairs. Technically just one part of the state bureaucracy, the NKVD, like all other commissariats, was nominally subordinated to Sovnarkom. In reality, the NKVD was a state within the state—a commanding position that also found expression in the political geography of Magnitogorsk.

Although the gorkom building was allowed to be the city's most conspicuous, it was physically overshadowed by the nearby NKVD building. Only two-stories tall, the NKVD building, finished in 1934, was strategically perched above the rest of the city on a hill (just off the main square, in the direction of Socialist City). The newspaper pointed out, furthermore, that the NKVD had "perhaps the single building in Magnitogorsk completed without 'unfinished parts' [*nedodelki*] [and] in an extraordinarily brief time."[28] The NKVD also had its own lock-up in the basement (a compliment to the main city prison across the industrial lake)[29] as well as one of the best equipped multipurpose clubs in town. It was in this club that important party meetings usually took place, since the gorkom building was completed only in 1937 (seven years after the factory administration building).

Even after the party headquarters was completed, however, the gorkom remained under the watchful eye of the security police. This was a striking reversal of the party's basic relationship with all other institutions (as discussed below) but in keeping with the mandate of the NKVD, or self-described "sword of the revolution." The NKVD performed the same inquisitorial tasks for the whole society that the party did on itself, creating more than a little ambiguity since the party, too, was part of society. In fact, the terror could be said to have truly begun when the NKVD assumed *complete* control over the process of political vetting *within* the party—but this is jumping ahead. First it is necessary to disentangle the nature and operation of the USSR's system of authority.

By law the city soviet was Magnitogorsk's highest governing body, the embodiment of "Soviet power." Comprising a policy-making chamber of popularly "elected" deputies and a policy-enacting executive committee elected by the chamber, city soviets in the early 1930s added planning commissions and a number of "sections" staffed by volunteers.[30] The Magnitogorsk newspaper emphasized the soviet's wide mandate, pointing out that "there is no area of life they miss."[31] Yet the examples of the soviet's work put forward most often by the newspaper—combating drunkenness, addressing family problems, checking up on the operation of stores and the city's market—suggested a more limited role as a repository of citizens' complaints[32] and a grassroots social welfare agency,[33] as well as a bureau for collecting trade and other statistics. At full strength the city soviet met intermittently (only when summoned by the executive committee or by at least half the deputies); in between sessions it was run by a presidium consisting at various times of anywhere from six to fifteen people, including the chairman of the soviet but mostly officials whose authority derived from positions they held in other agencies.[34]

Day-to-day administration of Magnitogorsk's urban affairs was carried out by the factory, through its KBU, or department of everyday life, which in effect usurped the functions of the city soviet's executive committee. The factory, not the city soviet, built the city's schools, nurseries and daycare centers, and the bulk of its housing stock. The factory also built and owned the urban transport system, the city's baths and laundries, the water supply, and the electric power station. The urban food supply and the distribution of dry goods, although technically controlled by separate trade agencies, were largely dependent on the factory's actions. Even the air breathed by the urban inhabitants, although not legally owned by the plant, bore the unmistakable influence of the factory.[35]

In terms of staff size, the KBU surpassed all the other departments of the factory administration taken together. For some time the Magnitogorsk newspaper carried urgent calls for "relieving" the already overburdened factory administration of responsibility for the management of the city. The city soviet, it was argued, should exercise its duties. But the proposed transfer of urban property and administration from one agency of the state to another never occurred, not even after a direct order from Moscow in 1939.[36] Even if a transfer of Magnitogorsk's infrastructure to nominal city soviet ownership and/or management had been carried out, however, it would have had little practical effect.

Making steel entailed more than securing raw materials or acquiring particular technologies; it required assembling a large pool of people and providing for their needs, which meant finding and training not just steel workers, engineers, and managers, but also doctors, store clerks, and school teachers. Making steel necessitated creating a city—a task that, because of the prohibitions against private property and hired labor, was assumed by the state. And the part of the "state" that had power over the country's resources and thus the wherewithal to carry off such a task were the industrial commissariats, especially NKTP. City soviets did not even have the authority to regulate the factories that operated within their territory. The literal meaning of "Soviet power," in other words, did not amount to much in the face of near absolute corporatist (*vedomstvennyi*) rule.

If in order to make steel, members of the factory administration understood that they had to provide for and manage the lives of a large urban population, they also knew that making steel was a political as well as an economic task: each steel rail produced was thought to "strengthen socialism." In practical managerial terms, this meant simply producing greater and greater quantities. But politically speaking, there turned out to be far more to making steel than just making steel, as every Soviet industrial manager came to understand. There was, in fact, an entire organization devoted exclusively to the purpose of expounding and acting upon the complex relationship between politics and industrial production. That organization was, of course, the Communist party.

Contemporaries thought of the Communist party as the key to the Soviet Union's political system and the backbone of the country. But the party, far from guaranteeing stability, turned out to be a source of near continuous turmoil. In fact, the more complex the political situation inside and outside the country seemed to become, the greater was the turmoil in and around the party. This unforeseen instability connected with the party grew out of the nature of its special role, which in turn was a consequence of its revolutionary origins.

In tsarist Russia the Bolshevik party had justified its existence on the grounds that workers, if left to their own devices, were capable of developing only trade-union consciousness. To make a socialist revolution, the argument went, there had to be a vanguard of revolutionary consciousness, which the Bolshevik party claimed to be. But once the revolution occurred and power was transferred to the workers (and peasants), what would be the party's role? Soviet Russia had a government, Sovnarkom, and state organs, the soviets, so why did it need a parallel structure of party organizations? The answer to this question was far from obvious. In the early years of the revolution there were suggestions to abolish the party.[37]

Far from being abolished, however, the Bolshevik party, which in 1918 renamed itself the All-Russian Communist Party (of Bolsheviks), achieved a "monopoly" on power through the repression of other parties. This notorious turn of events occurred during the complicated Civil War, and remains a matter of historiographical dispute.[38] Whatever the important historical processes involved in the Bolsheviks' startling achievement of a monopoly, such an outcome was consistent with the party's origins and self-perception as the advanced guard of the working class.[39] In fact, no less profound a development during the Civil War than the achievement of a monopoly was the party's discovery of a rationale and model for its postrevolutionary existence in that status as the vanguard of revolutionary consciousness.

In 1918, when the new regime found itself forced to enlist the skills of former tsarist officers whose allegiance was considered suspect, the party leadership, on Trotsky's initiative, introduced political commissars to work alongside the military specialists and ensure their loyalty. On an analogous principle, in the judiciary, schools, industry, trade unions, soviets, and government the equivalent of political commissars—party "fractions," made up of party members who worked in these bodies—were formed. By "shadowing" the gamut of institutions, the party sought to verify (*kontrolirovat*) that their operation conformed to what was defined as the "interests of the working class," determined by the party leadership. Thus was born a structural division between expertise and "proper" ideology, with the latter becoming the duty of the party and the justification for its prominent postrevolutionary role.

It was not long before the party leadership tried to systematize the practice of loyalty verification by compiling lists of what were considered key administrative posts—the so-called *nomenklatura*, or nomenclature—to be filled by Communists. Beginning with the Twelfth Party Congress in April 1923, the *nomenklatura* system of appointing personnel to designated "key posts" was extended to state-controlled industry and reproduced on the local level.[40] Using the *nomenklatura* mechanism, the party functioned as an ever-expanding personnel machine, placing Communists from its appointment lists in positions of responsibility throughout industry and government, or requiring those already in such positions to join the party. Improving the educational level and competence of its own members, as well as validating their loyalty (*predannost*), became, logically enough, the primary preoccupations of the party.

Although individual party members could possess managerial and scientific skills, the party's raison d'être remained ideological, not professional or technical. Accordingly, the party's systematic permeation, or shadowing, of institutions with party cells to safeguard political loyalty and "correct" decision making did not signify that the party would replace, say, factory administrations or soviets. Rather, the party would imbue such bodies with *partiinost*, or party spirit, by which was meant a historical and political understanding derived from ideology. Party "verification," in other words, institutionalized a permanent dualism in the Soviet political system, which appropriately came to be called a party-state.

To decide any single set of issues, almost all officials had to meet twice: the first time they usually assembled in the guise of party members, the second as executives of a state institution. Because the party was not an administrative organ, this practice of duplication remained the case long after the notion of providing ideological guidance lost its luster. Binding decisions had to be issued and implemented, at least formally, in the name of the government or the state (soviets).[41] In short, both parts of the party-state were functional, but their functions were different: whereas the state's role was defined in terms of competent technical and economic administration, the party's was defined in terms of ideological and political guidance. Such a bifurcated political system, with the party analogous to a church, resembled a kind of theocracy.

In relation to events and its own internal dynamic, the party's organizational structure evolved, and its membership composition changed. But what remained constant was its ideological raison d'être, derived from its origins and institutionalized in every organization, giving the country a duplicate set of administrative structures, party and state. The consequences of having a theocratic system, which gradually acquired a corresponding religious aura, were profound, beginning with the sacralization of all affairs, great and small, and ending with the party's self-immolation.

THE STRAINS AND BURDENS OF THEOCRACY

The terror began in the party, whose unique attributes presented a many-sided challenge to contemporaries. The party was neither a governmental body nor a political party in the traditional sense, and its legal status long remained ambiguous. With the new constitution of 1936, the party was finally designated a "public organization" (*obshchestvennaia organizatsiia*) formed as an expression of the will of its members (the party was not mentioned in the sections dealing with organs of state power and administration). Unlike other "public organizations" named in the constitution, however, the party was empowered as nothing less than "the leading core of all organizations of the working people, both public and state."[42] In practice, this paradoxical nongovernmental yet omnicompetent status meant that the party could arrogate to itself the authority to intervene in any and all matters.

Of course, the party fell far short of "directing" all institutions, but it struggled incessantly—and from its self-definition quite properly—to do so.[43] Nothing was beyond the party's purview.[44] As a result of the party's auto-universalization, the entire space in which Soviet life took place was politicized. Any activity, even thinking or speaking one's mind, became a political act. Every citizen, but especially party members, had to measure his or her thoughts and actions against the goals and pronouncements of the party leadership. Whether the task at hand was selling vegetables or making steel, "proper" politics became not simply a means but an end in itself, at enormous cost to society.

For the party, living up to its own mandate was far from easy. Ironically, the industrialization drive, heralded as the wise policy of the party, unexpectedly threw the party's self-assigned "leading role" into confusion. The suppression of capitalism and the building of socialism empowered the state—the legions of officials acting in its name—to manage the mushrooming noncapitalist industrial economy. The vast economic apparat, in contrast to the party, possessed the technical and administrative skills required to run modern industry. With so many economic and technical matters awaiting resolution, party meetings could seem not only superfluous but detrimental, "interference" rather than "guidance," although it was dangerous to say so openly and thereby question the country's most sacred institution.

At the same time, "party work" proved to be highly intricate and labor-intensive, consuming enormous energy and resources. In the localities no less than in Moscow, party organizations had to arrange continual public celebrations of their own rule in the form of meetings. These opened and closed with familiar rituals, including the invocation of the latest doctrinal truths, an abject homage to the Leader, and a collective singing of the "Internationale." The hallowed color of red predominated. Iconic portraits of party leaders looked down on the proceedings, and the "presence" of these high priests was often reinforced by their honorary inclusion on the presidium elected by acclamation to preside over each meeting. Unity of will and purpose was the overriding goal, and through incantations of the party's achievements, often called miracles (*chudesa*), assembled Communists publicly reaffirmed their absolute faith and devotion to the party and to its "sacred cause" (*sviatoe delo*), building socialism and, ultimately, Communism. These ceremonies, at which often considerable business also had to be transacted, took place with great frequency.[45]

No less elaborate was the process of entering the party, which meant becoming part of a diligently cultivated revolutionary tradition (the underground, Siberian exile, October, the Civil War, Lenin, Stalin). A prospective member had to be recommended by current members, make a full confession of his or her (presumably appropriate) social background and life history, and go through an apprenticeship as a "candidate" before being welcomed into "the ranks" and taking on the "high title" of a "Bolshevik" and "Communist."[46] Once admitted, a Communist stood above the law, subject to arrest or criminal investigation only after the party had taken up the matter and rendered a decision. To maintain what was called the "purity" (*chistota*) of the ranks, periodic "purges" (*chistki*) were undertaken. Unworthy members were expelled, underscoring for those remaining the "special calling" involved in being a Communist after what were rather exhausting procedures.[47]

Individual Communists were encouraged to consider themselves part of an elect and to shoulder appropriate responsibilities. Perhaps the most important duty deriving from membership in a movement founded on a shared universal faith cast as the one true theory was familiarity with that theory (the revolutionary "scripture"—the works of Marx-Engels-Lenin, the speeches of Stalin—whose interpretation was entrusted to party theologians, called "ideologists"). Communists were also expected to be well versed in the recent decisions of the Central Committee, current events, and the background of the revolutionary movement, and to improve their knowledge continually—no small assignment! Every member had to keep party secrets, or as it was sometimes put, "observe the conspiracy" (*sobliudat konspiratsiiu*).

Keeping secrets was a part of the oath party members took to uphold "party discipline," which in effect meant submitting without question to all decisions of the party. Indeed, Communists were expected to carry out the party's directives "tirelessly," thereby demonstrating their political "activeness" and ability to lead by example.[48] Lenin had called the party "the mind, honor, and conscience of the epoch," and these words were often displayed on banners in the local party headquarters, party clubs, and other gathering spots. Those were very high ideals to live up to, but living up to them was part of what it meant to be a church.

As is well known, the church-like party was organized according to a strict, military-like hierarchy, built from the bottom up. All party members were affiliated with the party organization at their place of work (or at a neighboring one, if theirs was too small to have one). The lowest level organizations were called party fractions (*fraktsii*) or cells (*iacehiki*) until 1934, when they were officially named primary party organizations (PPOs). PPOs were subordinated to district committees, called raikoms, which were in turn subordinated to gorkoms (city committees). City committees came under the supervision of the provincial committees, or obkoms, which were subordinated to the Central Committee of the USSR in a pyramid.[49] Such centralization of the party was christened "democratic centralism," which despite appearances was not without friction and even open confrontation.[50]

Orders came down the chain of command, to be carried out without question, provoking resentment and subtle forms of resistance. At the same time, on many matters a formal motion had to begin at the bottom and then be "confirmed" at each successive level up the hierarchy. Leadership positions, for example, were usually assigned from above, but even so, candidates to them were formally "elected" at meetings by the rank and file. Between these poles of democracy and military-like centralism a certain tension persisted under the surface, and could sometimes burst through, momentarily reversing the pyramid. This tension within the hierarchy became a vital part of the process of the terror.

By far the greatest source of tension, as well as conflict, arose from the parallelism of party and state. Obkoms, equivalent to episcopates, were in some ways the linchpins to the Soviet political system. Like the Central Committee, the authority the obkoms exercised was rooted in the regulation of personnel appointments. By the 1930s an obkom *nomenklatura* included the staff of the gorkoms and raikoms, soviets, trade organizations, directors of scientific institutes and universities, state farm chairmen, and factory directors within its territory.[51] With the industrialization drive, however, the central apparatus came to depend on the obkoms more for control of rural areas than for control of urban ones or substantial urban pockets within rural provinces. Where large factories were located, Moscow asserted its prerogatives largely by means of "the state," that is, through the economic commissariats.[52] Thus, local factory administrations often eclipsed the corresponding obkoms as the critical battlegrounds in

Moscow's quest for hegemony.[53] But the obkoms continued to assert "their prerogatives."

Although the Magnitogorsk plant administration was subordinated directly to Moscow—both the city soviet and gorkom were subordinated to Cheliabinsk, where the provincial, or oblast, soviet and obkom were located—shops bosses, the factory director, and his deputies remained on the obkom's *nomenklatura*. As a result, struggling to assert itself in the face of Moscow's accusations of evasion or subversion of central directives, the obkom fought just as tenaciously to maintain influence over industrial enterprises, concentrations of wealth and resources that were outside the obkom's day-to-day control but still nominally within its territory.

Within Magnitogorsk, battles for supremacy were waged between the party's first secretary, who controlled the local press, and the factory director, who controlled local economic resources (from housing to food supply) and was usually a man of greater stature in the national party organization than the local party secretary.[54] There were similar rivalries all the way down the parallel hierarchies, as well as throughout the factory administration.[55] The everyday functioning of the dual apparats brought forth suspicions, grudges, webs of alliances—in short, everything from petty squabbling to bureaucratic warfare, which, although mostly invisible, was quite real and was compounded by the parallelism.

In this bureaucratic Leviathan, throughout which authority was perpetually contested, infighting, intrigues, and provocations were the modi operandi. This kind of strife, endemic to bureaucracies and organizations, was perhaps not particularly worrisome, except that it took place on a vast scale—the apparats managed all the affairs of the entire country—and within a highly charged political atmosphere. Added to this were the tensions arising from the unlimited jurisdiction of the GPU/NKVD,[56] whose clandestine operations were independent of local control.[57] If only to protect itself, the Magnitogorsk NKVD had no choice but to keep a close watch on the local party organization and factory administration.[58]

Strict military hierarchy combined with various democratic practices, deliberately overlapping jurisdictions derived from the theocratic structure of the party-state, and the hypervigilance of the NKVD were not the only sources of tensions in the Soviet political system. Communists professed an ethic of devoted service for the people, but that ethic often clashed with their methods. To administer party matters, for example, many Communists—the staff of the raikoms, gorkoms, and obkoms, and the secretaries of the largest primary party organizations—were "released" from the duty to hold a regular job.[59] These were the so-called apparatchiks, who in some cases could appear to be performing no other function than lording over other people's lives—people who may have been party members and thus had to participate in party matters, but who also held full-time jobs.

In fact, the party *nomenklatura* was set up as a literal ruling elite. Members of the *nomenklatura* could be and were appointed in any official capacity, regardless of their particular skills, because they were thought to have the general capacity to rule (*pravit*). Inevitably, with even low-level positions came the spoils of office: not always a motorcar with driver, telephone, and secretary, but probably at least the pick of scarce clothing, some extra sausage, and a real apartment. Such were the conditions of Magnitogorsk life that the perquisites of the *nomenklatura* and its favored associates could not remain entirely inconspicuous. On the contrary, elite lifestyles emerged as a central theme of the terror, as we shall see.

The party's activities as spiritual guide turned out to be a source of strength but also a deadly burden for both the party and the country. Life in the party was characterized alternately by feelings of omnipotence and utter vulnerability, by a smug complacency shattered by periods of unremitting tension, by proclamations of ironclad "truths" amid threatening uncertainties. To be sure, the party was deadly serious about its ideological mission (indeed, to act or think otherwise was to open up troublesome questions about the nature of the socialist revolution and the legitimacy of the Soviet regime).[60] Yet the more the party tried to live up to its role, the more strident and brittle it appeared to become. Predictably, a self-declared vanguard organization that was also a movement founded on iron discipline, absolute purity, and supreme personal sacrifice had a difficult time remaining true to its own ideals. But try it did, laying the basis for the terror.

THE PARTY COMES ALIVE:
THE SEARCH FOR THE ENEMY WITHIN (I)

The first party affiliate in the Magnitogorsk region was formed in June 1929, and consisted of around twelve members.[61] By the beginning of 1933, less than four years after its establishment, the local party organization claimed an apparently robust membership of 8,200.[62] Over the next five years, however, it shrank to less than 2,000 members and candidates (only 300 of whom were women).[63] This massive contraction in the Magnitogorsk ranks began with the unionwide party "purge," regulated by a central directive sent in April 1933—the first of a series of increasingly violent political shocks sent to the provinces along the party's communications fault line.[64]

Periodic "cleansings" of incompetents, drunkards, and thieves, as well as "oppositionists," had occurred virtually since the party came to power, the last and largest one having taken place in 1929. But well more than half the membership in Magnitogorsk had joined since 1929, so 1933 was their first experience of a purge. The close scrutiny must have looked like a drastic change from the open-arms reception that had propelled the rapid growth of the early 1930s, when the regime strove to convert the "pathos of socialist construction" into a greater political base of support.[65]

From the regime's point of view, however, the wholesale expansion necessitated a careful, albeit ex post facto, screening of new members. Membership in the party, considered a unique honor available only to certain classes and earned and continuously affirmed by deeds, also brought various privileges amid scarcity and hardship. And beyond the issue of privileges, the political reliability of party members needed to be ensured, especially since the 1933 purge was being prepared under unprecedented circumstances:[66] the upheaval of collectivization and the famine, which together provoked a crisis in the regime and considerable second-guessing around the country. Already unsure of itself and its grip on the country, the regime appears to have been inundated with complaints regarding the abuses, high-handedness, and "moral degeneracy" of low-level officials.

Particularly troublesome from the regime's point of view were the instances whereby apparatchiks swore allegiance to the party but supposedly refused to carry out or even make public its decisions. "An enemy with a party card in his pocket," the party's main newspaper noted ominously in late 1932, "is more dangerous than an open counterrevolutionary."[67] It was just such a formulation, occasioned by the trauma of collectivization, that made the purge, however much a response to legitimate housekeeping and security concerns, the beginning of a process comparable in some ways to the Inquisition, but in the end far nastier.

Yet another complicating factor in the 1933 purge also connected with collectivization were the muted doubts expressed toward the end of 1932 about the leadership of Stalin. Stalin had triumphed over the other pretenders to become Lenin's successor, but he was blamed for having led the country into near ruin and was conducting a curious foreign policy branding social democrats as more dangerous than fascists.[68] A bumper harvest in 1933 set the country on the path of recovery. But misgivings about the regime's rash policies and Stalin's authority persisted, constituting the unspoken background to the party purge.[69]

Within the dictatorship of the party Stalin *achieved* a personal dictatorship, and from his position atop the party apparat, or secretariat, he oversaw the purge, as well as all information sent via party channels. Untrusting to the point of paranoia (he listened in on wiretaps of aides' conversations) and ambitious to the point of megalomania (he became avidly involved in the rewriting of history and his role in it), he had already demonstrated with the launching of collectivization that even if he did not always have his way at plenary meetings, for all intents and purposes he was beyond the control of the Central Committee and the politburo. Within ruling circles, the need for a party purge does not appear to have been a matter of dispute, but there may well have been concern that Stalin would simultaneously pursue his own personal agenda.

And so the purge. One by one party members were called in front of an ad hoc commission formed by representatives of local party leaderships. Approaching the front of the room, Communists placed their party cards on a red-draped table and, with portraits of the party's leaders in the background, recited their political biographies and prepared to answer questions. Commission members, occasionally joined by an audience of invited "party activists" and the "nonparty mass," then explored the depths of a Communist's political sophistication and sometimes challenged the veracity of the autobiographical presentations. Many party members had only an elementary education and were ignorant of political theory and history, decisive areas of knowledge for a Communist. Moreover, in the buildup to the purge, special receptacles had been installed inside all institutions for the collection of signed or more often anonymous testimony about the Communists in that organization. No party member could be certain of what the commission had managed to find out or might ask. The atmosphere in the hall could turn hostile or friendly, depending on the disposition of the commission toward the particular party member before it.[70]

Members who passed the interrogation were handed back their party cards, frequently with an official reprimand (*vygovor*) entered into their dossiers for one or another "shortcoming" discovered about them. Anyone whose case seemed "suspicious" had his or her card "detained," pending further investigation. Some were "expelled" outright, their cards unconditionally "confiscated," for what was viewed as an inappropriate social background or political biography, or for misconduct. A large number of Communists whose understanding of ideology was deemed rudimentary were expelled; others so judged were allowed to remain in the ranks but were issued reprimands for "political literacy."

All expelled Communists who hoped to be reinstated, and even many of those not expelled, were required to offer public acts of repentance, or "self-criticism" (*samokritika*), and to redouble their efforts at political education in party schools and circles for the study of history and theory. Since there were procedures for overcoming one's shortcomings and achieving reinstatement, neither a reprimand nor even an expulsion appeared to be cause for undue concern, however disappointing or disagreeable for the one purged. Expelled Communists were not supposed to be dismissed from their everyday jobs.[71]

Those for whom party work *was* their everyday job constituted a special case. Accountability of apparatchiks before the regime and the public was a serious concern. During the purge, "self-criticism" by the rank and file of the "situation" in their party organizations was promoted as a way to combat the "bureaucratism" of lazy, unresponsive, or recalcitrant officials. With apparatchiks in charge of the purge, however, criticism of them by subordinates seemed an unrealistic goal. True, in Magnitogorsk the purge did lead to the removal of First Secretary Spirov, who was replaced in July 1933 by Beso Lominadze.[72] But this transpired only as a result of a visit to the site by People's Commissar of Heavy Industry and politburo member Sergo Ordzhonikidze, in whose weighty presence criticism of local officials "from below" was possible. More often, such "criticism" came anonymously, in the form of denunciations incited by bureaucratic jealousies and infighting. Such denunciations were not necessarily acted upon, yet even when set aside they could still become part of an apparatchik's file.[73]

Along with a change in the local party leadership, one of the chief consequences of the purge in Magnitogorsk, as elsewhere, was a staggering reduction in membership. More than two thousand Magnitogorsk Communists were expelled.[74] Predictably, the expulsions were not primarily from among the apparat, which conducted the purge, but from the rank and file, who were recent entries and whose presence in the party could be seen as perhaps superfluous, just so much extra "ballast" that could be tossed overboard without upsetting the ship. Somewhat unexpectedly, but in apparent confirmation that there had been a need for the purge, at least two thousand more party members simply disappeared from the rolls. Some of these were self-described Communists who turned out not to be members.[75] The vast majority were those who evidently declined to admit they were members, rather than face the scrutiny of the purge.[76]

The purge dragged on for quite some time. Originally scheduled to end in November 1933, it was still not officially complete in May 1935, when the party leadership in Moscow decided to extend the process with what was called a party document "verification" (*proverka*).[77] The verification was directed at "party economy" (*khoziaistvo*), by which was meant record keeping (*uchet*), for some time said to be in disarray. While many party cards had been lost or stolen, or were defective, without official seals and signatures, or forged, corresponding personnel files at the local level rarely kept pace with frequent transfers and rapid expansion. The power of the top of the party pyramid—the secretariat and Central Committee apparat—was predicated on the appointment system, which required accurate information on personnel. The more ambitious the central authorities were in making or supervising appointments, the lower they searched in the party pyramid for data on "cadres."

For the localities, reliable documentation on each Communist was deemed important because it served as the basis for evaluating the flood of petitions requesting reinstatement and because the verification, like the purge, was intended to expose not just the sots, swindlers, and "moral degenerates" who discredited the party, but Communists who showed no outward signs of disloyalty yet who entered or remained in the party by means of deception (*obmannym putem*) and may also have been hidden "class aliens."[78] A less than impeccable "proletarian" past and the act of having concealed this or any other information from the party were both targets of the procedure.[79] Indeed, the verification appeared to be designed to catch those who had "slipped through" the purge.[80] With new entrances into the party suspended as of January 1933, the verification portended a further reduction in membership, not to mention ample work for the apparat.[81]

Local party secretaries were given responsibility for the labor-intensive process, and so it appeared that the apparats would again determine which additional Communists might be expelled or reprimanded, or which might be reinstated. To an extent, however, the power of apparatchiks was counterbalanced by the reinforcement in December 1934 of the concept of the "party active" (*aktiv*). This device was designed to increase participation at party plenary meetings, which in violation of party rules were often conducted with only officials present but now had to be more inclusive.[82] In what was yet another manifestation of the longstanding tension between "democracy" and "centralism," members of the "active" were encouraged to discuss and thus "check" the decisions routinely taken behind closed doors by small circles of apparatchiks. The verification process was billed as a vehicle to "activate" the "party mass" and raise its political consciousness.

For all party members, the anxiety inherent in the scrutiny of the verification was heightened by the assassination of politburo member Sergei

Kirov back on 1 December 1934 at Leningrad party headquarters by someone in possession of a party card. At first the Kirov murder was treated as a limited though evil plot perpetrated by "White Guardists."[83] But on 23 December, to an audience of thousands in Magnitogorsk, Beso Lominadze reported the additional "findings" of the NKVD regarding the existence of a "Leningrad Center," a group of former top Bolsheviks accused of creating an atmosphere conducive to the killing.[84]

The announcement one week later in the central press of death sentences for all the accused was followed by a notice of the discovery of a "Moscow Center," comprised of more former Bolsheviks accused of directing the Leningrad Center and having ties to White Guard organizations.[85] The second trial testified to the sharpening of the political atmosphere in the aftermath of the Kirov murder. Equally momentous in this regard was the 1933 ascension to power in Germany of Adolf Hitler, whose hostile and expansionist rhetoric began to be taken seriously in 1934 and led to a dramatic change in Soviet foreign policy, which now belatedly formed a "united front" with socialists and other leftists against fascism.[86]

That there was a link between the assassination of a member of the Soviet leadership and the advent of an aggressive regime in Germany that called itself "National Socialist" yet singled out leftist socialists as its death enemy no doubt seemed plausible enough. In any case, such a suspicion was persistently reinforced by Soviet propaganda, which was based on the assumption—again plausible—that numerous "agents" of hostile "forces" were constantly being recruited from among the legions of internal enemies generated by the deliberately adversarial nature of Soviet industrialization. German National Socialism, in other words, was not only a real threat but a powerful context that reinforced and made more concrete already widespread apprehensions.

On 16 January 1935, five- and ten-year sentences in the Moscow Center trial were handed down, and two days later the Central Committee dispatched a secret letter on the treacherous role in the assassination of masked former "oppositionists" that called on all party organizations to be on guard for further signs of their activity.[87] Lominadze, responsible for delivering speeches and organizing public discussions in Magnitogorsk of the party's secret communication, was himself a former "oppositionist," "exiled" to the city after having served in far higher posts.[88] Perhaps in anticipation of his arrest, on 18 January 1935, the date of the secret Central Committee letter, he attempted suicide, dying later that night.[89] There was no mention of this newsworthy event in Magnitogorsk newspapers, although rumors circulated throughout the city.[90] What transpired in the immediate aftermath, as Lominadze was buried, remains mysterious.[91]

On 20 January, an outsider, Rafael Khitarov, the party secretary in Stalinsk (Novokuznetsk), was dispatched to Magnitogorsk. He was formally "elected" the new first secretary at a hastily called gorkom plenum on 5 February.[92] That same day, a ferocious article appeared in *Pravda* attacking several people said to belong to a "Lominadze group," including deputy factory director Iosif Alperovich and city newspaper editor Fedor Bezbabichev, who were soon removed and arrested for what was termed "double-dealing" (*dvurushnichestvo*).[93] Factory director Avraamii Zaveniagin, who had recently become a candidate member of the Central Committee, was not implicated.[94]

The parallel with the Leningrad and Moscow Centers was unmistakable. In Magnitogorsk, those who had observed Lominadze and his closest associates knew them to be eminently qualified and dedicated, but they also knew that the cause shone brighter than any individual.[95] Some people reasoned that if Lominadze were not "guilty," he would not have taken his own life; others understood that it was none of their business.[96] But in either case, the charge of "double-dealing" could be taken literally.

Contemporaries could scarcely deny that the history of the party, from its foundation up through the early 1930s, seemed to have been a continuous "struggle" to uphold what was called "the general line" or the "Leninist path" against one "opposition" after another. And even though Stalin declared at the Seventeenth Congress that the various oppositions had been defeated and that there was no one left to fight, this did not eliminate the need for "revolutionary vigilance." In fact, the following year the party's "enemies" were said to have resorted to "lying, political jesuitry and double-dealing."[97] "Opposition" had not disappeared; rather, divested of the possibility of carrying on open struggle, it had been forced "underground." This was the logic of the party's struggle for unity: precisely because of the party's *success* in achieving unity, "conspiracy" had become the only way to fight it.[98]

Such "conspiracies" were difficult to detect, but not completely fanciful. Lominadze's "opposition" to collectivization was well known; it had gotten him into trouble and landed him in Magnitogorsk. By the accepted rules of party discipline, neither he nor anyone else was permitted to disagree publicly with party policy. But what of his nonpublic views? Notwithstanding his "repentance" at the Seventeenth Party Congress in January-February 1934, it was plausible to reason that Lominadze may not have changed his mind and therefore could be understood to have put on a duplicitous face to "mask" his inner feelings.[99] How dangerous this might be was another matter, especially since Lominadze discharged his duties with distinction, but the authorities in Moscow had pronounced it cause for alarm. And they had the palpable threat posed by fascism to back them up.

The imputation of double-dealing would have made no sense in the absence of the party's obsession with orthodoxy as well as the appearance of unanimity, an obsession that was made operational by Stalin's relentless drive for absolute power.[100] But orthodoxy and outward unanimity could have become necessary only because the party's authority was based on absolute claims, meaning that even a single dissenting voice became dangerous as the potential ground for an alternative orthodoxy. Such were the implications of the party's church-like status which every Communist, especially those who disagreed with specific party policies, had to confront and which almost always elicited their capitulation.[101]

It should be kept in mind that Lominadze was not accused of perpetrating any specific acts. Thus, the charge of "double-dealing" against him was for a kind of thought-crime analogous to medieval heresy. For the medieval inquisitor, according to a leading historian, "the crime he sought to suppress by punishment was purely a mental one—acts, however criminal, were beyond his jurisdiction."[102] This was essentially the jurisdiction of the party purge as well. But like the Inquisition, the party could and did rely upon the "secular arm," or state, to enforce its judgments against heretics. If the party's inquisition was grounded in the nature of the party's identity and the logic of its struggle for unity, it was nonetheless the threat of arrest by the NKVD that made the party's inquisition so fearful.

In Magnitogorsk Lominadze's posthumously declared "objective" guilt contaminated others like an infection from the grave—but this seemingly bizarre turn of events also had a certain logic. If conspiracy was the method of struggle against the party, close association with a known enemy could be taken as prima facie proof of complicity. Thus, once Lominadze had been pronounced a heretic, anyone who had consorted with him had much to fear, regardless of how well they were known to have performed their duties. There was no undoing past contacts.[103] Those who defended him, moreover, automatically incriminated themselves.

In late March, at a local party conference called to ratify Rafael Khitarov's assumption of the position of first secretary, several more of Lominadze's associates, including the first secretary of the city Komsomol committee, Aleksandr Epeltsveig, were inculpated, thrown out of the party, and arrested.[104] But in the infectious atmosphere, accusations against party members not associated with Lominadze also proliferated, confronting

Khitarov with the unenviable task of sanctioning a wider bloodletting, or risking charges of protecting enemies.[105] Khitarov's position was further complicated by the fact that he had known the capable and dedicated Lominadze since their days together in the Caucasus in the 1920s.[106] Between 19 and 21 June 1935, obkom First Secretary Kuzma Ryndin visited Magnitogorsk, and spoke of the "difficult ordeals" of the Lominadze period. The really difficult ordeals for Ryndin, Khitarov, and the Magnitogorsk party organization, however, were still ahead.[107]

Under such anxious circumstances, the party verification went forward in Magnitogorsk, until by mid-summer 1935 it seemed to be coming to a close. Altogether only ninety-two party cards were withheld, and a mere eighteen Communists expelled, a stark contrast to the purge.[108] But in August, the Central Committee unexpectedly annulled the results of the verification across the country, and announced the necessity of repeating the entire procedure.[109] Through the intervention of the obkom, the co-chairmen of the Magnitogorsk verification commission, Matvei Larin (the city soviet chairman and former chairman of the defunct city Control Commission) and Umanskii (the arrested Bezbabichev's replacement as editor of the city newspaper), were given reprimands for allegedly permitting known White Guardists to retain their party cards.[110] In September 1935, after a struggle with the obkom, Umanskii was removed as editor of the Magnitogorsk newspaper. Both he and Larin were soon expelled from the party, sending a powerful message to their replacements.[111]

The Cheliabinsk obkom, itself under pressure from Moscow, oversaw an intensification of the verification within the Magnitogorsk party organization and a widening of its scope beyond a dozen ill-starred associates of Lominadze and a handful of rogues, to a past, and possible future "White Guard" said to be in possession of party cards.[112] As the obkom authorities were aware, during the Civil War large portions of the country, including the entire Urals, had been held by the Whites for a considerable period. For the many local people who later rose to positions of authority in Magnitogorsk, some contact with the arch-counterrevolutionaries had been unavoidable. Now, more than fifteen years after the events and despite any loyalty demonstrated in the interim, anything less than heroic resistance to the occupying Whites could be judged retrospectively as collaboration unworthy of a Communist.[113]

If a person had once failed to fight against or even fought for the "restoration of capitalism," what was to prevent him or her, when the moment was propitious, from doing so again? In conditions of capitalist encirclement, "forgiveness" meant a possible invitation to disaster. Compelling logic dictated vigilance and, presumably, further expulsions from the party. No party secretary could assert that there were *definitely* no hidden White Guardists inside his or her primary party organization without inviting denunciation for, at best, political blindness.[114] But having so spoken, each official then had to find such concealed former White Guards, or at least some hidden "class aliens." Scapegoating was unavoidable.

Discussions of the verification, like the purge, combined the rhetoric of hygiene with that of inquisition.[115] Under the slogan "Know Every Communist," Magnitogorsk's new verification commission, which included First Secretary Khitarov and an obkom representative, collected denunciations, both anonymous and signed, about party members and their families that served as the basis for inquiries sent to a party member's birthplace or previous place of employment. At the interrogation itself, which like the purge began with the placement of one's party card on the table but unlike the purge was without an audience, the questioning could become intense. Statements made by each member during the first verification, the 1933–34 purge, and other occasions were compared, as party members' biographies, and the way they had been previously reported, became potential traps.[116]

Some Communists refused to say where they first joined the party, and this was by itself considered incriminating.[117] Others told personal stories that seemed on the surface suspicious,[118] or unknowingly contradicted previous statements they had made.[119] Those who tried to be flip were punished.[120] Even people who came forward with "corrections" of their autobiographies, in an attempt to preempt damaging revelations, could well suffer the same fate as those who offered no assistance in the uncovering of inconvenient facts.[121] And unlike the 1933–34 purge, a Communist could not "disappear" by concealing party membership. For everyone in possession of a party card, the verification was inescapable. Verification commission members had wide latitude in the treatment of individual members whom they favored, but those in charge felt pressures to investigate everyone. Writers of denunciations sometimes sent copies to the obkom, Central Committee, Stalin, and the NKVD. Rivalries among apparatchiks at all levels, many of whom cultivated ambitions, increased the flow of information. And primary party meetings, where issues could be publicly aired under the slogan of "self-criticism," continued throughout.

Within the party conspiracy, no one could be completely sure of his or her position. The deference usually shown to members of the party hierarchy coexisted with an all-around vulnerability, even among top local officials. Seemingly unassailable party chieftains in the localities were kept off-balance by the secretariat in Moscow, which, in its persistent pursuit of tighter supervision of regional party machines, frequently resorted to populist appeals to the "party mass" to exercise "control." For local officials this meant that precisely those Communists most apt to question or denounce their rule had to be either placated or thoroughly destroyed. *Pravda* reported that there was some grumbling in the ranks about the verification being a "repression" of party members.[122]

The intensification of the verification in Magnitogorsk imposed by the obkom increased the number of expulsions. By October 1935, after 97 percent of the Magnitogorsk membership had undergone the second verification, there had been 234 expulsions, representing 8.6 percent of the total membership, considerably more than the first time around.[123] But even more important, having become an ex-Communist a person ceased to be above the law, and in some instances expulsions were now followed with arrest by the NKVD. In two top-secret reports to Procurator General Andrei Vyshinskii, dated 19 October 1935 and 7 January 1936, Magnitogorsk Procurator Petr Kefala wrote that criminal charges were brought in twenty-eight cases of expulsion: twelve for hiding service in the White Army, twelve for hiding a kulak past, three for "Trotskyism," and one for "counterrevolutionary activity."[124] The fate of these excommunicated Communists had passed from party bodies to the "secular authorities." Such were the potential stakes of having deceived or challenged the party.

In Moscow the verification was declared officially completed on 25 December 1935, when Nikolai Ezhov, chairman of the Commission of Party Control, addressed a plenum of the Central Committee on its results.[125] In Magnitogorsk, however, the second verification continued after Ezhov's report. Sometime in early 1936 a special obkom brigade arrived to further investigate individual cases. As a result the number of expulsions seems to have risen to 334 (which represented 12 percent of the membership). No explanation was offered for the 100 additional expulsions, a figure exceeding the entire total from the first verification and apparently effected in just two months. Pressure on the obkom from Moscow appears the likely cause although for reasons that remain unclear.[126]

In his report on the verification to a Magnitogorsk party plenum, Khitarov followed Central Committee directives and made a point of going beyond the matter of expulsions, declaring that the Magnitogorsk organization had discovered badly inadequate record keeping and a whole layer of "passive" Communists. "It is one thing to expose alien people, deceivers of the party," explained Khitarov. "The verification had another goal of seeing how each Communist works, how he works in political matters, in order to help him grow, in order to improve the entire party's mass work."[127] It was just such a radical revival of the party's ideological mission that served not only to justify but to necessitate the expulsion of "alien," illiterate, and passive Communists.[128]

The need for an ideological revival in the party could scarcely be denied.[129] It was regime policy to offer higher and faster promotions for party members, and the verification established what anyone could have guessed: that careerism served as one of the principal motivations for seeking party membership.[130] Nor did it require the verification to know that many comrades did not read the party press, let alone study revolutionary theory. One Communist, Bukov, allegedly protested that "I fought against the Whites and will still fight them, but I just can't study."[131] In the party schools, the subjects included Russian language and spelling, for native speakers too.[132]

Despite a mandatory attendance rule, moreover, the verification "revealed" that many Communists regularly missed party meetings, and that the party was overwhelmed trying to mobilize resources for construction and industry, notwithstanding the existence for that purpose of a separate economic administration. Such failings were not just lamentable, they were dangerous. If the redundant party machine did not uphold higher ideals or an ideological mission, it was nothing more than a parasitical stratum of apparatchiks lording over a rank and file burdened by apparently irrelevant extra responsibilities and resentful of the apparatchiks' "ruling class" privileges and lifestyles.

Thanks to the verification the rampant political "passivity" said to have gripped the party was reportedly being replaced by renewed activeness (*aktivnost*) and a rediscovery of the party's revolutionary calling. In Magnitogorsk's central electric station, for example, attendance at party meetings had been averaging 75 to 80 percent, but with the verification it was said to have risen to 100 percent, while the meetings were said to have become very lively. Party school attendance, which had been 70 to 80 percent, also rose, to 95 percent. And the electric station's wall newspaper was issued more frequently.[133] Such an apparent revitalization supposedly swept all Magnitogorsk shops, further stimulated by a general reorganization of party work.[134]

In February 1936, Khitarov could conclude that "the verification of party documents to a significant degree revived [*ozhivila*] internal party work and party mass work." But he added, as was customary for a Bolshevik who practiced "self-criticism," there was more to be done.[135] Khitarov was right, of course. Ezhov, in his December 1935 report on the verification, had announced that after a purge and two document verifications that had together dragged on for more three years, there would be yet another operation, an exchange (*obmen*) of old party cards for new ones. More than a technical matter of replacing worn documents, the 1936 exchange served in effect as a third verification, just when a relaxation might have been expected to set in.[136]

Although central directives stressed that the exchange was designed chiefly to reinforce the revitalizing effects of the second verification by rooting out remaining "passive" elements and was not to be another hunt for enemies, it was governed by even tighter procedures than the verification.[137] Magnitogorsk Communists were sternly advised to know all the facts about their lives and avoid making any mistakes, either when they gave oral presentations or filled in new personnel forms.[138] Only the local first secretary was to hand out the new cards, which were to be received directly from the Central Committee by NKVD field courier and to be filled out in special ink provided by Moscow.

"Not one card in the hands of the enemy!" warned the Magnitogorsk newspaper, which carried such a barrage of stories about fascism—"Fascism is the open terrorist dictatorship of the bourgeoisie"; "Japan occupies Manchuria, which borders on the Soviet Far East"; "Fascism is War!"— that one might have assumed it had in mind Germans, Italians, or Japanese. But as an example of an "enemy," the newspaper cited the case of a Magnitogorsk Communist, Tsarev-Ivanov of mill 300, who had claimed to be an old revolutionary. During the verification, in the preferred party euphemism, "documents came forward" characterizing him as a "class-alien element." When the Magnitogorsk apparat contacted the city from which Tsarev-Ivanov hailed, it discovered that he had been an artisan who had once employed hired labor, for which "he was known far and wide as a kulak." The "enemy" Tsarev-Ivanov was expelled from the ranks.[139]

Khitarov, quoting from the Central Committee instructions, remarked during the verification that "never before has the title of a party member been so high."[140] For that very reason, however, the purity of party members also had to be higher than ever.[141] The upshot of this inference, although derived from the party's self-understanding and the circumstances of the time, was self-destructive. As the party struggled in an uncertain international situation to put its house in order and reclaim its revolutionary mission, that mission came more and more to resemble an all-consuming witch-hunt for "enemies" within.

Party propaganda openly emphasized the inquisitorial aspect of the document "exchange," which coincided with the May 1936 release of the film

Party Card, a thriller about the collaboration of internal and external enemies. In the film, Pavel, the son of a former kulak who has become a shock worker, secretly works for a foreign intelligence agency, from which he receives the assignment of obtaining a party card to facilitate diversionary activity. Owing to a lack of "vigilance" (*bditelnost*) by his party-member wife, Anna, this enemy disguised as a peasant lad is initially successful, although in the end the hypervigilant NKVD uncovers and foils Pavel's plot. Although they love her, Anna's comrades at a party meeting rise one by one with "Bolshevik frankness" to speak about her lack of vigilance. Attention is devoted to the sacred calling of being a Communist, as members recall the heroic struggle in the underground and Civil War. But the overriding message is that no one can be trusted, that everyone should be on the lookout for suspicious behavior, and that given the supposed value for enemies of a party card, Communists especially have to be thoroughly verified. Enough examples from "real life" appeared in the press, dating back to the Kirov assassination, to reinforce the film's lessons. [142]

In such tense circumstances the party-card exchange continued throughout the spring and summer of 1936. On 17 August, approximately four months after it had begun, Khitarov reported to a gorkom plenum that the exchange could be considered finished, even though around one hundred Communists, most of whom were away, had yet to participate. [143] He maintained that the process, although not perfect, had been carried out with a high degree of care (only two blank cards were said to have been invalidated by accidental mutilation). He also disclosed that the eradication of what he now called Magnitogorsk's "Trotskyite-Zinovievite Center" had required an enormous amount of time owing to the leadership of the double-dealer Lominadze. [144] It was the first time Lominadze had been accused of anything in the Magnitogorsk newspaper and only the second time his name had come up since his death nineteen months earlier. Something had happened.

On the day before the city plenum announced the end of the exchange, the Magnitogorsk newspaper carried a notice that a demonstration trial for a "Trotskyite-Zinovievite Bloc" in Moscow had been set for 19 August 1936. Sixteen former oppositionists (eleven of whom were Jews), in cahoots with the arch-oppositionist and publisher of the émigré *Biulleten oppozitsii*, Leon Trotsky (since 1929 living in exile abroad), were now said to have carried out the Kirov assassination as well as to have plotted the murder of most of the party leadership, including Stalin. The "transcript" of the trial proceedings, during which the accused terrorists confessed, took up virtually the entire Magnitogorsk newspaper several days running. The verdict, execution by shooting, was reported on 24 August, accompanied by cries of "death to the evil dogs" and "no mercy for the vile enemies." It was the first time the death penalty was used against former Communists, signaling a further intensification of the "class struggle." Trotsky was convicted in absentia.[145]

Three weeks before the trial, on 29 July 1936, the Central Committee had dispatched a top secret letter to party organizations that explained how the "bloc" had formed in 1932, when the defeated oppositionists, without any chance of regaining power by ordinary political means, made contact with émigré Trotskyites and adopted a course of terror and assassination. According to the letter, the special danger of the bloc stemmed from its class base—it was said to be the "force for the remnants of smashed classes" and "the leading detachment of the counterrevolutionary bourgeoisie"—and from its successful covert penetration of the party apparat. Notwithstanding the trial and conviction, this ominous state of affairs would persist and required the highest vigilance. "Under present conditions," the letter concluded, "the inalienable quality of every Bolshevik must be the ability to detect an enemy of the party, however well he may be masked."[146]

Discussion of the trial and accompanying materials was mandatory for all primary party organizations, as a result of which accusations against "masked enemies" within the party multiplied.[147] In Magnitogorsk several more former associates of the "oppositionist" Lominadze, such as Margarita Dalinger, the party secretary in the dining hall trust, were "unmasked." Dalinger had evidently stated that there were no Trotskyites or Zinovievites in her organization—the surest possible evidence of their presence and her own guilt! Excoriated by the newspaper for such a "lapse of vigilance" and accused of being a close associate of "the double-dealing Lominadze," she admitted that she had "often visited him in his apartment." For this Dalinger was immediately arrested.[148] Others expelled from the party and arrested for having been associated with Lominadze included Magnitogorsk's highest legal official, City Procurator Petr Kefala, who had sanctioned the arrests of all previously identified members of the Lominadze "group."[149]

The setting for such accusations were the now boisterous primary party organization meetings, attended at Moscow's insistence by the mass of Communists who had been given official reprimands by their superiors and even many Communists who had been expelled. Suppressed grievances came to the fore; taboo subjects were broached. Something of the concealed "opposition" that the self-criticism campaign was designed to expose did indeed surface—but much of this "opposition" was directed at the unmasking campaign itself. At one meeting in August 1936 to discuss the Moscow trial of Zinovievites and Trotskyites, an economist, Inozemtsev from factory supply, evidently made a motion to vote against the government's recommended death sentence.[150]

Statements implicitly and explicitly criticizing Stalin appear to have been made. According to a Soviet journalist who in the period of glasnost gained access to party archives, a "sympathizer" named Zologarev remarked at a party meeting in 1936 that "if Lenin were alive, he would show us the correct path—NEP. But Lenin died, and so they repealed it." Tit Zyk, a former party member in the mechanical shop who had been expelled in 1935 for being a "self-seeker who refused to help collect the harvest," was said to have "condemned centralism, according to which 'they issue directives from above and we implement them without thinking. Collectivization was launched in 1929 by Stalin, and this is considered correct. . . . We are the bottom rungs [*nizy*].'"[151]

Neither Zyk's outburst nor Inozemtsev's suggestion to vote against the proposed death sentence was quoted in the local press. The factory newspaper did, however, report the comments of Mikhail Vasilev, the party organizer in the boiler repair shop, who supposedly claimed that "during the study of the materials of the trial of the counterrevolutionary band in our shop, under the guise of asking seemingly naive [*nedoumennye*] questions, certain people conducted manifest counterrevolutionary conversations." Vasilev offered only one example, accusing an economist of having remarked, "to plan, that means to finagle [*fokusnichat*]."[152] With the help of such acrimonious verbal exchanges, something of a leveling atmosphere was created in which the charges of "Trotskyism" and "double-dealing" could not be concentrated solely on Lominadze associates.

As the Magnitogorsk party became engulfed in a flood of accusations that touched management personnel, a few officials, such as Evgenii Kudriavtsev from the city soviet, tried to flee. But there was little chance to escape the pressure: Kudriavtsev was located and ordered to return.[153] Some idea of the atmosphere of the time comes across in the words of the young steel smelter and party stalwart, Aleksei Griaznov, who, when asked by the factory newspaper what to do with enemies, reportedly remarked: "Give them to us, we'll burn them in the open-hearth ovens."[154]

Griaznov could offer what may well have been a sincere suggestion in part because of an unshakable confidence about his own absolute loyalty, a feeling that the majority of Communists no doubt shared. But those making accusations could have other opinions, or ulterior motives. In such an environment, the normal interaction among Communists that arose during the course of party work became a source of possible incrimination and as such, a way to do in rivals, settle scores, or vent frustration.

"It happened that [Emil] Bekker [the chief of rolling mill construction] was connected to Lominadze, and [Moisei] Ioffe [chief of the steel plant's administrative-economic department (AKhU)] to Bekker, but Bekker remained in the party and Ioffe was expelled," wrote the factory newspaper, implying that by this reasoning Bekker too should have been expelled. Moreover, the newspaper asked, "Why didn't they also expel people who were tied to Ioffe?" commenting that "in this manner you can keep going a very long way."[155] If the factory newspaper could reason thusly, so could the ambitious or rancorous within the lower levels of the apparat and among the rank and file.

The Magnitogorsk apparat evidently endeavored to contain this internal convulsion. Some Communists were said by the gorkom to have been "wrongly" expelled because they were on the obkom *nomenklatura* (and as such could be removed only with the obkom's approval) and also because the charges against them were false. The three examples cited were city soviet chairman Dmitrii Snopov, expelled for being close to Evgenii Kudriavtsev and helping him escape (called true, but exaggerated); Ermolai Prokhorovich, chief of the city health department, expelled for giving Lominadze medical treatment (said to have been his duty); and Ioffe, who was accused of taking part in the burial of Lominadze (he was said not to have been in Magnitogorsk at the time).[156] To be sure, according to party statutes, primary party organizations were charged with the responsibility for voting expulsions. But everyone knew that these low-level bodies did not normally take action on such major questions without written or verbal instructions from above. Thus the "unauthorized" expulsions were a sign that Moscow's frequent calls to the "party mass" to become "active" were being heeded.

The obkom accused gorkom officials of shielding their own, a charge that in all likelihood was accurate.[157] Magnitogorsk party officials may have been frightened by where all this "activism" and "vigilance" from below was leading.[158] It was one matter to accept or even assist the destruction of a handful of the deceased Lominadze's associates, a few former officers in the White Army, and some supposedly better-off peasants who at one time might have been "exploiters." It was quite another to preside over the expulsion, and possible arrest, of one's own trusted friends and colleagues, not to say oneself. But short of a complete reinterpretation of the political situation by Moscow, the process could not be stopped.

Meetings could not be suspended or avoided, and accusations, once publicly stated, acquired a kind of irrefutability regardless of how implausible they might be. Denials were often seen as incriminating, and anyone who spoke on behalf of an accused Communist risked denunciation for "protecting enemies" or "defending vile murders and bandits."[159] Even when not immediately acted upon, the denunciations ensured that some "negative" information about a large number, perhaps a majority, of Communists was introduced into party files.[160]

The party in Magnitogorsk was enmeshed in a process whose premises and justifications all made sense, but one that was nonetheless becoming more and more bizarre as well as personally threatening. Yet precisely because the internal search for enemies was so logical—indeed necessary—from a party point of view, Communists could scarcely avoid participation in it. The continuation of the inquisition, in other words, appeared to be dictated by the fundamental tenets and basic political language of the worldview that party members held dear. At the same time, however, many apparatchiks no doubt began to feel that their only defense lay in attacking others.

In this highly uncertain mood within the party, after a few dozen arrests and a deluge of denunciations by Communists and ex-Communists of each other, the Sixth Magnitogorsk City Party Conference took place. It was late December 1936, and the Stalin constitution had just been formally adopted in Moscow. With the entire body of conference delegates standing, Magnitogorsk school children sang "Shiroka strana moia rodnaia," afterward calling out "thank you comrade Stalin for a happy childhood." Obkom First Secretary Ryndin gave a two-hour opening report, which was reportedly "greeted with a rousing ovation."[161] The principal topic of discussion appears to have been expulsions and "enemies."[162]

In what was described as an effort to improve party work, the Magnitogorsk gorkom was divided into three raikoms, or district committees—named for Kirov, Ordzhonikidze, and Stalin, the latter replacing the factory party committee.[163] What else the conference accomplished remains unclear. Outside the main hall, lavish buffet tables groaned under the weight of otherwise scarce food and drink supplied gratis to the delegates. But for many of those in attendance the conference would in retrospect come to look like a kind of last supper. As the year 1936 came to a close, the party inquisition in Magnitogorsk and localities around the country acquired a new character as a result of further decisive intervention by the party's top leadership.

THE PARTY COMES ALIVE:
THE SEARCH FOR THE ENEMY WITHIN (II)

In the main *political* task said to lay before the party and the country—the "struggle" to deploy Bolshevik "self-criticism" to "unmask" concealed internal enemies—Moscow effected a dramatic radicalization in November 1936 with *Pravda's* report of a trial in Novosibirsk for industrial sabotage. To be sure, charges of wrecking and sabotage dated from the first days of the new regime (serving as the rationale for the establishment of the security police), and several high-profile trials of industrial saboteurs had been held before (the so-called Shakhty affair in 1928 and Industrial Party affair in 1930, for example). Now, however, the alleged perpetrators were not "bourgeois" engineers, or holdovers from the tsarist regime, but traitorous "Soviet-era" personnel.[164]

Six engineers and administrative cadres from the Kemerovo central mine, one of whom was a German, were charged with having arranged a series of explosions on 23 September that killed ten miners and injured fourteen others. Their actions were said to constitute a "subversive Trotskyite conspiracy," involving foreign industrialists and the Gestapo, to restore capitalism in the USSR. On the last day of the trial, all six defendants were shot. The announcement of the sentence was accompanied by outpourings of indignation from "leading" workers who were quoted as demanding "no mercy for the swine." "Stenographic" accounts of the proceedings were reprinted in local newspapers, including *Magnitogorskii rabochii*, to convey the trial's "lessons" regarding the supposed prevalence of subversion and to provide a guide for discussions at local party meetings.[165]

The events in Kemerovo were portrayed as signifying a transformation in "the enemy's" methods: from "double-dealing," a largely internal party affair that sometimes required the *subsequent* intervention of the "secular authorities," to "wrecking" (*vreditelstvo*), a matter that a priori fell within the jurisdiction of the "secular authorities." In a reflection of this declared change, on the eve of the Novosibirsk trial in late August 1936, Ezhov, one of Stalin's principal protégés and the person who had overseen the party verification, was transferred from the party apparat to the NKVD. Simultaneous with the trial, USSR Procurator General Vyshinskii, also a Stalin loyalist, issued a secret directive instructing local procurators to review all cases involving large-scale fires, breakdowns, and the production of defective goods for hints of counterrevolutionary wrecking.[166]

When it came to suspicions of industrial sabotage, Magnitogorsk, like all Soviet enterprises, was indeed rich in potential.[167] Altogether, industrial mishaps on the site numbered in the many thousands annually.[168] Even more serious, many of the "subversive" activities named in the Novosibirsk trial resembled everyday management practices in the planned economy. As was well known, in the efforts to fulfill the plan, numerous violations of procedures were knowingly made. This was especially true with Stakhanovism, whose deliberate adventurism led to numerous breakdowns and served as the basis for many of the concrete charges in cases of wrecking (even as the regime encouraged a revival of Stakhanovism to combat the wave of wrecking).[169] Given these circumstances, no engineer or manager was beyond accusation.[170]

The interpretation laid down in November 1936 that all unfortunate occurrences in industry were deliberate wrecking appears to have taken Magnitogorsk officials by surprise. A May 1936 gas poisoning in the coke shop resulting in twenty-two victims, including four fatalities (called "serious injuries" in the newspaper), had not been portrayed as "wrecking."[171] What is more, the first announced local case of "wrecking" following the Novosibirsk trial was a feeble one, involving the alleged poisoning of coke plant workers with contaminated milk by unnamed individuals.[172]

It was fully seven weeks after this dubious first report, and more than two months after the Novosibirsk trial, that a major instance of wrecking in Magnitogorsk with named perpetrators was announced in the local press. That case was also said to have occurred at the coke plant, whose former chief of construction, A. M. Mariasin, had been arrested in Moscow in connection with the January 1937 trial of Deputy Industry Commissar Georgii Piatakov and sixteen others (the so-called Parallel Anti-Soviet Trotskyite Center).[173] On 30 January, Piatakov was sentenced to death and executed.[174] Like the Novosibirsk case, discussion of the Piatakov trial and its "lessons" was made mandatory for all party organizations. This time, the effect in the localities appears to have been greater, although not immediately.

On February 9, N. Kartashov [Rafael Shneiveis], who at age twenty-seven was the Magnitogorsk newspaper's chief political correspondent, wrote a sharp piece about "wrecking" in the Magnitogorsk coke plant.[175] As "enemies" Kartashov named Manych, the former chief of the coke ovens shop who had left Magnitogorsk two years earlier and was now under arrest elsewhere, and Sazhin. Of the latter, Kartashov wrote that "in his time he was unmasked as an enemy and thrown out of the shop, only to reappear a few days later." In addition, Sazhin was said to have been given a new, equipped apartment in the second superblock. "Who sheltered the enemy?" Kartashov asked. "Who let him back into the plant? No one can say for sure." Of course, the only person with such authority was the shop chief, Vasilii Shevchenko, who only two years earlier had received the state's highest award, the Order of Lenin, and was now being indirectly impugned.[176]

Kartashov cast his account of wrecking in the coke plant as a revolutionary breakthrough in activism. "What is most evident in the coke shop today is that the trial of the Trotskyite band has generated considerable activeness," he wrote, adding that "one gets the impression that only now have the flood gates of self-criticism been opened." What made such "self-criticism" remarkable was that it was directed at top management. Workers, said to have been "afraid to open their mouths for fear of being fired," were now allegedly coming forward. The one "worker" cited by name, however, Maleev, said to be a foreman, offered only metaphors. He was quoted as saying that he could keep silent no longer "because if I keep silent and others do too, then the enemy will worm his way back in. The enemy hides himself in the burrow, and then comes out into the light and will wreck and ruin." Maleev pledged to unmask the enemy because "my shop is dearer than my life."[177]

Whether a "revolutionary breakthrough" in activism had yet been achieved seems doubtful. A similar exposé on the problems in the open-hearth shop by Aleksei Griaznov had appeared even earlier, on 6 February, but no wreckers were identified.[178] Considerable pressure from above was visible in the press, however. On 10 February, the *Magnitogorskii rabochii* had carried the lead editorial from *Pravda*, dated two days earlier: "Bolshevik Self-Criticism—The Basis of Party Action" (the entire rest of the issue was devoted to the Pushkin centenary).[179] On the eleventh, the obkom newspaper accused the Magnitogorsk gorkom of having limited trial discussions to those organizations where serious wrecking had already been unmasked (i.e., the coke plant).[180] Comparable pressure was no doubt also being applied behind the scenes.

Within two weeks of the obkom newspaper's published exhortation, "revelations" were announced concerning the discovery of wrecking in fire-clay production,[181] the construction trust,[182] coal storage,[183] rail transport,[184] steam generation,[185] rolling mills[186]—indeed, in virtually every corner of the Magnitogorsk plant. By the second half of February 1937, moreover, what had been only intimations of the culpability of top managers became direct accusations. Judging by the stories in the city newspaper, one could almost conclude that wrecking had suddenly become the most frequent activity engaged in by Soviet managers and engineers.[187]

Vasilii Shevchenko of the coke plant was the first to fall. In the obkom newspaper, he was denounced for having resisted firing people who had been "unmasked," for having relented only after pressure had been applied, and for having fired personnel in a way that was most advantageous to them (i.e., "let go in accordance with personal wishes"). Shevchenko was also accused of defending Manych, who had been arrested as a wrecker. Such actions led to Shevchenko's expulsion from the party.[188] Meanwhile, his assistant, Ivan Gavrilin, had apparently defended his boss at party meetings of the coke plant on 4 and 14 February (for which he, too, was expelled from the party).[189] No longer protected by party immunity, Shevchenko and Gavrilin were soon arrested by the "secular power" along with almost two dozen others—in the coke shop alone.[190] There were similar cases in other shops with comparable numbers of arrests.[191]

Committees to "liquidate the consequences of wrecking" were founded in each shop, and the supposed "lessons" of the many instances of "exposure" were endlessly analyzed and publicized.[192] In a follow-up piece on the coke plant, Kartashov wrote that "what yesterday was unclear, what earlier seemed mysterious and incomprehensible, today has become completely clear and transparent."[193] The exposure of wrecking in the coke plant, in other words, provided not only the definitive inducement to activism, but also a comprehensive explanation for the factory's well-known ills. Kartashov reiterated this "message" again, in greater detail, a few days later.[194]

To contemporaries, repeated mishaps and routine problems might seem to have resulted from carelessness arising out of worker inexperience or negligence on the part of foremen and other lower-level supervisory personnel, but some problems obviously stemmed from faulty design. Among the latter were the system of factory transport between shops and the facilities for loading and unloading raw materials, whose inefficient set-up and operation led to unnecessary work and expensive waste. More seriously, most "hot shops" at the steel plant were characterized by dangerously high temperatures, thick concentrations of dust, and the absence of ventilation, resulting in periodic gas poisonings.[195] Was such manifestly harmful design an accident? Was negligence really careless, or could it also be deliberate? Why were almost sixty workers a year being killed on the job?[196]

The many troubles and often poor performance of the steel plant and its auxiliary factories served as apparent confirmation that some people were indeed engaging in "sabotage," yet these wreckers were portrayed not as aggrieved persons acting individually, but as spies and agents engaged in conspiracies. The charge of wrecking may have seemed credible, but did the saturation of the USSR by enemies working for the foreign bourgeoisie really make sense? Stalin tackled this question directly in his published and widely disseminated report at the watershed Central Committee plenum in February-March 1937 (cited at the beginning of this chapter) devoted to the so-called right opposition and to wrecking.[197]

"Why should [bourgeois states] send fewer spies, wreckers, diversionaries, and murderers into the Soviet interior than they send into other bourgeois states?" Stalin asked rhetorically. "Wouldn't it be truer, from the point of view of Marxism, to suppose that into the interior of the Soviet Union bourgeois states ought to send twice and thrice more wreckers, spies, diversionaries, and murderers?" Mimicking doubters, he continued:

> Capitalist encirclement? Oh, that's rubbish! What significance can some kind of capitalist encirclement have if we fulfill and surpass our economic plans? New forms of wrecking, the struggle with Trotskyism? All nonsense! What significance can these trifles have if we fulfill and overfulfill our plan? Party rules, elections to party organs, the accountability of party leaders before the party mass? Is there a need for all this? Is it worth bothering with these trifles if our economy grows, if the material situation of workers and peasants improves more and more? Trifles, all of it! The plans we overfulfill, our party is not bad, the party's Central Committee is also not bad, what the hell more do we need? Strange people sit there in Moscow, in the Central Committee of the party: they think up all sorts of questions, instigate about some kind of wrecking; they themselves don't sleep and don't allow others to.

Such an attitude Stalin called a "glaring example" of the dangerous "political blindness" among those carried away by "dizzy excitement over economic successes."[198]

This was the same infamous formula Stalin had hit upon to deflect blame from himself during the disastrous opening stages of the collectivization campaign in 1930, when he ridiculed local officials for "laughable attempts to jump over themselves," attributing such missteps to "the fact that the heads of certain of our comrades are dizzy with success."[199] In 1937, the consequences of such giddiness were said to have been far more serious, having allowed traitorous Soviet engineers and managers to launch a countrywide wrecking campaign. The only answer could be to "raise vigilance" against Communist party officials, who, even if not deliberate enemies, could be held criminally accountable for their de facto encouragement of "wrecking." The plenum itself demonstrated this severe approach.[200]

Behind this probe for "objective" abetters of industrial saboteurs in the party apparat lay the presupposition that economic advances were nothing without commensurate strides in "political consciousness." This was after all the rationale for the party's role in the industrialization. Why did the party exist, if not to exercise political vigilance? But the party was being accused of being the main culprit in a general lapse of vigilance. Notwithstanding the previous several years' efforts of raising the party's ideological level, there was apparently more to be done. Aided by the press's incessant goading—"more self-criticism, comrades"—the linkage of industrial "wrecking" to "political carelessness" by the party laid down at the February-March Central Committee plenum finally seemed to bring about the party's long-sought total activization—as demonstrated by the spirited gathering of the Magnitogorsk "party active," held from 22 to 25 March 1937 to discuss the Moscow plenum.[201]

The ground for the Magnitogorsk meeting had been prepared a few days prior. On 20 March 1937, the Magnitogorsk newspaper printed a summary of a highly critical obkom plenum, held from 14 to 16 March, along with a vicious attack on the Magnitogorsk gorkom signed by A. Zakharov that had appeared in the *Cheliabinskii rabochii* on 18 March 1937.[202] The obkom's heavy-handedness toward the gorkom had been prompted largely by the obkom's own vulnerability, since even earlier it had been subjected to heavy fire in *Pravda* and again at the Central Committee plenum.[203] By means of the party press and public discussion, the grim instructions contained in internal communications sent from above were publicly fortified, reaching all the way down to the lowest levels of the party pyramid, no matter how far from Moscow.

According to the account in the city newspaper, the first day of the four-day Magnitogorsk plenary meeting was taken up with a report on the Central Committee plenum by Vladislav Shurov, second secretary of the Cheliabinsk obkom (filling in for First Secretary Ryndin, who was presiding over an obkom "party active" at the same time). The rest of the Magnitogorsk session was given over to discussion of Shurov's report, normally a pro forma exercise of slavish endorsement, and now anything but that. Indeed, the newspaper's account of the discussion following Shurov's report began with stinging charges by Aleksandr Lopaev, the director of the local branch office of the state bank, that Kasperovich, chief of the factory's Department of Capital Construction (OKS), had concealed the steel plant's true financial picture at a recent city soviet plenum.[204]

In this no doubt common practice, which impinged directly on the bank official's job and may have involved him in unavoidable financial shenanigans, Lopaev also implicated the former plant director, Avraamii Zaveniagin, who had just been promoted to first deputy commissar of NKTP.[205]

"After the[ir] deception," Lopaev was quoted as saying, "I asked in an article, 'Whom are the construction people tricking?' Because of this comrade Zaveniagin pounced on me, promising to 'wipe me from the face of the earth.'" Lopaev added that the gorkom and its secretary, Khitarov, also "knew about the false figures a year before from written reports," but had kept quiet. It is not clear what set Lopaev off. Given the steel plant's messy financial condition, perhaps he anticipated being held criminally accountable and concluded that going on the offensive was the best way to save his own skin. In any case, such a public attack against the highest local officials *while they were still in power* was unprecedented, and set the tone for the rest of the newspaper's report of the meeting.[206]

In the published version of the party meeting, after Lopaev came A. Goltsev, director of the sewing factory, who underlined the "historical significance" of the Central Committee plenum, then directed sharp words toward obkom First Secretary Ryndin, one of the seventy-one full members of the Central Committee, as well as Shurov, for their rude "bossing" (*administratirovanie*) of the Magnitogorsk party organization. The assault by members of the gorkom on the top party officials in the oblast—one of whom, Shurov, was present—may have been a survival tactic. All the same, it was in keeping with the logic of the process: those "below," after chafing under the millstone of "iron party discipline," were "activated" by "signals" in *Pravda* and secret party circulars to voice their accumulated grievances in the name of "inner-party democracy."

Fedor Savelev, party secretary for Magnitogorsk's Kirov raikom, followed Goltsev and adopted a different tactic. Although Goltsev too underscored the importance of the Central Committee plenum, he went on to malign not the obkom but the Magnitogorsk gorkom. Savelev was himself a prominent member of the gorkom, yet he did not admit his own part in the failures. He instead singled out First Secretary Khitarov, suggesting that the charges leveled at the gorkom ought to be directed at the top person, not his lieutenants. As Savelev's denunciation of Khitarov demonstrated, the apparat had a large hand in its own undoing.

At this point in the text, the chief of the construction trust Magnitostroi, Konstantin Valerius, condemned the deferential and rigidly hierarchical relations of power characteristic of economic and political administration. But of the thirteen people directly quoted in the newspaper's account of the meeting, Valerius was the only one not to attack others—for the time being. After Valerius, L. Rudnitskii, the city Komsomol secretary, also criticized the cultishness of the local party leadership and flattery, including his own. He faulted Khitarov for failing to put an end to these practices and then "brought up examples of the arbitrariness [*proizvol*] of certain local workers [*rabotnikov*]," as the newspaper observed. Rudnitskii named "deputy complex director Khazanov, also the chairman of the city sports club 'Metal Worker,' [who] acquired for himself a hired football squad." According to Rudnitskii, "the city committee of the Komsomol struggled against this." As a result, he claimed that "Khazanov forbade his employees to go to the Komsomol. We turned to the member of the bureau of the city committee comrade Kolbin, who remarked: 'Are you serious? Khazanov is the deputy director of the complex. You can't push this.'" Rudnitskii added that "the pattern of servility reached the point that there appeared in the city a settlement named after Khazanov." Having apparently staked his own survival and that of the rest of the city Komsomol leadership on criticism of even higher local officials, Rudnitskii directed a final barb at Kariaev, the editor of the city newspaper, for failing to criticize the mistakes of the gorkom.

A. Zakharov of the obkom spoke next in the published sequence, accusing Khitarov of having painted a rosy picture of the situation in Magnitogorsk to the obkom. Zakharov also noted that during December and January alone, seven or eight photographs of Khitarov had appeared in the Magnitogorsk newspaper (previously considered de rigueur). After Zakharov spoke, deputy factory chief Khazanov blasted his own administration, in extremely general terms, using the now stock phrase, it was "cut off from the masses." He repeated a question that may have been posed to him: why, since there were so many enemies in the factory, had he not known about them? Khazanov gave no answer, although he implied that shop bosses—his subordinates—were at fault.

Echoing the earlier remarks by Goltsev, two prominent members of the Magnitogorsk gorkom lashed out at the obkom. Lev Berman, the secretary of the city's Ordzhonikidze raikom, accused the obkom of mutual-protection (*semeistvennost*) and cliquishness (*artelshchina*). "Comrade Berman pointed out," the newspaper wrote, "that the newspaper *Magnitogorskii rabochii* struggled to criticize the gorkom." The paper's editor, Kariaev, followed this self-serving paraphrase by bashing the obkom for "toadyism, nepotism, squelching self-criticism, and violating and perverting internal party democracy." Unlike Berman, however, Kariaev also criticized the gorkom and admitted in careful language that the newspaper was "not on the level it should have been on" with respect to criticism of the gorkom's mistakes. Kariaev's appeared as one of the more adroit performances, considerably more sophisticated than Khazanov's.

Golushkin, second secretary of the gorkom, admitted the correctness of the criticism leveled at the gorkom, acknowledging that it had not paid enough attention to "party" matters. "I, for example, can more or less exactly say, what the situation regarding plan fulfillment is in construction, what is going on in the open-hearth shop, the blast furnace shop, what materials are lacking, how finished products are shipped, because every day five to six expediters [*tolkachi*] visit me," Golushkin revealed. "But about the situation in party organizations of this or that shop, about party organizers, I, very likely, don't know anything." The utter lack of embellishment or guile in Golushkin's self-criticism seems striking, as does his blunt admission that for him, the second highest Magnitogorsk party official, party work was really the same as factory administration. The party was made to appear redundant.

The voice of the police was printed next. Dorozhko, the deputy chief of the city NKVD, delivered a tirade against wreckers in the form of innuendo and slogans: "Wreckers are everywhere"; "We must maintain our vigilance"; "Not for one minute lessen your revolutionary vigilance." In what the city newspaper printed of his speech, there was little that was concrete, although according to the obkom newspaper, "the party active listened with great attention to the speech of comrade Dorozhko, who told of facts of wrecking work on the blast furnace, blooming, and railroad construction." His comments reflected the NKVD's broad-brush approach in the panicky political situation that they had deliberately strived to create.

Next, in a speech that must have lifted the spirits of the Magnitogorsk comrades, Syrkin, the editor of the obkom newspaper *Cheliabinskii rabochii*, added force to the charges leveled by the Magnitogorsk gorkom against the obkom. Made vulnerable by the collapse of its own solidarity, some members of the Magnitogorsk gorkom exploited the cleavages in the obkom. "Comrade Syrkin spoke about comrade Ryndin's incorrect selection of cadres according to nepotism and cliquishness," wrote the Magnitogorsk newspaper, "as a result of which in and around the obkom bureau there turned out to be not a few reticents [*malchalnikov*] and along with them blatant toadies." With this fortified grenade tossed at the obkom by Syrkin, who named several names, the report of the first day of discussion came to a close.

The newspaper's account of the second and third days' discussion began with a speech by Rafael Khitarov, who endeavored to meet the challenge of self-criticism. Having accepted blame, however, Khitarov soon redirected his comments toward the obkom, accusing it of squelching self-criticism. "Self-criticism," he quipped, "was on vacation." Although faulting obkom First Secretary Ryndin for intimidation (*zapugivanie*) and bossing (*ko-*

mandovanie), Khitarov acknowledged having known of the unsatisfactory state of affairs in the obkom and yet having failed to point it out. Of Khitarov's harsh appraisal of the obkom someone remarked that his criticism of the gorkom ought to have been as sharp.

Nikolai Saraikin, secretary of the Stalin raikom (the steel plant party committee), spoke in scandalous tones of how the arrested former coke plant director Vasilii Shevchenko "was praised until the last days, his portrait was published in the newspaper and in the collection published for the fifth-year anniversary of the factory, which was edited by Zaveniagin and Kariaev. They did not see that Shevchenko was an enemy." At the end of the account of the day's events the newspaper enigmatically noted that "Saraikin presented a statement acknowledging the erroneousness of his remarks," without specifying which remarks were erroneous and why. Leonid Vaisberg, then chief of mill 500, criticized Valerius and Khazanov, both of whom had been named by many others, but omitted any reference to Zaveniagin, Magnitogorsk's former director. Vaisberg was followed by Ivan Sorokin, the city procurator and the man with the power to sanction arrests. Sorokin was accused in editorial comments of not having discussed his own mistakes, but no details of his speech were offered. After Sorokin, Valerius spoke again, this time going mildly on the offensive.

Valerius claimed that Khitarov had strongly recommended he relate to Mrs. Zaveniagin, the president of the Council of Engineers' Wives, "with respect toward rank [*chinopochitanie*]," even though the work of the council was judged "very, very unsatisfactory." This was the one instance he accused anyone by name. For the next several months Valerius was savagely attacked, but he always defended himself without damaging others. Like many others in high positions, he probably hoped to ride things out. (A month later, in April 1937, the newspaper wrote that Valerius thought "the criticism of the construction trust had gone too far, but he also considered this 'unavoidable,' for it was now that kind of 'time' [*seichas takoi 'moment'*]." Meanwhile, he evidently protected people, for he was accused of sending "doubtful people" away on business trips or securing them posts elsewhere.)[207]

Following Valerius came Dmitrii Gleizer, secretary of the party committee in open-hearth shop no. 1, whose remarks were paraphrased. "He pointed out, allegedly," wrote the newspaper, "that the *Magnitogorskii rabochii*, squelching criticism, at the time of the city party conference did not publish in the summary account that part of his speech in which he had criticized the *Magnitogorskii rabochii*."[208] "After the speech by Gleizer," the newspaper added, "the discussion period was cut off [and] obkom secretary comrade Shurov gave the final word."[209]

In apparent confirmation of Gleizer's charges, what Shurov had said in closing was not reported, perhaps because he had berated the gorkom.[210] The newspaper, the organ of the gorkom, was understandably reluctant to use its own pages to destroy itself as well as the rest of the gorkom. But such self-destruction had become unavoidable. If the principal support for enemies was the suppression of "self-criticism," to suppress self-criticism was to incriminate oneself as a collaborator. The only choice was to practice self-criticism, thereby incriminating oneself anyway. Having struggled to limit the damage of the March meeting, the city newspaper ended up doing just that, publishing a devastating lead editorial on 27 March that was far sharper in tone and more focused on the gorkom, especially on the *Magnitogorskii rabochii* and its editor, Kariaev, than the account of the meeting itself had been.

The unsigned editorial could only have been written by someone familiar with the internal mood of the local party hierarchy. It accused the gorkom of having fallen into a period of "complacency, heedlessness, and light-heartedness" after the unmasking of Lominadze, the event that had been used by Moscow as a means for radicalizing the process begun with the 1933 party purge. In an indirect disclosure of the tension that had come to envelop Magnitogorsk party circles, the editorial related how following the completion of the 1935 exchange of party documents many members of the gorkom had come to feel that the party was "completely clean" and that the situation was "safe." But "all of a sudden," the editorial continued (tellingly emphasizing the surprise), new wreckers "were found." The reason given for this lamentable turn of events was analogous to the one Stalin put forth at the Central Committee plenum: at the top of the Magnitogorsk apparat, in the gorkom bureau itself, "there was no self-criticism," only "nepotism, toadyism, and complacency," which had allowed wreckers a free hand.[211] (The same analysis was applied to the factory administration.)[212]

That the party leadership in Magnitogorsk pursued the search for internal enemies only with considerable prodding from above, that it had hoped to control the process and limit its effects to people tied to Lominadze, and that it had then been caught unawares when Moscow further radicalized the campaign and directed it at the local leadership itself seems credible. For the local apparat, in March 1937 the world was suddenly turned upside down. What a cunning and unpredictable practice Bolshevik self-criticism had turned out to be! The more it was deployed, the more it still needed to be deployed, and the higher up the local hierarchy it went.

Self-criticism had come to mean outright condemnation, but much like the Inquisition, the "self-criticism" campaign of the party spoke of "saving" people, not destroying them. An article in the central press explained that "the real way to protect and preserve party officials is to be ruthless in the criticism of shortcomings, to expose them ruthlessly to the public opinion of the party." The article concluded that "one has to correct a man at the right moment, to save him for the party." In such a way were political denunciations made to appear altruistic.[213]

It also must be kept in mind that the search for internal enemies was conducted under the banner of "party revival" and "democratization." These concepts were not only accepted by all party members; they were also far from abstract, for as specified by the Central Committee at the February-March plenum, throughout April there were unprecedented secret-ballot elections to leadership positions in primary party organizations. This process led to a dramatic turnover of lower-level officeholders.[214] In Magnitogorsk, the city newspaper reported that in the Kirov raikom, 50 percent of party secretaries and organizers were new. Similar results were reported for the city's other two raikoms, and were confirmed at the Seventh Magnitogorsk Party Conference, held in late May 1937.[215] Previously, "voting" for such positions meant applying a rubber stamp to appointments made from above—a practice that was now "exposed" and condemned, further intensifying the atmosphere of "democratization."

When asked by the newspaper how he got involved in party work, Cherenkov, the secretary of the party committee in the KBO (the Kirov district branch of the KBU), reportedly responded that "once, comrade Savelev [of the raikom] summoned me and the chief of the KBO Tabunov and said to him: 'For party secretary I think I'll send you this here guy (he nods toward me). What do you think?'" Tabunov, of course, accepted raikom Secretary Savelev's "suggestion." Such a picture of the relationship between the raikom and primary party organizations was elaborated by another Magnitogorsk Communist, Likhachev, who was quoted to the effect that "the secretary of the Kirov raikom Savelev showed up at the KBU party committee, informed them that their party secretary, Larichev, was being summoned for work in the raikom and recommended Efimov in his place." According to Likhachev, "some members of the KBU party committee objected, but the secretary of the raikom insisted. And so they 'agreed' with him." In the recent secret-ballot party election, however, Efimov was not reelected.[216]

Elections were but one part of the process of "democratization." During and after the March meeting of the party "active" and the subsequent April party elections, political bombs continued to be detonated in the city newspaper. In addition to the charges of wrecking up and down the steel plant, "counterrevolutionary bands" were said to have been unmasked in the Komsomol, the city's medical department,[217] and the mining institute.[218] Group arrests by the NKVD shook these and other organizations. Such was the grim backdrop to the talk of democratization and "renewal." Within a few months of the March party "active" meeting, most of the fourteen gorkom speakers cited in the newspaper were expelled from the party and arrested; at least seven were executed.[219] As for the three obkom representatives at the meeting, two were expelled and arrested; the third escaped arrest but not death.

On 11 May 1937, six weeks after the "party active" meeting in Magnitogorsk, came the spectacular announcement that Vladislav Shurov of the obkom had "died" the previous day. He was thirty-seven years old. No cause of death was disclosed. Suicide seems likely.[220] Although the obkom and First Secretary Ryndin had been slammed by *Pravda* back in February, with the approach of the Second Cheliabinsk Obkom Party Conference, scheduled for June, the attacks grew fiercer.[221] The obkom leadership seems to have survived the conference,[222] but not long thereafter Magnitogorsk's A. Kariaev, despite having been mercilessly attacked by the obkom, was promoted to the editorship of the obkom newspaper, replacing Syrkin, who was arrested.[223] And a few months later, in October 1937, Khitarov was moved up to second secretary of the obkom, evidently to replace someone just arrested.[224] Before the end of the year, Khitarov too was arrested along with Ryndin (both were soon executed). In January 1938 new second and third secretaries, sent from Moscow, were named, but no first secretary.[225] In May 1938, when Dmitrii Antonov arrived from the Central Committee apparat to take over as first secretary, the rout of the obkom was complete.[226]

Back in Magnitogorsk, after Khitarov had moved to the obkom, he was replaced by the city's second secretary, Lev Berman. But at a gorkom plenum in December 1937, attended by K. M. Ogurtsov, the new acting obkom second secretary, and Pavel Chistov, the new chief of the oblast NKVD, Berman was relieved of his post as first secretary for "failing in the deployment of the struggle against enemies of the people"—a formulaic charge that can perhaps be taken literally. Soon expelled from the party, Berman was arrested and executed. (Konstantin Ivanov of the steel plant administration took over as acting first secretary of the gorkom.)[227] Several other ranking Communists were also removed from the gorkom plenum, including the secretaries of all three raikoms. There is reason to believe that most, if not all, were also arrested.[228]

Such a turn of events was a long way from the limited arrests by the "secular arm" in connection with the purge, verification, and exchange of party documents that had begun in 1933. But even amid the mass arrests and routing of both the obkom and gorkom, the party's self-criticism campaign retained its rhetoric of renewal. Moreover, scapegoats for the devastation were found when a January 1938 plenum of the decimated Central Committee issued a warning that the campaign to unmask enemies was being distorted by "hostile maneuvers."[229]

Energetic unmasking had been encouraged at every turn by Moscow's relentless calls for activism, yet now it could be taken as evidence of wrecking. Of the situation in Magnitogorsk the obkom newspaper reported that "many Communists were expelled as a result of provocational petitions by enemies of the people, slanderers, and careerists."[230] As examples of what were euphemistically called *perestrakhovshchiki* (those who play it safe, literally, "the over-insurers") the newspaper pointed to the ex-Communist Kekin, who was accused of having "slandered" twenty-seven party members. By such means, concluded the obkom paper with a ring of authenticity, "enemies of the people introduced uncertainty in the ranks of party organizations."[231] To make matters worse, the city newspaper complained that the Communists expelled by what were now categorized as unsubstantiated rumors were being treated like pariahs, shunned by colleagues and friends fearful of incrimination by association.[232]

The Central Committee plenum's decree on "mistakes in expulsions" and "the criminal treatment of the fate of party members," whatever the maneuvers and motivations in the capital, placed the responsibility for creating a situation conducive to mass expulsions, recriminations, and arrests on embittered enemies rather than on Moscow. While skillfully deflecting blame, the decree did nothing to stop the arrests by the NKVD. But it did set off a reinstatement frenzy within the party.

In Magnitogorsk the appeals process for expelled Communists started slowly (the official reason given was that documents had to be collected from primary party organizations), but by April the three Magnitogorsk raikoms held mini-party conferences to consider the matter of "groundless" expulsions. In the city's Stalin raikom, there were forty reinstatements (said to be about half the number of recent expulsions there). But the city newspaper complained that some of these reinstated Communists were in fact enemies, implying that the raikoms were trying to take advantage of the Central Committee resolution.[233] Nonetheless, up to a quarter of the Communists expelled in 1937–38 may have been reinstated, although some were again expelled.[234]

Adding to the confusion, alongside the reconsideration of expulsions the January Central Committee plenum ordered the review of all recent admissions to the party. Entrance to the party, which had been closed since January 1933, was reopened as of 1 November 1936 (by a 29 September 1936 Central Committee decree).[235] By the end of 1937, however, only 40 people had been admitted to the party in Magnitogorsk, and the entrance of even these few was now called into question. The drive for new members was renewed in early 1938, and by the middle of the year, 180 people were enrolled in the party as candidate members (against what was viewed as a potential recruit population of 8,000 Stakhanovites, 5,012 Komsomols, and 572 sympathizers).[236] Also, some 90 party candidates (of more than 750) were promoted to full membership.[237] But in terms of sheer numbers, neither the new enrollments nor the reinstatements compensated for the steep decline initiated in 1933, although they did contribute to the confusion and may have sowed what for many people turned out to be false hopes of survival.

With the reinstatement frenzy underway, a Magnitogorsk gorkom plenum took place in late February 1938 at which Konstantin Ivanov, acting first secretary, was demoted to acting second secretary, the position of first secretary remaining unfilled. Except for Ivanov, the entire gorkom bureau was also changed in what again appears to have been a group arrest.[238] On 23 March, Aleksandr Semenov arrived to take over as the city's new first secretary. Like Antonov, his recently arrived counterpart in the obkom, Semenov was a "plenipotentiary" sent by Moscow. A hereditary proletarian and veteran of the GPU troops, Semenov was graduated from the Leningrad Industrial Academy in 1937, after which he served as secretary of the Kirov factory party committee, the largest PPO in the country, before his assignment to Magnitogorsk.[239]

Semenov's appointment was voted at the Eighth Magnitogorsk Party Conference in June 1938, during which Magnitogorsk NKVD chief Aleksandr Pridorogin delivered a thunderous although nearly incoherent speech about wreckers in industry and the party.[240] Behind what were by now ritualistic incantations lay a political minefield requiring complicated maneuvers and countermaneuvers.[241] After the seemingly unassailable Semenov was blasted by Factory Director Pavel Korobov and by the obkom for not being sufficiently "self-critical," lesser figures joined in the fray, attacking not Semenov but people who had or could threaten them.[242]

Goltsev, director of the sewing factory, accused two members of the gorkom leadership, Prokhorchik and Kuznetsov, of making telephone calls to order expulsions of certain Communists and acting Second Secretary Ivanov of having gone along with them—all without ever holding a meeting of the gorkom bureau (as if the bureau, and not the primary party organizations, decided on expulsions). Ivanov, for his part, charged City Procurator Ivan Sorokin with defamation after the latter had accused Ivanov of showing up unannounced at a meeting of the Kirov raikom and demanding that the raikom officials submit to a "verification."[243] Vicious infighting between the gorkom and the three raikoms was also apparent.[244]

Semenov's closing words to the conference—"Communism is invincible! Communism will live eternally!"—were said to have been "drowned out by a rousing ovation and voices shouting 'Long Live Comrade Stalin!'" which was followed by the singing of "the anthem of the proletarian socialist revolution, the Internationale." After this, the newspaper reported that there were "again shouts: 'Long Live the Stalinist Commissar of Internal Affairs, Comrade Ezhov!' 'To the Comrade in Arms of Stalin, the Commissar of Heavy Industry, Comrade Kaganovich, Hurrah!' 'Long Live the Communist Party of Bolsheviks and its Leader, Comrade Stalin!' These words are drowned in a rousing ovation and shouts of 'Hurrah!'"[245]

Notwithstanding the appearance at the conference of great "activism" and of the party's having rediscovered its revolutionary mission, however, newspaper reports indicated that attendance at party school was back down to minimal levels.[246] And although great fanfare accompanied the publication in 1938 of the short course history of the party, Communists admitted having no time to study it, or anything else, owing to the need to attend perpetual gatherings (one apparatchik in the Ordzhonikidze raikom during nineteen days in November 1938 was said to have attended thirty-three meetings).[247] Meetings of the gorkom bureau as a rule were said to be conducted from 10 P.M. until 7 A.M.,[248] while the gorkom plenary meeting prior to the June party conference lasted twelve hours, from 4 P.M. to 4 A.M. "Some comrades slept," the newspaper reported.[249] "Activism" had paradoxically become an impediment to party work.

Pursuing the chimera of hyperactivism, the party had become consumed by itself. The endless petitions for reinstatement and the waves of denunciations stirred by "activism" swamped officials, even as arrests disorganized the ranks. On top of all this, the party was still unsure of its proper role. "We're listing from side to side," remarked V. Kotov, first secretary of the Ordzhonikidze raikom, at the June 1938 conference in Magnitogorsk. "If we take up political work, then we forget economic work, and vice versa." The revival, in other words, landed the party back where it had begun: still uncertain of how to fulfill its role as an omnicompetent political and ideological guide.[250]

In the meantime, the party revival had served as the vehicle for the search for a nonexistent enemy within that, with the involvement of the NKVD, devoured hundreds of Magnitogorsk Communists, including much of the apparat. This self-immolation of the party was effected by the recasting of commonplace industrial ills as deliberate wrecking, combined with the assertion that party officials—responsible for maintaining political watchfulness—had failed to keep up their guard owing to their preoccupation with successes. Such a formulation involved an expansion though not a redefinition of the category "enemy" as laid down on the eve of the party purge that followed collectivization.

To the "double-dealers" and concealed "oppositionists" holding party cards were added "wreckers" and "spies" among industrial managers and engineers, along with "bureaucrats" and "toadies" in the party apparat who suppressed self-criticism, the all-important weapon for unmasking. Yet having multiplied, the enemy was still viewed as internal, and still working for the foreign bourgeoisie. Supposedly, however, the enemy's tactics had changed. With the building of socialism achieved in its foundations, the enemy had reputedly united for a desperate, all-out final battle under the covenant of Trotskyism, the satanic incarnation of class-based, and therefore ideologically implacable, anti-Soviet counterrevolution begotten by the revolutionary movement itself, and nurtured by capitalist encirclement. The wise leader of the party had himself supplied this credible "analysis" of the confounding and dreadful events that cast a pall over the heroic socialist construction.

Although the search for presumed internal enemies was widely approved within party circles and employed methods, such as Bolshevik self-criticism, whose value was beyond question, it was strategically manipulated by Stalin. In that endeavor Stalin was assisted by several underlings at the top and a handful of zealous collaborators, aided by many more reluctant accomplices and unwitting pawns, in each locality around the country, including Magnitogorsk. In the name of carrying out their mission and ultimately of defending the revolution, party members participated in the destruction of each other, and often of themselves.

THE "SECULAR ARM"

The terror grew out of the party's self-understanding and rationale as a political or "spiritual" guide whose ideological level had to be raised if it were to fulfill its role and meet the political challenge of building socialism against the background of capitalist encirclement. But the party structure alone was insufficient to transform the prolonged verification of party members into the terror. The terror was the result of the appropriation of the party's inquisition by the "secular arm," or the NKVD. Any account of the terror as a process, therefore, must make some attempt to take the measure of this still largely obscure organization.[251]

The NKVD had undergone a chaotic expansion in size and influence with the collectivization and industrialization drives, and the terror brought still more growth as well as an organizational challenge. In July 1937, after it had begun to make widespread arrests, the NKVD issued an internal order to its branches extending the sentencing powers of its ad hoc boards, called troikas, which had been created in 1935 to expedite judgments in absentia for crimes involving "counterrevolution." Thus bolstered, these extrajudicial bodies served—until they were abolished in November 1938—as the processing mechanisms for "mass operations" conducted by the Soviet state against its own people.[252]

From a purely bureaucratic point of view, the extent of these mass operations was impressive. Precise figures on the number of arrests for "political crimes" (article 58) in Magnitogorsk are not available, but scattered data convey the order of magnitude.[253] As of 27 June 1937, City Procurator Sorokin reported that the Magnitogorsk remand prison, whose capacity was 400, held 675 people (265 of whom were still under investigation and therefore relatively recent arrests).[254] In another communication dated 5 May 1938, Sorokin reported that the same prison held 1,900 people.[255] It is unclear how many of these 1,900 inmates were "political" cases, or how many "politicals" had already been executed or turned over to Gulag for shipment to remote labor camps. Moreover, some people charged with crimes under article 58 were not taken to the overcrowded prison but, instead, were compelled to turn over their passports and to sign a document promising not to leave town.[256] Still, it is likely that John Scott was roughly correct when he wrote that "thousands were arrested" and "no group, no organization was spared."[257]

On such a scale, the execution of the terror was perforce sloppy. Documents from the Magnitogorsk procuracy (about its work and that of the NKVD) reveal that incompetence and confusion were rampant. A few individuals designated to be arrested or to be witnesses managed to skip town. Some remained in Magnitogorsk but still could not be located. And functionaries in the punitive apparatus could not explain to themselves why some people were hauled in and others were not.[258] Yet disorganized as its assembly-line enactment turned out to be, the terror cannot be said to have been the result of a mysterious process that somehow spun out of control. Indirect evidence suggests that the Magnitogorsk branch of the NKVD, which was led by Captain Aleksandr Pridorogin and his deputy, Major Aleksei Pushkov, received broad directives from controlling bodies in Moscow, via Cheliabinsk, to maximize the quantity of arrests. In 1938, the Magnitogorsk NKVD even began "arresting" large numbers of convicts in the city's labor colony (ITK).[259]

Procurator Sorokin wrote to Moscow of the discovery behind the ITK's barbed wire of a counterrevolutionary organization "dedicated to the overthrow of Soviet power" and connected to the "Polish Military Organization" (Polskaia Organizatsiia Voiskova). Many of the members of the Magnitogorsk affiliate of this "Polish" organization were Georgians, while the local leader was said to be Izrail Zolotovskii, a Jew from the Ukraine who had been arrested in 1937 and was serving an eight-year sentence for Trotskyism.[260] Such a preposterous nationality medley under the catchall category "Polish" was no more absurd than the absence of country designations in the cases of many convicts who were rearrested, both individually and in groups, as foreign spies.[261] In another letter to Moscow, for example, Sorokin wrote that "the city branch of the NKVD had uncovered a counterrevolutionary insurgent, espionage-diversionary organization active in the city of Magnitogorsk on assignment from one of the foreign states." Although he neglected to specify which one of the foreign states they served, Sorokin dutifully reported the NKVD's arrest totals: "with my sanction on 1 and 2 April two hundred forty participants of this organization were detained."[262]

Naturally, the existence of so many counterrevolutionary organizations within the ITK could not be considered "accidental." Having invented these counterrevolutionaries, the NKVD then had to explain how it was that their existence could have gone undetected until the moment they were unmasked. The answer was provided on 29 April 1938, when Aleksandr Geineman, chief of the labor colony, was arrested. He was accused of being an agent of German intelligence—a "logical" charge, for he had a German-sounding name.[263] Geineman's "accomplices," the heads of the labor colony administration's various subdivisions, were also arrested. In such a way did the terror snowball.[264]

Arrests during the terror were often "arbitrary," but even in dealing with convicts rearrested to pad totals there was a certain preoccupation with juridical procedure and the appearance of legality.[265] An arrest by the NKVD required the sanction of the procurator (depending on the status of the accused, this could mean requested approval via telegraph from the USSR procurator general). Any materials confiscated during arrests were inventoried, and a receipt was given. Charges were brought under specific articles of the Criminal Code. For those in custody, pretrial detention was limited to three months, and an extension required the written permission of the procurator (a rule that generated a massive correspondence between the NKVD and procuracy). Alongside the use of torture, which under the euphemism "physical measures" was apparently permitted by secret internal directives, there were cases in which suspects were released owing to NKVD violations of proper investigation procedures.[266]

Although such rules and procedures were frequently circumvented or flouted, the very need to do so, amid great pressures for quantitative results, raises the question of why people were not just rounded up and shot or deported without the labor-intensive formalities, especially the endless rounds of interrogations and accompanying minutely detailed protocols of defendants' confessions. Cases were decided in absentia, the content of confessions was invented, signatures on them could have been forged—if they were to be required at all. In short, the problem posed by the confessions is less why people who were tortured and blackmailed chose to make them than why the NKVD required confessions even from people whose arrests were not reported publicly and who would never be heard from again.

Certainly there was the convenience of receiving the names of others who could be arrested and added to the totals. Some scholars have also suggested that because the cases were manufactured, the only "evidence" for conviction was testimony (*pokazaniia*) by accessories and, above all, a confession by the accused. True enough, but this does not explain where the need for evidence came from. To understand that, we should keep in mind that the NKVD's work was based on the righteousness of the cause and their duty to uphold it. Working according to ostensibly juridical criteria and securing apparent confessions underscored both the just cause and the NKVD's "professionalism" to the rest of Soviet society, the outside world, and the NKVD operatives themselves. The NKVD as an institution, and the USSR as the champion of a superior civilization, recognized a need for the confessions.[267] At a more basic level, however, the impulse to extract confessions derived from the nature of the crime the NKVD sought to expose and eradicate: counterrevolution.

Counterrevolution was a state of mind—as much as any particular action—deemed contrary to "the revolution." As such, counterrevolution bore a striking resemblance to the religious heresy of the Middle Ages.[268] Such a parallel, noted above, has been remarked on by a few scholars, usually in passing, and was also noted by contemporaries (especially those victimized by the terror). But the significance of the inquisitorial mind-set and techniques for the NKVD's conduct of the terror, as well as the extent of the parallel with the Inquisition, remain to be clarified.

In the USSR, as in medieval Europe, "errors" in interpretation or the wholesale rejection of fundamental dogma was considered by the authorities to be not just morally wrong but dangerous, yet such "errors" need not be manifest. In fact, because of the penalties, most "potential" or "actual" counterrevolutionaries, like heretics, could scarcely be expected to admit their "heresy" flat out. So it was necessary to employ clever and forceful methods to probe suspected people's consciences, thereby exposing a suspect's true inner thoughts. From such propositions was the brutal work of the NKVD justified: they were doing the equivalent of "God's work."[269]

The NKVD "blue caps" were evidently taught to expect all manner of prevarication or other "tricks" from counterrevolutionaries, especially proclamations of innocence (in this regard, it would be interesting to compare the training manuals for the NKVD interrogators with those for the inquisitors). Just as in the battle against heresy, zealotry could seem an indispensable weapon for rooting out counterrevolutionary zealots. Little wonder that most NKVD interrogators, their expertise on the line no less than that of medieval inquisitors, spared nothing in the extraction (*dobytie*) of confessions, recording their "yields" in protocols signed by the accused.[270]

Yet although by encouraging "heretics" to build up cases against themselves the NKVD interrogator resembled the medieval inquisitor, in medieval times a genuine confession brought conversion, repentance, and forgiveness.[271] A repentant heretic could be imprisoned for suspected insincerity but was never burnt at the stake. Only heretics who refused to abjure and return to the Church with due penance were turned over to the "secular authorities" and executed—a relatively rare occurrence, for this reduced the likelihood of the person dying in a state of grace, meaning a soul was lost to the devil. Private scores were settled, coveted property confiscated, and fines accruing to the authorities were levied, but for all its abuses, the Inquisition was directed at reclaiming souls.[272]

By contrast, counterrevolutionaries were "outlawed" even though they confessed; they were either banished to perform forced labor in remote regions or executed (privately shot in the back of the neck, rather than publicly burned at the stake). Many were shot almost immediately after having been arrested and confessing.[273] "Acquittals" were rare, and when they occurred it was often because of whim or accident, not "repentance." As for "conversions," they could not have been induced because there was no alternative "church" for the Soviet population to convert from, Trotskyism notwithstanding. Thus, whereas most heretics who suffered did so because they refused to relinquish beliefs contrary to the teachings of the Catholic Church, "counterrevolutionaries" often confessed *because* of their abiding faith in the Communist party—and were executed all the same.

If the similarity of the terror to the Inquisition was limited to the nature of the crime, the resultant need to extract confessions, and the methods employed in doing so, the precondition for the terror remained, like the Inquisition, the existence of an organization imagining itself to be a universal "church" staunchly determined to enforce its self-proclaimed universality throughout "its" territory.[274] Such a circumstance did not "compel" the terror any more than the existence of heresy "compelled" the Inquisition. But the Communist party's church-like status offered a rationale for imagining how people who seemed not to have committed any criminal acts could nonetheless somehow be guilty. The inherent possibility, even likelihood, of the existence of counterrevolution reinforced the truth of the confessions, which in turn gave substance to the category of counterrevolution.

It should not be thought that the way of thinking that helped account for the institutional dynamics of "the secular arm" was abstract. Cases arose within the context of industrial breakdown at home and fascist aggression abroad. Both the internal and external aspects of this conjuncture drove the terror process, once it was underway. By no means did fascism necessitate the terror, but fascism did make concrete the endless talk about "enemies" and served as an inescapable frame of reference for guiding any particular person's thoughts and actions, whether that person was asked to collaborate in a single instance or was one of those responsible for conducting the terror locally.

The role of specific individuals within the "secular arm" during the terror remains obscure, but documents from one case shed a degree of light on the actions of the city's procurator, Ivan Sorokin. The case in question arose in the blooming mill. On 17 February 1937, after strong pressure from the obkom, a story appeared in the Magnitogorsk newspaper retrospectively declaring an incident in the mill "an act of conscious wrecking." The act had occurred on 31 January—the steel mill's fifth anniversary—and resulted in a six-day shutdown.[275] Having been prodded, the city newspaper named senior blooming operator A. G. Terekhov, a Stakhanovite, as the main culprit.[276]

This announcement was then followed by a meeting of the Stalin raikom at which others were implicated, including the shop chief, Fedor Golubitskii, a party member since 1928 who lived in the elite section of town, Berezka. Unlike Shevchenko, his thirty-nine-year-old counterpart in the coke plant, the thirty-four-year-old Golubitskii was apparently popular.[277] He also seems to have resisted the scapegoating of subordinates, as a result of which he evidently incurred the antipathy of Procurator Sorokin.[278]

As far as Sorokin was concerned, a convincing pretext for the inference of wrecking was provided by the lamentable circumstance, mostly a result of Stakhanovite adventurism, that "during 1936 and 1937 the blooming was systematically in a state of breakdown." To "nail" the shop chief, whose arrest technically required the sanction of Vyshinskii, Sorokin and the NKVD had to obtain testimony from those below Golubitskii in the blooming mill to the effect that they had caused the state of disrepair on his orders. This was easy enough. Terekhov, along with another award-winning operator, V. P. Ogorodnikov, and a labor colony convict employed by the blooming mill were arrested and tortured. Their statements—complete with minute technical details—about the deplorable state of the mill rang true, except for the attribution of criminal design.[279]

More than a year into the investigation, on the early morning of 12 March 1938, after two more breakdowns had occurred that month, the NKVD arrested Golubitskii with Sorokin's sanction, which the procurator gave without having secured the prior approval of Vyshinskii, in willful violation of regulations. Sorokin then wrote a long letter to Vyshinskii, dated 16 March 1938, to explain why he had sanctioned the arrest of a shop chief without prior approval from Moscow.[280] (Factory Director Korobov issued an executive order removing Golubitskii as shop chief the day *after* his arrest, 13 March 1938, demonstrating that this was a matter for the police to decide.)[281] Whether their superiors in Moscow had concurred beforehand or not, Sorokin and the Magnitogorsk NKVD had their case. Convicted on 29 July 1938, Golubitskii was shot that same day. Ogorodnikov, the labor colony convict, perhaps Terekhov, and no doubt others from the blooming mill were also executed.[282]

As the Golubitskii case demonstrates, the terror was propelled by the ambitions and grudges of the men of the NKVD and procuracy—including the competition and enmity between the two agencies. In this vein, Sorokin wrote to Vyshinskii in 1938 that "supervision of the UGB [Department of State Security in the NKVD] by the procuracy in charges brought under article 58, points 8, 9, 11 of the Criminal Code is unsatisfactory." This was an indirect way of acknowledging that the NKVD in Magnitogorsk was beyond his control. Reminding Vyshinskii of the laws whereby only the procurator can sanction an arrest and, moreover, must verify that the arrest is well-founded, Sorokin complained that he had been asked to give his sanction sometimes knowing only general phrases about a case. He also protested being cut off from the interrogations and further development of a case once he had signed an arrest order. "The procurator should be active and full of initiative in the struggle with wreckers, diversionists, and other similar enemies," he wrote.[283] Angered at his estrangement from cases of counterrevolution beyond formally sanctioning arrests, Sorokin fought a continuing turf battle with the NKVD.[284] Perhaps for this reason, on 25 July 1938 Sorokin himself was arrested "as a participant in a counterrevolutionary Trotskyite organization," evidently on testimony provided by the Magnitogorsk NKVD.

Sorokin's arrest followed an investigation into his work by the oblast procuracy.[285] According to an internal report by the oblast representative sent to examine the Magnitogorsk procuracy files, "Sorokin, to conceal his hostile activity, used the method whereby work on a case was only just begun, and he began to make noise and shout about the work already done." But "in actuality, the work begun was not consolidated, and collapsed." The investigator claimed that "Sorokin himself admitted in testimony given to the organs of the NKVD that he conducted his wrecking work by the disorganization of the city procuracy apparat, hiding behind 'pretense'—commotion."[286] Of course, the sacrifice of efficiency and proper procedure to zealotry was an integral aspect of the conduct of the terror, especially the pursuit of "high volume," and in this the hyperactive Sorokin may well have been exemplary. But such actions were easily turned into evidence of wrecking.[287]

Sorokin's arrest and subsequent expulsion from the party at a meeting of the Kirov raikom on 2 August 1938 appear to have introduced panic into the procuracy, where following the raikom gathering, a party meeting took place. "As you know," the new acting procurator, I. M. Sokolov, told those assembled, "Sorokin has been imprisoned as an enemy of the people." The implication for those remaining was plain. But Kirov raikom Secretary

S. Z. Zhemerikin, whose jurisdiction included the procuracy, acknowl-edged the "confusion" in the party organization of the procuracy yet tried to impose calm. "For Sokolov immediately the question arose, 'I worked with Sorokin, and so . . . , '" remarked Zhemerikin, who advised, "Let's not talk about this. You are members of the party; today, courteously fulfill and with confidence fulfill" the party's directives. Whether such efforts at reassurance dispelled the sense of terror within this part of the terror ap-paratus is unclear.

The meeting in the procuracy indirectly attested to the reduction of the procuracy's role to observer of the terror and supervisor of the local prison. Evidently meaning to cast aspersions on Sorokin, Sokolov spoke of several hunger strikes inside the Magnitogorsk lockup and one case of someone condemned to death (a party member without reprimands in his record) who was detained in the death cell but who wrote a petition to Vyshinskii, as a result of which his case was dismissed for lack of evidence. Sokolov also reported that there was tuberculosis in prison cells, but prisoners' requests to see a doctor had been denied. One procuracy employee, Zhiltsov, claimed that people came to work at the procuracy when they felt like it, left when they wanted, and sometimes did not show at all. Another, Tiu-tionnikov, claimed that "very important criminals were convicted of incon-sequential crimes or their cases were closed." A third, Soldatikov, evidently meaning to cast aspersions on Sorokin, remarked that "many are held for absolutely nothing."[288]

Sorokin was still in custody when the terror was abruptly halted in late 1938, around the time Stalin removed Nikolai Ezhov as People's Commis-sar for Internal Affairs. After the fall of Ezhov in Moscow, the leadership of the Magnitogorsk NKVD was routed in early 1939. This turned out to be a stroke of good fortune for Sorokin, who was released from prison and reinstated in the party.[289] His place in prison was taken by his former ac-cusers, Captain Pridorogin and Major Pushkov, who were arrested on charges that "they had grossly violated socialist legality, conducted mass arrests of citizens without foundation, themselves used and gave their sub-ordinates orders to use physical measures on those arrested, and falsified investigatory materials." This of course had been their mandate.[290]

Arrests continued after Pridorogin and Pushkov were incarcerated, especially in the labor colony, but many more people seem to have been released.[291] Even before the debacle of the Magnitogorsk NKVD, more-over, two central decrees were issued in late 1938 that reestablished the procurator's control over the NKVD and eliminated the NKVD's extrajudicial sentencing boards.[292] With the scapegoating of the "secular arm," the terror was ended.[293]

ENEMIES OF THE PEOPLE: THE TERROR AS PSEUDO–CLASS WAR

The ferocity of the terror can be attributed largely to the dictates imposed on the NKVD by Stalin and his inner circle, by the nature of the NKVD as an institution, and by the inquisitorial rationality that justified the NKVD's work on behalf of the revolution. But the terror also had something of a "popular" dimension, linked to resentment. Without access to the NKVD reports on overheard conversations, the existence of such resentment can only be inferred from the strategy adopted by the official press to appeal to such feelings during the height of the terror, and from the circumstances of the revolution's trajectory by the mid-1930s.

The October revolution, in the famous words of the "Internationale," meant that those "who had been nothing would become everything." In a speech outlining the need for the new constitution in 1936, Stalin explained that the class structure of Soviet society had indeed changed since 1917—only not precisely as foreseen. What were called "the exploiting classes"—landowners (*pomeshchiki*), capitalists in industry, kulaks in agriculture, merchants (*kuptsy*) and speculators in the sphere of trade—were said to have been "liquidated." According to Stalin, there remained only two classes, workers and peasants, and a stratum (*prosloika*), the intelligentsia, each radically transformed owing to the elimination of exploitation. Stalin made no mention of a new class that was created, but behind the awkward formulation of the "stratum" lay just such a reality.[294]

Industrialization had brought forth a colossal number of managers, technicians, and white-collar employees who, in the performance of their duties, exercised a kind of de facto "ownership" of the country's property. Thus arose the so-called "new class," a term for a Communist system's elite later popularized by the Yugoslav apostate, Milovan Djilas. Most commentators reject Djilas's attempt to attribute the origins and every policy of the Communist system to the class-conscious actions of a ruling elite, but there can be no doubt about the creation under the Communist system of such a social group or the far-reaching consequences of this fact.[295]

Here was a fundamental contradiction of the Soviet system: a "proletarian" revolution had created a literal ruling class, and, moreover, one whose operational authority was extensive yet whose existence could not be admitted, and thus whose relationship with the rest of society could only be highly problematic.[296] Communism had created its own class of "exploiters," or "blood-suckers" (*krovopiitsi*) as they were colloquially known. These ranged from mid-level white-collar workers to the large number of upper-level engineering and managerial positions with comparatively high salaries and various perquisites.[297]

These "new men" were young and often inexperienced, yet their difficulties in coping with their colossal responsibilities were matched not by a sense of humility but of arrogance. When passing simple directives to subordinates those in positions of power did not hesitate to pound their fists and use threats, such as "I'll have you fired," "I'll arrest you," or "I'll turn you over to the courts."[298] Factory chiefs set the tone, commanding with a decided heavy-handedness, and their underlings followed suit. But virtually the entire corpus of administrators, while treating the public purse with less than complete scrupulousness, frequently delivered oily speeches about their great sacrifices on the public's behalf.

With this consideration in mind we can better understand the highly publicized demolition of the KBU chief, Lukashevich, who in April 1937 was expelled from the party and, in the newspaper's almost gleeful words, "turned over to the investigative organs" (see chapter 6).[299] Among the various components of the bureaucracy in Magnitogorsk, the KBU (responsible for living conditions) was no doubt the most unpopular, and the press campaign against Lukashevich was especially vicious.

"It is impossible to describe all the outrages perpetrated by Lukashevich in one article," the newspaper wrote, adding that "many employees know about them, but they are silent before the 'all-powerful' Lukashevich." That silence was, of course, broken by his arrest. One underling, Uss, the chief of the KBU's department of workshops, was quoted as having remarked, "I am a toady [*podkhalim*]. It's true, comrades. But consider: Why did I become a toady to Lukashevich? You want to achieve something the honest way, but it doesn't work. So, you start toadying." A codefendant, the bookkeeper Serman, was said to have organized "a two-day drinking bout" in November 1936 attended by Efimov (KBU party secretary), Lukashevich, and others, after which Serman allegedly exclaimed: "Now they won't fire me from the KBU."[300] Following several months of such disclosures, a public trial of Lukashevich and several of his associates was finally held in November 1937. The charges were malfeasance, "collective coverup" (*krugovaia poruka*), and "mutual aid."

It is highly probable that behind the credible accusations of bureaucratic tyranny and crass self-interest lay a palpable social anger directed at local representatives of "Soviet power" who resembled a new gentry more than selfless servants of the people. In the buildup to the trial and during the actual proceeding, the newspaper reported that members of what it called "the KBU gang" were said to have awarded themselves and their friends choice apartments, received special food supplies at state prices or gratis, rode around in chauffeur-driven automobiles on private business, built personal cottages at state expense, taken frequent "business trips" to the capital, and helped themselves to petty cash for pocket money. Their wives were said to have been showered with hard-to-obtain fashions and cosmetics. This damning portrait of the elite's way of life was not included in the official indictment, but it was subtly accentuated and may have underlay the public reception of the charges of incompetence and malfeasance.[301]

In the public exposure of Lukashevich and "his cronies" we can see the resonance that the category "enemy of the people" (*vrag naroda*) could well have acquired.[302] The probable social tensions generated by the appearance of a new elite, by that elite's authoritarian method of rule (against a background of bureaucratic incompetence), and by the elite's immodest, "non-Communist" lifestyle meant that when encouraged from above, radical populism could become a powerful force. And encouragement was indeed forthcoming, especially from the country's premier "defender of the people."

At a reception on 29 October 1937 for management personnel and Stakhanovites in the steel and coal industries also attended by party and government leaders, Stalin offered brief but telling remarks on the terror that was underway. Proposing several toasts to those gathered in the hall, the USSR's supreme leader (*vozhd*) pointedly contrasted Soviet leaders (*rukovoditeli*) with economic managers and bosses in old times, who he said had been hated for being the "dog chains of capitalist masters." Stalin pointed out that Soviet managers had a chance to earn high honors and the trust of the people, but he speculated that officials didn't "always understand to what heights they have been raised by history in the conditions of the Soviet system." "The people's trust is a great matter, comrades," he emphasized. "Leaders come and go, but the people remain. Only the people are eternal. The rest is transient."[303]

In closing his speech, Stalin saluted Magnitogorsk's Pavel Korobov, the son of a blast furnace operator who, after following in his father's footsteps had risen to become the chief of the blast furnace shop in Magnitogorsk, then the director of the entire steel plant, and finally deputy commissar for ferrous metallurgy, in just a few years.[304] The message was unmistakable: sitting bosses were expendable, given that there were capable replacements, sons of the proletariat, at the ready.[305] With Stalin directing such pointed barbs at bosses and juxtaposing them against "the people," the terror came to resemble a kind of "socialist" class war, even if such a direct formulation was precluded by the official ideology.[306]

All bosses, no matter how seemingly powerful, could be reduced to nothing by even bigger bosses above them. Among the big "pine cones" at the Magnitogorsk steel plant, no one remained immune from denunciation, not even the supremely powerful Avraamii Zaveniagin (although he was attacked only after he had been transferred to Moscow).[307] By one incomplete official reckoning, in 1937–38 seventy "leading officials" in Magnitogorsk were executed and another fifty-seven were sent to labor camps.[308] These were substantial numbers (a July 1936 list of the top factory management personnel (*nachalstvo*) carried only fifty-four names).[309] To be sure, in the cases against bosses, lesser fry were usually caught up.[310] But it was almost always the downfall of the top person, along with his immediate underlings, that occasioned the greatest interest and clamor. That bosses did in fact have much to answer for was yet another factor contributing to the rationality of the terror.

UBIQUITOUS CONSPIRACY, SOCIAL SOLIDARITY

Alongside what appear to have been genuine social tensions, the terror, much like the Inquisition, revealed the evident insecurity of the aggrandizing authorities. In a way, the terror exposed not just their innermost fears but their worldview. On that score, the accusations leveled by the NKVD were most revealing.

In one typical case, Magnitogorsk's Mikhail Ubiivolk was accused by his interrogator of having "conducted anti-Soviet terrorist, defeatist agitation." He allegedly "spread malignant slanderous rumors about food difficulties in the country and blamed the party leadership and Soviet power." Ubiivolk was apparently denounced by Galina Iakovlena, whom he supposedly told that "if there's a war, he'll be the first to line up to shoot Communists." Similar charges were brought in many other cases, usually accompanied by allegations of conspiracies with highly militarized foreign adversaries to prepare plots against Stalin's life.[311]

That a supposed desire to strike against the party-state, which was imputed to many thousands of people, was usually assumed to be accompanied by a desire to assassinate Stalin is less absurd than it might seem. To the extent that the invented charges were a kind of projection, the schemes to murder Stalin made sense, for he had been made the party-state's personification. Similarly, the supposed ubiquity of plots could be seen as a mirror image of actual Soviet politics, which was after all a universe of intrigue and conspiracy. Widespread allegations of wrecking, meanwhile, could be read as confirmation of the feeling of vulnerability felt by a recently and far from fully industrialized peasant country, even as the propagandists loudly trumpeted the country's advances.

To the extent that the terror revealed a sense of inferiority, as well as a corresponding proclivity to overcompensate, such feelings no doubt extended beyond ruling circles. In the charges advanced by the NKVD, the telling defensiveness that emerged was also tinged with a certain xenophobia. A "foreign-sounding" (non-Slavic) name was often taken as ipso facto incriminating. Such a prejudice was related to the apparently genuine popular fear of being encircled, which whatever its geopolitical dimension was also partly derived from the population's ignorance of and inexperience with foreign cultures. In short, the NKVD interrogations inadvertently gave expression to deep-seated anxieties that were shared to an extent by the regime and the people. With such considerations in mind, the bizarre spy mania characteristic of the terror appears less preposterous.

It is important to remember that unlike the early period of the revolution, in 1937–38 the press did not speak of a campaign of terror but of "vigilance against spies and wreckers." Such "lessons" of the extraordinary times in which the people of the USSR lived were inculcated persistently. Magnitogorsk's 1937 theater season, for example, opened in October with *The Confrontation (Ochnaia stavka)*, a drama "about espionage and the diversionary work of fascist intelligence agencies." In the play, the USSR was depicted as locked in a life-and-death struggle with cleverly cloaked adversaries, such as the Gestapo agent Mark Walter, alias Ivan Ivanovich Ivanov, who was prepared to resort to any measures.[312] According to John Scott, the action gripped the audience and powerfully communicated the play's moral of the need for constant hypersuspicion in the face of great peril.[313]

To be sure, there were apparently limits to the population's acceptance of the spy-mania. On 11 June 1937, *Pravda* reported that Deputy Defense Commissar, Marshal of the USSR, Mikhail Tukhachevskii and seven other army commanders had been arrested and executed for organizing a "military conspiracy."[314] The announcement that treason had been committed by the USSR's best-known and most popular military leaders stunned the country. Nina Kondratkovskaia recalled during an interview in Magnitogorsk in May 1987 that "people worried that Stalin had been duped by Hitler into thinking these men were traitors, when of course such crystal clear people could not have been." With war approaching, she added, this kind of "serious mistake" was "very dangerous." In her refusal to accept that

Tukhachevskii was guilty and to find an explanation for the accusation, however, Kondratkovskaia revealed a basic belief in the authenticity of other conspiracies and plots. Interviews with other people elicited similar presumptions.[315]

In the late 1930s, everything could be (and was) explained by recourse to conspiracy. The arrests of those in charge of the terror as enemies of the people pointed to the ultimate "conspiracy": the deliberate fabrication of conspiracies by wreckers within the procuracy and NKVD. In fact, the entire terror was essentially one enormous, invisible conspiracy. Except for a handful of public trials and accompanying press accounts, almost all proceedings took place behind closed doors or otherwise out of sight. There were no public executions, let alone displays of severed heads or mutilated bodies. This was a terror of abductions, the symbol of which became the NKVD patrol wagons known as the "black marias" (*voronki*). The Black Marias combed Magnitogorsk and the surrounding district, the NKVD men got out, knocked on doors, and people disappeared. Some returned; most did not.[316]

Virtually all the arrests around the city were carried out at night, a practice that greatly magnified their fear-inducing effects. The secrecy and uncertainty fueled the tension still more.[317] "People were arrested when they least expected it," wrote John Scott, "and left alone for weeks when they expected every night to be taken"—a reflection of overwork and disorganization as much as intention, but terrifying all the same.[318] Inside the prison, meanwhile, most interrogations were conducted at night. "Everything was much more horrifying than people write," recalled the poet Mikhail Liugarin (who shared a cell with Komsomol Secretary Rudnitskii and was accused of conspiring to blow up the blast furnaces and murder Stalin).[319] Only several weeks or months after an arrest did the family receive any information, and even this was usually in the form of terse instructions to bring clean underwear, warm clothes, sugar, onions, and garlic (to combat scurvy) to the prison at a specified time—a sign of imminent departure for the labor camps of the North, conveyed indirectly and without explanation.[320]

The Soviet terror was, in other words, deliberately obscure, yet even when transparent, terror becomes effective as much through popular narration as spectacle.[321] There were those who sought refuge in denial, refusing to believe it could happen to them or accepting that those arrested were "probably" guilty. John Scott reported that among the Magnitogorsk population there was a laconic saying: "It's good to be a telegraph pole." But despite the apparent desire of some people to distance themselves psychologically from the terror, as well as the deliberate veil of secrecy drawn around the terror by the NKVD, the inhabitants of Magnitogorsk appear to have been more or less informed about specific events that were taking place.[322] Above all, the city seems to have been caught up talking about the terror.[323]

An episode from the summer of 1936 recorded by John Scott provides eloquent testimony to the process of continual interpretation that evidently surrounded the terror. A. Selivanov, the editor of the Magnitogorsk newspaper, was arrested without announcement, but the whole city soon learned it had happened and the ostensible reason why: a photograph in the issue of 28 June 1936 in which the glass stars hovering above the Kremlin gate-towers bore a faint resemblance to Nazi swastikas. The issue in question was quickly ordered withdrawn, but not all copies could be easily tracked down: many people defiantly held onto them. And those without their own copies inquired among friends to discover if they could see the swastikas. Some people speculated that it was the work of the Gestapo; others that it was just an accident, or a plot by the NKVD to justify its existence.[324] Such discussions of Selivanov's arrest demonstrate the curiosity of the populace and the prevalence of rumors and oral networks.[325]

There were ample opportunities for collecting terrifying stories and retelling them. Information spread from arrests made in the presence of a neutral witness, who signed a copy of the arrest report and could become a source of information. Rooms and apartments of those arrested were sometimes sealed shut by wax, an unmistakable sign even for skeptical neighbors. And absence from work could not be missed. From these as well as other sources, indirect knowledge of events could be gleaned. Direct knowledge, too, was possible to come by. When necessary to obtain a confession from the accused, family members were permitted visits to the prison, from which knowledge was gathered and then spread. Even details of far-off camp life filtered back, as some convicts were recalled from Gulag to provide testimony against others.[326] One prison guard, Fedor Budanov, was arrested and charged with mailing prisoners' letters (and getting drunk with the money he received as payment).[327]

The role of family members in the collection and dissemination of information about the terror can scarcely be exaggerated. In Magnitogorsk as elsewhere around the country, the overwhelming majority of people rounded up were able-bodied men (much like what happens during an occupation by a foreign army), but many women were also arrested, usually as the "wives of enemies" accused of having failed to denounce their husbands.[328] Before they, too, were incarcerated, wives, as well as sisters and mothers, gathered outside the NKVD headquarters or the city prison hoping to learn the fate and perhaps catch a glimpse of their loved ones. Besides sharing what they had managed to find out, these women supported each other and formed informal networks.

Such informal networks of enemies' wives exemplified the process by which fear was elaborated through tales of all-night interrogations, torture, screams and gunshot noises, and deportation to frozen wastes. But they also showed the emergence of bonds of social solidarity on the basis of a common predicament. According to Vera Kozhevnikova, for example, her husband, Micheslav Seratskii, who worked in a local state farm, was first arrested in November 1936, then released in March 1937. When he was again summoned by the NKVD, she accompanied him. "There was a big crowd at the NKVD, mostly women. My husband said to me that if they take him up to the second floor, it means he's arrested. When they led him upstairs, I began to scream. The women took me aside to quiet me."[329] Similar tales of a suddenly discovered social solidarity have been recounted by others.

In 1988, Iurii Pisarenko told the story of the arrest in 1937 of his father, G. A. Pisarenko, a noted surgeon, to a Magnitogorsk journalist. "The arrest of my father was preceded by months of tense waiting," Pisarenko explained. "In the ITR-settlement (near Berezka) they continuously came to haul people in. Each sound of a motor in the night brought forth dread and expectation—where is it going to stop? And so the turn of my father came." Because of fears that his mother would also be arrested, Iurii was taken in and cared for by a family friend, Ekaterina Almazova, the manager of the children's bone-tuberculosis dispensary, until his father was unexpectedly released, apparently in 1939. He also noted that Valeriia Biriukova, a nurse and party member, submitted a written defense of G. A. Pisarenko after he had been arrested. The terror brought out both the basest and the noblest instincts of the population.[330]

THE ENDURANCE OF PIETY

Overall, the effects of the terror, as John Scott observed, were paradoxical. Industrial production declined dramatically, and literal chaos often ensued (in 1937, coke plant construction did not fulfill its plan for a single month, sinking to a low of 27 percent in December).[331] But as Scott also noted, "officials and administrators who had formerly come to work at ten, gone home at four-thirty, and shrugged their shoulders at complaints, difficulties, and failures, began to stay at work from dawn till dark, to worry about the success or failure of their units, and to fight in a very real and earnest fashion for plan fulfillment, for economy, and for the well-being of their workers and employees, about whom they had previously not lost a wink of sleep."[332]

For these reasons Stalin was long held in high esteem, the leader who knew how to deal with provincial bosses and bureaucrats, ruling with an iron fist and keeping them in check through fear. Herein lay no doubt one of the principal effects of the terror, an effect that was connected to the terror's class aspect. But at the same time, many people appear to have been appalled at such methods and at the general leveling tendency that Stalin allowed free reign. This leveling tendency and its rueful consequences were apparent in the senseless disappearance of the Magnitogorsk's well-known poets, Boris Ruchev and Mikhail Liugarin, as well as the secretary of the local writer's union branch, Vasilii Makarov—the chief figures in the local "artistic intelligentsia."[333]

The terror rent deep and lasting divisions within the society and shook Magnitogorsk to its foundations. But many—perhaps most—people tried to prevent it from undermining everything else that had taken place.[334] Their country had been through a great deal and had achieved much, signs of which were there to see. Plebiscitary elections, complete with celebratory mass marches, continued to be held.[335] And hundreds of workers and lower-level officials continued to receive medals and awards, from the Order of the Red Banner to the Order of Lenin, the state's highest honor.[336] Even more crucial in this regard was the irreplaceable experience of the decade-long socialist construction.

In February 1938 the city newspaper published the following commentary of a Magnitogorsk engineer, Burylev, the new deputy chief of open-hearth construction:

> Soon it will be seven years that I'm working in Magnitogorsk. With my own eyes I've seen the pulsating, creative life of the builders of the Magnitogorsk giant. I myself have taken an active part in this construction with great enthusiasm. Our joy was great when we obtained the first Magnitogorsk steel from the wonderful open-hearth ovens. At the time there was no greater happiness for me than working in the open-hearth shop. Work in the open-hearth shop of the Magnitogorsk factory for me, a Soviet engineer, has been and is a new wonderful school. Here I enriched my theoretical knowledge and picked up practical habits, the Stakhanovite experience of work. Here as well I grew politically, acquired good experience in public-political work. I came to Magnitogorsk nonparty. The party organization of the open-hearth shop was able to give me access to an active public life, accepted me into a group of sympathizers. Not long ago I entered the ranks

of the Leninist-Stalinist party. Year by year the work of our open-hearth shop improves. New cadres of Stakhanovites, engineering and technical personnel, grow and are forged. They bring the country newer and newer victories. I love my hometown Magnitka with all my heart. I consider my work at the Magnitogorsk factory to be a special honor and high trust shown to me, a Soviet engineer, by the country. And in practical work I try to justify that trust in deeds. I love, I'm proud of Magnitka, the industrial colossus of our beloved motherland.[337]

The publication of such attempts to boost morale and convince *oneself*, above all, bespoke both the crushing impact of the terror and a powerful desire to overcome it, faith intact.[338] This was no mean feat.[339]

On 6 October 1939, the Magnitogorsk newspaper appeared with a startling photograph of Commissar of Foreign Affairs Vyacheslav Molotov on the first page signing a "pact of friendship" with a group of men dressed in Nazi uniforms. There also appeared the text of a speech to the Reichstag by the USSR's arch-enemy, Adolf Hitler, and an interview with Nazi Foreign Minister von Ribbentrop. For those who read the newspaper regularly over the last several years, news of the Hitler-Stalin pact, or as it was called the Molotov-Ribbentrop pact, must have come as a jolt. Many people recalled having interpreted the pact as a deliberate chess move, but others admitted having been puzzled.

In the end, perhaps the only certainty for the inhabitants of Magnitogorsk was the inevitability of war, whether with Germany in the West, Japan in the East, or both. Throughout 1938 and 1939 tens of thousands attended protest meetings held in the city center in response to border skirmishes with Japan. According to the oblast newspaper, one such meeting in 1938 reportedly drew more than twelve thousand people. Those gathered were said to have celebrated the building of socialism and the shining sun of the Soviet constitution, and expressed their readiness to increase industrial output and respond to "the enemy," as the country had done during the intervention and Civil War.[340] These were the same pledges that had been made on the eve of the terror, and meant no less now than they had then.

THE TERROR

Magnitogorsk was built, owned, and managed by "the state," which in principle meant the system of soviets but in practice meant the People's Commissariat for Heavy Industry and, beginning in 1939, its successor, the People's Commissariat for Ferrous Metallurgy. These commissariats exercised a kind of colonial domination over "their" provincial steel center.

The democratic promise of the formula "Soviet power" was belied by one of the most rigidly corporatist administrative structures history has ever seen.

Magnitogorsk's "administration" by the colonizing state apparatus was also enveloped in Communist party politics. The party maintained a very high profile, immoderately assigning itself all credit for everything. The size of the local party organization contradicted these improbable claims. Even before the convulsive and sharp contraction in membership between 1934 and 1938, the party in Magnitogorsk comprised no more than a small fraction of the population. Yet the party expressed a revolutionary purpose, and it was this purpose, rather than the number of its members, that constituted the party's strength and, paradoxically, its undoing.

John Scott regarded the Communist party as a useful organizing force but disapproved of what he viewed as its "unnecessary intriguing and heresy-hunting."[341] In one sense, Scott was on the mark: for those who knew how to use the galvanizing effects of revolutionary aura and the organizing techniques of political mobilization, the party could move a mountain, as it did in Magnitogorsk. But in another sense, Scott missed the point: intriguing and heresy-hunting in the pursuit of political purity may have appeared unnecessary, but they were rooted in the party's origins, nature, and identity. The party was not a booster club. It was a political conspiracy "shadowing" all organizations, including the state, that laid claim to the definition of acknowledged reality, a claim put forth as scientific truth embodied in and made functional by the cult of a Supreme Leader.

If the party's principal function was to exercise political guidance, its ability to cope with such a task did not always inspire confidence. After the launching of the industrialization drive and the collectivization of the countryside, the party leadership understandably attempted to secure greater order and consistency in the vital organization charged with monitoring institutions and guaranteeing political loyalty. Such efforts logically took the form of a sustained scrutiny of the entire membership, carried out in the name of a reassertion of the party's revolutionary mission, against the background of a threatening international context. That context deepened but did not create the ingrained sense of insecurity characteristic of this aspiring socialist great power.

The protracted search for internal enemies helped foster a mood of absolute intolerance and deep suspicion that gripped party circles. Inflammatory rhetoric, moreover, became an important component of the politics of violence when pandemonium broke out in 1937. But it required the displacement of the party by the NKVD as the principal agency for identifying and not just punishing internal enemies to transform the campaign to purify the party's ranks—which had resulted in mass expulsions, much anxiety, yet limited arrests—into the terror. This displacement occurred between the November 1936 Novosibirsk trial, which proclaimed the pervasiveness of wreckers in industry, and the February-March 1937 Central Committee plenum, which connected the spread of industrial wrecking to complacency within the apparat, said to be giddily excited by economic successes and thus inexcusably distracted from maintaining "vigilance."

Although consistent with the logic of the search for internal enemies and with the conspiratorial regime's basic structure and operation, neither of these perverse formulations were "inevitable" or "necessary." Impotently contested by local party officials, these centrally imposed determinations concerning wrecking and complacency could only have been instituted by an office that exercised control over the NKVD and procuracy, as well as the agenda for Central Committee plenums. Such an office was the party's administrative apparat, or secretariat, controlled by General Secretary Stalin and run by a coterie of individuals loyal to him, including Nikolai Ezhov, who was moved from the party apparat to manage the NKVD on the eve of the Novosibirsk trial. It is indeed striking how much pressure Moscow exerted on Magnitogorsk affairs, despite a distance of 1,200 kilometers and comparatively primitive communications, as well as how quickly a return to "normalcy" was achieved.

After Ezhov was removed in late 1938, the terror acquired the epithet "Ezhovshchina," a reflection of the success Stalin achieved in scapegoating Ezhov for the terror. Ezhov had done his part, to be sure, and in Magnitogorsk so did the newspaper correspondents and "activists" N. Kartashov [Rafael Shneiveis] and Aleksei Griaznov, the procurator Ivan Sorokin, and the NKVD officers Aleksandr Pridorogin and Aleksei Pushkov. The terror was realized through the misplaced zeal of these individuals (as well as the often reluctant complicity of many others). That a limited group of people could have propelled a massive firestorm testified to the multilayered nature of the terror.

But the execution of the terror required, and in the event received, wide participation. The reasons behind that participation, laid out in this chapter, included the political language and way of thinking characteristic of a party member's worldview, both of which were part of the institutional dynamics of the party. Additionally, there was the specific nature of the NKVD as an organization, its mission, and its operatives' way of thinking. Beyond the special characteristics of the party and the existence of an extensive police apparatus equipped to arrest and sentence in assembly-line fashion, the terror was also made possible by the adversarial nature of Soviet industrialization, which dictated the use of massive force and presupposed the creation of armies of enemies; by the existence of an extensive police apparatus equipped to arrest and sentence in assembly-line fashion; by the threatening international environment, assiduously exploited by the regime's strict control of information and promotion of certain ways of thinking; by the endemic malfunctions in the socialist economy that cried out for explanation; by the general resentment of the lifestyle and behavior of the new elite, whose mere existence pointed to unacknowledged contradictions; by the popular conspiratorial mentality and the Stalin cult of the "good tsar"; and by the widespread belief in a grand crusade, building socialism, in whose name the terror was conducted.

Stalin's conspiracy within the party drove the entire process, but it arose out of the fact that the party was itself a conspiracy, a "movement" operating in secrecy and revealing only unanimity, which struggled to live up to its self-assigned role of ideological watchdog in what was a redundant, theocratic political structure. The presence of the Communist party, alongside the fully functional state administration, turned out to be something of a time bomb, planted in 1917, and detonated in the second half of the 1930s. As to why the bomb was set off, this remains mysterious, but one traditional explanation seems unfounded.

Many have speculated that the terror was aimed at compelling "orthodoxy." Yet despite the insecurities that lay behind the vehemence with which the party asserted its monopoly, orthodoxy as such does not appear to have been in question. Although on the eve of the terror, before the mass arrests, various degrees of "doubt" may have been widespread, open defiance of the regime was rare. The shroud drawn around party affairs limited inside knowledge at any level of the hierarchy to a very narrow circle, an obvious disinvitation to challenges. Compliance with "the general line" was further obtained through party discipline, buttressed by the apparent righteousness of the cause and the threat of arrest by the NKVD, which cultivated a reputation for tireless execution of duty in the protection of "the revolution."[342] Anyone who attempted some form of even indirect questioning was caught and duly punished.[343]

For party members especially, disagreement was not just pointless; it was dangerous. And with Communists required to demonstrate repeatedly their conformity at party meetings and other occasions, having even private misgivings brought the risk of their public detection through one's subtle expressions and mannerisms. But beyond the threat of coercion, the worthiness of the cause, as opposed to certain negative manifestations associated with it, was not in dispute. If anything, the terror seems to have provoked people into privately reexamining their commitment to the Soviet regime and the grand crusade. Confessing to crimes they did not commit, some people were broken mentally, while those not arrested struggled to hold onto their cherished beliefs.[344] The clarity reimposed by the war against the Nazis came none too soon.

33. The factory administration building.

34. Headquarters of the city Communist party committee (tallest structure), with Socialist City in the background.

35. Magnitogorsk director Iakov Gugel (third from left) talking to officials, 1933. Chingiz Ildrym (second from left) is partially obscured.

36. Deputy Director Chingiz Ildrym (third from right) showing Industry
Commissar Sergo Ordzhonikidze (white coat and mustache) the interior of
a rolling mill, 1933.

37. Newspaper exhortation: "For Stalinist revolutionary norms."

38. Stakhanovite Mikhail Zuev.

39. Blooming mill operators, featured in the newspaper. Left to right: Ogorodnikov, Chernysh, Bogatyrenko, and Tishchenko.

40. Newspaper illustration, captioned "My factory."

41. Delegates to the city's Sixth Party Conference, December 1936. *(Above)* In the hall listening to a speech. *(Below)* In the lobby admiring the cornucopia.

42. Party lessons, 1930s.

43. Advertisement for the 1936 film *Party Card*, directed by I. Pyrev.

44. Local Party Secretary Beso Lominadze: as a youth; with parents and brother (standing); while working in Magnitogorsk.

45. On the reviewing stand, hands raised in salute: Party Secretary Rafael Khitarov (left) and Factory Director Avraamii Zaveniagin, 1936.

46. The party active of the internal transport shop listening to a broadcast of a speech by Stalin, November 1936.

47. Discussion in the blooming mill of Stalin's speech, 1936.

48. Newspaper caricature of shop bosses Golubitskii, Shevchenko, Zaitsev, and Kogan, depicting large quantities of unusable output, September 1936.

49. Newspaper illustration, August 1937: "General Franco has achieved new 'heights.'"

50. Newspaper illustration, October 1936: "The base and superstructure of the
'Third Reich,'" depicting freedom of speech, the press, and assembly, women's
right to work, freedom of belief, and the independence of the courts, all bound
and gagged.

51. Newspaper illustration, "The defense of China is in 'trusty' hands," in answer to a statement by the Japanese consulate in Moscow, 1937, that Japanese policy was aimed at "defending" China from Western aggression.

52. Newspaper illustration: "War: Japan and Germany in alliance."

53. Marching in gas masks, 1937 or 1938.

54. Discussion in the blast furnace shop of the Moscow trial of the Trotskyite-Zinovievite Bloc, 1938.

55. Voting in the open-hearth shop to approve the verdict of execution.

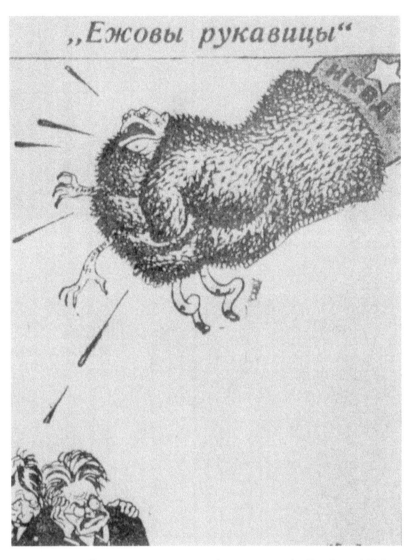

56. Newspaper illustration, August 1937, depicting a spy for Trotsky and Hitler, caught in the clutches of the NKVD, which was headed by Ezhov. Reprinted in *Magnitogorskii rabochii*, from *Isvestiia*.

57. Eyeless bureaucrat of the KBU, oblivious to the disrepair as fall begins to give way to winter.

58. Newspaper illustration depicting the queue to see KBU chief Tabunov.

Сов-секретно.

Н-ку ОМЗ УПРАВЛЕНИЯ НКВД
Копия: ПРОКУРОРУ ОБЛАСТИ.

На 5/V - в Магнитогорской тюрьме содержится
1900 чел. вместо лимита в 400 чел.

В камерах исключительная теснота.

В связи с этим прошу разрешить принимать
непосредственно в Магнитогорскую колонию, минуя тюрьму, всех
лиц осужденных по бытовым преступлениям нарсудами города
Магнитогорска и соседних районов: В.Уральск, Полтавка,
Кизильский, Брединский, Нагайбакский, Варненский.

О принятых Вами мерах прошу сообщить.

Горпрокурор _Исакович_ /СОРОКИН/.

59. Top secret internal letter to Moscow from Magnitogorsk procurator Ivan Sorokin informing central authorities that the Magnitogorsk prison, with a capacity of 400 inmates, was holding 1,900 people. Dated 5 May 1938.

60. The 1936 "Stalin" constitution.

„В результате пройденного пути борьбы и лишений приятно и радостно иметь свою Конституцию, трактующую о плодах наших побед" (СТАЛИН)

61. Wise father of the revolution, 1936.

62. May Day in Magnitogorsk, 1938.

63. Pupils in front of their school, 1930s.

64. First graduating class of the Mining and Metallurgical Academy, November 1937.

65. "Lucky Soviet youth boldy and cheerfully march under the banner of the Stalin Constitution": students of the pedagogical institute return after voting in the 1937 Soviet election.

66. Recently appointed factory director and soon-to-be People's Commissar of Metallurgy, Pavel Korobov, facing camera, 1938.

67. The workers.

Afterword: Stalinism as a Civilization

Although the Communist revolution may start with the most
idealistic concepts, calling for heroism and gigantic effort, it sows
the greatest and most permanent illusions.

Milovan Djilas[1]

In the 1930s, the people of the USSR were engaged in a grand historical endeavor called building socialism. This violent upheaval, which began with the suppression of capitalism, amounted to a collective search for socialism in housing, urban form, popular culture, the economy, management, population migration, social structure, politics, values, and just about everything else one could think of, from styles of dress to modes of reasoning. Within a steadfast but vague noncapitalist orientation, much remained to be discovered and settled.

Did planning mean centralized decision making in absolutely all matters? Or could a planned economy also permit forms of direct, ostensibly market-like, relations between firms, which remained state-owned? In factories designed and partly built by capitalist firms and containing capitalist-invented technology, were there socialist forms of labor? If so, what were these forms and how did they manifest the purported moral superiority of socialism? In terms of the municipal economy, if there was no private property, would there be no trade? If there was such a thing as socialist trade, how was it to be organized? And what of the law? Was there a specifically socialist justice, and how were socialist courts supposed to function?

What did a socialist city look like? Did a rejection of individualism and a commitment to collectivism mean that socialist housing should not be built to accommodate the family, or was the family compatible with socialism? What of socialist culture: did it signify workers writing poetry, or workers becoming "cultured" by reading Pushkin? Should socialism permit popular entertainments, and if so, what kind? Was jazz socialist, capitalist, or neither? If capitalist, could jazz nonetheless be permitted, provided there were enough other cultural activities that were unambiguously socialist, whatever those might be? And, perhaps the most difficult question of all, could a socialist revolution create a new elite, and if so, was this just?

Of course, the Soviet regime was a dictatorship and on these questions, unconditionally binding decisions backed by the threat of coercion were handed down from Moscow, without discussion beforehand and with little opportunity to give direct voice to reservations afterward. Yet, from the shop-floor production campaigns to nonprivate trade, from domestic living arrangements to organized recreation, the realization of socialism in practice involved the participation of people, affording ample opportunities for the circumvention of official strictures, spontaneous reinterpretations of the permissible cloaked by professions of ignorance, and myriad other forms of indirect challenges, as well as the discovery of unintended realms not envisioned by the decrees. No one except perhaps certain labor colony inmates with nothing to lose had a completely free hand to act as he or she saw fit, but even leaving aside calculated petty transgressions, living socialism according to the perceived rules made for its share of surprises.

Indeed, one of the most striking aspects of life in the Magnitogorsk of the 1930s were the constant efforts to name and characterize the many surprising, as well as mundane, phenomena encountered in daily life, and then explain their relation to socialism, from the machinations of the shadow economy to the endless search for political enemies. New categories of thinking suddenly appeared, old ones were modified; nothing stood still. This inescapable tangle of discussion and explanation—followed closely in this monograph—was made especially complex given the periodic shifts in policies and laws, sometimes of 180 degrees, such as the reversals on abortion and divorce in the mid-1930s.

Abrupt policy changes have usually been taken as evidence that, contrary to the regime's claims, there was no single ideology, and that in general, ideology had less influence over the shape of events than other, "more practical" considerations. To argue thusly, however, is to overlook both the process of searching for socialism, rooted in an "ideological" rejection of capitalism, and the enormous commitment of resources by the regime to maintain a single ideology and relate all events to that ideology, a struggle that the inhabitants of Magnitogorsk had no choice but to take part in. Life in the USSR under Stalin was enveloped not merely in constrained experimentation but in perpetual explication where neither mistakes nor reversals could be admitted, and where socialism, understood as noncapitalism, served as a universal point of reference.

Further misunderstandings surround the shift on abortion and the family in the mid-1930s because it was accompanied by a conspicuous revival of the Great Russian past, hitherto anathema. These developments (in combination with the rehabilitation of the Orthodox Church during World War II) have been interpreted as constituting nothing less than a "great retreat" from the original goals of the revolution, if not a counterrevolution.[2] But proponents of the great retreat interpretation of Stalinism fail to consider that there was no comparable "retreat" on private ownership of land and the means of production or on the hiring of wage labor, whose absence was seen as the defining characteristic of socialism. It was in this unwavering repudiation of "exploitation" that the USSR's claims to have brought about a civilization distinct from capitalism were grounded, whatever the other vacillations.

At bottom, the notion of a great retreat has always been based on the assumption that "true" revolution and an imperial state are inherently incompatible, an historically indefensible tenet. From the beginning of the revolution, Great Russian domination coexisted uneasily with the striving for a multinational identity, a tension exacerbated by the circumstance that socialism was, in the language of the day, built in one country. By and large, however, the great retreat interpretation removes consideration of the fate of the revolution from that geopolitical context. Soviet socialism formed part of the same historical epoch as Nazism and fascism, against which it was locked in a deadly competition.

In that light, the strengthening of the family and the promotion of Great Russian nationalism are better appreciated as, on the one hand, part of the groping for an understanding of what constituted socialism and, on the other, as indicative of a strategic shift from the task of building socialism to that of defending socialism. This shift became noticeable with the anxious attention given to the civil war in Spain, where Hitler supported Franco's "counterrevolution," and to Mussolini's imperialist war in Abyssinia. It was around this time, 1936, that socialism in the USSR was declared built in its foundations, and yet the external threat, rooted in what was called capitalist encirclement, appeared more menacing than ever.

This paradoxical combination of triumph and heightened vulnerability was used as one of the principal devices to stoke the terror of 1936–38, a bizarre episode that contemporaries struggled with little effect to comprehend and accept. Not even the enormously dysfunctional terror, however, proved capable of invalidating the USSR's claim to being a socialist society and therefore the fulfillment of October. Such a claim continued to make sense and motivate people the world over until the very end in 1991—a circumstance that the historian may or may not find abhorrent but has no right to dismiss and every obligation to explain. One can argue that millions of people were ignorant or deceived. Or one can try to understand how so many people could have reasoned the way they did, holding apparently contradictory views, fearing terror yet believing that they had built, and lived under, socialism.

. . .

Inside Stalin's USSR, the appeal of socialism had several layers, including the prospect of a quick leap, not simply into modernity but a superior form of modernity, the corresponding attainment of high international status, a broad conception of social welfare, and a sense of social justice that was built into property relations. Despite the long, vicious political struggle for power, rampant opportunism and careerism, and the violence and hatred that were unleashed, the USSR under Stalin meant something hopeful. It stood for a new world power, founded on laudatory ideals, and backed up by tangible programs and institutions: full employment, subsidized prices, paid vacations for workers, child care, health care, retirement pensions, education, and the promise of advancement for oneself and one's children.

To be sure, life in Magnitogorsk and around the USSR was characterized by gradations of commitment—particularly in the willingness to suspend disbelief. Put another way, belief in Soviet socialism, as in all matters of faith, was never without ambivalence, confusion, and misgivings. Even the truest of true believers appears to have had regular bouts with private doubt. But few could imagine alternatives. Nor was anyone encouraged to do so. Sealed borders and censorship did their part—especially considering that Soviet censorship was not merely the suppression of information, but also the hyperactive, indefatigable dissemination of certain kinds of information, as well as the inculcation of specific ways of understanding that information.

That such activist censorship proved effective need not be seen as solely a matter of manipulation, however. To be effective, propaganda must offer a story that people are prepared at some level to accept; one that retains the capacity to capture their imagination, and one that they can learn to express in their own words. As we have seen, the process of articulating the sanctioned vocabulary and values of the new society in one's own words was far from entirely voluntary, linked not merely to access to food and housing but to one's safety and the safety of one's relatives. But the presence of coercion, subtle and unsubtle, does not mean the absence of a high degree of voluntarism any more than the holding of genuine ideals precludes the energetic pursuit of self-interest.

Even when they found a niche in the new society, the inhabitants of Magnitogorsk did equivocate and evade, cry and curse—and with good reason. Constantly told that in material terms much of the promise of socialism remained in the future, they were compelled to endure enervating bureaucratic indifference and arbitrary repression. Only the most dogmatic refused to acknowledge the hardships, as well as the staggering waste, corruption, recourse to intimidation, and widespread fear. But no matter how suspect matters might come to seem, the contrast with the apparent progress made since the tsar and, above all, with the recognized evils of capitalism—unemployment, exploitation, endemic economic crises, and imperialism—was available to quell even the deepest of doubts.

It needs to be recalled, moreover, that in the 1930s a parade of authoritative foreigners willingly came to the USSR, making pilgrimages to shrines such as Magnitogorsk, denouncing capitalism and praising socialism. Volumes were spoken, too, by the trumpeted borrowings undertaken by socialism's friends, and preemptive imitation by its foes, in Europe, the United States, Japan, and elsewhere. Whether within the framework of parliamentary democracy or under an alternate model of overt authoritarianism, the aim of achieving what the USSR had apparently achieved by way of national purpose, economic development, and overcoming class divisions preoccupied the world community in the interwar period. Socialism addressed real problems and seemed to offer real solutions. As long as capitalism was mired in crisis, socialism retained a powerful appeal.

.   .   .

Some sixty years after Magnitogorsk was founded, the writer Veniamin Kaverin recalled a visit he had made to the famous construction site as a youth in 1931. He recalled having been bowled over by the speed with which the factory and city were rising in the wide-open steppe. In retrospect, though, he also claimed to have been overwhelmed at the time by the sight of starving women, the wives and widows of the thousands of peasants deported to Magnitogorsk and forced to live in tents through the winter. "The cemetery grew faster than the steel works," Kaverin now wrote, confessing that back then, having seen "the direct connection between the growth of the cemetery and the growth of the steel works, I tried not to see this connection—and, it came to pass, I walked the construction with closed eyes."[3]

In 1931, Kaverin walked the construction not with closed eyes but with eyes eager to gather in the promised new world. And that new world, centered on the technologically advanced factory, was easy to see. Decades afterward, when he came to question his once firmly held beliefs, Kaverin did so by remembering what he had in fact seen with his own eyes. The same history in the making that filled him with hope and a powerful sense of progress—his progress, the country's progress—subsequently filled him with shame for his country and himself. Kaverin expressed the dynamic whereby Soviet socialism unraveled: insight came, disillusionment set in, repentant confessions were made—not by everyone, to be sure, but by many, very many.[4]

The widely remarked disappointment in Soviet socialism reveals what had once been a powerful faith: to become disillusioned one had to have believed in the first place. And the greater the belief, the greater the disillusionment. Feelings of guilt were often so powerful that they became the basis for a fervent opposite reaction—no doubt in large part because socialism as a faith was also a source of identity. The story of socialism was nearly indistinguishable from the story of people's lives, a merged personal and societal allegory of progress, social justice, and overcoming adversity—in short, a fable of a new person and a new civilization, distinct because it was not capitalist, distinct because it was better than capitalism. This was socialism's original strength; it also turned out to be a crushing burden.

Soviet socialism collapsed from within, but it did so because it existed as an anti-world to capitalism. It was from capitalism that socialism derived its identity and against which it constantly measured itself. Over the long haul, however, socialism proved incapable of meeting the challenge that it had set of besting capitalism. At a certain point, the competition with capitalism—in military technology, in living standards, in ideas about politics and society—began working to the disadvantage of the USSR. This dynamic, which in a different form had helped precipitate the downfall of the tsarist regime and the onset of the revolutionary process, impelled the Soviet regime on a path that also culminated in that regime's dramatic self-liquidation.

Veniamin Kaverin did not say what induced his re-remembering of incidents he once willingly suppressed, but a changed perspective on the outside world—capitalism—probably played a critical role. For many, it was this altered context that enabled, even demanded, a reassessment of socialism and their own association with it. That reevaluation naturally focused on the icons of the new world. Magnitogorsk, what many had reasoned would "be the best propaganda for socialism,"[5] turned out to be effective propaganda against socialism—but effective propaganda all the same.

Under socialism there was little room for neutrality. It demanded spiritual commitment and constant affirmations of that commitment, even when people felt ambivalent, indifferent, or hostile, and even after socialism's claims of surpassing capitalist civilization had become seriously strained. By adopting a confessional mode and using personal experiences to evaluate the legitimacy of their country's political system, Kaverin and others were following the same procedures they had learned as youths, only with the exact opposite result: socialism as a matter of faith, but now the loss of faith; autobiography as politically meaningful, but now delegitimizing.

■ ■ ■

In the almost six decades between Kaverin's visits to Magnitogorsk, evaluations of the baseline for measuring socialism—the outside world—changed; so did the ability to make such evaluations. Part of this could be attributed to the increased availability of information, part to a heavy-handed but nonetheless humanistic education that promoted *both* outright falsehoods *and* a real commitment to the truth; a vision of merciless class struggle *and* of universal good.

In the Magnitogorsk of the 1930s, more than forty thousand people were enrolled in full- or part-time education programs, ranging from beginning and middle schools, regular or technical high schools, and institutions of higher learning (such as the Mining and Metallurgical Institute and the Pedagogical Institute) to so-called workers' academies (*rabfaks*). Another twelve thousand individuals were enrolled in literacy courses, part-time trade courses, or night school (with an additional several hundred students at a school for classical music).[6] Virtually everyone in the city who could study was studying.

Magnitogorsk schools suffered from chronic problems with facilities.[7] Only a handful of the almost forty elementary schools were located in what were designated as permanent buildings; the rest were housed in broken-down barracks that lacked not merely adequate classrooms or laboratories but heat and running water. Furniture, such as desks and chairs, was in critically short supply, as were books and paper.[8] Owing to delays in planned construction and repairs, each September classes invariably started late—but they always managed to get underway.[9] What ensured the onset of each school year despite the daunting obstacles was the devotion to education, one of the primary values associated with the new world that Magnitogorsk incarnated.

Curriculum combined the basics—reading, writing, and arithmetic—with a very strong emphasis on civics and politics. Students were trained in what was called the "spirit of socialism," by which was meant the traditions and myths of a revolutionary legacy inherited and advanced by the USSR. This inculcation of the spirit of socialism was supposed to carry over even to technical subjects (on which great emphasis was placed). First-year students of the Mining Institute, for example, were accused of being culturally illiterate for not knowing the dates of the French revolution, or when fascism began. They were also taken to task for not reading the "classics" of Marxism. [10] But these students had to know the same science that "capitalists" studied and used, not to mention the novels of Tolstoy and the music of Tchaikovsky.

In the processes of socialization the greatest attention and resources were bestowed upon Magnitogorsk's youngest pupils, who in addition to class-time activities participated in a countrywide children's organization known as the "Pioneers," where civic training in the spirit of socialism was especially pronounced. [11] Aspirations for this next generation were high. One concerned pamphleteer complained that in a Magnitogorsk kindergarten, the children did not know what a shock worker was, who Voroshilov was, or what was meant by the term *kulak*. [12] By the end of their education, however, every one of these pupils could be expected to have been taught all this—and much more, including the sometimes condemned but mostly admired values of European civilization and its "highest achievements," as well as native values and forms of sociability that predated the revolutionary epoch.

■　　■　　■

It was taken for granted by the above pamphleteer that information about Magnitogorsk kindergartens should be broadcast, not only so that the situation there could be "corrected" but because the whole world should know. Such missionary zeal in the propagation of the minutest details of the city's life recalled the example of Magnitogorsk's famous American predecessor, Gary, Indiana. When Gary was founded during the first decade of the twentieth century, contemporaries engaged in shameless boosterism, replete with poetry, and began immediately to collect documents on the city and its factory, in part to sell land, but also with the aim of rearing the present generation in the spirit of the values Gary supposedly represented, and passing these values on to the next generation.[13]

What Magnitogorsk and Gary shared was a sense that they constituted not merely a single city, however important, but an entire civilization, *and* that their civilization could rightfully lay claim to being the vanguard of progressive humanity. It was no accident that Gary became the model for Magnitogorsk, for after the revolution in the Russian empire there was an enormous amount of admiring discussion of the United States as the world's most advanced civilization, and of a kind of "Soviet Americanism" as history's next stage.[14] This Soviet cult of America—a young, dynamic country that appeared to have made itself—took many forms, from the worship of industrial technology to a sense among large segments of the population that they had inherited from the Americans the mantle of civilization and enlightenment, even as their envy and imitation persisted.

Many of the large number of Americans who made pilgrimages to the USSR after the revolution, John Scott among them, enthusiastically confirmed this passing of the torch from the United States to the USSR. Their interest in Soviet socialism demonstrated yet again that socialism in the Soviet Union took shape as, and for a long time remained, a deeply felt aspiration, much like the so-called American dream—only ostensibly far better. But most of these foreign champions of Soviet socialism came to reject their admiration. Several became avid adversaries, tirelessly warning against the dangers of socialism's allure while becoming strident about the superiority of American civilization and adamant in their refusals to acknowledge any positive influence of Soviet socialism on themselves or their country. Such repudiations from outside, much like the earlier affirmations, eventually found an eager audience among once true-believing Soviet citizens, including Veniamin Kaverin. The circle became complete, ironically concealing the full extent of interconnectedness and reciprocal influence.

■　　■　　■

In the world after 1991, Soviet socialism may seem little more than a bizarre nightmare best condemned and forgotten, or if remembered, then only as a cautionary tale about political despotism and dangerous ideas. But even though it was rooted in a rejection of capitalism, the story of the USSR needs to be recognized as an integral part of the course of European history.

At the very least, Europe and the United States are complicit in the Russian revolution. It was, after all, the senseless war among the Great Powers that provided the indispensable context for the all-important politicization of the tsarist army, the seizure of power by conspiratorial revolutionaries, and the legitimation of transcendental socialism as an alternative to death and destruction. Moreover, Lenin and other exiled members of the Bolshevik conspiracy had been provided refuge in various European capitals and were able to return to Russia from Switzerland only through the maliciously intentioned assistance of the German high command. Remember, too, that although the revolutionary authorities had been compelled to cede enormous territories to the Germans at the risk of internal collapse, the entrance of the United States into the war on the side of the allies turned the tide against the Germans, allowing the Soviet regime an opportunity to rebuild the Russian empire.

During the Civil War, ineffective military intervention in Soviet Russia by Britain, France, the United States, and Japan provided an important impetus for the establishment of Bolshevik hegemony over the revolutionary process. During the 1920s, the Germans provided critical technical assistance to the USSR, including to the Red Army. During the 1930s, a veritable "Who's Who" of leading capitalist firms, the originators of the culture of Fordism, advised and aided Stalinist industrialization. Above all, what we call Stalinism was consolidated in the USSR against the background of, and as an answer to, the Great Depression that spread throughout the advanced capitalist countries, as well as the aggression that coincided with it.

In the end, though, the main reason that the USSR needs to be reincorporated into European history is that Stalinism constituted a quintessential Enlightenment utopia, an attempt, via the instrumentality of the state, to impose a rational ordering on society, while at the same time overcoming the wrenching class divisions brought about by nineteenth-century industrialization. That attempt, in turn, was rooted in a tradition of urban-modeled, socially oriented utopias that helped make the Enlightenment possible. Magnitogorsk had very deep roots.

■   ■   ■

In the early part of the seventeenth century, Tommaso Campanella (1568–1639), a Dominican friar from near Naples, composed what may perhaps be regarded as the quintessential urban-modeled, socially oriented utopia. It took the form of a dialogue between an inquisitive innkeeper and a garrulous Genovese sailor (one of Columbus's crew), who has purportedly returned from a wondrous place known as "the City of the Sun."[15] At the time Magnitogorsk was being built three centuries later, this dialogue was mobilized as part of the efforts to situate the Russian revolution historically, a goal that in retrospect can be seen to have been perhaps even more successful than intended.

In a brief introduction to the Russian-language edition of Campanella's text that was reissued in 1934 (the first had appeared in 1918), the scholar V. P. Volgin placed the monk within what he identified as the tradition of "communist utopias," singling out especially "the absence of private property, the universal obligation of labor (which is considered a matter of honor), the social organization of production and distribution, and the training through labor of the inhabitants." Volgin might also have underscored the importance in the City of the Sun of the development and proper use of science, the vigorous efforts to ensure the welfare of the population combined with equally vigorous defensive preparations for the inevitability of war, the fusion of spiritual and temporal power in a kind of theocracy, the frequency of individual confession or self-criticism, and the assumption that state power rests on the nature of everyday life—all core aspects, as we have seen, of the society in which Volgin himself was living.[16]

These were not the only remarkable parallels called to mind by Campanella's text that Volgin overlooked. In the course of comparing Campanella's work with Plato's and that of the early Christian fathers, for example, Volgin delicately touched on the idea of the undemocratic "rule of the wise," but he did so without invoking the "leading role of the Communist party." Volgin also made no mention, not even indirectly, of the resemblance between Campanella's portrait of the supreme ruler, Sun, and the emerging cult of Stalin. What Volgin did do, however, was to recognize a more than passing affinity between Soviet society and an avowedly utopian document in which social welfare was made the state's foremost duty and the key to its international standing.

However circumscribed the circle of people in the USSR who were acquainted with Campanella's work might have been, it was in effect the ideal of a City of the Sun—a city-based society engineered and regulated so as to ensure the utmost well-being, productivity, and hence state power—that served as the sublime vision from which the real-life Stalinist microcosm, Magnitogorsk, derived and into which it fed. Placing Magnitogorsk within the context of Campanella's text helps explain why a single Soviet city, especially one built in near isolation at a previously almost uninhabited site, could serve as such a potent symbol for the self-proclaimed new civilization of socialism.

Magnitogorsk was conceived and built as a utopian experiment—a socialist earthly paradise—but this vision, as well as the actual construction, embodied a way of thinking and a set of practices that, notwithstanding the rejection of capitalism, shared a great deal with other industrial countries, all of which developed forms of social regulation and the welfare state. In the lands of the former USSR, the welfare state centered on large factories has outlasted the institutionally redundant Communist party, but it is in deep crisis. Rather than as a cause for comfort or self-congratulation, this crisis might better be seen as also our own.

Note on Sources

Pervyi blin—narkomom.
An untranslatable Soviet-era
variation on a Russian proverb

Stalinism could not stop speaking about itself. It produced an almost endless flow of words about what it was trying to do, why, how, and with what results. The advent of Stalinism brought one of the greatest proliferations of documents the world has ever seen. Of course, it was also true of Stalinism that not all of these documents have been, or are, available. But when I began this study, a very large number had long been accessible, and more and more became so each year.

Documents generated during the early Stalin years can be conveniently divided into those published and those that remain unpublished. It is perhaps best to take up the former first, for the quantity and variety of published materials is not well appreciated, given the regime's notorious hypersecrecy. Secrecy there certainly was, but no less indicative of the worldview that drove Stalinism was the fact that many people worked tirelessly to issue volumes of information.

Published sources from the 1930s range from detailed statistical compilations, journals (both popular and scholarly), and official materials reprinted from archives to pamphlets and various enthusiastic first-person remembrances, as well as an array of broadsheet newspapers.[1] Of the latter, Magnitogorsk had more than a dozen, led by the daily *Magnitogorskii rabochii* (Magnitogorsk Worker), whose circulation rose from 3,000 in 1930 to 20,000 by 1932 and 30,000 by 1934. Almost every extant issue of Magnitogorsk's many newspapers from the 1930s, as well as those of the main provincial (oblast) newspaper, *Cheliabinskii rabochii* (Cheliabinsk Worker), were consulted for this book.[2]

Every Soviet newspaper had institutional (*vedomstvennaia*) status, that is, it was owned and run by a particular organization, whose concerns and condition it generally reported in detail, whether the organization in question was a labor colony or the local branch of the Communist Youth League. Magnitogorsk's main daily was no exception: it was "the organ" of the Communist party city committee, or gorkom. For coverage of party affairs, the daily is therefore indispensable. In addition, because the party understood its mandate to include all spheres of city life, the gorkom newspaper's coverage of local issues was unlimited. Like the party, it tended to poke its nose into everything.[3]

The Magnitogorsk daily also took up matters of national concern under such ru-

367

brics as "From Around the USSR" and "A Day of Our Motherland." And it re-printed articles and official speeches from other Soviet newspapers, both central and provincial. More often than not, however, the city newspaper was packed full with news of life in Magnitogorsk. This was at least equally true of the rest of the local papers, even if they were published less frequently.

As these newspapers demonstrated time and again, Magnitogorsk officials were not very good at the critical task of waste disposal, but when it came to disseminating the official point of view they excelled. Indeed, everything published during the Stalin period was imbued with the most shameless forms of boosterism and subject to strict censorship—two characteristics which might seem to limit the usefulness of such "official sources." Yet even when they understood themselves to be following proper guidelines in their loud proclamations and equally conspicuous silences, Soviet newspapers revealed a great deal, both directly and indirectly. The bad harvest of 1936, for example, was a taboo topic, but the hoarding and resale of bread throughout Magnitogorsk was publicly condemned in article after article.

Soviet censorship, moreover, was not merely an act of suppression; its chief goal was to inculcate values. This process was entirely open and readily visible, as for instance when the main daily chastized the mine's paper, *Gorniak* (Miner), for using foreign words—*depressiia, monopoliia, stabilizatsiia*—in its attempt to explain a speech by Stalin to the Seventeenth Party Congress in early 1934.[4] Such publications were the epitome of the much misunderstood phenomenon of agitprop (agitation and propaganda), which often meant detailed statements of goals and revealing examinations of the efforts undertaken to meet these goals, including enumerations of shortcomings and exhortations to overcome them. Agitprop was a revealing window onto the struggle to realize socialist ideals and "perfect" society.

Magnitogorsk newspapers made no pretense of merely reporting events. Instead, they intervened actively by sending warnings when something was thought to be amiss, chastized those deemed responsible, and goaded everyone, but especially the officials and agencies spotlighted, to do better. In the main daily there was a rubric entitled "Signals" and a follow-up section "In the Footsteps of Our Work." Often the "signals" amounted to demagogy, but sometimes the newspaper investigations, such as those of bureaucratic snafus or obvious injustices, were resolvable and produced results.

The newspapers' interventionism was guided by a belief that "the masses" should, and in fact would, also take an active part if given the opportunity. To these ends, collective readings of newspapers, followed by general discussion, were organized in most shops of the steel plant and many other organizations. Newspapers also frequently printed communications demanding a response from so-called worker correspondents (open informants), as well as irate readers' letters, many of which appear to have been written without prompting, even if they were carefully selected and edited. During the first three months of 1936, the newspaper reported receiving 1,781 letters, almost 20 per day, of which 3 or 4 would be printed. The second most widely read paper, *Magnitogorskii metall* (the organ of the steel plant), received 15 letters a day.[5]

Although almost no letters printed voiced disapproval of regime policies, most contained searing criticism of local officials and agencies. These were forwarded for a response to the appropriate organizations (e.g., the city health care department, the procurator, and so on). Of the letters forwarded in a three-month sample from 1936, 248 were said to have been answered, while 659 were not. In one case it was discovered that the chief of personnel for the trade agency Magnittorg had tossed the forwarded letters into the trash. The trade official expressed dismay that the newspaper "interfered" in other people's business, a sentiment for which he was harshly criticized. Officials of some local agencies, such as those of Magnittorg, were far more likely than others, such as the ones staffing the mighty steel plant administration, to be publicly assailed in this way, but the foibles of the latter were finally subjected to scathing exposés during the terror, when for a time the newspapers reported on numerous taboo subjects.[6]

Much of the Magnitogorsk readership seems to have paid attention to what the newspapers had to say, if only because people usually had a direct stake in most of the matters under consideration. Not all local papers were widely read, however. *Magnitostroi*, the organ of the construction trust, had a nominal circulation of only 2,184. When the authorities leaned on the trade union organizers to round up more subscriptions among the construction union's nearly five thousand members, the union responded by simply ordering more copies, which were said to have been found still bundled up on the floor of the paper's editorial office. Nonetheless, the construction trust's affairs, especially its deficiencies and the lack of faith in its trade union, were covered in those papers.[7] Even if they were sometimes justifiably ignored by contemporaries, Stalin-era Soviet newspapers remain valuable primary sources.

Surviving unpublished documents on the history of Magnitogorsk are for the most part distributed in two separate but overlapping archives corresponding to the dual or "theocratic" nature of the country's political structure, made up of both party *and* state (see chapter 7). These two parallel archives are very similar, with one important difference: all matters of state find expression in both, but information on internal party matters—which was neither a state nor a governmental body, but rather something analogous to a church—is limited to the party archive. Such redundancy, whose consequences turned out to be far-reaching, was combined with a strict administration hierarchy. As a result, multiple copies of the same document can usually be found not only in both the party and state archives, but up and down each side of the parallel pyramids: at the all-union (USSR), republic, and provincial (oblast) levels.

For the purposes of a local study, the value of these overlapping collections varies. In the case of the party, there was no republic-level structure in the Russian republic (where Magnitogorsk was located), and the USSR Central Committee was preoccupied with the many dozens of RSFSR regions, not to mention the rest of the republics. For Magnitogorsk party matters, therefore, the provincial archive in Cheliabinsk remains by far the most important document collection. Much the same could be said for the state structure, except that the largest collection of materials of Magnitogorsk state administration turns out to be a city affiliate of the provincial state archive, for which there is no party archive equivalent.

With the exception of some materials consulted at the Central Committee archive in Moscow and a handful of important documents from the oblast party archive that were made available to me by local scholars, unpublished materials on the Magnitogorsk party organization proved to be inaccessible. To a great extent, the rich coverage of party matters in the local press, as well as the many party documents published since 1985, compensated for this lack of access. In the end, however, some key questions regarding the functioning of the party in Magnitogorsk, in particular its relation to Moscow and the oblast (see chapter 7), could not be resolved.[8]

By contrast, my access to the state archive affiliate located in the city itself (MFGAChO) was almost unrestricted. In the materials of the city soviet and planning commission one can see the travails of urban life. Officials expended great efforts to take stock of the growing society under their jurisdiction, carrying out inventories of water supply, electricity, transport, baths, fire department capacity, hotel rooms, and especially the trade and distribution of goods. They also struggled to keep track of marriages, divorces, births, and deaths (rarely did the various sets of data match). What emerges from these urgent and detailed documents compiled by hard-working people is a sense of their mobilizational, crisis-management approach to administration, and of the daunting catalogue of problems and sometimes self-imposed obstacles they faced.

The city affiliate of the state archive also contains documents from the local metalworkers' trade union committee and the steel plant administration.[9] For the latter, however, no less important a collection is the archive of the vast planned economy, RGAE, located in Moscow. There, one can find the files of decision-making bodies, particularly the People's Commissariat of Heavy Industry (NKTP) and its subdivision, the Main Administration of Metal Industry (GUMP), as well as the frequent reports made by the Magnitogorsk steel plant to these agencies. To a limited extent, dealings between Moscow and Magnitogorsk were also filtered through the intermediate level of the provincial state archive, many files of which were also made available to me in Moscow. Those materials are chiefly useful for the history of the city construction.

In the 1930s, private property's elimination (the cornerstone of the new society formed during the Stalin years) meant that everything which transpired in any given community (outside of internal party matters) would theoretically be reflected in the state archive; there were no private entities (corporations, clubs, etc.) that could legally conduct their business beyond the purview of the state. The enormous significance of this circumstance for would-be historians was brought into relief by the reluctance of the Arthur McKee Corporation, one of the principal foreign firms involved in the design and construction of Magnitogorsk, to answer my written and telephone inquiries regarding access to the firm's internal archive. As the problem of secrecy diminishes, the near complete statization and extreme centralization of Soviet reality have proven to be remarkable aids in its study.

Unfortunately, however, although all institutions except for the party were technically part of the state in the USSR, several state institutions did not turn over their documents to the state archive but instead maintained their own institutional (vedomstvennyi) archive. The two most important state institutions that did not turn over their documents to the state archive are the KGB—in the 1930s, the NKVD—and the procuracy. I did not see either of these institutional archives, which like the party archive are located not in Magnitogorsk but in the provincial capital of Cheliabinsk. A handful of valuable files from the Magnitogorsk procuracy during the 1930s, however, hidden over the years by a conscientious procuracy employee long after they were supposed to have been either transferred to Cheliabinsk or destroyed, were made available to me in Magnitogorsk. Although few in number, these documents convey a great deal about the nature and operation of this institution and, to a lesser extent, that of the NKVD during the terror of 1936–38.

My failure to gain access to the NKVD archive is especially regrettable given that institution's centrality in Soviet history and the fact that it operated in secret (unlike the party, the NKVD's newspaper did not circulate and cannot be consulted outside the building of its successor agency, the former KGB). Besides materials on the functioning of the NKVD and its relation to other institutions, this archive also contains periodic assessments of the public mood (*operativnye svodki*) based on informants' reports. Such assessments no doubt incorporated the fears harbored by officials and the ingratiating tendencies of those reporting, but insight into the fears of the authorities and knowledge of who did the reporting, and under what circumstances, would be enlightening. These materials would also have been valuable in the analysis of popular attitudes, made with considerable difficulty in this monograph (particularly in chapter 5).

In contrast to Smolensk, the only other locality for which a detailed case study of the Stalin period (based exclusively on party archives) exists, Magnitogorsk was a strategically important industrial center to which great attention was devoted and thus for the study of which there is a greater depth and range of source materials. In addition to the pamphlets, statistical literature, and newspapers mentioned above, there was a countrywide project to write the histories of the USSR's biggest industrial enterprises, some two dozen in all. Drawing on a tradition of local studies (*kraevedenie*), on-site teams of researchers, directed by a central editorial agency, collected enormous volumes of scattered documents, interviewed and surveyed great numbers of workers, and wrote numerous manuscripts. Only a few of these were published before the project and its leadership were "liquidated" in 1938. Fortunately, however, the materials gathered were deposited in the State Archive of the Russian Federation (GARF, fond 7952).[10] Those pertaining to Magnitogorsk are among the most extensive.[11]

These documents naturally reflect the goal that inspired the project. Put simply, that goal was to highlight the supposed contrast between the slave-like existence of workers under the tsarist regime and their presumably much improved lives since the October revolution. The materials collected tended to concentrate on the prerevolutionary period, however, and even when the Soviet period was covered, the documents rarely got past the years immediately after the October revolution. But some factories, such as Magnitogorsk, were built only in the 1930s; there was no tsarist past in which to become bogged down. Thus, not only are the files on Magnitogorsk extensive, they also cover a period otherwise ignored in the collection (from 1930 to the end of 1936).

Among the more time-consuming tasks for the Magnitogorsk history project researchers was the search for documents from various archives. Requests went out to the local party committee, the courts, and the procuracy as well as to many other organizations. Judging from the files left behind, the results of these efforts were mixed. One researcher complained that documents were too abundant and in poor order (only the Sovnarkom USSR archive was said to be well organized).[12] Another commented, however, that materials of the party and state inspectorate (TsKK-

RKI) were particularly valuable, writing that "there doesn't seem to be a question which was not the subject of an investigation by the RKI." Several of these excellent files were in fact obtained and are available in the 7952 collection.[13]

By far the most valuable materials assembled by the history project are the interviews and memoirs, more than one hundred of which survive. Most of these are from 1933, when various "evenings of remembrances" were conducted,[14] or from the so-called Stakhanovite movement of 1935–36 (see chapter 5). Sometimes questionnaires were handed out (one such form, dated 1933, contained a list of sixteen questions for people who worked on the blast furnace construction).[15] Just as often people sat around in groups or alone with someone who recorded their remarks. In a few cases, manuscripts, read aloud to workers, served as a basis for further discussion.[16] These and other instances of workers describing their own lives were central aspects of the new society that arose during the 1930s.

In ferreting out documents and tracking down people for interviews, the individuals involved in the Magnitogorsk history project went to great lengths. They also managed to draft a large number of chapters, and readied for publication a two-volume collection of documents.[17] But neither the document collection nor the book was published. Major complicating factors were the authors' truly grand ambitions, and their indecision over whether to pursue a comprehensive chronological approach and tell the story of the entire factory's construction, or write the history of each shop separately and hope they added up to something whole.[18] In effect, both approaches were adopted, which resulted in a conception for a work stretching to several dozen volumes.

This proposal was subjected to sharp criticism by Moscow supervisory personnel, after which the on-site editorial board was changed and a second version of the proposal commissioned with strict guidelines to be followed.[19] In the summer of 1934, a brigade of writers was dispatched from Moscow to take over.[20] The authors in Magnitogorsk objected to this appropriation of the project by Moscow, but in the face of a central command, there was nothing they could do.[21] In the event, the Moscow group found itself confronting the same difficulties of scale and approach.[22] Moreover, by early 1937 many of the people associated with the construction of Magnitogorsk had been named enemies of the people. It became impossible to mention them and thus very difficult to write intelligibly about the city's history.[23]

Even though some eleven chapters (devoted to the various shops) existed in draft, only a few excerpts were published. These appeared in the newspaper beginning in January 1937, and were tailored to the Trotskyite wrecking trial then taking place in Moscow.[24] A history of the Magnitogorsk factory was not issued until 1978, in connection with celebrations of the city's fiftieth anniversary the next year. Not only did this formulaic book rely on a far narrower source base than had the writers of the 1930s, it exuded none of the exhilaration and sense of promise that had distinguished the earlier efforts.[25]

At bottom, the unrealized 1930s history project demonstrated the extent to which the construction of Magnitogorsk was enveloped by a sense of participation in world-historical events. Those involved evinced a powerful desire to record as much of what they were doing as possible. On the site, people began collecting memoirs as early as 1931, less than two years after the first settlers arrived and before central instructions to do so were issued.[26] Locals also collected clippings from many newspapers, closely following what was being said about them around the USSR and abroad (sometimes indignant telegrams were sent in response to news items).[27] Parallel to these efforts, one enthusiast, P. Petrazhitskii, started a museum of the Magnitogorsk steel plant in his apartment. The collection included film clips, photographs, slides, drawings, and news clippings.[28] For contemporaries, Stalinism was a grand crusade, and Magnitogorsk its embodiment.

The excitement surrounding Magnitogorsk was shared by the large group of foreigners who came to the site and in some cases spent the better part of the decade. Many left behind their impressions. These widely scattered but valuable sources range from simple travelogues contained in alumni newsletters to the unpublished papers of William Haven, the on-site representative of the American firm that initially contracted to design the steel plant. By far the most important source on Magnitogorsk produced by a foreigner, however, is the memoir written by John Scott, an American college student who left depression America in 1932 to take part in the Soviet experiment and spent five years living and working in Magnitogorsk.[29]

Scott's vivid account of his time "behind the Urals," published in 1942, remains the classic memoir on Soviet life in the 1930s. The existence of such a superb study by a keenly observant eyewitness might seem to preclude the writing of the present monograph. Yet, far from discouraging me, the existence of Scott's account and the many otherwise unknowable details it provides, when used in conjunction with the rest of the sources outlined above, ultimately convinced me that it was possible to carry out a closely focused ethnographic investigation of a Soviet city, despite the limitations in access to police archive materials.

In the end, with or without John Scott, the greatest deficiency in the source base of the present monograph is less the absence of NKVD materials than the failure to uncover any diaries or personal letters, and thus to reach people's intimate thoughts. When interviewed, a few survivors from the 1930s told me of having produced such documents but of having failed for one reason or another to preserve them. Perhaps the majority of diaries and intimate letters disappeared, along with a good many of their authors and recipients, in the terror. That would seem to make the efforts to recall these people and to write the history of the mentality of the 1930s all the more important. Yet despite the energies that went into my study of Magnitogorsk and its inhabitants, I come away feeling that I have only managed to scratch the surface.

Notes

ABBREVIATIONS

CR   Cheliabinskii rabochii
GAChO   Gosudarstvennyi arkhiv Cheliabinskoi oblasti
GARF   Gosudarstvennyi arkhiv Rossiiskoi Federatsii
GASO   Gosudarstvennyi arkhiv Sverdlovskoi oblasti
MFGAChO   Magnitogorskii filial gosudarstvennogo arkhiva Cheliabinskoi
            oblasti
MR   Magnitogorskii rabochii
PAChO   Partiinyi arkhiv Cheliabinskoi oblasti
PASO   Partiinyi arkhiv Sverdlovskoi oblasti
RGAE   Rossiiskii gosudarstvennyi arkhiv ekonomiki
RTsKhIDNI   Rossiiskii tsentr khraneniia i izucheniia dokumentov noveishei
            istorii
TsGAKFD   Tsentralnyi gosudarstvennyi arkhiv kinofotodokumentov

INTRODUCTION

1. As quoted in Avril Pyman, *The Life of Alexander Blok*, vol. 2 (Oxford: Clarendon Press, 1980), p. 282; cited in Richard Stites, *Revolutionary Dreams: Utopian Vision and Experimental Life in the Russian Revolution* (New York: Oxford University Press, 1989), p. 38.

2. For a popular theory on the formation of the Urals range and the history of the various analyses of the ore content at Magnetic Mountain, see the interview with the geologist Palkin, taken on 1 December 1934, in GARF, fond 7952, opis 5, delo 312, listy 31–50. Before the October revolution, ownership of the iron-ore deposits was disputed. Grigorii Mishkevich, "Delo ob Atach-gore," *Ural*, 1963, no. 11, pp. 149–59.

3. Just such a broad-based approach to understanding Stalinism—more familiar for monographs on the history of early modern France—has sometimes been advocated by Soviet émigrés. The writer Andrei Siniavskii, for example, composed a kind of literary memoir in which he developed the thesis that the USSR was a

civilization entailing a way of life, a language, and a set of values. Siniavskii's efforts to demonstrate the validity of these insights were deliberately unsystematic, although highly suggestive. Siniavskii, *Soviet Civilization: A Cultural History* (New York: Little Brown, 1990).

4. Merle Fainsod, *Smolensk under Soviet Rule* (Cambridge, Mass.: Harvard University Press, 1958). On the origins and uses of the concept "totalitarianism," see Leonard Schapiro, "The Concept of Totalitarianism," *Survey* 73 (1969): 93–115. Perhaps the best short guide to the historiography on Stalinism is Giuseppe Boffa, *The Stalin Phenomenon* (Ithaca: Cornell University Press, 1992). Contrary to Boffa, I believe there are two primary understandings of Stalinism, the first being the Stalinist self-presentation, as codified by the short course history of the party of late 1937 and, with the values inverted, in the writings of the totalitarian school. Like the totalitarian interpretation, the short course stressed an essential continuity with Leninism and Marxism, placed the Communist party at the forefront of everything that took place, made ideology causal, and recognized a prominent role for terror (as class war). The other principal understanding, put forth by Stalin's rival Trotsky, asserted that Stalinism was in important ways discontinuous with Leninism (and hence Marxism) and that Stalinism constituted a counterrevolution. The seeming interpretation normally identified as "Russia's revenge," by which Stalinism is traced to the long history in Russia of autocratic rule, also derives from Stalinism's self-presentation, specifically the deliberate efforts to legitimize the Soviet state by reclaiming an imperial Russian history going back to Ivan the Terrible (but not to Novogorod). For further discussion of the term *Stalinism*, see note 25 below.

5. Alex Inkeles and Raymond Bauer, *The Soviet Citizen: Daily Life in a Totalitarian Society* (Cambridge, Mass.: Harvard University Press, 1959); see also Inkeles' earlier study, *Public Opinion in Soviet Russia: A Study in Mass Persuasion* (Cambridge, Mass.: Harvard University Press, 1950).

6. One book issued just as de-Stalinization began argued that terror was the central feature of the Soviet system. Zbigniew Brzezinski, *The Permanent Purge* (Cambridge, Mass.: Harvard University Press, 1956). In a review of the political science literature, George Breslauer has pointed out that the totalitarian school was far more sophisticated and diverse than generally portrayed, and that underneath the rhetoric of party control individual scholars often described varieties of social behavior whose very existence appeared to contradict their basic model, a predicament that some self-styled "Sovietologists" did acknowledge. Breslauer neglected to mention, however, that in their groping to come to grips with Soviet society, almost the only social data these scholars consulted were interviews with émigrés. Soviet sources were considered to be virtually useless. Breslauer, "In Defense of Sovietology," *Post-Soviet Affairs* 8, no. 3 (1992): 197–238.

7. While the U.S. debate in the 1950s on Stalinism was largely framed by research carried out within the totalitarian school, in Britain the research of E. H. Carr and Isaac Deutscher was conducted within an avowedly socialist framework. The latter put forward a modified version of the Trotskyite narrative; the former, a modified version of the Stalinist narrative (without the opprobrium of the totalitarian school, and with massive empirical detail). Both concurred in taking a far more sympathetic view of the USSR than was current in American academic cir-

cles. During the Khrushchev thaw, when the notion of discontinuity between Stalinism and Leninism seemed to have been confirmed, Deutscher was invited to give at least one presentation at Harvard's Russian Research Center (the heart of the totalitarian school). Sheila Fitzpatrick—an Australian educated in Great Britain who for a while taught at Columbia University's Russian Institute—can be said to have been the person who finally brought Carr's perspective firmly into American universities.

8. Following Fitzpatrick's lead, some self-styled revisionists even appeared to take the position that large numbers of people had pressed the regime "from below" for the launching of the revolution from above. A further corollary to this supposition was that terror, and thus fear, was not as widespread as previously claimed, or even widespread at all. These were erroneous judgments that have properly been discredited and abandoned (at least by Fitzpatrick). Sheila Fitzpatrick, "New Perspectives on Stalinism," *Russian Review* 45 (1986): 352–73. Because the revisionists believed that the advocates of the totalitarian thesis had assumed there was complete unanimity within the regime, demonstrating the existence of any divisions or tension among top political figures could be heralded as a scholarly breakthrough. Similarly, because as part of its pattern of total control the state supposedly knew what it was doing at all times, the discovery of an instance when the state appeared confused, acted at cross-purposes, or reversed itself was put forward as a major analytical innovation. What should have been basic assumptions with which to begin serious analysis became "major findings," loudly and acrimoniously proclaimed.

9. Although other scholars, including Fainsod, had made reference to this important historical development, it was Fitzpatrick who first used it as the organizing principle for systematic research. Sheila Fitzpatrick, *Education and Social Mobility in the Soviet Union, 1921–1934* (Cambridge: Cambridge University Press, 1979).

10. Sheila Fitzpatrick, ed., *Cultural Revolution in Russia, 1928–1931* (Bloomington: Indiana University Press, 1978). Fitzpatrick chose the year 1932 as the end point of her overview on the revolution. Fitzpatrick, *The Russian Revolution, 1917–1932* (New York: Oxford University Press, 1983).

11. Fitzpatrick, *The Cultural Front: Power and Culture in Revolutionary Russia* (Ithaca: Cornell University Press, 1992), pp. 13, 89–90, 213. Nicholas Timasheff, *The Great Retreat: The Growth and Decline of Communism in Russia* (New York: Dutton, 1946); Leon Trotsky, *The Revolution Betrayed* (New York: Pathfinder, 1972; originally published in Russian, 1937). The best statement of the Trotskyite view on the revolution remains George Orwell's brilliant satire, *Animal Farm* (New York: Penguin, 1989), originally published in 1945. For a survey of the others, see Robert McNeal, "Trotskyite Interpretations of Stalinism," in Robert Tucker, ed., *Stalinism: Essays in Historical Interpretation* (New York: Norton, 1977), pp. 30–52.

12. Fitzpatrick, *The Cultural Front*, pp. 118, 159, 197, 216, 218–19, 233.

13. Fitzpatrick, *The Cultural Front*, pp. 213–14. See also her positivistic introduction to *A Researcher's Guide to Sources on Soviet Social History in the 1930s*, ed. Sheila Fitzpatrick and Lynne Viola (Armonk, N.Y.: M. E. Sharpe, 1990).

14. Consideration of the important work of the British Soviet Industrialization Project led by Robert W. Davies at Birmingham University, because of its primarily

economic focus, has been placed in chapter 1, which treats the problem of the formation of the planned economy. For a time Lewin's work was carried out under the auspices of the Birmingham Project.

15. Moshe Lewin, *The Making of the Soviet System: Essays in the Social History of Interwar Russia* (New York: Pantheon, 1985), pp. 286–314. See also "Moshe Lewin, Interview with Paul Bushkovitch," *Radical History Review*, 1982, p. 301 and the juxtaposition in the title of Lewin's principal monograph, *Russian Peasants and Soviet Power* (Evanston: Illinois University Press, 1968). In support of his argument that the "social structure [was] breeding authoritarianism," Lewin cited Barrington Moore's thesis on the alleged agrarian origins of modern dictatorships. Lewin did not, however, address the forceful criticisms that have been leveled at Moore. Lewin, *The Making of the Soviet System*, pp. 295, 310 ff.; Moore, *The Social Origins of Dictatorship and Democracy* (Boston: Beacon, 1966).

16. As brilliant as his characterizations of the bureaucratic apparatus have been, Lewin has tended to exaggerate the peasantry's "backwardness" and to underestimate the extent to which the incompatibility of the peasantry with "modernization" had less to do with the peasantry and more with the Bolshevik party and its particular vision of modernity. Indeed, although he catalogues as well as anyone the misperceptions and policy errors of the Bolshevik leadership, Lewin seems to assume that the Bolsheviks' preferred strategy of modernization—creating a predominantly heavy industrial economy on the basis of state ownership—was the optimal one, even if it was implemented egregiously. Lewin wrote often of "the *muzhik*, a headache again," but he does not appear to have suggested that the Bolshevik party's monopoly on power was a problem. See the remarks by Roland Lew, "Grappling with Social Realities: Moshe Lewin and the Making of Social History," in Nick Lampert and Gabor Rittersporn, eds., *Stalinism: Its Nature and Aftermath. Essays in Honour of Moshe Lewin* (Armonk, N.Y.: M. E. Sharpe, 1992), pp. 1–24.

17. Lewin, *The Making of the Soviet System*, pp. 209, 220–23. Lewin did not write comparable essays on the nature of society during the second or third Five-Year Plans.

18. Lewin, *The Making of the Soviet System*, p. 274. In writing of the bureaucratization of society and the thoroughgoing statism of the Stalinist system Lewin seemed to echo the conclusions of the totalitarian model. In contrast to the totalitarian thesis, however, he has always insisted that far from being the consequence of political or ideological determinism, such statization was a kind of trap that Soviet Russia unnecessarily fell into in its misconceived haste to overcome its nature, and moreover, that the resulting statism began to come undone even at its height (pp. 284–85).

19. To many, Lewin's work has seemed to constitute a "social interpretation" for the advent of Stalinism. During a presentation to the Princeton University Davis Seminar in April 1990, however, Lewin maintained that this had never been his intention. Rather, he stated that his contribution lay in providing a new political interpretation with a heretofore missing social dimension. This statement constituted an important clarification. For example, Nicholas Lampert, a scholar who has acknowledged being among those strongly influenced by Lewin, had thought it necessary to point out that "the emergence of the 'Stalinist' state in the 1930s"

could not "be accounted for solely in terms of the social upheavals involved in industrial expansion and collectivisation. The fact that a 'revolution from above' was possible at all suggests that in one sense 'politics' was already 'in command' in the NEP period." Lewin would not disagree with this statement, yet at the same time he has concentrated on demonstrating that the assumption "politics was in command" turned out to be something of a delusion shared by the Bolsheviks. Lampert, *The Technical Intelligentsia and the Soviet State* (New York: Holmes and Meier, 1979), p. 149.

20. Lewin, *The Making of the Soviet System*, pp. 26–30, 35, 302 ff.

21. In Lewin's words, Stalinism was a "blockage" or temporary "obstruction" in Russia's path to modernity, which he assumed to be a still unrealized humane form of socialism linked not to Trotsky but to the Lenin of the early 1920s. Lewin accorded exceptional significance to the obscure suggestions offered by the dying Lenin, some of which were later taken up and developed by Nikolai Bukharin, before the latter was crushed in political infighting by Stalin. Moshe Lewin, *Lenin's Last Struggle* (New York: Monthly Review Press, 1968). Without ever directly repudiating the so-called Bukharin alternative, Fitzpatrick and her followers have concentrated on the forces pushing the country toward radicalism.

22. Moshe Lewin, *The Gorbachev Phenomenon: A Historical Interpretation* (Berkeley: University of California Press, 1988). Lewin's argument about the long-term political consequences of the regime's promotion of urbanization, which resulted in an educated society, clearly has more in common with Fitzpatrick's upward mobility thesis than he allowed. In fact, Lewin's essay "Society, State, and Ideology during the First Five-Year Plan," was originally published in Fitzpatrick's Cultural Revolution volume (1978). Later, in the introduction to his own collection of essays (1985), however, Lewin expressly rejected the thesis that there had been a Cultural Revolution between 1928 and 1932. He did so, moreover, without mentioning or citing Fitzpatrick's work. Her name did not appear in the index to his collected essays (neither did his in the index to her collected essays, published in 1992). Having once also rejected Fitzpatrick's social mobility thesis, on the grounds that although hundreds of thousands of new people did indeed rise to high positions there had been as much downward as upward movement during the terror, Lewin subsequently wrote in the introduction to his essay collection that "an impressive social mobility, often upward, was a key feature" of the Stalin period. But diminishing the significance of this point, he added the clause, "as in any other case of industrialization," while also stressing what he deemed to be the more relevant social crisis that accompanied this mobility.

On the problem of culture under Stalin, Lewin had written in an essay originally published in 1977 of "a deep cultural retreat and the demeaning of culture," maintaining tentatively that "the cultural trends of the Stalinist era were not necessarily responses to what the peasants wanted to get but rather an expression of the psychic and mental tensions and values of the officials and leaders of the state machinery." This surmise resembled the basic premise of Fitzpatrick's work, first published almost at the same time. Lewin never returned to it in his later essays. As to how such a view on the elite's "counterrevolutionary" cultural proclivities meshed with his notion of the primarily rural influence on the formation of Stalinism, Lewin suggested somewhat enigmatically that there had been an "indirect influence of the rural milieu on the peculiar backward way of moving forward." Lewin, *The Making of the Soviet System*, pp. 33, 38–41, 276.

23. Writing in language strikingly reminiscent of Trotsky—for example, that Bolshevism "acquired a social base it did not want and did not immediately recognize: the bureaucracy"—Lewin has rarely cited him. At the same time, in his critique of the USSR under Stalin, Lewin went much further than Trotsky ever did. Lewin, *The Making of the Soviet System*, pp. 261, 267, 283. By contrast, Fitzpatrick has frequently cited Trotsky, and with approval. Yet she has refused to accept the negative connotations of Trotsky's Thermidor thesis. No doubt this refusal reflects in part the influence on her of E. H. Carr. In his monumental work on Soviet Russia, Carr had argued that the Bolshevik revolution, following the interregnum of Lenin's unexpected death, was transformed by circumstances—above all the international situation—into the necessity of building socialism in one country, a recognition of reality made by Stalin over Trotsky's objections. For Carr, the creation of the planned economy was thus the logical outcome of the revolutionary process. Fitzpatrick's work might best be understood as an attempt to unite the seemingly irreconcilable positions of Trotsky and Carr. Carr, *A History of Soviet Russia*, 13 vols. (New York: Macmillan, 1951–64).

24. As Leszek Kolakowski has written, "fascism was not a Communist-invented bogeyman, but a very real and tangible threat to civilizations and nations." He added that "the ambiguous and at times timid policy of the Western powers in the face of this threat was skillfully exploited by the Communists." For Kolakowski this did not "mean the communists have in any way, or even partially, resolved these problems. On the contrary," he argued, "virtually all their efforts to solve the social, cultural, national, and international issues which they once championed have ended in disaster." Kolakowski, "Communism as a Cultural Formation," *Survey* 29, no. 2 (1985): 136–48. When the USSR signed the pact with Nazi Germany in 1939, people were shocked precisely because, until then, they had believed that for all its faults, the Soviet Union did in fact represent the cause of progressive humanity. The Nazi-Soviet pact, even more than the terror, hurt the USSR's credibility abroad. Wolfgang Leonhard, *Betrayal: The Hitler-Stalin Pact of 1939* (New York: St. Martin's, 1989).

25. In the USSR, the term *Stalinism* was not used. Rather, the USSR claimed to be a socialist country based on the ideology of Marxism-Leninism and under the rule of the Communist party, also known as the Bolsheviks. Contemporaries did employ the adjective *Stalinist* to describe themselves and their accomplishments, but never as a substitute for Leninism and Bolshevism. It was the opponents of Stalin's leadership and policies who derided the USSR of the 1930s as "Stalinism," so as to differentiate Stalin's rule, which they repudiated, from that of Lenin and the October legacy. Stalinism as an "ism" has thus always implied a political judgment of discontinuity in the revolution. As is well known, numerous scholars have made this assertion of discontinuity the basis of their research. From the historical point of view, however, an analysis of Soviet society in the 1930s should try to make sense of the predominant terms and categories used by those living in the society at the time. In this monograph precisely such a course has been followed, with the single exception of the term *Stalinism*, which has become so widely accepted in English that to have refused to use it would have appeared strange. My usage of the

term, however, is not meant to imply discontinuity. In analyzing the Russian revolution, the historical task remains to explain not only how the Stalin revolution emerged from October—including possible alternatives and why they were not taken—but also how Stalinism was able to present itself effectively as a continuation of the October legacy. To claim that there was no such thing as a Stalinist Bolshevik is to deny millions of people their identity. Stephen F. Cohen, *Bukharin and the Bolshevik Revolution: A Political Biography*, 1888–1938 (New York: Knopf, 1973).

26. Keith Baker, *Condorcet: From Natural Philosophy to Social Mathematics* (Chicago: University of Chicago Press, 1975), pp. 385–86. Baker notes the important role that Condorcet reserved for the "scientific elite," who were charged with guiding social progress—a mission reminiscent of the one assumed in Russia by the Bolshevik party. According to Condorcet, the elite, made up of people of "superior intellect," was somehow to be bound by the principle of democratic consent, but no mechanism was specified. The centrality of the Enlightenment and Condorcet for understanding the Russian revolution was impressed upon me by Martin Malia.

27. Lynn Hunt, *Politics, Culture, and Class in the French Revolution* (Berkeley: University of California Press, 1984), p. 3.

28. George Lichtheim, *The Origins of Socialism* (New York: Praeger, 1969).

29. The pamphlet, an extract from the polemic commonly known as *Anti-Dühring* (1878), can be found in Robert C. Tucker, ed., *The Marx-Engels Readers*, 2d ed. (New York: Norton, 1978), pp. 683–717.

30. Leszek Kolakowski, *Main Currents of Marxism*, vol. 3 (New York: Oxford University Press, 1981), pp. 523–30.

31. Alexis de Tocqueville, *The Old Regime and the French Revolution*, trans. by Stuart Gilbert (New York: Dutton, 1955), p. 1.

32. No satisfactory account of the origins of the Russian revolution, comparable to the work by William Doyle on France, exists. For the closest approximation, see the challenging synthetic treatment by Tim McDaniel, who reproduces the trends of the historiography, focusing on the relation between labor and the autocracy while omitting consideration of the army, the countryside, and the nationalities. McDaniel recognizes, however, that the autocracy was the demiurge of revolution. McDaniel, *Autocracy, Capitalism, and Revolution* (Berkeley: University of California Press, 1988). For a critique of McDaniel and the secondary literature upon which he relies, see Stephen Kotkin, "One Hand Clapping: Workers and 1917," *Labor History* 32, no. 4 (1991): 604–20. It might be noted that the social interpretation of 1917 derives almost all its categories of analysis and modes of explanation from the social democratic vocabulary, whether in its Menshevik or Bolshevik variant. Investigations are framed in terms of what are taken to be classes, especially the working class but also sometimes the peasantry, and their relationship to political parties and programs.

33. Some people still adhere to the thesis that the revolution in the Russian empire can be explained as nothing more complicated than a typical authoritarian pattern of modernization historically dictated by the pressures of the international situation. The classic statement of this view was made by Theodore von Laue, who in addition to downplaying the significance of differing modernization strategies, tended to underestimate the extent to which the burden of modernization, although not self-imposed, was markedly colored by Russian ambitions and self-

perceptions. Von Laue, *Why Lenin? Why Stalin? A Reappraisal of the Russian Revolution, 1900–1930* (Philadelphia: J. B. Lippincott, 1964). In relegating socialism and property to at best secondary importance in order to stress a supposed universal process of development, the modernization approach becomes in effect an unwitting demonstration of Stalinism's roots in the Enlightenment.

34. A similar model of the outbreak of the Russian revolution was put forth by Theda Skocpol, who focused on the combination of external challenges and crippling internal constraints (supposedly derived from the agrarian social structure) that led to the collapse of the tsarist state. Unfortunately, Skocpol chose to take for granted the most striking aspect of imperial Russian development: namely, the formation of a "public," meaning the ability, not to mention desire, of various social groups to mobilize for the goal of effecting political change. *States and Social Revolutions* (Cambridge, Mass.: Harvard University Press, 1979).

35. This point has been made, in slightly different form, by William Rosenberg, "Russian Labor and Bolshevik Power: Social Dimensions of Protest in Petrograd after October," in Robert Kaiser, ed., *The Workers' Revolution in Russia, 1917: The View from Below* (Cambridge: Cambridge University Press, 1987), pp. 106–11.

36. R. John Rath, "The *Carbonari*: Their Origins, Initiation Rites, and Aims," *American Historical Review* 69, no. 2 (1963–64): 353–70.

37. This point is eloquently stated by Edvard Radzinsky, *The Last Tsar: The Life and Death of Nicholas II* (New York: Arrow, 1993; originally published in Russian, 1992), pp. 183–84, 213–15. See also Robert Daniels, *Red October: The Bolshevik Revolution of 1917* (New York: Charles Scribner's Sons, 1967), pp. 3–17.

38. Trotsky recognized as much when, despite his deeply Marxist understanding of history as a developmental process with underlying laws, he concluded soberly that without Lenin there would in all probability have been no Bolshevik seizure of power. Trotsky, *The Russian Revolution* (New York: Doubleday, 1959), pp. 261–303, esp. 291.

39. Alexander Rabinowitch, *Prelude to Revolution: The Petrograd Bolsheviks and the July 1917 Uprising* (Bloomington: Indiana University Press, 1968).

40. The bungled Kornilov putsch transformed the revolution into an armed conflict, galvanizing the revolutionaries into taking the defensive actions that made them able to stage a coup. Moreover, although the "right" failed to mobilize in the immediate aftermath of the Bolshevik coup in October, the threat of counterrevolution, made concrete by Kornilov's ill-conceived putsch, remained a powerful organizing principle, shaping events and popular attitudes. George Katkov, *Russia 1917, the Kornilov Affair* (New York: Longman, 1980). The importance of the Kornilov affair in the Bolshevik narrative of the revolution is reflected in a popular book issued under the auspices of the project on the history of the party (Istpart): Vera Vladimirovna, *Kontr-revoliutsiia v 1917 g. (Kornilovshchina)* (Moscow, 1924).

41. Between February 1917, when the tsar abdicated, and the summer of 1918, the peasants eliminated the gentry class and divided up the land. Orlando Figes, *Peasant Russia, Civil War: The Volga Countryside in Revolution, 1917–1921* (New York: Oxford, 1989); John Keep, *The Russian Revolution: A Study in Mass Mo-*

bilization (New York: Norton, 1976); John Channon, "The Bolsheviks and the Peasantry: The Land Question during the First Eight Months of Soviet Rule," *Slavic and East European Review* 66, no. 4 (1988): 593–624. See also the unorthodox analysis of the relationship between the peasantry and political parties by Arthur Adams, "The Great Ukrainian Jacquerie," in Taras Hunczak, ed., *The Ukraine, 1917–1921* (Cambridge, Mass.: Harvard University Press, 1977), pp. 247–70. The peasant revolution of 1917–18 was undone in 1929.

42. For all the talk about the radical mood in the factories, Bolshevism took root above all at the front, where millions were massed and subjected to agitation. Bolshevism was spread, moreover, largely among and by soldiers and sailors. Viktor Shklovsky, *A Sentimental Journey: Memoirs, 1917–1922* (Ithaca: Cornell University Press, 1984; originally published in Russian in 1923); Allan Wildman, *The End of the Russian Imperial Army*, 2 vols. (Princeton: Princeton University Press, 1980, 1987); Evan Mawdsley, *The Russian Revolution and the Baltic Fleet: War and Politics, February 1917–April 1918* (New York: Barnes and Noble, 1978); Norman Saul, *Sailors in Revolt: The Russian Baltic Fleet in 1917* (Lawrence: University of Kansas Press, 1978). Characteristically, when Lenin was challenged in policy disputes and abandoned argumentation for intimidation, more often than not he threatened to appeal directly to the soldiers and sailors, not the workers.

43. The importance of 1918 has been argued by Martin Malia, *Comprendre la révolution Russe* (Paris, 1980), pp. 121–41. The processes whereby the Bolsheviks were able to assert a political monopoly over the revolution is not well understood. The basic work remains Leonard Schapiro, *The Origins of the Communist Autocracy: Political Opposition in the Soviet State, First Phase, 1917–1922*, 2d ed. (New York: Macmillan, 1977). In tracing the formation and consolidation of the one-party dictatorship, Schapiro focused not only on the actions of the Bolsheviks but also on those of the other parties, whose leaders, he argued, had failed to understand the course of events and to mount an effective challenge. Schapiro did not, however, pay much attention to the tensions and developments in the wider ranks of the Bolshevik movement, or to the symbols and language of the revolutionary process. Subsequent scholarship, although it has moved the discussion to the provinces, has not developed a more sophisticated view of the revolutionary process, often just restating, consciously or not, the discussion of the Bolsheviks put forth by contemporaries, in the very same analytical categories, as if the revolution was still being fought. For a compendium of the immediate reactions to Bolshevism that have set the terms of subsequent debate, see Jane Burbank, *Intelligentsia and Revolution: Russian Views of Bolshevism, 1917–1922* (New York: Oxford, 1986).

44. Significantly, after the October coup, but before the onset of the Civil War proper, there were large protest votes against Bolshevik candidates to local soviets that resulted in majorities for the Mensheviks or Socialist Revolutionaries in all provincial capitals where elections were held. Vladimir Brovkin, "The Mensheviks' Political Comeback: The Elections to the Provincial Soviets in Spring 1918," *Russian Review* 42 (1983): 1–50. There were also numerous workers' strikes, and a Conference of Factory and Plant Representatives in Petrograd that called for "the complete liquidation of the current regime." Ironically, the capitulatory peace signed with the Germans at Brest-Litovsk, which brought an end to the "imperialist war," served as one of the principal sources of disillusionment. But the Bolsheviks'

frequent resort to repression seems to have brought the greatest revulsion. Protests only elicited further repression. Rosenberg, "Russian Labor and Bolshevik Power," pp. 115–28.

45. The coup occurred, of course, in the capital, which in contrast to the rest of the empire, counted 400,000 industrial workers (employed in very large factories), as well as a permanent garrison of 110,000 soldiers, among its two million inhabitants. Imitative and Petrograd-assisted coups were attempted elsewhere, mostly in areas dominated by Great Russians, but not only did these coups usually encounter difficulties, they often did not succeed in establishing unambiguous "Soviet power" locally. Moreover, there was no Bolshevik coup in Kiev, Tashkent, or the Caucasus, where "Soviet power" was established later by an invading Red Army. In other places, such as Poland, Finland, and on the Baltic Sea, the Red Army proved incapable of establishing "Soviet power," or did not even try. For a discussion of the uniqueness of Petrograd, see Roger Pethybridge, *The Spread of the Russian Revolution: Essays on 1917* (London: Macmillan, 1972), ch. 6. The literature on events around the empire is extensive, but rarely incorporated into the master narratives of the revolution. Examples of the earliest monographs include John Reshetar, *The Ukrainian Revolution 1917–1920: A Study in Nationalism* (Princeton: Princeton University Press, 1952); Alexander Park, *Bolshevism in Turkestan, 1917–1927* (New York: Columbia University Press, 1957); and Firuz Kazemzadeh, *The Struggle for Transcaucasia (1917–1921)* (New York: The Philosophical Library, 1951). One of the few attempts to synthesize this literature, which does not, however, offer a completely convincing explanation for Bolshevik success, is Richard Pipes, *The Formation of the Soviet Union*, 2d ed. (Cambridge, Mass.: Harvard University Press, 1964).

46. In November 1920, the reenactment of the storming of the Winter Palace, the founding event of the "October revolution," was staged as a battle between Reds and Whites, demonstrating in graphic form the transformation of "the revolution." See William Rosenberg, ed., *Bolshevik Visions: First Phase of the Cultural Revolution in Soviet Russia* (Ann Arbor: Ardis, 1984), pp. 445–47; René Fülöp-Miller, *Geist und Gesicht des Bolschewismus* (Vienna: Almathea-Verlag, 1926), translated as *The Mind and Face of Bolshevism: An Examination of Cultural Life in Soviet Russia* (New York: Knopf, 1928), pp. 208–13. The February revolution was commemorated until 1927.

47. On the dilemmas involved in the collaboration of socialists with antisocialists in the struggle against Bolshevism, see Vladimir Brovkin, *The Mensheviks after October: Socialist Opposition and the Rise of the Bolshevik Dictatorship* (Ithaca: Cornell University Press, 1987), pp. 295–99. The Bolsheviks, too, entered into tactical alliances with nonsocialists, as in their linking up with the Jadids in the battle to overthrow the Khanate of Bukhara. But this was rare. See Hélène Carrère D'Encausse, *Islam and the Russian Empire* (London: I. B. Taurus, 1988), pp. 148–66. It might be mentioned that Bolshevik military victories in Central Asia, no less than those against the peasants in Russia, were usually accompanied by what the Bolsheviks viewed as concessions, such as the return of confiscated religious properties.

48. The Left Socialist Revolutionaries also captured the post and telegraph office, and sent telegrams around the empire that referred to themselves as "the party

in power." They do not, however, appear to have had a firm plan to seize power. George Leggett, *The Cheka: Lenin's Political Police* (New York: Oxford University Press, 1981), pp. 70–81; Robert Service, *The Bolshevik Party in Revolution: A Study in Organisational Change* (New York: Barnes and Noble, 1979), p. 2. It was around the time of the 1918 crisis that the imperial family, held in captivity in the Urals, was executed. Richard Pipes, *The Russian Revolution* (New York: Knopf, 1990), pp. 745–88.

49. The importance of the Civil War as a formative experience for the Bolshevik party has been cogently argued by both Sheila Fitzpatrick and Moshe Lewin. See their essays "The Legacy of the Civil War" (Fitzpatrick) and "The Civil War: Dynamics and Legacy" (Lewin), in Diane Koenker et al., eds., *Party, State, and Society in the Russian Civil War* (Bloomington: Indiana University Press, 1989), pp. 385–98 and 399–423. Lewin has observed that the Bolsheviks won because they created a state, "a dynamism that the other side lacked." For her part, Fitzpatrick has noted that the Civil War bequeathed to the Bolsheviks a military victory, a militant ethos that was retained despite the "retreat" of the NEP, and perhaps most importantly, a heroic myth about themselves. In an earlier article, she pointed out that "many Bolsheviks got their first administrative experience in the Red Army and the Cheka," and that "in the years following the Civil War, the party owed much of its coherence to the bonds forged among comrades in arms." Fitzpatrick, "The Civil War as a Formative Experience," in Abbot Gleason et al., eds., *Bolshevik Culture: Experiment and Order in the Russian Revolution* (Bloomington: Indiana University Press, 1985), pp. 57–76.

50. Witte's scheme relied heavily on foreign capital, a policy that became the source of a politics of resentment. Theodore von Laue, *Sergei Witte and the Industrialization of Russia* (New York: Atheneum, 1969).

51. Socialism, which emerged in Russia decades before there was a "proletariat," was the lifeblood of the intelligentsia. What began as a philosophy of life and personal ethics for a generation of rebellious individuals, and then became a popular movement founded on an idealization of the peasantry and countryside, by the end of the nineteenth century had become an ideology of development centered on the working class and industry. Martin Malia, *Alexander Herzen and the Birth of Russian Socialism* (Cambridge, Mass.: Harvard University Press, 1961); Leopold Haimson, *The Russian Marxists and the Origins of Bolshevism* (Cambridge, Mass.: Harvard University Press, 1955).

52. This was already becoming clear when the successful effort to reverse the Polish invasion of Ukraine and Belorussia turned into an attempt to bring about a revolution in Poland through invasion, an episode that greatly expanded the integration of the old tsarist officer corp into the Red Army. Norman Davies, *White Eagle, Red Star: The Polish-Soviet War, 1919–1920* (London: Macdonald, 1972).

53. The advent, evolution, and monumental impact of the Russian intelligentsia, despite its meager numbers, has been treated by Martin Malia. In elaborating the maximalist tendencies of the intelligentsia that the Bolsheviks inherited, however, Malia makes almost no attempt to account for the Bolsheviks' capacity to implement radical schemes, other than to reiterate Kliuchevskii's observation on the absence in Russia of a powerful middle class. Nor does Malia devote much attention to the impact of the revolutionary process on the Bolsheviks. Malia, "What is the

Intelligentsia?" in Richard Pipes, ed., *The Russian Intelligentsia* (New York: Columbia University Press, 1961), pp. 1–18.

54. Attempts to create a Red Army in January 1918 failed. Only the onset of the Civil War brought success, which was indeed remarkable. As Leonard Schapiro has observed, "the principal Communist achievement in the military field was perhaps not so much the military victory in the Civil War as the skill with which the Soviet Government succeeded in retaining to a sufficient degree for victory the loyalty of an army composed largely of ex-Imperial army officers and of reluctant peasants." Unfortunately, Schapiro offered little explanation for this success, aside from praising the brilliant organizational skills of Trotsky. Schapiro, "The Birth of the Red Army," in Liddell Hart, ed., *The Red Army* (New York: Harcourt, Brace, 1956), pp. 24–32. There was massive peasant desertion from the Red Army, but peasants rarely defected to the other side; they simply went home. In many cases peasants fought the Whites on their own, without joining the Red Army.

55. This point, remarked upon widely by contemporaries, especially the Bolsheviks who feared the "contamination" of the revolution by a class of petty-bourgeois clerks, was recently remade by Daniel Orlovsky, "State Building in the Civil War: The Role of the Lower-Middle Strata," in Koenker et al., eds., *Party, State, and Society in the Russian Civil War*, pp. 180–209. See also Robert Daniels, *The Conscience of the Revolution: Communist Opposition in Soviet Russia* (Cambridge, Mass.: Harvard University Press, 1961), p. 136.

56. Oliver Radkey, *Russia Goes to the Polls: The Election to the All-Russian Constituent Assembly, 1917* (Ithaca: Cornell University Press, 1990). Radkey points out that although the Bolsheviks lost the election, four-fifths of the electorate voted for socialists of one kind or another.

57. In ritual excoriations of the Bolsheviks it has become a commonplace to lament the fate of the Socialist Revolutionary party (SR), which won the elections in late 1917 to the Constituent Assembly but were then shunted aside. But when representatives of the Petrograd garrison went to the SR Central Committee with an offer to defend by force the convocation of the Constituent Assembly, the SR leadership declined, and the assembly perished at the hands of a small number of Red Guards. Perhaps even more tellingly, when the revolt of the Czech legion enabled the SRs to form an opposition government in Samara (their stronghold), they could not manage to form an army. The SRs were dependent first on the Czechs and then on the Whites, who finally did away with the SR government altogether, but not before the great peasant party had entered into an alliance with a Constitutional Democrat-led, avowedly pro-landowner government organized in Omsk. Oliver Radkey, *The Sickle under the Hammer: The Russian Socialist Revolutionaries in the Early Months of Soviet Rule* (New York: Columbia University Press, 1963).

58. The 1921 Petropavlovsk resolutions and formation of a "socialist commune" by the Kronstadt sailors once again vividly demonstrated the coherence of a popular vision of the revolution independent of the Bolsheviks. Although under threat of invasion, the sailors on principle refused offers of assistance by self-proclaimed White Guards. Yet both Lenin and Trotsky vehemently sought to characterize the anti-Bolshevik but thoroughly socialist Kronstadt rebellion as a White Guard counterrevolution. Here in stark form was the Civil War binary opposition—Bolshevik socialism or the Whites—through which the wider revolution was

Bolshevized. Israel Getzler, *Kronstadt 1917–1921: The Fate of a Soviet Democracy* (Cambridge: Cambridge University Press, 1983), pp. 205–45; V. I. Lenin and Leon Trotsky, *Kronstadt* (New York: Monad Press, 1979), pp. 44–53.

59. What might be called the cultural dimension of Bolshevism is belatedly being recovered (although it has yet to be made integral to the master narrative on politics, especially in comparison with the work on social history). See, for example, Nina Tumarkin, *Lenin Lives! The Lenin Cult in Soviet Russia* (Cambridge, Mass.: Harvard University Press, 1981); Gleason et al., *Bolshevik Culture*; and James van Geldern, *Bolshevik Festivals, 1917–1920* (Berkeley: University of California Press, 1993). An important source book on the cultural dimension of the revolution is available in English: William Rosenberg, ed., *Bolshevik Visions* (Ann Arbor, Mich.: Ardis Press, 1984). It is symptomatic that the collection is called "Bolshevik Visions," rather than, say, "Revolutionary Visions," and that the process whereby Bolshevism came to be identified with "the revolution" is not addressed in the introduction or the selection of documents.

60. Sviatlovskii quoted in Tamarchenko, "Nauchnaia fantastika i model revoliutsii," in Suvin, ed., *Twentieth-Century Science Fiction in Warsaw Pact Countries*, special issue of *Canadian-American Slavic Studies* 18, nos. 1–2 (1984): 43; cited in Stites, *Revolutionary Dreams: Utopian Vision and Experimental Life in the Russian Revolution* (New York: Oxford University Press, 1989), p. 168. See also Jerome Gilison, *The Soviet Image of Utopia* (Baltimore: Johns Hopkins University Press, 1975).

61. Perhaps the most infamous example of the condemnation of utopianism in politics, and the most powerful justification imaginable of the status quo, is J. L. Talmon, *Utopianism in Politics* (London: Conservative Political Centre, 1957), excerpted in George Kateb, ed., *Utopia* (New York: Atheneum, 1971), pp. 91–101. See also Mikhail Heller and Aleksandr Nekrich, *Utopia in Power: The History of the Soviet Union from 1917 to the Present* (New York: Summit Books, 1986; originally published in Russian, 1982).

62. Fülöp-Miller expressed a certain awe of Bolshevism, not as a form of political organization, but because he understood that Bolshevism encompassed the whole of existence of its adherents, who were destined to increase because of the Bolsheviks' commitment to cultural transformation and their successful exploitation of the public space and the category of "the masses." Fülöp-Miller, *The Mind and Face of Bolshevism*.

63. Moreover, despite what he saw as the essentially anarchist or at least rebellious strain in this utopian experimentation, Stites insisted on its harmonious coexistence with what he viewed as "tolerant" political authorities—until 1931, when Stalin launched what Stites calls a "war on the dreamers." Stites, *Revolutionary Dreams*, pp. 131, 252.

64. In a subsequent article Stites wrote that "there was a huge difference between the utopian experimenters of the 1920s who attempted to build a socialist counter-culture from the inside out and the hot-headed enthusiasts of the early 1930s who wanted to leap into modernization and Socialism." But in the article as in the book, Stites put forth no explanation of how or why the "utopianism" of the 1920s ended—as he contends it did—other than to appeal to the evil nature of Stalin (and Kaganovich) and to certain unspecified changes in the social composition

of the party. He also admitted that "euphoria, culture building, and visionary ide-alism are human attitudes that are hard to sustain over a long period—whether or not the environment is hostile or sympathetic." Stites, "Stalinism and the Restruc-turing of Revolutionary Utopia," in Hans Gunther, ed., *The Culture of the Stalin Period* (New York: St. Martin's, 1990), pp. 78–94; Stites, *Revolutionary Dreams,* p. 226. Given the emphasis in the scholarly literature, it should perhaps be reit-erated that the drive for unity, heresy-hunting, and the frequent resort to violence were obviously present from the beginning, part of the revolutionary iconoclasm and Manichean worldview that fed into Stalinism and made it possible, even if Sta-linism considerably deepened these tendencies.

65. In August–September 1920, after the Civil War was essentially won and the threat of a restoration of landowner rights ended, there had been a massive uprising by a peasant army against the Bolsheviks. This peasant or "Green Army" which mobilized around 20,000 troops and was similar in organization to the Red Army, was defeated by a Red Army force more than double its size. At the same time, central authorities also made concessions in Tambov, introducing a NEP *avant la lettre.* Oliver Radkey, *The Unknown Civil War in Soviet Russia: A Study of the Green Movement in the Tambov Region, 1920–1921* (Stanford: Hoover Institu-tion, 1976). The analogy to the capitulatory treaty signed with the Germans in March 1918—a desperate gamble that paid off when the Germans surrendered to the Allies in November—was made by Bukharin, and repeated by Riazanov dur-ing the debate on the tax-in-kind decree at the Tenth Party Congress. *Desiatyi s"ezd Rossiiskoi kommunisticheskoi partii: Stenograficheskii otchet* (Moscow, 1926), p. 255. In many regions, including Siberia, Central Asia, and Ukraine, the introduction of the tax-in-kind was purposely delayed for as long as a year.

66. The NEP was not introduced by a single decree. Laws and decrees were is-sued like an avalanche throughout 1922 and 1923. These were notable for the many restrictions they carried against trade in certain goods, and the many limitations they maintained on private manufacturing and the hiring of labor. In 1923, more-over, the regime began backing away from some of the provisions of the NEP, and though the NEP did receive something of a second wind in 1924–25, it was again partially rolled back in 1926. This ambivalence and grudging tolerance character-ized the entire existence of the NEP. It should also be kept in mind that during this time, the regime remained a dictatorship; there may have been a "cultural" NEP, but there was no "political" NEP. See E. H. Carr, *The Bolshevik Revolution, 1917–1923,* vol. 2 (New York: Macmillan, 1952), pp. 269–359.

67. Alan Ball, *Russia's Last Capitalists: The Nepmen, 1921–1929* (Berkeley: University of California Press, 1987); Roger Pethybridge, *One Step Backwards, Two Steps Forward: Soviet Society and Politics under the New Economic Policy* (Oxford: Clarendon Press, 1990).

68. On the question of what was deemed within and outside the realm of pos-sibility in the Russian context, see the perceptive comments by Silvana Malle, *The Economic Organization of War Communism, 1918–1921* (Cambridge: Cambridge University Press, 1985), pp. 495–96.

69. The contradictions of the NEP, especially when juxtaposed against the ap-parent certainties of the Civil War (at least in retrospect), are treated, along with the crucial importance of the institutional nexus of the Red Army, in Mark von

Hagen, *Soldiers in the Proletarian Dictatorship: The Red Army and the Soviet Socialist State, 1917–1930* (Ithaca: Cornell University Press, 1990).

70. The mood during the NEP both inside and outside party circles has been well-described by Nikolai Valentinov [Volskii], *Novaia ekonomicheskaia politika i krizis partii posle smerti Lenina* (Stanford: Hoover Institution Press, 1971).

71. Alexander Ehrlich, *The Soviet Industrialization Debate, 1924–1928* (Cambridge, Mass.: Harvard University Press, 1960).

72. Further discussion of the Great Break appears in the introduction to part 1.

73. Since the 1960s, there has been much talk in the historiography of the "alternatives" to Stalin, with attention focusing on Trotsky and Bukharin. Despite being a Jew, Trotsky did probably have the potential to become paramount leader following Lenin's death, but for a variety of reasons he lost out. Bukharin never had such a chance. Discussion of a "Bukharin alternative" is not simply a matter of whether he had an alternative "plan" of action, but whether Stalin might have chosen to follow it, for once Trotsky was defeated, there was no alternative to Stalin's rule, barring accidental death or assassination. For an analysis of the succession problem that represents a step forward, see Lars Lih, "Political Testament of Lenin and Bukharin and the Meaning of NEP," *Slavic Review* 50, no. 2 (1991): 240–52.

74. For a handy review of the explanations of Stalin's rise to supremacy, see Chris Ward, *Stalin's Russia* (London: Edward Arnold, 1993), pp. 7–38. Documents being released from formerly secret archives are liable to shed considerable new light on this critical problem.

75. I. V. Stalin, "Ob osnovakh Leninism," lectures at Sverdlov University published in *Pravda*, 26 and 30 April 1924; and 9, 11, 14, 15, 18 May 1924; reprinted in *Sochineniia*, vol. 6 (Moscow, 1947), pp. 69–188. In addition to systematizing Leninism (in strikingly defensive terms), Stalin apparently invented, and certainly popularized, the denigrating term "Trotskyism" (see *Sochineniia*, pp. 342–57), which sealed Trotsky's fate. It should be kept in mind that Leninism as an ideology was not formed automatically. Stalin's vigorous handling of the formulation of Leninism has been remarked on by Robert Tucker, *Stalin as Revolutionary, 1879–1929* (New York: Norton, 1973), pp. 316–18, 324. Significantly, although Lev Kamenev by virtue of his position as boss of the Moscow party organization was nominally in charge of the Marx-Engels-Lenin Institute, he gave it little attention. The institute and its critically important documents were assiduously controlled by aides to Stalin from inside the apparat. See Larry Holmes and William Burgess, "Scholarly Voice or Political Echo? Soviet Party History in the 1920s," *Russian History/Histoire Russe* 9 (1982): 378–98; Niels Erik Rosenfeldt, "'The Consistory of the Communist Church': The Origins and Development of Stalin's Secret Chancellery," ibid., pp. 308–24.

76. More serious were the considerations that (1) just such a course had been advocated by the so-called left opposition, which Stalin had vanquished as part of his bid for absolute power; and (2) that certain circles in the party, upon whom he had relied to destroy the opposition, were against the leftist course. Stalin rhetorically dismissed the resemblance of the Big Drive to the program of the left opposition, at the same time shifting attention onto those whom he castigated as the "right opposition."

77. Stalin's revolution has been called a "revolution from above," a characterization that was officially incorporated by the Soviet regime in the short course party history published in late 1937 as a description of collectivization. In fact, such a notion had been advanced by an émigré Orthodox Christian socialist, Georgii Fedotov, *Problemy budushchei Rossii* tom 1 (1931; St. Petersburg, 1991), p. 229. (I am grateful to Professor Wada Haruki for bringing this source to my attention.) Echoing such commentators, Robert Tucker has treated the oft-noted resemblance to past tsars invoked by Stalin not as the result of efforts to generate legitimacy for state policies by means of crafted historical analogies but as a factual model that inspired Stalin's actions and as an accurate characterization of the social, political, economic, and cultural order formed under him. Such a view tends to downplay considerations of property, class, and socialism. Tucker, *Stalin in Power: The Revolution from Above, 1928–1941* (New York: Norton, 1990). For a discussion of the concept "revolution from above" in Russian history, see E. H. Carr, *Socialism in One Country*, vol. 1 (New York: Macmillan, 1958), pp. 9–10.

78. A partial list of new Soviet cities built between the wars can be found in "Goroda postroenny pri sovetskoi vlasti," *Bloknot agitatora*, no. 1 (1948): 23–33. In some ways even Moscow had come to resemble Magnitogorsk. B. I. Nikolskii, artistic director of the Magnitogorsk theater, speaking at a party meeting of the city's Kirov *raikom* in 1936, remarked that "I am an old Muscovite. I lived forty years in Moscow. When the Maly theater suggested I go to Magnitogorsk, I must confess, my face did not express joy or great desire." But Nikolskii went on to assert that the difference between Moscow and Magnitogorsk was "not that great." He observed that "living in Magnitogorsk, you don't feel as you do living on Moscow's Kuznetskii Most, but as if you were living a bit farther out, in the outskirts, say, on the Boulevard of Enthusiasts, where gigantic construction is going on." *MR*, 21 December 1936.

79. Data from the suppressed 1937 census have finally become available, confirming the long suspected need to modify downward the total population in 1939. But such a correction would have little effect on the magnitude of the expansion of the urban population. Even considering that some of the urban growth was the result of reclassification, the USSR certainly underwent the largest urban expansion in a single decade that the world had known up to that time. See Chauncy Harris, *Cities of the Soviet Union: Studies in Their Functions, Size, Density, and Growth* (Chicago: Association of American Geographers, 1972), pp. 1, 61, 89–90; Adolf G. Rashin, "Rost gorodskogo naseleniia v SSSR (1926–1959 gg.)," *Istoricheskie zapiski*, no. 66 (1960): 269–77; E. Andreev et al., "Opyt otsenki chislennosti naseleniia SSSR 1926–1941 gg. (kratkie rezultaty issledovaniia)," *Vestnik statistiki*, 1990, no. 7, pp. 34–58; and V. A. Isupov, "Igra bez pravil: Perepisi naseleniia SSSR v 30-e gody," *Sovetskaia istoriia: Problemy i uroki* (Novosibirsk, 1992), pp. 149–67. An often unremarked point is that the population of Gulag sites was apparently classified as urban.

80. For an example and continuation of this tendency, see Jacques le Goff, "The Town as an Agent of Civilization," in Carlo Cipolla, ed., *The Fontana Economic History of Europe and the Middle Ages* (New York, 1972), pp. 77–106. A handy survey of the development of the social scientific study of the city in the United States, beginning with the writings of sociologists at the University of Chicago in

the first decades of the twentieth century, is provided by Ulf Hannerz, *Exploring the City: Inquiries toward an Urban Anthropology* (New York: Columbia University Press, 1980). Hannerz omits any comment on the fact that the analysts of the city live in it, or that his own advocacy of an urban anthropology is an artifact of city life.

81. As the great urbanist Lewis Mumford pointed out, until the late nineteenth century, discussion of the city was largely limited to utopian literature. "City," in *International Encyclopedia of the Social Sciences*, vol. 2 (New York: Macmillan and the Free Press, 1968), p. 448. Echoing Mumford, the literary critic Northrop Frye also pointed out that utopia "is primarily a vision of an orderly city and a city-dominated society." Frye, "Varieties of Literary Utopias," *Daedalus* 94 (1965): 323–47; quote from 328.

82. Lewis Mumford, *The City in History: Its Origins, Its Transformations, and Its Prospects* (New York: Harcourt Brace Jovanovich, 1961). Gwendolyn Wright and Paul Rabinow have asserted that the advent of the writings on cities was connected with the fifteenth- and sixteenth-century rise of administrative states (out of the great postfeudal territorial monarchies), and with the corresponding new problem then posed of administering not just territories but also inhabitants. Wright and Rabinow, "Spatialization of Power," *Skyline*, 1982.

83. To be sure, in recent years a streak of revisionism appeared that has questioned whether feudalization of the bourgeoisie, rather than *embourgeoisement* of the old regimes, should be the basic story line. In this vigorously argued challenge to the standard view, however, the interpretive categories do not change; only the emphasis does. Arno J. Mayer, *The Persistence of the Old Regime* (New York: Pantheon, 1981). Rather than focus on the bourgeoisie as a class, one scholar has advocated concentrating on private property, the market, the public sphere, law, and voluntary associations—in short, on what he calls "the silent bourgeois revolution," which might better be termed the civic revolution. David Blackbourn, "The Discreet Charm of the Bourgeoisie: Reappraising German History in the Nineteenth Century," in David Blackbourn and Geoff Eley, *The Peculiarities of German History: Bourgeois Society and Politics in Nineteenth-Century Germany* (New York: Oxford, 1984), pp. 174–205.

84. Further discussion of this and related issues can be found in the innovative analysis of urban planning and administration in French-controlled Morocco by Paul Rabinow. In contrast to the approach taken in this monograph, Rabinow focuses on the class of administrators (thus offering a kind of intellectual history), rather than on the social relations and contestations that the administrators' actions helped produce in the urban milieus in which they conducted experiments. Rabinow, *French Modern: Norms and Forms of the Social Environment* (Cambridge, Mass.: MIT Press, 1989), pp. 13, 145.

85. For an excellent critical review of the explanations for the rise of the welfare state, see George Steinmetz, *Regulating the Social: The Welfare State and Local Politics in Imperial Germany* (Princeton: Princeton University Press, 1993), pp. 15–40.

86. One study of pensions in Denmark, Sweden, Britain, France, and Germany that sought to demonstrate that welfare state practices normally attributed to labor movements originated in bourgeois politics took as its organizing principle the de-

velopment of what the author called risk communities. In this way, the author demonstrated that the development and functioning of the welfare state were based on a way of looking at the world, or social calculus. Unfortunately, this and virtually all other comparative studies of the development of the welfare state invariably overlook the case of the USSR. Peter Baldwin, *The Politics of Social Solidarity: Class Bases of the European Welfare State, 1875–1975* (New York: Cambridge University Press, 1990). See also Francois Ewald, "Insurance and Risk," in Graham Burchell et al., eds., *The Foucault Effect: Studies in Governmentality* (Chicago: University of Chicago Press, 1991), pp. 197–210.

87. The commitment of the Soviet state to social welfare was particularly dramatic given the prerevolutionary legacy. As one scholar has concluded, "welfare aid in Russia was never more than a palliative, and was rendered even more ineffective by the ravages of World War I." Yet although the USSR had less of a base to work with than other nations, and had to overcome great calamities, it "achieved more comparatively than any other nation." Bernice Madison, *Social Welfare in the Soviet Union* (Stanford: Stanford University Press, 1968), pp. 3–76, 230.

88. Few scholars have taken up, even in general terms, the influence of the USSR on Western Europe and the United States (as opposed to the third world). An important exception, although far too uncritical in its evaluation of Soviet realities, is E. H. Carr, *The Soviet Impact on the Western World* (New York: Macmillan, 1949).

89. Such a line of analysis, and its implications, have been set down in detail by Pierre Bourdieu, *Outline of a Theory of Praxis* (Cambridge, Mass.: Harvard University Press, 1977), esp. pp. 72–87; and ibid., "The Genesis of the Concepts of *Habitus* and *Field*," *Sociocriticism* 2, no. 2 (1985): 11–24. Bourdieu's imaginative approach to social action is ultimately embedded in a view of class domination achieved through successful manipulation of the state apparatus, a view whose adoption is not obligatory for those who seek to draw on his many insights.

90. Among Foucault's many works, the two that were most important for developing the approach adopted in this monograph are the essay "The Subject and Power," afterword to Hubert Dreyfus and Paul Rabinow, *Michel Foucault: Beyond Structuralism and Hermeneutics,* 2d ed. (Chicago: University of Chicago Press, 1982, 1983) and the lectures on Parrhesia (or the problem of truth telling in Ancient Greece), delivered at the University of California, Berkeley, in 1983, during and after which Foucault engaged in discussions of methodology. I also relied on the collections *Power-Knowledge: Selected Interviews and Other Writings, 1972–1977,* ed. Colin Gordon (New York: Pantheon, 1980) and *The Foucault Reader,* ed. Paul Rabinow (New York: Pantheon, 1984), including the valuable introductory essays by the editors.

91. On the problem of daily life, I follow the Foucault-inspired analysis by Michel de Certeau. Whereas studies of culture as a material practice (as opposed to a representation of underlying social forces) have usually been preoccupied with the producer (writer, city planner) and the product (book, city street), de Certeau focused his attention on the consumer (reader, pedestrian). Arguing that nothing exists until it is used, he viewed "consumption" as active, every bit a form of production, and argued that the result—achieved through "the art of doing" or "making do"—should be seen as "the invention of everyday life." Treating urban life as

a kind of strategic engagement in which even the weak have recourse to many effective stratagems, he celebrated the inventiveness of people whose tactics of living are usually ignored. He also suggested that "resistance" in everyday life should be understood less as a bid for power than as calculated circumvention. De Certeau's perspective on "the appropriation of the urban milieu" provided a healthy corrective to analyses of largely immutable "structures" and "institutions," even if one cannot share the full extent of his unapologetic Romanticism. *The Practice of Everyday Life* (Berkeley: University of California Press, 1984; originally published in French, 1980).

92. Foucault, *Power-Knowledge*, pp. 60, 122.

93. In the literature on the rise of social welfare in France, much attention has been devoted to the conceptualization in the early nineteenth century of a realm called the social, which was said to lie between the state and civil society (the economy). This domain became the target of intervention and regulation, and thus the basis for the welfare state, in societies based on private property. In the USSR, however, no such separate domain of the social was postulated, for the obvious reason that there was thought to be no division between the state and society. Jacques Donzelot, *Policing of Families* (New York: Pantheon, 1979), including the foreword by Gilles Deleuze, "The Rise of the Social"); and Donzelot, *L'Invention du Social* (n.p., 1984). A different view of the social that emphasizes not its separateness but its role in enabling the interpenetration of state and society is offered by Jürgen Habermas, *The Structural Transformation of the Public Sphere* (Cambridge, Mass.: MIT Press, 1989), p. 231.

PART I. BUILDING SOCIALISM

1. *Sochineniia*, vol. 7 (Moscow, 1952), p. 355.

2. The frontier has long been an important element in Russian history, both as a means of escape from the authorities and as the target for a state-led internal colonization drive. See Benedict Sumner, *A Short History of Russia* (New York: Reynal and Hitchcock, 1944), ch. 1.

3. "God velikogo pereloma," *Pravda*, 7 November 1929, reprinted in *Sochineniia*, vol. 12 (Moscow, 1949), p. 135. Stalin's speech, particularly the dread of backwardness and the emphasis on speed, carried echoes of the state-led industrial acceleration launched by Sergei Witte in the 1890s. Witte's scheme, of course, did not repudiate "capitalism." See von Laue, *Sergei Witte*. The potential for later developing nations to vault forward through the acquisition of ready-made foreign technology was the subject of a provocative 1952 essay by Alexander Gerschenkron, "Economic Backwardness in Historical Perspective," reprinted in his *Economic Backwardness in Historical Perspective: A Book of Essays* (Cambridge, Mass.: Harvard University Press, 1962), pp. 5–30.

4. Ending Russia's supposedly harmful dependence on "foreign" capital had always been one of the most pronounced elements of the Bolshevik critique of the tsarist regime (and an important strategic concern during the 1920s). Later, the decisive contribution of foreign economic assistance to the Soviet industrialization

drive was largely proscribed from Soviet accounts. See V. I. Kasianenko, *Zavoevanie ekonomicheskoi nezavisimosti SSSR, 1917–1940* (Moscow, 1972).

5. Milovan Djilas has argued that the Bolshevik party's success in 1917, despite the existence of many other parties, consisted in the fact that the Communists were revolutionary in their opposition to the status quo as well as staunch and consistent in their support of the industrial transformation. Djilas, *The New Class: An Analysis of the Communist System* (New York: Praeger, 1957), p. 15.

6. *Piatiletnyi plan razvitiia narodnogo khoziastva*, 3d ed., 3 vols. (Moscow, 1930). The best analysis remains Naum Jasny, *Soviet Industrialization, 1928–1952* (Chicago: University of Chicago Press, 1961), part A.

7. *Sochineniia*, vol. 7, pp. 353–63. Lenin had written that "the war taught us much, not only that people suffered but especially the fact that those who have the best technology, organization, discipline and the best machines emerge on top; it is this the war has taught us. It is essential to learn that without machines, without discipline, it is impossible to live in modern society. It is necessary to master the highest technology or be crushed." *Polnoe sobranie sochinenii*, 5th ed., vol. 26 (Moscow, 1970), p. 116.

8. Alfred Meyer, "The War Scare of 1927," *Soviet Union/Union Sovietique* 5, no. 1 (1978): 1–25; Sheila Fitzpatrick, "The Foreign Threat during the First Five-Year Plan," ibid., pp. 26–35.

9. "O rabotakh aprelskogo ob"edinennogo plenuma TsK i TsKK," *Pravda*, 18 April 1928, reprinted in *Sochineniia*, vol. 11 (Moscow, 1949), p. 54. See also the words Stalin addressed to the delegates of the Sixteenth Party Congress in June 1930, *Sochineniia*, vol. 12, p. 331.

10. The Soviet acquisition in the 1930s of "capitalist" technology, controversial when it occurred, became the source of even greater gnashing of teeth after World War II. One of the most vituperative treatments was by Werner Keller, who boasted that his book was "part of the Cold War." Keller, *East Minus West Equals Zero: Russia's Debt to the Western World 862–1962* (New York: Putnam, 1962; originally published in German, 1960), p. 7. In the sixteenth century, the King of Poland wrote to Queen Elizabeth in protest against English trade and friendship with Ivan IV: "We seemed hitherto to vanquish him only in this, that he was rude of arts and ignorant of policies. . . . We that know best and border upon him, do admonish other Christian princes in time, that they do not betray their dignity, liberty and life of them and their subjects to a most barbarous and cruel enemy. . . . The Muscovite puffed up in pride . . . and made more perfect in warlike affairs with engines and ships will make assault this way on Christendom." As cited in Jesse Clarkson, *A History of Russia* (New York: Random House, 1961), pp. 129–30.

11. See, for example, the primer written for school children by Ilin Marshak, *Rasskaz o velikom plane* (Moscow, 1930); translated as *New Russia's Primer: The Story of the Great Five-Year Plan* (Boston: Houghton Mifflin, 1931), it was a Book of the Month Club selection. The plan's martial vocabulary has been underscored by Moshe Lewin, *Stalinism and the Seeds of Soviet Reform: The Debates of the 1960s* (Armonk, N.Y.: M. E. Sharpe, 1991), p. 112. This is a retitled reprint of his *Political Undercurrents in Soviet Economic Debates: From Bukharin to the Modern Reformers* (London: Pluto Press, 1975).

12. Carr, *The Bolshevik Revolution 1917–1923*, vol. 2, pp. 360–83; see also

Charles Maier, "Between Taylorism and Technocracy: European Ideologies and the Vison of Industrial Productivity in the 1920s," *Journal of Contemporary History* 5, no. 2 (1970): 45–54.

13. A similar characterization of Soviet industrialization, with somewhat less emphasis on the international context, is offered by Hiroaki Kuromiya, who argues that "the class-war ideology of the industrialization drive created a basis for the survival of the regime." Kuromiya ended his study in 1932. *Stalin's Industrial Revolution: Politics and Workers, 1928–1932* (Cambridge: Cambridge University Press, 1988), pp. xiii–xiv. A fuller argument for the regime's "basis of survival," also incorporating class war, will be made in this book, especially in chs. 4–7.

14. Lewin, among others, has argued that there were two possible "models" of Soviet economic development—the accidentally discovered "war communism" and the pragmatically introduced NEP—and that the Soviet leadership mistakenly re-introduced the former model in the late 1920s. What both "models" had in common, however, was the assumption that capitalist development was not the answer to the contry's industrialization needs. The "Soviet industrialization debate" of the 1920s was about the optimal path to socialism, which meant noncapitalism. The disagreement was about the pace of industrialization and what short-term expedients (e.g., "concessions" to the peasantry) resembling capitalism but ultimately somehow leading to socialism should or should not be permitted. Stalin decided, repeating the arguments of the left opposition, that continuing the expedients then in place (the NEP) would inhibit the pace of industrialization and, moreover, would not lead the country to socialism. Such a conclusion was based on the universally shared premise that state-controlled heavy industry was unambiguously socialist (i.e., noncapitalist). Lewin, *Stalinism and the Seeds of Soviet Reform*, esp. chs. 4 and 5.

15. This is a paraphrase of Lewin, *The Gorbachev Phenomenon* (Berkeley: University of California Press, 1987), who refers to Soviet Russia as "a country in a hurry."

16. Gerschenkron made a similar point, writing that "the stress on heavy industry and oversized plant is . . . by no means peculiar to Soviet Russia. But what is true is that in Soviet Russia those common features of industrialization processes have been magnified and distorted out of all proportion." True enough, but Gerschenkron never explained why this was so, except to assert that the Soviet government could be described as a product of the country's economic backwardness, which permitted the seizure of power by a dictatorship; and that because of its supposedly problematic legitimacy, the Soviet government could maintain itself in power only by making the people believe that it performed an important social function. Such an argument is questionable, and in any case completely neglects the importance of Soviet industrialization's expressly socialist nature, which ruled out shopkeeping, private trade, and all other forms of "capitalist" economic activity, thereby imparting a powerful sense of uniqueness to the grand undertaking. Gerschenkron, "Economic Backwardness," pp. 28–29.

17. A list of the sixteen metallurgical factories that were to be built and the twenty that were to be reconstructed can be found in Aleksandr I. Gurevich, *Zadachi chernoi metallurgii v 1932 g.* (Moscow, 1932), pp. 8–9.

18. "The huge Magnitogorsk iron and steel plant . . . is at once the greatest, the

most dramatic, and the most symbolic enterprise carried out under the Five-Year Plan," wrote William Chamberlain, the Moscow correspondent for the *Christian Science Monitor* from 1922 to 1934. "It might well be regarded as the Five-Year Plan incarnate." Chamberlain, *Russia's Iron Age* (Boston: Little, Brown, 1934), pp. 48–49.

19. One Magnitogorsk pamphleteer, paraphrasing Clausewitz, wrote that "construction in our conditions is a continuation of war, only by different means." A. Baranov, *Magnitogorskaia plotina* (Sverdlovsk, 1931), p. 4.

20. E. Korin, "Step otstupaet za gory," *Buksir: Rabochii literaturno-khudo-zhestvennyi zhurnal* [Magnitogorsk], 1931, no. 3, p. 14.

21. An enormous literature on the "urban question" and the problem of the city under socialism poured forth, the bulk of it in periodicals and pamphlets, too numerous to list. This literature has been the focus of a substantial body of scholarship, which has examined the supposed benefits of comprehensive planning, the work of individual architects and architectural institutions, the evolution of various styles, the importation of ideas from the West and in turn the contribution by Soviet architects to the "modernist movement." Paradoxically, the attention bestowed upon prominent individuals and architectural institutions has shed little light on Soviet urban life during a period of profound construction. For an introduction, see S. Frederick Starr, "Visionary Town Planning in the Cultural Revolution," in Sheila Fitzpatrick, ed., *Cultural Revolution in Russia, 1928–1931* (Bloomington: Indiana University Press, 1978), pp. 207–40; Starr, "Writings from the 1960s on the Modern Movement in Russia," *Journal of the Society of Architectural Historians* 30, no. 2 (May 1971): 170–78. A penetrating analysis that calls into question the assumptions and conclusions of the existing literature has been made by Boris Groys, who demonstrates the close relationship of the avant-garde of the 1920s to the purveyors of socialist realism in the 1930s. Groys, *The Total Art of Stalinism: Avant-Garde, Aesthetic Dictatorship, and Beyond* (Princeton: Princeton University Press, 1992; originally published in German in 1988).

22. The Soviet leadership could scarcely ignore the countryside, where the majority of the population lived, but socialism was an urban-based vision. In this book, the Magnitogorsk countryside will be addressed only in passing.

23. There was no shortage of dazzling projects, even if none included any discussion of which building materials would be used and where they would come from (or whence the builders, tools, and machines). Most of these sketches were published, thereby amplifying the architect's international stature and the image of the Soviet Union as a leader of "modern" culture. See, for example, the designs of M. Barshch, V. Vladimirov, M. Okhitovich, and N. Sokolov in *Sovremennaia arkhitektura*, 1930, nos. 1–2, pp. 38–56; of I. Leonidov and the OSA brigade, in ibid., 1930, no. 3, pp. 1–4; and of the architects of LIIKS, in V. I. Kazarinova and V. I. Pavlichenkov, *Magnitogorsk* (Moscow, 1961), p. 17.

24. In 1929, under the initiative of the State Planning Commission (Gosplan), a two-day symposium was held on "the problem of the socialist city." One of the chief purposes of the published volume was to demonstrate that the problem of the city under socialism was not soluble either by architects or engineers, those traditionally involved in town planning and construction, but required the expertise of

the entire range of social and political agents and agencies. *K probleme stroitelstva sotsialisticheskogo goroda* (Moscow, 1930).

25. *Magnitostroi: Biulleten*, 1930, no. 1, p. 4.

26. The previous population census had been taken in 1926, before Magnitogorsk was founded. In 1936 Doctor S. Grossman, the city's medical chief, admitted that "there were no hard data on the total number of inhabitants" of Magnitogorsk. *MR*, 18 May and 1 June 1936.

27. *MR*, 6 January 1937, 22 September 1936. A clear reflection of the state's recognition of the importance of demography occurred even before the census. As part of a campaign begun in 1936 to increase the aggregate population, motherhood was promoted and most abortions were prohibited. In Magnitogorsk, where the formation of a large population in a brief period strongly hindered the establishment of family patterns, the demographic "shortfall" was of particular moment. This issue is treated in chapter 4.

28. The technique of the population census was developed during the Renaissance. As one historian has written of the census back then, "although it was still primarily for tax and military purposes, more and more frequently [man], rather than his land as a tax unit, was the object of counting." Hyman Alterman, *Counting People: The Census in History* (New York: Harcourt, Brace, and World, 1969), p. 37.

29. V. G. Davidovich, *O razvitii* (Moscow, 1959), p. 59.

30. W. H. Parker, *An Historical Geography of Russia* (London: University of London Press, 1968), p. 13.

31. J. M. Hooson, *A New Soviet Heartland?* (Princeton: D. van Nostrand, 1964), pp. 7, 30; idem., *The Soviet Union: A Systematic Regional Geography* (London: University of London Press, 1966). The United States benefitted from waves of immigration, far more hospitable natural conditions, and relative insulation from formidable competing powers. Moreover, the USSR carried out a United States-like boom in territory on the same latitude as Canada, and with borders on Europe, the Middle East, South Asia, China, and Japan. For the comments of one American policy analyst studying the USSR on the similarities and differences in the two countries' parallel frontier settlement experiences, see Jack Underhill, *Soviet New Towns: Housing and National Urban Growth Policy* (Washington, D.C.: U.S. Department of Housing and Urban Development, 1970), pp. 1–2.

32. As Russia's greatest historian wrote, "the history of Russia is the history of a country which is being colonized. Its regions of colonization expanded together with its state territory. Now rising, now falling, this age old movement has continued to our times." V. O. Kliuchevskii, *Kurs russkoi istorii* (Moscow, 1911); reprinted in *Sochineniia v deviati tomakh*, vol. 1 (Moscow, 1987), p. 50. A law of 15 December 1928 established that all land on the territory of the USSR belonged to the Union, not the republics. *Sobranie zakonov i rasporiazhenii*, 1928, no. 69, items 641 and 642. See the commentary by Eugene Kulischer, *Europe on the Move: War and Population Changes, 1917–1947* (New York: Columbia University Press, 1948), p. 87.

33. Nikolai Mikhailov, *Soviet Geography*, 2d ed. (London: Methuen, 1937), p. xiv. The Bolsheviks claimed legitimacy, as Kendall Bailes has written, "not only as

the avant-garde of the industrial proletariat, but on the basis of their ability to transform nature and society." Bailes, *Technology and Society under Lenin and Stalin: Origins of the Soviet Technical Intelligentsia 1912–1945* (Princeton: Princeton University Press, 1978), p. 383. The many-sided conquest of the steppe was an integral part of the formation of a powerful state under Bolshevik rule. In this connection, the Bolshevik rulers' juxtaposition of a present state of "backwardness" with a utopian future to be achieved by means of the proper application of science and technology paralleled the justification offered by European imperial powers, the self-proclaimed bearers of "the most progressive and advanced civilization ever known," for their brutal colonial enterprises. Even though in the Soviet case the "colonization" was entirely internal, the legitimizing credo and, above all, the practices of exploitative rule by a metropole, coincided. Michael Adas, *Machines as the Measure of Men: Science, Technology, and Ideologies of Western Dominance* (Ithaca: Cornell University Press, 1989), p. 203.

CHAPTER 1. ON THE MARCH FOR METAL

1. A. Malenky, *Magnitogorsk: The Metallurgical Combine of the Future* (Moscow, 1932), p. 55.
2. *Tri goda raboty Gipromeza 1926–1929* (Leningrad, 1929), pp. 4, 8.
3. Anthony C. Sutton, *Western Technology and Soviet Economic Development, 1930–1945* (Stanford: Hoover Institution Press, 1971), p. 63. See also the recollections of an on-site Freyn employee, W. S. Orr, contained in the files "American Engineers in Russia," Hoover Institution Archives, Stanford, California.
4. I. P. Bardin, *Rozhdenie zavoda i vospominaniia inzhenera* (Novosibirsk, 1936), pp. 10, 13. Freyn and Co. remained at Gipromez until 1933.
5. Henry Freyn, "Iron and Steel Industry in Russia," *Blast Furnace and Steel Plant* (January 1930): 90–92, 99. See also H. J. Freyn and L. E. Thomas, "Russia Will Expand Its Iron and Steel Industry," *Freyn Design* (October 1927): 6–7; and Gordon Fox, "Diagnosing a Nation's Steel Industry," *Freyn Design* (January 1930): 1–3.
6. Actually, the Urals Design Bureau, which had been opened by Vesenkha in September 1925, simply changed its name to the Urals branch of Gipromez in July 1926. By February 1927, Gipromez employed 600 people, 240 in the central office and the rest in affiliates, including 156 in the Urals branch. By 1929 Gipromez had more than 1,000 employees. *Tri goda raboty Gipromeza 1926–1929*, p. 4.
7. Preliminary observations of the iron-ore deposits at Magnetic Mountain had been undertaken in 1828–29. The first major geological investigation was carried out in 1899 by a government commission. In 1911–12, the Russian geologist Zavaritskii estimated the total ore at 86.8 million tons. Another study done in 1926 raised the estimate to 275.2 million tons. V. Skazinskii, *Magnitogorskii gigant im. tov. Stalina* (Sverdlovsk-Moscow, 1930), pp. 16–18; GARF, f. 7952, op. 5, d. 349, ll. 10–11. The actual total turned out to be around 500 million tons.
8. Gasselblat may have chosen the site as early as 1925. GARF, f. 7952, op. 5, d. 350, l. 37.
9. Ibid., d. 348, l. 27. See also I. S. Koropeckyj, *Location Patterns in Soviet*

Industry Before World War II: The Case of the Ukraine (Chapel Hill: University of North Carolina Press, 1971); and idem., "The Development of Soviet Location Theory before the Second World War," *Soviet Studies* 19, no. 1 (1967): 1–28, and no. 2 (1967): 232–44. For a discussion of the various resources near the site, see *Magnitostroi: Stroitelstvo i ekspluatatsiia Magnitogorskogo metallurgicheskogo kombinata imeni tov. Stalina. 1929–1933 gg.* (Sverdlovsk-Magnitogorsk, 1934), pp. 6–7.

10. GARF, f. 7952, op. 5, d. 147, l. 4. See also Valentin Serzhantov, "Metallurgi Magnitki v borbe za osvoenie novoi tekhniki v gody vtoroi piatiletki," in *Iz istorii revoliutsionnogo dvizheniia i sotsialisticheskogo stroitelstva na iuzhnom Urale. Uchenye zapiski Cheliabinskogo pedagogicheskogo instituta,* tom 1, vyp. 1 (Cheliabinsk, 1959), pp. 90–91. On the extreme concentration of industry in a few areas, see R. W. Davies, *The Soviet Economy in Turmoil, 1929–1930* (New York: Macmillan, 1989), p. 26. Despite Mezhlauk's arguments, a number of pamphlets were published asserting how cheap Magnitogorsk metal would be, even with the long-distance energy supply problem.

11. Before the 1890s, the Urals accounted for more than 50 percent of Russia's pig iron production, but the region's ferrous metallurgy went into steep decline thereafter because of the lack of coking coal (which was required by the new metallurgical processes). By the eve of World War I, the Urals' share of pig iron had dropped to under 20 percent. *Metall,* 1929, nos. 5–6, p. 155. The first detailed plan to solve the Urals' energy problem by uniting West Siberian coal with Urals iron ore appears to have been drawn up in 1915. GASO, f. 339, op. 4, d. 672, l. 44.

12. A sea of pamphlets about the Ural-Kuznetsk Combine written to underscore the strategic benefits of such internal colonization were echoed by analyses from Siberian scientists stressing the expected boon to the country of economic development in comparatively underdeveloped regions. These themes were then taken up and championed in Gosplan and elsewhere. See *Uralo-Kuznetskii kombinat: Sbornik statei* (Moscow, 1931). A cheerful evaluation of the Ural-Kuznetsk Combine's supposed success that nonetheless fails to conceal its abandonment as an operational mechanism can be found in Petr Matushkin, *Uralo-Kuzbass: Borba kommunisticheskoi partii za sozdanie vtoroi ugol no-promyshlennoi bazy SSSR* (Cheliabinsk, 1966). See also Franklyn Holzman, "The Soviet Ural-Kuznetsk Combine: A Study in Investment Criteria and Industrialization Policies," *Quarterly Journal of Economics* 71 (1957): 368–405; and *Pesnia ob Uralo-Kuzbasse (dlia dvukh-golosnogo khora)* (Moscow, 1932). The great "shift" eastward in investment, to the extent that it took place, did so only beginning with the war and the evacuation of industry to the Urals and Siberia. In the 1930s, investment in established industrial regions (Leningrad, Moscow, the Ukraine) remained relatively greater than investment in the East. See M. Gardner Clark, *The Economics of Soviet Steel* (Cambridge: Harvard University Press, 1956), p. 237.

13. GASO, f. 225, op. 1, d. 104, ll. 1–2; *Magnitogorskii metallurgicheskii zavod: Materialy k piatiletnemu planu khoziastva Urala* (Sverdlovsk, 1928).

14. GARF, f. 7952, op. 5, d. 348, l. 50.

15. Ibid., ll. 1–71.

16. GARF, f. 7952, op. 5, d. 348, l. 71; and d. 148, l. 116.

17. *Magnitogorskii metallurgicheskii zavod: Proekt* (Leningrad, 1929).

18. In a sense, the Leningrad project could be read as a belated response to the doubters in the Ukrainian branch of Gosplan. An even more vigorous "response" awaited both the Ukrainian economists and the engineers of the Urals branch of Gipromez, namely the "trial" of the so-called Industrial party in 1930, the culmination of the campaigns against the pre-revolutionary technical intelligentsia. See the account by Bailes, *Technology and Society*, ch. 4.

19. Bardin criticized the Gipromez project for having too small a capacity, compared with the Gary Works. GARF, f. 7952, op. 5, d. 148, l. 39.

20. *Piatiletnyi plan*, vol. 1: 42–44; *Torgovo-promyshlennaia gazeta*, 17 December 1929; *Za industrializatsiiu*, 10 August 1930. For some "planners," the sky was the limit. In May 1931, Valerian Kuibyshev announced that a pig iron output of 60 million tons would be required by 1937, the final year of the second Five-Year Plan. (A year earlier Leonid Sabsovich had suggested 132 million.) Production in 1937 was 14 million; 60 million tons was not reached until 1964. See R. W. Davies, "The Emergence of the Soviet Economic System, 1927–1934," unpublished paper, University of Birmingham, Centre for Russian and East European Studies (1974): 13. Naum Jasny, who coined the term "bacchanalian planning," remarked that "it seems impossible to select the most unrealistic target of the era. . . . Again and again one stumbles on another, even more far-fetched." Jasny, *Soviet Industrialization*, p. 70.

21. *Torgovo-promyshlennaia gazeta*, 28 July 1929; *Pravda*, 1 November 1929; *Za industrializatsiiu*, 1 February 1930. The figure of 2.5 million was confirmed in a subsequent Central Committee decree. *Pravda*, 26 January 1931; see also V. N. Zuikov, *Sozdanie tiazheloi promyshlennosti na Urale* (Moscow, 1971), p. 127.

22. By the spring of 1930 the Five-Year Plan was thoroughly disrupted, but no new Plan was introduced to take its place. Davies, *The Soviet Economy in Turmoil*, p. 194.

23. Alexander Erlich, *The Soviet Industrialization Debate, 1924–1928* (Cambridge, Mass.: Harvard University Press, 1960), pp. 163–87; E. H. Carr and R. W. Davies, *Foundations of a Planned Economy, 1926–1929*, vol. 1, pt. 1 (London: Macmillan, 1969), pp. 312–32; Davies, *The Soviet Economy in Turmoil*, pp. 46–54; and Lewin, *The Making of the Soviet System*, pp. 91–120.

24. The six-year (1924–30) "delay" in the start-up of construction at Stalingrad offers an interesting parallel with Magnitogorsk. Moshe Lewin has argued that the delay, which was followed by highly wasteful crash construction, was linked to the series of ill-founded decisions that culminated in the disaster of collectivization, and to the country's administrative lack of preparedness. Norton Dodge and Dana Dalrymple took issue with Lewin's contention, arguing that there was no actual delay, simply a reasonable lapse of time to be expected with such an undertaking and that considering the end result, the work was completed rather quickly. Moreover, they argued that the experience of planning and designing Stalingrad Tractor helped in the planning of dozens of other industrial enterprises. The information Dodge and Dalrymple presented, however, seems compatible with Lewin's argument. In any case, their argument can be read another way: namely, that the homegrown ability to design a plant was lacking, so that the plant's fortunes (and thus its timing) hinged on securing the assistance of a capitalist firm, a goal that was pursued in earnest only after a dramatic expansion in the conception

of the plant's size and capacity. Lewin, *The Making of the Soviet System,* pp. 94–95, citing *Bolshevik,* 1930, nos. 11–12, p. 61. Dodge and Dalrymple, "The Stalingrad Tractor Plant in Early Soviet Planning," *Soviet Studies* 18, no. 2 (October 1966): 164–68.

25. Lewin, *The Making of the Soviet System,* pp. 3–45, 114–20.

26. Vladimir Andrle, *Workers in Stalin's Russia: Industrialization and Social Change in a Planned Economy* (Armonk, N.Y.: St. Martin's, 1988), ch. 3; and Lewin, *The Making of the Soviet System,* pp. 241–57.

27. Gregory Grossman, "Notes for a Theory of the Command Economy," *Soviet Studies* 15, no. 2 (1963): 101–23, reprinted in Morris Bornstein, ed., *Comparative Economic Systems: Models and Cases* (Homewood: Richard D. Irwin, 1965), pp. 135–56 (but omitted from the second and third editions); Oscar Lange, "The Role of Planning in Socialist Economies," in ibid., p. 200. It was Lange who popularized the notion that the USSR was a "war economy." James Millar has contested this view, arguing that "although it seems to be true that the prewar structure of the Soviet economy lent itself to rapid conversion to war economy status, the changes in priorities, in demand patterns, and in the extent of labor mobilization indicate unambiguously that the prewar economy was *not* a "war economy." Millar, however, appears to confuse an economy whose structure and operation resemble the workings of the military with the process of fighting a war. By his reasoning, the organization of the United States Pentagon does not constitute a "war economy" either, for when the Pentagon goes to war enormous shifts in priorities, as well as dramatically increased mobilization, take place. Millar, "Conclusion: Impact and Aftermath of World War II," in Susan Linz, ed., *The Impact of World War II on the Soviet Union* (Totowa, N.J.: Rowman and Allenheld, 1985), p. 286.

28. R. W. Davies, "Models of the Economic System in Soviet Practice, 1926–1936," in *L'industrialisation de l'URSS dans les années trente* (Paris, 1982), pp. 17–30.

29. One researcher has written an uneven history of the design and construction of Magnitogorsk in the form of an anti-Soviet polemic based on a limited number of sources that nonetheless contains valuable information and insights. Tatjana Kirstein, *Sowjetische Industrialisierung—geplanter oder spontaner Prozess? Eine Strukturanalyse des wirtschaftspolitischen Entscheidungsprozesses beim Aufbau des Ural-Kuzneck-Kombinats 1918–1930* (Baden-Baden, 1979; and idem., *Die Bedeutung von Durchführungsentscheidungen in dem zentralistisch verfassten Entscheidungssystem der Sowjetunion: Eine Analyse des stalinischen Entscheidungssystems am Beispiel des Aufbaus von Magnitogorsk (1928–1932)* (Wiesbaden, 1984); the second volume is largely a reworking of the first. A more satisfactory study that offers a thorough if overly generous review of the significance of the debate on the Ural-Kuznetsk Combine, and one on which Kirstein relied greatly, is Michael Rosenberg, *Die Schwerindustrie in Russisch-Asien: Eine Studie über das Ural-Kusnezker-Kombinat* (Berlin, 1938). Rosenberg was genuinely intrigued by Siberia's enormous *Lebensraum.*

30. "The Greatest Steel Plant in the World," *Iron Age,* 7 January, 4 February, 1 April, and 6 May 1909; "Gary: The Largest and Most Modern Steel Works in Existence," *Scientific American,* 11 December 1909, pp. 441–43, 450–1; "Gary Works—The World's Largest Steel Plant," *Blast Furnace and Steel Plant* (August

1937), special issue. The parallels between the building of Gary and Magnitogorsk are striking, and comparisons to the experience of Gary will be made in the notes whenever appropriate.

31. G. K. Ordzhonikidze, *Stati i rechi*, vol. 2 (Moscow, 1957), p. 481. A party member since 1903 and a member of the politburo since 1930, Ordzhonikidze enjoyed a reputation rare among high-level Bolsheviks for being approachable. According to Sheila Fitzpatrick, "Ordzhonikidze personally signed most of the . . . appointments, and made [the] Cadres Sector answer directly to him." Fitzpatrick, "Ordzhonikidze's Takeover of Vesenkha: A Case Study in Soviet Bureaucratic Politics," *Soviet Studies* 37, no. 2 (1985): 170, n. 83. Magnitogorsk's Avraamii Zaveniagin wrote that "people worked for Sergo not out of fear, but out of conscience." Zaveniagin, "Uchitsia rabotat, kak Sergo," *Za industrializatsiiu*, 28 October 1936.

32. According to an American engineer who was soon to become involved in the Magnitogorsk project, "the plant was indeed to be patterned after the Gary, Indiana plant of the U.S. Steel Corporation." Raymond W. Stuck, "First-Hand Impressions of Soviet Russia," *Case Alumnus* [Cleveland], October-November-December 1932/ February-April 1933, pp. 7–8.

33. Ordzhonikidze, *Stati i rechi*, vol. 2, p. 478.

34. GARF, f. 7952, op. 5, d. 140, ll. 7–8. According to Anthony Sutton, "the only iron and steel plant not covered by the Freyn contract was the Magnitogorsk complex." Sutton, *Western Technology*, p. 78. See also Davies, *The Soviet Economy in Turmoil*, pp. 210 ff.

35. GARF, f. 7952, op. 5, d. 350, l. 141. According to another Soviet source, Siemens-Bauunion asked for 7.2 million rubles, 6.2 million of which were to be in gold. This stipulation, if true, combined with the fact that the firm had never built a steel plant, no doubt convinced the Soviet government to look elsewhere (although it kept up the negotiations with Siemens, apparently aware of the leverage to be gained from competition among capitalist firms). Valentin G. Serzhantov, "KPSS—Vdokhnovitel i organizator stroitelstva i osvoeniia Magnitogorskogo kombinata im. tov. Stalina—Moshchnoi metallurgicheskoi bazy strany, 1929–1937 gg.," candidate's dissertation, Moscow, 1959, pp. 153–4.

36. One Soviet scholar familiar with the archival documents claimed (without citation) that McKee offered its services as early as the first half of 1929. V. N. Eliseeva, "Predislovie," in *Iz istorii MMK i goroda Magnitogorska, 1929–1941 gg.* (Cheliabinsk, 1965), p. 265, n. 2. On the general preference for American over German technology, see Kendall Bailes, "The American Connection: Ideology and the Transfer of American Technology to the Soviet Union, 1917–1941," *Comparative Studies in Society and History* 23, no. 3 (1981): 421–48; and Clark, who points out that "the Russians had shifted their attention from European to American blast furnace technique even before the revolution." Clark, *The Economics of Soviet Steel*, p. 64. Whereas Freyn's standard design for blast furnaces was based on a volume of 920–930 cu. meters, McKee called for 1,200. This may have been the reason Soviet authorities decided to experiment with McKee. Davies, *The Soviet Economy in Turmoil*, p. 203. Another factor in McKee's favor may have been his acquaintance with "Colonel" Hugh Cooper, the American advisor on the Dneprostroi project, whom McKee seems to have visited while he was in the USSR in 1929. GARF, f. 7952, op. 5, d. 337, l. 37.

37. V. N. Eliseeva, "Iz istorii proektirovanii i stroitelstva Magnitogorskogo metallurgicheskogo kombinata," *Iz istorii revoliutsionnogo dvizheniia na Iuzhnom Urale* (Cheliabinsk, 1959), pp. 136–37; see also a letter from Gurevich of the Foreign Department of Vesenkha, dated 10 December 1929, outlining the points of agreement between the American firm and the Soviet government: GARF, f. 7952, op. 5, d. 151, ll. 48–50, reprinted in Eliseeva, *Iz istorii*, pp. 59–61. Because of the high phosphorous content of Magnitogorsk iron ore, it was eventually decided to build open-hearth instead of Bessemer furnaces, despite the lower cost of the latter. K. Neilandt and Nikolai Zaitsev, *Martenovskoe proizvodstvo na Magnitogorskom metallurgicheskom zavode* (Sverdlovsk-Moscow, 1932), pp. 9–11.

38. GARF, f. 7952, op. 5, d. 412, ll. 14–15.

39. *Magnitostroi: Informatsionnyi biulleten*, February 1931, no. 2, pp. 28–29. Despite the Soviet desire to have Soviet firms supply as much of the plant's equipment as possible, most fundamental equipment was ordered abroad. Soviet factories simply could not fulfill the orders. See A. M. Mariasin, *Vtoroi gigant gory Magnitnoi* (Sverdlovsk, 1933), p. 402. A list of equipment suppliers for Magnitogorsk in an official Soviet publication reads like a "who's who" of capitalist engineering firms: Otis Elevator, General Electric, Demag, AEG, Krupp, Siemens, Trailer, and so on. *Stroitelstvo i ekspluatatsiia*, pp. 92–3. For the electrical work on the mine, Magnitostroi initially contracted with General Electric but could not afford their fees. So they turned to an Italian firm said to be "without much experience" but much cheaper. Evidently, an inexperienced Italian electrical firm was viewed as preferable to any Soviet organization. GARF, f. 7952, op. 5, d. 304, l. 102. When, as in the case of the Italian firm, the Soviet government turned to Europe to order equipment, McKee lost valuable commissions. Soviet officials claimed that they preferred to buy in Europe because it was cheaper, but it seems that they had trouble obtaining credit in the U.S., which did not recognize the Soviet government until 1933.

40. Eliseeva, "Iz istorii proektirovanii," pp. 133–36, citing GARF, f. 7952, op. 5, d. 140, l. 7.

41. Serzhantov, "KPSS—Vdokhnovitel," pp. 97–103, citing PASO, f. 4, op. 7, d. 205, l. 5.

42. GARF, f. 7952, op. 5, d. 350, l. 135.

43. Serzhantov, "KPSS—Vdokhnovitel," pp. 97–103.

44. Ildrym, who was said to have known Smolianinov since 1921, also knew both Ordzhonikidze and Sergei Kirov from the revolutionary underground in the Caucasus. Lev Polonskii, *Magnitka zovet: Stranitsy istorii velikoi stroiki i zhizni Chingiza Ildryma* (Baku, 1972), pp. 3, 13–14, 20, 65–68; I. F. Galiguzov and M. E. Churillin, *Flagman otechestvennoi industrii: Istoriia Magnitogorskogo metallurgicheskogo kombinata im. Lenina* (Moscow, 1978), pp. 23–26; *Iunost Magnitki: Dokumentalno-khudozhestvennaia kompozitsiia* (Moscow, 1981), p. 57. During the terror Smolianinov (1909–1962), who was then working in a Moscow metallurgical plant, was expelled from the party, reinstated, and then arrested, according to Victor Kravchenko. *I Chose Freedom: The Personal and Political Life of a Soviet Official* (New York: Scribner, 1946), p. 359. Zelentsov died in 1932. Leonid Akudinov, *Magnitostroi* (Cheliabinsk, 1979), p. 8.

45. *Slovo o Magnitke* (Moscow, 1979), p. 38; GARF, f. 7952, op. 5, d. 317, l. 72.

46. *Stroitelstvo i ekspluatatsiia*, pp. viii, 51–55.

47. Official plan fulfillment figures were as follows: October–December 1929, 51 percent; January–March 1930, 33 percent; April–June 1930, 19 percent. *Za industrializatsiiu*, 4 October 1930.

48. At one point, the train was held up half a day waiting for the clearance of a station master who was off playing the leading role in a local production of Gogol's *Inspector General*—just as the "inspectors" from Moscow pulled into his remote train station. Both Iakov Shmidt, who led the Soviet group heading for Magnitogorsk, and Sergei Frankfurt and his team heading for Kuznetsk, were on board. GARF, f. 7952, op. 5, d. 385, ll. 88–91.

49. Ibid., d. 308, l. 11.

50. Ibid., d. 385, l. 34. A list of some of the McKee personnel as well as that of the Koppers Company who were in Magnitogorsk is provided in ibid., d. 412, ll. 21–22, 200.

51. Ibid., d. 310, ll. 187–88. As per the contract, the Americans did bring several tons of tools, from which Soviet factories were supposed to begin making copies. Ibid., d. 304, l. 13. On the absence of machinery and supplies, see I. V. Antipova and M. I. Shkolnik, "Iz istorii sozdaniia Magnitogorskogo metallurgicheskogo kombinata (1929–1933 gg.)," *Istoriia SSSR*, 1958, no. 5, p. 42, n. 118; and Polonskii, *Magnitka zovet*, p. 51.

52. According to the recollections of G. N. Serebrianyi, a "bourgeois specialist" who arrived at the site in 1929 as deputy director of Tekstilstroi. GARF, f. 7952, op. 5, d. 312, l. 188–92.

53. *Stroitelstvo i ekspluatatsiia*, pp. 89–90; P. Zhigunov, *Udarnyi eshelon—Magnitostroiu* (Leningrad-Moscow, 1932).

54. The depth of scarcity was captured in a story told by a young worker named I. N. Mokhov, who was making his way from Moscow to Magnitogorsk by train in 1931. At a junction in the Urals it was necessary to change trains, which required an overnight stopover. Mokhov, who spent the night in a room rented from a cobbler and his wife, got to talking with his hosts about where he was going, about the gigantic new steel plant that was being built at Magnitogorsk. When the cobbler began to show interest in the fantastic tales of automated technology, it was too much for his wife to bear. She burst out at him: "You lousy old fart. You want to build blast furnaces and a city when you, a shoemaker, can't even buy a packet of nails anywhere!" GARF, f. 7952, op. 5, d. 317, l. 3. Nikolai Bukharin had argued that it would be absurd to undertake a massive construction program knowing in advance that the requisite materials would not be available. But Stalin and the rest of the leadership had decided that rather than wait for these materials to appear, not knowing when that might happen, it was necessary to will them into being. Bukharin, "Zametki ekonomista," *Pravda*, 30 September 1928, as cited in Lewin, *The Making of the Soviet System*, p. 115; and also Davies, *The Soviet Economy in Turmoil*, p. 96.

55. GARF, f. 7952, op. 5, d. 337, l. 18. The rumors regarding the lack of ore reached Stalin. Nikolai Zaitsev, the Magnitogorsk correspondent for *Rabochaia gazeta*, relying on the assertions of a Soviet "engineer" named Trubin who seems

to have been the chief of mine construction, sounded the alarm about the supposed lack of ore and the poor state of the mine to his editor, Filov. Filov then passed the accusations "upstairs" in May 1931, and again in July. Vasilii Goncharenko, secretary of the party cell on the mine, was said in Filov's report to have come to exactly the opposite conclusions as Trubin regarding the amount of ore and to have wanted Trubin removed for wrecking. Trubin evidently responded in kind, "exposing" Goncharenko's alleged wrecking, which meant condemning as many problems with the mine as possible. Zaitsev, who painted a picture of generalized chaos and of a local mine administration overcome with "class alien elements," recommended sending "an authoritative government commission." RTsKhIDNI, f. 558, op. 1, d. 2976, ll. 1–14. In September 1931, Klement Voroshilov paid a surprise visit to the site to check the allegations. Despite finding the ore to be there, Voroshilov supposedly refused to believe that no wrecking had taken place, according to an unpublished manuscript by Vladilen Moshkovtsev, "Magnitka (1743–1941)," (Magnitogorsk, 1988), pp. 99–101. Relying on testimony from Goncharenko, Moshkovtsev suggests that the entire incident over the ore and mine was occasioned solely by intrigue. The author provides little detail of what ensued, except to say that some arrests were made at Voroshilov's insistence. In the end, Trubin was apparently removed, for Goncharenko became chief of the mine.

56. GARF, f. 7952, op. 5, d. 381, l. 48. "At Magnitogorsk," wrote one journalist, "there are so many emergencies that it is simply impossible to imagine counting them." Semen Nariniani, *Na stroike mirovogo giganta: Opyt komsomola Magnitogorska* (Moscow, 1931), p. 28.

57. In 1931, there were already 850 people on the staff of the factory administration, of whom only 212, or 24 percent, were Communist party members, according to an investigation by Rabkrin. GARF, f. 7952, op. 5, d. 223, l. 4.

58. A discussion of the organizational maze can be found in *Stroitelstvo i ekspluatatsiia*, pp. 50–1, 71–2. In recollections recorded in the mid-1930s, Iakov Shmidt complained that "the urgent questions of the construction of the two giants [Magnitogorsk and Kuznetsk] were decided slowly. Interminable bureaucratic wranglings and fights took place. Innumerable commissions held discussions and took part in arguments with commissariats, bureaucracies, and *glavki*." *Slovo o Magnitke*, p. 38. A sense of the heaviness of the bureaucratic machinery, and the frustration felt by all those involved, can be found in the numerous appeals by Chingiz Ildrym to Ordzhonikidze directly, in letters and telegrams sent in 1931, often about trivial matters. RTsKhIDNI, f. 85, op. 28, d. 71, ll. 20–21.

59. GARF, f. 7952, op. 5, d. 149, ll. 5–6. Stalmost, which had specialized in building bridges and had no experience in assembling blast furnaces, was put in charge of blast furnace assembly work by Mezhlauk while he was visiting Magnitogorsk in May 1931. Ibid., d. 307, l. 141. Teplostroi was put in charge of fire-brick installation, of which it had no prior experience; yet it was subsequently elevated by 1936 into the "All-Union Trust for Fire-Brick Installation." Ibid., d. 312, l. 13. Shmidt had himself been a specialist in building textile factories. In November 1930 he wrote a letter to Stalin complaining about the lack of specialists: "I don't know if you are aware but the last five months I have been working without a chief engineer and in general without qualified metallurgists. . . . The biggest metallurgical giant in the world is being built, and at the site, aside from some specialists sen-

tenced to three years' forced labor for wrecking . . . there isn't a single experienced metallurgist." For Magnitogorsk he was given around one hundred specialists, but "none of them had any experience in metallurgy." Ibid., d. 381, ll. 3, 19, 102 (unpublished ms. by Shmidt, "Rozhdenie giganta," 1934). Sergei Frankfurt, appointed to head Kuznetskstroi, had also worked in building textile plants and had no prior experience in metallurgy. S. Frankfurt, *Men and Steel* (Moscow, 1935), p. 23.

60. GARF, f. 7952, op. 5, d. 312, l. 120. One foreman in blast furnace construction admitted that since he had never seen such imported equipment before, it was hard to supervise its assembly. But he desperately wanted to learn and began to try to figure out how to read blueprints. Ibid., d. 318, l. 43.

61. One journalist prefigured the eventual direction taken: "Transstroi, for example, was required by contract to perform earth-moving work and to lay rails only in the event that Magnitostroi provided the subcontractor with excavators, rails, and workers. One must ask, why was Transstroi needed if everything sits on the shoulders of Magnitostroi?" Nariniani, *Na stroike*, p. 19. See also *Stroitelstvo i ekspluatatsiia*, p. 57; and V. K. Korolkov, "Borba KPSS za sozdanie i osvoenie Magnitogorskogo metallurgicheskogo kombinata, 1929–1933 gg.," candidate's dissertation, Leningrad, 1955, p. 59.

62. *Sotsialistichekoe stroitelstvo SSSR: Statisicheskii ezhegodnik* (Moscow, 1936), pp. 52–53. A rough idea of the factory's size can be had from the specifications based on the original and on the final revised capacity:

	Original specifications	Revised capacity
Annual tons of pig iron	656,000	2.5 million
Coke ovens	3 batteries, 63 ovens	8 batteries, 69 ovens
Blast furnaces	4 furnaces (vol. 925 m³)	8 furnaces (vol. 1,210 m³)
Open-hearth ovens	5 ovens (100 tons each)	28 ovens (150 tons each)
Rolling mills	1 blooming, 1 rails, 3 sorting	2 blooming, 1 rails, 3 sorting

From Korolkov, "Borba KPSS," p. 99, citing PAChO, f. 234, op. 4, sv. 3, d. 21, l. 84. By comparison, the Gary Works, with a capacity of 2.4 million tons of pig iron and 3.75 million tons of steel, had 16 blast furnaces and 84 sixty-ton open-hearth ovens.

63. The best description of the metallurgical process at Magnitogorsk is Malenky, *Magnitogorsk*.

64. According to Haven, the auxiliary shops were to include: "a machine shop, iron, steel, and brass foundries, pattern storage, garage and automobile repair shop, locomotive repair shop, car repair shop, and ingot mold foundry." William Haven, "The Magnitogorski Mines and Metallurgical Plant," *Blast Furnace and Steel Plant* (January 1931): 144. Some sense of just how revolutionary the giant Magnitogorsk complex was can be gleaned from the fact that at the beginning of the Five-Year Plan, there were only two cement factories in the entire Urals region. Zuikov, *Sozdanie tiazheloi*, p. 113. Most of the repair shops, however, were not built.

65. *Stroitelstvo i ekspluatatsiia*, p. vii; William A. Haven, *Magnitostroi: Informatsionnyi biulleten*, 1931, no. 2, p. 27.

66. "The Magnitogorsk project," wrote Haven, "represents one of the few opportunities which have been given to American engineers to plan a steel plant of such capacity complete in every respect as a unit of design and construction." Haven, "The Magnitogorski Mines," p. 121. Haven was said to have remarked further that "Magnitogorsk was an opportunity that comes but once in the lifetime of an engineer. The magnificent setting provided by nature of this enterprise made possible a general plan that for completeness, symmetry, utility and even beauty, from an engineering and operating viewpoint, has rarely been equalled." Quoted in Miles Sherover, "Magnitogorsk: Epic of Soviet labor," *Current History* 36 (July 1932): 406. Similar enthusiasm had been expressed by professionals over the Gary Works. *The Iron Age*, 7 January 1909, p. 1. For an account of a commercially daring gamble by an American steel company—the Nucor Corporation in Crawfordsville, Indiana—to build a highly advanced steel plant in a great hurry and against all odds, see Richard Preston, *American Steel: Hot Metal Men and the Resurrection of the Rust Belt* (New York: Prentice Hall, 1991).

67. GARF, f. 7952, op. 5, d. 385, ll. 17–26. According to Haven, "when word was received one day in February 1930 that the Russian engineers would arrive in Cleveland within a few days, the top management was in a dither. This job was many times larger than any McKee had previously handled. There were neither men nor drawing rooms available. Hurriedly, an unused top floor of the building at 2422 Euclid Avenue was cleared out, partitioned into offices and drawing rooms, and dozens of drawing boards and desks were bought and moved in." Haven Papers, 1916–1972, Case Western Reserve Historical Society, Cleveland, Ohio, container 1, folder 2; unpublished autobiography, January 1960, ch. 7.

68. At first McKee refused to allow the Soviets do deal directly with Koppers, but when Koppers refused to subordinate itself to McKee and signed a contract for the coke plant directly with the Soviet government, McKee was forced to relinquish its claim on a $150,000 fee. McKee also lost commissions for equipment purchases, which the Soviet government decided to make primarily in Germany, not the United States. GARF, f. 7952, op. 5, d. 385, ll. 17–26. Koppers' famous coke plant design, which replaced the old beehive ovens and revolutionized the steelmaking process, was first installed in 1908, in Joliet, Illinois. See *By-product Coke and Gas Plants* (Pittsburgh, 1921).

69. Under the new terms, McKee was responsible solely for the blast furnace shop, the ore-enriching plant, and rail lines for the blast furnace shop and the mine. Galiguzov and Churillin, *Flagman*, p. 26.

70. According to an unpublished manuscript by a Soviet historian, the chief Soviet negotiator with the American firm, Stanislav Kosior, was well aware that the deadlines imposed on McKee were absurd. Ford had been allowed more than six months for the design of the Gorky Auto Plant, which was far smaller and considerably less complicated than Magnitogorsk. But if this was in fact Kosior's opinion, he never revealed it to McKee. GARF, f. 7952, op. 5, d. 337, l. 6. Several factors contributed to the "delays" in the reception of drawings at the construction site, including its distance not only from Cleveland but from Moscow. For reasons that remain unclear, McKee adamantly turned down persistent Soviet requests to transfer the design work to the site itself. Ibid., d. 385, l. 92; d. 143, l. 45. Ordzhonikidze was evidently convinced that the firm was not fulfilling its contract. See RGAE, f.

3429, op. 1, d. 5195, ll. 204–5 (Vesenkha order dated 24 December 1930), as cited in Davies, *The Soviet Economy in Turmoil*, pp. 216–17. For its part, McKee, to prepare for possible litigation, began documenting the failure of its Soviet partners to supply promised data and used the lack of data to answer Soviet accusations of delay. GARF, f. 7952, op. 5, d. 385, ll. 19–21. For the extensive correspondence between the firm and the Soviet government, see Ibid., d. 233a.

71. McKee's relations with its Soviet partner may have been contentious, but they were not unique. As one Soviet commentator remarked, "even Freyn, which had worked with Soviet firms, saw in each suggestion of the Soviet negotiating commission a desire to trick the firm." GARF, f. 7952, op. 5, d. 385, l. 12.

72. Ibid., d. 304, ll. 83–84 and d. 309, l. 215. Magnitogorsk management complained often to GUMP that Soviet factories supplied Magnitogorsk with defective parts. See, for example, an early report in RGAE, f. 4086, op. 2, d. 42, ll. 6–25. In this report GUMP was urged to send, among other items, a 100-ton crane, apparently to hoist an overturned locomotive.

73. Raymond Stuck, a McKee employee, relates the story of a Russian engineer in Germany who arbitrarily decided to purchase gas-cleaning equipment for Magnitogorsk larger than that specified in the designs, but did not inform anyone. When the equipment arrived, it was discovered that the designs prepared for the structure that was to house the equipment had been rendered obsolete even before they were begun. With a useless structure partially completed and the expensive equipment without shelter, it was necessary to produce a new design "on the fly." Raymond Stuck, "Russia As I Saw It," ms., Hoover Institution Archives, American Engineers in Russia, pp. 45–47. See also the detailed letters by Arthur McKee, dated 29 May 1931, and William Haven, dated 15 June 1931, in GARF, f. 7952, op. 5, d. 233a, ll. 28–33, 55–57.

74. The 1 October 1931 date had been laid down by Kuibyshev in 1928 as the deadline for completion of the entire factory. See *Torgovo-promyshlennaia gazeta*, 11 December 1928.

75. Iakov Gugel later wrote that the first McKee chief at the site was always drunk. His replacement, Raymond Stuck, was judged more solid but inexperienced in metallurgy (he had primarily supervised bridge and airplane hanger construction). Not until William Haven arrived did McKee have in place someone experienced in building a steel plant who commanded the respect of the Soviets. GARF, f. 7952, op. 5, d. 351, ll. 32–33, 34a. According to Iakov Shmidt, Vitalii Gasselblat felt that overall the Americans had provided little for the money. Ibid., d. 381, l. 63. The author of several unpublished chapters on the history of Magnitogorsk offered the following characterization: "Among the Americans who came there were some decent (*neplokhie*) engineers. But with very few exceptions, these were people of a not very high cultural level, with limited horizons, who to a great extent were not curious and not especially interested in their work. They were not fired by the enthusiasm of the builders, they did not enter into the heated technical debates, and the attempts to draw them into socialist competition were greeted with condescending smiles. . . . With the [Americans'] arrival and departure from work people checked the accuracy of their watches." Ibid., d. 366, ll. 20–21.

76. GARF, f. 7952, op. 5, d. 310, l. 187; and d. 381, l. 70. Most of McKee's

warnings were borne out in subsequent investigations by Rabkrin. See, for example, ibid., d. 241, ll. 3–13.

77. Shmidt was said to have laid the first brick, his deputy Chingiz Ildrym the second, Konstantin Valerius the third, and an American the fourth. GARF, f. 7952, op. 5, d. 200, l. 71; and d. 316, l. 50. Work at Kuznetsk also began without a completed project. "In America they were still discussing details [of the project]," wrote Frankfurt, "but we, convinced that there was no other way, were already building the plant." He explained that "we had strict instructions that the principal departments of the plant were to be put into operation by the end of 1931. For this it was necessary to utilize fully the building season of 1930. What were we to do?" Frankfurt, *Men and Steel*, p. 30.

78. Valerius, whose recollections were recorded by the journalist Z. Ostrovskii, called this example "very characteristic." GARF, f. 7952, op. 5, d. 305, l. 202.

79. Ibid., d. 412, ll. 14–5.

80. In January 1931, Shmidt (1897–1937) gave a report about Magnitostroi to the politburo, after which he was replaced by Iakov Gugel (1905–1937), who was mobilized to Magnitostroi from Mariupol. Ibid., d. 381, ll. 102, 115. Shmidt's deputy, Chingiz Ildrym, remained as Gugel's deputy, but the two did not enjoy good relations. Ildrym was frequently sent to the USA by NKTP to purchase industrial equipment. After one such trip in 1933, he returned to discover that Avraamii Zaveniagin had been named Magnitogorsk director. The two did not hit it off, and Ildrym was reassigned to Krivoi Rog. Polonskii, *Magnitka zovet*, pp. 76–77, 83–86, 136, 140; Iurii Elfimov, *Marshal industrii: Biograficheskii ocherk o A. P. Zaveniagine* (Cheliabinsk, 1982), pp. 5–6.

81. GARF, f. 7952, op. 5, d. 347, ll. 15 ff. The ore-crushing equipment, from the American firm Trailer was installed without a crane. Robbins, the on-site Trailer representative, was said by Iakov Gugel to have considered this situation lunacy, a position Robbins held even after the work was done. Ibid., d. 351, l. 36. For the Central Committee decree, "O stroitelstve Magnitogorskogo metallurgicheskogo zavoda," see *Pravda*, 26 January 1931; excerpted in Eliseeva, *Iz istorii*, pp. 76–81.

82. "Although it was written everywhere," our eyewitness continued, "it was completely obvious that we were not going to finish the blast furnace by 1 October." GARF, f. 7952, op. 5, d. 309, l. 32.

83. G. Printsmutil, *Magnitogorskie bolsheviki v boiakh za tekhniku* (Moscow, 1932), p. 25; A. I. Seredkina, "Rozhdenie Magnitki," *Magnitka: Kratkii istoricheskii ocherk* (Cheliabinsk, 1971), p. 60; *Za industrializatsiiu*, 29 September 1931. The transfer of some eight hundred workers from the open-hearth construction to the blast furnace appears to have been resented. GARF, f. 7952, op. 5, d. 339, l. 31. With the near total statization of employment, a series of regulations was introduced governing the transfer of employees by their principal employer to other work. These rules were designed to protect the rights of the employee, as well as to give management flexibility in the "deployment" of labor power. *Izvestiia NKT SSSR*, 1930, no. 13 and 1932, nos. 22–23, reprinted in *Sbornik zakonodatelnykh aktov o trude* (Moscow, 1956), pp. 64–65.

84. According to one candid official assessment, "If the lack of necessary design, serious insufficiency of workers, interruptions in the supply of construction ma-

terials and general inadequate supply of equipment and metal constructions had an influence on the failure to fulfill the plans for 1929 and 1930, then for the failure to fulfill the 1931 construction plan we must add to this list the woeful inadequacy and ill-preparedness of subsidiary shops and organizations for mastering such a huge volume of work, which 1931 presented." *Stroitelstvo i ekspluatatsiia*, p. 56. The construction of the Gary Works, which began in March 1906 after more than one year of intensive design work, was said to have been half completed by December 1909. *Scientific American*, 11 December 1909, p. 44. In 1911, a sheet and tin plate mill was added to the Gary complex, and in 1913, just seven years after construction began, the steel plant was considerably expanded. "By 1913," one historian has written, "Gary was truly a world steel center." Isaac James Quillen, "Industrial City: A History of Gary, Indiana to 1929," Ph.D. dissertation, Yale University, 1942, pp. 248–49.

85. A sensational article in the *Chicago Tribune* in 1931 about how the whole project was going under was quickly translated into Russian and circulated. A clipping can be found in GARF, f. 7952, op. 5, d. 337, ll. 65–71. Around this time, John Calder, an American specialist who worked as a "troubleshooter" in the Soviet steel industry, was asked to travel to Magnitogorsk to work his magic. The results of his trip, if any, could not be ascertained. See Walter Duranty in the *New York Times*, 2 June and 26 August 1931; and Maurice Hindus, "Pinch-Hitter for the Soviets," *The American Magazine*, April 1932, pp. 31–33, 135–37.

86. His telegram read: "We hereby grant permission to blow in the blast furnace. We wish you success and victory. We await the first pig iron for the opening of the Seventeenth Party Conference." As quoted in Iurii Petrov, *Magnitka* (Moscow, 1971), p. 58.

87. Haven Papers, container 1, ms. of autobiography, ch. 8. The precise timing of the cable is unclear. According to one Soviet source, "*after* blast furnace no. 1 was put into operation, the McKee firm forbade its engineers to give any instructions or advice. . . . The Americans officially refused to give instruction, but they gave them secretly, coming to the blast furnace at night" (my italics). GARF, f. 7952, op. 5, d. 310, l. 254. While he represented McKee, Haven cost the Soviet government 25,000 dollars a year, according to Chingiz Ildrym, Iakov Shmidt's deputy who served as acting on-site chief while Shmidt was in Cleveland. RTsKhIDNI, f. 85, op. 28, d. 71, l. 15. Stuck appears to have been paid 800 dollars per month, plus 1,000 rubles. GARF, f. 7952, op. 5, d. 310, l. 196.

88. Iakov Gugel, "Vospominaniia o Magnitke," in *God vosemnadtsatyi: Almanakh shestoi* (Moscow, 1935), pp. 326–27.

89. Ibid. According to N. Savichev, an eyewitness asked about the first pig iron decades later, "everyone shouted 'hurrah'; people were hugging and kissing each other; women cried with joy." As quoted in Moshkovtsev, "Magnitka (1743–1941)," pp. 104–5.

90. Galiguzov and Churillin, *Flagman*, p. 39. The first pig iron at the Gary Works was produced on 21 December 1908, some 22 months after construction began. The first Gary steel followed almost immediately, in February 1909. Quillen, "Industrial City," p. 196.

91. The termination of *valiuta* specialists came amid a severe crisis in foreign trade. Soviet historians claim that their government took the initiative. According

to Haven, interviewed in Harbin after he had left by the anti-Soviet émigré publication *Zaria* (19 March 1932), the contract was annulled "because the Soviet government was too inaccurate in its payment provided for by the contract." U.S. National Archives, decimal file 861.5017/452. Whoever took the initiative to discontinue commercial relations in 1932, this was not the end of the relationship between the USSR and the American firm. One Soviet historian has written that "in spite of the lack of conscientiousness of the McKee Co. in producing drawings, business relations with the firm were not broken off." Eliseeva, "Iz istorii proektirovanii," p. 130. McKee himself wrote in 1933 that "I should not hesitate to return to Russia again if the Russian government should offer to our company another contract comparable to the one which we have already concluded." In fact, on 10 July 1936 McKee signed a new contract to expand the Baku petroleum refinery. "American Engineers in Russia," box 3; Sutton, *Western Technology*, p. 82.

92. Duranty, *New York Times*, 17 March 1932. Haven was no doubt sincere. After his forced return to the U.S., he sent letters and telegrams to various Soviet officials whom he knew offering his services but apparently never received a reply. He went on to supervise important work for McKee in more than a dozen countries. Haven Papers, passim.

93. *MR*, 20 May 1931.

94. *Stroitelstvo i ekspluatatsiia*, pp. 119–22. The breakdown is well described in the unpublished memoirs of Kolbin, who was party secretary of blast furnace construction. GARF, f. 7952, op. 5, d. 309, ll. 26–27. The first blast furnace at Kuznetsk was blown in at the beginning of April 1932. During the triumphal celebrations, the temporary water main burst, necessitating a shutdown. Frankfurt, *Men and Steel*, p. 87.

95. Raymond Stuck estimated that blast furnace no. 1 was only three-quarters complete when it was put into operation. Stuck, "Russia As I Saw It," p. 41; see also Fred Hays, "Five Great Power Plants Rise at Magnitogorsk," *Power* 76, no. 2 (August 1932): 83; and GARF, f. 7952, op. 5, d. 199, ll. 27–29 (an investigation by the Control Commission-Workers' and Peasants' Inspectorate, TsKK-RKI, dated 5 May 1932). Already back on 29 May 1931, Arthur McKee had written to Bogdanov, the head of Amtorg offices in New York, that "the blast furnace foundations for numbers 1 and 2 furnaces were ready for steel work over four months before furnace columns arrived and when they came [they were] merely a lot of I-beams, angles, and plates carelessly punched and not assembled. This made it necessary to assemble the columns in the field where it was simply impossible to properly rivet them and as no milling machine was available it was impossible to machine the top and bottom surfaces of the columns. For these reasons the load carrying capacity of these columns is much less than was estimated for them." Ibid., d. 233a, l. 30.

96. These lines were written *after* the very disaster that Haven and others had predicted and struggled so hard to prevent. GARF, f. 7952, op. 5, d. 351, ll. 34–35. See also Gugel, "Vospominaniia," p. 336. This sad episode was described for a Soviet audience in the historical novel by Anatolii Rybakov, *Deti arbata* (Moscow, 1988), which is based in part on Magnitogorsk. It was also briefly mentioned by Lev Polonskii, who recreated the following conversation, apparently on the basis of correspondence, between Haven and Ildrym: "'Two workers, I heard, are in the hospital. Burned, fractured . . . and you are in pain.' Haven shook his head, 'Tell me,

Mr. Ildrym, was it worth it to make such sacrifices. Couldn't you have allowed for three months more. . . . '" *Magnitka zovet*, pp. 104–5. See also Printsmutil, *Magnitogorskie bolsheviki*, pp. 25–26.

97. *Historical Statistics of the United States, Colonial Times to 1970* (Washington, D.C.: Bureau of the Census, 1975), p. 693; Douglas Fisher, *Steel Serves the Nation, 1901–1951: The Fifty-Year History of United States Steel* (New York: U.S. Steel, 1951), p. 224.

98. See Richard Julius Meister, "A History of Gary Indiana: 1930–1940," Ph.D. dissertation, University of Notre Dame, 1967. Soviet newspapers gave wide coverage to the problems of unemployment, social unrest, and the difficulties of the New Deal. See, for example, *Pravda*, 15 September 1933.

99. Discussions over announcing the early fulfillment of the Five-Year Plan took place back in 1930, when the economy was in deep crisis. Davies, *The Soviet Economy in Turmoil*, p. 96.

100. *Summary of the Fulfillment of the First Five-Year Plan for the Development of the National Economy of the USSR*, 2d ed. (Moscow, 1935), pp. ix, 8–9. As should be evident, the chronology of the first Five-Year Plan had little to do with the timing of the planning and construction of the Magnitogorsk factory. What was written about Magnitogorsk in the published text of the Five-Year Plan, moreover, bore little resemblance to the plant that was eventually built. In addition, when the Plan was published, there was as yet no operative plan for the Urals. One Soviet historian revealed that the Central Committee requested Vesenkha to submit a Five-Year Plan for the Urals no later than 1 August 1930, although he failed to say when it complied with the request. Zuikov, *Sozdanie tiazheloi*, p. 43. When the fulfillment of the Plan was announced at the end of 1932, the Magnitogorsk plant was not only far behind schedule, but the one shop that had been put into operation—the blast furnaces—had already suffered one major disaster and would just then undergo a second. This same basic picture has been drawn for the whole country by Jasny, *Soviet Industrialization*; see also Davies, *The Soviet Economy in Turmoil*.

101. GARF, f. 7952, op. 5, d. 200, ll. 87–93. *MR* reported on the disaster all through January and February 1933. During the same winter of 1932–33 there was an explosion in the blast furnaces of Kuznetsk. Frankfurt, *Men and Steel*, p. 189. In Magnitogorsk the problems stemming from the weather continued. Scott, "Heavy Industry in the Soviet Union East of the Volga; A Report Prepared for the Board of Economic Warfare," Washington, D.C., 1943, declassified, Library of Congress, pp. 364–65.

102. Gugel was reassigned to the Ilich plant in Mariupol, then served as chief of Azovstal before being promoted to deputy chief of GUMP. In 1937, after more than a decade of managing metallurgical enterprises, Gugel began studying for an engineering degree. He was arrested and executed that same year. *Slovo o Magnitke: Otvet metallurgov tovarishchu Stalinu* (Moscow, 1936): *Za industrializatsiiu*, 5 July 1937. The year before he was executed, Gugel was remembered as "a sort of dictator at Magnitka," who overruled others' decisions at will. GARF, f. 7952, op. 5, d. 304, l. 5.

103. GARF, f. 7952, op. 5, d. 200, ll. 87–93.

104. Plagued by shortages of locomotives, many of which were in disrepair and

out of commission, the mine was not fulfilling its plan. (This was what had led to the rumors that there was no more ore in the mountain.) Also, a several-year delay in the construction of the agglomeration factory had an adverse effect on the quality of the iron ore. GARF, f. 7952, op. 5, d. 409, l. 3; MFGAChO, f. 10, op. 1, d. 243, passim.

105. In a report for a special Gosplan commission prepared back on 18 January 1931, one inspector had issued a stern warning: "At the present moment we are facing a major catastrophe. Today at Magnitostroi in place of the construction of rolling mills and open-hearth shops we have empty sectors on which no work is being conducted. . . . For all the millions of rubles invested all we will get is pig iron. . . . Let's put an end to this parading [*paradnost*]. One must approach the construction of such a factory seriously." Notwithstanding the report, all energies were still concentrated on the blast furnace. GARF, f. 7952, op. 5, d. 137, ll. 74–76.

106. Eliseeva, "Iz istorii proektirovanii," p. 138; *Za industrializatsiiu*, 15 May 1931. The design of the mine and the supervision of its construction and operation had been thrown into disarray already in February 1931, when the clause in the McKee contract for the mine was canceled. In April the design bureau on the site that had been opened in December 1930 by the McKee engineer McKechney was closed. One eyewitness recalled that "after the office was liquidated the huge mass of design materials, including those received from McKee, were and still are in horrendous condition. There is no account of them and they are not used in the construction work. . . . At the present moment [July 1931] we have not received a single mining specialist and so cannot open a new design office." GARF, f. 7952, op. 5, d. 409, l. 77.

107. In published Soviet accounts, the Americans' contribution was downplayed to the point that they were later accused of having been wreckers. Valentin Serzhantov, "Stolitsa chernoi metallurgii," in *Liudi Stalinskoi Magnitki* (Cheliabinsk, 1952), p. 264. Vladimir Kizenko, then chief of blast furnace construction, offered the following unpublished remarks concerning the Americans in interviews conducted in the mid-1930s: "It must be said . . . that they knew an awful lot. I picked up a great deal from them from a technical point of view. It must be said that there was a great deal positive from their work. . . . They supplied us with superb blueprints. These drawings were so finely executed that, despite the fact that they were in English, . . . we preferred the American drawings to our Russian ones. Their drawings were so well worked out that an ordinary assembly worker could comprehend them without any written explanations. . . . Moreover, they did more than 3,000 drawings for the blast furnace, and not a single one was based on a new or different standard: all 3,000 had the exact same scale. Meanwhile, our Russian drawings for the blowing station had a different scale on each separate blueprint." GARF, f. 7952, op. 5, d. 310, ll. 187–93.

108. In an unpublished manuscript, one Soviet historian admitted that the Soviet design staff was having trouble copying Donbas factory designs for mill 500 in Magnitogorsk. M. E. Churillin, "Zaveniagin na Magnitke," in the Magnitogorskii kraevedcheskii muzei, inv. no. 105. When Vesenkha "turned over" the design work from McKee to the "Soviet" agency Stalproekt, Vesenkha allowed Stal proekt to hire one hundred German engineers and instructors. GASO, f. 1150, op. 1, d. 28, l. 1. Also, since Freyn was charged with both the development of standardized de-

signs and the project for the Kuznetsk plant, it seems likely that many of Freyn's drawings were available as substitutes when contracts with foreign firms were discontinued.

109. "In fact," one Soviet historian has written, "while concentrating on having the design work done in the USSR, the Soviet government did not reject the use of foreign experience." This statement, unusual for its candor, appears in a Khrushchev-era volume. All the same, the author claims that the foreigners did no more than a fifth of the design work, but she offers no indication of how she arrived at such an estimate. Eliseeva, "Iz istorii proektirovanii," p. 139. According to the entry for Arthur Glenn McKee in the *National Cyclopedia of American Biography*, vol. 45 (New York: J. T. White, 1962), p. 378, "about half" of the project for the Magnitogorsk Works was built by the McKee firm. This can be considered the firm's view. Whatever the precise quantitative assessment of the number of drawings executed by foreigners, the key question was the advanced technology, all of which came from foreign concerns, whether supplied directly or somehow copied by the Soviet side. As Anthony Sutton has argued, "no amount of Soviet investment, within a politically acceptable time period, could have replaced importation of the latest Western smelting and rolling mill technologies." Sutton, *Western Technology*, p. 61.

110. "The peculiarity of the design of the Magnitogorsk factory," the leading Soviet historian of its design has written, "consisted in the fact that it was conducted parallel with construction." Eliseeva, "Iz istorii proektirovanii," p. 139.

111. "In normal conditions," Iakov Shmidt later wrote, without taking the time to explain why normal conditions did not obtain, "it would have made sense to interrupt all construction work on the factory and begin from the beginning with the preparation of the site, the construction of housing, services, roads, and infrastructure, auxiliary shops, and so on. Only then should we have proceeded with the construction of the actual factory. But the ruthless deadlines for putting the factory into operation did not permit such an approach." GARF, f. 7952, op. 5, d. 381, l. 32.

112. Ordzhonikidze, "Completion of the Technical Reconstruction of the Entire National Economy," in *Socialism Victorious* (New York, 1934), p. 599. At the Central Committee and Central Control Commission Joint Plenum in April 1933, Stalin, explaining the results of the Five-Year Plan, boasted that "the party whipped the country onwards, accelerating its race forward." That it did. I. V. Stalin, *Sochineniia*, vol. 13 (Moscow, 1952), p. 183.

113. "We thought we could erect Magnitka in two or three years," Ordzhonikidze confessed at the Central Committee Plenum in October 1932. "It didn't come off. We strained every nerve, but it didn't come off. . . . What an undertaking [the construction of an iron and steel industry], what a terribly serious undertaking; we are in torment, we bang our heads, and we learn." Ordzhonikidze, *Stati i rechi*, vol. 2, pp. 417–19.

114. Kendall Bailes expertly reconstructs the complicated debates over the plan targets and the process of planning within the highest levels of the political and economic bureaucracies, revealing how conflicts and alliances formed within the expanding management apparatus. Bailes, *Technology and Society*, ch. 11, esp. pp. 272 ff. See also the historical novel by Aleksandr Bek, *Novoe naznachenie* (Mos-

cow, 1989), and the introduction by Gavriil Popov, "S tochki zreniia ekonomista." Popov popularized the euphemism "administrative-command system."

115. In the 1930s the USSR fell into a state of economic insulation that was unparalleled by any industrial economy at peace, as Michael Dohan has observed. (Socialism, to put it another way, was built in one country.) But more questionable is Dohan's contention that the 1930s collapse of Soviet foreign trade was rooted solely in the pre–World War I structure of the Russian economy and its foreign trade sector (keyed to agricultural exports), which absorbed an unanticipated body blow from collectivization (in other words, autarky came about—at least initially— largely unintentionally). As Dohan himself conceded, after 1934 many factors "worked against" a revival of foreign trade. Although he did not make the point directly, prominent among such causes was surely the recognition by the country's leadership that the goal of economic "self-reliance" was a "good in itself," a goal that resonated strongly with the Soviet public. At bottom, the impulse toward autarky within the planned economy—which was not geared to responding to constantly shifting demand, supply, and prices—was very strong. Indeed, however important a role the collapse of Soviet agriculture played in the precipitate plunge of foreign trade, in a different kind of economy a variety of responses would have been possible, including finding other avenues for trade. Dohan, "The Economic Origins of Soviet Autarky, 1927/28–1934," *Slavic Review* 35, no. 4 (December 1976): 604– 35.

116. *Pravda*, 6 September 1933. Whereas the assembly of blast furnace no. 1 required almost 7,000 workers, on no. 3 there were fewer than 3,000. GARF, f. 7952, op. 5, d. 200, l. 97.

117. GARF, f. 7952, op. 5, d. 312, ll. 128–29. Work on the open-hearth shop was conducted with the consultation of two American advisors from the Morgan Company.

118. GARF, f. 7952, op. 5, d. 306, l. 176.

119. This is the prelude to the interval (1934–36) that Jasny, in his bid to substitute an alternate periodization for that of the Five-Year Plans, christened "three 'good' years." *Soviet Industrialization*, pp. 13–15. In Soviet parlance, this period marks the time when the economy was "normalized." See V. I. Kuzmin, *V borbe za sotsialisticheskuiu rekonstruktsiiu, 1926–1937 gg.* (Moscow, 1976), pp. 201 ff.

120. Molotov was in Magnitogorsk on 13 May 1932. He was accompanied by Andrei Andreev, then people's commissar for railroads. *Stalinskaia stroika* (Magnitogorsk, 1939), p. 25; *Piat let Magnitogorskogo*, p. 35. Stalin, who traveled seldom, appears never to have visited.

121. Lewin, *The Making of the Soviet System*, p. 27. The second Five-Year Plan, although it began in January 1933, was not officially ratified until the end of 1934. Jasny, *Soviet Industrialization*, p. 7.

122. E. H. Carr and R. W. Davies scrupulously detail the step-by-step replacement of the market by planning up to 1929. *Foundations*, vol. 1, pt. 1, ch. 16. See also Davies, *The Soviet Economy in Turmoil*, pp. 46–54, 96; and Nove, *An Economic History of the USSR* (New York: Penguin, 1982), pp. 188–96.

123. Grigorii Vylomov later recalled that "Sergo Ordzhonikidze came with Ivan Kabakov [Urals oblast party secretary]. At that time our party secretary was Spirov. He opened the meeting and began his speech. . . . but he said nothing of

substance. Sergo rose and said, 'Let's talk heart to heart. Have your secretary get up and say what is going on here, and we'll listen and then discuss it.' Spirov did not anticipate this. He claimed he forgot the text of his report. Basically, he got all mixed up. Nevertheless, he was forced to make a speech extemporaneously. Some other fellow from the party organization spoke after him and also said nothing of substance. After this comrade Sergo delivered sharp criticism." GARF, f. 7952, op. 5, d. 305, l. 215.

124. *MR*, 4 August 1933; excerpted in Eliseeva, *Iz istorii*, pp. 160–62. Several officials emphasized the inspirational quality of Sergo's presence and his apparently sincere desire to hear his subordinates' true feelings. GARF, f. 7952, op. 5, d. 309, l. 93; Churillin, "Zaveniagin na Magnitke," pp. 23–24.

125. GARF, f. 7952, op. 5, d. 289, l. 34. Although it is not clear how Myshkin's alleged deception was uncovered, it is possible that if someone within the factory administration did not report the "irregularities" to higher authorities, then perhaps the independent industrial inspection carried out by the security police (GPU) did. The extensive role in economic management that the security police came to play is treated by Kuromiya, *Stalin's Industrial Revolution*, pp. 171, 295.

126. According to one Soviet historian, Ordzhonikidze brought with him a sizable group of specialists, and dozens more arrived soon thereafter. Petrov, *Magnitka*, pp. 70–71. Myshkin was evidently transferred to the Commissariat of Light Industry (NKLP). His subsequent fate could not be ascertained. GARF, f. 7952, op. 5, d. 309, l. 86.

127. At the Moscow Mining Academy, which had been opened in 1919, Zaveniagin (1901–1956) was named assistant rector for academic affairs under rector Ivan Gubkin and bore a heavy burden of administrative work while only a first-year student in the metallurgy department. Through Gubkin's connections in Vesenkha, Zaveniagin began to develop contacts in that important industrial bureaucracy. In 1929 Zaveniagin became party secretary of the Mining Academy. He met Ordzhonikidze for the first time in February 1931, while visiting Moscow. In January 1933 Ordzhonikidze appointed his new protégé director of the Dzierżyński steel plant, located in the Ukrainian city of Dnepropetrovsk. At that time "Dzerzhinka" was undergoing a total overhaul. Not long after posting Zaveniagin to Dzerzhinka, Ordzhonikidze awarded him a Packard motorcar. *MR*, 20 February 1937 and *CR*, 20 November 1937.

128. At first Zaveniagin was apparently resented by Magnitogorsk officials already on the site. He was considered too young, and was also not from the Urals. But he evidently soon came to impress people with his managerial style and effectiveness. Churillin, "Zaveniagin na Magnitke," p. 6; Debola Alkatsev and Zhores Troshev, *Avraamii Pavlovich Zaveniagin: Ocherki zhizni i deiatelnosti* (Krasnoiarsk, 1975), pp. 36–37.

129. I. S. Peshkin, "Stanovlenie sovetskoi metallurgii," in *Byli industrialnye*, 2d ed. (Moscow, 1973), p. 202. In a January 1934 speech at the Seventeenth Party Congress, Ordzhonikidze singled Zaveniagin out as the prime example of an up-and-coming specialist in the ferrous metallurgy industry. Ordzhonikidze, *Stati i rechi*, vol. 2, p. 547.

130. GARF, f. 7952, op. 5, d. 364, l. 2 (essay by I. I. Ivich, "The Stakhanovite Year"); and d. 306, l. 45. In November 1936 Golubitskii claimed that he became

chief of the blooming mill after "a very large wrecking group" there had been exposed and sentenced in 1935. He mentioned several names. In fact, when he arrived he was named chief of mill 300 no. 1, taking over the blooming later, after the arrest in August 1936 of Vasilev (see ch. 5). Golubitskii, born in 1904 in the Northern Caucasus, joined the party in 1927 and was a student at the Moscow Mining Academy from 1925 to 1930 (along with Zaveniagin). Upon graduation, Golubitskii worked in Mariupol (where Gugel also worked). He claimed that he was summoned to Magnitogorsk by Zaveniagin, through Ordzhonikidze, and that he set off for the new factory "without much enthusiasm." But he supposedly managed to drag fifty people with him. Golubitskii said he dreamed about leaving his job as head of the mill and studying to become a professor. Ibid., ll. 84–87, 90, 99, 105–07. His subsequent arrest is discussed in ch. 7. Bekker, who also came from the Ukraine, was promoted to a position in NKTP in June 1936. *MR*, 12 June 1936.

131. Vaisberg, who was born in 1907, joined the party in 1924, and went on to study in the Dnepropetrovsk Mining Institute. He claimed to have passed all his exams, except the one for Ukrainian language (his native language was apparently Yiddish), and to have been graduated in January 1930. He quickly became a shop chief, learning on the job. He was briefly sent to Germany in 1931 to get a sense of foreign technology and work methods. In 1933 he was awarded a piano; in 1934, a motorcar. The next year he received the state's highest medal, the Order of Lenin. GARF, f. 7952, op. 5, d. 305, ll. 3, 68–80, 92.

132. Zaveniagin was born on 14 April 1901 at the Uzlovaia railroad settlement near Tula, the son of Pavel Ustinovich Zaveniagin-Sleptsov, a peasant who had left the village for the railroad depot, and Pelateia Vladimirovna, also a peasant. Pavel and Pelateia had nine children (three of them died very young). Avraamii's older brother, Ivan, who took the last name Sleptsov, early on became a member of the Russian Social Democratic Workers' party and gave political speeches to the workers at the Uzlovaia depot. It was through Ivan that Avraamii got involved in radical politics, joining the Bolshevik party in 1917. In 1921, when the Civil War was winding down, Zaveniagin, still only twenty, was elected to the Central Committee of the Ukrainian Communist party, although he suffered a temporary setback after a run-in with Georgii Piatakov. Zaveniagin entered the Moscow Mining Academy in 1923. After his stint in Magnitogorsk, he rose to the furthest heights of the Soviet system. In 1938, he became the director of a Gulag nickel-mining venture on the Arctic Circle in Norilsk, the northernmost settlement ever to attain a population of 100,000 people. Sometime during the war, he was elevated to chief of strategic minerals in the Gulag administration, a jurisdiction that included the vast gold-mining operations of Dalstroi in the Kolyma. In 1943, he was additionally named Beria's deputy and the director of operations for the Soviet atomic project. He died, reportedly of a heart ailment, in 1956 at the age of fifty-five, and was buried in the Kremlin wall. Alkatsev and Troshev, *Avraamii Zaveniagin*; Elfimov, *Marshal industrii*; *Bolshaia Sovetskaia Entsiklopedia*, vol. 9 (Moscow, 1972), p. 267; Boris Nicolaevsky, "The Land of White Death," in David Dallin and Boris Nicolaevsky, *Forced Labor in Soviet Russia* (New Haven: Yale University Press, 1947), p. 134. In addition to heading Gipromez, Zaveniagin served as deputy chief for technical matters in the State Administration for Metal Industry, GUMP.

133. Lewin, *The Making of the Soviet System*, pp. 252–54.

134. For example, Reizer, Gugel's chief of open-hearth construction who had also come to Magnitogorsk from Mariupol in January 1931, Poverennyi, the chief of blast furnace construction, and Popov, the chief of factory production, all lived in the same cottage in Berezka, the elite part of town described in ch. 3. "Very frequently we tried to help each other independently of the factory administration with materials," Reizer recalled in March 1936. "Let's say I would give Poverennyi construction materials and labor power, then next time he would compensate with what I needed. Thus we lived and worked in a friendly way." Reizer had replaced the "prisoner specialist" Vorobev, who had hung himself. In April 1934, after the sixth open-hearth oven was put into operation, Reizer was transferred by NKTP to Dzerzhinka. He eventually became USSR minister of construction. GARF, f. 7952, op. 5, d. 312, ll. 118, 127, 139, 140–42; Galiguzov and Churillin, *Flagman*, p. 48. The fate of the other two could not be ascertained.

135. Kuromiya, *Stalin's Industrial Revolution*, p. 54.

136. The archival finding-aid (*opis*) for GUMP (RGAE fond 4086) gives an overview of its establishment and operation, listing almost 5,000 files covering dozens of factories around the country and giving a vivid picture of one corner of the planned economy. As for the U.S. Steel Corporation, it was world famous for being a fully integrated industrial empire with its own ore, coke, and transportation, as well as iron and steel producing facilities. Quillen, "Industrial City," pp. 15–34.

137. One Soviet manager from nearby Magnitogorsk recalled an incident during Ordzhonikidze's visit to the coal trust Cheliabugol in 1933 when he was upbraided by the people's commissar for having turned to the GPU for help in procuring excavators and dumpcars to ready a mine by deadline. The GPU turned around and asked NKTP for equipment—this for a mine under NKTP jurisdiction—which infuriated Ordzhonikidze. This manager also pointed out that Ordzhonikidze did not appreciate industrial managers appealing for assistance through party channels. I. V. Paramonov, *Puti proidennye*, 2d ed. (Moscow, 1970), pp. 317–19.

138. John Scott described the state of affairs well: "Supplying the job with lumber was an even knottier problem. In winter lumber disappeared by the ton to be used as fuel in workers' homes. There was nothing to build scaffolds with. An incoming carload of lumber became the subject of telegrams to Ordzhonikidze, and sometimes even to Stalin, to decide which of the many competing organizations was to get the precious material." Scott, "Heavy Industry," p. 363.

139. When making a request of the central authorities, Lominadze wrote letters both to Stalin (as head of the party) and to Ordzhonikidze (as head of industrial management). See, for example, Lominadze's urgent appeal for more money for housing and factory construction. RTsKhIDNI, f. 85, op. 28. d. 454, ll. 1–4.

140. MFGAChO, f. 99, op. 10, d. 1090, l. 209.

141. Lewin, *The Making of the Soviet System*, pp. 29–30; and more generally, Janos Kornai, *Economics of Shortage* (New York: Elsevier-North Holland, 1980).

142. GARF, f. 7952, op. 5, d. 289, l. 2.

143. R. W. Davies, "The Socialist Market: A Debate in Soviet Industry, 1932–33," *Slavic Review* 42, no. 2 (1984): 201–23. It was at this time the so-called collective farm markets were introduced, allowing a certain amount of direct trade in agricultural goods.

144. *Industrii*, 9 February 1938.

145. For further elaboration, see Grossman, "Notes for a Theory of the Command Economy," pp. 101–23. Soviet industrial management has been the subject of several studies, including those by David Granick, *Management of the Industrial Firm in the USSR: A Study in Economic Planning* (New York: Columbia University Press, 1954); and Joseph Berliner, *Factory and Manager in the USSR* (Cambridge: Harvard University Press, 1957). See also Vasilii Grossman's novel, written during the Khrushchev era and later published abroad, in which a Siberian construction superintendent gives blunt but commonsense views on the functioning of the Soviet economy, emphasizing the need to break the law to survive. Grossman, *Forever Flowing*, (New York: Harper & Row, 1972), p. 3.

146. As cited in Sergei Ikonnikov, *Sozdanie i deiatelnost ob"edinennykh organov TsKK-RKI v 1923–1934 gg.* (Moscow, 1971), p. 221. Of course, it was Ordzhonikidze's offices that repeatedly stressed the importance of record keeping (*uchet*), requiring volume after volume of information about each factory's performance.

147. Lewin, *The Making of the Soviet System*, pp. 237–40.

148. *Stroitelstvo i ekspluatatsiia*, p. xi.

149. "Designing," he added, "was done everywhere and therefore nowhere: Gipromez, Giprokoks, Gipromash, Giproruda, etc. etc., to say nothing of the design department of the Magnitogorsk complex itself." *MR*, 15, 16, and 17 January 1934. As party secretary, Lominadze supervised all propaganda, including the work of the newspaper, which he clearly viewed as a platform from which he could show off.

150. GARF, f. 7952, op. 5, d. 309, l. 173.

151. *MR*, 25 June 1938. This is the same mill described by John Scott, *Behind the Urals: An American Worker in Russia's City of Steel* (Bloomington: Indiana University Press, 1989), pp. 145–53.

152. *MR*, 28 July 1936. Meanwhile, in one of the many newspaper pieces excoriating the factory's financial chaos, it was revealed that the complex owed more than 10 million rubles to its suppliers, who refused to ship anything more until payment was made. One of the firms owed money by Magnitogorsk was Gorlovka, the supplier of the crane girders. If and how they ever got the crane was never revealed in the press. Ibid., 9 August 1936.

153. *MR*, 2 February 1938. Kuzma Ryndin, secretary of the Cheliabinsk *obkom* (created in 1934 when the Urals oblast was divided in three), complained of the Magnitogorsk plant that "in 1936 not a single installation was finished by the deadline and that which was completed as a rule needed to be redone." *MR*, 8 January 1937.

154. Three more open-hearth ovens went into operation in 1934, bringing the total to seven, as did two more rolling mills: mill 450 and a medium structural-shapes mill (mill 500). The next year another four open-hearth ovens, a sorting mill (mill 300 no. 1), a light sorting mill (mill 250), and a strip and light angle iron mill (mill 300 no. 2)—the first of its kind in the USSR—were started up. In 1936 the twelfth open-hearth oven and the chemical by-products and rectification plant finally went into operation. In 1937 and 1938 two more sorting mills were added (mill 300 no. 3 and a heavy wire mill, mill 250 no. 2). A complete inventory of the

factory as of the end of 1938 can be found in RGAE, f. 4086, op. 2, d. 4546. In 1939 and 1940 four more open-hearth ovens, a powerful second blooming mill (the biggest in the USSR), and a fourth coke battery were built, while construction resumed on blast furnaces 5 and 6 (the foundations of which had been dug in 1937 before construction had been halted). The furnaces were completed during the war. See Galiguzov and Churillin, *Flagman.*

155. Scott, "Heavy Industry," p. 353.

156. Scott, *Behind,* p. 78.

157. *MR,* 20 October 1933.

158. Ordzhonikidze visited the site again in early September 1934. An interesting and frank discussion followed his remarks delivered to an assembly of the "party active." After delineating the many factors inhibiting better performance, Zaveniagin noted that "we are still accustomed to working by onslaughts and campaigns, in the Asian way. We have yet to accustom ourselves to the present, to work by industrial methods with full use of mechanized construction work." RGAE, f. 7297, op. 28, d. 327, l. 31.

159. In October 1936 construction activity was split off from the factory administration. The Construction Department of the Magnitogorsk Complex was liquidated and replaced by an independent trust named "Magnitostroi," the original name for the agency charged with building the factory. In addition to all construction work, the new trust was responsible for the brick factory, gravel pit and cement factory, and the lumberyard. *MR,* 1 September and 4 October 1936. Like the MMK, Magnitostroi was subordinated to GUMP.

160. "In 1936, 65 percent of all earth-moving work in Magnitogorsk was accomplished by hand, the remaining 35 percent with mechanization," revealed the newspaper. "The huge park of excavators, which cost around two million rubles, was used 30 percent" of capacity. "In other branches of construction," the newspaper lamented, "the situation is still worse." The construction trust owned 7.5 million rubles worth of machinery, but only around 25 percent of it was being used. The machines, much of them imported, were lying under snow drifts, many of them broken. In 1936 more than 1 million rubles were spent on repair work, yet out of 1,111 different machines, 780 still needed repairs. In such circumstances, the presence of a large force of convict laborers (see ch. 2) comes as no surprise. *MR,* 3 April 1937. Nonetheless, the availability of machinery at Magnitogorsk surpassed that of other large new construction sites. V. N. Eliseeva, "Borba za kadry na stroitelstve Magnitogorskogo metallurgicheskogo kombinata v gody pervoi piatiletki," in *Uchenye zapiski Cheliabinskogo pedagogicheskogo instituta* (Cheliabinsk, 1956), p. 217.

161. He listed numerous examples of the faulty designs holding up construction work. RGAE, f. 4086, op. 2, d. 933, l. 7.

162. Scott, "Heavy Industry," p. 363. Swearing at supply personnel was a frequent if ineffective response. GARF, f. 7952, op. 5, d. 309, l. 212.

163. For example, *MR,* 12 December 1934.

164. *MR,* 23 and 24 June, 6 July 1936.

165. This was also true of the plant in Kuznetsk, where it was said that "construction interfered with operation, operation interfered with construction." Frankfurt, *Men and Steel,* p. 188.

166. For this and other problems cited, the Southern Urals Railroad was blamed along with the steel plant. *CR*, 6 March 1935. Three years later, another article repeated many of these themes, estimating that the steel plant was supplied with only 55 percent of the railroad stock it needed to operate properly. Ibid., 12 February 1938.

167. Almost every day in 1935 an article in the newspaper would catalogue the woes of this shop. The problem was partly the complicated technology, partly the shop's large size. In 1936 it was divided into two separate shops of six ovens each and thoroughly renovated. Some improvement was seen, but the open-hearth shops continued to lag others. Attempts to achieve "record" production totals during some shifts put a severe strain on the ovens, and a shortage of quality fire-brick did not help. *MR*, 22 July and 26 August 1936. See also Clark, *The Economics of Soviet Steel*, p. 84. Pavel Kogan, chief of Magnitogorsk's open-hearth shop no. 1, claimed in an unpublished interview in November 1936 that the shop had not gotten any new equipment for more than a year. GARF, f. 7952, op. 5, d. 310, l. 389.

168. For countrywide production totals, see *Sotsialisticheskoe stroitelstvo SSSR* (Moscow, 1936), p. 133; *Itogi vypolneniia piatiletnego plana razvitiia narodnogo khoziaistva SSSR*, 2d ed. (Moscow, 1934), p. 105; and *Promyshlennost SSSR* (Moscow, 1957), p. 106.

169. Indeed, different data can be found in other official sources: *Stroitelstvo i ekspluatatsiia* (Sverdlovsk-Magnitogorsk, 1934), p. 103; *Piat let Magnitogorskogo*, p. 8; Galiguzov and Churillin, *Flagman*, p. 59, citing Tekushchii Arkhiv MMK: Kombinat v tsifrakh, p. 3; and *Iunost Magnitki* (Moscow, 1981), p. 80; as well as in John Scott, *Behind*, p. 273, app. 8, and p. 277, app. 21; idem., "Heavy Industry," p. 359. Scott relied on official sources.

170. Production targets were as follows: pig iron, 1,725,000 tons; steel, 1,450,000; rolling stock, 1,135,000—meaning that the actual production achieved represented only 92, 97, and 99 percent of the plan, respectively. *Obzor raboty zavoda za ianvar 1937 goda* (Magnitogorsk, 1937) p. 1.

171. *MR*, 11 May 1939.

172. Between unusable pig iron and excessive fuel use, the blast furnace shop showed a loss (*ubytok*) of nearly 3 million rubles for the first quarter of 1937. *MR*, 26 April and 6 May 1937. In 1939 the chief engineer at Magnitogorsk complained that "on modern technical equipment grandfatherly methods of work are employed." This was only one small part of the problem. Eliseeva, *Iz istorii*, p. 208.

173. *MR*, 26 July 1936. The Magnitogorsk open-hearth shop had only four casting cranes for twelve ovens. By contrast, Makeevka had four cranes for only six ovens, and Kuznetsk had six cranes for thirteen ovens. Grigorii Bobrov, who had been mobilized from Beloretsk in June 1934 and became a steel smelter in the open-hearth shop, commented in November 1936 that the biggest problem in the shop were the cranes. GARF, f. 7952, op. 5, d. 304, ll. 186–92. Another problem was that during a six month period in 1938, the critically important fire-brick shop produced only 40 to 50 percent of plan. *CR*, 18 November 1938. Magnitogorsk rolling mills were supplied with raw steel (*slitki*) from the Kuznetsk complex, but even this did not make up for the shortfall arising from the poor work of the Magnitogorsk open-hearth shop. Four new open-hearth ovens said to be under construction in Magnitogorsk were being built slowly, according to a 1938 report in the oblast

newspaper. In February, the local cement factory did not deliver any cement to Magnitostroi's division of open-hearth assembly, evidently because the construction trust was not paying for deliveries, causing a delay in the payment of wages at the cement factory. Meanwhile, Magnitostroi continued to write out orders for more cement. *CR*, 1 March 1938.

174. *MR*, 26 April 1937. A spot check of the blooming mill operation for four days in 1936 showed that of the 19,000 tons of steel produced, 5,400 tons were rejected. "It must be added," the newspaper reported, "that, of the metal considered by us to meet all standards, a considerable part is rejected by our customers as not meeting analytical standards." This was said to have resulted in "a severe financial loss for the factory." Ibid., 20 September 1936. More details were provided by the factory newspaper, which noted that during a period of around three months in 1936, a total of 16,247 tons of unusable steel, valued at more than 7 million rubles, had accumulated in the blooming mill. *Magnitogorskii metall*, 2 October 1936. And the oblast newspaper asserted that not only were many blooms said to be unmarked, and thus of unknown quality, but the central laboratory was incapable of coping with its evaluative tasks. *CR*, 8 February 1938.

175. *MR*, 11 October 1936. In June 1938, the chief of the factory's "special department" recommended that the large assemblage of inoperative rolling stock be removed from the factory's books to eliminate a serious financial drag. MFGAChO, f. 99, op. 10, d. 1096, l. 39.

176. *MR*, 17 July 1936. Insight into both the importance of transport and the sense of desperation resulting from equipment shortages is provided by a report of the "Case of the Stolen Engine." On 28 December 1935 the chief of the construction of the second dam borrowed a locomotive from the trust Soiuztransstroi, which he then refused to return. The Office for Disputes of the Cheliabinsk Branch of the People's Commissariat of Heavy Industry ordered the return of the locomotive and assessed a fine of 100 rubles per day for non-compliance. The Magnitogorsk complex preferred to incur the fine and retain use of the locomotive. By the time the newspaper report was published, the complex had run up a bill for more than 15,000 rubles, most of which had already been paid. All the same, the dam—whose water was vital to the steel plant—remained years behind schedule. *MR*, 5 July 1936.

177. *CR*, 12 October 1938.

178. *MR*, 26 April 1937.

179. Scott, "Heavy Industry," p. 351.

180. According to a blistering exposé of Magnitogorsk's rolling shops that appeared in the oblast newspaper, quality considerations were ignored in the shipping of orders, although some customers apparently refused to accept what they were being sent. At the same time, many factories that had contracted for Magnitogorsk rolled steel received either much less than specified or nothing at all. Meanwhile, the warehouse for finished product, "equipped with fabulous crane mechanisms," was said to "have been transformed into a chaotic rubbish heap of thousands of tons of disparate metal. There is no order, no system." *CR*, 9 March 1935.

181. *MR*, 23 December 1936.

182. In 1939, for the economy as a whole, defective output was officially said to account for 25 to 30 percent of all production, and to be characteristic even of the

armaments industry. *Vosemnadtsatyi s"ezd VKP (b): Stenograficheskii otchet* (Moscow, 1939), pp. 230, 267–68, 465.

183. For an insider account of the Soviet industrial bureaucracy, its strangling red tape, inefficiency, intrigues, and waste, see *An American Engineer in Stalin's Russia: The Memoirs of Zara Witkin, 1932–1934,* ed. by Michael Gelb (Berkeley: University of California Press, 1991).

184. In a careful survey of the growth claims made by the Soviet government and the counterassessments by Nutter, Seton, and Hodgman, R. W. Davies concludes that most Western economists, who offer figures for an increase in output by the conclusion of the second Five-Year Plan (1937) of from 249 to 370 percent of 1928 levels (an annual rate of 10.5 to 16 percent), underestimate the rate of growth and thus the extent of the Soviet achievement. But despite the precision and care Davies demonstrates, one may wonder what meaning such statistics of growth could have, given the notorious problems of double-counted output, defective and low-quality goods, and prodigal waste we have encountered at Magnitogorsk, and that were characteristic of the entire country. Davies, "Soviet Industrial Production, 1928–1937: The Rival Estimates," unpublished paper, University of Birmingham, Centre for Russian and East European Studies, no. 18 (1978); and S. G. Wheatcroft, R. W. Davies, and Julian Cooper, "Soviet Industrialization Reconsidered: Some Preliminary Conclusions about Economic Development between 1926 and 1941," *Economic History Review,* 2d ser., 39, no. 2 (1986): 264–94.

185. In effect, the USSR, much like its European and Asian neighbors, was engaged in the establishment of a war-making economy, although unlike its neighbors, the USSR seemed to be doing so for strictly defensive aims. The military nature of industrialization entailed two primary considerations: the formation of a multibranch defense industry (aircraft, tanks, ships, arms and ammunition), and the organization of civilian industry in such a way as to facilitate the growth of military industry. Many nominally civilian plants were to be built or reconstructed to allow for easy expansion of capacity and ready conversion to military purposes, while priorities in the all-important centrally controlled supply network were to be placed on military or militarily oriented enterprises.

186. Julian Cooper, "Defence Production and the Soviet Economy, 1929–1941," unpublished paper, University of Birmingham, Centre for Russian and East European Studies, no. 3 (1976): 41.

187. The emerging planned economy's near total disregard for consumption in favor of investment was the subject of a stinging published critique by M. I. Birbraer, a member of the staff of the leading newspaper for industry: "Why all these mountains of metal, machines, etc., for which so much labor has to be spent, crawling into the bowels of the earth and so on and so forth, if all this leads to such a relatively low level of consumption. Have we not turned man in these plan variants into a slave of all these things? The legitimate question arises: ultimately is man for socialism, or socialism for man?" *Za industrializatsiiu,* 29 and 30 May, 1930, as cited in Davies, "The Socialist Market," p. 206.

188. *MR,* 16 August 1937. The exception, of course, was for anyone deemed politically suspect. (For a fuller discussion of this theme, see ch. 5.) It is worth remarking just how unusual the permanence of employment was in an industrial city, as seen in David Crew's account of Bochum, a German town at the turn of the cen-

tury. Crew shows that notwithstanding the widespread moralist rhetoric on the advantages of a stable existence, a surprisingly high percentage of the jobs available to Bochum's residents were in effect "temporary" and subject to unpredictable but common fluctuations in what would come to be called the "business cycle." This inherent uncertainty was soon much magnified by the grandest of all business cycles, the Great Depression of the 1930s. Crew, *Town in the Ruhr: A Social History of Bochum, 1860–1914* (New York: Columbia University Press, 1979).

189. *CR*, 12 October 1938. According to John Scott, "while an American blast furnace of 1,000 cubic meter volume was tended by 70–80 men, in Magnitogorsk it took 165"; similarly, while "in America 150-ton [open] hearths are manned by 45–50 men, in Magnitogorsk it took 100–110 men." Scott, *Behind*, pp. 142, 167. This was generally known at the site. One Soviet author, for example, wrote that there were more than 200 Soviet workers on each blast furnace, versus only 128 on an American blast furnace. Rafael Shneiveis, "Gigant chernoi metallurgii," in *Piat let Magnitogorskogo*, p. 31.

190. As of 1 January 1939, the work force of the Magnitogorsk steel complex, including auxiliary shops (but not rail transport), stood at 31,193 people, of whom 13,164 worked in steelmaking shops proper, with the rest in the factory's numerous "repair" shops, dining halls, state farms, and so on. In the blast furnace shop, there were 1,099 people; open-hearth, 1,644; blooming mill, 667; mill 500, 687; power station, 657; coke and chemical, 1,411. MFGAChO, f. 118, op. 1, d. 80, l. 115. The breakdown according to category was as follows: workers, 22,625; engineers and technical personnel, 2,649; "white-collar" employees, 2,184; young service personnel and students, 3,745. Another 3,748 people were employed in rail transport. Ibid., f. 9, op. 1, d. 173, ll. 6, 8. Despite the huge size of the work force, complaints of insufficient labor power persisted. For example, in a report of 31 December 1938, factory director Pavel Korobov lamented "large shortfalls of labor power in certain shops of the complex." Ibid., f. 99, op. 10, d. 1099, l. 1. Uneducated, Korobov cultivated a crude management style, constantly threatening subordinates with "severe measures" for noncompliance. To one shop manager he wrote: "I will be forced to remove you and turn you over to the courts." This presented a sharp contrast with the style of Zaveniagin, who was no less authoritarian but far better educated and perceived as far more "cultured," despite his frequent recourse to unprintable language.

191. Angered by the uncontrolled expansion of its enterprises' work force, NKTP strove to enforce greater payroll discipline. In 1936 total wages for the Magnitogorsk Metallurgical Complex were set at 8,011,000 rubles. But the factory administration ignored these strictures and budgeted for 9,672,000 rubles. Nor did the complex seem squeamish about exceeding even this budget. The local newspaper did its job and deplored the system whereby everyone was awarded prizes and bonuses, but it had to know that the factory administration had little choice. *MR*, 10 August 1936 and 10 February 1938.

192. As of January 1937, after deep cuts had been made, there were still more than 3,000 white-collar employees and technical personnel in the metallurgical complex alone. *Tekhniko-ekonomicheskie pokazateli raboty zavoda za desiat mesiatsev 1936 goda* (Magnitogorsk, 1936), p. 12. Indeed, despite the deep cuts, especially in 1936 and 1937, NKTP continued to issue complaints, for a while. Accord-

ing to a study by the Moscow Institute of State and Law, in the decade between 1926 and 1935, almost two hundred brochures and articles were published in the Soviet press about "the struggle with bureaucratism." For the period 1972–81, the corresponding total was nine. *Nauchnyi kommunizm*, 1988, no. 4, p. 30. See also V. P. Makarenko, *Biurokratiia i stalinizm* (Rostov-na-Danu, 1989). In 1936 the Magnitogorsk newspaper carried its only spotlight on an employee (*sluzhashchii*), Stepan Korostylev, an economist of the factory's planning department. The fifty-two-year-old economist had thirty years of experience working in various bookkeeping posts in the Urals. He was cited for his thorough, flawless work, for never being late to work or with his reports, which were commended as detailed and many-sided, and for keeping up diligently with the literature in his profession. Korostylev was the first bookkeeper at Magnetic Mountain, having arrived with the original party of settlers in 1929. *MR*, 10 June 1936.

193. See Gardner Clark, who to the foregoing adds that "when the Soviets tried to transplant the Gary Works from the neighborhood of South Chicago and set it up in the barren mountains of the southern Urals, they failed to appreciate that Gary, Indiana, is located on the edge of the highest concentration of metal-fabricating plants in the world." Of course, one of the reasons behind locating the steel plant in Magnitogorsk was to develop that region and those still farther from the European markets, but this ambitious strategy required colossal investment in rail transport and several decades to create corresponding industry. The problem of isolation was even more acute for Kuznetsk, which shipped more than 15 percent of its beams and channels to Leningrad, a distance of some 3,500 kilometers. Clark, *The Economics of Soviet Steel*, pp. 90, 94.

194. According to party secretary Rafael Khitarov, as of November 1936 Magnitogorsk steel cost only 76 rubles per ton, supposedly 28 rubles cheaper than at Makeevka. GARF, f. 7952, op. 5, d. 313, l. 35.

195. Interpreting the results of such efforts, however, did not come easily. Everything depended on which prices were used in the calculations. In principle prices were fixed by the planners—which was problematic enough—but in practice matters were further muddled, for industrial prices tended to rise dramatically throughout the 1930s as a result of the enterprise bidding-war for the ever-increasing category of "extraplan" raw materials and supplies. "Unplanned" expenditures associated with the constant pressure to retain a large repair staff and to maintain the wherewithal to "storm" at the end of a quarter combined with higher than anticipated wastage to raise industrial costs still further. The state's only recourse, aside from fruitlessly attempting to clamp down on firms hemorrhaging money, was to extend greater and greater amounts of credit, and thus essentially to lose control over the money supply (permitting bankruptcy or closing a firm was considered beyond the realm of possibility). In such a way did an inflationary spiral develop. See the excellent technical discussion in R. W. Davies, *The Development of the Soviet Budgetary System* (Cambridge: Cambridge University Press, 1958), esp. chs. 7, 8 and 9; see also Arthur Arnold, *Banks, Credit and Money in Soviet Russia* (New York: Columbia University Press, 1937).

196. To explain the factory's violation of its financial plan, the newspaper disclosed that the blast furnace shop alone exceeded its budget for coke consumption by 9 million rubles and that the accumulation of unsalable products meant a decline

in income even greater than the disappointing plan fulfillment of only 89.7 percent would have caused. *MR*, 1 March 1939. All the same, Soviet economic terms and categories, however contradictory or even absurd, not only made sense to contemporaries but were indispensable for the functioning of the planned economy. See Lewin, *Stalinism and the Seeds of Soviet Reform*, p. 114. There was evidently a large "soft" budget. The factory director, for example, had at his disposal a special account. In 1936 the director's account held 2,897,000 rubles. Notwithstanding the guidelines for managing the account, the director exercised wide discretion in the dispersal of funds, some of which, for example, went to the Komsomol. *MR*, 9 May 1937.

197. RGAE, f. 4086, op. 2, d. 933, ll. 31–33.

198. The construction of the famed Metal Workers' Club, discussed in chapter 3, had been budgeted for 2.68 million rubles. By the end of 1936, it had already cost 6.95 million, and was not even completed. RGAE, f. 4086, op. 2, d. 3081, ll. 37–38.

199. *MR*, 1 April 1936. This article by Aleksandr Lopaev was one of several aimed at the chief of the construction trust, Kasperovich, whose response was published on 15 April 1936. Ignoring all the direct charges of Lopaev, Kasperovich resorted to the argument that the results for 1935 were superior to those for 1934, but neglected to compare the results for 1935 with the plan targets—Lopaev's main point. Kasperovich was removed as chief of the construction trust. Lopaev too was replaced not long thereafter (see ch. 7).

200. *MR*, 1 April 1936. Lopaev added that the celebrated 1935 cost reduction of 14 percent was "shameless eyewash"—in reality, costs rose by 4.3 percent—and he branded as blatant fabrication the claim of 97 percent fulfillment for the 1936 construction plan, divulging that the real figure was closer to 86 percent, including only 54.1 percent for blast furnace construction and 79.4 percent for the open-hearth shop. These dreary figures, Lopaev angrily wrote, were "raised" to an average of 97 percent by the inclusion of "capital repairs," work which had been necessitated by the shabbiness of the original construction work. As another executive in the banking system put it in reference to the construction plan fulfillment statistics for the first quarter of 1936, "only naive people could believe in those figures." *MR*, 6 May 1936.

201. The article further disclosed that "Leningrad factories supplying important steel constructions sent telegrams demanding payment," while a "construction workers' delegation went to the bank demanding an explanation as to why they were not being paid." *MR*, 8 August 1936.

202. *MR*, 9 August 1936. Other newspaper reports indicated that the construction trust lost 16.5 million rubles in 1937, and another 3.1 million during the first half of 1938. *MR*, 26 February, 1 March 1938, and 15 September 1938.

203. *Stalinskaia stroika* (Magnitogorsk, 1939), p. 11. Investment only through late 1931 was estimated at 204.7 million rubles. *Pravda*, 6 November 1931.

204. *Stroitelstvo i ekspluatatsiia*, pp. x–xi. Total costs for the plant, including the city, were estimated at 2.5 billion rubles, of which 607 million rubles had been spent by 1 January 1934. The project was being financed, according to this publication, through "the magic of the state budget" (p. 94). Scott himself admitted that of the 2.5 billion rubles, 700 million were so-called gold rubles, and that "expenses

in gold for foreign equipment were reckoned in these figures according to the nominal ruble value in gold, which gives no real idea of what it cost the Soviet Union to buy and install foreign equipment for Magnitogorsk." Scott, "Heavy Industry," p. 360.

205. And as one bank executive lamented, many expenditures made during construction were never recorded. *MR*, 24 June 1938.

206. One scholar has tried to estimate the cost of steel plants in the USSR. He comes up with a figure for a generic plant of around 1 billion rubles, only to write that "no one knew the costs of things being built or how much money was spent." Sergei Koptewski, "The Costs of Construction of New Metallurgical Plants in the USSR," East European Fund, Inc. Research Program on the USSR, mimeo series, no. 19 (1952).

207. Of the party's Five-Year Plan, Georgii Piatakov, then chairman of the State Bank and future deputy commissar of heavy industry, enthused in late 1929 that "the heroic phase of our socialist construction has begun." *Torgovo-promyshlennaia gazeta*, 5 October 1929.

208. The recklessness of the "race against time" is discussed by Lewin, who dismisses motivations for it on the basis of the external threat and appears to attribute the impulse to Stalin and his maneuvering against the middle peasants who were withholding grain. Lewin, *The Making of the Soviet System*, pp. 107–8. The title of Kataev's novel is taken from the Mayakovski poem, "Marsh vremeni." See *Literaturnai gazeta*, 1947, no. 57. For more background on the novel, see L. Skorino, *Pisatel i ego vremia* (Moscow, 1965); T. N. Sidelnikova, *Valentin Kataev: Ocherk zhizni i tvorchestva* (Moscow, 1957; *Rost*, 1933, nos. 11–12, p. 10; and *Pravda*, 28 September 1933.

209. GARF, f. 7952, op. 5, d. 309, ll. 36–37. "At first, nothing made sense," wrote one worker. "It looked queer: digging a huge circular ditch. We thought it was for containing a wild animal, but it was the foundation for open-hearth ovens." Ibid., d. 313, l. 11. Similar comments were made by engineers and specialists. Ibid., d. 312, l. 181; and d. 307, l. 183. Raymond Stuck of McKee wrote that "it is impossible for the layman to picture the magnitude of such an undertaking." Stuck, "First-Hand Impressions of Soviet Russia."

210. GARF, f. 7952, op. 5, d. 305, l. 48.

211. *Pravda*, 2 February 1935.

212. Ordzhonikidze, "Dognat i peregnat," speech delivered in Magnitogorsk, 26 July 1933, abridged and reprinted in *Stati i rechi*, vol. 2, p. 481. Of the Gary Works it was remarked: "Until industry waved its magic wand over the land upon which the vast steel mills of Gary now stand, the place was none other than a bleak, sandy waste, a strip of prairie with virtually no habitation." *Blast Furnace and Steel Plant* 25, no. 8 (August 1937): 823. Of course, the ecology of Indiana's Calumet region, no less than that of the area surrounding Magnetic Mountain, was for centuries home to hundreds of species of wildlife. Moreover, the Calumet at one time was inhabited by Native Americans, who were forcibly removed from the land in the 1830s and resettled in "reservations" in what is now Kansas.

213. *MR*, 1 January 1937. The figure of seventy-two shops includes the factory proper—mine, coke plant, and steel plant—as well as repair shops and so-called auxiliary shops located at or near the steel plant. For example, the nearby Katav-

Ivanovskii metal factory, which was founded in 1755 with samovar-like furnaces and which by the mid-1930s was composed of one small open-hearth shop and a cement factory, was declared to be a shop of the Magnitogorsk complex in 1935. *MR*, 29 August 1936.

214. The steel plant's annual capacity (in tons) as set by Gipromez in 1933 was as follow: pig iron, 2,750,000; steel, 3,050,000; rolling stock, 2,485,000. These capacities were for eight blast furnaces, thirty-four open-hearth ovens, and eighteen rolling mills. As of 1938 only four blast furnaces, four coke batteries, twelve open-hearth ovens and ten rolling mills were in operation. *Stroitelstvo i ekspluatatsiia*, p. 4.

215. *Buksir*, June 1932, no. 4, p. 2. At a 1934 meeting of Moscow Communists, Kulakov, from the factory Elektrozavod, had tied Magnitogorsk and the industrialization to the belated recognition of the Soviet government by the United States in late 1933. "The American sirs, convinced of our power and especially of the victories of the first Five-Year Plan, were compelled to recognize us," asserted Kulakov. "Our Magnitostrois, our giants of industry, our tremendous growth forced the capitalist countries to take note of us." *IV Moskovskaia oblastnaia partiinaia konferentsiia i III gorodskaia konferentsiia VKP (b): Stenograficheskii otchet* (Moscow, 1934), p. 65. For further discussion of the relationship between technology and political legitimacy, see Bailes, *Technology and Society*, esp. ch. 14.

216. John Scott, although not alone in praising Stalin's purported genius at ruthlessly compelling the country to industrialize as fast as possible, did so as eloquently as anyone. Scott, *Behind*, pp. 253–63.

217. Pierre Dominique [P. Lucchini], *Secrets of Siberia* (London: Hutchinson, 1934), pp. 114–15, 107–8. Writing of a similar steel plant erected during the first Five-Year Plan, one former Soviet manager concluded that "the amazing part of it, looking back, . . . is that somehow, miraculously, a large part of the metallurgical complex was built. More slowly, more expensively than planned, at an almost incalculable cost in life and suffering, but it was built." Kravchenko, *I Chose Freedom*, p. 81.

218. An examination of the factory as a crucible for new thoughts and behavior is taken up in ch. 5.

219. *Piat let Magnitogorskogo.*

CHAPTER 2. PEOPLING A SHOCK CONSTRUCTION SITE

1. R. Roman, *Krokodil v Magnitostroe* (Moscow, 1931), p. 5.

2. Their travails were reported in *Torgovo-promyshlennaia gazeta*, 28 July 1929. The recollections of the group's leader, Andrei Sulimov, can be found in *Magnitostroi: Informatsionnyi biulleten*, June 1931, pp. 55–56. Long celebrated as the person who received the first *putevka* to Magnitostroi, Sulimov was later accused of Trotskyism and arrested.

3. *Uralskii rabochii*, 2 July 1929.

4. In 1928 the population of the entire *raion* in which Magnetic Mountain was located, then part of Troitsk okrug, was about 12,900. GARF, f. 7952, op. 5, d. 308, l. 83.

5. "Back then [1930]," wrote one young worker in the mid-1930s, "it seemed to me and others in the train that Cheliabinsk, which we were seeing for the first time, was a large rich village, and not a city." He added that this was not his impression of Sverdlovsk, the "capital" of the Urals, where he had just been. GARF, f. 7952, op. 5, d. 317, l. 28.

6. *Pravda*, 25 October 1932. This seems to have been a slight exaggeration. Throughout the remainder of the 1930s semi-official estimates put the population at between 200,000 and 220,000. *MR*, 17 August 1934, 9 February 1936, 18 December 1936, 9 January 1937. Between 1929 and 1932 the population grew quickly but unevenly. In September 1929 there were 30,000 people at the site; in December 1929, 60,000, according to estimates given by the city planning commission chairman. *MR*, 11 July 1938. In October 1930 there were some 72,000. At the time of the first local census, January 1931, the population was given at 70,386. MFGAChO, f. 16, op. 1, d. 5, l. 13. In March 1931, within two years of the arrival of the first party, there were 83,200 people. By May 1931, the population passed 100,000, and another 50,000 were added the following June alone. By the end of the summer in 1931 the population approached 195,000, *Magnitostroi v tsifrakh: Statisticheskii otchet za 1931 g.*(Magnitogorsk, 1932), p. 327. A different estimate put the population in January 1932 at 175,000. RGAE, f. 4086, op. 2, d. 116, l. 21. The same figure was given in *Magnitogorskii komsomolets*, 10 September 1931. In February 1932, however, the journal *SSSR na stroike*, 1932, no. 1, estimated 165,000. These differences arose because of the high mobility and the inconsistency in including or excluding prisoners in official statistics.

7. Lewin, *The Making of the Soviet System*, pp. 44, 221.

8. Fitzpatrick, *The Russian Revolution*, p. 8.

9. V. P. Polonskii, *Magnitostroi* (Moscow, 1931), p. 78. Polonskii, a founder and editor of the journal *Pechat i revoliutsiia*, died in the Magnitogorsk hospital barracks on 24 February 1932 of typhus, as reported in the local literary journal, *Za Magnitostroi literatury*, 1932, no. 1, p. 19.

10. The office was opened in 1925 as the Urals planning bureau, which was changed in 1926 to the Urals branch of Gipromez, and again in 1928 to "Magnitostroi." Serzhantov, "KPSS—Vdokhnovitel," p. 121, citing PAChO, f. 343, op. 3, d. 4, l. 115. The building, the famous Sverdlovsk Passage, had belonged to a merchant, Pachinskii. *Iunost Magnitki*, p. 37. The new office at the site was a little log cabin on which was written the grandiose designation: "VSNKh SSSR. Kontora Magnitostroia." Iurii Petrov, *Magnitka* (Moscow, 1971), p. 30. About 170 people made the move, according to Leonid G. Ankudinov, a member of the group. Ankudinov, *Magnitostroi* (Cheliabinsk, 1979), p. 9.

11. Polonskii, *Magnitka zovet*, p. 25. After having permitted Magnitostroi's office to be comfortably lodged far from the site in the "capital" city of the Urals for over two years, the central authorities ordered its immediate relocation, which for no apparent reason, had to be carried out in the greatest haste. One contemporary recalled: "Step by step the offices of Magnitostroi grew larger and larger until they occupied a huge area of the Sverdlovsk Passage. It was all very cultured. No one felt as if he was at a construction site. It was marvelous. The construction task itself was chic, the largest in the Union. They ordered a sign made from gold letters—Magnitostroi—for the Passage building. Everything was wonderful.

Everyone came to work at 9 A.M. with his briefcase and left around 3 P.M. Then came the announcement: 'Everybody's going to the site tomorrow!' Imagine what that meant! Just to pack up the files we needed took at least a week. . . . Everyone was in a panic. What is this?" GARF, f. 7952, op. 5, d. 308, l. 78. Another participant provided the answer: "an evacuation." Ibid., d. 342, l. 1. The impatience of the central authorities was made a mockery of, however, when the train ride carrying the offices and personnel from Sverdlovsk to the site—a distance of less than 800 kilometers—took six days. Ibid., d. 311, l. 6.

12. Polonskii, *Magnitka zovet*, p. 25. On the day of departure there were many tearful faces at the platform in Sverdlovsk. GARF, f. 7952, op. 5, d. 308, l. 78. The offices of Kuznetskstroi were initially located in Tomsk, a two-day train ride from the construction site. Frankfurt, *Men and Steel*, p. 26.

13. GARF, f. 7952, op. 5, d. 315, l. 40.

14. Ibid., d. 316, l. 18.

15. Ibid., d. 306, l. 13.

16. Ibid., d. 315, l.46; and d. 314, l. 16.

17. Serzhantov, "KPSS—Vdokhnovitel," pp. 101–4. In December 1929 another 270 former Red Army soldiers arrived at Magnitostroi. Valentin Serzhantov, "KPSS—Vdokhnovitel," p. 168. See also Antipova and Shkolnik, "Iz istorii," p. 33, citing PAChO, f. 344, op. 3, d. 111, l. 425.

18. GARF, f. 7952, op. 5, d. 309, l. 136.

19. Aleksandra Seredkina, *Borba Magnitogorskoi partinnoi organizatsii za sozdanie giganta chernoi metallurgii - MMK: V pomoshch lektoru* (Magnitogorsk, 1958), p. 10, citing PAChO, f. 349, op. 3, sv. 2, d. 7, l. 1 ob. Skilled production workers, such as Mikhail Zuev, an open-hearth furnace operator sent to Magnitogorsk from Mariupol, were told that they were "not allowed to leave." GARF, f. 7952, op. 5, d. 300 ll. 61, 70.

20. GARF, f. 7952, op. 5, d. 309, ll. 6–7.

21. Ibid., d. 318, l. 65.

22. Ibid., d. 313, l. 1.

23. To his wife's comments, Tomilov added that "truthfully, all you saw here were convicts [*itekovtsy*]." These were common criminals sentenced to forced labor in Magnitogorsk's Corrective Labor Colony, or ITK (see chs. 3 and 5). Tomilov, who at one point left Magnitogorsk for Kuznetsk, turned up at Magnitogorsk several years later, a veteran steel smelter, complaining in the factory newspaper: "Before Magnitka I worked at the Karl Marx Dnepropetrovsk factory. There, there was more concern about living people [*sic*]. Here, in my three years of work in the open hearth shops, for example, no one has asked, 'How's your health, comrade Tomilov, how are things at home, how are you spending your time off from work, how are you raising your kids, and maybe there's something you need?'" Tomilov did not stop there, adding that he could not find any coats, hats, or shoes for his children, who were about to start school, or any firewood for heating, and that there were two broken windows where he lived that needed to be replaced before winter set in. *Magnitogorskii metall*, 28 August 1935.

24. John Scott counted about twenty-five such prisoner specialists. Scott, *Behind*, pp. 286–88.

25. Nikolai Markevich, *Rozhdenie giganta* (Moscow, 1930), pp. 9–12.

26. Later, as the completion of various factory shops neared, a number of mobilizations of managers and skilled operating personnel from Donbas factories were ordered.

27. GARF, f. 7952, op. 5, d. 342, ll. 12–14. The same scenario was reenacted in 1933 when Avraamii Zaveniagin became the new chief of the factory.

28. GARF, f. 7952, op. 5, d. 312, ll. 118–19. Once pried loose, mobilized skilled workers and officials went to Moscow, to the famous offices at Ploshchad Nogina of the People's Commissariat of Heavy Industry (the former Delovoi Dvor), where they made the rounds of officials in charge of the nation's industry: Gurevich, the head of GUMP; Moskvin, the head of personnel at NKTP; Semushkin, Ordzhonikidze's secretary; and finally "Sergo" himself, who delivered legendary five-minute pep talks before sending his "troops" off as if into battle.

29. GARF, f. 7952, op. 5, d. 305, l. 84.

30. Scott estimated that "there were approximately 2,000 Poles, mostly Jews; 200 Finns, mostly ex-smugglers; 50 Bulgarians; 30 Germans; and a few Rumanians and Turks." Scott, *Behind*, pp. 288–89.

31. U.S. National Archives 861.5017/569. Of the various company contingents, the McKee group, by far the largest, had some thirty engineers at any one time. Engineers of the McKee group were changed frequently, so that as many as eighty may have come and gone. Ibid., 861.5017/452. Another American company, Koppers, had about fifteen or eighteen in its party.

32. *Moscow News*, 26 May 1933. Soviet authorities did attempt to keep some of these specialists by signing them to ruble contracts, and some foreign specialists did in fact stay on under the new terms. Virtually all of the most qualified foreign engineers and technicians, however, were gone by the middle of the 1930s, although short-term visits by foreign consultants continued.

33. One Soviet eyewitness later recalled an incident in the early 1930s: "The party and trade union organizations, together with the economic leadership, called a meeting of foreign workers and specialists at which there were twenty-six Germans. Many foreigners came to the meeting with books of Marx and Lenin and began to cite the texts in order to show the incorrect treatment of the working class by our organizations." What, if anything, resulted was not clarified. GARF, f. 7952, op. 5, d. 306, l. 16.

34. In general, workers tended to stay longer than specialists and engineers. Some workers married Soviet women, adopted Soviet citizenship, and hoped to remain permanently. But by 1938 a foreign worker in Magnitogorsk was an anomaly. During the witch hunts of 1937 and 1938, those who retained their foreign passports were forced from their jobs and had to leave the city, while those who had become Soviet citizens in many cases were arrested and disappeared.

35. One Soviet source put the number as of February 1932 at 310 (131 specialists and 179 workers) plus another 180 family members (or a total of about 500), representing seventeen countries. Matushkin, *Uralo-kuzbass*, pp. 299–300. A different source indicated that during the years 1929–35, 752 foreign specialists at one time or another lived and worked in Magnitogorsk, of whom approximately two-thirds were highly skilled and more than one-third were Communists or socialists. About half were Germans, the next largest group were Czechs and Slovaks, then came Americans, Italians and others. A. T. Kolotilin, "Inostrannye trudiashchiesia

na Magnitostroe," in *Tvorcheskaia deiatelnost rabochego klassa Magnitki*, Magnitogorskii Gorno-Metallicheskii Institut, Sbornik no. 49 (Magnitogorsk, 1967), p. 20, citing MFGAChO f. 99, op. 8, d. 1–777 (this material on the foreign specialists remained classified through 1991). A later article, in *Iunost Magnitki*, p. 76, also gave a figure of 752, citing unspecified Cheliabinsk oblast archives. And yet a third source claimed there were 992 foreigners in Magnitogorsk by 1932–33, of whom 434 were Communists (174 of foreign parties, 260 Soviet). N. P. Sharapov, "Ob uchastii inostrannykh rabochikh i spetsialistov v sotsialisti-cheskom stroitelstve na Urale (1930–1934)," *Voprosy istorii KPSS*, 1966, no. 3, p. 78. By the middle to late 1930s there were perhaps as many as 7,000 foreigners in the Urals (this number must include deported refugees). P. G. Matushkin, *Druzhba, solidarnost* (Cheliabinsk, 1960), p. 29. The number of foreigners throughout the USSR during this time was large. One Soviet source reported in 1936 that 6,800 foreign specialists were working in heavy industry in 1932. *Handbook of the Soviet Union* (New York: American-Russian Chamber of Commerce, 1930), p. 347. According to a contemporary German periodical, by the summer of 1932 there were some 10,000 foreign *Mitarbeiter* in the USSR, of whom 7,000 were workers (half of these Germans) and the rest specialists. This seems to be an underestimate. *Osteuropa*, June 1932, pp. 509–21, and July 1932, pp. 591–99. That same source indicates that Amtorg had yet to process the applications of 100,000 Americans seeking work in the USSR. (In the absence of diplomatic relations, it was far more difficult for Americans than for the Germans to go to the USSR for work.) In any case, the total number of foreigners working in the USSR during the 1930s certainly exceeded 10,000 and, judging by the number employed at Magnitogorsk, may well have been many more.

36. V. N. Eliseeva, "Istoriografiia voprosa o soiuze rabochego klassa i krestianstva v khode stroitelstva MMK," *Istoriografiia istorii sozdaniia i razvitiia soiuza rabochego klassa i krestianstva na Urale* (Sverdlovsk, 1982), p. 141, citing Gosudarstvennyi arkhiv Voronezhskoi oblasti, f. 1439, op. 4, d. 267, ll. 55–60; and GARF, f. 5515, op. 17, d. 375, l. 103; and d. 533, ll. 230–31.

37. Zuikov, *Sozdanie tiazheloi*, pp. 226 ff., citing RGAE, f. 4372, op. 28, d. 243, l. 28.

38. Magnitostroi could recruit in the Urals, the Ukraine, and selected parts of Ivanov and Moscow oblasts. V. N. Eliseeva, "O sposobakh privlecheniia rabochei sily v promyshlennost i stroitelstvo v period sotsialisticheskoi industrializatsii SSSR (1926–1937 gg.)," *Izvestiia Voronezhskogo gosudarstvennogo pedagogicheskogo instituta* (Voronezh, 1967), tom 63, p. 57.

39. Antipova and Shkolnik, "Iz istorii," p. 34. I saw some of them in the documentary film archives in Krasnogorsk at the Tsentralnyi gosudarstvennyi arkhiv kinofotodokumentov.

40. Serzhantov, "KPSS—Vdokhnovitel," p. 101.

41. *Iunost Magnitki*, p. 44.

42. GARF, f. 7952, op. 5, d. 303, l. 20. One memoir contains an example of what advice was given to those arriving at the site by people who had already been recruited:

A group of pitiful fellows who were sitting with drooping expressions began to look at us new arrivals.

"Hey, you new guys, you're clean. Where are you from?"

"From Dneprostroi."

"Well, get out of here as quick as you can."

As we shall see, many people took the advice. Ibid., d. 308, l. 55.

43. "Gigant i stroitel," *SSSR na stroike,* 1932, no. 1. Kalmykov was shown arriving at the site in primitive *lapty,* or bast sandals, with all his worldly belongings. His first residence, a communal barrack, was also depicted, as was a reenactment of his marriage at the civil registration office (ZAGS) to a German woman. In the Komsomol document exchange of 1932, Kalmykov had ceremoniously received the first new card. *Koordinaty podviga: Iz istorii Cheliabinskoi oblastnoi komsomolskoi organizatsii 1918–1968* (Cheliabinsk, 1968), p. 163. Selected as the Magnitogorsk delegate to a Moscow conference of shock workers, he came back in a fashionable new coat and cap. Petrov, *Magnitka,* p. 83. In 1938 Kalmykov was arrested and shot as a German spy. His wife and children were ostracized, then arrested and exiled.

44. *Slovo o Magnitke,* pp. 48–51.

45. Excerpts from seven letters, apparently written to friends and relatives at the behest of authorities, can be found in Zinovii Ostrovskii, *Magnitostroi* (Moscow, 1931), pp. 41–45.

46. Quoted in Pearl S. Buck, *Talk About Russia (with Masha Scott)* (New York, 1945), p. 91. Sometimes enthusiasm for city life was mixed with other motivations, such as the desire to avoid famine. One man from the Northern Caucasus received several enthusiastic letters from his brother at Magnitostroi. When the latter came home to the Caucasus for a brief visit in 1931, the younger brother decided to go back with him to Magnitogorsk. Later the younger brother himself returned to the Caucasus in 1933 to fetch the rest of the family. "I had heard nothing from my family, and 1933 in the Caucasus was an alarming time," he wrote, explaining why he went home that year. "I worked that summer and sent my mom and sister on to Magnitogorsk, then followed." GARF, f. 7952, op. 5, d. 300, ll. 129–44.

47. In Sverdlovsk, for example, industrial enterprises were supposed to send 1,000 workers to Magnitostroi by June 1930 but sent only 300. Eliseeva, "Borba za kadry," pp. 205–8.

48. GARF, f. 7952, op. 5, d. 312, l. 285.

49. *Stroitelstvo i ekspluatatsiia,* p. 83.

50. Eliseeva, "O sposobakh," pp. 47–49, citing RGAE, f. 7446, op. 8, d. 83, ll. 68–70.

51. Eliseeva, "O sposobakh," p. 55.

52. GARF, f. 7952, op. 5, d. 300, l. 49.

53. For example, E. A. Goncharov was sent to Magnitostroi in December 1929 along with the whole trade union and party "active" of his technicum. In March 1930 Goncharov was sent back to his native Tambov guberniia to recruit: "I went to Voronezh, found my former comrades there and got them to sign up. I went to the Labor Distribution Department from which I got unofficial permission to recruit 500 people. . . . I recruited 300 from Kalinka village and 186 from Gudovo:

... many of these workers had worked with me earlier, . . . so that my workers came with me out of trust. The village soviet also helped me, as I was recognized as a former worker and a local. . . . Within the course of a month, I brought them to Magnitostroi. Everyone to the last person went the distance—no one bolted along the way." Goncharov claimed that he earned 1,500 rubles for his efforts, then a hefty sum. GARF, f. 7952, op. 5, d. 306.

54. Without documents, they could have been taken for fleeing "kulaks." Indeed, it is possible that this entire story was concocted by the narrator to explain why two-hundred men arrived at the site without documents. GARF, f. 7952, op. 5, d. 315, l. 80.

55. N. A. Ivnitskii, *Klassovaia borba i likvidatsiia kulachestva kak klassa, 1929–1932* (Moscow, 1972), p. 178.

56. Lewin, *Russian Peasants,* pp. 482–513.

57. Robert Conquest, *The Harvest of Sorrow* (New York: Oxford University Press, 1986), p. 123.

58. GARF, f. 7952, op. 5, d. 200, l. 98. The first peasant exiles began arriving in Kuznetsk in the fall of 1930. According to Frankfurt, they were primarily from within Siberia. Later, in July 1931, "several thousand" peasant exiles arrived in Kuznetsk from the central regions of the USSR. Frankfurt, *Men and Steel,* pp. 139–40.

59. *Magnitostroi v tsifrakh,* p. 321.

60. GARF, f. 7952, op. 5, d. 306, l. 8. The speaker is E. A. Goncharov.

61. John Scott wrote of the difficult conditions and high mortality rate of the exiled peasants, estimating that by the end of 1933 the colony "was composed of about 35,000 persons." He added that "the four or five thousand who died during the winter of 1932–33 were replaced by newcomers who were mostly runaway peasants from other colonies. The total population of the Magnitogorsk colony, about 30,000 or 40,000, thus remained constant." (At the time, the total population at the site numbered around 190,000.) Scott, *Behind,* pp. 281–84. Other foreigners present in the city when the dekulakized arrived and in some cases holding positions of high responsibility unanimously confirm Scott's estimates of around 40,000 peasant exiles, or about one-fifth of the total population at the site. For example, Stuck, "Russia As I Saw It," p. 65; and Stadelman, in a 30 November 1932 debriefing at the U.S. Embassy (Berlin), 861.5017/569. Both the dekulakized and the prison population of the ITK were at the disposal of the steel plant. According to data from the factory administration, the Magnitogorsk Works employed 3,680 dekulakized peasants as of 25 December 1936. MFGAChO, f. 118, op. 1, d. 106, l. 6; and f. 99, d. 59, l. 103.

62. Magnitogorsk procuracy: Archival file "Nariad 21," l. 61. These particular dekulakized peasants were held in the Corrective Labor Colony (ITK), not the Special Labor Settlement. Beyond their "class alien" background, they had been convicted of crimes and sentenced to deprivation of freedom in a labor colony.

63. Quillen, "Industrial City," pp. 151–52; John Appleton, "The Iron and Steel Industry of the Calumet District: A Study in Economic Geography," *University of Illinois Studies in the Social Sciences,* 13, no. 2 (1925): 92–93. Gary's permanent population was far smaller than Magnitogorsk's. In 1910, Gary had 16,802 people, and in 1920, 55,378. More than thirty years after it was founded, it still had no

more than two-thirds as many people as Magnitogorsk. *A Study of the Social and Economic Conditions of the Negro Population of Gary, Indiana* (Washington, D. C.: The National Urban League, 1944), p. 3.

64. Unemployment was a volatile domestic political issue in the USSR during the 1920s, when it appears to have been increasing. With the industrialization drive, mass unemployment disappeared completely at the latest by the end of 1931 (but probably before), according to R. W. Davies, "The Ending of Mass Unemployment in the USSR," in David Lane, ed., *Labour and Employment in the USSR* (New York: New York University Press, 1986), pp. 19–35; see also L. S. Rogachevskaia, *Likvidatsiia bezrabotitsy v SSSR, 1917–1930 gg.* (Moscow, 1973). Although by the fall of 1929 in the Urals oblast there were only 1,491 registered unemployed and shortly thereafter the category disappeared altogether (registered unemployment ended in the Urals even earlier than in the USSR as a whole), in 1928 there had been only 42,908 registered unemployed. Eliseeva, "O sposobakh," pp. 39–40, citing GASO, f. 88, op. 2, d. 432, l. 277. The end of unemployment came as a surprise. As late as the spring of 1929, officials believed that unemployment would continue for many years. Davies, *The Soviet Economy in Turmoil*, pp. 66, 126.

65. N. V. Efremov, "K voprosu o roli kollektivizatsii v perekhode k orgnaboru rabochei sily dlia promyshlennosti Urala," in *Iz istorii zavodov i fabrik Urala: Sbornik statei* (Sverdlovsk, 1963), vyp. 2, pp. 208–9. One must wonder about how such statistics were gathered. One reliable scholar has suggested that attempts to register and direct *otkhod*, through such places as the *korrespondentskie punkty*, proved futile. Eliseeva, "O sposobakh," pp. 43–44.

66. See Panfilova, *Formirovanie*, p. 8, n. 6, for a bibliography of contemporary sources.

67. One scholar examined the relevant Soviet sources thoroughly, only to conclude that the data are contradictory and confusing. Nobuaki Shiokawa, "The Collectivization of Agriculture and Otkhodnichestvo in the USSR, 1930," *Tōkyō Daigaku: Shakai Kagaku Kenkyūjo, Annals,* 1982–83, pp. 129–58. While some of those on the move were not peasants but traders, shopkeepers, and urban artisans, many of those peasants included in the statistics must have been fleeing collectivization (rather than looking for seasonal work).

68. *MR*, 30 December 1932.

69. Efremov, "K voprosu," p. 212, citing GASO, f. 922, op. 1, d. 150, l. 191.

70. A. I. Paiskova, "Nekotorye dannye po voprosu formirovaniia rabochego klassa Urala v gody pervoi piatiletki," in *Iz istorii zavodov i fabrik Urala* (Sverdlovsk, 1963), vyp. 2, pp. 228–30, citing GASO, f. 1812-r, op. 1, d. 19, ll. 115, 101.

71. Efremov, "K voprosu," p. 214.

72. Incomplete data for 1933 arrivals, asked their region of origin during the residency registration, or *propiska*, are as follows:

Urals	14,001
Central Black Earth Region	9,369
Mid-Volga Territory	5,911
Kazakhstan	3,293
Bashkiria	3,101

Ukraine	2,033
Other	3,895
Total	41,603

The same source gives a figure for total arrivals for 1933 as 46,497, meaning that the places of origin of more than 5,000 people are inexplicably missing from the table. Taking the data in the table, only slightly more than one-third of all arrivals would seem to have begun their journey to Magnitogorsk from within the Urals. MFGAChO, f. 16, op. 1, d. 29, l. 40; and d. 42, l. 92.

73. *Istoriia Urala* (Perm, 1965), tom 2, p. 258. This number seems extremely small. In Kazakhstan, with about half the population (but where the political situation admittedly was different), some 40,000 households were dekulakized, while another 15,000 fled or "self-dekulakized." B. A. Tulepbaev, *Torzhestvo Leninskikh idei sotsialisticheskogo preobrazovaniia selskogo khoziaistva v Srednei Azii i Kazakhstane* (Moscow, 1971), p. 199.

74. Scott, *Behind*, p. 281; GARF, f. 7952, op. 5, d. 306, l. 14.

75. Soviet historians ritualistically praise the great number of nationalities present at Magnitostroi, with some sources claiming thirty or even forty (without providing detailed data). For example, Galiguzov and Churillin, *Flagman*, p. 28. Similar vague assertions can be found in contemporary pamphlets and propaganda literature.

76. A. Zverev, *Na stroike giganta* (Sverdlovsk, 1931), p. 78.

77. *MR*, 2 November 1936. It is highly likely that they were forcibly brought in. In one memoir the Kazakhs are called "special resettlers," as were the dekulakized. GARF, f. 7952, op. 5, d. 304, l. 5. There was also a sizable contingent of Kazakhs at Kuznetsk, an even greater distance from Kazakhstan. Frankfurt, *Men and Steel*, pp. 136–39.

78. Another chance piece of evidence indicates that as of May 1930, there were only 500 *natsmen* (*natsionalnoe menshinstvo*) workers at Magnitostroi, but that by July 1931 there were 11,000 (out of 65,000). GARF, f. 7952, op. 5, d. 384, l. 324; and *MR*, 10 July 1931. Reflecting the presence of sizable groups of such nationals, the local newspaper for a while was issued in a Bashkir-Tatar (1931–35) and a Kazakh (1934–36) edition. One source indicates that the Tatar-Bashkir edition had a *tirazh* of 3,000 copies (it was apparently also made available outside Magnitogorsk). Eliseeva, "Borba za kadry," pp. 223–24. Reductions over time in the number of a particular nationality within the aggregate *natsmen* population cannot be excluded, although the discontinuation of the non-Russian versions of the local newspaper can be explained by the fact that the Tatars learned Russian while the Kazakh edition was absorbed by a national newspaper.

79. P. N. Stepanov, *Uralskaia oblast* (Moscow, 1928), p. 36.

80. Ihor Stebelsky, "Ukrainian Peasant Colonization East of the Urals, 1896–1914," *Soviet Geography: Review and Translation* 25, no. 9 (November 1984): 681–94.

81. The recollections of G. M. Glushkov, a Komsomol mobilized to Magnitostroi, quoted in *Iunost Magnitki*, p. 59.

82. *Profsoiuznaia perepis 1932–33 gg.* (Moscow, 1934), pp. 75, 98–99. The

percentage of peasants in ferrous metallurgy for the USSR as a whole was given as 43.6.

83. Eliseeva, "Iz istorii proektirovanii," p. 147.

84. *MR*, 6 March 1932.

85. *Stroitelstvo i ekspluatatsiia*, p. 82. Impressionistic accounts unanimously agree that youths were everywhere in evidence. "There was not one person in the barrack over 35 years old, and not many over 25," according to John Scott. "Magnitogorsk was built by young people." John Scott, "'Magnetic City,' Core of Valiant Russia's Industrial Might," *National Geographic* 83, no. 5 (1934): 546.

86. According to the January 1931 census, of the 70,386 people found to be at the site, only 27,840, or around 35 percent, were women (this included the population of the city proper and the adjacent villages, where more than 11,000 women were recorded and the ratio of men to women was one to one). MFGAChO, f. 16, op. 1, d. 5, l. 13. Data for 1932, contained in a statistical report sent to the center, show a population at Magnitostroi of 155,000, of whom 71,300, or 46 percent, were women. Data for 1935 show a population of 204,234, 101,444 of whom (almost half) were women. These were called "working" figures; other, conflicting numbers are given elsewhere in the same document. MFGAChO, f. 16, op. 1, d. 34, l. 2; and d. 40, l. 53. According to official sources, the number of women workers reached 5,000 in December 1931, by which time there were some 40,000 working men. By 1941 women workers totaled 8,311, almost 30 percent of the labor force. As reported in *Tvorcheskaia deiatelnost rabochego klassa Magnitki* (Magnitogorsk, 1967), p. 28, citing MFGAChO, f. 99, op. 10, d. 1119, l. 1; see also *Magnitostroi v tsifrakh*, p. 270.

87. On this point, in addition to Panfilova, *Formirovanie*, see the work of Rashin, Goltsman, and many others, summarized and discussed in John Barber, "The Composition of the Soviet Working Class, 1928–1941," unpublished paper, Centre for Russian and East European Studies, Birmingham, 1978.

88. Eliseeva, "Borba za kadry," p. 210.

89. Eliseeva, "Iz istorii proektirovanii," p. 145.

90. Serzhantov, "KPSS—Vdokhnovitel," pp. 108, 200.

91. Ibid., p. 204.

92. V. Bulgakov, *Za obraztsovoe kultobsluzhivanie novostroek: Ocherki po kultrabote v Magnitogorske* (Moscow, 1932), p. 33.

93. The journalist Semen Nariniani offered an analogy to understand the maturation of workers: "childhood"—earth moving, when they are still people of the land; then "adolescence"—cement work, when they are already former people of the land; and finally "youth"—steel assembly, when they have become people of the future. Nariniani, *Doroga v sovershennoletie* (Moscow, 1934), p. 22.

94. Eliseeva, "Borba za kadry," p. 221.

95. Ibid., p. 226.

96. Serzhantov, "KPSS—Vdokhnovitel," p. 209, citing MFGAChO, f. 99, op. 9, d. 18, l. 31. Experience was a good teacher, but as John Scott wrote, "obviously many of the [unskilled] laborers had to do the work of skilled workers. The result was that inexperienced riggers fell and untrained brick layers laid walls that did not stand." These were also "new men." Scott, *Behind*, p. 73.

97. Eliseeva, "Borba za kadry," p. 233.

98. E. Korin, *Na novykh putiakh* (Sverdlovsk-Moscow, 1931), p. 14.

99. GARF, f. 7952, op. 5, d. 309, ll. 88–89. See the study by David Hoffman, "Urbanization and Social Change during Soviet Industrialization: In-Migration to Moscow, 1929–1937," Ph.D. dissertation, Columbia University, 1990. Hoffman demonstrates that during the first Five-Year Plan artels were widespread and argues further that they persisted for years and continued to influence worker attitudes and organization. While the former point seems indisputable, the latter point needs to be assessed against the background of the political confrontation that the artels' existence brought on.

100. Two years later, in July 1933, one-quarter of all construction workers were still not being paid individually. *Stroitelstvo i ekspluatatsiia*, p. 83.

101. GARF, f. 7952, op. 5, d. 309, l. 140.

102. By June 1931, what had been the site's 850 artels had "become" 530 brigades. Antipova and Shkolnik, "Iz istorii," p. 37. See also the recollections of former Komsomol A. Grebenishchenko, as cited in A. P. Orlova, "Rol komsomola v organizatsii i razvitii massogo sorevnovaniia na stroitelstve Magnitogorskogo metallurgicheskogo kombinata (1929–1933 gg.)," in *Iz istorii KPSS za pobedu sotsialistichekoi revoliutsii i postroenie kommunisticheskogo obshchestva* (Moscow, 1971), vyp. 2, pp. 161–62.

103. Membership in the Urals Komsomol increased from 132,000 in 1929 to 248,000 in 1932. *Istoriia Urala*, p. 278.

104. Orlova, "Rol komsomola," pp. 159–60, citing PAChO, f. 525, op. 12, d. 679, l. 167; and f. 1101, op. 1, d. 16, l. 50.

105. Valentin Zuikov, "Komsomol na stroitelstve i osvoenii Magnitogorskogo metallurgicheskogo kombinata imeni Stalina (1929–1933 gg.)," candidate's dissertation, Sverdlovsk, 1950.

106. T. N. Reshetko, "*Komsomolskaia pravda* na Magnitostroe: Iz istorii Komsomola strany na stroitelstve Magnitogorskogo metallicheskogo kombinata," in *Deiatelnost KPSS po sozdaniiu materialno-tekhnicheskoi bazy kommunizma (po materialam Urala)* (Cheliabinsk, 1976), vyp. 10, pp. 131–32.

107. Gugel, "Vospominaniia," p. 326. The heroic role of the Komsomol in "socialist construction" has been mythologized in several films, such as the 1943 "Komsomoltsy" (TsGAKFD 1–9689). It would seem that the trade unions also experienced rapid growth at Magnitostroi, but, curiously, not a single source contains statistics on trade union membership or exalts the role played by them.

108. There was an uproar over the dam's design. The original "Soviet" design for an earthen dam, supposedly better able to withstand the low temperatures, was scrapped in favor of the proposal by McKee, which advised building a concrete dam like the ones in Minnesota (a cold-weather region). The fight between the American and "Soviet" designs, which took the form of a debate over the technical merits of each plan, became a matter of pride, as Soviet "specialists" resented having to accede to the greater expertise and experience of the American specialists. It took numerous telegrams and ultimatums from Moscow to get the authorities at Magnitostroi to follow the American design. Ironically, the so-called Soviet design, for which the local authorities lobbied, was the work of one Vaida, who, as it turned out, was not a Soviet but a Hungarian enthusiast, brought to Magnitostroi from Dneprostroi. Vaida was later arrested and sent to the great Gulag dam project Be-

lomorstroi, where he finally got the chance to supervise construction of an earthen dam. GARF, f. 7952, op. 5, d. 336, ll. 40–42, 60; d. 402, l. 10. The Ural River, which originates in the swamps of the southern half of the mountain range, winds its way through the steppes and desert, emptying into the Caspian Sea.

109. Korolkov, "Borba KPSS za sozdanie," citing PAChO, f. 349, op. 3, sv. 2, d. 6, l. 170.

110. Nariniani, *Na stroike*, pp. 21–24; Galiguzov and Churillin, *Flagman*, pp. 34–35.

111. Korin, *Na novykh*, pp. 54–5.

112. Baranov, *Magnitogorskaia plotina*, pp. 11–36.

113. Nariniani, *Na stroike*, p. 22.

114. Korin, *Na novykh*, p. 51.

115. Baranov, *Magnitogorskaia plotina*, p. 22.

116. Korolkov, "Borba KPSS za sozdanie," p. 131.

117. As workers noted, the construction had been made a political test of allegiance, and there was no avoiding the political implications of one's actions. GARF, f. 7952, op. 5, d. 366, ll. 20–21.

118. The recollections of A. Grebenishchenko, as quoted in Orlova, "Rol komsomola," p. 161, from *MR*, 27 April 1966.

119. Baranov, *Magnitogorskaia plotina*, pp. 31–32.

120. Bulgakov, *Za obraztsovoe*, p. 17.

121. Gugel, "Vospominaniia," p. 322.

122. Korin, *Na novykh*, p. 52.

123. RGAE, f. 4086, op. 2, d. 42, l. 5.

124. GARF, f. 7952, op. 5, d. 412, ll. 6 ff.

125. Part of the reason may have been that in early 1934, dam construction was given over to the labor colony. *Borba za metall*, 5 January 1934. According to internal factory documents, even after having been officially completed in 1938, the second dam suffered what were called *nedodelki* ("unfinished sections"). MFGAChO, f. 99, op. 10, d. 1096, l. 205.

126. The number of shock workers was as follows:

February 1930	1,090
September 1930	1,635
October 1930	6,064
January 1931	10,000
January 1932	18,927

The total number of workers in January 1931 was 18,865; in January 1932, 32,666. Orlova, "Rol komsomola," pp. 164–65, citing PAChO, f. 1101, op. 1, d. 17, l. 38; *Stroitelstvo i ekspluatatsiia*, p. 82.

127. Here are the purported words of the young shock worker, Viktor Kalmykov: "Inside something burns, something you can't express in words. For example, our right bank is engaged in competition with the left. I always go on over there to have a look, how're things with them. I look over at the shore and I see Levitskii. . . . That little Levitskii is bypassing us again. So what. Me and the boys just go at it that much harder." As quoted in Korin, *Na novykh*, pp. 55–56.

128. Gugel, "Vospominaniia," p. 32. This theme was given wide expression in

pamphlets and newspapers, eventually becoming a shibboleth of Soviet historiography. Ivan Kabakov, the Urals obkom first secretary who visited Magnitogorsk many times, was said to have related the following story from the early 1930s: "In one of the barracks I was conversing with a Komsomol. I asked, 'How is it living here?' The young man answered, 'Well, what do you want? Difficulties abound, sometimes quite grave. But we are not depressed. We are bringing a factory into being, then we will live better. . . . ' How much energy they had. How much enthusiasm! They lived life as builders of Magnitka. Magnitka became their dream, the substance of their lives." As quoted in Vasilii Romanov, *Ivan Kabakov* (Sverdlovsk, 1965), pp. 65–66. In 1934, the Urals oblast was split in three, and Kabakov, after whom the Magnitogorsk mine was (temporarily) named, became party secretary of the Sverdlovsk oblast. Magnitogorsk was included in the newly formed Cheliabinsk oblast.

129. Nariniani, *Doroga*. With the storming and the socialist competition on the dam project, Soviet historians subsequently wrote, "the authority of the party soared." Antipova and Shkolnik, "Iz istorii," p. 37. The relentless pressure and great efforts of the press seemed to indicate a longing for legitimation. To be sure, there was never a question of an alternative form of government, but even indifference seemed to scare the leadership.

130. Petrov, *Magnitka*, pp. 63–64.

131. Scott, "'Magnetic City,'" p. 544. Scott wrote that Magnitogorsk was built "with a mass heroism seldom paralleled in History." Scott, *Behind*, pp. 91–92.

132. Korin, *Na novykh*, p. 61.

133. Nariniani, *Na stroike*, pp. 57–58. Leon Banks, an American engineer who worked briefly in Magnitogorsk during the early 1930s, did not deny the existence of enthusiasm, but was circumspect in assessing its scope. "A certain percentage were fanatically and faithfully endeavoring to do all they could for the success of the Five-Year Plan," Banks wrote. "The remainder, the overwhelming majority, were passive, indifferent, inefficient, and mainly refrained from doing anything that could be construed as counterrevolutionary. . . . The greatest resourcefulness observed was in the attempt to secure food or housing." "American Engineers in Russia," Hoover Institution Archives, box 2.

134. In the spring of 1932 it was rumored that a human finger had been found in a meat pie (*pirozhok*). This was followed by "reports" that one person had bought two kilos of meat at the market and that a doctor had verified they were human flesh. Then word went around that all those who were dealing in human meat would be shot at the market on a particular evening. According to one eyewitness, despite the protestations and pleas of the authorities, at 7 P.M. many left work and went to the market to see the "executions." A short time later, while riding on a train outside Magnitogorsk, a Magnitogorsk inhabitant overheard three men who claimed not merely that human flesh was on sale in Magnitogorsk, but that they themselves had purchased it. "I fulfilled my duty in the struggle for the general line of the party," he piously claimed. "I turned them in to the GPU at the station, and they arrested them right out of the railroad car." GARF, f. 7952, op. 5, d. 319, ll. 35–36. This rumor seems to have begun as a story that someone was going to "cut up" all Tatars and Bashkirs. The rumor is mentioned in the memoirs

of several others; for example, in ibid., d. 305, l. 216. In Kuznetsk there were also rumors that Kazakhs ate human flesh. Frankfurt, *Men and Steel*, p. 137.

135. The first "counterrevolutionary group" in Magnitogorsk was "unmasked" in the office of communications. The evidence cited of counterrevolutionary activity was far from unequivocal—20,000 undistributed newspapers bundled up on the floor along with an unspecified number of undelivered letters—but the cries of danger were not. *Rabochaia gazeta*, 26 January 1931; Serzhantov, "KPSS—Vdokhnovitel," p. 261, and Eliseeva, "Borba za kadry," p. 215. Another instance of counterrevolutionary activity supposedly took place at the brick factory, one of the first enterprises on which construction began at the site, where in 1930 there were allegedly "leaflets" being printed that read: "How long are we to endure Bolshevik power?" and "The GPU is our enemy. Leave the job." GARF, f. 7952, op. 5, d. 308, l. 22. The problems at the brick factory were linked to the Industrial party trial in November–December 1930. Vitalii Gasselblat, the chief engineer for Magnitostroi, was accused of membership in the fictitious party and arrested, charged among other things with responsibility for the many fires occurring at the site. He died in a camp in the Pechora coal basin in January 1932, at the age of fifty-two. *MR*, 29 November 1988. Another prerevolutionary specialist working in Magnitogorsk, Vasilii Vorobev, received a six-year sentence in the Industrial party trial. Shortly thereafter, he hung himself in the bathroom with a belt. GARF, f. 7952, op. 5, d. 312, l. 84; d. 385, ll. 127–28; d. 381, l. 30; and d. 342, ll. 9, 35. A third case of counterrevolution uncovered in March 1931 involved a group of Komsomols who allegedly perpetrated "diversionary acts," such as handing out leaflets and agitating among newly arriving youth about the construction site's problems. *Magnitogorskii komsomolets*, 21 March 1931; Zverev, *Na stroike giganta*, p. 67; Antipova and Shkolnik, "Iz istorii," pp. 49–50.

136. Here, for example, is how entrances to the Komsomol were sworn: "Official notice of a young brigade of assembly workers. Having heard the report and the uncovering of a counterrevolutionary group at Magnitostroi, which was trying to foil our construction, in answer we ask to be received into the ranks of the Komsomol, in order, under the leadership of the party, to fight for socialism." Zuikov, "Komsomol," p. 197, citing Arkhiv Magnitogorskogo GK VLKSM, d. 50, l. 13.

137. *Uralskii rabochii*, 12 February 1933.

138. A. F. Khavin, *Karaganda—Tretia ugolnaia baza SSSR* (Moscow, 1951), pp. 81–82. At the beginning of 1931, the population at Karaganda was around 5,000.

139. *Kuzbass: Rezultaty perepisi gorodskogo naseleniia 1931 g.* (Novosibirsk, 1931), p. viii.

140. In 1928–29, according to then Urals oblast Party Secretary Shvernik, 300,000 people came to industrial enterprises in the Urals and another 260,000 left. As cited in V. V. Feldman, "O nekotorykh voprosakh formirovaniia sotsialisticheskogo rabochego klassa Urala," *Iz istorii rabochego klassa Urala: Sbornik statei* (Perm, 1961), pp. 306–19, citing GARF, f. 5451, op. 14, d. 15, l. 8.

141. Reprinted in Polonskii, *Magnitka zovet*, p. 23.

142. Z. Chagan, *U podnozhia Magnitnoi gory* (Moscow-Leningrad, 1930), p. 7.

143. It is important to emphasize that these figures are for Magnitostroi and

not for the parallel organization, Koksostroi. Since Koksostroi had approximately 4,000 workers, at a rate of ten times the total, we could increase the numbers of those who came another 35 to 40,000. The mine also had a separate administration, and so its workers, a thousand or so, were not included. Nor are so-called cadre workers included, that is, those workers who were relatively skilled and had been sent on order by other factories. Alternative figures are given in *Magnitostroi v tsifrakh*, pp. 242–43; and *Stroitelstvo i ekspluatatsiia*, p. 83. Yet another set of data from oblast archives (GAChO, f. 1373, op. 1, d. 69, l. 7) are given in Eliseeva, "Iz istorii proektirovanii," p. 147. Despite the differences in these figures, the order of magnitude remains constant throughout.

144. GARF, f. 7952, op. 5, d. 342, l. 10.

145. Ibid., d. 300, l. 50; and d. 311, l. 36.

146. *Magnitostroi v tsifrakh*, pp. 250–51. Slightly different figures are given in RGAE, f. 4086, op. 2, d. 119, ll. 25–26: total registered exit, 30,755; less than six months on site, 27,914. The differences are minuscule.

147. RGAE, f. 4086, op. 2, d. 119, ll. 21–22.

148. Ibid., ll. 25, 26. For the total white-collar employees: *Magnitostroi: Informatsionnyi biulleten*, 1931, no. 2, p. 43.

149. *Magnitostroi v tsifrakh*, pp. 250–51.

150. *Magnitostroi*, 1931, nos. 9–12.

151. *Magnitostroi v tsifrakh*, pp. 250–51.

152. Eliseeva, "O sposobakh," p. 70.

153. GARF, f. 7952, op. 5, d. 309, l. 38; and d. 300, l. 44. A third memoir says that "interruptions in supply began in the fall of 1932." Ibid., d. 312, ll. 296–97.

154. GARF, f. 7952, op. 5, d. 301, l. 69.

155. *Magnitogorskii komsomolets*, 10 January 1932.

156. *MR*, 20 January 1934.

157. GARF, f. 7952, op. 5, d. 309, l. 39.

158. Ordzhonikidze, *Stati i rechi*, vol. 2, pp. 411–12; and Lewin, *The Making of the Soviet System*, pp. 221–22. Compare the accumulated misery at train stations in the Donbas, where famine still raged: V. Budrov, "U vorot Donbassa," *Za industrializatsiiu*, 2 February 1933.

159. Eliseeva, "O sposobakh," p. 58, citing GARF, f. 7952, op. 5, d. 72, ll. 36, 29.

160. Serzhantov, "KPSS—Vdokhnovitel," p. 184.

161. GARF, f. 7952, op. 5, d. 361, l. 28.

162. Ibid., d. 304, l. 11.

163. Ibid., d. 309, l. 45. Workers were also given money to purchase cows, which around this time cost just under 2,000 rubles. Ibid., d. 315, l. 64.

164. Korolkov, "Borba KPSS za sozdanie," pp. 139–40.

165. GARF, f. 7952, op. 5, d. 307, l. 145.

166. *MR*, 12 and 15 February 1933.

167. *MR*, 17 February 1933.

168. According to one newspaper report, in 1934, 35,262 three-year passports were issued, while 34,678 five-year and 14,320 three-year passports were issued the following year. But there is no indication of what percentage of the total number these figures represented. *MR*, 21 October 1936.

169. Orlova, "Rol komsomola," pp. 153–72, citing PAChO, f. 234, op. 1, d. 243, l. 208. In a speech a few months later, Beso Lominadze asserted that 52,000 people without the right to a passport were deported (*vyslany*) from Magnitogorsk during the passport campaign. *MR*, 15 January 1934. This figure was repeated (without reference) in an unpublished manuscript by V. Shklovskii, "Poezdka v Magnitogorsk." It is clearly an exaggeration. GARF, f. 7952, op. 5, d. 380, l. 4.

170. For example, Narpit, the city food trust, as of 1 March 1933 had 4,360 employees, 3,812 of whom presented themselves for a passport (meaning that 548 people, around 12.5 percent, simply fled). Passports good for three years were issued to 657 people; for one year, to 1,495; and for three months, to 1,566. Another ninety or so Narpit employees were denied passports, of whom twenty had their files turned over to the courts for further investigation. It should be emphasized that more than one-third of Narpit's employees who received passports faced reexamination after only three months, and more than three-quarters after one year or less. Narpit was notorious as a supposed refuge for unsavory elements, but although more passports of greater duration were issued in other organizations, the bulk of the city's population still had to be reissued passports within only three years. And complaints or denunciations that needed to be checked out during that interval could pile up. GARF, f. 7952, op. 5, d. 294, ll. 39–42.

171. *MR*, 11 April 1936.

172. Of course, the authorities claimed just the opposite. Vladimir Tiurin, for example, was said to have used false papers, obtained from a village soviet to disguise the fact that he was the son of a kulak so he could enter the Red Army. When he saw how "thoroughly everyone was checked," according to the city newspaper, Tiurin gave himself in. He was tried, and received a sentence of three years. *MR*, 9 March 1936.

173. This was particularly true in the construction industry. "Some leaders of enterprises and organizations hire people who have not yet been registered to live in Magnitogorsk, or have been registered temporarily," wrote the city newspaper. "Sometimes people who are not supposed to be permitted residency in Magnitogorsk are supplied with 'official invitations' and other similar 'documents.'" The newspaper singled out the chief of cadres for heating construction, Slavutskii, who was fined and to be brought to trial. Someone else, not named, was also fined. *MR*, 16 February 1938. See also GARF, f. 7952, op. 5, d. 366, l. 15.

174. *MR*, 9 August 1936.

175. *MR*, 6 March 1936. A decree of 27 December 1932 equated the crime of forging of passport applications with counterfeiting money. *Sobranie zakonov i rasporiazhenii*, 1932, no. 84, excerpted in *Sbornik dokumentov po istorii ugolovnogo zakonodatelstva SSSR i RSFSR*, ed. Ivan Goliakov (Moscow, 1953), pp. 337–38.

176. *MR*, 27 January 1938. And this process did not happen immediately, judging by the complaints made by officials that managers inside the shops, where the photographing was to take place, were not enforcing compliance. MFGAChO, f. 10, op. 10, d. 1096, l. 259.

177. *MR*, 9 May 1936.

178. *MR*, 6 April 1936.

179. *MR*, 16 May 1936.

180. Ivan Kozints, for example, wrote himself out a diploma from the Kharkov Technical Institute and passed himself off as an engineer (which in those days [1931] was not overly difficult). He worked in that capacity at various factories, ending up as an engineer in the Mining Administration at Magnitogorsk, until he was "unmasked." Significantly, he also claimed to have served in the Red Army. *MR*, 20 March 1931.

181. *MR*, 16 March 1936.

182. For example, one woman who had allegedly stolen the daily receipts from a dining hall and fled Magnitogorsk turned up in the city again and was nailed by the militia during the mandatory *propiska*. *MR*, 20 November 1936. In 1936 the militia initiated sixteen criminal investigations for violations of the passport regime. Magnitogorsk procuracy: Archival file "Nariad 34/C. [Untitled] 1936 g.," l. 22.

183. *MR*, 26 January 1936.

184. *MR*, 21 October 1936. At first the longest duration passport had been three years. In 1935, a five-year passport was introduced.

185. *MR*, 16 February 1938.

186. In 1933, as the passport system was being introduced, 32,852 people came to Magnitogorsk and another 21,421 left. During 1934, the first full year of operation of the passport system, 53,369 people arrived in Magnitogorsk, and 33,333 left—a net gain of over 20,000 people. MFGAChO, f. 16, op. 1, d. 42, l. 92. In 1935, 29,900 arrived and 21,020 left; in 1937, 24,501 arrived and 25,564 left. In the first six months of 1938 (no yearly data were available), there were 7,663 registered arrivals and 10,783 departures, and in 1939, the figures were 20,248 and 19,673, respectively. Ibid., d. 72, ll. 21, 45; d. 73, l. 21,; and d. 102, ll. 2–53. Different figures are given in RGAE, f. 4086, op. 2, d. 933, l. 22. The main point is that movement persisted after the passport campaign; whatever the precise figures, the number of people entering or leaving the city was in the tens of thousands. Still, caution seems advised by the discrepancy in the numbers reported by officials as well as by indications that the registration system (particularly in the case of departures) may not have been perfect. Magnitogorsk statisticians conducted a survey of two buildings to ascertain the accuracy of the migration data. In one building with 219 registered residents (in 32 apartments), only 166 people were discovered to be residing there. Sixty-seven people had left the city without registering their departure and another 14 people were living in the unit without having registered (presumably recently born children). In the other building surveyed, of the 217 registered residents, all but one was actually in residence, and no one was living there without registration. Unfortunately, the report of the survey made no indication of the representativeness of the buildings and hence the significance of the findings. MFGAChO, f. 16, op. 1, d. 72, l. 31.

187. *MR*, 1 January 1936. Whereas during the first nine months of 1936 "several thousand" workers (not tens of thousands) left the construction trust, in the last four months of 1937, only around 1,500 construction workers were lost. *MR*, 18 December 1936 and 25 January 1938. There seems to have been a constant shortage of construction workers, a problem made more acute toward the end of the decade when large-scale construction was renewed. In early 1940 it was reported

that 1,000 Belorussian families had been imported to Magnitogorsk, with another 1,000 to come later. Ibid., 1 and 5 January 1940.

188. This is reflected in the language used by management officials, for example MFGAChO, f. 16, op. 1, d. 42, l. 62. Compare the data published for Kharkov, whose population between the censuses of 1926 and 1939 doubled (as did that of Moscow and Leningrad) in M. V. Kurman and I. V. Lebedinskii, *Naselenie bolshogo sotsialisticheskogo goroda* (Moscow, 1968), pp. 27, 64.

189. Horace Davis, "Company Towns," *International Encyclopedia of the Social Sciences*, vol. 4 (New York: Macmillan, 1931), pp. 119–23. This aim extended well beyond the shop floor, and was not limited to considerations of maximizing profit. In the industrial town of Bochum during the late nineteenth century, to take one example, one historian has demonstrated that employers spent considerable time and energy strategizing about how best to exercise social control over "their" labor force, for the supposed moral benefit of the workers. Crew, *Town in the Ruhr*, ch. 4.

190. John Reps, *The Making of Urban America: A History of City Planning in the United States* (Princeton: Princeton University Press 1965), p. 436.

CHAPTER 3. THE IDIOCY OF URBAN LIFE

1. My translation from the 1979 Russian edition published in Cheliabinsk, pp. 134–35.

2. Semen Nariniani, "Kak eto bylo," in *Slavnye traditsii: Sbornik dokumentov, ocherkov, vospominanii,* 2d ed., Moscow, 1960, pp. 136–42; *Koordinaty podviga* (Cheliabinsk, 1968), pp. 146–47. By the late 1930s, the train trip to Moscow usually took around four days. Nariniani, the Magnitogorsk correspondent for *Komsomolskaia pravda* who rode around Magnitogorsk on a horse whom he called "Katia," was said to speak about himself in the third person. He often told the story of how upon arrival at the site he had been assigned a "future room in a future barracks." He actually lived relatively comfortably in the Central Hotel. *Slovo o Magnitke,* pp. 70–71.

3. GARF, f. 7952, op. 5, d. 385, l. 1.

4. It bears keeping in mind that when Magnitogorsk was constructed, city planning was still a relatively new notion. As one historian of city planning has written, "the terms *urbanización, urbanisme,* town-planning, *Städtebau,* were formulated for the first time during the second half of the nineteenth century." Françoise Choay, *The Modern City: Planning in the Nineteenth Century* (New York: Braziller, 1969), p. 7.

5. See the analysis by Andrew Bond of the Arctic city of Norilsk, founded in 1935 (for nickel mining and processing). Bond argues "that the Soviets embarked upon the settlement of the territory with little specific knowledge of its environmental constraints, and with few firm goals other than boosting mineral production to a high level as soon as possible." He characterizes Soviet development as a combination of three approaches: a) bootstrapping, defined as making low-budget improvements derived from experience (rather than large capital outlays) and making-do with resources "leftover" after establishing industrial production; b) trial

and error; and c) crisis management, or triage. These seem to be three ways of saying the same thing, but the point is well taken. Bond, "Norilsk: Profile of a Soviet Arctic Development Project," Ph.D. dissertation, University of Wisconsin, Milwaukee, 1983. The nickel plant at Norilsk, a Gulag enterprise under the jurisdiction of the NKVD, today carries the name of Magnitogorsk's Avraamii Zaveniagin, who served as its director from 1938 to 1941 before going on to direct strategic mineral operations for all of Gulag. Elfimov, *Marshal industrii*, pp. 134–35. Back in December 1934, during a special reception for "metallurgists" held at the Kremlin, Zaveniagin, speaking in his capacity as director of Magnitogorsk, had told the assembled notables, most of whom worked in the European part of the Soviet Union, that "work in a new economic region of the country is immeasurably more interesting." Avraamii Zaveniagin, "Magnitogorskii zavod im. Stalina," *Otvet metallurgov tovarishchu Stalinu* (Moscow, 1936), pp. 72–91.

6. Unraveling the story of the attempt to design and build the city of Magnitogorsk presents some challenges. Although there are three published accounts by Soviet scholars on the planning and architecture of Magnitogorsk, they deal primarily with the postwar period, for reasons addressed in the main text. (They are Z. N. Nesterova, *Magnitogorsk* [Moscow, 1951]; L. O. Bumazhnyi and M. G. Morozov, *Magnitogorsk* [Moscow, 1958]; and V. I. Kazarinova and V. I. Pavlichenkov, *Magnitogorsk: Opyt sovetskoi arkhitektury* [Moscow, 1961], which is the most substantial and even has a few footnotes.) Moreover, important archives—those of the Ministry of Municipal Economy (Minkomkhoz) and those of the Magnitogorsk Urban Design Department—remain inaccessible, if only for technical reasons (they are not designed to receive researchers). Fortunately, however, many key details of the story are contained in one of the best unpublished manuscripts on Magnitogorsk in the archival collection Istoriia fabrik i zavodov (GARF, f. 7952, op. 5, d. 361, ll. 1–34). Entitled "Stroitelstvo goroda," the manuscript is signed I. Ivich, a pseudonym for Ignatiem Ignatievich Vernshtein (see ibid., d. 330, l. 43). As with all the unpublished manuscripts contained in this collection there are several variants, for example d. 362, 363, 365, and 366; I have used the version which, based upon editorial changes, seems to be the last. Written as events were still unfolding—though undated, it was clearly written between 1934 and 1936—Vernshtein's splendid essay offers the advantages of a lively firsthand memoir that also displays a terrific sense of humor. But it remained unpublished, and in fact there are some inaccuracies regarding dates and other matters. Accordingly, the manuscript is used with caution and, when possible, in conjunction with corroborating materials, especially contemporary newspapers and pamphlets and foreigners' accounts. A special issue of *Arkhitektura SSSR* in 1979 devoted to Magnitogorsk was also helpful, as were discussions in 1987 with Magnitogorsk's then chief architect, Vilii Bogun.

7. Lewin, *The Making of the Soviet System*, pp. 220, 258–85, 298–300.

8. As Boris Ruchev, the poet of Magnitogorsk (who also spent many years in the Kolyma), proclaimed in an oft-quoted passage from one of his poems, the new city would be "without churches, without pubs, and without prisons." Ruchev, *Sobranie sochinenii v dvukh tomakh*, vol. 2 (Cheliabinsk, 1979), pp. 36–46. Similar hopes can be found in the pamphlet literature, e.g., V. P. Polonskii, *Magnitostroi* (Moscow, 1931), pp. 42–3.

9. GARF, f. 7952, op. 5, d. 361, l. 7.

10. There seems to have been not two, but several competitions, but the sources are unclear. *Stroitelnaia promyshlennost*, 1930, no. 3, pp. 195–99, carries an announcement for what appears to be a different contest, for which there was no first-place winner. A different competition was announced by the trade union council, VTsSPS, in December 1929 for an "industrialnyi gorod-poselok" of 50,000 people. It is not clear if this competition took place. GARF, f. 5451, op. 13, d. 225, l. 3.

11. GARF, f. 7952, op. 5, d. 361, l. 12.

12. GASO, f. 241, op. 1, d. 1320, ll. 14–19; and GARF, f. 7952, op. 5, d. 160, l. 24. Neither of these files contains the actual designs. Only one plan, that of V. G. Davidovich (not even the winning one), was published in the Magnitogorsk newspaper, "O proekte goroda Magnitogorska," *MR*, 28–30 October 1930. Already on 2 October 1929, Chernyshev made a presentation in Moscow on a proposal for Magnitogorsk; a transcript of his presentation and the subsequent discussion reveal a stark primitiveness in the understanding of what such an undertaking involved. At a follow-up meeting attended by representatives from a range of state institutions (but dominated by Leonid Sabsovich), discussion focused on how planners needed to mold and shape social realities through the sizes and shapes of buildings, and to arrange buildings to maximize efficient childrearing and ensure health. Controversy centered around the question of whether to keep family units together. To support his argument for collectivized living, Sabsovich cited the *Communist Manifesto*. GARF, f. 7952, op. 5, d. 179 passim; and d. 180, ll. 15–51. An analysis of the issue of collectivity can be found in chapter 4.

13. Kazarinova and Pavlichenkov, *Magnitogorsk*, p. 17.

14. GARF, f. 7952, op. 5, d. 361, ll. 7–8.

15. With copious funding, public building organizations, and a large labor pool, the city of Frankfurt began in 1925 what has been hailed as "one of the most remarkable city planning experiments in the twentieth century." John R. Mullin, "City Planning in Frankfurt, Germany, 1925–1932: A Study in Practical Utopianism," *Journal of Urban History* 4, no. 1 (November 1977): 3.

16. By the early 1930s, some 15,000 new dwelling units had been completed. If nothing else, May's work helped alleviate the housing shortage. But more than that, "he viewed his assignment as extending beyond the actual planning and development of the physical city," as one admiring historian biographer has written. "The plans and programs created under his direction were to serve as stimulants in support of creating a new social milieu," as his magazine, *Das neue Frankfurt*, suggested. Justus Bükschmitt, *Ernst May* (Stuttgart, 1963), p. 5.

17. Bükschmitt, *Ernst May*, p. 59.

18. Hans Schmidt, "Die Tätigkeiten deutscher Architekten und Spezialisten des Bauwesens in der Sowjetunion in den Jahren 1930 bis 1937." *Wissenschaftliche Zeitschrift der Humboldt-Universität zu Berlin. Gesellschafts- und Sprachwissenschaftliche Reihe* 16, no. 3 (1967): 383 ff. The group of about twenty, called "May's brigade," was later joined by other German-speaking architects (such as the Swiss-born Schmidt), and also included a Dutchman (Mart Stam), a Hungarian, and some Soviet co-workers. See Walter Schwangenscheidt, *Baukunst und Werkform*, 1956, no. 9, p. 477; and Kurt Junghanns, "Deutsche Architekten in der Sowjetunion während des ersten Fünfjahrplans und des vaterländischen Krieges," *Wissenschaftliche Zeitschrift der Hochschule für Architektur und Bauwesen* 29

(Weimar, 1983), heft 2. A nearly complete list of foreign architects associated with May in the USSR can be found in Milka Bliznakov, "The Realization of Utopia: Western Technology and Soviet Avant-Garde Architecture," in William Brumfield, ed., *Reshaping Russian Architecture: Western Technology, Utopian Dreams* (Washington, D.C.: Woodrow Wilson Center and Cambridge University Press, 1990), pp. 158, 174. See also Hans Blumenfeld, *Life Begins at 65: The Not Entirely Candid Autobiography of a Drifter* (Montreal: Harvest House, 1987), ch. 6.

19. Ernst May, "Sotsgorod," in *Magnitostroi: Informatsionnyi biulleten*, 1931, no. 2, p. 39. According to Bükschmitt, in 1929 May made a preliminary trip to the Soviet Union and conducted negotiations with the Central Communal Bank (Tsekombank) and in January 1930 signed a contract and set off for Moscow (*Ernst May*, p. 59). If this is true, May returned to Frankfurt to do some of the work, for another source indicates that he left for the USSR in September 1930. "Stadtrat Mays Russland Pläne," *Bauwelt*, 1930, no. 36, p. 1156, trans. and published in El Lissitzky, *Russia: An Architecture for World Revolution* (Cambridge, Mass. MIT Press, 1970), pp. 173–75; see also Junghanns, "Deutsche Architekten in der Soviet Union." May's political naiveté (he described himself as "apolitical") can be gauged from his report on the early experiences of his group in *Frankfurter Zeitung*, 30 November 1930, trans. and published as "Ernst May, Moscow: City Building in the USSR," in El Lissitzky, *Russia*, pp. 175–79.

20. Ernst May, "Bekenntnise des Stadtbauers," in *Das neue Russland*, 1930, nos. 5–6, p. 53. As one Swiss architect who also traveled to the USSR wrote, summing up the attitudes of May and his collaborators at the time, "with the West in depression, the Soviet Union looked like the land of the future." Schmidt, "Die Tätigkeiten," p. 383. In the 1960s May recalled that he had had "no hesitation" in accepting the Soviet government's offer. See Ernst May, "Cities of the Future," in Walter Laqueur and Leopold Labedz, eds., *The Future of Communist Society* (New York, 1962), p. 179.

21. Working in various Soviet organizations—1930–32 in Tsekombank, 1932–33 in the Organization for the Standardization of City Design (Standardproekt), and from 1933 the Organization for City Design (Gorstroiproekt)—May also participated in projects for the Stalingrad Tractor Settlement, Nizhnii Tagil, Orsk, Makeevka, Karaganda, Novokuznetsk, and the reconstruction of Moscow. The Magnitogorsk commission turned out to be the largest.

22. GARF, f. 7952, op. 5, d. 361, ll. 8, 11.

23. Bükschmitt, *Ernst May*, pp. 63–64; May, "Cities of the Future," in El Lissitzky, *Russia*, p. 179; Schmidt, "Die Tätigkeiten," p. 386. An illustration of Soria y Mata's concept appeared in the book published in German in 1930 by the Soviet architect El Lissitzky. Nikolai Miliutin, then the recently appointed chair of the study committee on new city construction and a leader among Soviet architects, published a reworking of the linear city concept in 1930, entitled *Problema stroitelstva sotsialisticheskikh gorodov*, translated into English as *Sotsgorod: The Problem of Socialist Cities* (Cambridge, Mass.: MIT Press, 1974). May expressed his approval for the linear city idea in an article that appeared in *Das neue Russland*, 1931, pp. viii–ix, which was translated and published in the expanded English-language edition of El Lissitzky, *Russia*, pp. 188–203, and includes a diagram (p. 193).

24. Kazarinova and Pavlichenkov, *Magnitogorsk*, p. 17; Ernst May, "K proektu generalnogo plana Magnitogorska," *Sovetskaia arkhitektura*, 1933, no. 3, pp. 17–25. A further complication arose when, belatedly, the population target for the proposed city was raised to 80,000 with a long-term perspective of 120,000, a grudging admission that the number of people already massed at the site was a good indication of the city's future population. "Ernst May: From Frankfurt to the New Russia," in El Lissitzky, *Russia*, p. 178.

25. Ivich wrote that Chernyshev "had failed to consider the local relief, so that the magnificent central boulevard of his project would be transformed on the current site into a crooked horn. And in this way the best project turned out to be abstract." Ivich dates the arrival of Chernyshev as July 1930. GARF, f. 7952, op. 5, d. 361, l. 9. Ivich's vignette is confirmed by Frolov, "Gorod Magnitogorsk," *Magnitostroi: Informatsionnyi biulleten*, 1931, nos. 4–5, p. 90. An authoritative source dates the initial arrival of Chernyshev at the site as June 1930, indicating that he was accompanied by a German architect (but not May). *Pravda*, 14 December 1930. Chernyshev's rejection of his own plan, whether in June or July, did not, of course, mean that the authorities would not use it. According to May, however, when confronted with a choice between his project and Chernyshev's, a commission of Sovnarkom chose May's. See "Ernst May, Moscow," pp. 188–203.

26. GARF, f. 7952, op. 5, d. 361, l. 12; Leonid G. Ankudinov, "Trudovoi podvig stroitelei Magnitki," in *Cheliabinskaia oblast za 40 let Sovetskoi vlasti* (Cheliabinsk, 1957), p. 437.

27. So reasoned an on-site engineer familiar with the issues in the spring of 1931, reiterating a widely held view. *Magnitostroi: Informatsionnyi biulleten*, 1931, nos. 4–5, p. 94.

28. As it turned out, the only data on the wind direction in Magnitogorsk initially made available to central planners were observations made several decades earlier at the weather station of a town fifty kilometers away. Ironically, these data on supposed southwesterly winds had been used to argue against the right-bank city on sanitation grounds. With construction of the factory underway and more accurate data "blowing in," and in light of the astronomically greater quantities of smoke, soot, and chemicals that the fully completed factory would emit once it was put into operation, many people began to wonder if the city should not be shifted to the other bank. See Ivich: GARF, f. 7952, op. 5, d. 361, l. 10, whose account is confirmed by Frolov, "Gorod Magnitogorsk," pp. 89–95; and *Magnitostroi: Informatsionnyi biulleten*, 1931, nos. 4–5, pp. 89–95.

29. When the order to relocate the city was received, Mart Stam, the foreign architect in charge of city construction at the site, was called on to defend moving the left-bank city so far away that it would complicate the fundamental goal of easy movement to and from the steel plant. Stam reasoned that the noise of the factory might bother the workers were they to live too close to it; that there was a great number of temporary barracks in the area adjacent to the factory whose removal would strain the already difficult housing situation; and that the incline of Karadyrka hill a few kilometers back from the factory might afford some nice possibilities for recreation. GASO, f. 241, op. 1, d. 1310, l. 135.

30. GARF, f. 7952, op. 5, d. 361, l. 13.

31. Ibid., d. 180, ll. 1–12.

32. In May 1930 a commission of Rabkrin's decided to locate the future city on the left bank. While this decision allowed local officials to lay the first stone ceremoniously, far from settling the question of the city's location, it only heightened the uncertainty, for the Urals oblast planning commission preferred a right-bank variant and drew up some preliminary proposals. Then, on 20 March 1931, Sovnarkom RSFSR, on the basis of a report from its own special commission, decided to rescind the original decision of Rabkrin and relocate the socialist city on the right bank. But immediately after this decision, Sovnarkom USSR sent yet another commission to the site which ruled in favor of the left bank. Sovnarkom RSFSR was in turn encouraged to "rethink" its right-bank recommendation, which it did, supporting the conclusions of its superior. As we shall see, however, this was not the end of the story. *Uralskii rabochii*, 13 February 1931; May, "K proektu," p. 18; GASO, f. 241, op. 2, d. 3066, ll. 29–30; GARF, f. 7952, op. 5, d. 361, ll. 20–21; MFGAChO, f. 10, op. 1, d. 28, ll. 1–2, reprinted in Eliseeva, *Iz istorii*, pp. 223–25.

33. R. Roman, *Krokodil v Magnitostroe: Nedostatki v stroitelstve* (Sverdlovsk, 1931), pp. 35–36.

34. *Sovetskaia arkhitektura*, 1933, no. 3, p. 25. According to one Soviet account, Chernyshev lobbied for the right bank, and it is implied that May advocated the left. See Kazarinova and Pavlichenkov, *Magnitogorsk*, p. 17. A cryptic newspaper article gives an indirect impression of May's preference for the left bank, and May's own presentation of his proposals, published after the decision had been taken, indicates he was comfortable with the selection of the left bank. *MR*, 9 February 1931; *Sovetskaia arkhitektura*, 1933, no. 3, pp. 17–25. That May had favored the left bank was also the impression of the then chief architect for the city of Magnitogorsk, Vilii Bogun, a man familiar with the original planning materials, whom the author interviewed in Magnitogorsk in May 1987. In any case, May reported that the special government commission chose the left bank because this variant meant that workers' housing could be ready roughly at the same time as the startup of the factory, but that it rejected his "layout schema," meaning, apparently, the northern satellite. But, as we have already seen, the southeastern triangle was too small for the whole city, which means that the commission either did not understand May's proposal—which cannot be excluded—or it had decided not to try to house the entire population in the socialist city. *Sovetskaia arkhitektura*, pp. 17–18.

35. Permanent apartment buildings in a "northern satellite" were not built until after the war—and this at the site of the railroad workers' settlement, which turned out to be situated a far greater distance from the original left-bank socialist city than was envisioned in May's drawings.

36. "Ernst May, Moscow," p. 199. May's standardized apartment buildings were called the "INKO A" design. MFGAChO, f. 10, op. 1, d. 4, l. 1.

37. GARF, f. 7952, op. 5, d. 149, ll. 1–4; reprinted in Eliseeva, *Iz istorii*, pp. 219–20.

38. GASO, f. 241, op. 1, d. 1320, ll. 2, 3.

39. GARF, f. 7952, op. 5, d. 361, l. 19.

40. They enlisted Stam to form a "brigade" to reorganize the woodworking. *Magnitogorskii komsomolets*, 5 August 1931.

41. GARF, f. 7952, op. 5, d. 361, l. 19. In 1933, a special decree had to be issued

by the People's Commissar for Heavy Industry to mobilize materials, transport, and workers to install toilets in Magnitogorsk apartment buildings. *MR,* 17 November 1933. But when plans shifted in 1935 and 1936 back to the right-bank variant, work on the left-bank sewage system was halted, and was not rescheduled until 1937. MFGAChO, f. 9, op. 1, d. 152, ll. 27–29.

42. GARF, f. 7952, op. 5, d. 366, l. 30; and d. 361, l. 17. That Molotov and Postyshev sent telegrams regarding the construction and that nothing would have been built without such prodding is confirmed by another source: Ibid., d. 309, l. 35.

43. *MR,* 26 April 1932.

44. The approval of Ordzhonikidze or his deputies, for example, was doggedly sought to build something as simple as a children's nursery not originally specified in the approved plan. And dozens of letters and telegrams went back and forth between the site and Moscow over a request to build an eight-car garage. See GARF, f. 7952, op. 5, d. 160, ll. 120 ff. Other examples could be added.

45. Ibid., d. 361, l. 16.

46. *MR,* 5 April 1931.

47. *MR,* 26 August 1932.

48. GARF, f. 7952, op. 5, d. 361, l. 25.

49. RGAE, f. 4086, op. 2 d. 42, l. 26.

50. *Izvestiia,* 29 March 1933. Back in 1931 May had written, no doubt out of frustration, that "no general plan for Magnitogorsk was possible, because the planning of the industrial plant was done before that of the residential city." *Magnitostroi: Informatsionnyi biulleten,* 1931, nos. 9–12, p. 40.

51. *Magnitogorskii komsomolets,* 10 August 1931, reprinted in Eliseeva, *Iz istorii,* p. 226. An entire settlement of these lattice-wood or "carcass" buildings, as they were sometimes called, was built much more quickly than the stone and brick buildings. Sometimes the designation "socialist city" included this Lattice-Wood Town. Housing data for 1 January 1934, for example, list seventy-eight buildings in the "socialist city," of which twenty-one were in the first superblock and fifty-seven were of lattice wood. MFGAChO, f. 10, op. 1, d. 20, l. 7.

52. Moreover, most of them had just one communal kitchen for as many as eighty families, and the kitchens were located outside the residential buildings. See the report by city Party Secretary Semenov in 1938, as quoted in Eliseeva, *Iz istorii,* p. 250, citing PAChO, f. 241, op. 1, d. 544, ll. 1–4.

53. In Magnitogorsk, virtually everything was built without the proper materials and needed immediate repair. Repairs often needed repair again immediately. And how long repairs took! After having been open for only five years, the famous sound movie theater that was heralded as holding enormous political significance was closed two full years for repairs. In comparison with some other buildings, this was not a long time. *MR,* 26 September 1939.

54. GARF, f. 7952, op. 5, d. 180, ll. 1–12. With his return to his native Germany blocked by the Nazi regime, May went to Africa, working as a farmer and architect in Kenya and Uganda. In 1940 he was interned for two years as an alien in South Africa. After almost two decades in Africa, he returned in 1953 to West Germany. He died in Hamburg in 1970. See Rosemarie Hupfner and Volker Fischer, eds., *Ernst May und das neue Frankfurt, 1925–1930* (Berlin: Ernst und

Sohn, 1986), p. 159. According to the architect Vilii Bogun, interviewed in Magnitogorsk in 1987, May visited Magnitogorsk briefly in the 1960s. Bogun claimed that upon seeing the right-bank city that had been built after the war, May conceded that in retrospect the right-bank variant was obviously the better alternative.

55. D. E. Shibaev, "Za sotsialisticheskii gorod Magnitogorsk," *Sovetskaia arkhitektura*, 1933, no. 3, pp. 25–30. In 1937, criticism of May became rabid. See A. Mostakov, "Bezobraznoe nasledstvo arkhitektura Maia," *Arkhitektura SSSR*, 1937, no. 9, p. 62; and the comments by Anatole Kopp, "Foreign Architects in the Soviet Union during the First Two Five-Year Plans," in Brumfield, *Reshaping*, pp. 179–80, 186–87. One-sided criticism of May, along with inaccurate descriptions of his work in the USSR, continues. See Andrei Ikonnikov, *Russian Architecture of the Soviet Period* (Moscow, 1988), pp. 113–14.

56. GARF, f. 7952, op. 5, d. 361, l. 20.

57. MR, 5 September 1935. In May's defense, it must be remembered that there was as yet no definitive understanding of the socialist city, except that it was somehow to be different from a capitalist city. All that May, or anyone else for that matter, knew was that he had to plan for the whole lives of the people and employ a good deal of communalization, which he had carried out in his own way and true to his principles. After seeing how that principle operated in a situation constrained by the lack of adequate communal facilities and by people's preferences, the Soviet planners retreated and designed for individual kitchens and for apartments of more than one small room—something May clearly could have done if asked. Moreover, the decision to build on the left bank, a decision that Avraamii Zaveniagin would refer to as a "horrible mistake," was, of course, not May's. GARF, f. 7952, op. 5, d. 354, l. 21. In Magnitogorsk May made his share of mistakes, but his efforts were conscientious and, given the conditions in which he was compelled to work, bordered on the heroic. Lazarev of Giprogor admitted as much. MR, 5 April 1931.

58. *Magnitostroi: Informatsionnyi biulleten*, 1931, no. 2. On May's frustrations with the Soviet bureaucracy and gradual disillusionment, see the memoirs of Zara Witkin. Witkin knew May well and wrote a scathing report, on request by the GPU, outlining the architect's reasons for leaving the USSR. Witkin claimed he wrote in his report that May's reasons were fully justified. *An American Engineer*, pp. 232–35.

59. GARF, f. 7952, op. 5, d. 361, l. 28.

60. RTsKhIDNI, f. 85, op. 29, d. 52, ll. 2–4, 11, 13.

61. PAChO, f. 234, op. 1, d. 623, ll. 80–81, published in Eliseeva, *Iz istorii*, p. 261. Unfortunately, Ivich did not continue his account of the design of the city beyond the visit of Ordzhonikidze and the change in the local leadership in the summer of 1933, by which time, Ivich asserts, everything miraculously changed for the better. The new local leaders (Zaveniagin and Lominadze) were still in power when Ivich was writing.

62. Working under Lengorstroiproekt, the architects B. V. Danchich and A. A. Shtange outlined how within eighteen to twenty years right-bank Magnitogorsk, a city of 300,000 people, would be built and what it would be like. To be constructed along a planned embankment on the industrial lake, the city would be oriented to face the factory. All along the embankment there would be tall apartment buildings

anchoring the space and answering the factory's impressive industrial physique across the way with a proud residential facade. On the embankment's lower part (south) there would be a park and a stadium. There would be three wide north-south arteries in the city's interior, around which the bulk of the residential units would be arranged. At the end of one of the arteries would be the passenger train station. The city would have two large squares, one right on the water, another directly inland a bit. All this was reported in a sober, professional tone, and, what is more, it was an exclusively architectural treatment, with no social engineering—a visual expression of socialism in stone without the winged rhetorical flights about a socialist city of the future. *MR*, 29 July 1936; see also *CR*, 11 October 1935. The plan was finally carried out in the 1950s, with admirable results, although on a scale that did not meet the ever-increasing demand for housing.

63. Lominadze added that "the project, according to which the [right-bank] city is being built, is beneath any possible criticism." *MR*, 20 January 1934.

64. *CR*, 6 June 1935. Dozens of prefabricated buildings were erected beginning in the 1960s.

65. *MR*, 9 May 1937. The newspaper reported that, as of June 1937, the city had only one skilled architect with a small staff of young trainees, since all the other architects had "simply left." The newspaper failed to say where they went (most likely they had been arrested). In any case, no one was designing the city. *MR*, 5 June 1937. Continuing its reportage on this saga, in early 1938 the newspaper summarized as follows: "after three years of construction, there is not a single finished objective." *MR*, 15 January 1938. Ominously, the newspaper added that the situation had been investigated by two commissions in late 1937, one on 2 November, the other 15 December, the conclusions of which it summarized as follows: "you can't call it anything but wrecking." Zverev was arrested in 1937 (although released in 1939).

66. PAChO, f. 234, op. 1, d. 594, ll. 1–4, excerpted in Eliseeva, *Iz istorii*, p. 250. According to an official report for 1949, only that year did the construction trust Magnitostroi "for the first time begin seriously the comprehensive bringing to order of the superblocks and streets under construction in the right-bank city." *Otchet o deiatelnosti ispolkolma Magnitogorskogo gorskogo soveta za 1949 g.* (Magnitogorsk, 1950), p. 6.

67. *MR*, 21 May 1937. No doubt city construction remained so poor because much of it was carried out by inmates of the labor colony. *Borba za metall*, 27 November 1933.

68. Accordingly, the three Soviet books devoted to the history of architecture and city planning in Magnitogorsk deal almost exclusively with the postwar period.

69. In this regard, the primitiveness of a discussion following a presentation by Professor Chernyshev in Moscow on 2 October 1929 was highly revealing. GARF, f. 7952, op. 5, d. 179.

70. See Ivich: GARF, f. 7952, op. 5, d. 361, l. 14. His humorous rendition of this point is matched by a straight-faced one in some pamphlets, e.g., G. Puzis, *Magnitogorsk* (Moscow, 1930), where such calculations are carried out and a figure of 47–48,000 is presented.

71. Semen Nariniani, *Magnitogorskii metallurgicheskii kombinat* (Moscow, 1931), p. 16.

72. *Magnitostroi: Biulleten*, 1930, no. 1, p. 4.

73. GARF, f. 7952, op. 5, d. 361, l. 12.

74. According to the newspaper and published documents, in 1935 the housing construction plan for each bank was fulfilled at about 33 percent. In 1936 only 48 percent of the planned housing was built, while many buildings begun two years earlier had not been finished. In 1937 the civil construction plan, measured in terms of rubles spent, was fulfilled at 55.6 percent, while in the first seven months of 1938 the rate was 40.3 percent. Rubles spent, of course, did not mean actual housing, as invariably the costs of each square meter were far in excess of the planned costs. *MR*, 27 February 1936 and 5 February 1937; PAChO, f. 234, op. 1, d. 594, ll. 1–4, in Eliseeva, *Iz istorii*, p. 250. An unpublished report gives only slightly different percentages: 40.7 for 1935, 45.2 for 1936, 58.5 for 1937. MFGAChO, f. 9, op. 1, d. 170.

75. For a description of the first superblock, see Scott, *Behind*, pp. 209–11.

76. Ibid., pp. 90–91. The central food emporium (*gastronom*) of the first superblock is to this day called the "German store."

77. *MR*, 9 January 1936 and 17 February 1937.

78. *MR*, 26 November 1936. One of the building's residents was Dmitrii Bogatyrenko. Bogatyrenko, who was born in 1906 and arrived in Magnitogorsk in 1932, had come a long way. He worked as a skilled operator in the blooming mill from the moment it was launched in July 1933. "When the blooming was put into operation," he recalled in November 1935, "I lived in the Fifth Sector in a barracks without windows, without doors—street no. 18, barracks no. 9. There were five of us, all buddies [*vse svoi rebiata*], from Konstantinovka. We all lived in a single room. We came on our own. My family joined me after a year. We knew that there were no apartments. You lie down to sleep, then you wake up, and the bed is full of snow. There were no mice, but bed bugs were plentiful [*do chorta*]." GARF, f. 7952, op. 5, d. 310, ll. 288, 291.

79. Vera Dunham has used the expression "middle class" to characterize a large segment of the Soviet population. *In Stalin's Time: Middleclass Values in Soviet Fiction* (Cambridge: Cambridge University Press, 1976). The problem of class in Soviet society is addressed in chs. 5 and 7. For a parallel example of the strategy of making skilled employees utterly dependent, see the analysis of Gary, Indiana, by Edward Greer, *Big Steel: Black Politics and Corporate Power in Gary, Indiana* (New York: Monthly Review Press, 1979), pp. 65–66.

80. GARF, f. 7952, op. 5, d. 176, l. 6.

81. Ibid., d. 336, l. 80. "Certainly a sincere effort was made by the Russians," wrote William Haven, "to give the Americans living conditions that would approach American standards." Haven Papers, container 5, folder 2. This did not mean that the Americans were entirely satisfied. In a letter dated 8 February 1931 one McKee employee wrote that "the conditions at the colony still promote inconveniences, such as no water for weeks at a time, no lights after night, and no transportation to and fro. . . . The food has been fairly good, but as you know, is costing us so much that the balance of our ruble account is practically nil. Of the fourteen Ford cars possessed here, only one is now operating, and the boys are using horses to a great extent." GARF, f. 7952, op. 5, d. 233a, ll. 91–92.

82. Scott, *Behind*, p. 86.

83. GARF, f. 7952, op. 5, d. 312, ll. 296–97.

84. Stuck, "Russia As I Saw It," box 4, pp. 132–33.

85. Kizenko appears to have been fascinated by the Americans. He claimed that "generally we were struck with curiosity at each American marvel [*dikovinki*]. For example, they häd these wonderful pencils. . . . with all colors: green, red, black, in a word, the whole assortment. They turned the pencil, and automatically a new color appeared." He also claimed to be shocked to discover that they always worked the same shift (daytime), for six months or longer, leaving precisely when the shift was over. He added that the Americans were supplied with alcohol, and that they knew how to drink (a sentiment echoed by many others). Kizenko had been part of a group of thirty specialists mobilized to Magnitogorsk in February 1931, not long after Gugel arrived, from Mariupol. Like Gugel, Kizenko also worked in Azovstal. GARF, f. 7952, op. 5, d. 310, ll. 170, 176, 197–98.

86. Ibid., d. 342, l. 14.

87. Scott, *Behind*, pp. 231–32. In 1987 I stayed in one of these spacious cottages, which today is maintained as a guest house by the Magnitogorsk Metallurgical Complex.

88. As quoted in Elfimov, *Marshal industrii*, p. 117. Zaveniagin's unpublished "autobiography," apparently preserved with the surviving members of the Zaveniagin family, was entitled "Garden. Trees. Observations. Remarks." In it he wrote that "all my life fruit trees, a garden, its growth, ripening, and . . . the introduction of new brands, the secret life and birth of apples, berries, have attracted me. But almost never have I been able to follow up on this fascinating and noble pursuit." Mikhail Kolpakov, "Odnoi sudboi," *Sovetskaia Rossiia*, 25 October 1987.

89. Even the rent for these palaces—calculated by space and thus relatively high—was paid out of the factory budget as an administrative expense. Scott, *Behind*, p. 233.

90. In summer, some fifty to seventy favored workers each day were also allowed to use the facilities of the resort. But the vast majority of the city's population was dependent on irregular bus service to the lake, had no place to spend the night, could not use any equipment, and for the most part were without the opportunity to purchase food or drink once there. Even so, people lined up at the bus stops to go to the lake, and drivers were invariably forced to turn many away. *MR*, 8 June and 5 August 1936; GARF, f. 7952, op. 5, d. 309, l. 217. On the privileges of the elite, see Lewin, *The Making of the Soviet System*, p. 236. According to local lore, the lake near Magnetic Mountain was named Bannoe because Emilian Pugachev, the leader of a late eighteenth-century peasant and cossack rebellion, bathed there.

91. *MR*, 8 and 21 April 1936.

92. *MR*, 22 September 1936.

93. *MR*, 10 June 1936. The local Council of Engineers' Wives was founded in June 1935, although its organizers had been active before then. As of March 1936, it counted 202 members. That month, the council held a conference in Magnitogorsk, attended by their counterparts from Cheliabinsk and Kuznetsk, at which they discussed their involvement in a range of public and philanthropic activities, including health care, tree-planting, general cleanliness, and education. They also planned numerous dinner parties, and could follow the activities of similarly sta-

tus-conscious, civic-minded women around the country in the new national journal, *Obshchestvennitsa*, founded in 1936. See *My aktivno uchastvuem v sotsialisticheskom stroitelstve* (Magnitogorsk, 1936), pp. 1–31. Most of the wives of the
men who made up the local elite performed unpaid labor, such as ad hoc investigatory and supervisory commissions, but some were given official posts. The wife
of Aleksandr Pridorogin, the local NKVD chief during the terror, for example, was
named chief of the steel plant's complaint bureau in 1938. MFGAChO, f. 99, op.
10, d. 1095, l. 4.

94. *MR*, 1 and 4 May 1936.

95. See the open discussion of stratification and reward, for example, in *Magnitogorskii komsomolets*, 9 January 1932. That such efforts did not always amount
to much in practical terms does not vitiate the main point: privilege was considered
as an acceptable aspect of Soviet life.

96. The legitimacy of these "petty-bourgeois" attitudes and lifestyles (*mesh-
chanstvo*) was later ratified in Soviet novels of the 1940s and 1950s. Dunham, *In
Stalin's Time*, pp. 19–21.

97. Lacking "culture" themselves, these individuals supposedly made a "deal"
with the intelligenstia (possessors of the coveted *kulturnost*), and this deal, Fitzpatrick has claimed, accounts for the intelligentsia's elevated status within the
USSR, despite the harassment and censorship, as well as the philistine tastes of the
elite. As to what made possible the merger of "petty-bourgeois" or "middle-class"
values with the revolutionary and socialist traditions, Fitzpatrick pointed to the
doctrine of socialist realism, which, following Siniavskii, she treated as a mentality,
or way of thinking, corresponding to the proposition, "life as it will be"; those who
already possessed *kulturnost* enjoyed the deserved privileges of an abundant life
that would eventually accrue to others when they, too—indeed, when the whole
society—acquired "culture." Fitzpatrick, *The Cultural Front*, pp. 9, 13, 41, 146,
213, 247, 256. Notwithstanding the suggestiveness of these arguments, Fitzpatrick's conclusion that by the middle of the 1930s, *kulturnost* entirely replaced "class
war" as the dominant note of Soviet life (except for the quasi-populist episode of
the terror) seems questionable. The continued centrality of (an admittedly transformed) notion of class analysis is treated in ch. 5; the accent on *kulturnost* is discussed in ch. 4.

98. Scott, *Behind*, p. 86.

99. Nina Kondratkovskaia, interview by author, Magnitogorsk, May 1987.
Typical stories that made the rounds were of lavish drinking bouts and banquets,
some of which appear to have had some basis in fact. It was said of the chief of the
coke construction A. M. Mariasin, who was evidently a large man, that during one
such banquet in Berezka in late 1931, on the occasion of the startup of the first gas
furnace, "he got drunk and, dressed in a Russian-style long shirt like a merchant,
. . . danced on the table. We just about died from laughter." GARF, f. 7952, op. 5,
d. 308, l. 33.

100. *MR*, 23 July 1938.

101. *MR*, 31 December 1939.

102. *Magnitostroi:Biulleten*, 1930, no. 1, pp. 12–13.

103. *MR*, 20 November 1938. In 1932 the official boundary was widened to include the limestone quarry at the village of Agapovka, twenty kilometers to the

south (the city already included the "village" settlement of Sredne-Uralsk). In addition to a limestone quarry, the Agapovskii raion contained several state and collective farms, three machine tractor stations, and a timber mill. In 1935 the urban boundary was widened again to include the area across the industrial lake on the right bank. *MR,* 27 August, 17 October, 14 November, 11 and 15 December 1936, 3 January and 15 June 1937.

104. *MR,* 8 August 1936.

105. According to one eyewitness, "the city party committee . . . required that all lower (primary) party organizations, in cooperation with economic and trade union organizations, help distribute the population territorially, that is such that construction workers of the open-hearth shop live in one sector, in specific barracks, and the construction workers of the blast furnace live in their own sector and barracks, in order to allow the social organizations to work with their workers." GARF, f. 7952, op. 5, d. 306, l. 15.

106. The official added that "we had the opposite results, that is, turnover on the site was high, and the turnover from shop to shop was also high." GARF, f. 7952, op. 5, d. 306, l. 15; see also *Stroitelstvo i ekspluatatsiia,* p. 51.

107. According to one contemporary observer, "people arriving on one train were settled in one barracks. They went to work in different sectors. From the barracks to the place of work it was often necessary to walk several kilometers. And adjacent to the place of work stood other barracks. But here other people were living who worked on the opposite side of the construction site." GARF, f. 7952, op. 5, d. 385, 1. 2.

108. This road, as important as it was, suffered from crippling defects. When it was built, instead of laying the norm of 32 centimeters of asphalt, they "saved" materials and put down only 18 centimeters' worth. (Even more materials were "saved" by building the road completely without a roadbed.) After the first layer was put down, it got dirty, so that between the first and second layers there was poor contact. And there was no drainage funnel. The result was that the road needed constant repairs. By 1938 the total cost of laying and repairing the troublesome and dangerous but nonetheless vital road had reached almost 20 million rubles, more than a million rubles per kilometer. *MR,* 15 August 1938.

109. MFGAChO, f. 10, op. 1, d. 139, l. 7.

110. Even the direct "road" linking the Kirov district's "cultural center" and the factory gates, named Pushkin Prospect in 1937, was little more than a dirt trail. *MR,* 16 February 1937. Movement on these paths was inhibited by various factors, depending on the season. In winter, blanketed with snow and subject to periodic blizzards that could bury entire barracks, Magnitogorsk completely froze, making traveling treacherous. With the spring thaw the city turned into a nonnegotiable mud patch. Summer brought its own special plague—the blinding dust storms from which there was no shelter in the open steppe—and revealed the many deep craters of the hardened-earth avenues. GARF, f. 7952, op. 5, d. 306, ll. 19–20.

111. *MR,* 17 November 1936.

112. *MR,* 11 June 1936; GARF, f. 7952, op. 5, d. 313, l. 8.

113. By 1941, the KBU owned fifteen vehicles (and 163 horses) for use by the city. This "fleet" was occupied mostly with the hauling of trash and waste. *Materialy o rabote Magnitogorskogo soveta deputatov trudiashchikhsia za 1940 god*

(Magnitogorsk, 1941), p. 9; *MR*, 21 February 1936. As of 1939 there were apparently some taxis, but it is unclear for whom. Ibid., 2 December 1939.

114. *MR*, 26 September 1936; MFGAChO, f. 9, op. 1, d. 170. Built in 1930, Magnitogorsk's grain elevator served more than one hundred collective and state farms of the surrounding region, including parts of Bashkiriia. Soviet authorities deliberately chose to build such facilities in cities, rather than the countryside where the grain was harvested. In 1938, 50 percent of the grain collected in Magnitogorsk was still being stored in poorly built, temporary structures. *MR*, 3 April 1938.

115. *MR*, 4 March 1936.

116. Accidents were reported either when people crossing the tracks tried to beat an oncoming tram, or when drivers violated the speed limit. *MR*, 27 April 1936.

117. *MR*, 16 April 1938. Like the tracks of the factory railroad system, the tracks of the tram were often snowed under, so that in winter many people were employed in track clearing. Ibid., 2 February 1936.

118. GARF, f. 7952, op. 5, d. 313, l. 8.

119. *MR*, 18 January 1935. The first electric tram appears to have been introduced in the Berlin suburbs in 1881 (the cable car was introduced in San Francisco in 1873). In the Russian empire, the first tram began operation in Kiev in 1892. Initially, streetcars were opposed in Europe on aesthetic grounds. The overhead wires were seen as unseemly, particularly in historic city centers. Soon enough, however, trams ceased to be a luxury and became a necessity in most large cities. They were used extensively by the workers of Krupp in the town of Essen, and were viewed as a panacea for alleviating crowded living conditions by allowing greater dispersion. John McKay, *Tramways and Trolleys: The Rise of Urban Mass Transit in Europe* (Princeton: Princeton University Press, 1976), pp. 35–56, 85–86, 193, 203–5.

120. *MR*, 8 August 1936. Population figures for the various settlements not included in the table vary. A reference in the city newspaper put the population of Fertilizer Settlement at 15,000. Another gave a figure of 17,000 for the Cement and Fertilizer Settlements, the Twelfth and Fourteenth Sectors, and Sredne-Uralsk combined. *MR*, 27 September 1938 and 4 March 1937.

121. *MR*, 10 August 1936, 5 September 1938 and 18 January 1939. Kazakhs and Tatars could also be found in other parts of the city.

122. By contrast, the published results of a January 1931 census conducted in the Kuzbas explicitly states that the dekulakized peasants deported to Stalinsk (Novokuznetsk) lived in a "concentration camp." Unfortunately, from the way the data were published it is impossible to know the size of the concentration-camp population there. Interestingly, of those living in Kuzbas cities for less than three years before the census, 83 percent came from the Sibkrai. Unlike the Urals, the Kuzbas did not draw a huge influx of people from the European part of the USSR in the early 1930s. See *Kuzbass: Rezultaty perepisi gorodskogo naseleniia 1931 g.* (Novosibirsk, 1931), p. 42.

123. *Izvestiia Magnitogorska*, 21 April 1934 and 5 February 1936.

124. One official report from 1932 estimated that the number may have been

as high as 50,000, of whom more than 30,000 were said to live in the five Special Labor Settlements proper. MFGAChO, f. 10, op. 1, d. 1, ll. 80–86.

125. *MR*, 15 February 1933.

126. Migration from the city was not open to the exiles. Few were granted internal passports, which beginning in 1933 were required for travel within the country. John and Mariia Scott's maid, Vera, the daughter of dekulakized parents, was packed off and sent by the police to Cheliabinsk in 1938, "along with several thousand other disfranchised minors," on twenty-four hours' notice. Scott, *Behind*, p. 131.

127. Magnitogorsk's Special Labor Settlement technically belonged to what Solzhenitsyn called the Gulag Archipelago. But there was a vast difference between a restricted settlement for peasants sentenced to "exile with forced labor" and "political" prisoners sent to mine gold in the frozen tundra. Solzhenitsyn, *The Gulag Archipelago*, vol. 3 (New York: Harper and Row, 1978), pp. 350–68.

128. RTsKhIDNI, f. 85, op. 29, d. 52, l. 3.

129. In the early years conditions in the colony were frightful. A four-page letter written in 1932 by an inmate, Aleksei Vafolomeev, and mailed to Stalin detailed the colony's abominable conditions. The letter was redirected to the Magnitogorsk procurator, B. Krepyshev, for a response. Indicating that many of the problems singled out by Vafolomeev belonged to the colony's initial organizational period, Krepyshev's assistant prepared a reply acknowledging that of the colony's sixty barracks, thirty-eight had no stoves or floors; that there was not enough water in the colony, or transport to deliver what little water there was; that in the winter for weeks at a time there was no light in the barracks; that the colony had linen for only 30 percent of the more than 10,000 convicts; and that not only warm coats but even short half-jackets were in critically short supply. Magnitogorsk procuracy: Archival file "Delo No. 14 po ITK za 1932 g.," l. 26 (dated 13 December 1932). A follow-up report in the same file dated 4 January 1933 disclosed that the barracks with dirt floors held more than 2,500 convicts, and that more than 5,000 convicts lived in garages until 15 October 1932, when the barracks were completed (Ibid., ll. 30–40). With time the colony improved. By 1935 even the medical situation stabilized, according to the chief of the colony's medical unit, N. Lizogub. He claimed that the cases of typhus numbered only one or two per year, and that these were brought in from elsewhere. *Borba za metall*, 27 June and 6 August 1935.

130. It is unclear what the administrative relation was between the ITK and the Special Labor Settlement, although they seem to have been separate. Sergei Frankfurt made a sharp distinction between the dekulakized and the prisoners of the ITK in Novokuznetsk. See Frankfurt, *Men and Steel*, p. 173.

131. In the USSR, according to the then chief of the Urals oblast ITK administration, Korovin, there were four types of facilities for those convicted of crimes and sentenced to forced labor with deprivation of freedom: houses of detention, punishment colonies, closed-regime colonies, and open-regime colonies, where convicts came and went (presumably in connection with their job assignments), except for those confined to solitary for finite periods and recidivists detained in the special section (the eleventh). Magnitogorsk became a "closed-regime" ITK. *Borba za metall*, 6 March 1933.

132. In August 1932, a month after the colony was formed, there were nearly

3,000 escapes. In September 1932, officials estimated the colony population at 13,700, but a month later the figure given was 11,000. A report by the assistant to the city procurator dated 4 January 1933 gave a figure of 5,609 escapes, roughly half the number of convicts received, in the five months of the colony's existence; only a few hundred were caught. Magnitogorsk procuracy: Archival file "Delo No. 14 po ITK za 1932 g.," ll. 4, 7, 40, 45–46.

133. Ibid., ll. 86, 91.

134. Scott, Behind, p. 285.

135. A 1931 report on the procuracy listed sixteen reported murders during the fourth quarter of 1930, nine in the first quarter of 1931 and another thirteen in the second quarter of that year. (The number of murders was exceeded by fatal industrial accidents.) One of the crime categories listed was anti-Semitism, eight instances of which were recorded over the nine months covered by the report. MFGAChO, f. 10, op. 1, d. 18, l. 152. According to unpublished reminiscences, the first city militia, located in a First Sector barracks shared with the city soviet, was formed by people sent by the oblast authorities. At first, the Magnitogorsk militia had one vehicle, which frequently did not work, and very poor communications. Rotanov, "Rovesnitsa Magnitki," unpublished ms., Magnitogorsk, 1979, p. 13.

136. One contemporary wrote of the situation at the brick factory, for example, that "the very atmosphere among the workers was un-Soviet. . . . Here in the summer there were mass drinking bouts, knife fights, even pistol shootouts and rapes of women. . . . The atmosphere was such that public institutions were deeply terrorized even to question the behavior of these people. One fellow, Kollarov, who was an active worker and a good worker correspondent, wrote three or four notes about what was going on, and for that he was knifed and lay in the hospital two months." GARF, f. 7952, op. 5, d. 308, l. 12; see also ibid., d. 200, l. 78. Women assigned to construction of the brick factory refused to work the night shift. Nariniani, Na stroike, pp. 55–56. Before censorship began to blank out such reporting, one journalist wrote that women were abused, threatened, and even spent the night where they worked, afraid to go home to the barracks at night. Moreover, women's barracks were frequent targets of "hooliganism." Chagan, U podnozhia, p. 9. In 1930, males outnumbered females at the site 31,314 to 16,381; by 1932, females outnumbered males 83,700 to 71,300 (not including exiled peasants and prison laborers), according to official data. MFGAChO, f. 16, op. 1, d. 34, l. 2. A similar state of affairs predominated in Gary, Indiana, which attracted "tramps, fugitives from justice, gamblers." There were not many women or wives, drinking was widespread, and the population was said to be a rough lot. Quillen, "Industrial City," p. 108.

137. One retired militia officer recalled that "the work conditions in the militia were especially difficult. The staff was small. The offices were located in a barracks. There was inadequate transport. Often it was necessary to hitch a ride from passing cars." To assist the militia Soviet authorities created a parapolice. In 1937 militiamen were no longer permitted to carry weapons. MR, 19 October 1937. Of the Fourteenth Sector (out beyond the Fertilizer Settlement on the way to the grain elevator), the newspaper wrote that it had but one "road," and "only the brave" ventured by it on foot or horse-drawn cart. "The inhabitants of the Fourteenth Sec-

tor rarely attend the theater or circus," the paper added. "They can only go in big crowds, so that the return trip home is not so scary." MR, 29 February 1936.

138. In 1936, for example, three men, in violation of colony rules, were allowed to go swimming without convoy. They ran away and hid but were caught four days later having done minimal damage. On another occasion, however, two prisoners released for two hours to go to the baths managed to get hold of some vodka. They "tied one on," and then broke into some apartments. Escapees from other colonies sometimes turned up in Magnitogorsk, their identities discovered after they had been apprehended locally for perpetrating a crime, almost always burglary or robbery. MR, 18 August 1936.

139. According to a report submitted by the colony chief A. A. Geineman to Beso Lominadze in September 1933 (when the latter took over as Magnitogorsk party secretary), the ITK had 8,480 convicts. A total of 6,580 were listed as working. In the report Geineman explained the colony's operation and aims, and complained that supervisory personnel, in addition to lacking recreational activities, were sometimes forced to live in the same barracks as the convicts. Magnitogorsk procuracy: Archival file "Perepiska: Tsirkuliary sekretnye po mestam lisheniia svobody za 1933–34 gg.," ll. 31–41. Scott estimated the number of ITK convicts at 20,000 to 35,000. But in testimony given to the United States embassy in 1938, he had written "fifteen to eighteen thousand." And in an earlier draft of his memoirs, he gave a figure of 27,000, noting further, without explanation, that by 1938 "a mere 2,000 petty criminals" remained, although "five years before the number of these prisoners in Magnitogorsk was 10 or 15 times as large." This passage was deleted before publication. Scott, Behind, pp. 85, 285; Scott Papers, State Historical Archives, Madison, Wisconsin, yellow-page draft, p. 235.

140. MR, 18 October 1936; Scott, Behind, pp. 284–86. The locations of the installations were given in scattered references in the newspaper; for example, MR, 15 May 1931 and 3 February 1936; see also GARF, f. 7952, op. 5, d. 306, l. 13. These locations were confirmed in my private conversations in 1987 in Magnitogorsk with people who had lived in the city during the 1930s.

141. MR, 22 January 1937.

142. In Magnitogorsk itself, many difficulties confronted the passengers who wished to leave the city. The first train station in Magnitogorsk was a parked railroad car, conveniently located just north of the main factory entrance, but in 1932 a real station was built several kilometers farther north (and west) at the base of the factory railroad yards. This was more than five kilometers from the factory gates and eight kilometers from the Kirov district. The tram was not extended two additional kilometers from the end of the line at Berezka to the train station, perhaps in order that an exit from the city not be too easy. In any case, arriving and departing Magnitogorsk were trying ordeals, which often necessitated lugging baggage on foot at least to and from the last tram stop. By way of comparison, the first "train station" in Gary, Indiana was also a box car switched to a siding with the word "Gary" emblazoned on its side. Quillen, "Industrial City," p. 100.

143. Many letters were discovered to be wrongly delivered or not delivered at all owing to disorganization. There were also periodic shortages of stamps for sale. MR, 20 September and 5 October 1936.

144. In the early years, communication links with the outside world were frag-

ile. "A telegram from America to Moscow arrives faster than one from Magnito-gorsk," grieved one journalist. "Telegrams from Moscow to Magnitogorsk arrive on the fifth day." Moreover, he reported that "on the site, where some 15,000 peo-ple are working, there is one post office, in which one person sells stamps, accepts all correspondence, telegrams, money transfers, and thousands of letters marked 'general delivery.'" Markevich, *Rozhdenie giganta*, pp. 3–4. With time the post system expanded and telegram service was improved. Although both were still plagued by confusion over addresses, not to mention semiliterate letter carriers and office workers, they appear to have gotten extensive use. In 1936, for example, the city sent and received more than 16,000 telegrams a day. *MR*, 24 February, 14 May, and 17 December 1936. The factory, of course, used the separate governmental tele-phone and telegraph systems, while the NKVD had their own transmission and re-ception equipment, as well as a system of field couriers (also used by the party). As for the local telephone network, there were said to be around 2,000 "subscribers" (*abonenty*), but virtually all were in offices. Home telephones went only to im-portant administrative staff, and at home only the factory director had a direct line to Moscow. Everyone else had to place interurban calls in advance. The city's cen-tral telephone station had six operators, who were said to handle upwards of 32,000 calls (local and long-distance) every twenty-four hours. It was said to be highly overburdened. The lines themselves were "party" lines, which meant that there were crowds of people on them—moving one journalist to quip: "This is not a tele-phone, but a multivoice bazaar." He also claimed that the cables were poor and sub-ject to induction in damp weather. *MR*, 16 June, 29 August, and 21 October 1936.

145. The comments of Semen Ragozina, GARF, f. 7952, op. 5, d. 300, l. 131.

146. *MR*, 21 April 1936.

147. *MR*, 9 May 1937. There were no public lists of the organizations operating in the city, and since they often lacked signs on their buildings (or still carried the signs of the previous occupants), some organizations were said to be nearly impos-sible to find. In 1936 the city soviet issued a decree that all organizations had to paint their buildings, put up signs indicating their function and address, and hang flags on holidays. *MR*, 9 March and 6 May 1936.

148. *MR*, 15 January 1937. In 1934 more than 7,000 medical emergencies were called in. In 1936 the number rose to almost 20,000, and in the first month of 1937 there were almost 2,000, or over 60 per day. Many of the calls turned out to be for drunks. The emergency service had only five vehicles (*karety*), two of which carried infected and critically ill patients from the ambulatory to the hospital, leaving only three to serve the entire city of over 200,000. *MR*, 12 May 1936 and 9 May 1937.

149. *MR*, 30 January 1938. All four hundred school-age children were said to be attending school.

150. Scott, *Behind*, p. 233.

151. *MR*, 30 January 1936.

152. *CR*, 17 July 1938.

153. Official reports complained that the housing in Socialist City proper was being ruined by tenants who kept animals, fuel, and garbage on the balconies. MFGAChO, f. 10, op. 1, d. 168, l. 1.

154. These supplicants were not just the "unrepentant peasants" of mud-hut settlements. The barracks of steel workers were surrounded by small plots. GARF,

f. 7952, op. 5, d. 309, l. 46. In January, 1934, Beso Lominadze proudly announced that almost 25,000 workers were engaged in some form of cultivation, with very satisfactory results. *MR*, 20 January 1934. An official source claimed that in 1939 almost 2,500 hectares in or near the city were under cultivation and tended by 15,000 gardeners (*ogorodniki*). *Materialy o rabote*, p. 26. Another source from 1939 put the number of local cultivators at 18,450 *households. Stalinskaia stroika*, p. 54. Whatever the precise totals, the number of cultivators certainly ranged in the tens of thousands. The allocation of land was largely by shop, as was the provision of tools, seed, and transportation to the outlying plots. There were conflicts over mistaken or multiple assignments. *Magnitogorskii metall*, 12 and 15 May, 1935.

155. *MR*, 2 December 1939.

156. *MR*, 9 March 1936.

157. *MR*, 1 March 1936.

158. Because the Magnitogorsk steel plant required a large constant power supply, Magnitogorsk had its own high-capacity electric power station, one of several score across the country. The 100,000 kilowatt power station also supplied Zlatoust and Beloretsk in addition to its own giant steel works and city, placing severe strains on the system's capacity. In 1936, the city got its own substation, but the total power generated was still inadequate. Some institutions sought to insulate themselves from the overtaxed and therefore unreliable urban energy grid with their own generators, but these too were subject to periodic breakdowns. Various attempts to conserve energy in the steel plant and city were hindered by the lack of meters for over a third of all energy users. *MR*, 21 May, 5 August, and 2 September 1936. In 1938 the authorities imposed "blackouts" for all residents during the day (9 A.M. to 5 P.M.) and the early morning (2 A.M. to 5 A.M.).

159. *MR*, 2 February 1936.

160. *MR*, 7 February and 3 March 1936.

161. The kerosene store was located in the Kirov district, far from where the people who needed it lived, yet it was forbidden to transport the substance on the tram or bus. Nonetheless, demand was evidently high. On one October 1936 morning the newspaper reported that several hundred people were standing outside the store at 8 A.M., in anticipation of kerosene going on sale at 10 A.M. *MR*, 3 April, 3 September, and 18 October 1936.

162. *MR*, 14 January 1935. The city's twelve boilers (*kotelnye*) served a total of 134 buildings. *Stalinskaia stroika*, p. 35. Newspaper reports humorously described how half the people were freezing while the other half sweated—a familiar complaint of urbanites the world over. *MR*, 5 April 1936.

163. *MR*, 6 January 1936.

164. Scott, *Behind*, p. 37.

165. *MR*, 6 January 1936.

166. It could be especially cold in schools, many of which were located in barracks. Scott, *Behind*, p. 15. Fuel provisioning for 1940 was as follows: schools, 84 percent of plan; hospitals, 82 percent; baths-laundries, 77 percent; and the city population, 42 percent. The plan targets were not likely to have been generous on the side of providing heat. Inside the barracks it was often so cold that people preferred when possible to spend the night in the heated offices, even if that meant sleeping on a wooden table. GARF, f. 7952, op. 5, d. 300, l. 3.

167. GARF, f. 7952, op. 5, d. 389, l. 16.

168. *MR*, 22 May 1934. A plumbing system for the mine was finally completed in 1937, at a cost of 300,000 rubles, but it never worked properly, and when investigations uncovered the shoddy workmanship, it was decided to cover the system over rather than correct the problems. *MR*, 11 April 1939. According to the city planning commission, as of 1 January 1939, 15.6 percent of the city's housing had both sewage and running water; 79.2 percent had neither. The same report listed 16.3 percent of the housing stock as brick, 60.5 percent as carcass and barracks, 6.3 percent as wooden, and 16.9 percent as mud huts. MFGAChO, f. 9, op. 1, d. 170, passim.

169. *MR*, 16 February 1936.

170. *MR*, 21 May 1938.

171. Each year the costs of hauling sewage exceeded 2 million rubles; estimates put the cost of building a real sewage system at 12 million rubles. *MR*, 2 June 1937. In the spring of 1937, the newspaper reported that of 1,349 cesspools (*pomoinye iamy*) citywide, 320 were overfull. The situation, warned the newspaper, would get much worse because of the forty-two vehicles equipped to haul the refuse, only fifteen were running. The rest could not be repaired, owing to the lack of spare parts and other problems. In 1937 the chief of the city auto park was fired and arrested, but nothing changed. Ibid., 6 May 1937.

172. *MR*, 17 April 1936.

173. *MR*, 21, 23, and 26 May 1938, and 23 June 1936.

174. *MR*, 11 August and 14 September 1936.

175. *MR*, 17 March 1937.

176. *MR*, 8 August 1936 and 8 March 1936. In such circumstances fires were especially treacherous. In 1936 six homes burnt down because there was no water main nearby, and by the time water was brought in cisterns it was too late. *MR*, 17 May 1936. "On the site there were fires virtually everyday," according to Valentin Serzhantov, but "many parts of the site were not supplied with water." The fire department under the NKVD had its hands full battling the fires inside the factory. Serzhantov, "KPSS—Vdokhnovitel," pp. 172, 178.

177. The Urals oblast party committee issued an emergency decree and sent a special "sanitation train" with medical personnel who went around to barracks and gave injections. A number of the medical personnel contracted the disease and died. *MR*, 10 September 1932; Serzhantov, "KPSS—Vdokhnovitel," pp. 259–60, citing RTsKhIDNI, f. 17, op. 21, d. 3787, ll. 41–43; *Magnitogorskii komsomolets*, 4 and 10 September 1936. According to the unpublished memoirs of a leading Magnitogorsk physician held in the city archive, in 1931 there were 1,989 reported cases of typhoid fever and another 1,174 of spotted fever. In 1932, the number of cases were 905 and 5,725, respectively. A. A. Baryshev, "Zdravookhranenie Magnitogorska: Istoriia stanovleniia i razvitiia s 1929 g. po 1975 g." (Magnitogorsk, 1976), pp. 36, 40, 41.

178. The report, dated 17 January 1932, was signed by Shuette, identified as the chief of the city health department. MFGAChO, f. 10, op. 1, d. 1, ll. 80–86, 140, 202.

179. The stream of Bashik to the north, a swamp on the Fifth Sector, a lake on the Sixth, and numerous trenches throughout the city were identified as the primary sources for the spread of malaria. *MR*, 30 May 1936.

180. Baryshev, "Zdravookhranenie Magnitogorska," pp. 36, 40–41.

181. *MR*, 4 and 10 September 1936.

182. The factory was even more unsanitary. *MR*, 26 May and 3 June 1938.

183. The beds were full, people were lying in the corridor, and there was just one little room for all operations. "The prosecutor should investigate," demanded one newspaper, in yet another example of the supercharged atmosphere of the day. *Magnitogorskii komsomolets*, 6 July 1931.

184. Scott, *Behind*, p. 219. In an earlier draft Scott wrote that the Magnitogorsk hospital "was and probably still is the most disgraceful blemish in the face of the city." Scott Papers, earlier draft of "Behind the Urals." The hospital was supplemented by other medical facilities. By 1937, according to Petr Tambovtsev, chief of the city's health department, there were seven outpatient polyclinics, ten women's and children's consultations offices, fourteen pharmacies, and thirteen medical stations in the factory and mine. There was a maternity ward (*rodilnyi dom*) located in the Kirov district, with a statue out front of a mother cuddling a baby. In 1936 the newspaper triumphantly announced the first anesthetized birth. A veterinary ward was opened in Fertilizer Settlement in 1936 (forty families were evicted from a barracks to make room for it). As for the steel plant, it too had some medical facilities. But O. I. Ivanova, the chief of medical facilities for the factory, disclosed that only the blast furnace shop had a real facility. All other shops had a formally designated medical "station," without running water or toilets. *MR*, 20 February 1936 and 16 February 1937.

185. The 963-person hospital staff, of whom 51 were "doctors" and another 205 nurses and midwives, literally had its hands full. The number of doctors citywide, already inadequate, declined inexplicably in 1936, from around 200 to 170. (There were also 400 nurses.) The city had just eleven acting pediatricians, only four of whom were actually specialists in children's medicine. One analysis revealed that the ratio of doctors to population, which in Moscow was 1 to 450 and in industrial cities 1 to 750, in Magnitogorsk was one doctor for every 1,700–1,800 people. *MR*, 11 March 1936 and 27 May 1937. The city also had a psychiatric facility—across the industrial lake in Old Magnitnyi Settlement—which was founded in July 1933 by Anna Vitkovskaia, a graduate of Moscow University's medical faculty. She was the only staff doctor. In 1937, it had sixty patients (against a capacity of forty). *MR*, 27 October 1937 and 5 September 1936.

186. "Ten Years of the Magnitogorsk Hospital," written by G. I. Drobyshev, for whom the first permanent hospital in Magnitogorsk, built after the war, was named. *MR*, 11 November 1939.

187. *MR*, 22 January 1937.

188. *MR*, 26 January 1938.

189. *MR*, 26 September 1939. The article originally appeared in *Pravda*, 25 September 1939.

190. Scott, "'Magnetic City,'" p. 550.

191. *MR*, 21 October 1937.

192. Even from this viewpoint Magnitogorsk appeared chaotic. John Scott flew over Magnitogorsk in 1933 and described it as "a wide construction camp which looked dirty and disorganized even from the air." Scott, *Behind*, pp. 113–14. This was early on and, moreover, Scott was remarking on the contrast between Magnitogorsk and the main cities of the Urals, Sverdlovsk and Cheliabinsk.

193. A. M. Gasparian, "Magnitogorsk," *Planirovka i stroitelstvo gorodov*, 1933, no. 2, pp. 3–8.

194. *MR*, 1 January 1937. Although the smokestacks spewing out multicolored smoke were a source of pride, data on pollution in Magnitogorsk were collected. The Department of Industrial Sanitation and Labor Hygiene of the Institute of Health conducted tests on dust accumulation during all four seasons in 1935. They found that in the Fifth Sector, squeezed between the mine and the factory, 3–4 grams of dust accumulated every 24 hours. In the Kirov district, 1.4, in Berezka, 1.2, and on the right bank, 0.7. *MR*, 11 February 1936. Sympathy for those living on factory grounds, in the Sixth and Seventh Sectors, was expressed once in the local newspaper, on 28 April 1937.

PART II. LIVING SOCIALISM

1. *Sobranie sochinenii*, vol. 1, pp. 92–95.

2. Marshak, *New Russia's Primer*, p. 154.

3. By 1940 Sovnarkom was made up of thirty-four commissariats, twenty-four of which were engaged in economic management. See Alexander Baykov, *The Development of the Soviet Economic System: An Essay on the Experience of Planning in the USSR* (New York: Macmillan, 1948), pp. 297–99.

4. In fascist Italy new towns, founded on an average of one a year, also formed part of an ambitious internal colonization drive (in the Italian case, the goal was redirecting people from the overpopulated North to the underdeveloped South). The fascist program was put forward as a state-sponsored effort to achieve social progress while upholding the interests of the people. Not the state, however, but newly established "public" organizations, as well as private companies, were given near dictatorial control over the building and governance of the new towns, largely without laws or regulatory supervision. Such a form of "planning," which resulted in badly inadequate housing, medical care, and even food supplies, resembled the Soviet state ministerial approach whereby the "interests" of the bureaucracy override all other considerations and in fact betray the public interest that the state supposedly existed to protect. Lucia Nuti, "Public and Private Interests in New Town Planning: The Case of Italy, 1922–1942," *Planning Perspectives* 3 (1988): 81–98.

5. Gugel, "Vospominaniia," p. 321.

6. R. A. French, "The Individuality of the Soviet City," in French and F. E. Ian Hamilton, eds., *The Socialist City: Spatial Structure and Urban Policy* (Chichester: Wiley, 1979), pp. 101–2.

7. One of the contributors to the conference argued elsewhere, in a textbook on the Soviet city, that "the very essence of the planned socialist city is the ability to predetermine growth and adequately accommodate it." But he also outlined the

many constraints that in practice rendered this goal problematic. This contradiction served to call into question the existence of a specifically socialist city, notwithstanding the book's aims. James H. Bater, *The Soviet City: Ideal and Reality* (Beverly Hills: Sage, 1980), p. 30.

8. Denis J. B. Shaw, "Some Influences on Spatial Structure in the State Socilaist City: The Case of the USSR," in Lutz Holzner and Jeane Knapp, eds., *Soviet Geography in Our Time* (Madison: University of Wisconsin Press, 1987), pp. 201–27. Shaw recognized that planning alone could not account for the spatial form and land use that could be found in Soviet cities. He concluded that some account had to be taken of the role played by the urban inhabitants—a task that was attempted in part 1 of this monograph.

9. Lazar Kaganovich, *Za sotsialisticheskuiu rekonstruktsiiu Moskvy i gorodov SSSR, pererabotannaia stenogramma doklada na iiunskom plenume TsK VKP (b)* (Moscow, 1931).

10. Ironically, with the collapse of Communism in 1991, the post-Communist leadership initially took much the same approach regarding capitalism: what would be permitted as part of the restoration of capitalism was whatever had been forbidden under socialism.

11. *Grazhdanskii kodeks RSFSR s izmeneniiami do 1 Maia 1934 g.* (Moscow, 1934), p. 16. The decree on land can be found in *Sobranie Ukazov*, 1918, no. 62, item 674.

12. Interview with Roy Howard, *Pravda*, 5 March 1936, reprinted in Robert McNeal, ed., *Sochineniia*, vol. 1 [14] (Stanford: Hoover Institution Press, 1967), p. 126. Socialism, in the words of Milovan Djilas, was "a slogan and a pledge, a faith and a lofty ideal, and, in fact, a particular form of government and ownership which would facilitate the industrial revolution and make possible improvement and expansion of production." Djilas, *The New Class*, p. 18.

13. "Under Communist systems the people realize quickly what they are and what they are not permitted to do," wrote Djilas. "Everyone knows what can and cannot be done, and what depends on whom." Djilas, *The New Class*, pp. 70–71.

14. This model of historical analysis, adapted from Machiavelli, is employed with great skill by Adrian Lyttelton in his study of the onset of fascism in Italy. Lyttleton treats the rise of fascism as a political problem, and analyzes politics as a question of (1) the menu of options open to political actors at any given time, within the constraints imposed by social structure, institutions, traditions, and the historical conjuncture; and (2) the actions individuals take, given these constraints and options. As he emphasizes, all actions undertaken lead to a realignment of the correlation of forces and thus to a reconfiguration of the menu of options. Lyttelton, *The Seizure of Power: Fascism in Italy, 1919–1929* (Princeton: Princeton University Press, 1973; 1987), esp. p. 77. Lyttelton's study had the great merit of removing Mussolini's personality and psyche from the center of the story (he did not mention *il duce* until ch. 5). But because Lyttleton tended to underestimate the role of what might be called ideology or belief systems, his view of political action at times appeared unnecessarily instrumentalist.

CHAPTER 4. LIVING SPACE AND THE STRANGER'S GAZE

1. *Hope against Hope: A Memoir*, trans. Max Hayward (New York: Atheneum, 1970), p. 135.

2. GARF, f. 7952, op. 5, d. 300, l. 35.

3. Ibid., d. 309, l. 7.

4. Interview, Magnitogorsk, May 1987. Many people, however, continued to live in tents. In September 1930, with winter approaching, one local newspaper reported that 2,000 workers still lived in tents. GARF, f. 7952, op. 5, d. 385, l. 1. In 1931, for the 1,600 workers engaged in the construction of the first two blast furnaces, there was one barracks. At about the same time, 1,350 workers of the coke-chemical plant construction were still living in tents, and virtually all the blast furnace workers were living in tents. Ibid., d. 304, l. 11; *Magnitogorskii komsomolets*, 16 October 1931. Two Soviet historians wrote that in the summer of 1931 (i.e., after the dekulakized peasants had begun arriving in large numbers) "more than" 10,000 people were living in tents. Just how many more, however, remains unclear. Antipova and Shkolnik, "Iz istorii." A report by the city soviet dated 1 August 1931 gave a figure of 15,000 people in tents, of a total population of 170,000. MFGAChO, f. 10, op. 1, d. 18, l. 86.

5. During 1931 an average of 500 people were arriving at Magnitogorsk every day, and some days 1,200 or more would disembark from the train. People were also leaving the site, often because they had found no place to live. GARF, f. 7952, op. 5, d. 309, l. 9.

6. "Altogether on the site around 200 railroad cars are being used as housing," revealed one official report in early 1932, which added that skilled workers in the rail transport department, having the right by contract to an apartment, nevertheless lived for more than a year in such "accommodations." GARF, f. 7952, op. 5, d. 143, l. 51; and d. 137, l. 74. In the Donbas, workers slept on station platforms, according to Panfilova, *Formirovanie*, p. 33. In Kuznetsk some people lived in caves on the hillside. John Westgarth, *Russian Engineer* (London: Archer, 1934), p. 59. In Moscow a considerable number of workers of the Elektrozavod factory slept on the floor in the factory. Andrew Smith, *I Was a Soviet Worker* (New York: Dutton, 1937), p. 115. And in Asbest (in the Urals) some families "were living in a sort of earth hovel; others in huts half of which were hardly more than excavations in the ground rudely roofed over." Walter Rukeyser, *Working for the Soviets: An American Engineer in Russia* (New York: Covici, 1932), pp. 152–3.

7. GASO, f. 241, op. 1, d. 1320, l. 4.

8. Whereas in 1912 the average number of occupants per housing unit in Berlin was 3.9 and in London 4.5, in Moscow it was 8.5. See Joseph Bradley, "From Big Village to Metropolis," in Michael Hamm, ed., *The City in Late Imperial Russia* (Bloomington: Indiana University Press, 1986), pp. 14–15; and Bradley, *Muzhik and Muscovite: Urbanization in Late Imperial Russia* (Berkeley: University of California Press, 1985), pp. 211 ff. Soviet approaches to housing grew out of, but also in many ways transformed, the prerevolutionary understanding of the "urban question" in Russia as it had emerged in the nineteenth century. Then the issue was framed chiefly as a problem of rectifying the squalid, unhealthy, and unsanitary living conditions of the great bulk of the population. After October, the urban ques-

tion became one of transforming human consciousness and behavior, and augmenting the power of the state. See V. V. Sviatlovskii, *Zhilishchnyi vopros*, 5 vols. (St. Petersburg, 1902); and Michael Hamm, "The Modern Russian City: An Historiographical Analysis," *Journal of Urban History* 4, no. 1 (1977): 39–76.

9. The resemblance of Soviet notions of housing to the ideas of the nineteenth-century French thinkers Charles Fourier and Henri-Claude Saint-Simon, both of whom had an enormous impact in Russia, has been noted by Milka Bliznakov, "Soviet Housing during the Experimental Years," in William Brumfield and Blair Ruble, *Russian Housing in the Modern Age: Design and Social History* (Washington, D. C.: Woodrow Wilson Center and Cambridge University Press, 1993), pp. 93, 95.

10. *MR*, 20 February 1930.

11. See, for example, John Burnett, *A Social History of Housing 1815–1970* (London: Methuen, 1978); and Ann-Louise Shapiro, *Housing the Poor of Paris, 1850–1902* (Madison: University of Wisconsin Press, 1985). With housing as with other issues thought to concern what was called "the welfare of the population," the Great War was a formative experience for the further articulation of a field of social activity for the state. The Russian revolution, which of course took place during the Great War, not only accelerated this social articulation in Russia but also stamped the process with an ideological coloring (Communism) that rendered it considerably more problematic outside of Russia.

12. In regard to housing, the first order of business for the socially oriented and transformative Soviet state was to gain administrative control over the country's housing stock, which meant taking an inventory—a daunting task made more so by the onset of civil war (by the time hostilities drew to a close in 1920, much of the already inadequate prerevolutionary urban housing stock was unusable or nearly so). Various appraisals of the housing stock were attempted with little success, until the urban census of 1923 provided an opportunity for a systematic survey. See *Zhilishchnye usloviia gorodov po perepisi 1923 goda, po SSSR v tselom: Statisticheskii ezhegodnik 1922–1923 gg.*, vyp. 2 (Moscow, n.d.). The results were summarized in *Ekonomicheskoe obozrenie*, 1924, no. 5. The next urban housing survey was conducted during the 1926 census, partial results of which were reported in "Zhilishchnyi vopros v otrazhenii vsesoiuznoi perepisi," *Ekonomicheskoe obozrenie*, 1928, no. 9. For a brief introduction to the complex issue of statistics in the early Soviet period, see I. Iu. Pisarev, "Razvitiie sovetskoi statistiki (kratkii obzor osnovnykh rabot)," in *Ocherki po istorii statistiki SSSR: Sbornik vtoroi* (Moscow, 1957), pp. 297–326.

13. According to the decree on land, only the largest buildings in cities of more than 10,000 people were supposed to be confiscated outright and given over to "workers," but implementation of central directives varied from place to place, even from hour to hour, according to the strength and disposition of local authorities. The decree is translated in Timothy Sosnovy, *The Housing Problem in the Soviet Union* (New York: Research Program on the USSR, 1954), pp. 228–29. One contemporary Soviet specialist claimed that the process of expropriation was essentially completed by the spring of 1919, and that altogether 8 billion rubles' worth of housing was seized. D. Buzin, "Zhilishchno-kommunalnoe khoziaistvo za 20 let (1917–1937 gg.)," *Problemy ekonomiki*, 1937, nos. 5–6, pp. 171–96. Unfortunately, there is no way to verify such a figure. See also the discussion in Vladimir

Gsovski, *Soviet Civil Law: Private Rights and their Background under the Soviet Regime*, vol. 1 (Ann Arbor: University of Michigan Law School, 1948), pp. 287–92.

14. Many sequestered buildings had been abandoned by the previous occupants and were in no condition for use by anyone. Sometimes new "worker" tenants who had been granted "possession" of an expropriated apartment fled the city for the countryside without ever occupying their new living quarters. See the findings published in *European Housing Problems since the War, 1914–1923*, International Labour Office (London), Studies and Reports, Series G (housing and welfare), no. 1, pp. 454–55. Many of the best residential structures were taken over by official organizations that, despite rapid growth, showed little desire to relinquish control over their comparatively plush if soon overburdened quarters. According to an official survey, one-third of all nationalized buildings, residential and commercial, were occupied by institutions. See Sosnovy, *The Housing Problem*, p. 41, n. 13, citing the 1923 census.

15. Beginning in 1921, restrictions were placed on the grounds for summary eviction, and payment was reinstated for municipal services and rent, which along with money had been "abolished." Buildings with more than five dwellings became subject to demunicipalization, and some were either returned to former owners or leased, partly in the hope that an "owner" would become responsible for repair and maintenance. Many structures were simply taken over by state enterprises. Also, new housing construction, which had dropped off entirely, was encouraged as private persons and tenants' "cooperatives" received permission to construct housing with a guarantee of long-term ownership. Housing cooperatives were governed by a 1924 law that remained in force until 1937, when cooperatives lost their independent status. Anon., "The Housing Problem in Soviet Russia," *International Labour Review* 12, no. 2 (August 1925): 245–61; see also the official guidebook to cooperative housing: Iurii Katkovskii, *Zhilishchno-arednye i zhilishchno-stroitelnye kooperativy: Sbornik po zakonodatelstvu v voprosakh i otvetakh* (Moscow, 1936). It is not clear how many buildings underwent a change in ownership during the initial nationalization or the subsequent partial denationalization (with large state enterprises often assuming control over residential structures, demunicipalization did not necessarily mean denationalization). Moscow appears to be an exception, for municipally owned buildings there still constituted 72 percent of all structures in 1923, when the countrywide figure was 14.6 percent. *European Housing Problems*, p. 478. In 1928, according to Gsovski, who cites a contemporary Soviet source, privately owned houses in the Russian republic constituted 85 percent of all urban buildings and accounted for about one-half of housing space. With the onset of the Five-Year Plans, however, all of this changed radically. Gsovski, *Soviet Civil Law*, vol. 1, p. 287, citing *Chastnoe domovladneiie: Sbornik dekretov* (Moscow, 1928), preface. See also Buzin, "Zhilishchno-kommunalnoe khoziaistvo," passim.

16. See Elise Kimerling, "Civil Rights and Social Policy in Soviet Russia, 1918–1936," *Russian Review* 41, no. 2 (1982): 24–46. Through an examination of willfully discriminatory central electoral policy, as well as local confusion regarding the implementation of the laws, Kimerling highlights the contradictions of pre-Stalinist efforts at class-based social engineering. For the prerevolutionary legacy on civil

rights, see Olga Crisp and Linda Edmundson, eds., *Civil Rights in Imperial Russia* (Oxford: Clarendon, 1989).

17. Mervyn Mathews, "Social Dimensions in Soviet Urban Housing," in French and Hamilton, *The Socialist City*, pp. 105–18. Municipal and central authorities also asserted a responsibility for urban administration, including the construction and management of roads, sewage, and mass transit, all of which had been badly neglected under the old regime. In tsarist Russia, according to one historian, "fire was the principal instrument of urban renewal in city after city." Daniel Brower, "Urbanization and Autocracy: Russian Urban Development in the First Half of the Nineteenth Century," *Russian Review* 42 (1983): 377–402; quote is from 381. See also James Bater, "The Legacy of Autocracy: Environmental Quality in St. Petersburg," in French and Hamilton, *The Socialist City*, pp. 23–48. For a comparison of pre- and postrevolutionary approaches to urban infrastructure and management, see Buzin, "Zhilishchno-kommunalnoe khoziaistvo," p. 183.

18. This important process has not been researched and analyzed. Generally speaking, most large buildings had been, or were once again, taken over by city soviets, although some smaller ones continued to be privately owned. Even the latter were in many cases de facto expropriated, however, as can be seen from the comments of Nadezhda Mandelstam, describing Voronezh in 1934. Mandelstam, *Hope against Hope*, p. 129.

19. Soviet pamphleteers, of course, insisted on a sharp break between "socialist" and "capitalist" approaches to and results in city building. For example, L. Perchik, *Zhilishchnyi vopros pri kapitalizme i sotsializme* (Moscow, 1934). Although most of the same ways of looking at housing, and some of the same practices in housing organization and management, were current in Europe at the time, the pamphleteers' claims were largely justified. See Anon., "Housing as a Post-War Problem in Europe," *International Labour Review*, August 1924, pp. 277–95, and September 1924, pp. 452–69; and Ivan Szelenyi and Gyorgy Konrad, "Housing Systems and the Social Structure," *The Sociological Review Monographs* 17 (1972): 269–97.

20. See Alfred John DiMaio, Jr., *Soviet Urban Housing: Problems and Policies* (New York: Praeger, 1974); and Alexander Block, "Soviet Housing—the Historical Aspect: Some Notes on the Problem of Policy," *Soviet Studies* 3, no. 1 (July 1951): 1–15, and no. 3 (January 1952): 229–57. The best introduction to housing in the USSR remains Sosnovy, *The Housing Problem*, cited in n. 13. Even Sosnovy casts his study in terms of a housing shortage, but unlike all other commentators, he manages to cover a range of other aspects of "the housing question," including a chapter on "the impact on everyday life," and thus comes closest to the approach adopted here.

21. Housing issues were governed by the 1926 civil code until a comprehensive law on housing was issued in 1937. See A. M. Berzin et al., *Deistvuiushchee zhilishchnoe zakonodatelstvo: Sistematicheskii sbornik zakonov SSSR i RSFSR, vedomstvennykh postanovlenii Moskovskogo soveta* (Moscow, 1937); V. K. Khimev, *Sovteskoe zakonodatelstvo o zhilishche: Sistematicheskii sbornik vazneishikh postanovlenii* (Moscow, 1937); and John Hazard, *Soviet Housing Law* (New Haven: Yale University Press, 1939).

22. *Magnitostroi: Informatsionnyi biulleten,* 1931, no. 2, p. 43. One square meter is equal to approximately ten square feet.

23. *Magnitostroi v tsifrakh* (Magnitogorsk, 1932), pp. 322–27. A clearer demonstration of the drop in living standards accompanying the first Five-Year Plan would be hard to imagine.

24. At the time of Stalin's death, the average was still less than five square meters. By the late 1970s, the average had still not reached the original norm of nine. By this time, statistics were often expressed in *obshchaia ploshchad* (overall space), which in addition to *zhilaia ploshchad* (living space) included kitchens and washrooms. See Henry Morton, "Who Gets What, When, and How? Housing in the Soviet Union," *Soviet Studies* 32, no. 2 (April 1980): 235–59.

25. In the report submitted by the Magnitogorsk steel plant's chief accountant to the Metallurgy Trust (GUMP) of the People's Commissariat of Heavy Industry, the housing stock as of 1 January 1935 was characterized as follows:

	Number of residents		% of total living space
Permanent buildings	25,540	(16%)	21.1
Barracks	116,805	(75%)	71.3
Mud huts	12,445	(9%)	7.6
Total	154,790		

Given that the total population was probably closer to 200,000, the data are incomplete. In the distribution of residents by type of housing the accountant has probably omitted the housing of the Corrective Labor Colony (ITK) and the Special Labor Settlement, which were under NKVD and not GUMP jurisdiction and made up chiefly of barracks. Within the same report, data on the status of housing for workers indicate that only 10,837 people, or 14.4 percent of the aggregate working population, lived in permanent buildings. And 80 percent of those workers in permanent buildings (around 8,700) were production workers. But the other 25,811 production workers—the people for whom the socialist city was purportedly being built—still lived in barracks. RGAE, f. 4086, op. 2, d. 933, ll. 26–27.

26. The measurement of living space was clearly inaccurate, making exact comparisons impossible and inviting caution in the use of the statistics for anything other than approximating orders of magnitude. Notwithstanding small inconsistencies in the data, however, it is obvious that three or four years later the cramped conditions remained much the same. See *MR,* 11 July 1938, 3 April and 2 December 1939; and MFGAChO, f. 10, op. 4, d. 63, ll. 39–40, reprinted in Eliseeva, *Iz istorii,* pp. 245–47. The removal of barracks, made possible in part by a slight population decline, was facilitated by the increased availability of apartments in permanent buildings, but no overall increase in space resulted. By the outbreak of the war, the overwhelming majority, probably at least two-thirds, of the city's inhabitants were still living in barracks and mud huts. Data from 1940 and 1941 on aggregate living space are consistent with those from 1937 and 1938. GAChO, f. 804, op. 11, d. 105, l. 40; and *Materialy o rabote,* p. 8. The latter source gives an average per person in 1941 of 3.6 square meters—a slight decrease from the 1935 figure of 3.9, but a shift small enough to be virtually meaningless. The average for the USSR

as a whole in 1940 was around 4 square meters, whereas in the mid-1920s it had been around 6. See Sosnovy, *The Housing Problem*, pp. 105, 269.

27. The fact that buildings constituted 21 percent of the total living space but housed only 16 percent of the population indicates that some people within the catch-all category of buildings had comparatively more space than those living in either barracks or mud huts. The averages for people living in barracks (3.68) and mud huts (3.70) were almost identical. John Scott claimed that in the Kirov district in 1937 there were 3.34 square meters per person on average and that, normally, four to five people lived in a room. He cited no source. Scott, *Behind*, pp. 210–11.

28. The data in table 6 can be juxtaposed against those offered by John Scott (*Behind*, p. 234) on the distribution of population permanent apartment

Berezka and Central Hotel	2%
Kirov district and other permanent apartment buildings	15%
Permanent individual houses	8%
Barracks and other temporary houses	50%
Mud huts	25%

Combining Scott's data with those of the party archive, it emerges that about 33 percent of the city's space but only 15 percent of its population was in permanent brick buildings. Conversely, mud huts covered 17.5 percent of the city's space and housed 25 percent of the population.

29. Whereas the urban housing fund in the Soviet Union increased by almost 90 million square meters between 1926 and 1940, the total urban population increased by almost 30 million. For every new urban inhabitant, there were only 3 square meters of new living space. Moreover, much of that space did not meet even the minimum standards established by the Soviet government. When one takes into account the very small percentage of urban housing space provided with running water (cold), plumbing, central heating, and a bath, the picture becomes even bleaker. See Sosnovy, *The Housing Problem*, pp. 57, 66, 139, 144.

30. In 1931 a group of individuals in Magnitogorsk joined together to build cooperative housing. Money was collected and construction of one building began. Five years later, the building was less than one-fifth completed. Most members of the original cooperative had left the city. The city soviet sought the advice of the Urals oblast housing union on whether or not to liquidate the organization, the Workers' Housing Construction Cooperative Society. No information on its ultimate fate was reported. *MR*, 29 September 1936.

31. Hiring contracts often carried stipulations on the nature and size of the living space to be granted to the employee, but did not mention penalties for failure to do so. Many people nonetheless took a particular job for the sole reason that it meant acquiring living space. As with ration cards (see ch. 6), the allocation of living space was used to pressure people to work.

32. *Magnitostroi: Informatsionnyi biulleten*, 1931, no. 3, p. 38.

33. *MR*, 24 April 1936. Within a few years Makarov rose to become the chief of Magnitogorsk's coke batteries. In 1938 or 1939 he was transferred to Kuznetsk, where he became the chief of the coke shop. *Stalinskaia stroika*, pp. 19–34.

34. A population chart for October 1932 was divided into three residential dis-

tricts, none of which included the settlements of the exiled peasants. MFGAChO, f. 9, op. 1, d. 16, l. 51.

35. *MR*, 4 October 1934. The Magnitogorsk newspaper never said as much, but to characterize such situations people used the word *blat*, a slang term with multiple meanings ranging from "influence" and "pull" to "informal" and "illegal." As one Soviet factory worker from a Ukrainian city who fled to the Allied side during the confusing aftermath of World War II remarked, "You could do anything, if you knew the right people. We had a proverb which we used very often in our factory, 'Don't have two brothers [*brata*] but have two pulls [*blata*].' You see, this 'blat' was really great." Jay K. Zawodny, "Twenty-six Interviews," I/3.

36. *MR*, 16 December 1936.

37. *Magnitogorskii komsomolets*, 16 October 1931.

38. RGAE, f. 4086, op. 2, d. 933, ll. 26–27.

39. In American company towns, employers often succeeded in making housing contingent on employment, either by limiting the town's housing market to rental units they owned, or by controlling the local banking industry and thus the granting of mortgages. Davis, "Company Towns," pp. 119–23.

40. *Sobranie ukazov RSFSR*, 1932, no. 85, item 371, reprinted in *Kodeks zakonov o trude, s izmeneniiami na 1 iiulia 1938 g.* (Moscow, 1938), p. 22.

41. *MR*, 26 July 1939. According to John Hazard, whose monograph on Soviet housing law was written after a three-year stay in the USSR during the 1930s, "housing law is no mystery to Soviet citizens. The usual occupant of a room or apartment can answer in some detail questions about the law applying to his right of occupancy." Hazard, *Soviet Housing Law*, p. 122.

42. *Sobranie zakonov i rasporiazhenii SSSR*, 1932, no. 84, items 516 and 517. See also the discussion by Ivan Kunitsyn, "'Vot, tebe, babushka, Iurev den,'" *Iunost*, 1989, no. 4, pp. 56–61.

43. The city kept files on the commandants. A list of some, with short characterizations, can be found in MFGAChO, f. 10, op. 1, d. 139, ll. 26–27.

44. In 1936, for example, one reporter went to the so-called *adresnyi stol*—a public service, not the militia registration bureau—at which for 25 kopecks one could, theoretically, learn the address of anyone living in the city. The reporter inquired about sixteen friends whom he knew to be living in Magnitogorsk. Eight were not on the master list. When the reporter asked about himself (supposedly over the phone), he was allegedly told that such a person had left for Cheliabinsk five years ago. It leads one to wonder what the registration records at the neighborhood militia bureaus were like. *MR*, 29 March 1936. By the end of the decade, registration seems to have been much more reliable and systematic, at least in certain parts of town. An investigation of residence registration in the Fifth Sector and Socialist City conducted in April 1941 uncovered twenty-one unregistered people, twenty of whom were children. The twenty-first person had a registration stamp in his passport but was not recorded in the building's book. One person was found not to have a passport. MFGAChO, f. 16, op. 1. d. 134, l. 7.

45. "To live without police registration in Soviet cities was risky," wrote one former Soviet citizen. "If discovered, one might be sentenced to as much as two years." Valentina Kamyshina, "A Woman's Heart," in Louis Fischer, ed., *Thirteen Who Fled* (New York: Harper, 1949), p. 106. Public places in some cities, such as

Moscow, were subject to periodic, unannounced document sweeps. See S. Moros, "Ia esche vernus: Povest v dvukh chastiakh," unpublished ms., 8 November 1949, Hoover Institution Archives, Nicolaevsky Collection, series 236, box 3, folder 410–11, p. 35. It is unclear whether such sweeps were conducted in Magnitogorsk in the 1930s.

46. This was how, for example, Nina Kondratkovskaia, a member of the writers' union, a resident of Magnitogorsk for more than fifty years, and self-described patriot of Magnitogorsk was able to settle in the city in 1934. She met Valentin Serzhantov, a worker-correspondent for the newspaper *Magnitogorskii komsomolets.* "We both shared an interest in literature," explained Kondratkovskaia, "and anyway he had good documents. I was from the village and without a valid passport. He agreed to help me out. We were able to get an apartment in Socialist City (actually, Lattice-Wood Town), and we moved in together. Otherwise, I don't know what I would have done." The couple later divorced. Interview by author, Magnitogorsk, May 1987. Serzhantov, who lives in Cheliabinsk, refused repeated requests to speak with this author in 1987 and 1989. Kondratkovskaia died in 1990.

47. Freda Utley, a British citizen who lived in the Soviet Union during the better part of the 1930s, wrote that "even when both husband and wife wish to separate, it is almost impossible for them to do so because neither can find a room to move into. One couple of our acquaintance who had twice divorced each other always got together again because they had to go on living in the same flat. Since most families often have only one room to live in it is almost impossible to separate, just as young people are often unable to get married . . . because they cannot get a room to live in away from their parents. Often married couples have to share the one room occupied by mother and father and brother and sisters." Freda Utley, *The Dream We Lost: Soviet Russia Then and Now* (New York: John Day, 1940), p. 107. Conversely, one Soviet expatriate interviewed after entering the United States reported that "girls married men with a suitable room and vice-versa. They could then divorce and claim a part of the room they had married. It could often be heard said that someone had married a twenty square meter room. Then after two weeks or a month of marriage, the person concerned would divorce. The room would then remain in the possession of the least scrupulous one with the strongest nerves. He or she would proceed to organize parties every night in his or her section of the room. These parties would usually be very noisy, smoky and drink-filled. As a final recourse, if his ex-wife had by that time not yet decided to move out, the man would bring in women. The ex-owner of the room would then attempt to find a man with a suitable room and the cycle would begin all over again." From the Harvard Project on the Soviet Social System, life-history interviews, informant 43, as quoted in H. Kent Geiger, *The Family in Soviet Russia* (Cambridge, Mass.: Harvard University Press, 1968), p. 209.

48. The older the city, the higher the percentage of housing stock owned by the city soviet, which acquired buildings mostly through sequestration. Magnitogorsk started from scratch, so there was no prerevolutionary housing stock to confiscate. It bears remembering that the land on which a building stood was leased, not owned. By a 1932 law, state enterprises acquired the right to build on urban land by obtaining from the local soviet a so-called Act of Perpetual Use, or lease in perpetuity (technically, as long as the enterprise's property right in that building was

maintained). It was in this sense that they owned the buildings. See Hazard, *Soviet Housing Law*, pp. 14–15.

49. According to an official report of 1 January 1937, the steel plant was in charge of all municipal facilities and the entire housing stock, except for 5,000 square meters under the jurisdiction of the city soviet. MFGAChO, f. 10, op. 1, d. 243, l. 8. There was a parallel urban management organization, Gorkomkhoz, the city branch of the Commissariat of Municipal Economy, but it seems to have been overshadowed by the steel plant's KBU.

50. *Sobranie ukazov*, 1921, no. 6, item 47; and no. 56, item 355.

51. *MR*, 30 June 1935.

52. Paradoxically, in the case of the person with the most space, the relative increase was the smallest. It was only those in a space of over nine square meters per person who would be assessed triple the basic rate for each "excessive" square meter. But as we have seen in chapter 3, these people, living predominantly in the elite enclave of Berezka, charged their rent to the factory. *MR*, 2 August 1936. A law of 17 October 1937 provided for the private renting of living space in individual housing, including mud huts. The newspaper fumed that residents apparently took advantage of the opportunity, renting space for three times the state-calculated rent—and getting away with it. *MR*, 28 May 1937.

53. *MR*, 11 August 1936.

54. *MR*, 12 September 1933.

55. *CR*, 18 September 1935. In 1938 some barracks were said not to have been attended to since they were first built, back in 1932. *CR*, 9 May 1938.

56. *MR*, 16 March 1936.

57. *MR*, 5 August 1936.

58. *MR*, 20 August 1938. Lukashevich was initially replaced by Beloglazov, but soon the latter was also removed, and replaced by Tabunov; Tabunov was arrested and replaced three months later by Teplitskii, the fourth chief of the KBU in a span of five months. MFGAChO, f. 99, op. 10, d. 1091, ll. 56, 124. In July 1938 Ananenko became at least the fifth KBU chief since Lukashevich. *CR*, 3 December 1938.

59. By 1939, the number of barracks had declined to around six hundred. *MR*, 3 April and 2 December 1939.

60. *MR*, 11 February 1936. According to Beso Lominadze the very first barracks removed on the site had been taken down to make way for the slag dump. RGAE, f. 7297, op. 28, d. 327, l. 39. That slag heap is still there; more than fifty-five years later, it has grown to the size of the original iron-ore mountain, which is precisely what it is made of.

61. *MR*, 18 February and 30 March 1936.

62. In the winter of 1937–38, the approximately 2,000 inhabitants of the Third Sector, located on the territory of the coke and chemical plant, were told the barracks in which they lived would be torn down, as a result of which the collapsing barracks were not repaired. Then the inhabitants were informed that the barracks would be left standing another three years. Repairs, however, were still not scheduled. *MR*, 10 April and 8 June 1938.

63. *MR*, 27 July 1938. The KBU changed into the UKKh on 17 October 1937, in connection with the central decree "on the preservation of the housing fund." MFGAChO, f. 99, op. 10, d. 1096, l. 211.

64. *MR*, 11 July 1938.

65. At first the cost of riding the tram depended on the distance traveled. Most people traveled short distances, paying either 10 or 15 kopecks. In 1936 the cost rose to 20, regardless of the distance, and KBU revenues shot up. Whereas 1935 "profits" had been 200,000 rubles, for the first two months of 1936 after the fee change profits were already 60,000 rubles—360,000 per year, an increase of 80 percent. Lukashevich was rebuked for bringing in such high "profits." *MR*, 18 March 1936.

66. *MR*, 22 February 1936. As of 1 June 1937, the KBU was owed more than 2 million rubles in back rent. MFGAChO, f. 99, op. 10, d. 1091, l. 124.

67. *MR*, 3 October 1938.

68. *CR*, 3 December 1938.

69. Even in permanent buildings, residents thought nothing of chopping wood in common areas, whatever damage that caused. Nor did they shrink from removing the glass from the kitchen windows to replace broken or missing windows in their own rooms. *MR*, 16 December 1936.

70. GARF, f. 7952, op. 5, d. 300, ll. 42, 44–45.

71. Ibid., d. 304, l. 33.

72. *Magnitogorskii komsomolets*, 16 October 1931; and GARF, f. 7952, op. 5, d. 389, l. 16.

73. *Komsomolskaia pravda*, 15 June 1931. Nina Kondratkovskaia, speaking of the barracks around 1934, drew an even more vivid picture: "Dormitories without separate rooms, divided into four sections, tiny kitchen areas where it was impossible to turn around, stoves [*pechki*] thoroughly overrun with pots and pans, people in greasy work clothes (there were no showers at the steel plant), children in the hallways, water in columns, wretched 'furniture': metal cots, bedside tables, homemade desks and shelves." To this litany she added that "on each sector between the barracks there were common toilets," the memory of which also stood out in her mind. *MR*, 31 March 1989. Conditions at Magnitogorsk were typical. See the description by an Italian Communist who worked as a miner in the town of Bobrik (Donskoi) quoted, without citation, in Sosnovy, *The Housing Problem*, p. 224.

74. *MR*, 29 January 1936.

75. *MR*, 1 February 1938.

76. *MR*, 16 April 1934.

77. *Materialy o rabote*, p. 9.

78. *MR*, 11 January 1938.

79. *MR*, 9 June 1936.

80. GARF, f. 7952, op. 5, d. 318, l. 60.

81. One early official investigation of the public dining halls found "dirt, stench, filth, long lines, lack of spoons, forks, and knives; filth in the kitchen, food not fit to be served anywhere, unwashed or poorly washed eating utensils." As reported in Polonskii, *Magnitostroi*, pp. 46 ff. Polonskii mentions in passing that there was, of course, a nice setup for foreign specialists and administrative personnel, "as there should be."

82. GARF, f. 7952, op. 5, d. 389, l. 17.

83. Eating facilities inside the factory were superior to those in the city. The dining hall in the open-hearth shop, for example, which served over 3,000 people

daily, enjoyed an excellent reputation. Of course, one had to work in the shop to eat there. The best public-access dining hall, in the opinion of the newspaper, was in the basement of the cinema, Magnit. But aside from the problem that the cinema was located far from the chief residential districts, long queues necessitated a long wait before being served. For this, the newspaper attacked the service personnel (and not the ratio of dining halls to population, or their location). But one female employee, subject to rude remarks by impatient patrons, was reported by the newspaper to have shot back: "I don't have ten legs, wait a bit." MR, 2 October 1938.

84. Scott, Behind, p. 40. Even the great enthusiasts of collectivized living at the Moscow architectural institutes admitted that urbanites, especially families, preferred to eat in the confines of their own home, sometimes even carrying home the food they obtained at the canteens. See Moisei Ginzburg, Zhilishche (Moscow, 1934), p. 82.

85. In 1936 fewer than 1,000 children, aged two months to two years, appear to have been in the city's sixteen nurseries. Total staff was said to be 180, of whom 15 had special training. MR, 3 April 1936.

86. MR, 26 September 1936 and 29 January 1938; Scott, Behind, pp. 212–13. When it came to domestic chores at home, men took a far less active role than women. All six of the people I interviewed who lived in Magnitogorsk in the 1930s reported that women did the overwhelming majority of the housework; not one could recall a household where it was otherwise. Whereas the female children of the dekulakized provided a ready supply of maids for those who could afford the expense, for the majority of households the burden was carried by the women. Two early 1930s time-budget studies are reproduced in Susan Kingsbury and Mildred Fairchild, Factory, Family, and Woman in the Soviet Union (New York: Putnam, 1935), pp. 290–91. The first, based on the study of 841 men and women, is taken from "a manuscript report from Central Bureau National Economic Accounting [TsUNKhU], 1931"; the second, based on the study of 683 "factory" men and women, is taken from Trud v SSSR (Moscow, 1932), p. 169. According to the studies, women spent between double and triple the time men did on housework. Moreover, at least half of male household work consisted in "care of personal sanitation." At the same time, women also spent more time each day doing "productive" (i.e., paid) labor. Women must have simply slept less. Fifty years later the situation with housework remained pretty much the same. See L. A. Gordon and E. Klopov, Chelovek posle raboty (Moscow, 1975), ch. 3.

87. Indeed, one scholar has noted that "no one can fail to see the potentialities for disputes, grudges, insults, petty thieving, riotous children, and noise inherent in crowded Soviet housing conditions." Hazard, Soviet Housing Law, p. 110.

88. GARF, f. 7952, op. 5, d. 313, l. 140.

89. One former Soviet citizen (not from Magnitogorsk) offered the following testimony: "Our 'apartment' consisted of one small room in an eight-room house. A family lived in each room. There was a single kitchen which we were all supposed to use, but I preferred to prepare food in the room." Kamyshina, "A Woman's Heart," p. 103.

90. Originally, comrade courts were formed in work places. According to a 20 February 1931 decree, they could be established anywhere where there were one hundred or more employees. The justifications enumerated were "the struggle for

production discipline and the industrial plan, plus the struggle against drunkenness, hooliganism, mischief and other phenomena causing disorganization of production life." They had no jurisdiction over large cases, or administrative personnel. *Polozhenie o rabote tovarishcheskikh sudov* (Magnitogorsk, 1939), p. 7. According to an official report, production-comrade courts were said to be rare (around twenty), with few cases (261) in 1936. MFGAChO, f. 10, op. 1, d. 246, l. 13. Be that as it may, comrade courts were also established in residences, although it is unclear when. Such courts consisted of a president, a vice president, and a certain number of members (elected at a general meeting of all inhabitants) who sat in rotation, with no more than three on the bench at one time. No member could be related to either of the parties involved in a dispute. Interestingly, there was no right of appeal; a comrade court's order was final. But it is not clear how decisions were enforced. See Hazard, *Soviet Housing Law*, pp. 114–17. Writing of a later period, one scholar points out that "the jurisdiction of these courts extends primarily to petty cases of intra-apartment order, such as the manner in which dwelling [i.e., living] space is to be used by several families, the right of passage through a room occupied by another tenant, the resettling of persons occupying utility space (kitchens, corridors, pantries, etc.) into the dwelling space of individuals who have agreed to share their accommodations with them, the manner of utilizing useful non-dwelling [*obshchaia*] space in apartments, internal apartment discipline (the cleaning of space used in common by all tenants, the closing and opening of outside doorways, hours during which silence is to be observed), the keeping of animals in utility rooms, etc. The most frequent cases among the tenants involve disputes over how much tenants are to be assessed for repairs and the maintenance of collectively used facilities and for municipal utilities." Sosnovy, *The Housing Problem*, p. 215. Regulations governing the conduct of residents of communal apartments (such as quiet hours, playing of radios, etc.) were apparently first drawn up only in 1949. See *Spravochnik upravliaiushchego domom* (Moscow, 1951), pp. 19–20.

91. In a hilarious fictional account of communal apartment life under Stalin by a former Soviet citizen, the narrator explains that "the managers, the courts, the militia, are swamped with a sea of complaints, denunciations, declarations on 'the impossibility of living with citizen so and so,' . . . on 'the need to evict citizennes so and so,' . . . on the summoning to court for slander of citizens so and so." In the process, "every wretched little sign of civilization—a radio, plumbing, the telephone, the bath, electricity, everything created for a little comfort, is transformed by the tenants [of a communal apartment] into a weapon of torture with which they torment and hound each other to death." I. I. Ivanov [pseudonym], "I ia zhil v raiu imeni tovarishcha Stalina," [1950–51?], unpublished ms., Hoover Institution Archives, Nicolaevsky Collection, series 236, box 4, folders 411–15, pp. 71, 67. For additional vignettes of communal apartment life, see Sosnovy, *The Housing Problem*, pp. 213–14.

92. From Berzin et al., *Deistvuiushchee*, pp. 174–75. A study of 202 cases of hooliganism that had come up before the People's Court of Moscow in the mid-1920s revealed that 25 percent of the cases were "the result of the acute housing problem and overcrowding." See *Khuliganstvo i ponozhovshchina: Sbornik statei* (Moscow, 1927), pp. 66–67.

93. Initially, the authorities insisted that anyone building a mud hut receive of-

ficial permission to do so. A 1931 report by the city soviet listed 5,000 people living in mud huts "with permission" (*po razresheniiu*), with 20,000 "unauthorized" (*samovolnykh*). MFGAChO, f. 10, op. 1, d. 18, l. 86.

94. *MR*, 10 February 1936.

95. "O snose zemlianok," *MR*, 27 February 1936.

96. MFGAChO, f. 10, op. 4, d. 63, l. 22, reprinted in Eliseeva, *Iz istorii*, p. 269, n. 22.

97. *CR*, 29 November 1935.

98. "The barracks we knew were temporary, we needed them for a certain while and then they would be removed," recalled Nina Kondratkovskaia. "But the mud huts were unbearable: they were ugly, a symbol of backwardness, and quickly acquired a nasty reputation as places of filth and speculation." Interview by author, Magnitogorsk, May 1987. Victor Kravchenko wrote of a Ukrainian industrial town's "slums, called 'shanghais,' and they were, in fact, as filthy and swarming as the worst oriental anthills." Kravchenko, *I Chose Freedom*, p. 324.

99. This was shown if only by the fact that payments were made to the residents when one was scheduled to be removed.

100. GARF, f. 7952, op. 5, d. 309, l. 46.

101. Kataev, *Vremia, Vpered!*, p. 216. Ironically, such imaginative attempts to affix the litany of the authorities' and popular fears in a specific place recalled nineteenth-century European descriptions of the neighborhoods of the working classes. See the muddled but highly suggestive and important work on Paris by Louis Chevalier, *Laboring Classes and Dangerous Classes in Paris in the First Half of the Nineteenth Century* (Princeton: Princeton University Press, 1973; French ed., 1958).

102. *MR*, 22 January 1937.

103. *MR*, 30 January 1938.

104. *MR*, 9 February 1936.

105. *MR*, 12 June and 1 August 1936. The hiring of labor on individual constructions might have been allowed under what was by mid-1936 an outmoded addendum to article 1 of the Soviet Labor Code introduced during the collectivization drive. The addendum permitted the hiring of subsidiary (*podsobnyi*) workers by poor and middle peasant households, and even kulak households in areas where wholesale collectivization was not being conducted. Given the extent of collectivization, these decrees soon lost their practical significance, yet they were not removed from the Labor Code until sometime after December 1936, when article 9 of the 1936 constitution expressly forbade the "exploitation of others' labor" (*eksploatatsiia chuzogo truda*) by private individuals. *Sobranie zakonov i rasporiazhenii*, 1929, no. 46, item 402, and 1930, no. 15, item 161; *Kodeks zakonov o trude, s izmeneniiami do 1 iiulia 1934 g.* (Moscow, 1934), pp. 70–74; *Kodeks zakonov o trude, s izmeneniiami na 1 iiulia 1938 g.* (Moscow, 1938), p. 89; *Sbornik zakonodatelnykh*, p. 5.

106. *MR*, 5 January 1936.

107. GARF, f. 7952, op. 5, d. 309, l. 47. The official did not say so, but the petty officials of the agency in charge, helped themselves to the spoils of their office; this came to light later, in 1937 during the scandal revolving around the delivery and

use of scarce construction materials that resulted in the downfall of a half-dozen leading officials (see ch. 6).

108. *MR*, 11 May 1936.

109. *MR*, 15 November 1936.

110. As the newspaper repeatedly pointed out, individual housing construction was a mess. *MR*, 12 June and 1 August 1936.

111. See Roman, *Krokodil v Magnitostroe*, p. 31.

112. This was the figure reported in the 1939 census. The fertility rate was given as 44.3, overall mortality, 22.3. These data include the entire raion, meaning villages in the immediate vicinity. Soviet infant mortality rates did not include still-births. *Magnitogorsk v tsifrakh*, p. 5.

113. *MR*, 27 June 1935, 18 and 21 May 1936.

114. For the 27 June 1936 abortion-restricting decree, see *Sobranie zakonov i rasporiazhenii*, 1936, no. 34, excerpted in *Sbornik dokumentov*, pp. 390–92. Interestingly, it was apparently recognized, although not widely publicized, that men were often the cause of abortions. As one account in the factory newspaper put it, "A woman goes with a man, but she is not sure about the durability of his feelings. Now everything is OK, they love each other. But it still seems to her that it is not a strong love. They live together half a year and then break up. And what will she then do with the child?" *Magnitogorskii metall*, 17 August 1935.

115. For the decree, see *Sbornik dokumentov*, p. 393. The 5 October 1935 decree was reinforced by another issued on 9 April 1937. *Sobranie zakonov i rasporiazhenii*, 1937, no. 25, item 99, reprinted in *Sbornik zakonodatelnykh*, pp. 24–25.

116. *MR*, 18 May 1936. After the new laws went into effect in June 1936, official statistics promoted the notion that the city's birth rate increased, in part because the number of abortions supposedly declined precipitously, from 570 in the first half of 1936 to 56 during the second half. Bemoaning the laxity of the abortion commission, the newspaper complained that even this number was too many. At the same time, what were called "spontaneous abortions," that is, miscarriages, supposedly increased only slightly over the same time period, from 640 to 656. Many women, however, gave birth and underwent abortions outside the hospital. (Lists of those permitted abortions in hospitals after mid-1936 included mostly professional women.) Before the new law to limit abortions took effect, the newspaper carried stories of women who performed abortions in their barracks rooms for 15 rubles. No further reports of barracks abortions were carried after mid-1936, but the newspaper did deplore the fact that some women, when unable to obtain an abortion either legally or illegally, resorted to smothering their newborn babies. *MR*, 11 November 1936, 27 December 1936, 9 March 1937, 6 May 1937, and 1 January 1939. For a skeptical view of the impact of the law restricting abortions by a woman who in the late 1930s worked in hospitals of the People's Commissariat of Health investigating the conditions of women undergoing abortions, see E. Sadvokasova, *Izuchenie vosproizvodstva naseleniia* (Moscow, 1968), p. 210. Her conclusions are echoed by a British demographer, who argues that "by the end of the 1930s the incidence of abortions could scarcely have been much below what it was in the mid-1930s, although most of the operations were now carried out by private and presumably untrained personnel." S. G. Wheatcroft, "The Population Dy-

namic and Factors Affecting It in the Soviet Union in the 1920s and 1930s," unpublished paper, University of Birmingham, Centre for Russian and East European Studies (1976), pt. 1, p. 54.

117. For translations of the principal documents relating to Soviet policies toward the family, see Rudolf Schlesinger, ed., *Changing Attitudes in Soviet Russia: The Family in the USSR* (London: Routledge and Kegan Paul, 1949).

118. Scott, *Behind*, p. 40.

119. *Magnitogorskii komsomolets*, 5 January 1932.

120. Sheila Fitzpatrick has identified socialist realism as not just an aesthetic but a visionary mentality—a propensity to focus less on a perhaps less than ideal current state of affairs than on supposedly soon-to-be-realized prospects. She also noted that traces of this mentality could be found in every bureaucratic report and statistical compilation of the period. "In the socialist realist view of the world," Fitzpatrick explained, "a dry, half-dug ditch signified a future canal full of loaded barges, [while] a ruined church was a potential kolkhoz clubhouse." Fitzpatrick, *The Cultural Front*, p. 217. See also Abram Tertz [Andrei Siniavskii], *On Socialist Realism* (New York: Pantheon, 1960).

121. Such exhortations appeared almost daily in *Magnitogorskii komsomolets*. A particularly good example is the one by Valentin Serzhantov that appeared in the 26 April 1931 issue.

122. Markevich, *Rozhdenie giganta*, pp. 21–23. A constant lament was that "drinking bouts took the place of cultural work." *Magnitogorskii komsomolets*, 1 January 1932.

123. *MR*, 18 September 1936. In a related article entitled "Gloom in the Barracks," the newspaper wrote that "one could become depressed, especially at night, when there was no light and therefore no way to read or even to lounge around." Similarly, a nonparty engineer's assistant was quoted as saying that "you come home from work, feel like reading a newspaper, but there aren't any. The red corner is empty. So you lie down, or you take a walk, or sometimes you just sit down in front of a bottle." *MR*, 2 February and 18 September 1936.

124. John Scott offered the following description of "cultural" life in the barracks: "At about six o'clock a dozen or so young workers, men and women, gathered in the Red Corner with a couple of balalaikas and a guitar. Work was finished for the day, supper was on the stove, it was time for a song. And they sang! Workers' revolutionary songs, folk tunes, and the old Russian romantic lyrics. . . . The balalaikas were played very skillfully. I never ceased wondering at the high percentage of Russian workers who could play the balalaika." Scott, *Behind*, p. 41.

125. One barracks ditty has been preserved, and possibly sanitized, by a popular novelist of the time:

Tseluy menia, Betti	Kiss me, Betty
V poslednii raz:	For the last time:
Zavtra na rassvete	Tomorrow at dawn
Uidet barkas.	The launch departs.
Uidet na rassvete	It departs at dawn
V dalekii krai.	For a distant land.
Proshchai, moia Betti!	Farewell, my Betty!
Radost, proshchai.	My joy, farewell.

From Aleksandr Avdeenko, *Ia liubliu* (Moscow, 1933).

126. *Rezoliutsia pervoi Magnitogorskoi partkonferentsii po kultstroitelstvu na 1932 g.* (Magnitogorsk, 1932), p. 4.

127. *Magnitogorskii metall*, 17 July 1935.

128. *Materialy o rabote*, p. 13.

129. *MR*, 14 March 1936. This was a familiar refrain. See *MR*, 20 January 1936.

130. Construction of the club, begun in 1934, took a very long time, a circumstance that came in for repeated criticism by the newspaper. *MR*, 22 February and 6 April 1936.

131. The first public showing of a sound film in the USSR took place in Leningrad in 1929. As late as 1934, the country had fewer than 500 sound movie projectors. By 1939, however, the number exceeded 15,000. *Kino-slovar*, vol. 2 (Moscow, 1966), p. 471; *Istoriia Sovetskogo kino*, vol. 2 (Moscow, 1973), p. 122.

132. *Materialy o rabote* p. 13.

133. Although the clubs often had projectors, only Magnit showed first-run features. The newspaper campaigned for the opening of a second cinema in the northern part of town, where it said 25,000 people lived. According to the newspaper, this could be done by investing the proceeds of Magnit, said to have amounted to more than 220,000 rubles in 1936, but the oblast authorities in Cheliabinsk insisted on keeping Magnit's earnings, not even allocating funds for repairs. *MR*, 10 December 1936.

134. Chaplin, the film's producer and star who also wrote the screenplay and music, was praised as "a supremely talented individual." *MR*, 28 August 1936.

135. Many of these newsreels have been preserved and can be viewed at the documentary film archive, TsAKFD, in Krasnogorsk, just outside Moscow.

136. *MR*, 21 May 1936.

137. *Pravda*, 21 November 1934; R. Iurenev, *Kratkaia istoriia Sovetskogo kino* (Moscow, 1979), pp. 84–91; and Yuri Voronstov and Igor Rachuk, *The Phenomenon of the Soviet Cinema* (Moscow, 1980), pp. 76–79. The winning formula of *Happy Guys* was repeated, with even greater success, in the 1936 film *Circus*. See Richard Stites, *Russian Popular Culture: Entertainment and Society since 1900* (Cambridge: Cambridge University Press, 1992), pp. 85–94.

138. By the end of the decade, the popularity of Soviet film underwent further consolidation when studios were instructed to resurrect the legends of a great-power imperial past, and great-men heroes were allowed to join those of the common people. The significance of the reemergence of an imperial Russian identity is treated in ch. 5.

139. *MR*, 8 May and 21 December 1936; Scott, *Behind*, pp. 238–40.

140. *Magnitogorskii teatr imeni Pushkina* (Cheliabinsk, 1940). In 1936 the theater's main producer, B. V. Radov, wrote an article for the newspaper on the twenty-fifth anniversary on stage of the Moscow actor E. V. Svobodin. *MR*, 20 February 1936.

141. *MR*, 11 January and 12 October 1936. In summer, the group took its act on the road.

142. Such was the opinion of the Magnitogorsk writer Nina Kondratkovskaia, interviewed in 1987, and the conclusion contained in the recollections of deputy

theater director Mikhail Arsh, dated 20 November 1936. Arsh claimed that he had thought about leaving Magnitogorsk until Zaveniagin's arrival turned things around for the theater, no less than the rest of the city. GARF, f. 7952, op. 5, d. 304, ll. 30–51. Arsh may have met a bitter fate. According to an unpublished interview with Rafael Khitarov dated 26 November 1936, someone named Arsh (no first name) was said to have "turned out to be a counterrevolutionary." Since this is a very uncommon family name and the theater director appears to have been close to Party Secretary Beso Lominadze, whose many associates in Magnitogorsk were arrested either in 1935 or after the August 1936 Moscow trial, it appears likely that Arsh, too, was arrested. Ibid., d. 313, l. 31.

143. This is one of the principal arguments advanced by Sheila Fitzpatrick, *The Cultural Front*, pp. 14, 60–62.

144. *MR*, 15 December 1936 and 28 April 1937. The city also had a Ukrainian choir (perhaps inspired by the great Piatnitskii Choir in Moscow). The newspaper complained that it was always the same faces in the audience every time the group performed. *MR*, 5 April 1936.

145. *MR*, 17 October 1936.

146. *MR*, 4 August 1936. In 1936 the football club Metallurg won the oblast tournament, but it was discovered that they had used a "ringer" from another Magnitogorsk team, Construction Worker. As a result, first place was awarded to Cheliabinsk Tractor. *MR*, 15 August 1936.

147. *MR*, 27 July and 30 December 1936.

148. *MR*, 28 March 1936. During related events, such as fat-man wrestling, the circus was also said to be "full, indeed more than full." *MR*, 18 February 1936. The circus had a capacity of 2,451 people. *Stalinskaia stroika*, p. 44.

149. For years several organizations were worked very hard to "greenify" the rest of the city. Despite their efforts, however, the newspaper reported in 1937 that Magnitogorsk remained almost entirely without greenery. In fact, some areas had been turned into dust-plagued desert as a result of industrial and residential construction. *MR*, 28 February 1937.

150. In 1937, the park was equipped with loudspeakers through which the music played on Moscow radio could be heard. *MR*, 1 June 1936 and 28 March 1937.

151. Some people owned gramophones, although recordings were hard to come by. The public library was said to have a collection of more than six hundred records. Meanwhile, the manager of the record store allegedly sold records above the state-set prices and pocketed the difference, in this way earning more than 1,000 rubles. *MR*, 18 September and 26 August 1936. Jazz was extremely popular in the USSR during the 1930s. It was attacked and discredited in 1936, but not fully suppressed. S. Frederick Starr, *Red and Hot: The Fate of Jazz in the Soviet Union, 1917–1980* (New York: Oxford University Press, 1983), pp. 107–29.

152. In the 1970s the park fell into disuse and was allowed to deteriorate. As late as 1991, the statues and other artifacts recalling the park's original splendor could still be seen, but calls by a few historically minded individuals to restore it went unheeded.

153. *MR*, 28 November 1937. The article was written by Valentin Serzhantov.

154. *MR*, 20 October 1936.

155. Scott judged the performances "third-rate Barnum and Bailey quality," but claimed that they were popular. Scott, *Behind*, p. 240.

156. *MR*, 28 April 1936.

157. *MR*, 4 May 1936.

158. The newspaper did carry an article about anti-Semitism. In the report, a Jewish couple, the Khersonskii family, living in building no. 2 on Karadyr Prospect in the Kirov district, was said to have told the local militia that some of their belongings had been robbed. The militia was said to have done nothing, even though the family claimed they knew the culprit to be their next-door neighbor, who had done this once before. The neighbor was said to have struck the Jewish woman in the common kitchen and to have called them "kikes" (*zhidy*) and "kike faces" (*zhidskie mordy*). A witness to such a scene in front of the building sent a letter to the newspaper. The author of the newspaper piece, writing under the pen name N. Slonov, deplored the actions, but asserted that "the manifestations of anti-Semitism in our country are becoming a rarer and rarer phenomenon." *MR*, 3 July 1936. An earlier condemnatory piece on anti-Semitism without such an appended assertion appeared in *Magnitogorskii komsomolets*, 10 August 1931.

159. The authorities eventually relented. Construction of a church was sanctioned during the war, and completed just after. A second church was completed in the early 1980s. In the 1990s, city authorities belatedly gave permission for the building of a mosque.

160. In the days preceding the parade, the authorities in fact took care to stock local stores with extra supplies of holiday goods. As the day drew near, the newspaper did its part, airing complaints that highly anticipated supplies had yet to reach certain areas of the city.

161. In 1936, there were at least four such trials in less than two months. *MR*, 3 and 10 April, 5 and 28 May 1936.

162. The facts were described as follows: A man and a woman met and evidently married—the account does not specify whether the marriage was legalized—in Moscow in 1926. The woman was constantly subjected to the husband's drunkenness, insults, and physical abuse until 1930, when the husband enrolled in a Moscow institute and left her. At some point the wife discovered that he had relocated to Magnitogorsk, and she went there seeking him out. Upon seeing her, his alleged response was "What are you doing here? I didn't send for you!" He demanded that she leave at once. She did not have the money for the return trip, nor did it seem she wanted to leave. Continuing his old pattern, he abused her physically. One night she took an ax, killed him, and then calmly went to inform the militia of her deed. After the woman was convicted, her daughter was given over to her dead husband's sister. *MR*, 5 July 1936. In a different case, a German worker named Hans Gruber, who had been accused in one report of "fascist treatment" of his wife, was let off. He admitted that he had ripped his wife's dress, but promised never to do it again. The newspaper pointed out that he was "a Stakhanovite, one of the best workers in his shop, and respected by all the other workers." *MR*, 11 July 1936.

163. Korytov, an economist employed at mill 300, was singled out for public condemnation. Said to be "cultured and intelligent" at work, he often came home drunk and proceeded to beat his wife. When neighbors tried to intervene, he alleg-

edly snapped, "no one messes in my life." Another man, Ilia Nosov, was known far and wide for his oft-repeated refrain, "all women are prostitutes." *MR*, 26 October and 20 March 1936.

164. *MR*, 15 May 1936.

165. *MR*, 24 October and 12 December 1936.

166. See Polonskii, *Magnitostroi*, p. 42. One worker recalled that drivers were particularly popular, since they could go to the nearby town of Verkhne-Uralsk (some fifty kilometers to the north), where there was no dry law. In 1931, this worker claimed that a half-liter of vodka sold (discreetly) in Magnitogorsk for as much as 30 rubles. GARF, f. 7952, op. 5, d. 300, l. 45.

167. See, for example, GARF, f. 7952, op. 5, d. 304, l. 47. The struggle against vodka consumption provides a revealing window into the battle for cultural transformation in the barracks of Magnitogorsk. In barracks no. 9 in the Eleventh Sector lived a group of men, we are told, who had not been to work for two or three months but instead made a living selling vodka. Moreover, while the rest of the workers were thrown together in a big dormitory room (some even without beds), this group had their own private setup in the barracks' red corner itself. A twenty-four-year-old candidate member of the party decided to organize a "barracks soviet." He was elected as its chairman and began a fight to evict the vodka dealers. After two months, the young enthusiast finally succeeded in convincing someone with sufficient authority to dislodge the dealers. But they simply moved to another barracks. With the vodka dealers gone, the young party candidate member decided to organize a "comrades' court" to battle absenteeism. The court was charged with ensuring that all workers left the barracks in the morning when they were supposed to. After some initial resistance, recalcitrant workers did leave the barracks in the morning under the threat of expulsion. But the candidate party member soon discovered that although they departed at the appropriate time, they merely went off to amuse themselves. The semi-annual report of the Magnitogorsk court for the second half of 1931 concluded that the punishment of exile from the site (against convicted carousers) was ineffectual because the offender could simply change his or her address and stay. Likewise, sentences to "forced labor" at one's place of work (i.e., the same work at a reduction in pay) could not be enforced in the face of the absence of any registration of addresses or places of work. There was only one court investigator (*isponitel*) to follow up sentences. See Ibid., d. 143, l. 49, 52.

168. Popov, the deputy manager of the city's wine store, was accused of consuming, along with other employees, the store's wares on the premises without paying (*Popov pianstvoval, nado skazat, zdorovo*). They allegedly drank 1,132 rubles' worth but were evidently caught after an inventory was taken. Popov, who allegedly resisted arrest, was sentenced to three years' loss of freedom. *MR*, 12 July 1936.

169. *MR*, 17 and 18 April 1936.

170. For reasons that are unclear, the café closed "for repairs" only two weeks after opening, but it soon reopened. *MR*, 12 April and 21 May 1936.

171. *MR*, 5 June and 14 December 1936.

172. *MR*, 9 February 1937. Magnitogorsk featured a small number of evening "restaurants," meaning places to eat, drink, listen to music, and dance. One, called "Kushanii" (Eats), was located in the Central Hotel, adjacent to the main factory

gates. Open until 2 A.M., it featured live music, including jazz, and dancing. A second, less animated establishment at the train station was said to have a long and impressive menu, but one journalist reported that any attempt to order something from it was met with "We don't have that," until nothing remained to chose from. A third restaurant was opened in the Kirov district in 1937, more than four years after the facility it took over had been completed. First built as a school, the facility was then supposed to be turned into a club, and then a public cafeteria, but instead it long remained unused. "In Magnitogorsk one feels a great need for public buildings," commented the newspaper. "We do not have that many good facilities for stores, dining halls, and libraries so that we can allow one such large facility to be empty during the course of four years." When the restaurant finally opened, it turned out to be so full of drunks that the authorities soon ordered it permanently closed. By the end of the 1930s only one restaurant remained. *MR*, 17 February, 24 April, 8 and 16 October 1936, 28 April 1937, and 26 January 1939.

173. *MR*, 3 August 1936.

174. In this vein, the newspaper reported that when one mill was awarded a 5,000 ruble prize in December 1936, its workers voted to use the money to buy six season tickets to the Drama Theater and four to the circus. *MR*, 21 December 1936.

175. Another newspaper feature published the following year under the title "Magnitogorsk at Night," after enumerating the many clubs, theaters, cinemas, cafés, and restaurants, gasped that "everywhere one senses the big life of a big city." The article unwittingly showed, however, that the only place where "the pulse of a big city beat" until very late at night was the steel plant. *MR*, 5 March 1937.

176. *MR*, 15 September 1936.

177. *MR*, 3 March 1936 and 1 September 1936. Contemporary compilations of reading habits, whether from answers to surveys or from library records, need to be treated with caution because of the necessity for people to demonstrate not only an interest in reading but one in specific themes. For an intelligent discussion of this problem, although one that relies perhaps too readily on contemporary surveys, see John Barber, "Working-Class Culture and Political Culture in the 1930s," in Hans Günther, ed., *The Culture of the Stalin Period* (New York: St. Martin's, 1990), p. 7. Attendance at movies, on the other hand, may be a bit more indicative of what occupied workers' leisure time. At least in Magnitogorsk, workers seem to have gone to the movies far more often than Barber allows for the country as a whole.

178. A comparison of the Soviet state's attitude toward mass leisure with that of Mussolini's Italy is instructive. If in the Soviet Union under Stalin the question was chiefly how to create a "cultured" worker, in Italy the problem of organized leisure seems to have been how in a class society with an anti-working class regime to create a supraclass consensus. See the analysis of the Italian fascist leisure-time organization (*Opera Nazionale del Dopolavoro*) by Victoria de Grazia, *The Culture of Consent: Mass Organization of Leisure in Fascist Italy* (Cambridge: Cambridge University Press, 1981).

179. For his excellent work performance, Tishchenko also earned numerous prizes, including a hunting gun, a gramophone, money, and a motorcycle. He admitted, however, that he still did not know how to ride it. *MR*, 30 August 1936.

180. Article 128 of section 10. For a translation of the full text, see Aryeh Unger, *Constitutional Development in the USSR: A Guide to the Soviet Constitutions*

(New York: Pica, 1981), pp. 139–69. A need to enter homes for regular and emergency repairs was recognized. Section 3, paragraph j, of the model lease (based on the 1937 law on the preservation and improvement of the housing stock) required tenants "to permit repairmen sent by the house administrator to carry out repairs without hindrance, if three-days' notice has been given; and in the case of sudden serious damage, to permit their entrance irrespective of previous notice." From *Finansovyi i khoziaistvennyi biulleten*, 1938, nos. 8–9, p. 36, as translated in Hazard, *Soviet Housing Law*, pp. 127–30.

181. Commandants and house managers were frequently the targets of abuse by residents irate over the lack of repairs. *MR*, 1 April 1936.

182. All efforts to establish the number of NKVD operative personnel in Magnitogorsk during the 1930s proved fruitless. Their two-story building, still functioning in 1987, contained perhaps forty or fifty offices, although it is unclear how many people in the 1930s were in each office. And the point is not only how many agents were on permanent staff but also how many informants the NKVD had among the population. Without access to NKVD archives, there is no reliable way of estimating this number. Given what we know of the methods of recruitment, it is tempting to guess that the networks of "volunteer" secret operatives (*sekretnye sotrudniki*, or *seksoty*) were extensive. Under articles 58 and 59 in the section on counterrevolutionary crimes of the RSFSR Criminal Code, it was a criminal offense not to inform. False denunciation or testimony was also a crime, under article 95. *Ugolovnyi kodeks redaktsii 1926 g.* (Moscow, 1927), pp. 134–35, 155, 185–86. Further discussion of the NKVD can be found in ch. 7.

183. Benefiting from access to some surviving Gestapo archives, historians of Nazi Germany have been able to show how much of the Gestapo's power derived from its mystique. More precisely, they have demonstrated how the public's ignorance, deliberately fostered by the Gestapo, of the actual size, scope, and nature of Gestapo activities helped create a perception of ubiquity crucial for eliciting the public's cooperation, which in turn augmented the reach of the Gestapo, whose staff was far smaller than one might have imagined. It also seems to have been the case, however, that the Gestapo was nearly overwhelmed with denunciations, a great number of which were "spurious" but almost all of which were taken seriously and followed up. It is reasonable to assume that this picture broadly corresponds to what will soon be uncovered in long-closed Soviet security police archives. See Robert Gellately, *The Gestapo and German Society: Enforcing Racial Policy 1933–1945* (Oxford: Clarendon, 1990).

CHAPTER 5. SPEAKING BOLSHEVIK

1. Quoted in *Slovo o Magnitke* (Moscow, 1979), p. 104. Elena was the daughter of Aleksei Dzhaparidze, one of the twenty-six martyred Baku Commissars. She was raised in the family of Sergo Ordzhonikidze. After her experiences in Magnitogorsk, she went on to further "schooling" in the camps. See Solzhenitsyn, *Gulag Archipelago*, vol. 2 (New York: Harper and Row, 1975), p. 347. Interviewed by telephone in Moscow in 1989, Dzhaparidze expressed no bitterness.

2. The recollections of Cherneev, who added that they also put up a copy of Sta-

lin's "six conditions," as enunciated in his 1931 speech, plus some slogans, and issued a wall newspaper. GARF, f. 7952, op. 5, d. 319, ll. 28–29.

3. Reginald Zelnik, "Russian Workers and the Revolutionary Movement," *Journal of Social History* 6, no. 2 (1972): 214–37. For a review of the literature on labor and a sophisticated attempt at synthesis see McDaniel, *Autocracy, Capitalism, and Revolution in Russia.*

4. Donald Filtzer, *Soviet Workers and Stalinist Industrialization: The Formation of Modern Soviet Production Relations, 1928–1941* (Armonk, N.Y.: M. E. Sharpe, 1986), pp. 76–87, provides an overview of press reports that contain "negative" information. Filtzer's book is discussed in the text. The Jay K. Zawodny Collection of the Hoover Institution Archives contains interviews with former Soviet workers. Merle Fainsod, who studied the party archives from Smolensk, a predominantly agricultural region, noted that "the documents provide unimpeachable evidence of widespread mass discontent with Soviet rule." Fainsod, *Smolensk*, p. 449. It seems very likely that such evidence could be found in the Cheliabinsk oblast security police files, which as of 1991 remained inaccessible.

5. This view has been expressed by Solomon Schwarz, who wrote a number of well-informed pieces on workers under Stalin for the contemporary Menshevik émigré newspaper *Sotsialisticheskii vestnik*, and later developed his articles into the first major English-language study of the subject, *Labor in the Soviet Union* (New York: Praeger, 1951). Schwarz's book, written during the early years of World War II and meant to cover the period 1928–1941, was envisioned as an antidote to Soviet propaganda about the achievements of workers under socialism. The author thus gave detailed exposition to the draconian labor laws and their obviously repressive intent. At the same time, however, he documented the violations and circumventions of those same laws—without making it clear what such findings meant for his principal argument about the Soviet regime's "control" over labor. Not until Donald Filtzer's 1986 book did anyone attempt a synoptic reevaluation of labor under Stalin. Filtzer, in effect, sought to resolve the seeming paradox that had emerged in Schwarz's work whereby continued and severe repression by the regime was shown to have coexisted with effective circumvention of regime dictates by workers.

6. This is the position of Trotsky, who sought to pinpoint the "social base" of the usurping bureaucracy. Such a view was also espoused by the Mensheviks in *Sotsialisticheskii vestnik*. (Solomon Schwarz, one of the main contributors to the Menshevik publication, implicitly adopts this view in his book on Soviet labor, cited above.) John Barber, in his many unpublished but nonetheless influential essays for the Birmingham Centre for Russian and East European Studies, adopts a variant of it. Soviet historians have also promoted the notion that "backward" peasant workers adversely affected the "consciousness" of the working class. See A. I. Vdovin and V. Z. Drobizhev, *Rost rabochego klassa SSSR 1917–1940 gg.* (Moscow, 1976). In yet another variation, Vladimir Andrle ascribes the willingness of workers to denounce innocent people in exchange for rewards to the flux characteristic of an "unsettled and uprooted society." See Andrle, *Workers in Stalin's Russia.* It seems that no one likes to characterize admiration for dictatorship as a rational choice exercised by conscious individuals.

7. Fitzpatrick, *Education and Social Mobility.*

8. Filtzer, *Soviet Workers*, pp. 254–55. Expecting a proper "Marxist" response by exploited workers, Filtzer had trouble with actual manifestations of worker consciousness, reluctantly admitting that "expressions of discontent did not necessarily reflect a sophisticated political awareness of events or alternatives. Frequently they were couched in the most reactionary nationalist, anti-Semitic, and male-chauvinist terms." Unfortunately, he did not explore this point. Nonetheless, Filtzer's discussion of workers under Stalin has much to commend it, and we will draw on it at points in the discussion. Filtzer also offered an odd analysis of the formation of what he calls the "exploitative" elite, arguing that by 1935 the "emerging elite" had "consolidated" its position (pp. 80, 102). Just then, of course, the purges set in, decimating that elite. By contrast, Vladimir Andrle, whose analysis of workers in the 1930s is no match for Filtzer's, offers a far more nuanced view of the formation of the elite component of the "administrative-command system." See Andrle, *Workers in Stalin's Russia*.

9. *Pravda*, 30 March 1932, reprinted in Stalin, *Sochineniia* (Moscow, 1953), vol. 13, p. 133. A copy of the original can be found in RTsKhIDNI, f. 558, op. 1.

10. These strictures were set down in the 1936 constitution. Under article 12, work became compulsory. Under article 118, it was listed as a right.

11. Sentences of up to six months' forced labor were to be served at the convicted person's usual place of employment with a reduction in pay (not more than 25 percent). Sentences of more than six months were also served at one's regular place of employment, unless the sentence specified "deprivation of freedom," which meant relocation to a labor colony. A new RSFSR Corrective Labor Code was introduced in 1933, replacing the one from 1924. It is excerpted in *Sbornik dokumentov po istorii ugolovnogo*, pp. 367–78.

12. Kolakowski, *Main Currents of Marxism*, esp. vol. 3, chs. 1–3.

13. Paying more attention to the problem of class than most analysts, Sheila Fitzpatrick has argued that the Bolsheviks, clinging to their class-based view of the world, were compelled as a result of the disintegration and fragmentation of the Soviet working class during the Civil War to "reinvent" class-based politics during the 1920s. One wonders, however, whether a continual process of reinvention as she describes was underway even before the partial decomposition of what might be called the actually existing working class. No existing working class anywhere had the kind of characteristics, especially the mental outlook, that the Bolsheviks deemed "natural" for such a class. Moreover, Fitzpatrick notes the tension that developed in class definitions between a person's social genealogy and present class position, but she neglects another source of ambiguity, that between one's present class position and the "objective" class implications of the ideas one espoused. As a result of the latter tension, both hereditary members of the working class and recent workers were frequently found to be harboring class alien notions, for which they were "repressed." Fitzpatrick herself stresses that the idea of class could not be separated from that of struggle against class enemies, variously defined and sought out, indicating the operation of a dynamic far beyond the problem of a real sociological entity battered during the Civil War. That said, it was precisely the Bolshevik anxiety over the gulf between the actual Soviet working class and the kind they desired that led to the production of the voluminous documents making possible the kind of inquiry Fitzpatrick undertakes. Indeed, she reminds us that a mas-

sive statistical agency arose in the 1920s to study the problem of class in Soviet society. Sheila Fitzpatrick, "L'Usage Bolchevique de la 'class': Marxisme et construction de l'identité individuelle," *Actes de la recherche en sciences sociales,* dir. Pierre Bourdieu, no. 85 (November 1990).

14. The Plan foresaw an increase from 11.9 million employed in 1928–29 to 15.8 million by 1932–33, but in 1932 the actual number of people employed was 22.9 million. There were 6.5 million people in heavy industry proper in 1932 as against 3.1 million in 1928. In less than five years, both the number of people employed in general and the number of people employed in industry doubled. *Sotsialisticheskoe stroitelstvo SSSR* (Moscow, 1936), p. 508. After a brief period when the number employed decreased slightly, from 1934 on employment climbed again. By 1937, the end of the second Five-Year Plan, total employment reached 27 million. *Results of Fulfilling the Second Five-Year Plan* (Moscow, 1939), p. 104. Even though the latter figure fell short of the Plan target of 28.9 million, it capped an increase in the work force in one decade of over 15 million. When one recalls that by 1921–22, following years of war, revolution, and civil war, employment had shrunk to approximately 6.5 million, including only 1.24 million in industry, it becomes clear how far the country had come in providing a proletariat for the "proletarian revolution."

15. *MR,* 16 May 1938. This was down from the summer of 1936, when there were 25,882 people at the steel plant, of whom 20,749 were categorized as workers (*rabochie*), 1,273 as employees (*sluzhashchie*), 1,894 as engineers and technicians (ITR), 1,244 as young service personnel (MOP), and 723 as apprentices (*ucheniki*). The previous year, August 1935, the factory had employed 24,114 people. *Tekhniko-ekonomicheskie pokazateli raboty zavoda.* The example of Magnitogorsk was repeated in Eastern Europe after World War II, perhaps most famously in the outskirts of the old intelligentsia-center Cracow, where a new working class satellite town known as Nowa Huta was created in conscious imitation of Magnitogorsk (and with Soviet assistance), to create a proletarian "social basis" for the Communist regime and dilute the social significance of the old intelligentsia.

16. According to Scott, "The entire coke and chemical plant employed about 2,000 workers. Of these, some ten percent were so-called engineers and technical personnel, including foremen, superintendents, planners, and so on." Scott, *Behind,* p. 156; see also *MR,* 9 June 1937.

17. This figure included 21,500 in industry, of whom 10,589 worked in ferrous metallurgy proper. GAChO, f. 804, op. 11, d. 105, l. 37. In December 1931, there had been 54,600 workers on the site, virtually all of whom were employed in construction. RGAE, f. 4086, op. 2, d. 42, l. 28. The number of construction workers declined precipitously toward the end of the 1930s when little new construction was undertaken. By 1940, there were 4,200 workers in construction, whereas at the end of 1936, there had been 8,800. (The comparison is not exact, since the data for 1936 include engineers and technicians.) *MR,* 18 December 1936.

18. That many workers began as unskilled and illiterate "peasants" certainly affected how this training was conceived and implemented. But all workers, regardless of social origin, had to go through a "training" in life and work. Among the resolutions adopted at the 1932 first Magnitogorsk party conference on what was called "cultural construction" was one concerning the need for "the re-edu-

cation [*perevospitanie*] of the new strata of workers." *Rezoliutsia pervoi Magnitogorskoi partkonferentsii po kultstroitelstvu na 1932 g.,* p. 4. Statistics on the social composition of the Soviet work force are given in Adolf Rashin, "Dinamika promyshlennykh kadrov SSSR za 1917–1958 gg.," in *Izmenneniia v chislennosti i sostave sovetskogo rabochego klass: Sbornik statei* (Moscow, 1961), pp. 7–73. A discussion of published contemporary statistical sources can be found in Barber, "The Composition of the Soviet Working Class."

19. Writing about England, E. P. Thompson stressed the need to write histories not of inevitable technological change but of "exploitation and of resistance to exploitation," so as to avoid the moral desert of sociological accounts of industrialization. Thompson, "Time, Work-Discipline, and Industrial Capitalism," *Past and Present* 38 (December 1967): 56–97.

20. Such fears were expressed in a typical instructional pamphlet from 1929 on party membership purges: "These new workers . . . have never seen or known what class struggle means, or known why and how discipline is needed in the ranks of the proletariat. . . . For them the factory is neither the property of the working class that was taken by the working class from the capitalists, nor the child of the proletariat that has been erected by Soviet power, but rather a place in which they can earn a little extra to strengthen their own farms." I. I. Korotkov, "K proverke i chistke proizvodstvennykh iacheek," in E. M. Iaroslavskii, ed., *Kak provodit chistku partii* (Moscow, 1929), p. 83.

21. An excellent example of this thinking can be found in the children's book by N. P. Mislavskii, *Magnitogorsk* (Moscow, 1931). Such a vision captured the imagination of the artistic intelligentsia. In 1930, the architect El Lissitzky wrote that "by virtue of the exact division of time and work rhythm, and by making each individual share in a large common responsibility, the factory has become the real place of education—the university for the new socialist man." He added that "the factory has become the crucible of socialization for the urban population." Of course, in most places in the USSR people had first to build a factory. El Lissitzky, *Russia,* pp. 57–58.

22. "The construction of the Magnitogorsk factory," the Central Committee decreed in 1931, "should become a practical school for the creation of new methods and forms of socialist labor." See "O stroitelstve Magnitogorskogo metallurgicheskogo zavoda," *Pravda,* 26 January 1931; reprinted in *Partiinoe stroitelstvo,* February 1931, nos. 3–4, pp. 94–96.

23. Lewin, *The Making of the Soviet System,* p. 37.

24. According to Lewis Siegelbaum, "'Shock work' is a term that originated during the Civil War period to denote the performance of particularly arduous or urgent tasks. It acquired new meaning in 1927–28 when isolated groups of workers, primarily members of the Komsomol, organized brigades to fulfill obligations over and above their work assignments. These ranged from cutting down on absences and abstaining from alcohol to overfulfilling output norms and reducing the per unit cost of production." Siegelbaum, *Stakhanovism and the Politics of Productivity in the USSR, 1935–1941* (Cambridge: Cambridge University Press, 1988), p. 40.

25. Lewis Siegelbaum, "Shock Workers," in *The Modern Encyclopedia of Russian and Soviet History,* vol. 35, (Gulf Breeze, Fl.: Academic International, 1983),

pp. 23–27. In Valentin Kataev's novel about Magnitogorsk, one character extended the reasoning behind the rationalization of production to its logical conclusion, developing what he called a "theory of tempos": "An increase of the productivity of one machine automatically entails the increase of the productivity of others connected with it. And since all machines are connected with each other to a greater or lesser degree, and together represent a complex interlocking system, the raising of tempos at any given point in the system inevitably carries with it the unavoidable—however minute—raising of tempos of the system as a whole, thus, to a certain extent, bringing the time of socialism closer." In fact, as the novel makes clear, unsustainable superhuman exertions, rather than widespread and permanent rationalization, characterized the "battle" for higher productivity. Still, whatever the methods, the overriding goal remained reaching socialism as quickly as possible. Kataev, *Vremia Vpered!*, p. 166.

26. Rewards were individualized, but others could be carried along in the recipient's wake. Trade union lists of "workers" awarded special vacation trips because of outstanding performance, for example, almost always included the shift boss and shop chief where the worker was employed. MFGAChO, f. 118, op. 1, d. 80, ll. 96–101.

27. Scott, *Behind*, p. 72. The proliferation of bonuses followed a compelling logic. The regime could rail against overpayment of wages, but those individuals charged with enforcing output quotas and piece rates were under more pressure to meet production targets, and the only way to meet production targets was by enlisting the cooperation of the work force. The ability to regulate wages strictly, like much else, became hostage to the measurement of production in terms of quotas and the overriding concern to achieve those quotas, even if only on paper. See Filtzer, *Soviet Workers*, p. 232.

28. The wage schedule based upon norms was undermined by the uneven pace of production, which fluctuated in relation to interruptions in the supply of raw materials and the end of the quarter storms to fulfill plan. For a discussion of how the unpredictability of production was institutionalized, and thereby became predictable, see *Voprosy profdvizheniia*, 1933, no. 11, pp. 65–71 (a study of the Kulakov factory), as cited in Filtzer, *Soviet Workers*, p. 211.

29. Scott, *Behind*, p. 75.

30. For data on wage differentials in 1933, see Scott, *Behind*, p. 49; for data as of 1 January 1937, see *Obzor raboty zavoda za ianvar 1937 g.* (Magnitogorsk, 1937), p. 17. Over time average nominal wages generally rose, although they could be reduced, as demonstrated by data from the mine. *Stakhanovskii opyt Magnitogorskogo rudnika: Sbornik statei* (Moscow, 1939), p. 187. Increasing nominal wages were often put forward as proof of the progress that had been made possible by the revolution. One worker from Kazakhstan, who arrived illiterate in 1932, by 1936 was said to be earning 420 to 450 rubles/month. Such sums must have seemed fantastic, especially with older workers telling stories of the time before the revolution when they had worked ten hours or more a day for 75 kopecks. Of course, for the bulk of the population, real wages—and hence standard of living—declined precipitously. GARF, f. 7952, op. 5, d. 312, l. 295; and d. 319, l. 9.

31. See, for example, the incidents related in GARF, f. 7952, op. 5, d. 306, ll. 23–24. To an extent the popularization of shock work was inhibited by the tradi-

tional work-organization forms, such as cooperative artels, the breakup of which constituted one of the aims of the introduction of shock work, as discussed in ch. 2.

32. Foremen and brigade leaders also felt pressure to designate workers under their charge as shock workers, to demonstrate their leadership skills to the higher bosses, and to keep their workers happy. In a satire that appeared in the factory newspaper, a brigade leader said to have no time for socialist competitions or verifying norm fulfillment percentages nonetheless recognized the need to designate his charges as shock workers. In the satire, he assembles the brigade and begins reading off their names: "'Burnin!' he shouts. 'Enter into the ranks of shock workers?' 'Enter him,' someone yells out. Next to the name Burnin appears a mark and he becomes a shock worker." In such fashion the brigade leader goes through the entire list, and each time someone calls out "enter him." Those he accidentally passes over are named at the end and added. But he forgets about himself, as someone points out. By this time the rest of the brigade has left. No one remains to shout "enter him," so the brigade leader is left out, foiling his plans to make his whole brigade into shock workers. *Magnitogorskii metall*, 28 August 1935.

33. The factory party committee exercised considerable influence in the shops in relation to its members. For example, rolling mill worker Minokov, who saw one of his children die and had another on the verge of death, wanted to leave town, apparently because the city posed such a health risk. Vaisberg, the chief of the mill, offered Minokov a better housing situation and 250 rubles to send his wife and ill child to the South, but he still insisted on leaving. In retribution, the mill chief lowered his skill category (*razriad*), which angered Minokov, who did not show up for work for two days, as a result of which he was dishonorably discharged. But because Minokov was a party member, the party interceded, forbidding his summary release. All the same, Minokov was forced by the party to admit his guilt and to write an apology for his actions to be published in the city newspaper. GARF, f. 7952, op. 5, d. 305, ll. 52–5.

34. In late February 1936, the party organized a special meeting of agitators at which Secretary Rafael Khitarov delivered a report outlining the nature of their work. *MR*, 14 March 1936.

35. *MR*, 15 December 1936.

36. *Magnitogorskii metall*, 3 November 1935 and 30 June 1936. The reported comments took place during the grueling party card exchange (see ch. 7). At one so-called political day in the blast furnace shop in 1936, there was said to have been total silence after the main report. "No one wanted to ask questions, no one wanted to participate in discussions," the newspaper wrote. One worker complained that they had heard about the meeting only that day. Another said that he had not yet had a chance to read through the recent speech by Ordzhonikidze. A third added that "with us everything seems to be done impromptu." The paper concluded that "the manifest unpreparedness of the workers for such a meeting was felt." *MR*, 24 July 1936.

37. See the example given in Vladimir Andrle, "How Backward Workers Became Soviet: Industrialization of Labor and the Politics of Efficiency under the Second Five-Year Plan, 1933–1937," *Social History* 10, no. 2 (May 1985): 155, cited from *Voprosy profdvizheniia*, 1934, no. 7, p. 50. Andrle explains that "the practice

of carrying out 'social work' duties in work time had been specifically banned by a joint decree of the Council of People's Commissars and the Central Committee in March 1931. It was banned again by the industrial commissariats in September 1933. The factory meeting at which the above-quoted remark was heard in 1934 passed a resolution abolishing the practice." And yet such sessions continued.

38. Here is the breathless official report by the then head of the factory trade union committee, N. D. Larin: "Stalin's speech was received in Magnitogorsk on 22 November [1935] at approximately 10 A.M. Now in agreement with the editorial board of *Magnitogorskii rabochii* approximately 10,000 copies of a special 'extra' edition of the speech is being printed for the factory committee and being distributed to the shops. On this very day in all shifts and brigades discussions of Stalin's speech took place. Our entire trade union active was mobilized and the discussions were conducted by authoritative representatives of the factory committee. Male and female workers excitedly discussed the historic speech of comrade Stalin and brigade, entire shifts, brigades, and shops, as well as individual Stakhanovites, vowed to accept concrete obligations to introduce Stakhanovite methods more widely and in the perfection of mastering technology and fulfilling the production plan before the deadline." MFGAChO, f. 118, op. 1, d. 80, l. 112. The next year, the occasion of the new constitution became the subject of a reported 286 meetings, plus another 140 "individual conversations," involving 22,744 people. The meticulous records kept by agitators—the precise number of meetings, questions asked, and people encompassed (*okhvacheno*)—should not be taken as prima facie evidence of the formality and hence worthlessness of these occasions. Ibid., f. 10, op. 1, d. 139, l. 50.

39. He complained that the lack of a decent map hindered the sessions. *MR*, 4 March 1936.

40. See Scott, *Behind*, pp. 84–85. Scott's claim that "until 1935 . . . there were few arrests. But material was accumulating in dossiers" was echoed by, among others, the manager of a Soviet factory in the Ukraine who fled the country. See Kravchenko, *I Chose Freedom*, p. 75.

41. Ordzhonikidze, *Stati i rechi*, vol. 2, p. 458.

42. Scott, *Behind*, p. 36.

43. *MR*, 6 February 1938. Trade union politics, however, appears to have been another matter. In late 1937 the Central Committee of the Union of Metal Workers (East) sent a brigade to Magnitogorsk to "reconstruct" trade union work. In this connection, on 15 March a factorywide conference was held. Given its 20,000 official members, the local organization was required by law to have 1,500 delegates represent the membership at such a conference. On the first day of the proceeding, only 780 people showed up; on the second day, 524. The conference took place during the terror, which might help account for the poor attendance, but party meetings during the terror appear generally to have been well attended. *MR*, 24 February, 15 and 18 March 1937.

44. See particularly Siegelbaum, whose analysis of Stakhanovism as "both a state policy and a social phenomenon" takes full account of the many associations the word evoked: certain workers, certain methods of work, vocational schooling, and periods of intense work activity. Siegelbaum, *Stakhanovism*, pp. xii, 145. For a study more narrowly drawn than Siegelbaum's, see Francesco Benvenutti "Sta-

khanovism and Stalinism, 1934–1938," unpublished paper, University of Birmingham, Centre for Russian and East European Studies, July 1989, a condensed English-Language version of his *Fuoco sui sabotatori! Stachanovismo e organizzione industriale in URSS, 1934–1938* (Rome, 1988).

45. The central space of the city, Factory Administration Square, where holidays were publicly celebrated and political demonstrations were held, was (temporarily) renamed Stakhanovite Square. *MR*, 12 January and 4 May 1936.

46. GARF, f. 7952, op. 5, d. 313, l. 88.

47. *MR*, 1 March 1936. One Soviet historian of Magnitogorsk, writing soon after Stalin's death, disclosed that in just twelve days in January 1936, the number of Stakhanovites almost doubled, from 2,496 to 4,471. He added, however, that because there were not enough supplies, materials, or instruments, the efforts were not sustained but exhausted in "storms," while workers did not take sufficient care of machines. Serzhantov, "Metallurgi Magnitki v borbe," pp. 236–37. An identical assessment for the Soviet automobile industry is given in V. Sakharov, *Zarozhdenie i razvitie stakhanovskogo dvizheniia v avtotraktornoi promyshlennosti* (Moscow, 1979), pp. 144–45.

48. *MR*, 5 March 1936.

49. GARF, f. 7952, op. 5, d. 397, ll. 45–46, 50. By contrast, Boris Bogoliubov, a "prisoner specialist" who was deputy chief of the mine, claimed in unpublished remarks recorded on 28 November 1936 that "at the mine, all norms were mastered. This didn't happen very easily, but all norms were mastered." Ibid., d. 304, l. 113.

50. *Magnitogrorskii metall*, 3 November 1935.

51. GARF, f. 7952, op. 5, d. 313, l. 25.

52. Ibid., d. 312, l. 11.

53. Ibid., d. 306, ll. 84–87, l. 101. For further discussion of the pressures brought to bear on management by Stakhanovism, see *Za industrializatsiiu*, 18 January 1936; *Sotsialisticheskii vestnik*, 28 December 1935; and Kravchenko, *I Chose Freedom*, p. 188.

54. Bogatyrenko also pointed out that in the shop at the time of his article (August 1936) there was considerable idle time, equipment often gave out, and that cutting 215 ingots per shift was still unusual. He also revealed that "a few times I challenged the [other operators] to competitions," but there was "no support from the party or trade union, and no feeling of public support." *MR*, 14 August 1936.

55. GARF, f. 7952, op. 5, d. 312, l. 11.

56. *MR*, 14 August 1936.

57. *MR*, 28 January and 1 March 1936.

58. *Liudi Stalinskoi Magnitki*, pp. 104–5.

59. *MR*, 21 November 1936; GARF, f. 7952, op. 5, d. 300, ll. 61–81. In May 1936, Matiushenko, a sixty-one year old senior foreman (*obermaster*) in the open-hearth shop, was honored by a surprise reception in the shop's red corner. Asked to say a few words, Matiushenko was said to have been too choked up. Later, however, he explained how in 1934 the shop chief had first named him as foreman for all four ovens then in existence, with the proviso that another eight ovens were scheduled to be put into operation and that he should think about cadres. "I understood the conversation with the boss to mean that it was necessary to train steel smelters on

the spot," Matiushenko recalled. "As soon as I had a look around, studied people, I began to gather candidates for steel smelting positions from among the unskilled laborers [*chenorabochie*]." He added that contrary to assumed opinion, it took not ten to fifteen years to train a skilled smelter, but two. *MR*, 24 May 1936.

60. MFGAChO, f. 10, op. 1, d. 243, l. 3.

61. At the same time, four bosses (Zaveniagin, Bekker, Goncharenko, and Shevchenko) and one worker (Galiullin) received the Order of Lenin. *MR*, 11 December 1935.

62. MFGAChO, f. 99, op. 1, d. 1091, l. 81.

63. GARF, f. 7952, op. 5, d. 312, l. 14.

64. *MR*, 27 August 1936; GARF, f. 7952, op. 5, d. 313, l. 140. The newspaper also reported that books (and groceries) were being delivered to Stakhanovites' homes. Workers complained, however, that they had no time to read and that in place of the groceries they had ordered, substitutes of dubious quality were delivered. *MR*, 8 April and 17 June 1936.

65. *MR*, 30 August 1936.

66. Siegelbaum, *Stakhanovism*, p. 179.

67. As quoted in S. R. Gershberg, *Rabota u nas takaia: Zapiski zhurnalista-pravdista tridtsatykh godov* (Moscow, 1971), p. 321. Ordzhonikidze was referring to "Izotovites." Nikolai Izotov, a pickman in a Donbas mine, had exceeded his norm by 474 percent in the first three months of 1932. Essentially the first "Stakhanovite," Izotov was discovered by Gershberg. See Siegelbaum, *Stakhanovism*, pp. 54–61. In December 1938 the regime introduced a "Hero of Socialist Labor" medal. A recipient automatically received the Order of Lenin. *Vedomosti Verkhovnogo Soveta SSSR*, 1938, No. 23, reprinted in *Sbornik zakonodatelnykh*, p. 131.

68. In Khitarov's formulation, the Stakhanovite represented a "new type of person," with "wide horizons," "great *aktivnost*," and thirst for knowledge, all of which demanded more and better work from the party organization. But his characterization of party meetings before the advent of Stakhanovism was not particularly encouraging: "Previously, the party secretary, in preparing his summary report, would, with tender emotion, bend over the charts showing how many workers were involved in socialist competition—80 percent this year against 50 percent last year. . . . The production plan is still not being fulfilled, one can't escape that, but, no big deal; the majority of workers are shock workers; we've had such-and-such number of production meetings, so many hundreds or thousands of rationalization proposals. But how many conferences were actually lively, how many lead to a general discussion? How many rationalization suggestions were introduced, with real results? These matters the party secretary usually passed over in silence. . . . With agitprop the same thing happens: according to the tables, things are going fine: party study is up from 70 to 90 percent this year, even attendance is up, from 40 to 60 percent; so many wall newspapers were issued, so many discussions and readings held. But to what effect? With what results?" The problem of the formalism of party meetings held in the shops is discussed in ch. 7. *MR*, 10 March 1936. The article originally appeared in *Pravda*, 4 March 1936.

69. Stakhanovism was expressly connected with the exchange of party documents, which was being carried out simultaneously. For example, Nikita Paukov, a foreman (*master*) in the medium sorting mill with earnings above 1,000 rubles per

month and a record of norm-busting and prizes, had his name appear over a newspaper article entitled, "How I Prepared for the Exchange of Party Documents." Paukov, who came to Magnitogorsk in September 1934 and had joined the party in 1928, worked extra time as an agitator, conducting discussions in the shop, and studied in a circle for party history. He received his new party card in a special ceremony. That same year he also was awarded a motorcar. *MR*, 28 April 1936; and GARF, f. 7952, op. 5, d. 307, ll. 26–28; 312, l. 51.

70. GARF, f. 7952, op. 5, d. 312, l. 49.

71. The author was I. Ivich [Vernshtein], the same person who wrote the history of city construction used in chapter 3. GARF, f. 7952, op. 5, d. 364, ll. 58–61, 66. It was Leonid Terekhov whose left leg was shattered in a tangle of electric lines when the power was turned on by mistake. He lay in the hospital three months, after which he was sent to a resort, and then received back on the job with a suitable welcome. *MR*, 23 May 1936. For Terekhov's fate, see ch. 7.

72. Deputy Director Khazanov claimed that when shop chief Golubitskii gave Ogorodnikov orders, the latter replied, "What are you saying, you're here [in the mill] only one month, and I've been here a year and a half. I know better than you." GARF, f. 7952, op. 5, d. 313, l. 49. Ogorodnikov's hasty exit was apparently precipitated by a fine he was assessed by Golubitskii of 250 rubles for "endangering" the machinery. Angered by the fine and by the fact that no came to his defense, the operator left Magnitogorsk and went to the Makeevka blooming mill. When Magnitogorsk officials notified GUMP, Gurevich personally summoned Ogorodnikov from Makeevka to Moscow. On 3 May Ogorodnikov met with Gurevich and Ordzhonikidze, who rebuked him for not notifying the Commissariat of his problems and ordered him back to Magnitogorsk. Ogorodnikov claimed to have been surprised in his dealings with the famous commissar by the way "people are valued," but he admitted having not wanted to return and being nervous about the prospect. He arrived in Magnitogorsk on 10 May. The atmosphere in the blooming mill continued to be strained. *Za industrializatsiiu*, 12 April 1936; *Magnitogorskii metall*, 24 April 1936; *MR*, 12 May 1936; and GARF, f. 7952, op. 5, d. 312, ll. 5–11. In connection with this episode, Zaveniagin published a clever piece of self-criticism in *Za industrializatsiiu*, 25 April 1936, which was reprinted in *MR*, 27 April 1936. The factory director could not have been too pleased with the adverse publicity that this episode generated in the national press. For Ogorodnikov's subsequent fate, see ch. 7.

73. *MR*, 16 March 1936.

74. GARF, f. 7952, op. 5, d. 305, l. 59.

75. Ibid., d. 307, ll. 45–46 and d. 397, ll. 45–6, 50.

76. *MR*, 14 October 1936.

77. Avraamii Zaveniagin, "O peresmotre moshchnostei oborudovaniia i norm," *MR*, 9 March 1936.

78. *MR*, 5 April 1936.

79. Mysteriously, the newspaper made no mention of the Stakhanovite campaign, which at that time was in full swing, and must have had something to do with the fact that Vasilev "exceeded what was permissible." *MR*, 27 August 1936.

80. GARF, f. 7952, op, 5, d. 309, l. 74.

81. "In mill 300 No. 1 during the Stakhanovite ten-day in February [1936],"

the city newspaper wrote, "engineer Kudriavtsev (head of a shift), instead of mobilizing the workers' collective for the overfulfillment of the record of the shift of Makaev . . . adopted the stance of discrediting the shop chief and the shift of Makaev, announcing that the shop chief credited extra tons to Makaev's shift." The report further stated that "Kudriavtsev refused to conduct and lead countershift meetings, announcing that this was a matter of trade union and party concern and not of engineering personnel." Removed as shift boss, called a saboteur, expelled from the Engineers' and Technicians' Council (he was not a party member), Kudriavtsev was soon arrested. Makaev became the new shift boss. *MR*, 22 and 30 January, 9 February 1936; MFGAChO, f. 118, op. 1, d. 106, l. 23. It is unclear whether this Kudriavtsev was related to Nikolai or Evgenii Kudriavtsev.

82. John Scott, acknowledging that equipment and transport were overtaxed, repairs neglected, and machinery badly abused, nevertheless felt that "the Stakhanov movement in Magnitogorsk produced very marked results during the latter half of 1935 and almost all of 1936" and that "by and large, 1936, the Stakhanovite year, was a great success." Scott based his assessments on official data published in the newspaper in 1936. But in 1937, while Scott was away, these data were exposed as unreliable by the chairman of the Magnitogorsk affiliate of the state bank. Scott himself admitted that "it was difficult to credit" the factory's figures on profit, and that Magnitogorsk's steel "was expensive, both in terms of rubles and human lives." Scott, *Behind*, pp. 163–66. One Soviet eyewitness spoke the opinion of many people in Magnitogorsk when he testified that with Stakhanovism, one shift would produce above plan, the next shift nothing. GARF, f. 7952, op. 5, d. 306, ll. 77–78. Scott seems to be correct, however, that Stakhanovism, which was named after a miner, did have its best results on the iron-ore mine, whose work process was most amenable to speed-up. *Stakhanovskii opyt Magnitogorskogo rudnika*, pp. 22, 45.

83. MFGAChO, f. 118, op. 1, d. 106, l. 23. Another worker, Anton Vasilchenko of the medium sorting mill, who appears to have been dekulakized in 1931, was accused of refusing to help set up conditions for a record by the Stakhanovite Shevchuk. Vasilchenko was arrested, charged with counterrevolution under article 58, and dispatched to the Cheliabinsk oblast court. The details of his supposed crimes were not very convincing. He was apparently made a scapegoat in a case that was publicized in the newspaper under the title, "The Class Enemy in the Shop." *MR*, 30 January 1936.

84. This was in sharp contrast to American steel plants at this time, where minority groups such as blacks and Hispanics usually received the roughest and most dangerous jobs in the hot shops, indicating the low status of both the jobs and the workers. Greer, *Big Steel*, pp. 72–89.

85. According to a city soviet report, as of December 1936 there were 11,000 Stakhanovites and shock workers, or 51 percent of all workers at the steel plant. MFGAChO, f. 10, op. 1, d. 243, l. 3. As of September 1939, there were officially 11,150 Stakhanovites and shock workers at Magnitogorsk. The newspaper, which published this figure, commented that it was "eyewash" and had "nothing in common with reality." The paper no doubt had in mind the factory's production results, but the exigencies of reward-based categorization were strong. *MR*, 5 November

1939. In mid-1936 the steel plant's deputy director, Khazanov, revealed that according to factory administration data, there were 3,663 Stakhanovites at the steel plant, but according to the records of the trade union committee, there were 4,441. "In our shops," he commented, "there are insufficiently precise criteria for determining Stakhanovites." The Commissariat of Heavy Industry issued several instructions on classifying superior workers, most of which involved a system of quantitative norm fulfillment. By contrast, in one directive issued in August 1936, Gurevich, the chief of GUMP, wrote that Stakhanovites were differentiated from shock workers by the quality of their work and the conditions of their place of work and machinery. This was obviously an attempt to counter the tendencies of seeking quantity at the expense of quality and machinery. *Magnitogorskii metall*, 30 June and 4 August 1936.

86. Siegelbaum has argued that the principal goals of the state's promotion of Stakhanovism, in addition to raising productivity, were to undermine the autonomy of managers and to create a new proletarian culture supportive of the state. In the process, the working class was supposedly divided between a privileged stratum and a nonprivileged majority, with the former's weight and influence ensuring general adherence to regime values and the resulting intraclass tensions inhibiting the development of class solidarity. But Siegelbaum neglected the persistence of a "class outlook," or sense of common fate, among workers. Notwithstanding the extreme individualization and ostensibly successful stratification, workers knew that they were not bosses. According to Moshe Lewin, who was evacuated to the USSR from Poland during the war, "you couldn't come to a worker and tell him in private that he was a member of a ruling class. When I worked in the Urals, workers knew who they were and that it was the *nachalstvo* that had all the power and privileges." Siegelbaum, *Stakhanovism*, ch. 6; "Moshe Lewin, Interview with Paul Bushkovitch," *Radical History Review*, 1982, pp. 295–96. One former Soviet citizen testified that workers felt great fear, "but you know, we did like each other, I mean the workers. Everybody was in the same boat." "Twenty-six Interviews," I/2.

87. GARF, f. 7952, op. 5, d. 300, ll. 149–54.

88. Ibid., d. 315, l. 14; d. 300, l. 47.

89. Eliseeva, "Borba za kadry," p. 221.

90. Anatolii Dumkin, who arrived at the site in June 1931 and lived initially in a tent, had learned the trade of welding and moved into a dormitory barracks. He explained that most of the welding masks were hand held. A few were the kind that remained in place by themselves, but he said these made a worker extremely hot and had to be removed frequently anyway, so the work could be checked. Because several welders worked on the same sections in teams, it sometimes happened that one was temporarily blinded by the arc of the other's torch. Dumkin decided to take "a course" to become a fitter. This meant that he became someone's apprentice. GARF, f. 7952, op. 5, d. 300, ll. 40–41.

91. GARF, f. 7952, op. 5, d. 100, l. 110.

92. Aleksei Shatilin, a miner from the Donbas who came to Magnitogorsk in 1931, became one of Magnitogorsk's celebrated Stakhanovites after having been selected in 1934 to train for the position of blast furnace operator. Shatilin, *No domnakh Magnitki* (Moscow, 1953), pp. 4–5. Many Stakhanovites were experienced workers (although at less skilled occupations). According to 1936 trade union data

on 2,335 Magnitogorsk Stakhanovites, 1,028 had ten or more years' experience. Of 3,665 shock workers analyzed, 999 had three or less years' experience and 1,203 had ten years' or more. MFGAChO, f. 118, op. 1, d. 106, l. 4.

93. For Stakhanovites, the great dream was the Industrial Academy. Bogatyrenko, who had arrived in Magnitogorsk in August 1932, wanted to study further but could not because of language difficulties. An ethnic Ukrainian, he had studied three of his four years in primary school in Ukrainian, the other in Russian, and claimed to mix them up. Zaveniagin promised him a tutor to help get him ready for entrance into the Industrial Academy, but none was apparently supplied. Bogatyrenko noted that his fellow blooming operator Chernysh studied in the Tekhnikum. GARF, f. 7952, op. 5, d. 304, ll. 174–79. Ogorodnikov, who was the son of a Belorussian peasant from Smolensk *guberniia* and himself barely educated, also wanted to be allowed time off to study at state expense in the Industrial Academy. Ibid., d. 311, ll. 11–13, 15. Fedor Golubitskii claimed that Bogatyrenko was a superb worker, but fickle, moody, and prone to drinking, while Chernysh had "a very great craving for education" and studied all the time. Ibid., d. 306, l. 74. Rafael Khitarov noted that unlike some Stakhanovites, Bogatyrenko refused to become a special labor instructor, saying "myself, I'll work; let the others watch." Ibid., d. 313, l. 34.

94. V. F. Romanov, "Magnitogorskii metallurgicheskii kombinat," *Voprosy istorii*, 1975, no. 9, p. 108.

95. By the end of 1935, according to the city newspaper, 3,500 people had passed the state examination for the technical minimum in basic professions. *MR*, 2 February 1936; see also Scott, *Behind*, p. 218 and GARF, f. 7952, op. 5, d. 200, passim. More formally, the Factory Vocational School (*fabrichno-zavodskoe uchilishche*), or FZU, graduated 3,380 people in the first eight years of its existence. In 1939 the student body numbered more than 1,000. *MR*, 18 October 1939.

96. Improving one's work capacities went beyond simply acquiring a trade and honing one's skills. Workers were given instruction materials, such as small booklets that included metric tables, multiplication tables, and advice on behavior. GARF, f. 7952, op. 5, d. 301, l. 55. As the French historian Michelle Perrot has written, "industrial discipline represents only one form of discipline among others, and the factory belongs, with the school, military, penitentiary, and other systems, to a constellation of institutions which, each in its own way, contribute to the rule-making process." Perrot, "The Three Ages of Industrial Discipline in Nineteenth-Century France," in John Merriman, ed., *Consciousness and Class Experience in Nineteenth-Century Europe* (New York: Holmes and Meier, 1979), pp. 149–68; the quote appears on p. 149.

97. John Scott marveled at the "student body in Magnitogorsk night schools, [which was] willing to work 8, 10, even 12 hours on the job under the severest conditions, and then come to school at night, sometimes on an empty stomach and, sitting on a backless wooden bench, in a room so cold that you could see your breath a yard ahead of you, study mathematics for four hours straight." Scott, *Behind*, p. 49.

98. Although most of the production workers at the plant had helped to build it, some were imported from factories in the Urals and especially the Donbas. Yet even for them, production work required learning a new work culture. For exam-

ple, Grigorii Bobrov, a metal worker on open-hearth oven no. 9, came to Magnitogorsk in June 1934 from an older steelmaking factory:

> At the Beloretsk factory I trusted my eyes more than the laboratory. People said that the laboratory lies, that one's eyes are more trustworthy and exact. I arrived here and immediately began to work as I was accustomed. But here they said: 'Not that way, cart the steel over to the lab, work according to the lab.' I really liked this. I took courses here. I had to learn all over. Here I work with instruments, and work with instruments is of course more comfortable. I go over and check the ordometer—I no longer trust my eyes. . . . The lab gives you an analysis in five minutes. Now the lab is located in the middle of the shop.

GARF, f. 7952, op. 5, d. 304, l. 188.

99. Ibid., d. 305, l. 35.

100. Ibid., d. 300, l. 52.

101. *MR*, 28 October 1936. See also the volume on this theme, *Rabochie dinastii* (Moscow, 1975).

102. *MR*, 21 April 1936.

103. *Izvestiia*, 21 December 1938, reprinted in *Sbornik zakonodatelnykh*, pp. 20–21. In the apt words of one former Soviet manager from the Ukraine, "the labor book became for the rank and file workman what the party card was for the Communist. . . . the worker was condemned to drag the burden of his entire past with him always wherever he might go." Kravchenko, *I Chose Freedom*, p. 312.

104. One can find the rationale behind the labor book of 1938 already in the central press of 1931. See *Izvestiia*, 14 January 1931, as cited in Schwarz, *Labor in the Soviet Union*, pp. 96–97.

105. GARF, f. 7952, op. 5, d. 301, l. 83 (reverse). Similarly, a set of *kharakteristiki* for the "best Stakhanovites" in 1938 specified profession, when they began work, party affiliation, norm fulfillment, activism in public, and awards won. MFGAChO, f. 118, op. 1, d. 153, passim. And a set of *lichnye kartochki* for city soviet deputies included, in addition to name, sex, and nationality, the following points: *partiinost* (yes or no; if yes, year of entry), social ancestry (a choice among several), shock worker (yes or no), service in Red Army (yes or no), place of work, and home address. Ibid., f. 10, op. 1, d. 121, l. 1.

106. One form contained sixteen questions, almost all of which related to work experiences, although some sought to establish the social and geographical origins of the respondent, as well as the length of time spent in Magnitogorsk. Bosses were also interviewed. GARF, f. 7952, op. 5, d. 301, l. 79.

107. GARF, f. 7952, op. 5, d. 301, passim. Very few of the reminiscences left behind were by women. An exception was the case of Raisa Troinina. Ibid., d. 319, ll. 1 ff.

108. GARF, f. 7952, op. 5, d. 318, l. 20. There is internal evidence that the memoirs were at least partly written by workers themselves. Within the repetitious tropes, one can see considerable differences in style and emphasis. Moreover, many "delicate" or otherwise proscribed matters are openly discussed. And unlike most of the "worker letters" published in the newspaper, in the memoirs there was only one instance (out of more than one hundred) when the author concluded with

the exclamation: "Long Live the Party of the Bolsheviks, Long Live the Genius Leader Stalin, Long Live the World Giant [Magnitka]." Ibid., d. 318, l. 20.

109. As related to me by Louis Ernst, an eyewitness, in an interview in Doniphan, Missouri on 30 April 1986; confirmed by surviving dispossessed peasants interviewed in Magnitogorsk in 1987 and 1989.

110. *MR*, 29 April 1936.

111. *Magnitogorskii metall*, 4 January 1936; GARF, f. 7952, op. 5, d. 306, l. 204–22. Griaznov had worked in the Beloretsk factory (where his father also worked, for thirty-eight years), and in Magnitogorsk served as a worker correspondent, submitting investigatory material for the factory paper. In a March 1944 letter Griaznov sent from the front to Magnitogorsk journalists not long before he was killed (September), he supposedly wrote: "I hug you strongly, strongly. I'll kiss you after the war, you and my beloved open hearth. My furnace, my flame. I haven't seen it for three years. I miss it, I miss the shop, the metal, the noise, the dust, the salt on my shirt and face." Cited in Liudmila Tatianicheva and Nikolai Smelianskii, *Ulitsa stalevara Griaznova* (Moscow, 1978), p. 23. The full diary (1934–40) has never been published, although Tatianicheva and Smelianskii offer several more excerpts.

112. *MR*, 12 May 1936.

113. GARF, f. 7952, op. 5, d. 305, ll. 40–1.

114. Ibid., d. 303, ll. 3–5.

115. The dramatic and far-reaching Bolshevization of the Russian language— to say nothing of the many others that were spoken in the Soviet Union—was noted by contemporaries. Indeed, the four-volume interpretive dictionary issued between 1934 and 1940, *Tolkovyi slovar russkogo iazyka*, self-consciously set out to lay "the basis for a new phase in the life of the Russian language and at the same time to indicate the new norms that are being established for the use of words." A. M. Sleishchev, *Iazyk revoliutsionnoi epokhi: Iz nabliudenii nad russkim iazykom poslednykh let (1917–1926)*, 2d ed. (Moscow, 1928). See also Michael Waller, "The -Isms of Stalinism," *Soviet Studies* 20, no. 2 (October 1968): 229–34. An interesting comparison is furnished by Victor Klemperer, *LTI, Lingua Tertii Imperii: Die Sprache des Dritten Reiches* (Leipzig: Reclam, 1991; original ed., 1957). Part memoir, part detached analysis, Klemperer's book offers an amusing analysis of the Nazi penchant for acronyms, and links the specificity of "speaking Nazi" (*nazistisch sprechen*) with the goal of securing popular belief in an ersatz religion.

116. Cleverness and dissimulation, time-honored "peasant" attributes, perennially induced a sense of wonder in the authorities. See, for example, Daniel Field, *Rebels in the Name of the Tsar* (Boston: Unwin, Hyman, 1976).

117. This analysis of a variant on the Russian wife's traditional role as moralist with the husband as misbehaving drunk was suggested to me by Laura Engelstein.

118. One such spotlight fell on Nina Zaitseva, a brigade leader in the ore-crushing plant. *MR*, 8 March 1936.

119. *MR*, 11, 16, and 1 June 1936, respectively. These voices—published by the male editor—are unique not simply because they are female. Together they constitute the single instance of an unequivocal rebuke of official policies in the Magnitogorsk newspaper during the Stalin era, and would seem to indicate the deep dissatisfaction of certain women with the policy shift. For similarly critical letters

published in *Pravda* and *Komsomolskaia Pravda*, see Janet Evans, "The Communist Party of the Soviet Union and the Women's Question: The Case of the 1936 Decree 'In Defense of Mother and Child,'" *Journal of Contemporary History* 16 (1981): 757–75.

120. *MR*, 28 July 1936. His remarks were published as part of the celebration of the new constitution.

121. In 1938 the city had around 15,000 *natsmen*, or members of national minorities, a designation reserved primarily for non-Slavs, especially Kazakhs and Tatars. *MR*, 12 April 1938. Kazakhs, unlike the Tatars, did not seem to take well to the Russian language. One local petty official claimed that the Kazakhs spoke no Russian and wore their national clothes, which were difficult to work in. "They worked wonderfully in winter, but in summer they wanted to roam. So they roamed around the steppe, not with herds, but with their families, for they had worked and acquired a horse." GARF, f. 7952, op. 5, d. 309, ll. 38–43. The regime promoted a policy of instruction for minorities in their native tongue, but there was a severe shortage of qualified teachers who could conduct instruction in non-Russian languages. In the entire Magnitogorsk region, for example, there were only twenty Kazakh teachers. Only four had finished a seven-year school, while some had not made it past the third year. The newspaper found one school where Kazakh children were being taught in Tatar. *MR*, 29 September 1936.

122. *MR*, 17 March 1936.

123. During the first eight months of 1935, twenty-two suggestions were advanced in the coke-chemical plant, six of which were acted upon (although only five were realized). The other sixteen were declined. "In such a way," wrote the factory newspaper, "really only five rationalization suggestions, which benefit the shop, were advanced." The paper also pointed out that these were made by engineers and foremen, not rank-and-file workers. The spotlight provided by the newspaper sent a clear and unavoidable message to the plant's party and trade union organizers: in upcoming months results better be more substantial. *Magnitogorskii metall*, 23 August 1935.

124. Scott, *Behind*, p. 164.

125. An excellent case in point is the process of upward norm as described by Kravchenko, *I Chose Freedom*, p. 189.

126. Unequivocal evidence on the fear of informants comes from the testimony of former Soviet citizens (not from Magnitogorsk) in "Twenty-six Interviews" and from the Harvard Interview Project. During the same period, informants were widely used by American corporations, in violation of the law, which provoked Senate investigations and indignant denials by industrial executives. Frank Palmer, *Spies in Steel: An Exposé of Industrial War* (Denver: The Labor Press, 1928).

127. It was not that speaking out freely at any time was completely prohibited; one had to learn how and when to speak out. Scott described a worker's meeting in a large Moscow factory in 1940. "I saw workers get up and criticize the plant director, make suggestions as to how to increase production, improve quality, and lower costs," he wrote. "Then the question of the new Soviet-German trade pact came up. The workers unanimously passed a previously prepared resolution approving the Soviet foreign policy. There was no discussion. The Soviet workers had learned what was their business and what was not." Scott, *Behind*, p. 264.

128. According to the 1926 population census, *Vsesouiznaia perepis naseleniia 1926 goda* (Moscow, 1929).

129. See the analysis of the great American steel center, Pittsburgh, by Nora Faires, "Immigrants and Industry: Peopling the 'Iron City,'" in Samuel Hays, ed., *City at the Point: Essays on the Social History of Pittsburgh* (Pittsburgh: Pittsburgh University Press, 1989), pp. 3–31.

130. The rules governing these social welfare benefits were laid out in *Kodeks zakonov o trude, s izmeneniiami do 1 iiulia 1934 g.*, pp. 36–37, 85–92.

131. This is one of the chief arguments of Filtzer, *Soviet Workers*. See also Lewin, *The Making of the Soviet System*, p. 255. Whereas Filtzer treated all dysfunctional behavior by workers as resistance, John Barber contended that absenteeism or drunkenness did not constitute conscious or deliberate opposition. Yet although Filtzer may have gone too far in attributing motives to Soviet workers, surely the main point is that the regime's treatment of the kind of behavior Filtzer points to as a political problem, even when such behavior was more or less "innocent," had to make workers aware that being late or absent from work willy-nilly constituted a political statement and would be dealt with accordingly. Barber, "Working-Class Culture," pp. 10–13.

132. *Sobranie zakonov i rasporiazhenii*, 1932, no. 78, item 475; see also no. 45, item 244.

133. *MR*, 26 July 1939. In the first eleven months of 1936, 4,000 workers were said to have left their jobs at the steel plant and construction trust. *CR*, 30 December 1936. During the first four months of 1937, around 1,500 workers were said to have quit. Recruiters were said to be spending state money but recruiting no one, while little was being done to retain those workers already present. *MR*, 25 January 1938.

134. *MR*, 9 April 1934. For the repercussions of the labor shortage, see Filtzer, *Soviet Workers*, pp. 62, 261.

135. See David Granick, *Job Rights in the Soviet Union: Their Consequences* (Cambridge: Cambridge University Press, 1987). I am indebted to Kenneth Straus for directing me to this source and for fruitful discussions of Filtzer's work.

136. One former Soviet worker not from Magnitogorsk offered the following testimony: "In the early 1930s I and several of my friends used to drink a little bit of beer or wine together, and we used to gather in the same place on Saturdays. Sometimes, we drank vodka, sometimes we went to a movie. After a while, the party and the members of the Komsomol put pressure on us to break up our gatherings. They were afraid of *gruppovshchina* [group formation]. Let's say you write an application, and that you put in a request for something and several men sign it. That's *gruppovshchina*. Immediately, the local Communist party and trade union people will call one guy after another and reprimand him. But they will not call the whole group; they will deal with each individual, separately." "Twenty-six Interviews," II/14.

137. Gareth Stedman Jones has written that "there is no political or ideological institution that could not in some way be interpreted as an agency of social control. . . . Since capitalism is still with us, we can with impunity suppose, if we wish to, that at any time in the last three hundred years the mechanisms of social control were operating effectively." Similarly, he urged caution in the use of Gramsci's no-

tion of hegemony, which "can only give a tautological answer to a false question if it is used to explain the absence of a revolutionary proletarian class consciousness in the sense envisaged by Lukacs." When Stedman Jones attempted to put forth an alternative explanation for workers apparent "quiescence" under capitalism, however, he violated his own strictures regarding the place of culture and language, invoking—as he himself admitted in a critical reflection on his own essay—"the determinant place of relations of production . . . far too unproblematically." At the same time, he misinterpreted and dismissed Foucault, who, contrary to Stedman Jones's misreading, offered a way out of the dilemma that Stedman Jones has brought into sharp relief. Stedman Jones, "Class Expression Versus Social Control? A Critique of Recent Trends in the Social History of 'Leisure,'" in idem., *Languages of Class: Studies in English Working-Class History, 1832–1982* (Cambridge: Cambridge University Press, 1983), pp. 76–89.

138. "You simply had to be smart with them," explained one former worker, not from Magnitogorsk. "Very often you even felt good that you could outsmart all those restrictions." "Twenty-six Interviews," I/5. See also "Moshe Lewin, Interview with Paul Bushkovitch," pp. 294–96.

139. To paraphrase Febvre, one might argue that an analysis of *mentalité* in the Stalin years ought to be cast not as an investigation of any particular individual's beliefs measured against our own system for determining truth, but as a study of a range of possibilities within the given society's "regime of truth." Lucien Febvre, *The Problem of Unbelief in the Sixteenth Century: The Religion of Rabelais* (Cambridge, Mass.: Harvard University Press, 1982; originally published in French, 1942).

140. In 1936, a decree specified that crossing Soviet borders without passport and permission was punishable by sentences of from one to three years. *Sobranie zakonov i rasporiazhenii*, 1936, no. 52, reprinted in *Sbornik dokumentov*, p. 393.

141. Norman Davies, *Heart of Europe: A Short History of Poland* (Oxford: Oxford University Press, 1984), pp. 37–38. The mechanics of Soviet censorship are described in Fainsod, *Smolensk*, pp. 364–77. Strikes, although common in the 1920s, seem to have ceased sometime during the 1930s. Filtzer, *Soviet Workers*, p. 81.

142. As E. H. Carr has written, "Bolshevism has shown a remarkable capacity to inspire loyalty and self-sacrifice in its adherents; and this success is beyond doubt due in part to its bold claim—parallel to the claim of the Catholic church in countries where it is paramount—to be the source of principles binding for every form of human activity including the activity of the state." Carr, *The Soviet Impact on the Western World*, pp. 84–85.

143. Robert Tucker demonstrates convincingly that Stalin actively propagated his own cult, but he treats the cult chiefly as the outward manifestation of Stalin's megalomania rather than as a sophisticated technique of rule and an important dimension of Soviet popular culture. Tucker, *Stalin in Power*. A contrast is provided by the analysis of the Hitler cult by Ian Kershaw, who notes what he calls the Hitler myth's integratory function. Relying on surviving SS and Gestapo reports on popular moods, Kershaw argues that the Hitler myth developed at the expense of the Nazi movement, in compensation for the widespread and deep antipathy felt toward the Nazi party. Kershaw also shows how Hitler's popularity drew on the myth

of the "good tsar," whereby not the Führer but his henchmen were held accountable for any deficiencies or injustices, an impression that was enhanced by the unpopularity of the local Gauleiters or "little Hitlers." I suspect that these findings more or less apply to the Stalin cult, although the question cannot be resolved without recourse to NKVD reports on popular moods. But the popularity of the Bolshevik party was probably greater than that of the Nazis, if Kershaw is correct about the widespread revulsion (of course, the SS and the Gestapo were charged with rooting out and thus uncovering threatening or potentially threatening beliefs). Also, whereas the Hitler myth collapsed suddenly and ignominiously not long after the battle of Stalingrad, the Stalin myth remained alive for many millions of people until the devastating frontal assault against the dead leader's legacy conducted by the Soviet media during the summer of 1988, in connection with the Nineteenth Party Conference. In the contrasting endurance of the respective "myths" the outcome of the war was obviously pivotal, but I suspect there's more to it than this. Kershaw, *The Hitler Myth: Image and Reality in the Third Reich* (New York: Oxford University Press, 1987).

144. Mikhail Heller and Aleksandr Nekrich, *Utopia in Power* (New York: Summit, 1986; originally published in Russian, 1982), p. 281.

145. One study, which analyzes what is called the "cult of folklore" under Stalin, typically, but in my view too readily, dismisses the resulting outpouring of songs and tales about the Soviet leader as "artificial," the pseudo-creations of propagandists. Because Stalin-era "folklore" did not outlast the dictator, however, is no reason to suppose it had little resonance while he was alive. See Frank Miller, *Folklore for Stalin: Russian Folklore and Pseudofolklore of the Stalin Era* (New York: M. E. Sharpe, 1990).

146. The Stalin cult became functional after 1934, especially in 1936 in connection with the campaign for a new constitution, and not, as has been supposed, in 1929 with the celebration of his fiftieth birthday. In 1936 the Magnitogorsk newspaper's pages overran with praise and gratitude for Stalin, "our happiness," and with photograph after photograph of the "creator of the constitution." *MR*, 24, 26 and 27 November 1936. The shift to the warm fatherly figure occurred in schoolbooks addressed to children in the mid-1930s, at which time Stalin began to pose in the company of children. See James Heizer, "The Cult of Stalin, 1929–1939," Ph.D. dissertation, University of Kentucky, Lexington, 1977. Heizer speculates that Stalin probably enjoyed being with children, a hug being a welcome respite for him from all the spy and enemy hunting (p. 179).

147. The city of Magnitogorsk, for example, sent four delegates to the Extraordinary Eighth Congress of the Soviets in December 1936, at which the new constitution, celebrated during the course of most of the year, was given a ringing endorsement. Along with Factory Director Avraamii Zaveniagin and Party Secretary Rafael Khitarov, two workers were selected, one of whom was Marfa Rozhkova, who was known as "the best operator" of mill 500 (the factory newspaper noted that "during two years of work, not a single breakdown has been registered in her service record" *Magnitogorskii metall*, 6 July 1935). Upon returning from the Congress of Soviets, Rozhkova reportedly told an assembly in Magnitogorsk that "when Stalin emerged, all we could do was scream with joy." Under the headline "Enormous Joy," she proudly announced that she had voted in the affirmative on

every question before the Congress. She admitted that she had sat far away from the podium and had had a difficult time seeing, but nonetheless related the sense of joy she felt: "I lift my hand for the Constitution and Stalin lifts his hand for it. What happiness this is, comrades. Honestly, I feel like I'm eighteen years old." As for the other Magnitogorsk worker selected to attend, Mikhail Zuev, his remarks were more restrained. But Zuev stressed that "not one orator speaking during the discussion neglected the question of the strengthening of the military preparedness of the country. Numerous people spoke about the military danger." MR, 14 and 16 December 1936.

148. MR, 8 July 1936.

149. See the apt words on this concurrence by Arthur Koestler in his autobiography, Arrow in the Blue (New York, 1952), pp. 277–78, and in the collection of essays The God that Failed, ed. by Richard Crossman (New York: Harper and Row, 1950).

150. At the demonstration a presidium of the "best" Stakhanovites was elected and speeches were given by prominent local individuals from the platform attached to a statue of Stalin. The newspaper account of the proceedings counterposed the threat of fascism with the steel of Magnitka and the leadership of Stalin. The story was accompanied by photographs in which were visible many banners and portraits borne aloft by participants. Few of the banners mentioned Spain; instead they praised the Soviet leadership and especially its Leader. Almost all the portraits bore the same face. As was customary, a telegram, prepared beforehand by the local party leadership, was read aloud. It did not mention the Spanish Republic's struggle, the occasion of the gathering, but was instead taken up with praise and gratitude for the Great Leader. There were few clearer instances of Stalin's representation of the USSR's power and resolve. MR, 6 October 1936.

151. Barber also argued on the basis of émigré interviews that workers bought into the official ideology far less than did intellectuals, and that workers' attitudes toward the grand crusade fluctuated with their standard of living. This is an interesting hypothesis, considerable light on which is likely to be shed by surveys (operativnye svodki) prepared by the NKVD of the political mood among the populace. Barber, "Working-Class Culture," pp. 8–13. Of course, the contrast between the "proles" and the party members was one of the premises in George Orwell's 1984, first published in 1949. In another book, Orwell argued that "socialism in its developed form is a theory entirely confined to the middle class," rather than the worker, and that "one of the analogies between Communism and Roman Catholicism is that only the educated are completely orthodox." Orwell, The Road to Wigan Pier (New York: Harcourt, Brace, 1958), pp. 173–77.

152. This seems to have been the case even among the disaffected who later left the country, according to the analysis of conformity under Stalin based on the 1950s Harvard Interview Project by Alex Inkeles and Raymond Bauer. The authors argue that "regime policy for social control was designed to make the loyal and disloyal citizen behaviorally indistinguishable" by leaving "no viable alternative except to conform." This was achieved because "strong negative sanctions for nonconformity were complemented by a carefully structured system of rewards for conformity," and because having received a thorough political education in how to think, talk, and act "correctly," the populace was "expected on appropriate occasions

to indicate its acceptance and support of the system by politically 'correct' behavior and pronouncements." The frequency of these occasions, they point out, was "outstanding, especially for members of the intelligentsia." All true, yet Inkeles and Bauer never say why the "regime" compelled such manifestations from the people, except that Soviet leaders seemed to "crave" them. Such a view does not explain why shop foremen, agitators, petty officials and countless others participate in and enforce rituals of affirmation. As for why ordinary people went along, the authors argue that manifestations of loyalty were ultimately based on the perceived strength of the regime. That some level of genuine acceptance could coexist with intimidation appears not to have been considered by Inkeles and Bauer, who write that "whereas the stability of a liberal society is based on the loyalty of its citizens, it is probably correct to say that the loyalty of the Soviet citizen has been based on the stability of the system." This formulation, for all its unintended humor, still manages to convey the key point of difference: namely, that loyalty was *constantly at issue* under the Soviet regime. Inkeles and Bauer, *The Soviet Citizen: Daily Life in a Totalitarian Society* (Cambridge, Mass.: Harvard University Press, 1959), ch. 12.

153. As the historian of the ancient world Paul Veyne has argued in *Les grecs ont-ils cru à leurs mythes?* (Paris, 1983).

154. See the brilliant analysis of the phenomenon he called "Ketman" in postwar Poland by Czeslaw Milosz, *The Captive Mind* (New York: Vintage, 1981; originally published in Polish, 1951).

155. Timasheff, *The Great Retreat*.

156. Here we might take a cue from the valuable study of Eugen Weber. In an admittedly impressionistic work with what is arguably a simplistic model of change, Weber nonetheless expertly shows how during the nineteenth century the peoples of the disparate regions of France acquired a national identity, that of being Frenchmen. Weber unfortunately never defines this new "Frenchness," assuming "it" was "out there" just waiting to happen, and neglects to give a sense of its political content, which no doubt must have been strongly based in revolutionary republicanism. In that regard, the analogy with Soviet nationhood, which was grounded in revolution, is truly suggestive, although French nationhood clearly outlasted Soviet. Interestingly, much of Weber's most compelling evidence is linguistic. *Peasants into Frenchmen: The Modernization of Rural France* (Stanford: Stanford University Press, 1976).

157. As the narrator in a novel by Vasilii Grossman explains, "He, after all, believed, or, to be more precise about it, wished to believe, or, to be even more precise than that, was unable not to believe." Grossman, *Forever Flowing*, p. 75.

158. In an official report dated January 1933, the following breakdown by sentence length was given for 12,869 convicts; up to one year, 1,354; one to three years, 6,908; three to five years, 2,542; five or more years, 2,065. Magnitogorsk procuracy: Archival file "Delo No. 14 po ITK za 1932 g.," l. 65. Surviving files from the Magnitogorsk procuracy demonstrate that a large number, especially those with terms of five or more years, had been convicted under the seven-eights law for the theft of socialist property. The convictions of those serving time in the ITK ran the gamut of the articles of the Criminal Code. A parial list is provided in Magnitogorsk procuracy: Archival file "Nariad 34/C. [Untitled] 1936 g.," l. 17. John

Scott, who accurately noted that sentences ranged from a few months to a few years, with considerable time off for excellent work performance in most cases, reported that he was told by a friend who worked in the ITK administration that the offenses of perhaps as many as 90 percent of this group involved drunkenness. But there were many professional thieves, prostitutes, embezzlers, and murderers. Scott, *Behind*, pp. 86, 285.

159. For the most part the convicts seem to have been men under thirty years of age who were illiterate or semiliterate (in 1935 the colony newspaper reported that there were only 560 women in the colony). The paper also reported numerous instances of violence against women, particularly after drinking bouts. *Borba za metall*, 5 April 1934 and 6 August 1935.

160. Ibid., 8 January 1933. Much of the colony newspaper was taken up with information regarding the proper procedure for submitting requests to be released early (the single criterion was a proven record of superior work performance and public activity), examples of outstanding workers, complaints about horrendous living conditions, the "storms" around the holidays to clean the filthy colony. In honor of press day (5 May) in 1935, the paper discussed its work, admitting that it did not reach everyone, owing to its small print run (between 1,000 and 3,000), and that it did not know all its worker correspondents, who supposedly numbered more than 500. Ibid., 11 May 1935.

161. *Borba za metall*, 7 November 1934 and 30 March 1935. The wife of Nikolai Kudriavtsev, the chief of open-hearth construction, recalled that her husband "often phoned Geineman, chief of the ITK, asking for workers. Geineman is a good fellow, responsive." She added that among the local elite, Geineman was sometimes called a convict (*itekovets*) himself, as a joke. This was, as we shall see in ch. 7, no joke. GARF, f. 7952, op. 5, d. 309, ll. 214, 218.

162. When a colony health-care official who gave a positive assessment of one convict neglected to mention that the inmate was the son of a priest, i.e., a "class alien," everyone throughout the colony responsible for such assessments was advised "to determine above all the person's classness [*klassovost*]." Convicts were generally divided into the following categories: national minorities (*natsmen*), former members of the party and Komsomol, women, youth and teenagers, workers, collective farmers, and class aliens (kulaks, traders, priests, etc.)—the one category they struggled to avoid, if possible. The colony newspaper warned that former kulaks sought class designations of "middle peasant" or "poor peasant." *Borba za metall*, 5 December 1932, and 5 and 22 January 1934. Colony chief Geineman admitted, however, that in the colony it was nearly impossible to separate the "class friendly" from the "class alien." *Za novogo cheloveka*, 14 June 1934.

163. Revised rules for counting work days were periodically promulgated. The ones introduced in mid-1935 tied the calculation of work days exclusively to norm fulfillment percentages. *Borba za metall*, 30 August 1935.

164. *Borba za metall*, 5 January 1934.

165. *Blat*, or "pull" used to obtain extra rations, was said to be rampant in the colony's canteens. *Borba za metall*, 6 February 1933 and 5 April 1935.

166. *Borba za metall*, 17 April 1933.

167. Ibid., 2 December 1933.

168. Ibid., 16 January 1934. During the first five months of 1934, the Magni-

togorsk colony received 4,710 newcomers, or an average of 940 per month, and discharged 5,892, or 1,219 per month. "This turnover takes a great deal of time from the administration and does not allow it to fulfill its other tasks," Geineman wrote. *Za novogo cheloveka,* 14 June 1934. Back in December 1933 thousands of new convicts from all over the country were transferred to the Magnitogorsk colony. At a meeting for the newcomers, one of them reportedly offered a twist on a familiar formula for paying homage to the great construction site: "Magnitostroi is known to the whole world, its colony to all the colonies of the Union." In fact, as he indirectly disclosed, the Magnitogorsk colony had a nasty reputation: "For some reason everything I heard about the Magnitogorsk colony was bad, but when I arrived here I see the opposite." Another concurred: "What I see at the MITK has nothing in common with what I heard about it." *Borba za metall,* 5 January 1934. In September 1935 the colony was visited by a group of Austrians, who were greeted with shouts of "Hurrah!" As they departed their tour, the Austrians waved back from their open bus windows and called out "Red Front!" Ibid., 18 September 1935.

169. *Borba za metall,* 27 November 1933. The consequences of the difficulties in keeping accurate records were predictable. "Despite the fact that our newspaper has written about the disgraceful record-keeping," the colony publication complained, "we have [found] yet another example of a person living in the colony but listed among those escaped." Ibid., 27 January 1933.

170. At least one convict evidently read his case file. He submitted a petition to the procurator citing a governmental decree of 16 January 1936. It was discovered that the decree had not been made public, and an investigation was launched to determine how the inmate became aware of the decree and its contents. As it turned out, the decree was mentioned in prisoner case files. Magnitogorsk procuracy: Archival file "Nariad 34/C. [Untitled] 1936 g.," ll. 30–31.

171. The colony newspaper reported, for example, that in 1933, 4,294 convicts were "returned to society before their terms were up," and in 1936, more than 1,000 more were released early, with an even greater number still said awaiting final review. *Borba za metall,* 22 January 1934; Magnitogorsk procuracy: Archival file "Nariad 34/C. [Untitled] 1936 g.," l. 16. Cases were reviewed by the NKVD and handed over to the procuracy, which made recommendations to the court. The court had the final say. The paperwork involved was enormous and time-consuming. *Za novogo cheloveka,* 14 June 1934.

172. In what was virtually the only mention made of the Magnitogorsk ITK in the city newspaper, Valentin Serzhantov wrote a spotlight on Erkin, said to be a hard-core criminal turned into the "best known record-holder" working on the construction of the second dam. Enumerating Erkin's accomplishments, Serzhantov asserted that "in our young sunny country the greatest of deeds are being carried out. But the most remarkable phenomenon of our life is the education and reeducation of people . . . through the labor process." Erkin, who had been released early for his labor exploits once before, was quoted as claiming that this time "his previous life was past." *MR,* 18 April 1937. Similar stories were told of the dekulakized peasants in the newspaper for the Special Labor Settlement. *Izvestiia Magnitogorska,* 30 March 1935. Some issues of this irregular paper were printed partially in Tatar (viz. 30 December 1933 and 20 February 1934).

173. In this regard the colony paper referred glowingly to a collective volume—

the bible of corrective labor—by Soviet writers and Gulag officials on the construction of the Belomor canal. Translated into English, the volume was published as *Belomor: An Account of the Construction of the New Canal Between the White Sea and the Baltic Sea* (New York: Harrison Smith and Robert Haas, 1935). *Borba za metall,* 7 November 1934. The dekulakized peasants were also encouraged to follow the heroic example of Belomorstroi. *Izvestiia Magnitogorska,* 30 March 1935.

174. Scott, *Behind,* p. 285.

175. *Borba za metall,* 11 December 1935.

176. After rising at 6 A.M., the convicts were said to lose more than an hour beyond the allotted time to eat and arrive at the site. "Once there no one knows what they are supposed to do, because they are not told beforehand. They are shuffled from place to place, and lose still more time, in part because of a lack of tools. At one point they run out of nails, and then plywood. The authority of the brigadier is too weak to goad the workers. Workers do not know their norms." *Borba za metall,* 30 March 1935.

177. *Borba za metall,* 12 February 1933.

178. Ibid., 8 January 1933. One convict allegedly cut himself to get out of work. Ibid., 9 April 1933.

179. Ibid., 15 January 1933.

180. This impression emerges from a reading of the colony newspaper, and was also the opinion of John Scott, *Behind,* p. 285. Mariia Scott told Pearl Buck she once witnessed prison laborers marching back from a work site accompanied by a band playing "a very gay Soviet march." Buck, *Talk About Russia,* p. 93.

181. *Borba za metall,* 30 January 1934.

182. *Za novogo cheloveka,* 14 June 1934. As for the cultural choices of the dekulakized peasants, a play in the Central Settlement's club (*The Law of the First Night*) set in serf times pitted abused serfs against despicable landlords. The reviewer expressed dissatisfaction. *Izvestiia Magnitogorska,* February 1934.

183. *Za novogo cheloveka,* 14 June 1934.

184. Magnitogorsk procuracy: Archival file "Delo No. 14 po ITK za 1932 g.," l. 66.

185. Shilov, a colony convict said to have called shock work "total crap" (*sploshnoi blat*), one morning at 2 A.M. allegedly went in search of Communists to beat up. One near victim swore he was not a Communist and had no intention of becoming one. Finding no Communists, Shilov turned his attention to the cultural soviet of the barracks, shouting that it contained only fools and thieves, and that those who work never go to the cultural soviet or do public work. No one answered him, according to the camp newspaper, because everyone was intimidated by his size. *Borba za metall,* 18 December 1933. Notwithstanding this strong condemnation of Shilov by the colony newspaper, no report of his being disciplined ever appeared.

186. The paper published responses to many "letters" advising the anonymous writers that their accusations could not be investigated because they had failed to specify concrete facts. *Borba za metall,* 27 January 1933.

187. Ibid., 5 December 1932.

188. The city newspaper highlighted many cases of stigmatization, including

that of Luzhnetskii, who had worked in the NKVD's fire brigade but was sent to the labor colony for having caused a breakdown. Luzhnetskii served his sentence and obtained release with a favorable evaluation, but he was refused work as a former convict. *MR*, 1 April 1937. As of August 1935, work performed in a labor colony did not count toward pension calculations. *Sobranie ukazov RSFSR*, 1935, no. 20, item 192, reprinted in *Kodeks zakonov o trude, s izmeneniiami na 1 iiulia 1938 g.*, pp. 99–100.

189. *Borba za metall*, 5 December 1932.

190. Ibid., 12 February 1933.

191. *MR*, 17 August 1988. A 1933 investigation in the enterprises employing exiled peasants concluded that their work (largely construction) was organized poorly, that they were often idle for lack of materials and tools, that there were no "mass-cultural work," production conferences, or public displays of the results of their labor, and that their midday meals took too much time (more than three hours in one case, owing to a lack of soup bowls). By the November holiday in 1933, there were thirty-seven cultural-mass brigades comprised of 621 female peasant exiles. *Izvestiia Magnitogorska*, 27 June and 7 November 1933.

192. *CR*, 8 January 1989.

193. There were three schools in the city they could attend, but it is not clear if that was sufficient for all of the school-aged dekulakized children. Scott, *Behind*, pp. 282–83.

194. *Sobranie zakonov i rasporiazhenii*, 1931, no. 44, item 298, and 1934, no. 33, item 257, both reprinted in *Kollektiviizatsiia selskogo khoziaistva: Vazhneishie postanovleniia Kommunisticheskoi partii i Sovetskogo pravitelstva 1927–1935* (Moscow, 1957), pp. 391, 505.

195. Petitions by the dekulakized in Magnitogorsk to have their voting rights restored cited the amount of time they had performed "socially useful labor," their percentage of plan fulfillment, and the social and political activities in which they had participated. MFGAChO, f. 10, op. 1, d. 81, ll. 41–42; and d. 89, ll. 13–17.

196. Stalin issued his famous pronouncement, "the son does not answer for the father," in 1936, but already in 1933, Aron Solts, chairman of the Commission of Party Control, gave voice to such a policy toward the dekulakized in an article reprinted in the Magnitogorsk newspaper addressed to the exiled peasants. *Izvestiia Magnitogorska*, 29 October 1933 and 12 April 1936.

197. *Izvestiia Magnitogorska*, 1 and 11 May, 12 June 1934.

198. *Izvestiia Magnitogorska*, 25 June 1934. It is possible to imagine, if not to prove, that in an effort to overcome their tainted origins, some of the children of the dekulakized may have become fanatical.

199. As one perceptive Soviet journalist has written of the mood in the country on the eve of the war, "it was the prewar country that embarked upon the war, and the people brought everything with them to the front." He listed "the capacity for self-sacrifice and the suspiciousness, cruelty and spiritual unprotectedness, meanness and naive romanticism, the officially demonstrated loyalty to the Leader and the deeply hidden doubts, the dull sluggishness of bureaucrats and the overcautious, and the intrepid hope on the off-chance, the heavy burden of resentment and the feeling of the justness of the war." Vladimir Shubkin, "Odin den voiny,"

Literaturnaia gazeta, 23 September 1987, p. 13. The author, a sociologist, is recalling one day (23 August 1942) of the battle of Stalingrad, in which he took part.

200. "Beseda s nemetskim pisatelem Emilem Ludwigem," 13 December 1931, in Stalin, *Sochineniia,* vol. 13 (Moscow, 1952), p. 109. Note the date: five years before the "great terror."

201. A sizable number of people sent to Gulag as political prisoners did not always come to question the revolutionary truth, consoling themselves with such thoughts as "When Stalin finds out he will stick it to these NKVD butchers," or "They just made a mistake in my case; all these other people are guilty." For such people their continued loyalty to the revolutionary truth became a means to hold off the realization that their lives and actions in service to the cause had been not simply in vain but morally reprehensible. See the conversation about Magnitogorsk blast furnaces among Polish intellectuals in a Soviet prison reported by Aleksander Wat, *My Century* (New York: Norton, 1988; originally published in Polish, 1977), p. 67; Djilas, *New Class,* pp. 29, 98; and Kendall Bailes, who commented apropos the new intelligentsia that "even the horrors of collectivization, the famine and terror, could be explained away as necessities of the day." Bailes, *Technology and Society,* p. 259.

202. In the apt words of Eric Hobsbawm, "Peasants and Politics," *Journal of Peasant Studies* 1, no. 1 (1973): 3–22; the quote is from p. 13.

203. I follow Keith Gandal's interpretation of Michel Foucault writings on things said, or discourses, in "Prospects for Work," unpublished manuscript (1984), used by permission. See also Michel Foucualt, "Politics and the Study of Discourse," *Ideology and Consciousness,* no. 3 (1978): 7–26; originally published as "Réponse à une question," *Esprit* (1968).

CHAPTER 6. BREAD AND A CIRCUS

1. *The Thirteen Satires of Juvenal* (Hildesheim, 1966), vol. 1, p. 43, lines 78–80.

2. In his account of "one day" in the life of Magnitogorsk, John Scott captured the multisided importance of bread in the culture, diet, and economy. Scott, *Behind,* pp. 38, 42.

3. The words of Pierre Dominique [P. Lucchine], *Secrets of Siberia,* p. 123. By the fall of 1937, the newspaper complained that the rotting wooden building was raw, cold, and in need of serious mending—this despite the fact that the circus had been closed most of the previous summer for repairs. *MR,* 3 April 1936 and 6 October 1937.

4. Economic crimes were set down in chapter 5, part 2, of the 1926 RSFSR criminal code. *Ugolovnyi kodeks redaktsii 1926 g.,* pp. 266–82 (the 1926 code, although periodically amended, was in force until the adoption of a new one in 1960). Some of the economic offenses analyzed in this chapter were included in other sections of the code. For a discussion of economic crimes, see Harold Berman, *Justice in Russia: An Interpretation of Soviet Law* (Cambridge, Mass.: Harvard University Press, 1950); a second edition (1963) followed the adoption of the new code in 1960. It should be borne in mind that under the 1923 Soviet constitution the au-

thority to issue criminal codes fell to the republics; Magnitogorsk was in the Russian republic, or RSFSR. An analysis of the main differences between the RSFSR code and those of other republics can be found in *Sorok let Sovetskogo prava*, vol. 1 (Moscow, 1957), pp. 555–56. Military crimes (as opposed to regular offenses committed during wartime) were handled by separate courts operated under USSR jurisdiction. See *Sobranie zakonov i rasporiazhenii*, 1926, no. 57, item 413. So-called state crimes that were deemed major, such as counterrevolution, were also placed under USSR jurisdiction. Since the USSR as such did not have its own court system, responsibility for major state crimes fell to the security police, or GPU (after 1934 the NKVD), which combined investigative and sentencing powers. E. H. Carr, *Socialism in One Country, 1924–1926*, vol. 2, pp. 454–81.

5. *MR*, 8 October 1938. In the early years the circus was also used for award ceremonies. GARF, f. 7952, op. 5, d. 310, l. 53. It is tempting to view the spectacles as analogous to the medieval carnival, as analyzed by the Soviet literary critic Mikhail Bakhtin in *Rabelais and His World* (Bloomington: Indiana University Press, 1984). The function of the spectacles at the Magnitogorsk circus, however, was not comic laughter or inversion, but reinforcing an official reality, albeit with mass participation. Of course, it is still possible that despite the state's instigation and domination of the processes, the performances produced forms of belief that transgressed the state's intentions. Unfortunately, transcripts of the trials, if they were made, do not seem to have survived. What evidence from the circus trials there is— brief accounts in the official press—does not permit an analysis of the possible appropriation of the proceedings, in whole or in part, by the spectators. Bakhtin's text, it might be noted, was written during the Stalin era.

6. Typical of the uncertainty clouding private trade during the 1920s, the Soviet civil code of 1923 granted people the right to engage in private business even as the constitution of 1918 disfranchised anyone who exercised that right. An analysis of the subversion by the state of its own declared economic policy throughout the entire period of the NEP, with peaks of intensity in 1923 and again after 1926, is provided in the noteworthy study by Alan Ball. In addition to providing a compelling picture of the travails and absurdities involved in "ordinary buying and selling" under the Bolshevik regime, Ball details the perplexity within the party at the introduction of NEP and shows that its abandonment, although opposed by some party members, was easily explained within the framework of the revolution. Ball, *Russia's Last Capitalists*.

7. In announcing the "great break" at the end of the 1920s, Stalin, who positioned himself as Lenin's loyal and literal follower, nonetheless maintained, with a certain plausibility, that from the beginning NEP had always entailed two stages, an initial retreat followed by an offensive against the "bourgeoisie," and that the party had determined that the time had come for the country to enter the second stage of the offensive. No formal decree ever repealed the NEP, and throughout the first Five-year Plan officials denied that NEP had been abolished. In early 1935 Viacheslav Molotov announced to the Seventh Congress of Soviets that "NEP Russia had become Soviet Russia" (*Za industrializatsiiu*, 31 January 1935). But Stalin and others still referred to the continuation of NEP until the declaration in late 1936 that socialism was built in its foundations.

8. *Ugolovnyi kodeks RSFSR: Prakticheskoe posobie dlia rabotnikov iustitsii i iurideschikh kursov* (Moscow, 1934), p. 88.

9. It is a common mistake to call these small plots "private," but they could not be sold or inherited. All land was owned either by the state or by collective farms, and was made available under contractual terms with restrictions for household use (*polzovaniie*). See the decree "O sozdanii ustoichivogo zemlepolzovaniia kolkhozov" (3 September 1932), *Sobranie zakonov i rasporiazhenii*, 1932, no. 66, item 388, reprinted in *Istoriia kolkhoznogo prava: Sbornik zakonodatelnykh materialov SSSR i RSFSR 1917–1958 gg.*, vol. 1 (Moscow, 1959), pp. 225–26.

10. See the important article by Gregory Grossman, "The 'Second Economy' of the USSR," *Problems of Communism* (September-October 1977): 25–40. Grossman rejects the hypothesis that the term "second economy" arose in discussions by planners trying to devise and implement reforms of Soviet-type economies after Stalin's death. According to him, the term was apparently coined by K. S. Karol, in "Conversations in Russia," *The New Statesmen*, 1 January 1971, pp. 8–10. In any case, Grossman is largely responsible for its widespread acceptance. In official Soviet publications—whether those publicly available or those "for internal use"—the preferred term became "shadow" (*tenevaia*) economy, stressing the illicit or criminal nature of this kind of activity. But as Grossman points out, "the second economy includes much of the perfectly legal private activity which is possible in the USSR." He adds that "in many cases one cannot practically draw a line between legal and illegal private activity, since the former often serves as a front for the latter and both support one another." I follow Grossman's suggested definition (p. 25). Whatever definition one finally chooses, however, surely the key point is the ambiguity in the boundaries of the economic activity considered as legal or permitted by the state. On this point, in addition to Grossman see Valerii Khalidze, *Ugolovnaia Rossiia* (New York: Khronika, 1977), pp. 246–90.

11. In Merle Fainsod's study of the Smolensk region based on local party archives, the chapter on the legal system is the thinest. "The materials in the Smolensk Archive on the procuracy and the courts are spotty," he wrote. Fainsod, *Smolensk*, p. 173. A Magnitogorsk archivist informed me that to save space, records of trials, viewed as documents presenting little historical interest, were ordered destroyed in the 1970s. It is possible, however, that copies of such documents remain at the next level up, in the oblast archives. For a discussion of the formation of the Soviet legal system see John Hazard, *Settling Disputes in Soviet Society: The Formative Years of Legal Institutions* (New York: Columbia University Press, 1960). As Hazard points out, not just the acceptance of the need for a court system but the codification of the laws that lasted into the Stalin era and beyond, occurred in the 1920s, during the NEP.

12. In the early years, one official of the court complained of a lack of instructions for the lower levels of the justice system. As an example he cited an open-air session of a "comrade court" convened at the dam construction site in 1930 to handle the case of someone accused of negligence. Without regard to any laws, the "court" discussed the possibility of shooting the accused. GARF, f. 7952, op. 5, d. 143, l. 53. Although the newspaper never mentioned the existence of lawyers, the application of legal standards was revealed in a 1936 story about "the hooligan Povalikhin." When the prosecutor released him "because it [was] not established who

committed the act of hooliganism," Povalikhin seized the opportunity to flee Magnitogorsk, and the newspaper assailed the prosecutor for "protecting" hooligans. *MR*, 8 October 1936. The month before, the newspaper reported the case of a man who had been wrongly incarcerated for one and a half years, but was finally released. *MR*, 16 September 1936. Under the 1926 criminal code a person need not have committed a crime to be incarcerated. The law provided for detention of people who "represent a social danger because of their connection with a criminal environment or because of past activity." *Ugolovnyi kodeks redaktsii 1926 g.*, pp. 8–9, 29–31. In 1960, this provision was technically repudiated. See Berman, *Soviet Criminal Law and Procedure: The RSFSR Codes*, 2d ed. (Cambridge, Mass.: Harvard University Press, 1972), p. 21. The Magnitogorsk court also handled citizens' complaints, ranging from problems with housing to poor service in the dining halls, until 1936 when such complaints became the business of the procuracy. GARF, f. 7952, op. 5, d. 143, l. 51. Many of the cases handled by the militia and the courts involved drunkenness. *MR*, 20 September 1936.

13. One judge's biography was highlighted in the local newspaper. Ivan Dziubenko was said to have come to Magnitogorsk in 1930, upon being demobilized from the Red Army. He initially worked in the smithing shop, and in 1933 he became a brigadier in the coke shop, where he was "elected" a judge, evidently of a comrade court. On 15 December 1934 he began working for the Magnitogorsk raion court. In 1937 he admitted to the newspaper that at first he had "a poor knowledge of the laws." The newspaper neglected to specify what special training, if any, Dziubenko had received. Meanwhile, the paper casually mentioned that he "had jurisdiction over a large and serious sector—the Magnitogorsk factory." Moreover, despite his own lack of familiarity with the law, Dziubenko was responsible for training other judges, one of whom, Zoia Gavrilovna Veretnovaia, began working for the court in 1936. By late 1937 the new judge had already heard 870 cases involving "the rights of mother and child." *MR*, 29 August and 12 October 1937.

14. MFGAChO, f. 10, op. 1, d. 139, l. 158.

15. An exception for the years 1929–30 is Davies, *The Soviet Economy in Turmoil*, pp. 353–58.

16. De Soto, *The Other Path: The Invisible Revolution in the Third World* (New York: Harper, 1989), with a preface by Maria Vargas Llosa.

17. A. T. Kolbin, party secretary on the blast furnace construction, recalled that "at first the food situation was luxurious. In 1931 we gave out as much as people wanted. 'Come and take as much as you need'—this was especially so when there was so much shock work on the blast furnace construction. There were no ration cards for bread. Bread was sliced and put right on the table. When the workers came to eat, bowls of soup were already waiting for them on the tables. Right in the open air, right in front of the furnaces under construction." Beginning in the fall of 1931, however, "the food situation got tougher and tougher," according to Kolbin. GARF, f. 7952, op. 5, d. 309, l. 38. Other testimony by eyewitnesses confirms Kolbin's observation. Ibid., d. 319, l. 15.

18. *MR*, 12 November 1932.

19. In February 1931, he recalled, for a population approaching 100,000, there were only fifteen shoemakers. Gugel, "Vospominaniia," pp. 319–21.

20. In the mid-1930s, there were fifteen collective farms and ten state farms in Magnitogorsk raion, and many dozens more in adjacent Bashkiriia. MFGAChO, f. 10, op. 1, d. 139, l. 157.

21. There were periodic reports in the city newspaper on regional agriculture, but these brief articles were occasioned primarily by disasters, such as the deaths, in the absence of innoculations, of all but 243 of the 1,154 pigs on a state farm. *MR*, 7 February 1936. The only other occasion when the theme of agriculture came up was during harvest collection, when the newspaper issued a series of instructions and threats about the necessity of delivering all grain to the Magnitogorsk grain elevator by the deadlines.

22. They were located in the steppe, behind Lattice-Wood Town. *MR*, 24 February 1936.

23. GARF, f. 7952, op. 5, d. 318, l. 2.

24. In January 1934 city Party Secretary Beso Lominadze proudly announced that almost 25,000 Magnitogorsk workers were engaged in some form of cultivation with very satisfactory results. *MR*, 20 January 1934. Another official source asserted that in 1939 almost 2,500 hectares (more than 6,000 acres) in or very near the city were under cultivation by 15,000 individual gardeners. Yet another source from 1939 put the figure of urban cultivators at 18,450 households. *Materialy o rabote*, p. 26; *Stalinskaia stroika*, p. 54.

25. *MR*, 3 April 1938.

26. John Scott, who visited one state farm in 1933 along with a group of German and Austrian mechanics sent there to repair the agricultural machinery, painted an unflattering picture at the time of his visit. But four years later, visiting the same farm, he claimed to have found "astonishing changes." Scott concluded that "if a score of such farms could have been organized around Magnitogorsk, the city could have been provided with vegetables and dairy products from local sources entirely, thus solving one of the knottiest problems confronting the plant administration." Scott, *Behind*, pp. 95–98.

27. White-collar employees (*sluzhashchie*) were entitled to only 400 grams of bread per day according to the table for 28 October 1933 published in the newspaper. Another large group, nonworking dependents, likewise fell into the 400-gram category. *MR*, 4 November 1933.

28. According to John Scott, his rigger's card entitled him in 1932 to the following monthly allotments:

Bread	30 kilograms
Butter	½ kilogram
Meat	3 kilograms
Cereal grain	2 kilograms
Sugar	1 kilogram
Milk	15 liters
Potatoes	in proportion to supply

But Scott added that "during the entire winter of 1932–33, the riggers got no meat, no butter, and almost no sugar or milk. They received only bread and a little cereal grain." And riggers were in the most favorable supply category for workers. See also his description of how milk rations were distributed. Scott, *Behind*, p. 78, 37.

29. Who had the ultimate authority to assign or alter a category was unclear, opening the way for considerable manipulation by the industrious or unscrupulous. A bit later the newspaper condemned the "confusion" that characterized the determination of status in the rationing system and advocated that shops take over the assignment of categories from the state supply network. *MR*, 5 and 6 April 1934.

30. *MR*, 4 January 1933.

31. John Scott described a regular workers' outlet: "In the store to which they were attached [riggers] could buy, without the use of their cards, perfume, tobacco, 'coffee' (surrogate), and on occasion, when there was any, soap, salt, tea, candy. These latter products, however, were almost never in stock; and when a shipment did come in, the workers sometimes left their jobs, spud wrenches in their hands, to fight their way to half a pound of rocklike candy." Scott, *Behind*, pp. 78–79. With the arrival of Beso Lominadze in mid-1933, workers at the site four or more years were to be accorded preferential treatment in supply (as well as housing), as a way to discourage the general flight from the city. *MR*, 12 September 1934. It is not clear what effect, if any, the new booklets for four-year people might have had, or even what extra benefits four-year people received, but according to one original settler, the "party's undying concern for the welfare of the people" was widely publicized after Lominadze's arrival. Nina Kondratkovskaia, interview by author, Magnitogorsk, May 1987.

32. *Insnab*, according to Scott, "was stocked with a good quantity of all the necessary food products, such as meat, butter, eggs, milk, flour, bread, fish, canned goods, confectionery, and a fair variety of rather poor quality drygoods. The prices were lower, sometimes only one-tenth of those which the Soviet workers had to pay for similar goods in their stores." "Theoretically," Scott wrote, "no Soviet specialists were attached to the *insnab*; actually, however, the director of the steel complex and his assistants, the secretary of the city party committee, the chief of the GPU, and a half-dozen of the best prisoner specialists were on the list along with the foreigners." Scott, *Behind*, pp. 42, 87. Soviet higher-ups were already assigned to the best regular stores.

33. *MR*, 25 December 1932.

34. Scott, *Behind*, p. 282.

35. Ibid., pp. 30, 79.

36. The novelist Fedor Gladkov offered the following description of such outdoor canteens at the Dneprostroi dam project in 1930: "I go to the factory kitchen and am sickened by the very sight of the vile poison being made there. I go to the work sites, where the food is delivered in thermoses. The bluish swill stinks like a corpse and a cesspool. The workers prefer plain bread and water." Gladkov, *Energiia* (Moscow, 1936), p. 375.

37. One visiting foreign correspondent left behind this description: "At the top of this Magnitogorsk dining-room hierarchy was the eating place for high officials of the plant and famous foreign specialists. The food here, while it was a trifle monotonous, was substantial, with an abundance of meat. Somewhat lower in the scale was a dining room for Russian engineers and technicians. Then came the eating place for *udarniki* [shock workers]. . . . There was a big drop from the *udarniki* to the ordinary laborers, who were fed in crowded canteens, mainly on bread, cab-

bage soup, and *kasha*, with meat as a rare luxury." Chamberlain, *Russia's Iron Age*, pp. 112–13. Chamberlain's assessment was echoed by Louis Ernst, an American who was the deputy chief of the benzol department of the chemical by-products division of the Magnitogorsk coke plant during the 1930s. Interview by author, Doniphan, Missouri, 30 April 1986. See also Scott, *Behind*, p. 31. As for those working in the dining halls, they may have been paid comparatively less, but they were always assured of more food.

38. This irregularity became incorporated into the operation of the system. According to John Scott, "because foremen and administrators attempted to get their personnel to work better by giving them additional dining-room cards. In this way the welding trust was serving 2,000 dinners to 800 welders. However, inasmuch as the central supply office knew that the welding trust had only 800 workers and released them food enough for only 800 dinners, the dining-room director had to dilute. So the quality of dinners deteriorated. In the beginning of 1933 in Dining-Room No. 30 it was necessary to eat two or even three dinners to get a really adequate meal for a man working high at fifty below zero." Scott, *Behind*, p. 79.

39. Baryshev, "Zdravookhranenie Magnitogorska," p. 72.

40. MFGAChO, f. 118, op. 1, d. 81, l. 56. The distribution of scarce goods and favors in enterprises was handled by the trade unions. Not every worker was allowed to be a member. According to data for 12 December 1936, of the 21,358 people employed at the MMK, 3,680 did not have the "right" to trade union membership. Of the 17,578 who had such a right, 17,311, or 98.5 percent of those eligible, were said to be members. The tabulation unfortunately did not specify why 267 eligible people were not members, or why the 3,680 were excluded from consideration. Perhaps they had criminal records. Data for May 1937 showed a slight decline in membership among those eligible (19,227 out of 20,113). Ibid., d. 106, ll. 6, 37–47.

41. As John Scott explained, "everybody had money, but what one ate or wore depended almost exclusively on what there was to buy in the particular store to which one was attached." Scott, *Behind*, p. 42. Similar testimony can be found in "Twenty-six Interviews." Even after rationing was abolished, money would remain far less important than access to and connections in the official supply network.

42. *MR*, 10 August 1932.

43. No description of the Magnitogorsk bazaar could be found among the documents I consulted. One foreign traveler left behind a portrait of a Moscow market in 1932 whose sights and sounds could not have differed much from the one in Magnitogorsk. Julian Huxley, *A Scientist among the Soviets* (New York: Harper, 1932), pp. 46–48.

44. MFGAChO, f. 9, op. 1, d. 158, l. 22.

45. According to a city inspector, there were no industrial goods at the Fertilizer Market, only foodstuffs. The Fertilizer Market was known for its milk supplies, but most of the meat available was at the Central Market (the two were seven kilometers apart). At the Central Market there were many sales booths representing state stores. MFGAChO, f. 16, op. 1, d. 81, l. 31.

46. *MR*, 29 July 1936. Louis Ernst recalled that "the market . . . was nothing so mysterious or sinister. There were lots of ordinary people selling one or two items there. People working in the plant would sometimes trade clothes and shoes

to traveling peasants for food. In fact, there was plenty of food in the city [i.e., on sale at the market]. It was just expensive." Interview by author, Doniphan, Missouri, 30 April 1986.

47. The authorities constantly surveyed prices at the market. One such survey in 1937 revealed the following prices:

	28 March	5 April	15 April
Beef, frozen (rbls/kg)	8.00	8.00	8.00
Pork (rbls/kg)	9.00	—	12.00
Milk, fresh (rbls/l)	1.50	1.50	1.80
Butter (rbls/kg)	16.00	13.00	—
Potatoes (rbls/kg)	0.25	0.31	0.31

See MFGAChO, f. 16, op. 1, d. 81, passim. Prices varied according to quality. A similar official source revealed that in 1938 the best quality meat at the market sold for 26 rubles per kilo. Ibid., d. 96, l. 4.

48. John Scott told the story of how sometime in 1933 he accompanied a fellow welder to a drygoods store where that worker, Popov, hoped to buy a pair of inner-gloves, but that they discovered the store was empty and resigned themselves to going to the bazaar. Scott, *Behind*, p. 39.

49. *MR*, 9 December 1934.

50. *Magnitogorskii metall*, 20 August 1935.

51. *Magnitogorskii metall*, 27 September 1935.

52. The dining halls continued to be run by a single large trust, Narpit. Magnitogorsk's Narpit had been formed after central authorities created Glavnarpit in August 1931. For the decree see *Spravochnik partiinogo rabotnika*, vyp. 8 (Moscow, 1934), pp. 734–37.

53. John Scott wrote that the "quality of manufactured goods was generally low (shoes, suits, and materials were usually poor), though some things, the new short-wave radio sets, for example, were of comparable high quality." He added that during the changeover *insnab* was liquidated, "but the foreigners missed it only in that prices there had been lower. Similar grocery products and dry goods could be bought in 1935 and 1936 in open stores, often without the inconvenience of a queue." Scott, *Behind*, pp. 87, 126–27, 243. Despite having access to *insnab* and receiving packages from abroad sent by his father, Scott experienced the exceptionally lean years 1932 and 1933. To him, and to many others who had been far less privileged than he, 1935 and 1936 must have seemed like a relative cornucopia. The department store (*univermag*) opened in 1936 must have made an impression. According to official data, it accounted for 16.5 percent of all city trade, meaning that the authorities kept it stocked. If back in July 1931, the city had only 16 stores and 10 less formal shops, along with 49 "distribution outlets," by 1936 there were 134 stores and 42 smaller shops. MFGAChO, f. 10, op. 1, d. 243, l. 26, 42.

54. Store managers appear to have resisted the "raids" when they could. For example, two women deputies from the city soviet took it upon themselves as representatives of the public interest to investigate store no. 12 in the Kirov district. The store manager refused to permit the women to familiarize themselves with the store's operation, insisting that he needed to be shown more than their city soviet

documents. In most cases, however, inspectors were more powerful officials representing institutions that commanded more respect (fear) than the city soviet sections, and could not be so easily brushed aside. Moreover, in the case of the manager from store no. 12, the newspaper's intervention on behalf of the two women deputies may have attracted the interest of party or police officials. *MR*, 3 February 1936.

55. *MR*, 11 January 1936. Many items, such as musical instruments, were never available through the state stores and could only be purchased at the market. Even there, however, the newspaper conceded that instruments were not always seen, to say nothing of their price. *MR*, 21 February 1936.

56. *MR*, 28 January 1936.

57. *MR*, 24 May 1936.

58. Scott, *Behind*, pp. 242–43.

59. *MR*, 1 August 1938. In the language of an official report, there were "massive interruptions in the trade of goods exceeding demand" while warehouses contained certain goods "in more than sufficient quantities." MFGAChO, f. 9, op. 1, d. 170, l. 9. Trade, like everything else, was subject to "plan" targets, although what such targets meant and how they were established remains unclear. In any case, virtually none of the targets were recorded as met in 1936. For what it is worth, the lowest percentages listed were those for eggs, vegetables, potatoes, cooking oil, and kerosene; the highest, margarine, salt, herring, and tea. Ibid., f. 10, op. 1, d. 243, l. 46. Store inventories varied according to location. In 1937, according to a city soviet deputy from the Central Electric Station whose constituents lived on the Sixth and Seventh Sectors, as well as in Sredne-Uralsk, "if our wives want to buy a piece of soap or something else they go through the Fertilizer Settlement to the Fifth Sector." Ibid., d. 270, l. 111.

60. *MR*, 22 September 1936. For a related anecdote from émigrés sources, see "Twenty-six Interviews," I/15.

61. People were also said to "stand in line for hours even for bread" because "the schedule for bread deliveries to stores is violated day in and day out." *CR*, 21 July 1938.

62. *MR*, 4 October 1936. There were various tricks to queuing. It became common practice, for example, to wait in more than one queue simultaneously by asking someone in one queue to hold one's place while skipping off to another. Informal networks among relatives, friends, and acquaintances also sprung up. Amusing anecdotes illustrating these and many other queuing tactics can be found in an unpublished fictional account of life in the USSR during the Stalin years signed I. I. Ivanov, "I la zhil," p. 44.

63. The 22 August 1932 decree "on the struggle with speculation" was incorporated into a revised article 107 of the RSFSR criminal code. *Ugolovnyi kodeks RSFSR: Prakticheskoe posobie*, pp. 87–88. For the decree, see *Sobranie zakonov i rasporiazhenii*, 1932, no. 65, item 375, reprinted in *Sbornik dokumentov*, p. 336. Originally, article 107 of the RSFSR criminal code covered what was called "malicious raising of prices." *Ugolovnyi kodeks redaktsii 1926 g.*, pp. 219–21. See the remarks by Berman, *Soviet Criminal Law and Procedure*, p. 29. Many prior decrees in the years between 1918 and 1921 and again after 1928 had mentioned speculation; this one offered a succinct definition and hardened the penalties.

64. Stalin, speaking at a joint plenum of the Central Committee and Central Control Commission in 1933, remarked that "in the most recent period we have been able to throw private traders, merchants, and middlemen of all sorts completely out of trade. Of course, this does not exclude the possibility that private traders and speculators may again appear in trade according to the law of atavism, taking advantage of an especially favorable field for them—collective farm trade. Furthermore, the collective farmers themselves are not averse to engaging in speculation, which of course does them no honor. But to combat these unhealthy developments the Soviet government has recently issued measures for the suppression of speculation and the punishment of speculators. You know, of course, that this law does not suffer from softness. You understand, of course, that such a law did not and could not exist during the first stage of NEP." *Pravda*, 10 and 17 January 1933, reprinted in *Sochineniia*, vol. 13, p. 204, as cited in Ball, *Russia's Last Capitalists*, p. 186, n. 60.

65. *MR*, 28 January 1936.

66. Warm clothing was one of the major categories of nonfood goods traded at the bazaar. One women said to have several aliases was alleged to be speculating in felt boots, which she was "importing" from a nearby village. A search of her apartment and those of her accomplices uncovered eleven pairs, mere possession of which was said to be illegal. But it was never established whether the boots were homemade, meaning they could be legally sold, albeit not at "speculative" prices, whatever the authorities determined these to be. *MR*, 28 January 1936.

67. Under no circumstances, for example, was it permitted to resell new or nearly new items purchased in state stores, but people did so anyway. One of the hotest items at the bazaar were bicycles, which could be purchased in state stores only with official permission (to ensure that only the most "deserving" could obtain them). The newspaper reported that one factory worker granted such a reward paid 254.50 rubles, then promptly resold the bike to another worker in the open-hearth shop for 425 rubles. This worker then resold the bicycle to someone else for 475 rubles. *MR*, 4 August and 6 September 1936.

68. According to an official report, in one instance the militia permitted shoes scooped up at state stores to be resold at the market for the same prices. The militia was trying to ensure the sale of the shoes to those who "truly" needed them but had not been able to purchase them when they first went on sale. The report carried no word of how successful the militia were in this case or whether in general they had enough staff to perform such operations. MFGAChO, f. 16, op. 1, d. 81, l. 64.

69. *MR*, 23 October 1936. The activities of speculating housewives are well described in a humorous fictional account: "These women spend several days battling in queues, buy up everything sold by 'hard' [fixed] prices, and then carry their spoils to the flea market where they gouge the collective farmers, who tomorrow morning will gouge the women even worse for milk and potatoes. Dialectics!" Ivanov, "I Ia zhil," p. 44.

70. *MR*, 20 April 1936.

71. *MR*, 18 April 1938.

72. *Magnitogorskii metall*, 3 June 1936.

73. *MR*, 23 February 1936.

74. It was not simply a question of Magnitogorsk citizens traveling outside the

city in search of goods; people streamed into Magnitogorsk for the same purpose. Not only were shoppers coming from the surrounding countryside, but people were coming from remote smaller towns to buy up goods that could be resold very profitably back home. *MR*, 5 and 6 August 1936.

75. Complaining about employees taking business trips at state expense, the newspaper asserted they were doing so simply because they enjoyed traveling. But without denying the possibility of enjoyment, it seems that the desire to shop must be considered at least as important as an explanation for the frequent travel of those in a position to do so. *MR*, 9 January 1936.

76. *MR*, 4 September 1936.

77. *MR*, 24 February and 4 March 1936. Similarly, beginning in the spring of 1936 the newspaper carried many articles about the lack of vegetables for sale in the city. The newspaper explained that despite having signed contracts with local state farms, Magnitogorsk received no vegetables. In some desperation, and after having received official permission, Magnittorg scrambled to sign new contracts with state farms in neighboring regions (Kuibyshev, Kursk, Bashkiriia, Central Asia). But Magnittorg was without funds to make the necessary purchases, and the wary local branch of the State Bank refused to grant the floundering trade organization an advance. In early August some vegetables—cabbage, carrots, onions, potatoes, cucumbers—finally arrived. No sooner did the vegetables appear than long queues started forming. *MR*, 9 and 10 August 1936.

78. *MR*, 6 January 1938.

79. *MR*, 11 May 1936.

80. Many people were apparently caught in sweeps at the market. One woman detained while selling shoes was found to have no passport, no place of work, and no registered residence. She received a two-year term, though the newspaper neglected to mention the charges. *MR*, 30 August 1936. In another reported case, the militia, after receiving a phone call from a man who reported that a suit of his had just been stolen, raced to the bazaar. Within forty minutes of the theft, the thief was apprehended trying to sell the stolen suit. *MR*, 9 May 1936. In one passage John Scott implied that theft, not speculation, was considered the real problem. He wrote that the bazaar was a place "where anybody could go and sell anything he had for as much as he could get while the police watched for stolen goods." Scott, *Behind*, p. 241. This seems to be less a statement about the authorities' intentions than about their capacities.

81. *MR*, 20 May 1936. The newspaper bristled at the fact that these thieves were not detained until trial, meaning they often disappeared, as "those without a place of residence or work cannot be summoned to court."*MR*, 11 May 1936.

82. Until 1947 the theft of personal property was punishable by incarceration for a period of only up to three months. Berman, *Justice in Russia*, p. 82.

83. Lewin, personal communication, 1991. There were many other variants, including *obespech, ranshe, svoikh* and *ostalnoe razdavai sosedam.*

84. GARF, f. 7952, op. 5, d. 294, ll. 39–42. In 1935 a sizable group in the central payroll department of the steel plant was found to have stolen more than 90,000 rubles before being caught. Several suspects fled prior to arrest; those taken into custody were said to have admitted their guilt. Magnitogorsk procuracy: Archival file "Nariad 34/C. [Untitled] 1936 g.," l. 8 (dated 11 November 1935).

85. Dora Wiebenson, *Tony Garnier: The Cité Industrielle* (New York: Braziller, 1969), p. 19. Garnier's unrealized plan, a kind of remade Lyons, laid down the basic principles—emphasis on industry, separation of functions, and importance of circulation—that came to underlay Soviet planning, at least as conceptualized, if not always as practiced.

86. *MR*, 10 April 1938.

87. Grossman, "The 'Second Economy,'" p. 29.

88. Workers at state enterprises helped themselves to raw materials and tools, which they put to use, usually on their own time and for private gain—a practice by no means limited to a fully state-owned economy, except that in the Soviet case there was almost always no other way to obtain such supplies and tools, even if the workers were willing to pay for them. It is possible that some people did not carry the materials home, preferring to make use of them at the job, and that they were concerned less with personal gain than exploring the pleasures of their craft. This is a complex subject, as underscored by Michel de Certeau in his discussion of what in France is called *la perruque* ("the wig"), defined as the workers' own work disguised as work for their employer. *La perruque*, he writes, "differs from pilfering in that nothing of material value is stolen. It differs from absenteeism in that the worker is officially on the job. *La perruque* may be as simple as a secretary's writing a love letter on 'company time' or as complex as a cabinetmaker's 'borrowing' a lathe to make a piece of furniture for his living room." Government bureaucracies are an especially conducive environment for such practices. De Certeau, *The Practice of Everyday Life*, pp. 25–26.

89. Haven Papers.

90. *MR*, 9 September 1936. Another example: Pirogov, who served out his sentence in the corrective labor colony, became, of all things, the colony's supply chief. In that capacity he contacted his friend Panfilov, the chief of supply for freight transport, and asked the latter to line up some buyers for certain metal parts that were being shipped to the labor colony. Through Panfilov's connections, Pirogov was able to sell these precious materials to a supply agent for a collective farm, who must have been overjoyed. But they were all caught, and Pirogov, who had split the profits with Panfilov, was given five years, while his partner got three. *MR*, 3 March 1937.

91. The title of the decree, issued during the collectivization drive, was as follows: "On the protection of the property of state enterprises, collective farms, and cooperatives and the strengthening of societal (socialist) property." For the text see *Sobranie zakonov i rasporiazhenii USSR*, 1932, No. 62, item 360, reprinted in *Sbornik dokumentov*, pp. 335–36.

92. In 1934, of the 2,360 cases in the court system, 51 were brought on the seven-eighths law. These involved 169 individuals. Only 2 were not sentenced to five or ten years. In 1933, 482 people were sentenced under the seven-eighths. MFGAChO, f. 10, op. 1, d. 139, ll. 154–59. During the lean year of 1932, a supply agent for the labor colony was said to have systematically pilfered bread, which with the aid of an accomplice was sold at the market for what were called "speculative prices." The Magnitogorsk people's court traveled to the colony for the trial with fanfare, and the accused was sentenced to ten (additional) years under the seven-eighths. *Borba za metall*, 23 December 1932.

93. One Soviet textbook retrospectively ventured that "the law of 7 August was excessively severe and insufficiently worked out from the legal point of view. Malicious embezzlers and those who committed utterly insignificant misdemeanors alike came under its provisions." True enough, but the need to protect socialist property was not questioned. See *Istoriia SSSR*, vol. 8 (Moscow, 1975), p. 584. According to the 1926 criminal code, the purpose of Soviet criminal law was "the protection of the socialist state of workers and peasants." *Ugolovnyi kodeks redaktsii 1926 g.*, p. 23.

94. For example, at the beginning of 1936 lower prices were decreed for butter, threatening a loss in revenue for trade organizations. But in response, butter advertised as "regular variety" disappeared from the shelves, "replaced" by a number of new varieties labeled "extra," "export," and "higher grade." Naturally, these special brands were priced higher than the regular sort was to be priced under the new decree. In fact, the newspaper noted with irony, the price of the new higher sorts closely resembled that of the regular sort before the price decrease. To avoid a loss in revenue, dairy stores had decided to circumvent the disadvantageous (to them) decree. The newspaper concluded that there had in effect been no decrease in prices. *MR*, 20 January 1936.

95. *MR*, 7 February 1936. To get an understanding of how profitable such artifices could be, see the testimony of a former Soviet citizen, "Twenty-six Interviews," II/17.

96. *MR*, 3 March 1936.

97. At store no. 17 in 1933, sales personnel allegedly sold nine women's coats for 108.50 rubles, versus a state price of 103.15—a total of 48.15 rubles skimmed. Other cases were said to involve much larger differentials. GARF, f. 7952, op. 5, d. 294, l. 23.

98. *Magnitogorskii metall*, 29 September 1935. For food prices in 1937–38, see Scott, *Behind*, p. 242.

99. *MR*, 6 May 1936.

100. *MR*, 21 December 1936. In light of the fact that she had three small children at home, the woman who accepted the merchandise was said to have been given a suspended sentence.

101. *MR*, 5 August 1936.

102. A bookkeeper from the offices of the Cheliabinsk regional trade organization made a deal with a trade inspector to visit store no. 5 after it had closed and pick up any goods not sold. The appearance of a large crowd of customers during the day, however, meant that nothing would be left, so an effort was made to close the store early—denying an untold number of people the chance to make purchases. This unpopular action elicited noisy protests and led to an inquiry. It was established that the bookkeeper and inspector had carted off 250 rubles' worth of fabrics and other scarce items. *MR*, 22 January 1936. An inmate of the labor colony volunteered to paint a locomotive for the upcoming November holiday. He promised that if given the materials, he would have the job done by 5 November, with two days to spare. On that day, however, the authorities found him using the paint on the floors and walls of the barracks in which he lived. *Borba za metall*, 5 December 1932.

103. *MR*, 20 January 1936.

104. *MR*, 24 April 1936. See also "Twenty-six Interviews," I/15 and II/26.

105. The same was true for the local labor colony. One inmate was accused of stealing a tent and making a suit out of it; others allegedly stole and then sold state linen, bread, and packages designated for fellow inmates. Those convicted invariably received "tenners." *Borba za metall*, 15 and 27 January 1933. In late 1933 the colony administration undertook an inventory of colony property, such as bed linen, whose worth was estimated at more than 1 million rubles. If there were results of the inventory, they were not published. The colony newspaper did report, however, that in the absence of accounting, employees of the colony supply department continued to trade in all manner of materials. Ibid., 21 November and 26 December 1933.

106. After Magnitogorsk was divided into three administrative districts, its raion people's court was also divided into three jurisdictions. The Kirov district court was in a barracks near Socialist City, while the Ordzhonikidze and Stalin district courts were located together in a building on the First Sector. *MR*, 11 March 1937. According to a list of judges presented at a meeting of the city soviet presidium two months later, however, there appear to have been six judicial districts, divided more or less equally by population. It is possible that each of the three administrative districts was split in two. See MFGAChO, f. 10, op. 1, d. 281, l. 304.

107. The procuracy and the courts were united until the law of 20 July 1936 separated the procuracy and investigatory organs from the People's Commissariat of Justice and made them directly subordinate to the Procurator General, an office that had been created by the law of 20 June 1933. See Samuel Kucherov, *The Organs of Soviet Administration of Justice: Their History and Operation* (Leiden: E. J. Brill, 1970), pp. 93–104.

108. Article 3 of the Judiciary Act of 1938 stated that "by all their activities the courts shall educate the citizens of the USSR in the spirit of devotion to the motherland and the cause of socialism, in the spirit of strict and undeviating observance of Soviet laws, of care for socialist property, of labor discipline, of honesty toward public and social duty, of respect for the rules of socialist common-life." Berman, *Justice in Russia*, p. 212. Echoing such thinking, Magnitogorsk's chief judge, Babikova, wrote that "the court should inculcate new socialist relations to public property, to work, to responsibilities, which every citizen bears in relation to the state, new socialist relations with each other, the family, public activity." In a bid for more support and resources, she complained that the Magnitogorsk courts were "not fulfilling their educational functions," owing to difficulties obtaining decent offices, furniture, and even paper. She added that "people are not learning to respect the courts." *MR*, 11 April 1937.

109. *MR*, 18 September 1938. Another evening demonstration trial was held in the Open-Hearth Club in 1936 for three persons accused of stealing socialist property. The ringleader was given ten years, the others seven. *MR*, 30 October 1936.

110. In most of these cases it was the person identified as the "ringleader" who was shot, although in the case of the nineteen, six people were sentenced to be executed. Those convicted who were not shot received the maximum prison term, ten years. Magnitogorsk procuracy: Archival file "Nariad No. 21. Sektrenaia perepiska," ll. 62–63.

111. *MR,* 29 August 1936. Similarly, a bookkeeper employed by the mining administration, Arkadii Pereberin, who was a "class alien" (his father had been a clergyman), was accused of paying workers who no longer worked at the mine and pocketing the cash (some 7,775 rubles during 1934 and 1935). In court, he was reported to have said that he stole the money "out of a desire to live the good life." *MR,* 4 February 1936.

112. Without offering any details the newspaper stated that a similar group was uncovered in the coke shop's accounting department. *MR,* 17 January 1936.

113. *MR,* 10 September 1933.

114. The number of known embezzlers was raised to 150. *Pravda,* 26 August and 3 September 1933. Clippings of these and other articles were made for the Magnitogorsk history project. GARF, f. 7952, op. 5, d. 294, passim.

115. Something of a struggle appears to have taken place. It was subsequently reported that because Bondarev had been in charge of ORS only since May 1933, his party punishment was commuted to a reprimand. The same had happened to Ershov. *MR,* 18 October 1933. The newspaper did not say, but Bondarev must have been re-expelled in connection with the trial and sentencing.

116. *MR,* 18 October 1933; GARF, f. 7952, op. 5, d. 294, l. 4.

117. Lominadze called the decisions by the Central Committee and the Urals obkom regarding the fate of the previous Magnitogorsk party and economic leadership "severe," but in the newspaper account of his speech no details of those decisions were offered. *MR,* 15 January 1934.

118. According to the *Pravda* correspondent, "Bondarev tries to create the impression that he is completely innocent, that he saw everything, knew everything, even tried to warn [about it all], but that unfortunately 'no one helped him.' The fundamental question is, is Bondarev guilty of the fact that the Magnitogorsk ORS has been turned into a bountiful field for thieves of all kinds—a question that he was asked again and again at the party purge by the commission and from the floor, but one he studiously avoided." GARF, f. 7952, op. 5, d. 294, l. 47. Magnitogorsk city soviet chairman, G. K. Rumiantsev, was also removed during the party purge. His case took place in the Miners Club, and evidently presented a spectacle as Rumiantsev was asked why Magnitogorsk workers were without decent housing. He was blamed for the abominable housing situation. *Pravda,* 14 September 1933. The party purge is treated in ch. 7.

119. *Pravda,* 26 August 1933.

120. As *Pravda* explained, "On 18 July [1933] three wagons of canned fish arrived [in Magnitogorsk]. They [ORS] needed 156,000 rubles to pay for the shipment. There was no money. Bondarev, Ershov, and Uvarov collected money from enterprises. One factory paid for one wagon of canned fish and bartered it to the Milk Trust for milk products. [The Milk Trust] sold the fish to whomever came along as quickly as possible, up to fifty cans at a time. The workers didn't get any fish." *Pravda,* 26 August 1933; GARF, f. 7952, op. 5, d. 294, ll. 35, 43, 46

121. RTsKhIDNI, f. 17, op. 21, d. 5657, ll. 145–47 (protocols of obkom meetings, July 1934).

122. The next year, 1935, the Magnitogorsk ORS was severely criticized in the oblast newspaper, and the *gorkom* pronounced the performance of the ORS in 1934

"unsatisfactory," singling out for special condemnation the chief of ORS, Aronson, who was given a party reprimand. *CR*, 16 March 1935.

123. *MR*, 30 October 1936.

124. *MR*, 5 February 1936. Store managers and trade representatives may have had extraordinary access to scarce goods, but they worked under a dark cloud and all too often became the victims of popular rage and political demagogy. One way for store managers to shield themselves was to dismiss sales personnel for corruption. The newspaper alleged that when caught, store managers "on the take" would find some way to pass on the responsibility for the irregularities uncovered in inventory or receipts to salespeople. The turnover in trade personnel was dizzying. During the first seven months of 1938, for example, 94 store managers were hired, while 41 were fired. As for sales help, 139 were hired and 100 were fired during the same period. *MR*, 8 October 1938. As of 1 January 1939, 4,354 people were employed in trade and food services. MFGAChO, f. 9, op. 1, d. 170, l. 44.

125. During one purge of the Central Workers' Cooperative in early 1931, of 764 people in the category of employees, 416 were the object of anonymous accusations (*zaiavleniia*). Most were accused of having been former merchants. *Magnitogorskii komsomolets*, 7 February 1931. In 1933, during the passport campaign, 586 of the 4,300 employees of the dining hall trust, Narpit, supposedly disappeared rather than submit documents for scrutiny. GARF, f. 7952, op. 5, d. 294, ll. 36–38. According to a 1938 report by the oblast newspaper, 426 people working in Magnittorg were convicted "embezzlers" (*rastratchikov*). "Losses" in Magnitogorsk stores for the first six months of the year were said to amount to around 400,000 rubles. *CR*, 21 July 1938.

126. *MR*, 30 October 1936.

127. *MR*, 20 September 1936.

128. *MR*, 18 November 1936. Mismanagement or thriftlessness (*bezkhoziastvennost*) was also an economic crime. Article 128 of the criminal code stipulated that "thriftlessness, based on a negligent or unconscionable attitude toward a matter entrusted to them, of persons who stand at the head of state or social institutions, which has resulted in the squandering of the property of [such] institutions and enterprises or irreparable damage to them, [shall be punished by] deprivation of liberty for a term of up to two years or corrective labor tasks for a term of up to one year." *Ugolovnyi kodeks redaktsii 1926 g.*, pp. 266–71.

129. In one case, a store clerk was fired for a shortfall in pails. The store where she worked had ordered and paid for 1,000 pails, yet the supplier had shipped only 200. The woman neglected to check the order when it arrived and was held personally responsible for the shortfall, since the supplier denied shortchanging the store. The woman was charged with peculation. *MR*, 17 July 1936. The words embezzlement (*rastrata*) and insider theft (*raskhishchenie*) were generally used as synonyms, but they corresponded to two different articles of the criminal code (116 and 129). *Ugolovnyi kodeks redaktsii 1926 g.*, pp. 242–49, 271–73. In its accounts of trials, the newspaper never specified what article of the criminal code was being invoked. Nor was the text of the code available for public consultation.

130. *MR*, 9 January 1936.

131. The same was true for those who worked in industrial supply. John Scott

wrote of one administrator of supplies in the blast furnace construction trust that "everybody had a bad word for him." Scott, *Behind*, p. 43.

132. *MR*, 4 April 1937.

133. In the same trial, Ivanov, a foreman on the individual home construction sector was given a sentence of ten years, with three-years' additional disfranchisement and confiscation of all property. And Zhelnov, a former state farm director, got eight years with two years' disfranchisement and property confiscation. Mentioned by name for a future trial were Panov, a former engineer in charge of observing fence construction, Bychkov, an accountant in individual home construction, two employees and the chief of the woodworking plant. *MR*, 20 April 1937.

134. Scott did not name the defendant, referring instead to "the director of construction organization engaged in building individual dwellings." Either he was referring to Lukashevich, or more likely, creating a composite out of several defendants at the trials that year. The KBU organization had several vehicles. Scott, *Behind*, p. 185. In the block with Lukashevich were Ivanov, the manager of the KBU garage, Bukin, described as a technician, Zhigulev, a foreman, and Ishchenko, a deputy to the KBU chief. At first, the city newspaper reported only that for his cottage in Magnitogorsk's Kashirin Settlement the KBU chief had paid just 300 rubles for what were said to be 1,200 rubles' worth of wood from a dismantled barracks. *MR*, 21 July 1937. Subsequent reports in November when the trial took place were far more damning (see ch. 7).

135. *MR*, 23 and 27 November 1937. Beginning in 1936, sentences for most crimes reported in the newspaper tended to be far longer than they had been in the earlier part of the decade. In a 1937 report that cited the "poor work of comrade courts," especially the failure to carry out "mass political work," the newspaper also disparaged the record of a judge, Petrova. Twenty percent of her decisions were said to have been overturned, which the newspaper called, in an analogy with steelmaking, an example of judicial "spoilage" (*brak*). Petrova was removed from her post for being "too lenient with hooligans." *MR*, 16 and 17 August and 6 October 1937.

136. A newspaper article in 1936, for example, told of a "suggestion" for improving trade. One collective farm supposedly had a surplus of agricultural goods. But it was too far for the collective farmers to go to the city and sell the much-needed produce at the bazaar. The suggestion was made to open a bazaar right in the "village," to which the nearby population could also bring its produce for sale. The newspaper supported the suggestion (which, after all, it published), noting that "there used to be a bazaar in the village." The paper did not say when or why the old bazaar was closed, who suffered as a result, and how ironic it must have seemed that reopening the old bazaar could be presented as an original solution to the problem that its closing may actually have created. *MR*, 1 March 1936.

137. *MR*, 22 March 1936.

138. *MR*, 27 March 1936.

139. *MR*, 10 August 1936.

140. *MR*, 24 April 1936.

141. *MR*, 21 September 1936.

142. *MR*, 5 January 1936. This was also a favorite theme of the oblast newspaper. In one report it claimed that more than 1.5 million rubles' worth of goods

were in Magnitogorsk warehouses, without explaining whether this was a lot or a little, normal or abnormal, but taking care to specify the amounts held of beef (fifty tons), pork (seventy tons), and sugar (eight tons)—an indirect admission of the relative rarity of these items in the stores. In addition, the warehouses of the ORS were said to have a significant amount of rabbits, but stores were able to sell only 640 kilograms. One deputy store manager was quoted as saying that "our rabbits are dark and dirty; they cost us four rubles thirty kopecks per kilogram, and we sell them for eleven to twelve rubles. At the market collective farmers sell good rabbits for seven to eight rubles." *CR*, 6 April 1935.

143. *MR*, 12 August 1936.

144. *MR*, 28 August 1936.

145. *MR*, 26 September 1936.

146. *MR*, 18 October 1933.

147. In December 1937 alone, more than sixty people were fired and fifty hired. During the first seven months of 1938, ninety-four new store managers were hired, and forty-one let go. *MR*, 16 January and 8 October 1938. As part of sentencing, the court was supposed to forbid convicted employees from working in trade or supply for certain periods. But given the perpetual staffing problems in what was a low-paying, low-status job, this rule could not be enforced. GARF, f. 7952, op. 5, d. 294, l. 46.

148. *MR*, 9 October 1936.

149. *MR*, 12 September 1936.

150. During the first half of 1935, for example, there were 1,252 criminal cases in the city, but only 30 were for speculation (compared with 114 for hooliganism). In the first half of 1936, the total number of cases declined to 485. Forty-one of these came under the heading speculation. MFGAChO, f. 10, op. 1, d. 246, l. 12.

151. He mentioned fabrics, shoes, silk, knitted garments, and bicycles. *MR*, 9 August 1936.

152. *MR*, 5 August 1936.

153. Between 1 July and 20 September 1936 there were 128 arrests of "speculators." Sixty-eight trials were scheduled, of which forty-six had already been heard, resulting in forty-four convictions, by the time of the news reports. *MR*, 11 and 27 October 1936. According to a Soviet newspaper for foreigners, in 1934 Walter Rudolf, identified as a party member and secretary of the Magnitogorsk *insnab* commission, was convicted of speculating with scarce goods from *insnab*. He was fined 10 rubles, lost his *insnab* privileges for four months, and was expelled from the *insnab* commission and from the comrade court where he was a judge—hardly a severe punishment. It was implied in the article, written by John Scott, that Rudolf was selling *insnab* goods meant for foreigners to Soviet officials. *Moscow News*, 17 April 1934.

154. *MR*, 29 July 1936.

155. *MR*, 10 August 1932. For the decree by the Soviet government, which also warned of speculation, see *Sobranie zakonov i rasporiazhenii*, 1932, no. 38, item 233.

156. *MR*, 17 August 1937 and 1 February 1936.

157. *Magnitogorskii metall*, 11 August 1935. An officer of the militia, asked if

there was a lot of speculation and hooliganism at the bazaar, supposedly remarked, "we don't even have the paper to register such facts." *MR*, 17 August 1937.

158. *MR*, 3 January 1936.

159. Gubanishchev, a turner of the mechanical shop, was quoted as saying that "life has become good. I earn 400–500 rubles, and have had shoes and clothes delivered. I don't refuse myself anything." *MR*, 17 May 1936.

160. Here one can see something of a parallel with consumption in market societies. Department store managers in late nineteenth-century Paris realized that successful merchandising was as much a question of theater as cut-rate prices, and that consumers shopped for self-realization and social prestige, not just bargains. In Magnitogorsk, the availability of consumer goods was significantly less than in nineteenth-century France, and purchases were regulated by official authorization in addition to money. But the connection between consumption and status comes through all the same. See Philip Nord, "Labor, Commerce and Consumption: Studies in Market Culture in Nineteenth-Century France," *Radical History Review* 37 (1987): 82–92.

161. At the Seventeenth Party Congress, Stalin, perhaps seeking to calm the party faithful in the aftermath of the famine, explained that "there would have been no point in overthrowing capitalism in October 1917 and building socialism all these years if we were not going to secure a life of plenty for our people. Socialism does not mean destitution and privation." I. V. Stalin, "Otchetnyi doklad XVII S"ezdu partii o rabote TsK VKP (b)," in *Sochineniia*, vol. 13, p. 357.

162. Arthur Koestler, a Hungarian-born Communist, reported the kinds of questions he was asked after delivering lectures to Soviet audiences in 1933–34:

> "When you left the bourgeois press was your ration card withdrawn and were you kicked out at once from your room?"
> "What is the average number per day of French working-class families starving to death a) in rural areas b) in the towns?"

These questions, which came not long after a Soviet famine, are noteworthy as evidence of a sense of dependency and a healthy curiosity about the outside world, despite the constant barrage of information through official channels. See Richard Crossman, ed., *The God that Failed*, p. 61.

163. *Magnitogorskii metall*, 29 September 1935. Detailed budget studies were apparently infrequent. In 1931, for example, local authorities kept writing to Moscow asking for instructions, receiving only outraged telegrams in response. Scattered results of such attempted studies for 1931 are contained in the archives, but not for later years. MFGAChO, f. 16, op. 1, d. 2, l. 1. John Scott claimed that the availability of consumer goods dramatically improved in the second half of the 1930s, but also that "prices of the manufactured goods were appallingly high. A good pair of shoes cost two hundred and twenty rubles in 1936 and three hundred in 1938. Good woolen suits were almost unobtainable, and when they did appear in stores, if one was lucky enough to get one while they lasted, one had to pay from five hundred to fifteen hundred roubles." Scott never explained how anyone could obtain such expensive goods. In any case, money by itself was not a sufficient means to secure a better standard of living, since many purchases could not be made without permission and housing was distributed. Scott, *Behind*, p. 243. Despite the

low cost of housing and the subsidized food prices, most workers, especially those with families, struggled to make ends meet, having little choice but to grow some of their own food, engage in "speculation" or even theft, and take on secondary jobs, legal or illegal, for supplemental income. No one went without a job or was homeless, but few became comfortably well-off. See the discussion for the USSR as a whole by John Barber, "The Standard of Living of Soviet Industrial Workers, 1928–1941," pp. 109–22.

164. "In the city it is difficult to get a hold of [*dostat*] not only vegetables from the new harvest, but even last years' potatoes, cabbage, and onions," according to a report in the oblast newspaper. Stores were said to trade in vegetables "with big interruptions," and that season even supplies at the market were called spotty. The factory's greenhouses, important as they were, could not supply the whole city. *CR*, 21 July 1938.

165. During the first five days in April 1936 no meat went on sale in any Magnitogorsk store owing to problems with deliveries. *MR*, 6 April 1936. This was by no means an isolated occurrence. According to an official report, there was a breakdown in 1938 at the sausage department of the meat factory, leading to a lack of sausage in the city, a problem compounded by the removal of some sausage from store shelves after it was found to have pieces of metal in it. MFGAChO, f. 16, op. 1, d. 96, l. 4. According to a different official report, the city produced ninety kilograms of milk products per person in 1937. The report pointed out that this was just 250 grams per day per person, assuming a population of 177,000. There was, moreover, a prohibition against transporting milk from afar. In 1938, when disease struck state farms in nearby Agapovka, the authorities called on city dwellers who owned cows to try to make up the difference. But even at the market, there was not enough milk. The same report revealed that there was a lack of feed, prices having shot up to 35 rubles per kilo, a situation whose effects on the local herd were much feared. Such shortages invariably drove prices up even higher. Fruit, too, remained a problem, despite shipments of pears and plums from Central Asia. Ibid., f. 9, op. 1, d. 154, ll. 2–3, 14, 245–47.

166. In 1937 the Magnitogorsk newspaper reported the apprehension of three men from the countryside who managed to buy up 148 loaves of bread in Magnitogorsk. *MR*, 6 February 1937. Why would someone from the countryside travel to a city to purchase 148 loaves of bread? The newspaper had already supplied the answer, albeit indirectly, by reporting stories of long queues for bread in Magnitogorsk. *MR*, 17 January 1937. One woman was said to have traveled about the city and bought up all the bread she could find. A search of her home revealed that she had accumulated more than forty loaves. *MR*, 4 February 1937. In response, it was announced that five bread stores had already been designated to be open around the clock, with three more to be so designated shortly. *MR*, 9 February 1937. More significant was the announcement that a limit on purchases to two kilos per person was being imposed. *MR*, 4 February 1937.

167. *Magnitogorskii metall*, 29 September 1935. See also Scott, *Behind*, p. 302.

168. I interviewed separately almost a dozen "labor veterans" in Magnitogorsk in 1987 and 1989; all remembered holding a positive view of rationing fifty years earlier (which they still held).

169. Scott, *Behind*, pp. 13, 43. Even displaced persons who chose not to return to the Soviet Union admitted to having willingly endured the sacrifices, out of conviction. Moreover, most people appear to have believed they had achieved a superior standard of living, as demonstrated by the actions of Soviet soldiers when they entered Poland in September 1939 and bought up everything in sight. See Peter Gornev, "The Life of a Soviet Soldier," in Fischer, ed., *Thirteen Who Fled*, p. 36.

170. *MR*, 8 January 1936.

171. Neither did the state grocery stores always stock the necessary ingredients to enable urban residents to bake bread themselves; to bake bread one had first to visit the bazaar in search of yeast.

172. *MR*, 14 October 1933.

173. *MR*, 1 January 1938.

174. *MR*, 26 April 1936.

175. *MR*, 17 January 1936.

176. According to an official report, bread production declined precipitously from 1937 to 1938. In 1938 the bread factory was said to have produced only 77.8 percent of its output target. It is far from obvious, however, what this figure could have meant. The target may have been set high, meaning there was plenty of bread. Conversely, a certain portion of the counted output may not have made been edible. MFGAChO, f. 9, op. 1, d. 170, l. 9. Two years earlier, the newspaper alleged that the daily demand for bread in the city was 100 tons per day (about 1.2 pounds, or less than 550 grams per person), while the large bread factory, with its nearly 500 workers, was producing 118–120 tons—ostensibly a sufficient amount. But the newspaper's reports of hoarding implied spot shortages, and the implication was that any shortages were solely attributable to problems in delivery and distribution. It remains questionable, moreover, whether the bread factory's supposed daily output of 118–120 tons translated into an equivalent weight of edible loaves. The newspaper did not address the issue of spoilage, either at the factory or in the warehouses and stores. The newspaper admitted to receiving numerous irate letters from its readers who were angry that much of the bread baked at the single bread factory was of poor quality—a problem not of distribution but of production. *MR*, 20 November 1936.

177. MFGAChO, f. 9, op. 1, d. 159, ll. 2, 14–15.

178. In its first fourteen months of operation the shoe factory managed to turn out only 4,850 pairs of felt boots which, the newspaper complained, "in no way satisfied the demand." The sewing factory, located in Lattice-Wood Town, had 160 workers (as of 1935), and continued to expand in the second half of the decade. But according to the newspaper, 80 percent of the sewing factory's output in 1935 went to the Magnitogorsk Metallurgical Complex, meaning it was not available in city stores. *MR*, 6 September 1934 and 24 April 1935.

179. MFGAChO, f. 10, op. 1, d. 20, l. 5.

180. *MR*, 27 August 1938. Artels of course had output targets, or production "plans." In 1938 none of them met their plans. Energiia was said to have produced only 60 percent of its target. For all artels the figure given was 82.6 percent. MFGAChO, f. 9, op. 1, d. 170, l. 1.

181. *MR*, 5 October 1936.

182. *MR*, 5 March 1936.

183. *MR*, 14 April 1936.

184. *MR*, 5 April 1939.

185. MFGAChO, f. 9, op. 1, d. 173, l. 2.

186. *MR*, 20 February 1939.

187. *MR*, 26 September 1939.

188. *MR*, 10 August 1936. See also "Twenty-six Interviews," I/1 and I/5. According to the Magnitogorsk labor colony newspaper, "at the site of building No. 11 of the Kirov district the brigadier of the joiners' workshop Iurev accepted a 'private order' for a handmade suitcase for some accounts clerk," and had the brigade do the work during normal work hours. Evidently someone squealed. *Borba za metall*, 5 June 1935.

189. "At night," wrote the novelist Vasilii Grossman "the tailor was engaged in making boys' and womens' coats; the repairman had an electric hotplate under the floor on which he baked wafers that his wife sold on the open market; the lathe operator . . . turned out to be a nighttime shoemaker, manufacturing women's shoes; and the widows wove not only bags but women's sweaters." Grossman, *Forever Flowing*, p. 95.

190. *MR*, 29 October 1936.

191. *MR*, 10 October 1936.

192. It could sometimes be just as dangerous not to participate in illegal activities. See "Twenty-six Interviews," II/21.

193. Frequently enough, the activities of the shadow economy were prominently detailed in the press, and the "entrepreneurs" cited by name. One woman, Dobrynina, allegedly bought suits at a state store and enlisted her neighbor Duko to sell them. If Duko got double the state store price, she kept 20 rubles; triple, she kept 40 rubles. Dobrynina was also said to buy up all the purchase limitation coupons for fabric from workers, and then sew dresses and suits, which Duko also sold at the bazaar. Another woman, Kartashova, was said "not to trail Dobrynina." The newspaper reported that "everyday beginning in the morning [Kartashova] does duty [*dezhurit*] at the stores, buying up fabric and with it sewing various things, which she sold for a nice profit at the bazaar." The correspondent complained that not only did these "speculators" use accomplices to sell their ill-gotten goods, but some, such as Dobrynina, "wore the mask of persons active in public activities [*aktivnykh obshchestvennikov*]." *Magnitogorskii metall*, 5 September 1935.

194. Consider the example of public dining hall managers, who under pressure to feed their patrons, periodically experienced difficulties obtaining supplies. The managers were forced to scramble, and according to the newspaper, some resorted to buying "unbranded" meat from "speculators." *MR*, 4 October 1931. What else were they to do, to avoid charges of mismanagement or even wrecking for failing to serve the lunches called for by the plan? To follow the path traveled by the dining-room manager was dangerous, but it was often just as dangerous not to take the risk and engage in whatever illegal activities were necessary to meet one's state-imposed obligations.

195. Scott Papers, "Behind the Urals," ms., p. 223.

196. *MR*, 15 September 1936. The newspaper's insinuation that all such self-made salespeople were "former merchants" and current inmates of the labor colony cannot be taken seriously.

197. This conflation of "market" and black market" is also characteristic of the odd mention of such activities found in secondary accounts. Even Fitzpatrick appears to fall into this trap. *The Cultural Front*, pp. 220–21.

198. In Russian, the expression is *khleb i zrelishche*, literally "bread and spectacle." During the war, in the areas of the Soviet Union occupied by the Germans, who, among other things, were trying to revive churches in an effort to rally the population against the Soviet regime, the following ditty was promoted by the loyal organizers of the Soviet resistance:

Doloi tserkov, doloi khram,	Down with churches, down with cathedrals,
Doloi Gitlera trista gram.	Down with Hitler's 300 grams [of bread].
Davai kluby i kino,	Let's have clubs and the cinema,
Davai Stalinskoe kilo!	Let's have Stalin's kilogram!

A clearer expression of the traditional bread and circuses formula would be hard to imagine. See Alexander Werth, *Russia at War, 1941–1945* (New York: Carroll and Graf, 1964), p. 612.

199. As a recognition of this failure, the city trade organizations tried to organize special "fairs" in 1936 to draw state and collective farmers to the bazaar. Overnight accommodations were provided for the incoming farmers, as well as a dining facility and a place to keep their horses. After the February fair was canceled owing to blizzards, much preparation and publicity went into the March fair. In addition to guaranteed accomodations, the farmers were enticed with large quantities of industrial goods. Nevertheless, the turnout proved very disappointing. The newspaper claimed to be at a loss to explain why so few collective farmers showed up. On the other hand, the paper did mention that at the fair a "savings bank" had been established for "accepting" deposits and for "verifying the payment of state loans." Such a situation could not but serve as a disincentive to collective farmers who were in no hurry to undergo such harassment to sell their goods at the officially organized fairs when they could continue to engage in their trade through unofficial channels, or not trade at all. *MR*, 11 August 1936. Three men from neighboring Bashkiriia brought three cows to Magnitogorsk for sale. With the money they received, they purchased 2,000 rubles' worth of goods and still had 2,500 rubles left over. They were arrested for speculation. If cows had been less valuable—something beyond the control of the three Bashkirs—would they have been speculating? On the other hand, if prices had not been so high, would they have bothered to bring the cows to market? On this as on all matters, signals from Moscow were contradictory and ambiguous. For the local authorities, to be sure, it was best not to take any chances; when in doubt, arrest. Still, the police could not arrest the entire citizenry, including themselves, for what was a universal component of life in Magnitogorsk. *MR*, 23 February and 14 March 1936.

200. As argued by E. P. Thompson, "The Moral Economy of the English Crowd in the Eighteenth Century," *Past and Present* 50 (February 1971): 76–136.

CHAPTER 7. DIZZY WITH SUCCESS

1. Anatolii Rybakov, *Deti arbata* (Moscow, 1987), p. 85.

2. A reflection of the transformation of Magnitogorsk into a city was its budget,

which grew from 680,000 rubles in 1930 to almost 28 million by 1937. Most of this money was spent on health and education. The basic source of revenue was a tax on local industry and trade. *MR*, 6 March 1937.

3. In the preparations for the 1936 report on the city soviet's activities, a very interesting discussion of all the city's problems, including trade, health, and education, took place. MFGAChO, f. 10, op. 1, d. 212; and d. 243 (for report itself).

4. MFGAChO, f. 10, op. 1, d. 212, passim; and d. 213, l. 220; *MR*, 24, 26 and 27 November 1936. The new constitution replaced one from 1924. It was adopted at the Eighth All-Union Congress of Soviets, which created a new state legislature, the Supreme Soviet. Unger, *Constitutional Development*, pp. 79–138.

5. I. V. Stalin, "O nedostatkakh partiinoi raboty i merakh likvidatsii Trotskitskikh dvurushnikov," in *Sochineniia*, vol. 1 [14], pp. 189–224. Stalin's report was published in *Pravda*, after an unexplained delay, on 29 March; it appeared in *Magnitogorskii rabochii* the next day. On 5 March he delivered the plenum's closing speech, published in *Pravda* on 1 April. He retreated somewhat, but reiterated his main arguments. The speech and its impact are discussed below.

6. This did not mean that Soviet foreign policy was particularly astute or effective. For an analysis, see Tucker, *Stalin in Power*, pp. 223–37, 338–65.

7. The Smolensk party archive, which covers the years 1921–37, runs to 200,000 pages yet is incomplete, a deficiency Fainsod noted but did not consider serious. He also acknowledged that as an agricultural region and relative backwater, Smolensk "tended to be neglected by the center," raising questions about its representativeness. Fainsod, *Smolensk*, p. 5.

8. Fainsod's study was dominated by the relationship between the "center," as Moscow was known, and the locality. He demonstrated that the center drove the locality, goading and threatening, sending endless circulars and often intervening directly with commissions. With the center often frustrated by the responses to its directives, particularly evasion, the locality, or obkom, was said to have existed "in perpetual fear and in perpetual motion." Although he documented the flux and tensions within the locality, Fainsod presented the center as a monolith. Fainsod, *Smolensk*, pp. 77–78, 92.

9. In one memorable passage he wrote of the emergence of a "full-blown totalitarian regime in which all the lines of control ultimately converged in the hands of the supreme dictator." Fainsod, *Smolensk*, p. 12.

10. "The [oblast] party secretariat sought to contain the whole life of the oblast," he wrote. "One searches in vain for any aspect of oblast activity which does not find its reflection and point of control in one or another division of the secretariat." Fainsod, *Smolensk*, pp. 66–67.

11. Fainsod also mentioned, but did not investigate, the importance of the consolidation by the late 1930s of a "new class of beneficiaries" whose "vested interests" had become "involved in the regime's survival." And he singled out a supposed "tradition of servility," which seemed hard to square with the strikes and uprisings that had brought down the autocracy and Provisional Government, let alone the widespread dissatisfaction with Communist-party rule the author himself emphasized. Fainsod observed that "the documents provide unimpeachable evidence of mass discontent with Soviet rule," and likened the party to "an army of occupation in hostile territory." But he seems to have equated the anti-Communist-

party sentiment he uncovered in this predominantly rural province with an anti-Soviet position. It is possible, however, to imagine deep-seated hostility to the rule of the Communist party, especially given the behavior of local functionaries, co-existing with an acceptance of "Soviet power." Fainsod, *Smolensk*, pp. 52, 123, 449, 450–53.

12. In a textbook on the Soviet political system published before his study of Smolensk, Fainsod had treated the terror as "a system of power" and an "instrument" in the hands of the "totalitarian dictator." He noted that Stalin's drive "to consolidate his own personal power appears to have been a driving force" behind the terror, but argued that ultimately the "system" required terror to function, owing largely to its supposed lack of legitimacy. The book appeared just after Stalin died, however, and carried a photograph of Stalin's casket being borne by his successors. Fainsod's thesis was undermined by the succession of Khrushchev and the apparent end of organized terror, a development that induced him to revise his work. Ironically, the second, revised edition appeared just after Khrushchev had been removed and the de-Stalinization campaign seemed to have been called into question. Fainsod, *How Russia is Ruled*, 2d ed. (Cambridge, Mass.: Harvard University Press, 1965).

13. T. H. Rigby, "Stalinism and the Mono-organizational Society," in Robert Tucker, ed., *Stalinism: Essays in Historical Interpretation* (New York: Norton, 1977), pp. 53–76. The article, far more subtle than the hyphenated formula implies, represents a sophisticated attempt to restate the "totalitarian interpretation." Rigby wrote, for example, that "the salience of coercive controls" had "an objective basis in the functional needs of the system and does not merely flow from the repressive attitudes of the leaders" (p. 58).

14. In a study of the first Soviet government, Rigby recovered a sense of the uncertainty over the party's role after the revolution had been accomplished. He showed that even though Lenin viewed the party as a trusted group of special individuals who could be dispatched to perform critical functions in emergencies, the Bolshevik leader envisioned the Sovnarkom, and not the party, as the main instrument of rule. Thus, although the party soon came to eclipse the government, this development was far from straightforward, and in any case the government continued to grow and function. Rigby, *Lenin's Government: Sovnarkom, 1917–1922* (Cambridge: Cambridge University Press, 1979).

15. Walter Batsell, *Soviet Rule in Russia* (New York: Macmillan, 1929).

16. The claim being made here is not that this parallelism has gone unnoticed—quite the contrary—but that its significance has not been fully understood. Rigby himself cited the existence of "parallel party and governmental hierarchies, with their overlapping jurisdiction and blurred division of labor" as one of the key characteristics that differentiated the Soviet "mono-organizational society" from a run-of-the-mill "bureaucratic model." Rigby, "Stalinism," p. 55. By contrast, Leonard Schapiro, another outstanding scholar of Soviet politics, wrote what he called a "biography of the party." He thus inadvertently reduced not just the Soviet political system but the revolution itself to a history of the Communist party, ironically mimicking Soviet practice. Schapiro, *The Communist Party of the Soviet Union* (New York: Random House, 1960; 2d ed., 1971). My remarks on these matters were stimulated by the brief discussion of the "peculiar dualism" of the party and

state by Solomon Schwarz, "The Communist Party and the Soviet State," *Problems of Communism* 2, no. 1 (1953): 8–13.

17. Few if any contemporaries understood the political events of the second half of the 1930s. Even John Scott, an extraordinarily penetrating analyst of Magnitogorsk in the 1930s, was at a loss. In an earlier draft of his memoir, he wrote: "in some years, perhaps, this and other mystifying incidents connected with the struggle for power in the Soviet Union and the purges will be clarified. I only know that Kirov's assassination for the Soviet Union and Lominadze's suicide for Magnitogorsk began long and devious chains of nefarious police activity." Scott Papers, loose-leaf draft of "Behind the Urals," p. 106.

18. What reads as a grotesque tale of sadism and only partial tragedy (owing to the victim's complicity in the creation of the system) is given added eccentricity by Conquest's apparent obsession to "prove," largely with citations of conversations overheard by defector Chekists or camp prisoners, the validity of high-end figures—"in the tens of millions"—for the number of arrests and the size of the camp population. He implies that the larger the terror's scale, the greater the proof of design behind it. In general, Conquest relies on often questionable evidence, defended on the suspect grounds that we have no other, and even on tendentious use of evidence, creating something of an impression that he would stop at nothing to advance his arguments. Conquest, *The Great Terror: A Reassessment*, 3d ed. (New York: Oxford, 1990); the book originally bore the subtitle "Stalin's Purge of the Thirties." A Soviet historian, Roy Medvedev, has also viewed the terror as a deliberate "assault" by a power-hungry Stalin, part of what Medvedev called Stalin's "usurpation" of power. Medvedev, *Let History Judge: The Origins and Consequences of Stalinism* (New York: Columbia University Press, 1989; originally published in Russian, 1967). See also the balanced reconstruction of events at the center by John Armstrong, *The Politics of Totalitarianism: The Communist Party of the Soviet Union from 1934 to the Present* (New York: Random House, 1961).

19. Getty challenges one of the standard account's premises that the victims of the terror were chiefly Old Bolsheviks, a point that ought to have been obvious on the basis of readily available published materials. Similarly, one of Getty's fundamental arguments—that Stalin did not initiate or control everything that happened—would seem scarcely worth making, except that this is what Conquest has claimed. But Getty goes much further in his revisionism, labeling Stalin a "moderate" who, while adjudicating among subordinates, always sought the "middle ground"—a view that only a highly selective use of evidence could support. By placing so much weight on the argument that Stalin was not the prime mover, Getty ends up distracting attention from his genuine contributions and driving people into the arms of Conquest. Getty's equivocation—admitting that in the end it might indeed have all been "part of a fiendish and devilish plot," but that thus far "the evidence for such a plot is lacking"—further undermines his overstated attempt at revision. Getty, *The Origins of the Great Purges: The Soviet Communist Party Reconsidered, 1933–1937* (Cambridge: Cambridge University Press, 1985), p. 203. See the trenchant critique of Getty by Jonathan Haslam, "Why Rehabilitate Stalin?" *Intelligence and National Security* 2, no. 2 (1967): 362–67; and idem., "Political Opposition to Stalin and the Origins of the Terror in Russia, 1932–1936," *Historical Journal* 29, no. 2 (1986): 395–418.

20. Getty makes much of the manifest disorder in party records without addressing the question of why such records were deemed so important and what this says about the organization in question. He suggests that the need to improve record keeping was "natural" and therefore benign, dismissing the view that such a campaign could have served as a convenient pretext for terrorizing the party. With faulty record keeping placed at the origins of the great purges, however, the mass arrests do not become more comprehensible. Ultimately, Getty provides no explanation for the terror. What he calls "radicalism" is said to have had a perverse effect: it "turned the political machine inside out and destroyed the party bureaucracy." The unanswered question is, of course, why? "Conflict," to quote Getty's phraseology, "erupted as the center tried to streamline, regularize, and ultimately control local political organizations." But the relationship of "conflict" to mass arrests by the NKVD is never explained. Even within the confines of his own argument, Getty assumes, rather than demonstrates, what constituted "resistance" by local party machines. Similarly, he claims local machines were anxious to protect their "autonomy" without demonstrating that such autonomy existed or what about it was threatened. He writes that the "center wanted to use [the considerable] resentment to force compliance by the officials," without specifying what the center sought compliance with. He argues that "the existence of high-level personal rivalries, disputes over development or modernization plans, powerful and conflicting centrifugal and centripetal forces, and local conflicts made large-scale political violence possible and even likely," as if factional disputes regularly resolve themselves in fantastic stories of wrecking, spying, counterrevolution, and mass arrests. Why a regime built on personnel management could not simply rotate through its own cadres from Moscow to the localities is not addressed. Finally, in Getty's account there is no discussion of the famine or the international situation, and no ideology. He tells us, for example, that the ostensible unanimity at the Seventeenth Party Congress was a deliberately fostered illusion, but he does not tell us why it was thought necessary to foster an illusion of unanimity, or how such a trick could be carried off. *Origins*, pp. 12, 156, 171, 198, 206.

21. Rittersporn suggests that the conflicts within the apparatus grew out of a fear of conflicts within society, because the inefficiency and tyranny characteristic of the apparatus provoked considerable hostility. But even more important for him, internal conflicts made "the system" incapable of functioning "normally." As to why this might be so, Rittersporn proposes that apparatchiks "were more interested in keeping their positions and advancing their careers than in facilitating the regular and controlled working of governmental mechanisms," as if the two goals must be entirely incompatible, or that some discrepancy between them was unique to the Soviet case. As to the nature of the dangers arising out of the system's inability to function, Rittersporn asserts that "the country ran the risk of breaking down into quasi-feudal divisions," but he offers no evidence for this sweeping and astonishing claim. In fact, the center-locality conflict is muted in Rittersporn, who never says how or why he disagrees with Getty. Like Getty (and Conquest), Rittersporn ignores foreign affairs—mentioning the Munich Agreement and the Anschluss only briefly—and ideology. His "inevitable process" is institutionally not ideologically driven, but the genesis of the institutions is not explained. Rittersporn, *Stalinist Simplifications and Soviet Complications: Social Tensions and Po-*

litical Conflicts in the USSR, 1933–1953 (Chur, Switzerland: Hardwood Academic, 1991), pp. 18–19, 211.

22. Despite rhetoric about an "uncontrollable process" Rittersporn admits of a certain historical agency by "factions" within the leadership that represent policy tendencies. These plausible factions remain largely unidentified and mysterious. Moreover, Rittersporn goes much further in his deliberate effort to overturn the standard account, reducing Stalin from supreme despot to "merely the leader, and at times in a quite disadvantageous position," of one of these loose factions—a position that in some ways resembles Getty's. But whereas Getty depicts Stalin as a "moderate," Rittersporn puts Stalin at the head of the radicals who wanted more terror and therefore concludes that the "relaxation" of the terror in 1938 signaled Stalin's "defeat." Ignoring the institutional context of Stalin's authority, Rittersporn reaches this conjecture "Kremlinologically," that is, on the basis of inferences drawn from opaque articles in the official press. Indeed, although he makes use of a wide range of published sources, Rittersporn often argues with such phrases as "in all probability," "there is a high probability," "it was probably no accident," and so on. Perhaps the surest statement in the book is that "obviously the dearth of full and reliable information on the personal maneuvers and about-turns of leading politicians makes any analysis . . . most uncertain." Rittersporn, *Stalinist Simplifications*, pp. 185, 170, 202. Of course, an acceptance of Stalin's supremacy is entirely compatible with the recognition of persistent and fierce bureaucratic infighting. See Armstrong, *Politics of Totalitarianism*, p. 104.

23. Unlike Getty, Rittersporn acknowledges the massive scale of the arrests, which has been substantiated since 1985 by published documents and treatments based on access to previously secret materials in the Russian-language press, many of which Rittersporn cites. But Rittersporn never addresses the issue of why some people survived and others did not. And he says remarkably little about the NKVD or procuracy as institutions and their relations with the Party Secretariat, subjects that have yet to be adequately studied (in part for lack of access to sources). Meanwhile, in a short book on the stunning turnover among top NKVD personnel during the terror, Conquest again showed himself oblivious to the notion that the organization had or pursued institutional interests, summarizing his "analysis" as follows: "everything that happened over these years must finally derive from the special mentality of Stalin and of the Stalinist ruling group." Conquest, *Inside Stalin's Secret Police: NKVD Politics 1936–1939* (Stanford: Hoover Institution Press, 1985), p. 3.

24. Before Getty and Rittersporn, revisionists had been accused of ignoring the terror. Sheila Fitzpatrick, the original revisionist, ended her brief textbook on the revolution in 1932 and called the terror "a monstrous postscript," arguing that "the institutional and social structure and the cultural norms that were to last throughout the Stalin period had been established before the Great Purge, and did not change as a result of it." Fitzpatrick, *The Russian Revolution*, p. 3.

25. The hotel was notorious for never having any rooms for guests visiting the city. As of 1940 it had 230 rooms, of which 177 were occupied by "permanent residents" (one since 1932). Nineteen other rooms had been converted into workshops and offices. *MR*, 8 March 1940.

26. Nikolai Markevich, *Rozhdenie giganta*, p. 7.

27. Iurii Chaplygin, "Lager pressy u gory Magnitnoi," *Sovetskaia pechat*, 1957, no. 10, pp. 46–48. The Soviet periodical press was flooded by features on Magnitogorsk. A typical example is the piece "Gigant i stroitel," *SSSR na stroike*, 1932, no. 1. In addition to being the setting of and or subject for a handful of novels, Magnitogorsk was prominently featured in contemporary Soviet newsreels. At the New York World's Fair in 1939 a special section on Magnitogorsk formed part of the Soviet exhibit.

28. Its entranceway sported proud sculptures of the Soviet state emblem and a Red Army soldier, done by Seregin, the same artist who did the busts of Stalin and Lenin in the foyer of the cinema Magnit. *MR*, 16 June 1935.

29. The city prison, at first referred to as the "house of detention" (*arestnyi dom*), was located in the basement of a converted storage facility (*kladovaia*) in the old village settlement to the southwest of the site, known as *poselok Magnitnyi*. A doctor's report dated 31 October 1930 on this prison commented that there was no light, no boiled water, no change of linen, and few visits to the baths, all of which promoted the spread of disease. He suggested moving the facility to a different locale and observing elementary sanitary conditions. The file contains no follow-up to the report on what measures, if any, were taken. MFGAChO, f. 10, op. 1, d. 4, l. 19.

30. The 1918 constitution declared soviets, in whose name power had been seized in 1917, to be the highest authorities in their territories. The specific powers and organizational structure of soviets underwent modifications over time. City soviets were revamped in 1933, when their role and structure were clarified. See *Spravochnik partiinogo rabotnika*, p. 204; Valerii Andreev, *Rukovodstvo kommunisticheskoi partii gorodskimi sovetami RSFSR (1926–1937 gg.)* (Tomsk, 1990), p. 57; and A. A. Nelidov, *Istoriia gosudarstvennykh uchrezhdenii SSSR 1917–1936 gg.* (Moscow, 1962), pp. 284–303.

31. *MR*, 20 October 1936.

32. Much of the city soviet's work involved handling "complaints," for which the city procurator, working with the city soviet presidium, was ultimately responsible, but which sectionists most often undertook to resolve. During 1936, the city soviet received 2,137 written letters of complaint, 926 of which were protests against fines imposed by the militia. In 240 cases the fines were removed, while in the rest they were lowered. During the first eight months of 1938 the city soviet received around 400 written complaints. The city newspaper grumbled that the "complaint office" of the society merely registered complaints with no follow-up. *MR*, 12 December 1936 and 10 September 1938.

33. In 1936 the city soviet contained eleven "sections": revolutionary legality, finance, municipal economy, industrial construction, trade-cooperatives, health, communications, transport, defense, education, and juvenile delinquency. But only two—orphans (juvenile delinquency), staffed entirely by women, and trade—were thought by city authorities to be working full time. The education section, for example, was composed of 120 people, but far fewer seem to have been active. At a May 1936 meeting of the education section only thirty sectionists were present. Moreover, this was just the sixth meeting in the entire history of the section. Part of the problem, as the newspaper pointed out, was that deputies learned of section meetings only through newspaper announcements, which could easily be missed.

Nor could a meeting's agenda be known in advance. Far more important than problems with publicity, however, was the city soviet's failure to claim real political authority. Still, at least a few people associated with the city soviet appear to have been extremely active. "Who doesn't know grandma Rudenko?" read one newspaper headline about a deputy to the city soviet who was involved in organizing block committees and committees for the protection of urban greenery, selling subscriptions to the journal *Rabotnitsa*, and checking the quality of residential repair work. She also organized the city's Ukrainian chorus. *MR*, 14, 15 and 20 July, and 14 September 1936; MFGAChO, f. 10, op. 1, d. 139, l. 95.

34. Of the eight people on a December 1933 list of the city soviet presidium, three (Zaveniagin, Lominadze, Kiselev) were members of the city party committee bureau (indeed, one was city party secretary and another was the director of the metallurgical complex). A fourth, Gruzdev, was not in the party bureau, but he was the local GPU chief. A fifth (Kefala) the next year was listed as the city procurator and a member of the gorkom; a sixth, Diadiukin, the next year became a member of the gorkom and was listed as "regional military committee." (The positions or status of the remaining two—Marakulin and Iarigorodov—could not be ascertained.) The city soviet chairman in 1933, Kiselev, like most of the early leaders in Magnitogorsk, was a local product, born in Orenburg guberniia in 1888. In late 1933 he was removed as chairman in a scandal, and replaced by Larin, the chief of the city Control Commission-Workers' and Peasants' Inspectorate (KK-RKI). *MR*, 15 December 1933 and 12 March 1934. By 1938 the city soviet had grown considerably in size, to around 250 deputies and 600 sectionists, but it still had trouble convening meetings. The newspaper called attention to a city soviet plenum scheduled for 21 August that could not take place since only 105 people turned out, leaving those assembled without a quorum. *MR*, 3 September 1938.

35. In 1939 the value of the urban infrastructure built and managed by the steel plant was estimated at 150 million rubles. *MR*, 28 February and 17 April 1939.

36. *MR*, 26 March 1937. In 1938, Lapshev, then chairman of the city soviet, explained in a newspaper article that "the buildings of health and educational institutions (hospitals, outpatient clinics, schools, kindergartens, theaters, libraries, clubs, nurseries, and so on), with few exceptions, are also on the books of the metallurgical complex, although practically they are not within the jurisdiction of NKTP and have separate budgets and finances." As a result of what he called the "abnormal situation" whereby the operators were not the owners of the facilities, Lapshev concluded that no one had ultimate responsibility. Maybe this was acceptable in 1929–33, he added, but by 1938 the factory could afford neither the time nor the resources. He suggested transferring everything to the city soviet, the true master of the city, in stages, and creating a separate residential construction agency. In April 1938 Lapshev made this case before the Russian republic government, Sovnarkom RSFSR, but at the time it was tabled and sent to Gosplan for "clarification." *MR*, 11 July 1938; *CR*, 5 June 1938. In early 1939 Fedor Merkulov, the people's commissar for ferrous metallurgy, ordered the transfer from the factory's control of all housing, urban infrastructure and services (roads, trams, water, electricity, urban agriculture) to the city soviet. MFGAChO f. 10, op. 5, d. 46, l. 1, reprinted in Eliseeva, *Iz istorii*, pp. 255–57. More than fifty years later, the steel plant still owned and managed the city.

37. Schapiro, *Communist Party*, p. 247. Apparently, in the aftermath of Stalin's death in 1953, Lavrenti Beria proposed eliminating the party as redundant and relying solely on the state. Beria was soon arrested and executed by the other members of the inner circle.

38. Robert Service, *The Bolshevik Party in Revolution, 1917–1923* (London: Barnes and Noble, 1979). The standard account remains Leonard Schapiro's *Origin of the Communist Autocracy*, whose analysis is distinguished by its examination of the roles played by "opposition" parties in their own demise. But Schapiro employs a simplistic model of politics (positing an almost unconstrained human will) and of the Bolshevik party (as a kind of telos suspended above society). Compare the analysis of Italian fascism in Adrian Lyttelton's *The Seizure of Power*, where politics is viewed as a continuously shifting correlation of forces in which both human will and "structures" are given a place, and in which the influence of the wider movement on events at the center is neither ignored nor simplified.

39. Other "parties" were not expressly proscribed by law, but the class rationale behind the Communist party's position supported an intolerant posture. In 1936, when a new constitution was adopted, Stalin explained that "a party is a part of a class, its most advanced part. Several parties, and, consequently, freedom for parties, can exist only in a society in which there are antagonistic classes whose interests are mutually hostile and irreconcilable." Stalin, "O proekte konstitutsii Soiuza SSR" (25 November 1936), in *Sochineniia*, vol. 2 [14], pp. 164–65. In the public discussions of the constitution, one official argued that "it would be absurd to grant freedom of assembly, meetings, street processions, for example, to monarchists of any sort; it would be incongruous to have people in our streets bearing Tsarist flags and singing 'God Save our Tsar' in the Soviet land. There can be no meetings of lunatics, just as there can be no meetings of criminals—monarchists, Mensheviks, SR's, etc." P. Kataian, "Svoboda sobranii," *Izvestiia*, 6 August 1936.

40. The push for systematization coincided with the beginnings of Stalin's assertion of control over the nascent central apparatus. T. H. Rigby, "The Origins of the Nomenklatura System," in Inge Auerbach et al., eds., *Felder und Vorfelder russischer Geschichte* (Rombach, 1985), pp. 241–54.

41. This dualism characterized the system from the bottom to the top. Stalin was the supreme leader or general secretary of the party, but not the head of state. That title fell to Mikhail Kalinin, the chairman of the Central Executive Committee of the Supreme Soviet, under which was subsumed the government's chief executive, the chairman of Sovnarkom, Vyacheslav Molotov. Only the Supreme Soviet could make laws, but decrees (*postanovleniia*) with the force of law were issued in the name of both the Sovnarkom and Central Committee of the party, and signed by Molotov and Stalin.

42. Chapter 10, article 126, as translated in Unger, *Constitutional Development*, p. 156; see also Schwarz, "The Communist Party and the Soviet State," p. 9. As Milovan Djilas observed, "The 'directing role' of the party in the 'building of socialism' is nothing but the old theory regarding the avant-garde role of the party with respect to the working class." Djilas, *New Class*, p. 71.

43. Protocols of meetings of the Urals obkom between 1930 and 1934, for example, extend to hundreds of pages, and treat every conceivable question concerning Magnitogorsk, from the need for more public baths and laundries to a request

for permission to begin a Komsomol newspaper. RTsKhIDNI, f. 17, op. 21, d. 3985–3986, 3904–3906.

44. To take a typical example, the problem of bed bugs became the subject of a special gorkom decree. In the pronouncement no sympathy was expressed for the sufferings of the tens of thousands of workers being assaulted by the pests. Instead, it was broadcast that "all guilty parties should be turned over to the courts." Presumably, this did not refer to the bugs themselves. Nor did it refer to those party and government leaders who demanded the construction of a huge factory without planning for even minimal housing, sanitary, and medical conditions for an urban population. GARF, f. 7952, op. 5, d. 389, l. 17.

45. Some of these points have been suggested by Milosz, *The Captive Mind*, pp. 76–78, 197–98, 207. By contrast, the Nazis expressed their purpose and public image—youthful energy combined with a rebirth of national pride and military glory—less through indoor meetings than outdoor rallies and marches. See William Sheridan Allen, *The Nazi Seizure of Power: The Experience of a Single German Town 1922–1945* (New York: Franklin Watts, 1984), pp. 42–52, 202–16. According to this case study of Northeim, except for the years leading up and immediately after the takeover, the Nazi party appears to have existed at a far lower level of political and ideological intensity than did the Bolshevik party in Magnitogorsk. Not only did almost all the locally prominent Nazis survive their own regime in Northeim, but virtually all the former Social Democrats did as well!

46. Stalin, in a 1924 address to the Second Congress of the Soviets on the occasion of Lenin's death, described the higher calling of being a party member. Stalin, "Po povodu smerti Lenina. Rech na II Vsesoiuznom s"ezde Sovetov, 26 ianvaria 1924 g.," *Sochineniia*, vol. 6 (Moscow, 1952), p. 46. See also Emilian Iaroslavskii, *Chego partiia trebuet ot kommunista*, 2d ed. (Moscow, 1936), pp. 10, 33. The obligatory "candidate" stage of membership, an educative and testing period, was introduced into the party rules, or *ustav*, in 1919 and waved only in exceptional cases. Graeme Gill, *The Rules of the Communist Party of the Soviet Union* (Armonk, N.Y.: M. E. Sharpe, 1988), pp. 23–24.

47. Although they did not of necessity acquire any special bodily marks to indicate their chosen status, many Communists were recognizable by their jackboots, leather jackets (*kozhanka*), and workers' caps or pointed hats with a red star (*budenovka*), sometimes covering shaved heads, "Civil War style"; others were identifiable by their dapper suits, lapel pins, and fedoras. Every Communist was distinguished by possession of a party card (*partbilet*).

48. According to the 1934 edition of the party rules (*ustav*), "a party member is anyone who accepts the party program, works in one of its organizations, submits to the decisions of the party, and pays membership dues," which were calculated as a percentage of salary. The rules specified further that party members were obliged to "observe the strictest party discipline, actively participate in the political life of the party and country, . . . tirelessly work at increasing his or her ideological competence [and] at mastering Marxism-Leninism, [and] . . . be a model in the maintenance of labor and state discipline." Gill, *The Rules of the Communist Party*, pp. 149–50.

49. Until 1990, the Russian republic was the only one without a republic-level

party structure, meaning that obkoms in the RSFSR were subordinated directly to the Central Committee of the USSR.

50. The principle of democratic centralism was first set down, although only vaguely, in the 1906 party rules. Ironically, it seems to have been intended as a way to curb the power of the Central Committee and make it more responsive to the lower-level party organizations. The 1934 edition of the party rules was the first to clarify the meaning of democratic centralism (Section IV, 18) as consisting of four points: (1) the election of all leading organs of the party from the top to the bottom; (2) the periodic report of party organs to their party organizations; (3) strict party discipline and the subordination of the minority to the majority; (4) the unconditionally binding character of decisions of higher organs for lower organs and all party members. Gill, *The Rules of the Communist Party*, pp. 18, 152–54.

51. Fainsod, *Smolensk*, pp. 45, 64–66.

52. Correspondence to and from central authorities concerning Magnitogorsk went by parallel routes of the economic bureaucracy (GUMP and NKTP) and party channels (through the obkom or directly to the Central Committee). In both cases, personal contacts played an important role. In 1934, for example, Magnitogorsk Party Secretary Beso Lominadze (through party channels) wrote to Stalin and Ordzhonikidze, both of whom he knew well, asking for more money for housing and factory construction. RTsKhIDNI, f. 85, op. 29, d. 454, ll. 1–4.

53. One of the principal drawbacks of Getty's work, and indeed of most scholarship based on the Smolensk archive, is that the generalizations about the operation of the Soviet system are based on a rural locality, but are put forth as representative of the whole. Where large factories subordinated directly to Moscow were located, the weight of the obkom was considerably less than in predominantly rural areas such as Smolensk. Had the terror been chiefly a result of center-periphery relations—instead of an outgrowth of the party's church-like status and watchdog role, which were part of the strange dualism of the political system—it most likely would have begun in the factory administrations.

54. In 1930, Magnitogorsk Party Secretary Rumiantsev "thought that the chief of the construction was obliged to carry out the decisions of the local party committee and that the local party committee was in charge of the construction," according to one informed contemporary. "He thought that the local party committee had the right to remove any engineer or worker on the site." When Rumiantsev removed the chief of the electric power station, Chernopiatov, Iakov Shmidt, the chief of Magnitostroi, protested to the authorities in Moscow, and the removal was rescinded. After Shmidt's protest, a note appeared in the local newspaper—controlled by the city party committee—to the effect that management "refused" to carry out the decisions of the party. When Rumiantsev was temporarily away from Magnitogorsk, Shmidt removed the editor of the newspaper, a party-appointed post. Both Shmidt and Rumiantsev were soon removed by Moscow. GARF, f. 7952, op. 5, d. 381, ll. 92–93, 109. Tension between factory directors and party secretaries persisted long after Shmidt and Rumiantsev were removed. Party Secretary Frants Karklin did not get along with Factory Director Iakov Gugel. Ibid., d. 305, l. 215. Nor did their replacements, Beso Lominadze and Avraamii Zaveniagin, enjoy smooth relations. *MR*, 7 November 1987 and 30 July 1988. This duality of power was temporarily resolved with Lominadze's death in January 1935, and then only

because of the growing power of Zaveniagin, a candidate member of the Central Committee. Lominadze's replacement as party secretary, Rafael Khitarov, apparently did not see eye to eye with Pavel Korobov, Zaveniagin's successor. "He is a big individualist," complained Khitarov in an unpublished interview just before Korobov became the Magnitogorsk director. "He entered the party [only] in 1934 [by special dispensation]. He doesn't have experience dealing with the collective. For this reason his methods of interaction with people are sometimes insufficiently collectivist." GARF, f. 7952, op. 5, d. 313, l. 28.

55. The chief of any institution often had to obtain the approval of the district party committee (raikom) before firing, promoting, or even shuffling around party members on the staff, while subordinates, using the authority of raikom, could sometimes make their own recommendations on personnel and other matters. Small wonder that "every Soviet organization," as Victor Kravchenko wrote, was "a hotbed of personal feuds, competing cliques, [and] festering jealousies." Kravchenko, *I Chose Freedom*, p. 343.

56. One Chekist writing soon after the revolution hit the mark when he explained that "the sphere of the Cheka's work is determined by the activity of counterrevolutionary elements. . . . And since there is no sphere of life that counterrevolutionaries have not penetrated and does not show some evidence of their destructive work, the Cheka must intervene in all areas of life." M. Latsis, as quoted in Lennard Gerson, *The Secret Police in Lenin's Russia* (Philadelphia: Temple University Press, 1976), p. 78.

57. In Smolensk, according to Fainsod, the obkom did not supervise the operational activities of the NKVD. Obkom supervision was limited to party matters within NKVD. Fainsod, *Smolensk*, pp. 74, 167. The same situation no doubt applied to the Magnitogorsk NKVD, which was even beyond the purview of the procuracy—the one organization technically required to monitor the NKVD's activities. An investigation of the Magnitogorsk procuracy conducted by oblast authorities in May 1936 concluded that the procuracy was "failing" to follow directives for monitoring the NKVD. Interestingly, the investigation also found that the procuracy was violating its instructions by pursuing investigations without the agreement of economic managers (*khoziaistvenniki*) and issuing sanctions for arrests without basis (15 percent of all cases had to be canceled). Furthermore, the quality of investigatory work by the NKVD was pronounced unsatisfactory: of twenty-five cases sent to the oblast from the Magnitogorsk NKVD in 1935, five were sent back. The NKVD was also accused of violating the time frames for investigations and not properly informing the oblast of cases brought under article 58. The existence of discrepancies between the documents of the NKVD and the procuracy was criticized. Magnitogorsk procuracy: Archival file "Nariad 34/C. [Untitled] 1936 g.," ll. 19–22.

58. In 1934 Party Secretary Beso Lominadze and City Procurator Petr Kefala received reprimands from the Cheliabinsk obkom, for supposedly failing to do anything to prevent the embezzlement and sale of 18,323 kilograms of flour, on information evidently provided by the chief of the Magnitogorsk GPU, Nikolai Gruzdev. Gruzdev's "vigilance" was praised at a meeting of the obkom where the matter was discussed. RTsKhIDNI, f. 17, op. 21, d. 5656, l. 33.

59. For PPOs with more than one hundred members, for example, the party

secretary was a full-time official "released" from the obligation of holding a "regular" job. Secretaries of PPOs became the base from which the gorkoms and obkoms could draw their staff (after 1939, PPO secretaries had to be confirmed by the Central Committee). Gill, *The Rules of the Communist Party*, pp. 37, 51.

60. Already in December 1925, Stalin had observed in his closing remarks to the Fourteenth Party Congress that the party's "leading role" in domestic and foreign policy was the surest basis of the country's successes. This meant, he concluded, that "the question of the composition of the party—its conceptual level, party cadres, its ability to lead in the posing of questions of economic and soviet construction, its relative weight in the working class and among the peasantry, finally, its internal condition generally—is the fundamental question of our politics." *Sochineniia*, vol. 7, pp. 353–63.

61. A local Komsomol organization was founded one month later, in July 1929. By December of that year, the Magnitogorsk Komsomol numbered more than two thousand. Serzhantov, "KPSS—Vdokhnovitel," pp. 111–15.

62. This figure included 3,814 full members and 4,386 candidate members. Serzhantov, "Metallurgi Magnitki v borbe," p. 191, citing PAChO, f. 234, op. 6, d. 31. An analysis of party membership composition in Magnitogorsk as of 1 December 1931 is presented in Eliseeva, *Iz istorii*, pp. 109–15, excerpting PAChO, f. 234, op. 1, d. 28, ll. 9–30. Between 1924 and 1933 the Communist party of the Soviet Union increased its membership from 470,000 to 3,555,000, with the addition of a million new members in 1931 alone. Even with this impressive growth, however, the party still encompassed only some 2 percent of the country's population. Party members were overwhelmingly concentrated in cities. As late as mid-1932 only one in five collective farms had a party cell. T. H. Rigby, *Communist Party Membership in the USSR, 1917–1967* (Princeton: Princeton University Press, 1968), pp. 52, 189.

63. *MR*, 2 September 1938. Unionwide the number of party members shrank to less than two million by 1938, after having risen to 3,555,338 in 1933 (from 1,677,910 in 1930). Rigby, *Communist Party* p. 52. By the mid-1930s the number of party members in Magnitogorsk was significantly smaller than the number of workers in the blast furnace shop, or any of the other large shops of the steel plant. Still, a large number of the city's 2,000-odd party members were in the industrial shops. In June 1936 Rafael Khitarov reported that the steel plant had 633 Communists, including 397 members and 296 candidate members (60 Communists had been expelled from the steel plant party committee during the verification). "This is, of course, not very much for a twelve-thousand-person collective," he remarked. But the percentage of party members in industry (around 5) was at least five times the citywide percentage. *Magnitogorskii metall*, 30 June 1936. In the construction trust, which had more than 5,000 workers, there were 149 Communists in 1938—less than 3 percent. *CR*, 26 April 1938.

64. A January 1933 joint plenum of the Central Committee and Central Control Commission (TsKK) approved the purge, directing the politburo and the TsKK presidium to handle the details of its organization. *Pravda*, 13 January 1933, reprinted in *KPSS v rezoliutsiiakh i resheniiakh s"ezdov, konferentsii, plenumov TsK*, vol. 5 (Moscow, 1971), p. 89.

65. As of January 1932, when Magnitogorsk claimed 7,376 Communists, including 3,346 full members and 4,030 candidates, 60 percent of the membership

was listed as having joined during the period 1929–31, according to Magnitogorsk Party Secretary Frants Karklin, who spoke at the Fourth City Party Conference. Karklin emphasized that in the half year since the Third Party Conference of June 1931, the Magnitogorsk organization had added more than 2,000 members and candidates. *Magnitogorskii komsomolets*, 20 January 1932; Serzhantov, "Metallurgi Magnitki v borbe," p. 191, citing PAChO f. 234, op. 6, d. 31. The Komsomol, too, grew rapidly. See M. F. Nenashev, "Detishche partii i naroda," in *Magnitka: Kratkii istoricheskii ocherk* (Cheliabinsk, 1971), p. 8; and Zuikov, "Komsomol," pp. 189–90. Figures for the Magnitogorsk party organization counted Communists in the entire raion, which included surrounding villages.

66. The text explaining the purge made a point of mentioning previous purges and legitimizing the party's right to conduct this kind of operation. The preamble to the directive was as follows: "The Communist party has continually demonstrated concern for the purity [*chistota*] of its ranks, replenished by leading representatives of the working class, toiling peasantry, and Soviet intelligentsia and freeing itself of people unworthy of the high title of a Communist. In the course of two and a half years (from the end of 1930 to the beginning of 1933) 1.4 million people entered the party. The majority of them were active participants of socialist construction. But in a number of cases enrollment in the party was conducted indiscriminately, without a thorough verification, as a result of which alien elements turned up in the party." *Pravda*, 29 April 1933, reprinted in *KPSS v rezoliutsiiakh*, vol. 5, pp. 98–103.

67. This statement appeared in a lead editorial, which emphasized the connection between covert opposition to collectivization and the need for a cleansing of the party ranks. *Pravda*, 11 December 1932.

68. In the fall of 1932, around the time of a Central Committee plenum, two small groups of party officials were discovered to have had conversations regarding the removal of Stalin. One group produced a revealing written document, the "letter of the eighteen Bolsheviks" or "Riutin platform," whose existence was widely rumored in Moscow at the time. The other was accused of forming an underground troika. All eighteen of one group, and two of the three in the other, were expelled from the party. Stalin evidently urged harsher penalties, including execution for Riutin, but was rebuffed. Although the threat from these actions to his leadership was minuscule, they seemed to have had a deep effect on Stalin, who was also apparently shaken by the "protest" suicide of his wife Nadezhda on the night of 8–9 November 1932. The events of this period of late 1932 have been plausibly seen as the basis for his launching of the terror four years later. See Haslam, "Political Opposition," pp. 396–98; *Sotsialisticheskii vestnik*, 7 September 1932; *Pravda*, 13 January 1933; *Iunost*, 1988, no. 11, pp. 22–26; *Izvestiia TsK KPSS*, 1989, no. 6, pp. 103–15; Medvedev, *Let History Judge*, pp. 327–34; Tucker, *Stalin in Power*, pp. 204–22.

69. Rumors in the émigré press of "widespread opposition" to Stalin, including the casting of hundreds of votes against his reelection to the Central Committee at the Seventeenth Party Congress in January–February 1934, betrayed an inclination toward wishful thinking. An examination of archival materials relating to the voting at the Seventeenth Congress failed to turn up evidence of falsified ballots. *Iz-*

vestiia TsK KPSS, 1989, no. 7, pp. 114–21. For the rumors: *Sotsialisticheskii vetsnik*, 25 February 1934; and *Biulleten oppozitsii*, 1933, nos. 33 and 34.

70. Victor Kravchenko, who himself went through the process, has left behind one of the best descriptions. Kravchenko, *I Chose Freedom*, pp. 132–47. During the Medieval Inquisition, advance notice was given of a visit by the inquisitor so that the population could be summoned and encouraged to come forward with information. As that episode's leading historian wrote, "No one could know what stories might be circulating about himself which zealous fanaticism or personal enmity might exaggerate and carry to the inquisitor." One pope, Gregory IX, "boasted that on at least one such occasion, parents were led to denounce their children, and children their parents, husbands their wives, and wives their husbands." Henry Charles Lea, *A History of the Inquisition of the Middle Ages*, vol. 1 (New York: Harper, 1888), pp. 369–73.

71. The proper attitude to take toward one's expulsion or demotion was presented in the Magnitogorsk newspaper under the heading "How the Communist Filatov matured." During the purge Filatov was said to have been demoted to candidate status on the grounds of political illiteracy. "From this Filatov came to the proper conclusion," explained the newspaper. He completed an evening course in the party school and continued his study in a circle on party history. "Politically he has seriously matured," and had become "very active" in working on the wall newspaper. Two and a half years later, Filatov was raised back to full member status. *MR*, 26 February 1936.

72. The initial first secretary of the Magnitogorsk party organization was Vlasov, whose tenure did not last very long. In February 1930, Vasilii Dudin was made first secretary. He, too, was soon replaced (neither Vlasov's nor Dudin's ultimate fate could be ascertained). In July 1930 G. K. Rumiantsev became party secretary, but in January 1931 he was dismissed along with the entire Magnitogorsk bureau for "right opportunism" (one memoir from 1936 remarked in passing that Rumiantsev was "now dead"). Frants Karklin, a Latvian from Pskov whom one official recalled as "politically knowledgeable," took over the local party leadership in January 1931. In August 1932, Karklin was promoted to the Sverdlovsk city party committee (he was arrested and executed there in 1937). Karklin's successor in Magnitogorsk was Spirov, who was remembered as "a big talker [who] did nothing." Spirov's ultimate fate could not be ascertained. GARF, f. 7952, op. 5, d. 38, l. 9. See also ibid., d. 311, l. 88; d. 381, ll. 31–32; d. 347, l. 15; d. 309, l. 138; and d. 305, l. 215; *MR*, 24–28 July 1933; and Galiguzov and Churillin, *Flagman*, p. 27.

73. In September 1933, the composition of the Magnitogorsk purge commission was changed following a visit to the site by representatives of the Central Control Commission (in the wake of Ordzhonikidze's July 1933 visit). The chairman of the local purge commission, A. Ia. Savelev, was removed from both the Magnitogorsk purge commission and the city control commission (GorKK) in connection with his alleged failure to investigate the 1933 ORS case properly (see chapter 6). Savelev was replaced on the purge commission by Matvei Larin, who also became chairman of the GorKK. *Pravda*, 7 September 1933. Back in July 1933, A. T. Kolbin, a member of the gorkom responsible for conducting the purge in the countryside surrounding Magnitogorsk, was said to have visited a village party organization to prepare them for the upcoming purge and to mobilize them for food

deliveries. According to a GorKK report, however, "Kolbin took an active part in a collective drinking bout organized by the leadership of the state farm under the guise of a hunting expedition in the woods." Kolbin denied the charges, but the GorKK stood by them, and he was expelled from the party. GARF, f. 7952, op. 5, d. 294, ll. 47, 51–52.

74. The purge was also said to have increased the number of Communists actually taking part—as opposed to on paper—in socialist competitions and shock work, and in technical education courses. Many Communists lost their shock worker rations. PAChO, f., op. 1, d. 188, ll. 190–96, as reprinted in Eliseeva, *Iz istorii*, pp. 165–71.

75. Here is the case of one person exposed as an impostor, according to contemporary testimony: "Stepanov worked in the technical department as a subordinate to the chief mechanic, a nonparty man (Khabovskii) who, knowing Stepanov was a party member, flattered him. We had a bad habit, particularly among specialists. If someone was a party member, you had to flatter him . . . and not look into his work. Such was the treatment of the 'Communist' Stepanov. This Stepanov got a nice sum of money, did nothing, and caroused. . . . Once his wife asked me casually why he had no party card. . . . That very night I went to our party organization and inquired. They couldn't find his name in the register. . . . [At first] Stepanov said he was in the register in Magnitogorsk. . . . Then he claimed he was in the party in the Donbas and that his party card was there, but the Donbas party organization had no record of him. . . . When we found out that he was nonparty, we called in Khabovskii and asked what kind of technician Stepanov was. Khabovskii said that Stepanov knew nothing and could not even pass a simple technical test." Stepanov was summoned by the GPU but was said to have fled the city. GARF, f. 7952, op. 5, d. 309, ll. 136–37.

76. In a Soviet dissertation reviewing the results of the 1933 party purge in Magnitogorsk, it was revealed that there had been 6,084 Magnitogorsk Communists when the purge began. Nothing was said, however, about the discrepancy between this figure and January 1933 membership totals, which had indicated more than 8,000 local Communists. The author of the dissertation, V. K. Korolkov, who had access to party archives, wrote that 2,591 Communists, or 40 percent of the 6,084 total, were expelled in the purge, leaving 3,489 members and candidates (4 are unaccounted for). Korolkov, "Borba KPSS," pp. 182, 188. Other data conflict with these totals. Lominadze, speaking at the Fourth City Party Conference in January 1934, claimed—according to the account of his speech published in the city newspaper—that of Magnitogorsk's 5,500 Communists, 1,340, or 24 percent, were expelled in the purge. Lominadze added that another 35 percent, or more than 1,800 Communists, were demoted to "sympathizer." Demotion to sympathizer effectively meant being dropped from the rolls, so that by Lominadze's account the Magnitogorsk party organization was reduced by 3,140 Communists, a figure slightly higher than that put forward by Korolkov. *MR*, 15 January 1934. Yet another figure was offered by B. A. Roizenman, chairman of the oblast purge commission, who did not reveal the total number expelled but asserted that the Magnitogorsk party organization shrank by 32 percent during the first eleven months of 1933. *Dvenadtsataia Uralskaia oblastnaia konferentsiia: Stenograficheskii otchet* (Sverdlovsk, 1934), p. 153. Whatever the precise totals, it is clear that during

the 1933 purge a large number of Magnitogorsk Communists were expelled, while many purposefully "vanished." J. Arch Getty has written that "during 1933–34 the party 'lost' as many members as it expelled. While 17 to 18 percent of the party was expelled, the party decreased in size by one-third. The extra 15 percent (or approximately 500,000 persons) apparently withdrew voluntarily or 'disappeared' without the knowledge of local authorities." Getty, *Origins*, p. 55.

77. The Central Committee sent a "closed" letter explaining the verification on 13 May 1935, "On disorders in the registration, issuance, and custody of party cards, and on measures for regulating this matter," which can be found in the Smolensk party archive, WKP 499. This directive specified that "enemies of the party and the working class enjoyed access to party documents, received party cards and protected themselves with them in their infamous work of undermining the cause of the party and the Soviet state." See Fainsod, *Smolensk*, p. 57. In an effort to paint the procedure as "nonpolitical," Getty has asserted on the basis of a Soviet secondary source that the verification was originally planned in October 1934, although he admitted that in any case it was not so named until the May 1935 circular. Certainly the concern with record keeping predated May 1935, but even if the verification had been planned prior to the assassination of Sergei Kirov, this would not make it "nonpolitical." The concern with record keeping was genuine, yet such concern was thoroughly "political," even leaving aside the Kirov assassination and its enormous effect on the atmosphere surrounding the verification. Getty, *Origins*, pp. 58, 232, n. 1. See also Rittersporn, *Stalinist Simplifications*, pp. 44–45.

78. A long article in the Magnitogorsk factory newspaper offered a detailed explanation for the verification:

> Our Communist party was organized and nurtured by the greatest people of humanity, Lenin and Stalin. . . . Our party commands the greatest love and trust of the working people. . . . because during the course of dozens of years all the thoughts of the party, all its actions, have been concentrated in the struggle against exploiters and for a happy life for millions of people. But into our party, which commands colossal authority among the masses, alien people try to worm their way, to wreck our cause while remaining unnoticed. . . . Sometimes aliens, thieves have managed to obtain a party card. This happened where class vigilance was blunted, where 'party economy' was treated carelessly and irresponsibly. Frequently there was an absence of exemplary order in the giving out of party cards and with personnel record keeping (all of this is party economy).

Magnitogorskii metall, 16 September 1935.

79. Many Communists were done in by sudden biographical revelations. See, for example, the case of Kolesnikov. *Magnitogorskii metall*, 1 June 1935 and 12 February 1936. The circumstances of the discovery of the "hidden past" of Shcherinov (secretary of the coke shop's party committee) were remarkable. One associate in the coke shop recalled that Shcherinov "didn't do a bad job, but later it came to light that, upon entering the party he hid the fact that his father had been a big kulak and, secondly, that his father had been a member of an investigatory commission under the White Russian general Kolchak. This became known because a journal appeared in which there were portraits of Shcherinov alongside [Viktor] Kalmykov. The moment when Kalmykov entered the party [in coke construction, Shcherinov's jurisdiction] was depicted. The journal was seen by those workers liv-

ing in the place that Shcherinov hailed from, and they sent a note to us about him. He was removed from his post and subjected to a heavy party penalty. He soon left Magnitka." GARF, f. 7952, op. 5, d. 309, l. 138. The journal was *SSSR na stroike*, 1932, no. 1.

80. In this regard, Krivenkov, of the Magnitogorsk fire-brick shop, was said to have been expelled from the party in 1933 but somehow to have retained his party card. In Magnitogorsk he even made it onto the gorkom plenum, until the 1935 verification of party cards belatedly revealed his two-year-old expulsion. Another Communist, Romanshev, claimed he was a party member since 1917, that he was a hero in the Civil War, and that he had once received the Order of the Red Banner. When asked to show his award, he claimed he had "misplaced" it. "Romanshev was taken at his word!" wrote the factory newspaper. "Then complaints began to arrive about him." He was investigated, records indicating that he became a party member in 1931. At this point, Romanshev allegedly refused to show his party card, creating the suspicion that he might have had it confiscated. *Magnitogorskii metall*, 17 July 1935.

81. When the verification began in Magnitogorsk, there were by one count 3,979 local party members and candidates (of whom 476 were women). Of that number, 2,879 were from the city proper, the remainder belonging to party organizations of the surrounding territory, or okrug (as it was named in a March 1935 reorganization). At that time there were eighty-three primary party organizations in the city. *MR*, 28 March 1935.

82. A. Gavrilov, *Vnutripartiinaia demokratiia v Bolshevistskoi partii* (Moscow, 1951), pp. 98–99, as cited in Getty, *Origins*, p. 98.

83. Within a week of Kirov's death, Lominadze gave what seems to have been a gloomy assessment of the political situation to 3,500 party members, candidates, and sympathizers gathered in the city circus (another 1,600 people listened to a live broadcast at the cinema). *MR*, 8 December 1934.

84. *MR*, 23 December 1934; *Pravda*, 21 and 22 December 1934.

85. *Pravda*, 30 December 1934 and 17 January 1935.

86. The "united front" policy begun in 1934 was officially endorsed at the Seventh Comintern Congress in August 1935. See Armstrong, *Politics of Totalitarianism*, pp. 33–50. The threat of fascism became a prominent theme of party agitprop pamphlets, such as the one by G. M. Dmitrov, *Nastuplenie fashizma i zadachi Kommunisticheskogo Internationala v borbe za edintsvo rabochego klassa protiv fashizma* (Moscow, 1935).

87. The letter, "Uroki sobytii, sviazannykh s zlodeiskim ubiistvom tov. Kirova," dated 18 January 1935 and apparently written by Stalin, was published in *Izvestiia TsK KPSS*, 1989, no. 8, pp. 95–100; see ibid., 1989, no. 7, p. 85, for the information concerning Stalin's authorship.

88. Vissarion "Beso" Lominadze, who was born 6 June 1897 in Kutaisi, Georgia, joined the party in March 1917 (i.e., before the October revolution). From 1922 to 1924 he was a secretary of the Georgian Central Committee, (the last two years first secretary). From 1925 to 1929 he worked in the Comintern as secretary of the Communist Youth International (KIM) and as a member of the bureau of the Central Committee of KIM. He was regarded as a Stalin protégé (according to Victor Serge, Lominadze may have been Stalin's cousin, but no other source makes

such a claim). At the Fifteenth Party Congress in 1929 Lominadze became a candidate member of the Central Committee; at the Sixteenth Congress in 1930, he became a full member. Around this time, Lominadze appears to have made his misgivings about collectivization known. On 1 December 1930 he was removed from the Central Committee along with Syrtsov, chairman of Sovnarkom RSFSR, for participation in what was called "a left-right bloc," after the two had apparently had a conversation. Lominadze was "exiled" to a post in the Commissariat of Supply. In 1932 he became secretary of the party committee at Moscow factory no. 24 for machine construction, where the previous leadership had been dismissed in a scandal. In August 1933, upon his transfer to Magnitogorsk, Lominadze was awarded an Order of Lenin for "energetic and skillful organization of party work at factory No. 24." At the Seventeenth Party Congress in January 1934 he and several other "oppositionists" were permitted to deliver repentant speeches. *Bolshaia Sovetskaia Entsiklopedia*, 3d ed., vol. 15 (Moscow, 1972), p. 7; Serge, *From Lenin to Stalin* (New York, 1973), pp. 48–49; *Pravda*, 2 December 1930; R. W. Davies, "The Syrtsov-Lominadze Affair," *Soviet Studies* 33, no. 1 (January 1981): 29–50; *MR*, 20 January 1934 and 30 July 1988; *XVII s"ezd vsesoiuznoi kommunisticheskoi partii (b): Stenograficheskii otchet* (Moscow, 1934), pp. 118–20.

89. According to a 1988 interview with a Magnitogorsk reporter, Elena Karelina, by Lominadze's surviving son, Sergei, Beso Lominadze was telephoned by obkom secretary Ryndin and ordered to Cheliabinsk. Somewhere along the road, he shot himself, but returned to Magnitogorsk alive. Sergei believes his father would have lived except that NKVD chief Genrikh Iagoda, on the phone from Moscow, ordered an operation to be performed during which Lominadze was given an overdose of anesthesia. I came across no corroborating evidence for this supposition. Mikhail Kopylov, Lominadze's driver, related to the same Magnitogorsk journalist that he drove Lominadze to Cheliabinsk, but because the road was snowed in, they had to turn back near Verkhne-Uralsk. Kopylov claimed that Lominadze told him that he felt sick, and after drinking some cognac, the usually talkative Georgian was said to have gone to lie down on the back seat. Kopylov then heard a shot and, seeing Lominadze slumped on the seat, hurried back to Berezka. Kopylov claimed that Lominadze was already dead when they arrived. Karelina made no attempt to account for discrepancies in these two accounts. *MR*, 30 June and 19 March 1988. One scholar published what he claimed were quotes from Lominadze's suicide note, allegedly read over the telephone to Moscow by the Magnitogorsk party secretary's deputy. No citation for this source was offered, however. Nor was the deputy named. Oleg Khlevniuk, *1937-i: Stalin, NKVD, i Sovetskoe obshchestvo* (Moscow, 1992), p. 119.

90. During an interview with this author in Magnitogorsk in May 1987, Nina Kondratkovskaia recalled several of the rumors then in circulation. John Scott's version of Lominadze's suicide, based on such rumors, appears to be largely correct. Scott, *Behind*, p. 181. See also Margaret Buber-Neumann, *Von Potsdam nach Moskau* (Köln-Lövenich, 1981; originally published, 1957), p. 385; and Joseph Berger, *Shipwreck of a Generation* (1971), pp. 167–69, who recounts a conversation he had in a labor camp in 1935 with someone he calls Mironov, Lominadze's "second in command" in Magnitogorsk, apparently Alperovich. Berger, who knew Lominadze during the 1920s, recalled him as "tall and well-built, exceptionally intelligent and

energetic" (p. 165). Scott, who knew Lominadze a decade later, recalled him as "an enormous Georgian, whose huge body was covered with rolls of fat" (p. 82).

91. Kopylov recalled that Lominadze was buried "without honor" in the Old Magnitnyi cemetery but that several close friends took the risk and accompanied the casket. The driver claimed he was interrogated that night and let go the next day. "I saw plenty during the war," Kopylov told Karelina, "but what I went through those days, I wouldn't wish on my worst enemy." *MR*, 19 March 1988. The burial commission consisted of Zaveniagin, Nikolai Gruzdev (Magnitogorsk NKVD chief), and Freiman from the obkom. *CR*, 15 September 1988.

92. Born in December 1901 in the Georgian village Telavi, Khitarov, an Armenian whose real name was Mkhitarian, grew up in the Georgian capital, Tiflis. He knew Lominadze since the 1920s, when both worked in the Caucasus Komsomol, and replaced Lominadze as the secretary of the executive committee of the KIM in 1929. Khitarov spent several years during the early 1920s in Germany, part of the time under the alias Rudolf Martin, and was also sent to China in 1927. In Magnitogorsk Khitarov evidently conversed periodically with some of the Germans living there, a fact that became the basis for accusations that he was a German spy. *CR*, 14 and 15 September 1988; Vladimir Dmitrevskii, "Rafael Khitarov," in *Vozhaki Komsomola: Sbornik* (Moscow, 1978), pp. 46–131.

93. The article singled out the former deputy secretary of the city committee, Polina Charomskaia, who was expelled as a Trotskyite and was said to have been associated with Alperovich. "At the meeting at which he was expelled," it was said of Charomskaia, "she did not speak out openly, but proceeded to work behind the scenes to warn certain comrades that 'in the matter of the expulsion of Alperovich, it is necessary to be cautious.'" *Pravda*, 5 February 1935. Charomskaia (born 1899) and Alperovich were both shot on 5 November 1937. Although removed from the editorship of the city newspaper in February 1935, Bezbabichev was not immediately expelled from the party. He was transferred to the editorship of the newspaper of the construction trust, *Magnitostroi*. In 1936, however, he was arrested and sent to labor camp, according to information from the Cheliabinsk party archives passed on to me.

94. Another person, Aronson, who had spent seventeen years in the Bund and was then chief of the Magnitogorsk ORS, was also accused of being a protégé of Lominadze. At a party meeting in the ORS on 17 February 1935, Aronson allegedly denied any ties to Lominadze or any wrongdoing. "There might have been suppression of self-criticism," he was quoted as saying, "but it was not conscious." At the primary party meeting his denial was supposedly accepted, but pressure from above led to his expulsion. *CR*, 16 March and 6 April 1935.

95. Scott conveyed what appears to have been the general impression that "in Magnitogorsk, from the first day of his arrival, Lominadze worked like a beaver. An excellent orator, he made speech after speech to functionaries, engineers, and workers, explaining, persuading, cajoling, and encouraging." Scott added that Lominadze "had been in many countries and was a thoroughly cultured person. He knew German literature well, was a fine critic, and something of a writer." Scott, *Behind*, pp. 82–83. See also the highly favorable recollections in *MR*, 2 June 1979.

96. This was the logic expressed to me by Mariia Scott, Nina Kondratkovskaia, and a half dozen other people who recalled the suicide. Rafael Shneiveis, then an

editor of the factory newspaper under the name N. Kartashov, stressed that even party members were kept in the dark, and not told anything of what Lominadze had or had not done.

97. *Partiinoe stroitelstvo*, 1935, no. 5, p. 7.

98. Gabor Rittersporn makes a similar point when he stresses the secretive character of the Soviet state, noting that "ever since the 1920s Soviet politics had been characterized by intricate covert maneuvering in the highest milieux." Politics in the USSR could be seen as a conspiracy, he seems to be saying (without ever actually doing so), because in the Soviet case *it was a conspiracy*. Rittersporn, "The Omnipresent Conspiracy: On Soviet Imagery of Politics and Social Relations in the 1930s," in Nick Lampert and Gabor Rittersporn, eds., *Stalinism: Its Nature and Aftermath. Essays in Honour of Moshe Lewin* (Armonk, N.Y.: M. E. Sharpe, 1992), pp. 101–20.

99. According to a history of the party published in the Khrushchev period, delegates to the Seventeenth Congress "did not believe in the genuine nature" of the capitulatory statements made by former oppositionists. *Istoriia KPSS* (Moscow, 1959), p. 462.

100. Stalin's drive for power could be read in the Soviet press, albeit indirectly. During the political trial of Kirov's supposed assassins in January 1935, for example, one defendant (Evgenii Evdomikov) confessed to having described collectivization as a mad adventure; to having suggested that the tempos of industrialization would turn the working class against the party; and to having asserted that there was no party anymore, since Stalin had usurped its governing role. *Pravda*, 16 January 1935, as cited in Haslam, "Political Opposition," pp. 409–10.

101. As the Polish poet Czeslaw Milosz wrote, "The enemy, in a potential form, will *always* be there; the only friend will be the man who accepts the doctrine 100 percent. If he accepts only 99 percent, he will necessarily have to be considered a foe, for from that remaining 1 percent a new church can arise." Milosz, *The Captive Mind*, p. 214. The Czech novelist Milan Kundera used the imagery of the circle to express a similar point. *The Book of Laughter and Forgetting* (New York: Penguin, 1981), pp. 63–66, 171 (originally published in Czech, 1978).

102. Lea, *A History of the Inquisition*, p. 400.

103. For example, Mikhail Pastukhov, the chief of factory auxiliary shops who joined the party in 1931, was purged in 1933, and during the verification wrote an exemplary act of "repentance." GARF, f. 7952, op. 5, d. 315, l. 19. But Pastukhov omitted a significant detail of his case, according to Rafael Khitarov, who divulged that Pastukhov had been a friend of Alperovich and others of Lominadze's circle and that Pastukhov went to Alperovich's apartment after what Khitarov called the "incident [*sluchai*] with Lominadze." (This was the first mention of Lominadze in the city newspaper since his death ten months earlier.) For his ties to the counterrevolutionary group, Pastukhov was expelled from the party. *MR*, 28 October 1935.

104. *CR*, 2 and 16 April 1935. At the conference the gorkom was replaced by an okruzhkom, with three departments (party cadres, culture-propaganda, agriculture) and a three-person secretariat. Party committees in shops were in some cases replaced by what were called party organizers. To avoid confusion, I will continue to refer to the Magnitogorsk "city party committee," or gorkom, rather than to the okruzhkom.

105. At a meeting of the gorkom bureau on 11 February 1935, Khitarov reportedly refused to endorse the accumulated accusations against a large number of Communists made at many primary party organizations. *CR,* 15 September 1988.

106. In the Magnitogorsk newspaper's account of the Fourth City Party Conference, Khitarov avoided any mention of Lominadze, referring only to "serious political ordeals." *MR,* 30 March and 2 April 1935.

107. *CR,* 22 June 1935.

108. These numbers were cited later, after the verification was annulled. At that time, Khitarov singled out the cases of four Communists denied party cards in the verification: Kulichenko, a locomotive driver in the open-hearth shop, who was found to be a former White Guardist; Danilova, the former chief of a department for children's institutions, who declared her solidarity with Lominadze; Edelshtein, of the factory administration, who in 1927 had lost the right to vote as the son of a kulak and merchant but who in 1930 allegedly bribed his way into the party, claiming that "a party card was necessary for my career, authority, and status"; and Kadoshnikov, who was on the 1933 local purge commission but who was found to have been expelled from the party in 1923. Kadoshnikov had evidently reentered the party in another place in 1924. *MR,* 28 October 1935.

109. *MR,* 4 August 1935. The corresponding order of the obkom was dated 10 August 1935. *CR,* 15 August 1935.

110. Examples of their "mistakes" included the case of Zakhar Prokhorchenko, who stood accused of having served under Kolchak from 1918 to 1920. Despite concealing this information from the party, Prokhorchenko got his party card back from Larin (he was later expelled and arrested). Another case was that of N. Eletskii, who claimed he worked as the chief of a village soviet from 1918 to 1921. "The question arises," wrote the factory newspaper, "what did he work as when the whites arrived in Troitsk okrug?" Larin gave Eletskii back his party card also. As for Umanskii, thirteen party members were said to have been passed by him in less than half an hour. He allegedly admitted that he did not always ask whether a person served in the White Army or was in the "opposition." *Magnitogorskii metall,* 17 August 1935.

111. Umanskii was said to have initially reacted to the obkom decision by announcing that the second verification would show his innocence—a response that was castigated by the obkom newspaper as an indirect indictment of the obkom's decision and thus a clear violation of party discipline. Under repeated and intense obkom insistence, however, Umanskii published a highly negative assessment of his own work in the Magnitogorsk newspaper in late August. On 8 September 1935, he was removed as editor and replaced by A. Selivanov. *CR,* 26 and 30 August, 9 and 10 September 1935; *Magnitogorskii metall,* 11 September 1935. Before his resignation Umanskii was also forced to admit his "errors" at a party meeting. He was defended at the gathering by Tishin, from mill 300, who was quoted as saying that "Umanskii was compelled to conduct the verification quickly in view of his responsibilities as editor of the *Magnitogorskii rabochii*." But Tishin, who also argued that it was necessary to look for aliens less in industrial production than in bureaucracies (*uchrezhdeniia*) and cooperatives, was himself severely criticized and forced to admit his "errors." The obkom newspaper reported that "Communists smashed his speech." *CR,* 26 August 1935. The account of Tishin's actions in the

Magnitogorsk newspaper was printed several months later, and ran as follows: "There's no need to look for alien elements [*chuzhakov*] here; we don't have them at the mill. You need to look for them in the cooperative." *MR*, 18 February 1936.

112. In October 1935 twelve people were removed from the city party committee plenum (but not yet from the party). Several appear to have been Lominadze associates. They were Nikolai Saraikin, Mikhail Eremeev, Petr Kefala, Sabatovskaia, Mordukh "Dmitrii" Gleizer, Aleksei Eremin, Ivan Kalagartsev, Viktor Kalmykov, Vasilii Orlov, Ptitsyn, Boris Abrosimov, and Elena Bibikova. *CR*, 27 October 1935. All were eventually expelled from the party, either that same year or in 1937.

113. The obkom's role in turning the verification into a hunt for former "White Guardists" was reprised throughout the oblast. *CR*, 27 and 30 August, 3 September 1935.

114. The factory newspaper wrote that one Magnitogorsk Communist, Lunaev, "at a meeting to discuss the closed letter of the Central Committee said that in the party organization of the ORS everything regarding party economy was favorable. Such a mood is rotten, and is nowhere acceptable. Such a mood can be lethal." *Magnitogorskii metall*, 17 August 1935.

115. "Our party organization is young and unquestionably more contaminated [*zasorenno*] than others," explained Magnitogorsk Secretary Rafael Khitarov. "People came here from different corners of the country; we know little about the past of many people who entered the party here." *Magnitogorskii metall*, 17 August 1935. Of the 2,384 Communists added to the Magnitogorsk organization during 1930, 634 joined the party for the first time. The remaining 1,750 had been members of party organizations elsewhere. Of the 3,430 added during 1931, a majority came from the site itself. Aleksandra Seredkina, *Borba Magnitogorskoi*, p. 48, citing PAChO f. 349, op. 2, sv. 7, d. 115, l. 125; and sv. 4, d. 35, l. 105.

116. *Magnitogorskii metall*, 10 September 1935.

117. Ibid., 6 September 1935. Four people who came to their appointments without their party cards were allowed in but were given official reprimands. Ibid., 21 August 1935.

118. Of Smarin, a bookkeeper in the blooming mill, the factory newspaper wrote, "he says he was the chairman of a village soviet and all of a sudden he turns up in Magnitka as a bookkeeper. . . . It became known that he had two convictions and did time in a labor colony." *Magnitogorskii metall*, 6 September 1935.

119. In mill 500, where several Communists had been "unmasked" as enemies of the people, Khitarov himself conducted the verification. There, candidate member Andrei Koptev was said to have stated that he served in the White Army for six months. But on his personnel card he had written two months, and during the first verification he said a month and a half. *Magnitogorskii metall*, 3 September 1935.

120. Leonid Riabchenko of the central electrical station, when asked why he was not active, allegedly answered, "I'm in a bad mood right now, so I can't conduct any party work." He once supposedly summoned all the staff of the central electric station for an emergency, and when they were all assembled he greeted them with a laugh, "Today is April 1, don't believe anyone." *Magnitogorskii metall*, 12 September 1935. A party member since 1920 Riabchenko was expelled from the party "as a self-seeker and Philistine who conducts demoralizing agitation," according to

information from PAChO provided to the Magnitogorsk gorkom in 1989 and shown to me.

121. Timofei Kharchenko of the central electrical station was said to have "submitted a clarification to the party organization in which he admits that he had served in the White Army longer than it said in his short-form personnel sheet. On his personnel sheet it says that he served two months, but now he says he served six to seven months." A final decision on Kharchenko's status was postponed, pending clarification of what was called his "social visage" and the truthfulness of his latest submission. In fact, he was expelled. *Magnitogorskii metall*, 21 August 1935. During the Medieval inquisition, those who came forward during the "time of grace" (fifteen to thirty days) and confessed their heresy were promised "mercy," meaning either immunity or lesser punishments. Lea, *A History of the Inquisition*, pp. 369–70.

122. The charges were mentioned in a report on the results of the verification in Saratov oblast by Central Committee Secretary Andrei Zhdanov. *Pravda*, 12 July 1935, as cited in Getty, *Origins*, p. 106.

123. At this time total membership was given at 2,810. *Magnitogorskii metall*, 28 October 1935. The reasons for expulsion were specified as follows: 84 for hiding service in the White Army, 72 for being class aliens, 14 for being Trotskyites and double-dealers, 6 for hiding their criminal records, 40 for moral reasons, and 4 for constituting "ballast." No reason was given for the remaining 14 expulsions; there was a note that 6 cases were still awaiting clarification. *MR*, 28 October 1935. It seems likely that with the notable exceptions of those accused of ties with Lominadze (the Trotskyites and double-dealers), most of those expelled were rank and file members. In Smolensk, according to Fainsod, the verification, like the purge, "made virtually no dent on the party apparatus itself." Fainsod, *Smolensk*, p. 230.

124. By way of illustration, Kefala cited three cases—those of Veniamin Edelshtein, Mikhail Smagin, and Vasilii Bogomolov—all of whom were sentenced to five years' loss of freedom. Kefala also reported that no one in the procuracy had a party card withheld, although one judge had, for giving two different dates of service in the White Army. Magnitogorsk procuracy: Archival file "Nariad 34/C. [Untitled] 1936 g.," ll. 6–7, 10.

125. According to the summary of Ezhov's report in *Pravda*, reprinted in the Magnitogorsk newspaper, the principal result of the verification was that party organizations "have to a considerable extent overcome their organizational laxity, have brought order into the registering of party members, have made a better study of Communists, and on this basis have promoted many new and capable persons to leading positions." *Pravda*, 26 December 1935; *MR*, 27 December 1935.

126. In December 1935 the oblast newspaper reported that 154 of Magnitogorsk's 1,741 party members and 92 of its 1,022 candidate members lost their party cards, a total of 246 people, 9 percent of the membership. *CR*, 16 December 1935. Then, in February the Magnitogorsk factory newspaper reported that the number of expulsions was 334, or 12 percent. *Magnitogorskii metall*, 16 February 1936. In the countryside, party cards were confiscated from 18 percent of the membership. "It is no secret to anyone," Khitarov commented, "that party life in village organizations is on a much lower level than in the city organization." *MR*, 14 February 1936.

127. *Magnitogorskii metall*, 6 September 1935.

128. Getty's chapter on "radicalism and revival" is perhaps his best (even though he does not relate these themes to the formation and history of the party prior to the 1930s). Particularly valuable is his analysis of the personalities and roles of Zhdanov and Ezhov. Getty, *Origins*, pp. 92–112.

129. In the fall of 1936 the newspaper reported what it condemned as an all too typical party meeting, which seemed to have no purpose, in the coke shop. *MR*, 3 October 1936.

130. Edelshtein, when asked during the document exchange why he had joined the party, allegedly responded, "Having gotten a party card I pursued the goal of creating for myself a career, and attaining a high official position." To the same question Mikhail Smagin, accused of having hid his kulak past, supposedly stated he had wanted to become a Communist "to enter into trust and receive a good post, since before entering the party I saw that partyites [*partiitsy*] live better, are trusted more, and advance more rapidly in their posts." Similarly, Vasilii Bogomolov, said to have hid his White Army past, allegedly remarked, "Being nonparty until 1932, I worked as a charge-hand [*desiatnik*] at the mine, but after my acceptance into the party as a candidate I was elevated to foreman [*shteiger*]." Magnitogorsk procuracy: Archival file "Nariad 34/C. [Untitled] 1936 g.," ll. 6–7, 10.

131. *Magnitogorskii metall*, 6 September 1935.

132. *MR*, 16 March 1936.

133. *Magnitogorskii metall*, 10 September 1935. Back on 22 August 1935 the Central Committee issued a decree stating that there was not enough party work in factory shops. Ibid., 22 August 1935.

134. *Magnitogorskii metall*, 24 February 1936. In February 1936 a reorganization of all circles and study classes was carried out. In a published list of participants in the circle for study of party history there were 263 names; in the one for the study of Leninism, 65, and another 154 for the one on "political literacy." It is not clear how many of these people ever attended the sessions. *Set partiinogo prosveshcheniia v partorganizatsii Magnitogorskogo metallurgicheskogo zavoda imeni t. Stalina* (Magnitogorsk, 1936).

135. *Magnitogorskii metall*, 10 February 1936.

136. Rigby, *Communist Party*, pp. 208–9.

137. *KPSS v rezoliutsiiakh*, vol. 5, pp. 248–49.

138. *Magnitogorskii metall*, 23 April 1936. There was also an exchange of trade union membership cards. Ibid., 9 April 1936.

139. *MR*, 5 April 1936.

140. *Magnitogorskii metall*, 30 June 1936.

141. Of the various document verifications and exchanges, Victor Kravchenko wrote that "the whole procedure looked like a police documentation rather than a record of members of a political organization." The point, of course, was that they were both. Kravchenko, *I Chose Freedom*, p. 306.

142. A critic for the city newspaper deemed the film a success for its resemblance to real life and its simplicity. *MR*, 6 May 1936; *CR*, 6 May 1936.

143. As a result of the exchange, 14 people had their party cards confiscated: 6 for passivity, 4 for concealing their background, 1 for a counterrevolutionary conversation, and 3 for unspecified reasons. Two members had their status reduced to

candidate, and 2 others were demoted to sympathizer. Altogether in the city 2,130 communists (1,342 members and 788 candidates) received new party cards. Another 9 were expelled in the okrug. Total membership in the Magnitogorsk party committee, including the okrug, was given as 3,107. Of the 977 Communists then outside the city, 656 were full members and 321 were candidates. *MR*, 22 August 1936.

144. According to Khitarov, dues were being paid, attendance at meetings was up, primary party organizations had a much better knowledge of their members, passive Communists were being made active, and a large pool of "promotable" Communists had been discovered. Less happily, Khitarov pointed out that three Communists had already lost their new party cards, that the production plan was not being fulfilled, that construction was even further behind, and that in gathering the harvest, Magnitogorsk okrug was last in Cheliabinsk oblast. In the course of the report Khitarov denied the allegation that it was impossible to live in Magnitogorsk, asserting that life there was wonderful. *MR*, 22 August 1936.

145. On the fabrication of the trial, see *Izvestiia TsK KPSS*, July 1989, no. 8, pp. 78–94. See also Medvedev, *Let History Judge*, pp. 354–57, 389–90; and Armstrong, *Politics of Totalitarianism*, p. 51. Noting that Trotsky did have some contact with a few sitting party officials (largely through his son Leon Sedov in Berlin), Getty concludes that he therefore had "a clandestine organization inside the USSR," without, however, providing any indication of its size and goals. Getty also neglects to say whether this "organization" plotted or had the wherewithal to carry out the political murders of which it was accused. Moreover, in an apparent contradiction, Getty himself notes that abroad, "Trotsky's and Sedov's staffs were thoroughly infiltrated, and Sedov's closest collaborator in 1936, Mark Zobrowski, is said to have been an NKVD agent." In other words, to the extent that a "clandestine organization" existed inside the USSR, in all likelihood it consisted primarily of NKVD provocateurs working to detect party officials with "Trotskyite" sympathies. Getty, *Origins*, pp. 119–22.

146. The letter, "O terroristcheskoi deiatelnosti Trotkistsko-Zinovevskogo kontrrevoliutsionnogo bloka," which contains lengthy excerpts from the defendants' interrogations, was published, along with a two-page facsimile of an earlier version showing handwritten editorial corrections made by Stalin, in *Izvestiia TsK KPSS*, July 1989, no. 8, pp. 100–115.

147. During such discussions problems with documents were said to persist. For example, minutes of party meetings at which expulsions had been voted were said to be missing. There was sometimes a lack of attendance records, and many petitions by Communists were sitting unanswered in files. Primary party organizations were said to be lacking elementary information about their members, such as the duration of party membership (*stazh*) and social position. And restricted access documents were supposedly being kept in unlocked desk drawers. Serious as the implications of such reports were, however, far more serious were the mounting accusations against party members. *MR*, 24 February and 23 September 1936. In 1938 the city newspaper continued to carry warnings of destroyed and stolen documents, and of documents unsafely kept in unlocked cabinets. Finally, an order was issued that all documents of primary party organizations were to be turned over for safekeeping to the gorkom. *MR*, 2 June 1938.

148. *MR*, 24 August 1936. During the Inquisition, because an accused heretic was assumed to be guilty, persistent denial of guilt and assertion of orthodoxy rendered a person an obstinate heretic to be turned over to the secular arm and burned at the stake. Lea, *A History of the Inquisition*, p. 407.

149. As of late August 1936, the Lominadze crowd was said to include Dalinger, Kefala, Andrei Sulimov (of the factory auto-transport shop who had evidently claimed to have headed the Bolshevik party organization in Beloretsk in 1918, but was said to have headed an SR organization), Evgenii Kudriavtsev (a city soviet official), Elena Bibikova (a judge), Grigorii Novikov (auto transport), Likhachev, Nikolai Zentsov (an assistant to the factory director), Buriavskii, Abram Blitshtein (manager of the city department store), Kozunina, Zhukov, "and others." *Magnitogorskii metall*, 28 and 29 August 1936. The obkom's journal of party affairs identified other members of the "Lominadze group" as Zhukov (industrial construction), Kurkumelis (auxiliary shop), and Kuprikov (electrical power station). *Partiinyi rabotnik*, nos. 9–10, August–September 1936, p. 72. In September 1936, an article appeared in the Magnitogorsk newspaper about a "Trotskyite band" that had been lodged in the paper's editorial offices, and was supposedly headed by Redak. Former editor Malyshev was accused of having defended Redak, forcing the latter out only reluctantly (after which Malyshev himself was removed). Malyshev's replacement, Bezbabichev, was accused of having reinstated Redak. Although Bezbabichev wrote articles after Lominadze's suicide unmasking Trotskyites, he was said to have let Redak take a vacation and thus leave Magnitogorsk. These developments were reported by R. Shneiveis and A. Selivanov. The latter had replaced Bezbabichev in February 1935 as editor of the city newspaper. *MR*, 2 September 1936. The subsequent fate of Redak could not be determined.

150. *CR*, 15 September 1988.

151. Ibid.

152. *Magnitogorskii metall*, 27 August 1936. Notwithstanding such shows of vigilance, Vasilev himself was expelled in 1938.

153. Evgenii Kudriavtsev was said to have asked to be allowed to go to Moscow to study. His request was granted. During the verification, however, it was discovered that the department in the city soviet he headed was in disarray. Moreover, he had come to Magnitogorsk with Lominadze, and for a time they shared an apartment. (For some unknown reason, Kudriavtsev was not expelled after the suicide.) His request to study in Moscow was interpreted as a wish to flee, abetted by his boss, Dmitrii Snopov, the chairman of city soviet. "In Magnitogorsk Kudriavtsev smashed his head," Snopov reportedly said. "Here he had no options. For this reason we decided to let him leave to study." *CR*, 21 August 1936. Expelled from the party and later arrested, Kudriavtsev (born 1907) was shot on 7 August 1938.

154. Griaznov named names, mostly former associates of Lominadze, including Popov, the former chief of the open-hearth shop who had been promoted to GUMP, about whom Griaznov remarked, "It's necessary to get him out of GUMP." *Magnitogorskii metall*, 28 August 1936. Griaznov had been the party secretary in the Beloretsk factory when he supposedly requested being sent to Magnitogorsk, where he was trained as a steel smelter (*stalevar*) in the open-hearth shop. He began in the shop as a *chernorabochie* on 5 March 1934, becoming a full-fledged steel smelter in a year and eight months. "At Beloretsk," he remarked, "apprentices

work twenty years and don't become steel smelters." *CR*, 14 November 1936. See also Tatianicheva and Smeliansnkii, *Ulitsa stalevara Griaznova*, p. 4. In 1935 Griaznov worked as a *rabkor*, or worker correspondent, for the factory newspaper. *Magnitogorskii metall*, 12 May 1935. By 1936 he had become one of the city's most visible and rapidly rising party "activists."

155. *Magnitogorskii metall*, 26 October 1936.

156. *CR*, 5 November 1936. For having tried to save Lominadze's life Prokhorovich was later arrested. *MR*, 29 October 1988. Moisei Iakovlevich Ioffe appears to be the person referred to by John Scott as Mikhail Jackovich Jaffe, a wheeler-and-dealer "in a perpetual whirl of petty intrigue" owing to the fact that he was responsible for "all plant administrative buildings, all hotels, living quarters, rest homes, together with all the furniture and other appurtenances, plant automobiles, roads, and so forth." Scott, *Behind*, pp. 183–84. Expelled and arrested in 1938, Ioffe was among those reinstated in 1939. After the war he rose to become a deputy minister in Moscow.

157. According to the obkom newspaper, "In a number of cases during the process of the exchange of party documents, certain party leaders tried to assign each Communist some kind of [activist] position . . . so that no Communists would be left 'unemployed.'" *CR*, 5 November 1936.

158. In his printed public pronouncements Khitarov struck a restrained, although still recognizably "Bolshevik" tone. *Magnitogorskii metall*, 23 October 1936.

159. Such was the verdict passed on Bishoff, of the factory administration, although precisely what he said, and whom he defended, were not specified. Ibid., 9 September 1936.

160. According to Fainsod, beginning with the meetings following the Kirov assassination, long lists of denunciations began to accumulate in the Smolensk party archives. Each round of meetings following the secret letters sent by the Central Committee occasioned further denunciations. Fainsod wrote of "a holocaust of denunciations" that "swept through party ranks" in response to the 29 July 1936 central Committee letter. Fainsod, *Smolensk*, pp. 57–58, 233–37.

161. *CR*, 30 December 1936. Born in 1893 in a village near Cheliabinsk, the son of a tailor, Ryndin joined the Bolshevik party in 1915. During the Civil War he worked as chairman of the Ufa Cheka and as a political worker in the Red Army, after which he returned to a party post in the apparat of his native Urals. In 1924 he became a candidate member of the Central Committee, and in 1927 secretary of the Urals obkom. The next year he was transferred to the Central Committee apparat. In 1930, he became second secretary of the important Moscow obkom, under Lazar Kaganovich, with responsibility for Moscow's large and strategic heavy industry. That same year, Ryndin was made a full member of the Central Committee. In the fall of 1933, for reasons that are unclear, he was sent to Nizhnyi Tagil, becoming party secretary of that raion, a post he had held ten years before. In 1934, when the Urals oblast was divided in three, Ryndin was named first secretary of the Cheliabinsk obkom. Both Nizhnii Tagil and Cheliabinsk were regions of developing heavy industry, Ryndin's specialty. *Bolshaia Sovetskaia Entsiklopedia*, 3d ed., vol. 22, p. 451; see also Nobuo Shimotomai, *Moscow under Stalinist Rule, 1931–1934* (New York: Macmillan, 1991), pp. 30–31.

162. In his report to the conference, Khitarov again cited the total of 334 Communists expelled during the course of the verifications (plus 14 more in the exchange), adding that another 10 had been expelled in the aftermath of the Trotskyite-Zinovievite affair. Whereas the membership had stood at 2,775 at the time of the previous local party conference back in April 1935, now (in December 1936) there were said to be 2,150 local Communists, 1,356 members and 794 candidates (as well as 638 "sympathizers"). Khitarov made no attempt to account for the full 625-person reduction. Some party members had no doubt been transferred to other locales. MR, 29 December 1936.

163. GARF, f. 7952, op. 5, d. 309, l. 83. The Kirov district included the first and second superblocks of the southeastern city, or original "socialist city," Lattice-Wood Town, and the many mud-hut and individual-home settlements in the vicinity. It had an approximate population of 100,000. The Ordzhonikidze district included the largest residential area, the Fifth Sector, along with the western and many northern settlements. It contained an estimated 120,000 inhabitants. The Stalin "district" was not a residential section of the city but encompassed the factory, mine, and railroad (all but the construction trust, which was made part of the Ordzhonikidze district). The city soviet was divided not in three branches but in two, between the Kirov and Ordzhonikidze districts. MR, 26 October and 18 December 1936, 9 January 1937.

164. Accusations of sabotage against Soviet-era officials began during collectivization, but were limited to agriculture. Sobranie zakonov i rasporiazhenii, 1933, no. 19, reprinted in Sbornik dokumentov, p. 339.

165. Pravda, 20–24 November 1936. See the excellent reporting from abroad by Solomon Schwarz, "Novosibirskii protsess," Sotsialisticheskii vestnik, 1936, nos. 23–24, pp. 13–14; and Kravchenko, I Chose Freedom, pp. 329–31.

166. N. V. Zhogin, "Ob izvrashcheniiakh Vyshinskogo v teorii i praktike sovteskogo prava," Sovetskoe gosudarstvo i pravo, 1965, no. 3, pp. 22–32. The output of poor quality goods was one of the "economic crimes" delineated in the 1926 criminal code. In November 1929 a revision of the code (the insertion of article 128a) called for sentences up to five years for "massive or systematic output from industrial or trade enterprises of poor quality goods." In December 1933, a further revision singled out managers and specified sentences of "not less than five years." The crime of wrecking, however, was covered by article 58. In July 1940, after the terror was over, the penalties for crimes charged under article 128a were stiffened and the output of poor quality goods was called an "anti-state crime equivalent to wrecking." See Sobranie zakonov i rasporiazhenii, 1930, no. 2, item 9; ibid., 1933, no. 73; and Vedomosti, 1940, no. 23, All three are reprinted in Sbornik dokumentov po istorii ugolovnogo, pp. 250, 340, and 406. See also Ugolovnyi kodeks RSFSR: Prakticheskoe posobie, p. 117; and Berman, Justice in Russia, p. 80.

167. Of all Magnitogorsk shops, the blast furnace had the nastiest reputation. In the mid-1930s, after another series of incidents involving falling objects, some people refused to return to work there. GARF, f. 7952, op. 5, d. 304, l. 11; ibid., d. 313, l. 15. One official publication on safety revealed that in 1932, 101 of 266 incidents resulting in injury in the blast furnace shop were attributable to fires, mostly caused by molten metal and slag. Apparently, the workers had difficulty operating the machinery. Even after they acquired more experience, workers still had

to contend with insufficient elementary safety equipment—such as goggles—clutters of garbage, the presence of dangerous gases, the absence of adequate ventilation, and the lack of safety training. The recommendations for improving safety given in official publications were highly revealing of the danger and disrepair in the shops. See *Voprosy tekhniki bezopasnosti i ozdorovleniia truda v domennom tsekhe Magnitogorskogo metallurgicheskogo zavoda* (Magnitogorsk, 1935). In Kuznetsk, the most dreaded shop was the coke plant, where in one incident, 26 people died and 75 were injured. Frankfurt, *Men and Steel*, p. 76.

168. A report from the city procurator to First Secretary Khitarov listed 3,545 "mishaps" (*avarii*) in 1935, 103 serious (*tiazhelykh*) and 40 fatal, and for the first eleven months of 1936, another 4,340 accidents, which resulted in 60 fatalities. Magnitogorsk procuracy: Archival file "Nariad 31/C: Sekretnye otchetnosti 1937 g.," ll. 1–3. One newspaper story from the summer of 1936 revealed that "according to by no means complete data, in the previous four months 15,200 work days were lost to injury [*travma*]. An average of 126 workers were out each day." It was not disclosed how long the average injury-related work absence was, nor how many individual workers were involved in the figure of 15,200 work days. Whenever such misfortunes happened, the injured workers' families received material compensation. *MR*, 4 June 1936.

169. In 1937, a new rubric appeared in the newspaper: "With Stakhanovist Labor Liquidate the Consequences of Wrecking." *MR*, 9 February 1937. The attempted revival of Stakhanovism failed, however, and in 1938 enemies and wreckers were held accountable for this too.

170. In the correspondence between the Magnitogorsk factory administration and GUMP, wrecking was often not mentioned, even in the year-end report for 1938. RGAE, f. 4086, op. 2, d. 4398, ll. 9–11; for earlier examples, see GARF, f. 7952, op. 5, d. 185 (Rabkrin reports, 1931 through 1933). Fires, power outages, and breakdowns had always been investigated by the GPU and its successor, the NKVD, but arrests were infrequent, even if, as John Scott observed, "material was accumulating in dossiers." Scott, *Behind*, pp. 84–85, 182 ff. Before 1936, arrests for another form of counterrevolution, anti-Soviet agitation, were apparently more frequent than those for causing breakdowns. In a letter sent to the GPU archives, Aleksandr Panfilov, one of the local writers involved in the Magnitogorsk history project, requested documents on a long list of individuals who had been convicted of counterrevolutionary agitation back in 1931. GARF, f. 7952, op. 5, d. 327, l. 24. A December 1931 investigation of the catastrophic health situation in Magnitogorsk by a Central Committee commission recommended the arrest of the leaders of the city health department. In the event, all were removed, although it is not clear if they were also arrested. The direct, unvarnished language of the investigation's report contrasts vividly with that of the press and pamphlet literature. MFGAChO, f. 10, op. 1, d. 1, ll. 69–79, 80–85.

171. In an internal report to Party Secretary Khitarov, City Procurator Ivan Sorokin concluded that the blast could have been avoided if the gas had been immediately turned off. Instead, a second blast occurred. The shop was said to lack proper ventilation, emergency instructions, and a telephone connection to the gas emergency crew. The three foremen were sentenced to six-, three-, and one-year terms.

Magnitogorsk procuracy: Archival file "Nariad 31/C. Sektrenye otchetnosti 1937 g.," ll. 1–3; MR, 23, 27–29 May 1936.

172. It was said that the coke workers' special milk ration had been delivered with gasoline and kerosene mixed in, a fact the newspaper cited as "a vile sally by class enemies." The newspaper omitted any discussion of what kind of containers the milk was normally delivered in, and for what other purposes they might have been used. MR, 21 December 1936.

173. A repented member of the Trotskyite opposition in the 1920s, Piatakov had evidently at first been appointed the prosecutor at the Novosibirsk trial. For an account of the fabrication of the case against him, see Izvestiia TsK KPSS, no. 9, September 1989, pp. 30–50. See also Fitzpatrick, The Cultural Front, pp. 170–76. In the charges against Mariasin, who had left Magnitogorsk to become chief of construction at the Nizhnii Tagil rolling-stock factory, the vast paper trail left behind by foreign engineers and specialists detailing the future problems likely to arise because of the failure to follow their technical instructions was culled for technically convincing evidence. GARF, f. 7952, op. 5, d. 402, ll. 11–12.

174. Piatakov had appealed for his life. "In a few hours you will pass your sentence," he reportedly told the court. "Here I stand before you in filth, crushed by my own crimes, bereft of everything through my own fault, a man who has lost his party, who has no friends, who has lost his family, who has lost his very self." Report of Court Proceedings in the Case of the Anti-Soviet Trotskyite Center (Moscow: People's Commissariat of Justice, 1937), p. 541.

175. Born in the Belorussian part of the old "pale of settlement" in 1910, Shneiveis/Kartashov made his way to Moscow in the 1920s, finding factory work and joining the Komsomol. In 1931 he was mobilized to Magnitogorsk, becoming a candidate member of the party in 1932. In 1935 he was expelled from the party organization of the printing works, the PPO for journalists, for failing to disclose his nonproletarian social background. At that time he worked as the deputy editor of the factory newspaper, Magnitogorskii metall. In December 1937 he was transferred to Kerch, narrowly escaping the terror in Magnitogorsk. Interviewed in 1989 in Cheliabinsk, where he worked as a journalist and editor for four decades after the war, he expressed no remorse for his actions. "Kartashov" was his wife's maiden name, which he used in place of his own Jewish surname.

176. He was one of five such recipients from Magnitogorsk. The others were Khabibulla Galiullin (a brigadier), Emil Bekker (chief of rolling mill construction), V. A. Goncharenko (chief of the mine), and Avraamii Zaveniagin. Eight others received the Order of the Red Banner. MR, 26 March 1935.

177. MR, 9 February 1937.

178. MR, 6 February 1937. In an internal party memorandum dated 16 January 1937 about a breakdown in the open-hearth shop, Griaznov wrote: "Commission [poruchit] comrades Pridorogin, Pushkov, and Sorokin to investigate the breakdown on the mixer and to inform the plenum of the city party committee about the results by 20 January 1937." The memo was signed "acting secretary of the gorkom Griaznov." Magnitogorsk procuracy: Archival file "Nariad 33/C [Untitled]," l. 1.

179. By contrast, a two-day factorywide trade union conference that took place on 15 and 16 March was poorly attended, failing to reach a quorum. Unlike the party meetings, nothing was at stake. MR, 18 March 1937. Several nasty city so-

viet meetings took place throughout 1937. *MR*, 3 April 1937. Between August and December 1937, there were at least six different chairmen or acting chairmen: Anokhin, L. S. Gapanovich, Maksim Gavrilov, Berg (chief of the militia), Ivan Seredkin, and Malikov. Gapanovich, Gavrilov, and Seredkin were arrested, and perhaps the others were as well. MFGAChO, f. 10, op. 1, d. 270, passim.

180. *CR*, 11 February 1937.

181. According to an article entitled "In Place of Vigilance—Shutting One's Eyes," "for a long time representatives of the German firms Krupp and Reisler, the engineers Braun and Bikker, and also the Trotskyite [Nikolai] Pilakh, bandied about in the fire-clay factory. The design and equipment of this factory belong to above-mentioned firms. It is clear that they tried as much as possible to wreck." The "evidence" adduced for this conclusion included the following facts: there were no spare parts, and the most expensive equipment was housed in a wooden building. Gurevich, the chief of GUMP, had ordered the immediate construction of a stone enclosure, but it would not be ready until the end of 1937. Moreover, there were frequent breakdowns. The shop was down 28 percent of the time, considered "normal" by the shop leadership. As for working conditions, "in tunnels through which the workers were supposed to drag wheelbarrows, there was no light." Who precisely was "shutting their eyes" to all of this was not stated. *MR*, 16 February 1937.

182. The spotlight turned on Konstantin Valerius, the chief of the construction trust Magnitostroi, who admitted at the meeting of the construction committee on 17 February that he had not understood the "political sharpness" of the situation in construction. *MR*, 26 February 1937.

183. The coal storage department was the scene of especially active wrecking, the newspaper wrote. Coal was unloaded "not in the storage area, but all over the shop, in places where it was impossible to move it." At the same time, the newspaper acknowledged that the coal storage shop was not mechanized. *MR*, 26 February 1937.

184. Leontii Metelskii, the chief of factory rail transport, was charged with wrecking for transferring railroad cars, locomotives, and the entire station Ugolnaia to the coke shop "on concession." Evidently, this was harmful, although the newspaper did not explain why. *MR*, 27 February 1937. Metelskii's boss, Ivan Kniazev, former chief of the Southern Urals Railroad (Cheliabinsk), had been accused of spying and wrecking. Arrested in late 1936, Kniazev was one of the defendants at the January 1937 Piatakov trial in Moscow. *CR*, 16 February 1937. Metelskii (b. 1899) was shot on 7 August 1937. *MR*, 24 October 1990.

185. At the steam generating station the ventilation did not work; in the blast furnace electric department cables were exposed and high and low voltage were mixed into one cable. *MR*, 28 February 1937.

186. *MR*, 28 February 1937.

187. "For centuries the people had built and created, always honorably, always honestly, even for serf-owners," marveled Aleksandr Solzhenitsyn. "But now, when for the first time all the wealth had come to belong to the people, hundreds of thousands of the best sons of the people inexplicably rushed off to wreck." Solzhenitsyn, *The Gulag Archipelago*, vol. 1 (New York: Harper and Row, 1973), p. 64. The degree of suspicion and the energies that went into the investigations are difficult to exaggerate. Victor Kravchenko, the manager of a pipe factory in the

Ukraine, reported that when a German-made machine in his factory broke down, "the police-minded swarm of officials . . . was less concerned with restoring operations than with finding culprits." The pressure on managers took a heavy toll, even when they were not arrested. Kravchenko, *I Chose Freedom*, pp. 192, 287. Of the fictional factory director Mark Riazanov, the novelist Anatolii Rybakov wrote: "The factory is he, Riazanov, his life, his death." *Deti arbata*, p. 155.

188. *CR*, 18 February 1937.

189. *MR*, 18 February 1937.

190. Shevchenko (b. 1898) was shot on 7 August 1937. *MR*, 24 October 1990. John Scott, who worked in the chemical shop of the coke plant at the time but soon lost his job, described Shevchenko as "a gruff man, exceedingly energetic, hard-hitting, and often rude and vulgar," and also as "at least fifty percent bandit—a dishonest and unscrupulous careerist." He nonetheless judged Shevchenko "not a bad plant director." Scott's insight into the situation inside the coke plant gives the impression that workers talked among themselves about even the most sensitive issues, and that rumors were rampant. Scott, *Behind*, pp. 175–80, 296–97. Louis Ernst, deputy chief of the tar-distillation plant who hired Scott, was also fired, although not arrested. In 1937 Ernst, under whose supervision the sulphate department, the benzol plant, and the rectification plant were put into operation, was simply told that "an American cannot be trusted in such an important position." Through the intervention of Industry Commissar Lazar Kaganovich, Ernst was reassigned to the Donbas. He spent the war years in the USSR, experiencing the evacuation east. Interviewed by the author, Doniphan, Missouri, 1986; see also Ernst, "Inside a Soviet Industry," *Fortune*, October 1944, pp. 116–19, 172–78.

191. In the blast furnace shop, thirty-three people were apparently arrested. Moshkovtsev, "Magnitka (1743–1941)," p. 180.

192. *MR*, 16 and 17 February, 18 April 1937.

193. *MR*, 17 February 1937. The delay in the completion of the coke plant's chemical shop until several years after the coke ovens had begun operation, which led to the loss of valuable chemicals, was also cited as prime evidence of wrecking, rather than a consequence of planning decisions dictated by circumstances.

194. *MR*, 20 February 1937, which bore the front-page headline, "Wrecking in the Coke and Chemical Plant—A Serious Lesson," carried a notice of Ordzhonikidze's death.

195. One doctor wrote an urgent article on the problem of factory ventilation for the local newspaper: "In the open-hearth shop there are cases of gas poisoning. At first glance, it is hard to believe that it is possible for anyone to be poisoned by fumes, because the building is not yet completed (it lacks a bracing wall on the south side through which air flows freely). But research conducted by the scientific station's inspection brigade in the summer of 1935 and the winter of 1935–36 showed that not only the inside of the shop, but even the exterior air around the building is saturated with dangerous gases." When the building was fully enclosed, the situation would only be worse. The doctor concluded by insisting that ventilation should be provided while a shop was being built. He did not mention wrecking. *MR*, 16 May 1936. See also *MR*, 11 April 1937.

196. In 1933, there were officially twenty deaths from industrial causes at Magnitogorsk; during the first quarter of 1934 there were another seventeen, and in the

second quarter of that year, fourteen more. Thus, in a span of eighteen months, there were more than fifty factory-related deaths. This grim outlook did not improve much. During the first four months and twenty days of 1937, there were twenty-two deaths, a yearly average of almost sixty. RGAE, f. 4086, op. 2, d. 1367, ll. 1–11; MFGAChO, f. 99, op. 10, d. 1091, l. 179.

197. Stalin's report delivered on 3 March, was reprinted in the Cheliabinsk and Magnitogorsk newspapers on 30 March, one day after it appeared in *Pravda*. The "delay" was not explained. An account of the plenum, apparently based on Central Committee archives, is given by Dmitrii Volkogonov, *Triumf i tragediia*, vol. 1, pt. 2 (Moscow, 1989), pp. 203–9.

198. Stalin, *Sochineniia*, vol. 1 [14], pp. 196, 207–8.

199. "Golovokruzhenie ot uspekhov," *Pravda*, 2 March 1930, reprinted in *Sochineniia*, vol. 12, p. 199.

200. When it came to industrial production, on which everyone knew the country's security was founded, "the numerous incidents of wrecking showed that it was not enough merely to master technology," wrote *Pravda*, echoing Stalin's plenum report putting forth a new slogan: "Master Bolshevism." A new rallying cry was needed, the central newspaper explained, for the "political education of cadres and the liquidation of political carelessness." *Pravda*, 29 March 1937.

201. What follows is based on the version of the Magnitogorsk meeting published in the city newspaper. There was broad similarity, although differences in emphasis, between this account and the one in the obkom newspaper, which was shorter. *MR*, 26 March 1937; *CR*, 27 March 1937.

202. Zakharov wrote that the gorkom had "a list for potential promotion on which there are one hundred thirty people," but that thirty people from the reserve long ago left Magnitogorsk, while others have even been expelled from the party." Zakharov further charged that there was poor attendance by the leadership at primary party organization meetings, and that of the last twenty-five admissions into the party, only two were workers (one of whom had already been unmasked as an alien), "in the largest worker's organization in the oblast." He singled out Konstantin Valerius for special condemnation, and claimed that at the exhibition for the five-year anniversary of the Magnitogorsk factory currently on show, a picture of Lominadze had been included, as one observant worker pointed out (the implication, of course, was that vigilance was not high). Finally, he faulted Magnitogorsk Communists for failing to interpret "signals" properly, specifically for failing to engage in criticism of MMK Deputy Director Kasperovich, "even though he has been attacked in the newspaper." The Magnitogorsk newspaper picked up the hint, not only in the case of Kasperovich, but also Valerius. Condemnatory exposés appeared immediately, including one on the long "tail" of people Valerius had brought with him to Magnitogorsk in 1935 from Tagilstroi. *MR*, 20 and 21 March 1937; see also *Partiinyi rabotnik*, February 1937.

203. *Pravda*, 9 February 1937. No response appeared in the *Cheliabinsk rabochii* until 14 February, when the *Pravda* article was quoted. *Pravda* repeated its attacks against the Cheliabinsk obkom in an article on 10 March, which was reprinted in the obkom the next day, and again on 13 March, which elicited a vague "acceptance" of the criticism by Ryndin. At an obkom plenum on 21 March, Ryndin delivered a report on the recent Central Committee plenum. Emphasizing at

length the charges against Bukharin and the rightists, he admitted having made errors himself but did not state what these were. The obkom was not about to cave in. *CR*, 22 March 1937. Rittersporn argues suggestively that the attacks against officials not only "intensified the activity of solidarity networks among cadres" but that their heightened "attempts to save each other reinforced the imagery of omnipresent 'plots.'" Rittersporn, "The Omnipresent Conspiracy," pp. 112–13.

204. An incautious remark haunted Kasperovich. He was quoted as having said to someone, "It is not your business to oversee my work. I am a proven person and I know what I am doing. I ask you not to intrude into my affairs." *MR*, 20 March 1937. The first mention of this remark in the obkom newspaper occurred a month earlier. In that version, Kasperovich was quoted as having said to the person questioning his performance, "You're a bit young to check up on me!" *CR*, 18 February 1937.

205. Zaveniagin, who was succeeded by Pavel Korobov, had been director since August 1933. His sudden departure must have added to the uncertainty. *MR*, 16 and 17 March 1937.

206. In the struggle between the leadership of the construction trust—whose necks were on the line for failing to complete projects on time, so no expense was spared—and the bankers—who sought to protect themselves from the consequences of the ensuing financial chaos by exposing the bankrupting practices of the construction management—both sides lost. The investigative organs, it turned out, also had their own agenda. *MR*, 21 and 26 March 1937.

207. *MR*, 18 April 1937. Valerius (b. 1894) was arrested in either 1937 or 1938, and shot on 27 July 1938.

208. This was the only time the word *allegedly* was used to describe the accusations of the various speakers; in this case, the accusation was directed at the newspaper.

209. There was also a two-day meeting of what was called the "economic active" of the factory in April 1937 (almost all the speakers identified were party members). "On the first day of the meeting of the active around five hundred people took part, but on the second day the number of participants scarcely exceeded one hundred fifty people," the newspaper reported, without offering an explanation. "Missing from the meeting were Stakhanovites and party workers of shops; there were few shift engineers." Even worse, from the newspaper's point of view, was that "a number of comrades spoke narrowly about factory matters such that the meeting of the active turned into an ordinary production conference. Only a few speeches were politically sharp and boldly uncovered the fundamental insufficiencies in the work of the factory" (as an example of a speaker who properly understood the nature of the meeting, the newspaper singled out Aleksei Griaznov). Golubitskii, the chief of the blooming mill, made some revealing remarks about the bureaucratic nature of factory management. "Only through Korobov," Golubitskii said, referring to the chief of the steel complex, "is it possible to secure from the rail transport shop a flat car for moving freight. . . . It is necessary to free the director of the complex from these trifles." Korobov gave the opening and closing speeches, but, curiously, his remarks were not printed. *MR*, 8 April 1937.

210. Shurov's comments were not the only ones omitted. During the four-day outburst of accusations and counteraccusations, 115 people were said to have signed

up to speak, of whom 48 were given the floor, but only the remarks of 17 speakers were excerpted or paraphrased in the newspaper. Revealing as it was, much was suppressed from the public account.

211. *MR*, 27 March 1937. In that same issue, it was revealed that the meeting lasted four days (it had been scheduled for three, and the published account gave no indication of the extra day).

212. Shneiveis/Kartashov published a scathing article, "Ingratiators and Toadies in the Factory Administration," in which he reported that A. Sukharev had written a letter of support for Kasperovich. This act took considerable courage on Sukharev's part, but Kasperovich had already admitted his mistakes, and Sukharev's action was self-incriminatory. It seems, however, that Sukharev was not the only one to come forward on behalf of Kasperovich. Charova, the director of the factory laboratory, allegedly made the following remark to a group of engineers in the lab: "Having heard that Kasperovich is leaving Magnitka [for Moscow], they loosened their tongues. But there isn't an ounce of truth in their criticism." Shneiveis made it clear that Charova was worthy of investigation. He also cited what he called the "mutual encouragement" of Shadrin, the chief of the supply department, and his deputy, Dmitriev. "It was pointed out that Dmitriev was a self-supplier, a drunkard, a fumbler, and generally a worthless leader," Shneiveis wrote. "Dmitriev impudently told his co-workers: 'So what, so what. Zaveniagin and I ate from the same pot. They won't do anything to me.'" Meanwhile, Shadrin, who had promised to remove his deputy, instead wrote him an excellent evaluation. "Open the window [*fortochka*] in the factory administration!" Shneiveis exclaimed. "Honestly, it's impossible to breath in here." *MR*, 3 April 1937.

213. *Pravda*, 19 April 1937.

214. *CR*, 15 March 1937. Twenty-eight of the Stalin raikom's thirty-five shop party organizers (partorg) and secretaries were said to have been named directly from industrial production the previous month. *CR*, 14 February 1937.

215. The obkom newspaper reported that of Magnitogorsk's 118 party secretaries and shop organizers, 83 were new, including 35 elected to such a post for first time. *CR*, 28 and 30 May 1937. The city newspaper's accounts of the local party conference were remarkably tame. *MR*, 28 and 30 May 1937. Early in the process, the party organizer of open-hearth shop no. 1, Dmitrii Gleizer, was accused of having run the elections "bureaucratically." What happened was unclear from the newspaper account. Gleizer may have tried to forestall a negative vote against his candidacy. *MR*, 30 March 1937.

216. Bastrikov, party secretary of the NKVD, was also not reelected, although "until now the bureau of the raikom had considered Bastrikov one of the best party workers." Others who failed to retain their posts included Kharin, the secretary of the city soviet party committee. *MR*, 24, 27 and 28 April 1937.

217. Several doctors, including the chief of the city's medical department Petr Tambovtsev (1906–1985), Tigran Mamveliants (chief sanitation doctor), M. A. Gluzikov (head surgeon at the city hospital), A. V. Glagolev (head pediatrician), and G. A. Pisarenko (a surgeon) were arrested. Tambovtsev's replacement, Olga Agenosova, was named head of a commission to investigate his "wrecking activities." After the commission reported finding no wrecking, she was reportedly told by the NKVD, "He himself has confessed and you write me that there was no

wrecking." Threatened with prison, Agenosova evidently stood firm, and then a "miracle occurred." In 1939 Tambovtsev was released from prison and reinstated in the party, for a while resuming his old job as chief of the city's medical department before going off to the war, after which he chose not to return to Magnitogorsk. Gluzikov and Glagolev were also released, although they both became ill and died. *MR*, 21 November 1987, 30 November and 10 December 1988; see also Baryshev, "Zdravookhranenie Magnitogorska," p. 74.

218. An unsigned article, "The Rotten Leadership of the Metallurgical Institute," accused the rector, Anton Upenek, of squelching self-criticism and surrounding himself with flatterers. The article relied exclusively on innuendo, citing the following "facts": Kasperovich, from the factory administration, was on the staff; one teacher, Sorokin, accused of delivering anti-Soviet lectures, had been arrested before in the Industrial party case of 1930; another teacher, Isakov, had been kicked out of the party for organizing a "kulak" collective farm and been removed from the Rabfak (Department of Worker Education) in 1934 for inciting antagonism and fights between Tatars and Kazakhs, and so on. After Upenek announced that he was leaving the institute, the newspaper asserted that he had fled to Moscow because he had been told that he must hold a party meeting in the institute to discuss the Central Committee plenum. His return, two weeks later, occurred as a general "students'" meeting had been called. At that meeting, Upenek allegedly concocted stories of wrecking by various people, all of whom had already departed the institute. His transparent attempt to avoid the devastation of the institute's staff only served to augment "student" ire, according to the newspaper. Arrested in 1938, Upenek (b. 1893) was shot on 30 September 1938. *MR*, 21 and 22 April 1937, and 24 October 1990. On 22 June 1938, arrests were made of what was called a "fascist group" of teachers at the technical school and Rabfak. Magnitogorsk procuracy: Archival file "Nariad 34/C. Perepiska s NKVD za 1938 g.," l. 5.

219. Lopaev (b. 1905) was shot 17 January 1938; Savelev (b. 1902) was shot on 26 July 1938; Rudnitskii (b. 1907) was shot on 7 January 1938; Saraikin (b. 1904) was shot on 28 December 1937; Berman (b. 1903) was shot on 25 July 1938; Valerius was shot (the date could not be ascertained); Gleizer (b. 1907) was arrested (his fate could not be ascertained); Vaisberg, who for a time became deputy factory director (replacing the departed Kasperovich), was arrested in 1938, and released and reinstated in the party in 1939. Khazanov was removed from steel plant management on 10 May 1937. It could not be ascertained whether he was arrested. Dorozhko's name does not appear in any subsequent references to the Magnitogorsk NKVD. *MR*, 24 October 1990; MFGAChO, f. 99, op. 1, d. 1091, l. 238. The four remaining speakers from Magnitogorsk were promoted to positions in the oblast center or in Moscow. Of these, only Khitarov is known to have been arrested and executed, but the others—Golushkin, Kariaev, Kasperovich—may have met the same fate. Zaveniagin, having become deputy commissar for heavy industry, may have interceded to protect Kasperovich by transferring him to Moscow. *MR*, 15 April 1937; MFGAChO, f. 99, op. 1, d. 1090, l. 47.

220. *MR*, 11 May 1937.

221. At the obkom conference both Ryndin and Khitarov were criticized by the obkom paper. Medvedev, chief of the Magnitogorsk NKVD, gave a speech, which was noted in the paper, but no details were disclosed. *CR*, 1 June 1937.

222. Khitarov evidently defended Ryndin. "Pointing to the existence among the leaders of the obkom of mutual-protection [*semeistvennost*] and 'cliquishness' [*artelshchina*]," wrote the obkom newspaper, "comrade Khitarov thinks that comrade Ryndin has understood the mistakes he committed and in Bolshevik fashion will correct them." In his closing speech Ryndin expressed his "complete agreement" with all criticisms of his work. Magnitogorsk's Aleksei Griaznov apparently delivered the sharpest speech, but in the obkom paper it was published only in abridged form. *CR*, 12 June 1937.

223. *CR*, 21 June 1937. Batalin replaced Ovchinnikov as the principal political correspondent.

224. *CR*, 29 October 1937. In August 1937 Major Pavel Vasilevich Chistov was promoted from deputy to chief of the Cheliabinsk oblast NKVD. (No mention was made of what happened to the former Cheliabinsk oblast NKVD chief, Medvedev; it is possible that this was Aleksandr Medvedev, who became NKVD chief in Bashkiria at about the time Chistov was promoted). In connection with his promotion, Chistov had been summoned to Moscow to meet with his boss, People's Commissar of State Security Nikolai Ezhov. Judging by the report in the obkom newspaper, Chistov had evidently feared for his life, but for the time being he survived to arrest others. Chistov, who had failed to complete middle school, worked in the organs since the age of eighteen (1923), serving in Moscow, Irkutsk, Novosibirsk, and Barnaul. Within a month after his promotion, the Cheliabinsk NKVD began unmasking a counterrevolutionary organization in each raion of the oblast. In most cases there were public trials, after which all the defendants were shot. "Believe me," Chistov was said to have told the obkom newspaper in November 1937, "of my fourteen years in the organs of the GPU-NKVD, for me this year has been the most full-blooded [*polnokrovnyi*]." *CR*, 16 and 26 November, 9 December 1937. Chistov left Cheliabinsk in mid-1938 to become NKVD chief in Stalino (Donetsk), where he remained until at least April 1940, evidently surviving (although perhaps only temporarily) the near complete destruction of provincial NKVD chiefs following Ezhov's downfall in December 1938. Chistov's replacement in Cheliabinsk was Fedor Lapshin. Conquest, *Inside Stalin's Secret Police*, p. 63.

225. *CR*, 11 January 1938. At the obkom plenum on 8 January 1938, forty-six of the sixty-one members and seven of the fifteen candidates were removed, including seven of the eight members of the bureau. K. M. Ogurtsov was named acting second secretary and M. P. Sobolev acting third secretary. Khitarov was arrested on 11 November 1937, and expelled from the party the next day. He was executed in 1938. According to Oksana Bulgakova, a Cheliabinsk journalist granted access to PAChO, at a meeting of the Magnitogorsk party active on 17 December 1937 oblast NKVD chief Pavel Chistov said in part: "Khitarov, who at this time sits in prison, and other like-minded types relate how under the slogan of careful treatment of people in order not to make mistakes, they curtailed the struggle with enemies of the people and in essence simply did not conduct this struggle, protecting enemy elements." Such a statement contained an element of truth, namely that Khitarov was not zealous in his pursuit of "enemies" in the Magnitogorsk party. *CR*, 14 September 1988. Ryndin was executed on 10 February 1938. In the destruction of the Cheliabinsk obkom, a decisive role may have been played by a visit from

Lazar Kaganovich, Ryndin's former boss from the days when the two were first and second secretaries of the Moscow obkom.

226. Born in 1896, the son of a Smolensk peasant who worked in the Donbas as an *otkhodnik*, Anotonov went to school for only three years. He joined the party in 1918. In 1930 he entered the Moscow Mining Academy. The Magnitogorsk newspaper conceded that at the time Antonov was not well-qualified, but it called him "not the worst student." In 1935 he was moved into the Central Committee apparat, where he remained until being assigned to Cheliabinsk. *MR*, 17 June 1938; *CR*, 6 May 1938.

227. Back in February 1937, after Zaveniagin moved to Moscow, Ivanov had been temporarily named acting deputy director of the steel plant. In 1938 he served as city soviet chairman and acting first secretary of the gorkom, then acting second secretary. Born in 1901, Ivanov had studied at the Urals polytechnique in Sverdlovsk, and came to Magnitogorsk in April 1931. In August 1933 he was named shift boss in the blooming mill, which was just opened. In September 1934 he became a shift boss in mill 500. In July 1936, he was named shop chief of mill 300 no. 1, replacing Golubitskii, who became chief of the blooming mill. *CR*, 1 February 1937; *MR*, 26 and 30 January 1939. In the early 1930s Ivanov was sent to the United States to learn American work methods. He served as one of the models— along with Avraamii Zaveniagin—for the character Mark Riazanov in Anatolii Rybakov's *Deti arbata*, according to the novelist himself, as related in an interview by the author, Boston, November 1987.

228. Besides Lev Berman, the list of those removed from the gorkom plenum included Nikolai Larin, Aleksandr Geineman, Aleksandr Kalagartsev, A. S. Goltsev, and Efanov. Larin was also removed as first secretary of Stalin raikom and expelled from the party for "ties to an enemy of the people." He was temporarily replaced by Aleksei Griaznov, because Kalagartsev, the Stalin raikom second secretary, was also arrested. Larin (born 1906) was executed on 26 July 1938; Kalagartsev (born 1904), on 28 July 1938. The fate of Goltsev and Efanov could not be ascertained. Geineman's fate is discussed below. *MR*, 21 and 22 December 1937, and 24 October 1990. Lev Zakharovich Berman may have been related to, but was apparently not, as many supposed, the brother of, Matvei Davydovich Berman, one-time chief of Gulag, and Boris Davydovich Berman, an interrogator in the Zinoviev trial who became chief of the Belorussian NKVD. Matvei was arrested in December 1938 and shot in February 1939; Boris was arrested around the same time and also executed. Conquest, *Inside Stalin's Secret Police*, p. 160.

229. *Pravda*, 19 January 1938 (reprinted in *KPSS v rezoliutsiiakh*, vol. 5, pp. 303–12), as cited by Rittersporn, "The Omnipresent Conspiracy," p. 113.

230. *CR*, 21 February 1938.

231. *CR*, 29 May 1938. In the Magnitogorsk Komsomol, it was reported, "somebody started a rumor that Bolshakov was a kulak hiding behind an assumed name. This rumor was not checked either in the raikom, or the gorkom. Bolshakov was expelled from the party." He was reinstated, but it was not established who began the malicious rumor about him. *CR*, 23 March 1938.

232. The city newspaper singled out the case of Kochevanova, who arrived illiterate in Magnitogorsk in 1930, first working as a cleaning lady in the bread factory. She attended a *likbez* (circle for the liquidation of illiteracy), soon entered the

Komsomol, and in 1932 took professional improvement courses, becoming a laboratory aid. In 1935 she became the manager of the laboratory at the bread factory, and then the factory's general manager for production. In 1937 she was elected chairwoman of the bread factory's trade union committee of bakers, and that same year was sent by order of the obkom to Voronezh for further special courses. While studying in Voronezh, however, Kochevanova was summoned back to Magnitogorsk. The director of the bread factory, Fedor Kuriapin, had been expelled from the party and arrested as an enemy of the people and information began to accumulate about her "ties" to him. Not only had she served directly under him, but Kochevanova had once defended Kuriapin in a paternity suit. On the basis of what the city newspaper called "these unproven rumors and allegations," Kochevanova was expelled from the Komsomol on 11 January 1938. She was then accused of causing a general breakdown of the bread factory and was thrown out of the trade union. "She had been trade union chairwoman for around two months, and in the factory's top management for about the same length of time," wrote the city newspaper, "and yet she was blamed for everything that was wrong." The newspaper called these "murderous decisions" constituting "inhuman treatment." When Kochevanova went to the new bread factory director, Moissenko, for a job, he gave her the runaround, telling her to find work elsewhere, with the explanation that "all the accusations thrown at Kochevanova were widely discussed at the bread factory, . . . so that if Kochevanova was permitted back to work it would be necessary to explain about her to workers from the exact opposite position." The newspaper concluded that Kochevanova "should answer for her actions" (*postupki*) but that she had been abused and called for an end to the abuse. *MR*, 5 February 1938. Kuriapin's paternity case (publicly tried in April 1937) involved his secretary, whom he set up in an apartment until she became pregnant. The court pronounced him the father of the child and ordered he pay child support. "How will the party treat his case?" asked the newspaper, ominously. That year he was expelled, leading to Kochevanova's problems. *MR*, 27 April 1937. Kuriapin was arrested on more serious charges in 1938. Magnitogorsk procuracy: Archival file "Nariad 32/C. Perepiska s vysshestoiashchimi organizatsiiami 1938 g.," ll. 33–35, 49.

233. *MR*, 16 April 1938. The obkom newspaper contrasted two cases of ex-Communists being considered for reinstatement. One involved Fomin, who was said to have delivered a load of bricks to the site of a future monument by order of the chief of construction, who was then unmasked as an enemy. Fomin was accused of "ties to enemies of the people" and expelled from the party. The newspaper supported his request. But in the case of Stepanov, the newspaper claimed that after being expelled from the party, he had managed to get reinstated until it was discovered that he had written "dozens of slanderous accusations" against other Communists. Stepanov's reinstatement was reversed. *CR*, 27 January 1938.

234. According to the Magnitogorsk newspaper, Semenov first worked in Petrograd at the Putilov factory, which he left for the village during the Civil War, returning in 1924. In 1926 he entered the GPU, serving in their military forces, and also joined the party. In 1929 he was demobilized and returned to Putilov. He studied in a *rabfak*, and then was sent to the Leningrad Industrial Academy, returning in 1937 to Putilov (now Kirov) with an engineer's diploma before being sent to Magnitogorsk on 23 March 1938. The newspaper called Semenov's "two years in

the ranks of the honored Chekists one of the most remarkable pages in his life." *MR*, 10 and 15 June 1938.

235. *Magnitogorskii metall*, 2 October 1936.

236. By way of explanation, an official report cited "red tape attending the consideration of petitions for acceptance into the party," but omitted mentioning the number of petitions not considered, if any, or the fantastic turmoil in the party's ranks caused by the arrests. *Rezoliutsiia VIII Magnitogorskoi partiinoi organizatsii po otchetnomu dokladu GK VKP (b) za period Iiun 1937 g. - Iuin 1938 g.* (Magnitogorsk, 1938), p. 3.

237. There were 747 candidate members in the Magnitogorsk party as of April 1938. *MR*, 12 April 1938. One reason for the slowness of the processes cited by the newspaper was that party documents sent by PPOs to the gorkom in connection with the reinstatements and new admissions were said to have remained there for months before being sent back to the PPOs to be filled out properly. Documents were also said to have been lost. New party cards were issued in 1938. They included detailed biographical data, a record of activities, rewards, punishments, and, for the first time, a photograph. One copy was sent to Moscow, another was kept locally. *MR*, 5 June 1938. In April 1938 there were around 5,000 Magnitogorsk Komsomols. During the first eleven months of 1938 another 2,636 people were admitted. *CR*, 28 April and 29 December 1938.

238. *MR*, 26 February 1938. In January Aleksei Griaznov had been temporarily promoted to first secretary of the Stalin raikom. He was soon demoted to second secretary. *CR*, 18 January 1938.

239. According to the obkom, nationwide there were 155,000 appeals as of August 1938, 85,000 of which had been investigated; 54 percent of these resulted in reinstatement. *CR*, 8 August 1938.

240. Material published in connection with the party conference revealed that from 1 June 1937 to 1 June 1938, the Magnitogorsk gorkom had promoted 49 new people to party posts, 138 to economic posts, 35 to Komsomol posts, 45 to posts in soviets, and 17 more to posts elsewhere in the oblast. Another article claimed 267 people had been promoted and that this "list was not complete." No mention was made of why so many positions had opened up so suddenly, but the answer was obvious: arrests had devastated the apparat. *MR*, 3 and 5 June 1938. Elections to posts in primary party organizations were held just prior to the conference. Of Magnitogorsk's ninety-seven primary party organizations, twenty-seven returned first-time first secretaries. In fifty-one cases the elected secretary was working in that PPO for the first time. Thirty-five PPO secretaries had an apparat seniority (*stazh*) of under six months. *MR*, 30 May 1938.

241. The obkom accused the Magnitogorsk newspaper of suppressing the sharpest worker correspondent submissions naming enemies of the people. Kariaev—apparently back as editor in Magnitogorsk after his replacement there, Selivanov, had been arrested—stated that Korobov and his new deputy, Leonid Vaisberg, did not especially welcome criticism by the newspaper. Vaisberg supposedly responded to the newspaper's signals by claiming that the problem in question had been resolved, and the guilty punished, but Kariaev said that this was not the case. Vaisberg was said to have been trying to deflect attention. *CR*, 6 and 8 June 1938. On 16 November at a Magnitogorsk party meeting, Kariaev was removed from the

gorkom for "rousing political doubts" owing to his close association with Khitarov, who had just been arrested. But he seems to have escaped expulsion from the party. *CR*, 20 September 1988.

242. *MR*, 6 and 8 June 1938. Back on 11 May 1938, at a meeting of what was called the "economic active," several speakers blamed Korobov for the widespread toadying, asserting that Korobov had failed to denounce this behavior. He was evidently not going to make the same mistake. *CR*, 15 May 1938. At the conference there were 125 voting and 51 nonvoting delegates; among the voting delegates were fifteen women; among the nonvoting, five women.

243. Ivanov refused to accept the criticism, and called Sorokin's accusation "slander without proof." But the newspaper added: "a verification of all the members of the plenum of the Kirov raikom in the presence of comrade Ivanov in essence took place." Ivanov was also said "to have gotten interested" in the work of Sorokin, when he should have been dealing with enemies of the people. *MR*, 8 June 1938. At the conference a teacher, Arkadii Demin, was accused of having "delivered a Trotskyite speech," but not a single detail was revealed. Moreover, Sorokin defended Demin. *MR*, 6 June 1938. Ivanov was made chairman of the city soviet on 16 June 1938. Sorokin was arrested on 25 July 1938. On 2 September 1938 Ivanov was promoted to deputy director of the steel plant.

244. *CR*, 5 June 1938.

245. *MR*, 9 June 1938.

246. *CR*, 11 August 1938.

247. *CR*, 21 November 1938.

248. *CR*, 29 May 1938.

249. *MR*, 6 June 1938.

250. *MR*, 6 June 1938.

251. The absence of a satisfactory history of the NKVD, given the source limitations, is understandable, if regrettable. The basic guide remains Simon Wolin and Robert Slusser, eds., *The Soviet Secret Police* (New York: Praeger, 1957).

252. Local "troikas" (of three NKVD officials) had been created by a 27 May 1935 decree and given the same powers as the central NKVD's "special board" (*osoboe soveshchanie*), meaning they were empowered to pass sentences of either internal administrative exile or incarceration in a labor camp for up to five years (but not expulsion from the USSR). After the 30 July 1937 order increasing their sentencing powers, two further orders were issued, introducing *dvoikas*. A 17 November 1938 joint Central Committee/Sovnarkom decree, "Ob arestakh, prokurorskom nadzore i vedenii sledstviia," led to a 26 November 1938 NKVD order to abolish *dvoikas* and troikas. *Izvestiia TsK KPSS*, 1989, no. 10, pp. 80–82.

253. For accounting purposes, arrests by the NKVD were tabulated by oblast, not city. According to the Cheliabinsk KGB (successor to the NKVD), some 37,000 people were "repressed" in Cheliabinsk oblast in the 1930s, 1940s, and 1950s. (To determine the precise number from Magnitogorsk, the KGB would have to examine each case.) Magnitogorsk was the second largest city in the oblast, slightly less than half the size of the oblast center. *MR*, 18 November 1990.

254. The rest were presumably awaiting transfer to Gulag. For that purpose prison personnel, especially convoy staff, were said to be severely overburdened. Magnitogorsk procuracy: Archival file "Nariad 34/C. Perepiska c NKVD i RKM

1936–1937 gg.," ll. 62, 64. Born in 1902 the son of a smith, Ivan Sorokin began working before the October revolution, while underage, in trade. After the Civil War this petty trader who had evidently acquired a measure of literacy became a court scribe and, at age twenty-one, a village investigator. At some point he was sent to take a few law courses in Perm, after which he worked as an assistant to the procurator in the city of Shadrinsk (Urals) from 1926 to 1930. That year he became district procurator in Kamensk (Urals), a position he held until 1934. During 1934 and 1935 he worked in the Cheliabinsk oblast procuracy. During 1935 and 1936, Sorokin was district procurator for Shadrinsk raion. He became procurator of Magnitogorsk okrug in mid-1936, when Petr Kefala was arrested.

255. Sorokin reported to Vyshinskii in 1938 that "in the Magnitogorsk prison are being held women charged under article 58-12, the investigation of whom was concluded six months ago or more. Their cases have been forwarded. Thus far there have been no results. The specified period of detention has lapsed. Some of the women charged under article 58-12 were not incarcerated; they signed written statements not to leave, and their passports and other documents were confiscated." Magnitogorsk procuracy: Archival file "Nariad 32/C. Perepiska s vysshestoiash-chimi organizatsiiami 1938 g.," l. 58.

256. Sorokin requested permission to transfer all those convicted of everyday crimes directly to the local labor colony. Magnitogorsk procuracy: Archival file "Nariad 32/C. Perepiska s vysshestoiashchimi organizatsiiami 1938 g.," l. 31. On 11 April 1938 Vasilii Govorukhin, the warden of the Magnitogorsk prison and a former officer in the Austrian army who ended up in Russia in 1916, was arrested. He was said to have admitted being an agent of German intelligence. In the document Govorukhin was mistakenly identified as Ivan Gavrilov (the name of an assistant to the chief of the chemical shop of the coke plant who had been arrested in 1937). Ibid.: Archival file "Naraid 33/C. Postanovleniia na prodleniia sroka 1938–1939 gg.," l. 159. For the purposes of the 1939 census, Magnitogorsk's "prison" population was said to include those held in the NKVD building's basement lockup or in prison no. 3 in Old Magnitnyi Settlement, the special resettlers, the ITK, and exiles (*vyslannye*) living throughout the urban territory. MFGAChO, f. 16, op. 1, d. 105, l. 229.

257. Having been fired from his job in the chemical plant for being a foreigner, Scott left Magnitogorsk in early 1937 and traveled to the United States, perhaps afraid for his life (one night the NKVD had come to the apartment directly above his in Socialist City to arrest the occupant). Maria Scott, pregnant with their second child at the time, related in an interview in 1987 that after John left she was convinced he would not return. Many months later, however, Scott did return, and after a brief trip to the Urals (Cheliabinsk, Sverdlovsk, and Magnitogorsk) in February 1938, he told a United States embassy official in Moscow that he saw "no signs" indicating that the terror's momentum was slackening. Scott, *Behind*, pp. 187, 194, 303–4. On 16 March 1938 Sorokin wrote to Vyshinskii that since he had taken over as Magnitogorsk procurator (on 12 October 1936) he had sanctioned the arrest of "hundreds" of enemies of the people charged under article 58. It is difficult to asses this vague statement. Also, when the letter was written, the terror was far from over. Magnitogorsk procuracy: Archival file "Nariad 32/C. Perepiska s vysshestoiashchimi organizatsiiami 1938 g.," ll. 5–7.

258. Magnitogorsk procuracy: Archival file "Nariad 34/C. Perepiska c NKVD i RKM 1936–1937 gg.," ll. 50, 66.

259. In 1988, a former Magnitogorsk NKVD operative allegedly told a Magnitogorsk writer, Vladilen Moshkovtsev, that "they demanded that we uncover conspiracies, shoot hundreds. It was better to destroy those already in custody than to go after construction workers and metal workers, who constituted the country's potential." All the same, the retired officer supposedly admitted that "in those years hundreds of construction and metal workers were also arrested and destroyed." Moshkovtsev, "Magnitka (1743–1941)," p. 163. In 1938 the NKVD also made a sweep of the surrounding state farms, arresting all the directors and bookkeepers. Magnitogorsk procuracy: Archival file "Nariad 34/C. Perepiska s NKVD za 1938 g.," l. 9. The various departments within the NKVD of Kirghizia declared a "socialist competition" for arresting spies and counterrevolutionaries (the fourth department won). *Izvestiia TsK KPSS*, 1989, no. 5, pp. 74–75.

260. Magnitogorsk procuracy: Archival file "Nariad 33/. Postanovleniia na prodlenie sroka po NKVD 1938–1939 gg.," l. 8.

261. Nikolai Gesler, for example, said to be a German born in Poland who immigrated to the USSR in 1917, was arrested as an "agent of foreign intelligence" as was Franz Kviatovskii, a Pole. The same could be said about people arrested for "bourgeois nationalism." Nigamedzhen Davletshina, for example, was arrested on 28 March 1938 for belonging to a "counterrevolutionary nationalist insurgent organization" of unspecified nationality. Magnitogorsk procuracy: Archival file "Nariad 33/. Postanovleniia na prodlenie sroka po NKVD 1938–1939 gg.," ll. 13, 26, 22.

262. The ringleader was said to be Ivan Svistunov (b. 1887), a party member since 1930 who worked in vehicular freight transport. In 1937, Svistunov was expelled from the party and arrested. In 1938, while serving a two-year sentence in the labor colony, he was rearrested as the "leader of a counterrevolutionary, diversionary wrecking terrorist organization of rightists." Magnitogorsk procuracy: Archival file "Nariad 33/. Postanovleniia na prodlenie sroka po NKVD 1938–1939 gg.," l. 1.

263. He was said to have been recruited by another "German agent," former Magnitogorsk First Secretary Khitarov, who knew German from his time spent abroad and conversed in that language with Germans living in Magnitogorsk.

264. According to a report dated 2 April 1939, and signed by NKVD Chief Pridorogin and Procurator Sokolov. Magnitogorsk procuracy: Archival File "Nariad 33/C. Postanovleniia na prodlenie sroka 1938–1939 gg.," ll. 44–46, 52. A further communication, dated 5 May 1938, gave details of Geineman's arrest. Magnitogorsk procuracy: Archival file "Nariad 32/C. Perepiska s vysshestoiashchimi organizatsiiami 1938 g.," l. 32.

265. The rules governing cases of counterrevolution had been greatly simplified in connection with the Kirov murder. A reproduction of the 1 December 1934 decree issued the day of the Kirov murder with Stalin's notations can be found in Volkogonov, *Triumf i tragediia*, vol. 1, pt. 2 (Moscow, 1989), between pp. 64–65; the decree was originally published in *Izvestiia*, 5 December 1934. Another decree along the same lines was evidently issued on 14 November 1937. See Zhogin, "Ob izvrashcheniiakh," pp. 26–27.

266. Magnitogorsk procuracy: Archival file "Nariad 34/C. Perepiska s NKVD za 1938 g.," passim.

267. F. Beck and W. Godin, *Russian Purge and the Extraction of Confession* (New York: Viking, 1951), p. 57. In the third edition of his book, Robert Conquest belatedly addressed the question of why confessions were deemed necessary, essentially reiterating the arguments of Beck and Godin, but adding his own characteristic touch by concluding that in the end, the idea "must have been Stalin's." Conquest, *The Great Terror*, pp. 130–31.

268. Like the terror, the Medieval Inquisition did not emerge full blown. It was Pope Gregory IX who, after being unsatisfied with the Church's episcopal inquisitions and experimenting with various procedures, decided to resort to special agents equipped with full powers from the papacy to conduct inquisitions of the population. And even after the Medieval Inquisition's basic structure was established, secular authorities continued to make inquiries regarding heresy. Moreover, the Papal Inquisition existed side by side with the episcopal one (although bishops also had other duties and when passing sentence were required to call in the papal inquisitor anyway). Relations between bishops and inquisitors were often strained, much like those between obkom secretaries and regional NKVD chiefs. Malcolm Lambert, *Medieval Heresy: Popular Movements from Bogomil to Hus* (New York: Holmes and Meier, 1976), p. 102. Bernard Hamilton, *The Medieval Inquisition* (New York: Holmes and Meier, 1981), pp. 35–38; Lea, *A History of the Inquisition*, pp. 324–32, 356–65. In contrast to the Medieval Papal Inquisition, inquisitors of the Spanish Inquisition were appointed by the sovereign, not the pope. Thus, the Spanish Inquisition was not an ecclesiastical tribunal but an instrument of royal absolutism, making it in some ways even more analogous to the Soviet terror mechanism. Cecil Roth, *The Spanish Inquisition* (London: Hale, 1937), pp. 72–73.

269. The best analysis of the NKVD officers' psychology is still Solzhenitsyn, *The Gulag Archipelago*, vol. 1, pp. 144–78; and idem., *The First Circle* (New York: Harper and Row, 1968).

270. Documentation was a crucial aspect of the work of the NKVD, which maintained files on each prisoner. (Immediately following the Nazi invasion, there appear to have been instances when the Zeks were executed but their documents were shipped East for safekeeping.) During the Medieval Inquisition, because all the proceedings were recorded, an enormous mass of documents accumulated that could be launched at any time (cross-indexing of the files was even practiced). In 1235, the citizens of Narbonne, in an insurrection against the Inquisition, destroyed all its books and records. Lea, *A History of the Inquisition*, pp. 378, 380, 408–15.

271. In the Middle Ages religious doubt did not constitute heresy. Doubt was "negative," heresy a matter of positive belief. Doubt was viewed as a temptation that could become a sin if allowed to persist, and not a crime. Hamilton, *The Medieval Inquisition*, pp. 14–16. But "suspicion of heresy" was punishable. Wives and husbands of heretics sometimes incurred suspicion of heresy for having failed to denounce their spouses, as did anyone thought to have extended hospitality or given alms to a heretic. Isolation of a heretic could be enforced by the threat of excommunication for anyone who associated with an excommunicate. And the truest

sign of a sincere confession was the denunciation of others. Lea, *A History of the Inquisition*, pp. 378, 387–88, 431–34, 461.

272. "Trials" for heretics were in camera (although not in absentia), but judgments were pronounced in public. The inquisitor had no power to pass sentence himself. Sentences were passed at an assembly, with episcopal concurrence and expert participation. The death sentence was never pronounced; the admitted but unrepentant heretic was said to be "relaxed" to the secular arm. Theoretically inquisitors had no power to inflict any punishment. Instead they proposed "penances," which were supposed to be voluntary and ranged from pious observances (prayers, extra church attendance, fasting, pilgrimages, and even fines for nominally pious purposes) to humiliation (wearing large yellow crosses for years, even life) and incarceration in special prisons (a "penance" of bread and water), often with confiscation of property. Banishment was also occasionally prescribed, and sometimes houses inhabited by heretics were designated for demolition and communities ordered to build chapels. Lea asserted that imprisonment was the most frequent remedy, but Bernard Hamilton claims that 90 percent of all cases were resolved with canonical penances. Hamilton, *The Medieval Inquisition*, pp. 51–58. In a later work Hamilton omitted percentages, asserting that the "vast majority" of accused heretics was dismissed with canonical penances, although he acknowledges that a "substantial minority" was imprisoned. Hamilton, *Religion in the Medieval West* (London: Edward Arnold, 1986), p. 177. Lea also wrote of the Inquisition's "saturnalia of plunder," a theme that Hamilton does not treat. Lea, *A History of the Inquisition*, pp. 462–500, 513, 541–42, 549.

273. Grigorii Semashin, the chief of the compressor station who lived in Berezka, was arrested on 29 November 1937 and shot on 2 December, according to information later provided to surviving members of his family. *MR*, 1 November 1988.

274. The Inquisition was far-reaching, but it did not extend to England, Denmark, Scandinavia, or Castile (until the fifteenth century, when it acquired a different character). Moreover, in areas where it operated the Inquisition was dependent on the support of secular authorities and lacked effective power when such support was not forthcoming. Hamilton, *The Medieval Inquisition*; Lea, *A History of the Inquisition*, pp. 352–53.

275. In the absence of hard information, the obkom paper conceded that all manner of rumors were going around, for which the partorg, Sorokin, was faulted, having failed to squelch them. The obkom newspaper also claimed that a "foreign diversionist" had been caught on factory territory not long ago, but gave no details. *CR*, 11 February 1937.

276. According to the city newspaper, "senior blooming operator Terekhov snapped the shafts of a motor on the first gap in the first handle of the wheeling [buksovka]. As a result the connecting spindle between the motor and the gear wheel of the blooming was broken, as was the motor's coupling and the coupling on the gear wheel." At this point Terekhov apparently made an error of judgment: "Having heard the snap, Terekhov did not shut down the blooming, but instead fired up the motor twice more, as a result of which the breakdown took on a more serious character." Observing that "the breakdown took place at the very moment that the trial of the Anti-Soviet Trotskyite Center ended, just after the results of

the trial had been discussed!" the newspaper found it "strange" that the party organization in the blooming mill "did not immediately discern" that what occurred on 31 January was "not an accident." At a shop party meeting on 14 February, Terekhov, was found to be two years behind in the payment of his Komsomol dues, and was expelled from the youth organization. *MR*, 17 February 1937. Back on 8 February 1937, plant director Zaveniagin had issued an order dismissing Terekhov for breaking a motor and other equipment in the pressing shop and instructing Golubitskii to supervise the shop more closely and to punish violators. The order said nothing of wrecking. MFGAChO, f. 99, op. 10, d. 1090, l. 212. Zaveniagin, in contrast to his successor Korobov, seems to have tried to protect some people. Moshkovtsev, "Magnitka (1743–1941)," pp. 138, 162–67; and *Sovetskaia Rossia*, 25 October 1987.

277. According to A. A. Raetskaia, who worked as a technician in the blooming mill, at the shop meeting following Golubitskii's arrest "many people rose to his defense." She also recalled that there was a rumor later that he had died in the Cheliabinsk prison. *MR*, 29 November 1988.

278. Reinforcing Sorokin's complaints, the obkom newspaper complained that "as became clear at the party meeting, the leadership of the blooming mill plainly liberalizes with enemies. In the shop squelching of self-criticism is evident. Communist Koshelev stated to the secretary of the party committee that he would not deploy self-criticism because he was afraid of being fired." *CR*, 18 February 1937.

279. Golubitskii had been named chief of the blooming mill on 27 May 1936, only nine months before the wrecking accusations began, having served as chief of mill 500. MfGAChO, f. 99, op. 4, f. 59, l. 125. It is not clear how much training in the process of rolling steel he had. But the record of Ogorodnikov's testimony unintentionally confirms that Stakhanovism wreaked havoc with the equipment. A member of the "Polish Military Organization," Anton Ostrovskii, who worked in the blooming mill, was quoted as testifying that "by assignment from Golubitskii I collected testimony about the mood of workers on the Magnitogorsk metallurgical complex and their material everyday life conditions." Testimony was added from Iakov Kisselgof, another arrested management official, that Golubitskii had wrecked in mill 300 no. 1 before moving over to the blooming. Magnitogorsk procuracy: Archival file "Nariad 32/C. Perepiska s vysshestoiashchimi organizatsiiami 1938 g.," ll. 11–13.

280. Sorokin's letter read in part:

> In accordance with the law of 17 April 1935 your sanction was needed for his arrest, but in this case I permitted a conscious violation by the following justifications: a) he is charged according to article 58, points 7, 8, 9, and 11 of the Criminal Code; b) sanction for his arrest was requested by the city procurator's office on 5 and 16 February, but since then no answer has been received; c) Golubitskii, as an enemy of the people, became definitively insolent and continued to wreck day in and day out, even after the arrest of his coparticipants—two operators of the blooming mill; moreover, on various momentous days of our motherland or special events he responded with wrecking: on the opening day of the Eighth Congress of Soviets, on the day of the announcement of the sentence in the case of the Parallel Trotskyite Center, and so on; d) Golubitskii continued to organize premeditated, wrecking breakdowns and produce poor quality output right through to March, that is, to the day of his arrest, and every breakdown

cost the factory dearly; e) given all these conditions, it was impossible to leave him in the shop, and I decided to commit a conscious violation of the law and sanction Golubitskii's arrest, equating this case to the arrest at the place of the crime.

Magnitogorsk procuracy: Archival file "Nariad 32/C. Perepiska s vysshestoiashchimi organizatsiiami 1938 g.," ll. 5–7.

281. MFGAChO, f. 99, op. 10, d. 1095, ll. 5–9.

282. According to a letter from the Cheliabinsk oblast procurator's office to the Magnitogorsk city party committee, dated 15 March 1989, and made available to me. The problems of the blooming mill, however, appear not to have gone away. On 13 September 1938 acting factory director Konstantin Ivanov complained that the pressing and preparatory shops were not supplying the sorting mills with the proper steel, forcing the latter to halt production. B. D. Trakhtman, Golubitskii's replacement, was warned but appears not to have been punished. MFGAChO, f. 99, op. 1, d. 1097, l. 10. The son of a poor peasant, Trakhtman had served in the Red Army, worked in a factory and studied at rabfak, before joining the party and being sent to study at an institute. In April 1936 he was promoted to shift boss in mill 500. *MR*, 24 April 1936. Not long after replacing Golubitskii as chief of the blooming mill, Trakhtman became chief of the factory's construction department (OKS), replacing the arrested Leonid Vaisberg. Vaisberg appears to have been subsequently released.

283. Magnitogorsk procuracy: Archival file "Nariad 32/C. Perepiska s vysshestoiashchimi organizatsiiami 1938 g.," ll. 5–7.

284. On 11 March 1938 Sorokin had requested clarification of the cases in which he was not permitted to sanction an arrest, following a secret circular dated 25 February 1938. Sokolov, Sorokin's replacement, also had trouble with jurisdiction, having sanctioned the arrests of transport personnel, for whom a separate transport procurator was responsible. This case was further complicated because by the time of arrest, the person arrested had already been fired. Still, it was the previous place of employment that determined jurisdiction. Magnitogorsk procuracy: Archival file "Nariad 32/C. Perepiska s vysshestoiashchimi organizatsiiami 1938 g.," l. 18, 82.

285. According to excerpts from the minutes of a meeting of the oblast procuracy on 27 and 28 June 1938, the oblast criticized the city procuracy for not fighting violations of technical safety or the theft of socialist property, as well as long delays in the processing of cases, the poor quality of its investigations, and its failures to supervise the work of the courts, which in the absence of proper supervision had handed down "improper" sentences. Magnitogorsk procuracy: Archival file Nariad 32/C. Perepiska s vysshestoiashchimi organizatsiiami 1938 g.," l. 74.

286. The charges against Sorokin were handled from Cheliabinsk, which requested information from Magnitogorsk, according to a memo dated 7 September 1938. Magnitogorsk procuracy: Archival file "Nariad 32/C. Perepiska s vysshestoiashchimi organizatsiiami 1938 g.," ll. 41, 73.

287. Sorokin was ever-vigilant. He wrote an indignant letter to the secretary of the gorkom reporting that someone had found in the Magnitogorsk library the book *Istoriia grazhdanskoi voiny* with portraits of Trotskyites and rightist wreckers, diversionaries and spies (he listed Bukharin, Zinoviev, and "even Trotsky").

This, of course, was an inadvertent recognition of the roles they had played in the critical episode. Sorokin ordered that all libraries be checked. Magnitogorsk procuracy: Archival file "Nariad 33/C," l. 8. In a letter to NKIu RSFSR dated 7 March 1938 Sorokin asked whether he should remove all publications by Nikolai Krylenko from the procuracy library. Ibid.: Archival file "Nariad 32/C. Perepiska s vysshestoiashchimi organizatsiiami 1938 g.," l. 4.

288. Magnitogorsk procuracy: Archival file "Nariad 33/C [Untitled] 1938," ll. 14–39.

289. Under interrogation Sorokin was said to have admitted his guilt, but then recanted. He seems to have been in a Cheliabinsk prison from the time of his arrest in 25 July 1938 until 5 December 1939, when he was released (following the arrests of Pridorogin and Pushkov). But according to a letter from the Cheliabinsk oblast procurator's office to the Magnitogorsk city party committee, dated 15 March 1989, Sorokin was said to have been released from prison on 29 February 1939. In any case, he was reinstated in the party in Magnitogorsk on 29 December 1939, although it remains unclear what job he obtained upon returning. PAChO, f. 288, op. 70, d. 82; ibid., f. 234, op. 14, d. 7.

290. They were sentenced to death by a military tribunal of NKVD troops of the Urals military district on 18 July 1941, twenty-six days after the German invasion, according to a letter of the Cheliabinsk oblast procurator to the Magnitogorsk gorkom, dated 15 July 1988 and shown to me. These were not the first arrests in the Magnitogorsk NKVD. One operative, Alfred Rinkis, was shot on 16 June 1938; another, Aleksei Sokolov, was executed on 19 November 1938. There are likely to have been others. MR, 24 October 1990.

291. In January 1939 Andrei Kapitanov, serving a five-year term since 1937, was "rearrested" and accused of being "an active participant of a counterrevolutionary terrorist insurgent and wrecker-diversionist organization operating in the Magnitogorsk prison." The organization, said to be dedicated to the goal of overthrowing the state apparat in the USSR, was led by "the Menshevik Smirnov." According to a report by the procurator, "in cell No. 21, [Kapitanov] conducted counterrevolutionary activities, directing agents to overthrow Soviet power and physically annihilating a party member." Kapitanov was also said to be preparing a prison uprising. Magnitogorsk procuracy: Archival file "Nariad 33/. Postanovleniia na prodlenie sroka po NKVD 1938–1939 gg.," ll. 23–25. A case of a counterrevolutionary Trotskyite organization in the labor colony was still being investigated in July 1939, when the period covered by the archival file ends. Magnitogorsk procuracy: Archival file "Nariad 33/. Postanovleniia na prodlenie sroka po NKVD 1938–1939 gg.," ll. 42–46.

292. A decree of 17 November 1938, "On arrests, procurator supervision and the conduct of investigations," urged the procuracy to get control of the NKVD by restoring the practice of procuratorial sanction for arrests and supervision of investigation procedures. A second decree, "On the procedure of agreement for arrests," dated 1 December 1938, specified that to arrest party members the NKVD needed the agreement of the local first secretary, or in his absence, that of the second secretary; to arrest military personnel, the NKVD needed to have the sanction of the People's Commissariat of Defense. Magnitogorsk procuracy: Archival file "Sekretnye tsirkuliary za 1938 g."

293. An account of the intense pressures to end the terror that were brought to bear from the localities in the preparations for the Nineteenth Party Congress can be found in Khlevniuk, *1937-i: Stalin, NKVD, i Sovetskoe obshchestvo.*

294. Stalin, "O proekte konstitutsii SSSR," 25 November 1936, in *Sochineniia,* vol. 14 [1], pp. 142–45.

295. For Djilas, the former number two man in the Yugoslav hierarchy who was expelled from the party and jailed for his heretical views, the Communist system, which purported to be based on collective ownership, was in reality an elaborate cover for a class that controlled all the country's property while concealing its own existence. Who was this class? Arguing that it was identical to neither the party nor the entire bureaucracy, Djilas conceded that "it is difficult, perhaps impossible to define the limits of the new class." Despite offering only a vague sense of who they were, Djilas credited the establishment and all further evolution of the Communist system to their class-conscious actions, which appeared to be motivated by an uncanny perception and defense of their class interests. Djilas, *The New Class,* pp. 39–42. See the discussion in Boffa, *The Stalin Phenomenon,* pp. 102–04. Djilas's search for the "social base" of Stalinism grew out of the tradition inspired by Trotsky discussed in the introduction to this book.

296. This is one of the principal themes explored by Rittersporn, who argues that "far from making the regime's functioning predictable and controllable, the political monopoly and the need to preserve it tended to render uncontrollable both those who were supposed to represent and defend it, and the relations they had to maintain with the rest of society." True enough, but Rittersporn offers no evidence for his additional claim that these social tensions were dangerous. Rittersporn, *Stalinist Simplifications,* p. 328.

297. In 1937, the metallurgical complex's administration, excluding the large department of capital construction, contained 181 engineers and technicians, 290 white-collar employees, 74 service personnel, and 12 blue-collar workers, according to the city newspaper. The newspaper implied that the factory administration was overblown, yet the administration insisted that it needed to add staff, as there was a severe shortage of skilled personnel. Both opinions had much to recommend them. *MR,* 22 April 1937. John Scott noted "the rising number of office workers" in Magnitogorsk, pointing out that "every industrial organization acquired a budget department, a planning division, an economic department, a technical bureau, a large supply department, and a tremendous bookkeeping staff"—all of whom enjoyed the comfort of office jobs, and the relative privileges deriving therefrom. Scott, *Behind,* p. 75.

298. According to the newspaper, when Matvei Larin (at the time chairman of the factory trade union committee) called the hospital emergency service because his wife had a stomachache, he threatened to have the staff shot if they did not arrive within five minutes. *MR,* 9 May 1937.

299. *MR,* 12 April 1937. Lukashevich was removed as KBU chief in an executive order dated 25 April 1937 and signed by Korobov, who noted the removal was carried out "according to the special department." MFGAChO, f. 99, op. 10, d. 1090, ll. 25–26. A public announcement of Lukashevich's removal was carried the day before the executive order (and twelve days after his expulsion from the party). *MR,* 24 April 1937. This was the first and only instance when the newspaper re-

ported the fate of a high-level local figure in negative terms. In all other cases, mention was made of the appointment of replacements, while the fate of the outgoing person would be passed over in silence, unless that person had been transferred to Moscow.

300. The newspaper cited an incident involving Lukashevich's eleven-year-old son, Anatolii, who back in 1936 had shot a thirteen-year old boy (Ilia Vdovenko) with a small caliber rifle while the two were playing. "Everyone knows about this," wrote the newspaper, "yet despite the fact that, above all, it is the father who is at fault, it passes Lukashevich by [emu eto skhodit]." The newspaper also published a letter from KBU employees, attaching a note to the effect that the names of the authors have been changed by their insistence, a circumstance that was said to testify to the "squelching of self-criticism in the administration of the KBU." In addition, the article criticized Teplitskii, the chief of tram construction, who was accused of helping himself to funds from the KBU cashier for a trip, a fact that Lukashevich allegedly knew but did nothing about (only after the intervention of Khazanov did Teplitskii receive a reprimand). MR, 4 and 9 April 1937, and 18 February 1936. Andrei Tabunov was arrested but evidently not executed. MR, 3 October 1936.

301. MR, 23 and 27 November 1937. Lukashevich's dismissal and trial engendered a series of intrigues by others within the KBU who sought to defend themselves by playing on the parallelism of party and state. In his first four months as KBU chief in 1938, for example, Ananenko accumulated four party reprimands. "Having taken over an organization ravaged by enemies of the people, Ananenko began to purge the apparat of self-suppliers, drunkards, and embezzlers of socialist property," wrote the oblast newspaper. "But at every step he encountered the resistance of the secretary of the [KBU] party committee, Efimov." When Ananenko fired Efimov for allocating apartments to friends, the raikom interceded to rescind the action and Efimov summoned a meeting of the KBU party committee, which issued Ananenko a party reprimand. At this point, the chief engineer (deputy director) of the metallurgical complex, Konstantin Ivanov, stepped in and refired Efimov. But Ananenko was given a second party reprimand for his "liberal treatment" of Efimov. When Ananenko complained to the gorkom, his petition was redirected to the Kirov raikom, which gave him a third reprimand. (He received a fourth reprimand for failing to provide the militia with a facility by an agreed upon deadline.) Ananenko's case was taken up at two meetings of the gorkom, which pronounced the facts as expressed in the oblast newspaper's account correct and called upon the factory administration to support Ananenko in his mission to clean up the KBU. CR, 3 and 23 December 1938.

302. Rittersporn has argued, admittedly without much evidence, that "the inefficiency and petty tyranny of a very large number of responsible officials within the economic and administrative apparatus w[ere] becoming blatant"; and that the "notion that officials wanted to or already had transformed their management responsibilities into virtual property rights almost like a bourgeoisie struck a chord." Rittersporn, Stalinist Simplifications, pp. 41, 101. See also Fitzpatrick, The Cultural Front, pp. 124, 173.

303. Pravda, 31 October 1937, reprinted in Sochineniia, vol. 1 [14], pp. 253–55.

304. Korobov was born in 1902 in Makeevka. He was said to have finished middle school, beginning his working career as an unskilled laborer at age fourteen. He worked in the Ukraine until January 1936, when he was sent to Magnitogorsk as chief of the blast furnace shop. In November 1936 he became deputy director, and in March 1937, director of the MMK. He entered the party in 1934 by special dispensation. *MR*, 14 November 1937. In January 1939, when Korobov was promoted to deputy commissar of the Commissariat of Ferrous Metallurgy (NKChM), Konstantin Ivanov became acting factory director. Not long thereafter, Ivanov was named chief of the trust Uraldrevmet. He was replaced as the chief of the MMK by Grigorii Nosov. Born in Katav-Ivanovskii in the Urals, Nosov worked in the open-hearth shop at Stalinsk (Novokuznetsk) from 1933 to 1938, rising to shop chief. In April 1939 he became deputy director of the MMK under Ivanov. Nosov joined the party in 1925. *MR*, 12 November 1939. Nosov remained Magnitogorsk director until his death in 1951.

305. In his report to the Eighteenth Party Congress on 10 March 1939, Stalin offered just such a retroactive justification for the terror. *Pravda*, 11 March 1939, reprinted in *Sochineniia*, vol. 1 [14], p. 398; see also Viacheslav Molotov's speech to the February-March 1937 plenum, "Uroki vreditelstva, diversii i shpionazha iapono-nemetsko-trotskistskikh agentov," *Pravda*, 21 April 1937, excerpted in *Bolshevik*, 14 April 1937, pp. 24–26 (also published separately as a pamphlet). Whether these considerations motivated the terror remains questionable, but they undoubtedly made the destruction of the existing elite more possible, as Sheila Fitzpatrick has argued. "Stalin and the Making of a New Elite," pp. 377–402, reprinted in idem., *The Cultural Front*, pp. 149–82; see also the comments by Kendall Bailes, "Stalin and the Making of a New Elite: A Comment," *Slavic Review* 39, no. 2 (1980): 286–89; and idem., *Technology and Society*, pp. 259, 279–87; and by Robert Thurston, "Fear and Belief in the USSR's 'Great Terror': Response to Arrest, 1935–1939," *Slavic Review* 45, no. 2 (1986): 232.

306. This is one of the principal arguments of Rittersporn, *Stalinist Simplifications*, pp. 53–55. See also Leonard Schapiro, who speculated that the elite feared society's vengeance so much it preferred Stalin's despotic rule. Schapiro, *Communist Party*, pp. 383, 387, 432.

307. In May 1937 the newspaper printed vague charges of irregularities in the use of the special director's account by former complex director Zaveniagin, accusing him of allocating the funds at his discretion in violation of the laws. As examples, the newspaper cited the facts that not a kopeck was spent on housing, and the bulk of the monies were given over for use by shop bosses. It seemed that Zaveniagin had done little more than allocate the funds where needed. *MR*, 9 May 1937. Pechenkin, an editor of the factory newspaper, attacked Zaveniagin at a 17 December 1937 meeting of the "party active." So did Procurator Sorokin, who accused Zaveniagin of protecting Pikovskii, a nonparty specialist, and Bulgakov, for whom Zaveniagin had allegedly appealed all the way to Vyshinskii, Sorokin's boss. Sorokin offered other examples of cases where he received telegrams from Moscow with instructions not to charge people he had already arrested as a result of Zaveniagin's interference. *CR*, 20 September 1988. No mention was made in the newspaper of the incident in late 1936 regarding insufficient coal supplies described by John Scott, *Behind*, p. 293.

308. *MR*, 24 October 1990. By no means were all bosses destroyed. Kogan, the chief of open-hearth shop no. 1, for example, survived the terror, becoming in 1939 a deputy commissar for ferrous metallurgy. *Stalinskaia stroika*, pp. 19–34.

309. MFGAChO, f. 99, op. 4, d. 59, ll. 62–63.

310. In the era of glasnost, the pages of the Magnitogorsk newspaper became filled with the stories of "simple people" who related how either they or their relatives had been arrested in 1937 and 1938. Viz. *MR*, 14 and 31 March 1989.

311. Magnitogorsk procuracy: Archival file "Nariad 34/C. Perepiska c NKVD i RKM 1936–1937 gg.," l. 52.

312. *MR*, 5 and 16 October 1937.

313. Scott, *Behind*, pp. 197–203.

314. For an account of the trial and Stalin's active role in it, see *Izvestiia TsK KPSS*, 1989, no. 4, pp. 42–80.

315. Mariia Scott expressed the same thought in nearly identical language. Interview by author, Ridgefield, Connecticut, February 1986. Even the level-headed John Scott was convinced that there were sufficient numbers of potential "fifth columnists" inside the USSR to justify some degree of purging. He also thought that there were real cases of wrecking. The few examples he adduces of victims expressing their grievances appear pathetic against the background of what the Soviet state did to them and others. Scott, *Behind*, pp. 188–89, 206, 282–83, 290–92.

316. The best description of the terror's psychological effects on an arrested party member remains Evgeniia Ginzburg, *Journey into the Whirlwind* (New York: Harcourt Brace Jovanovich, 1967).

317. In a forceful critique of some of Conquest's extreme claims on the general fear, Robert Thurston has made some questionable counterclaims. According to Thurston, there was no widespread "fear" before 1937, and even then it was circumscribed, so that "general fear did not exist in the USSR at any time in the late 1930s." Thurston must mean fear of arrest. This was not widespread before 1937 simply because mass arrests were not widespread, the deportations during collectivization notwithstanding. But beyond doubt, intimidation was very widespread well before 1937, and the population understood the consequences of speaking its mind. Thurston, "Fear and Belief in the USSR's 'Great Terror,'" 214–34.

318. Scott wrote, no doubt correctly, that "when one gets away from the circle of the middle and petty official and talks with the more or less average Soviet citizen in the trains, at home, and so forth, the terror appears to be *somewhat less than might be expected*" (my italics). But his claim that "the rank and file of the workers, with the exception, of course, of a great many foreign-born workers, do not appear to have been affected by the purge" seems mistaken, as does his contention that "only a small percentage of workers from the bench, so far as I have been able to ascertain, have been arrested." Scott also asserted that "the workers are often quite gleeful about the arrest of some 'big bird,' as they are termed by the laborers, whom they have not liked for one reason or another." Scott, *Behind*, pp. 190–93, 304.

319. *MR*, 2 July 1988.

320. Because the NKVD was not informing relatives of the fate of their arrested kin, and complaints poured in to the procurator, Sorokin wrote to Moscow requesting instructions on whether to respond, asking specifically for instructions on what to tell the relatives of those condemned to execution, such as sixteen-year-old Ev-

genii Gruzdev. The file contains no response to Sorokin's inquiry, dated 19 July 1938. The query was re-sent, but again the file contains no response. Magnitogorsk procuracy: Archival file "Nariad 32/C. Perepiska s vysshestoiashchimi organizat-siiami 1938 g.," ll. 64, 66.

321. See the discussion by Michael Taussig, "Culture of Fear—Space of Death. Roger Casement's Putumayo Report and the Explanation of Torture," *Comparative Studies of Society and History* 26 (1984): 467–97.

322. Scott heard of the arrest of labor colony chief Aleksandr Geineman, as well as that of the NKVD's Aleksei Pushkov, obviously from contacts he had among the local population. These events had not been divulged by the press. Scott, *Behind*, p. 196.

323. A certain gallows humor about the terror arose. One anecdote has been preserved in a collection of defectors' accounts: "Once, all the rabbits of the Soviet Union started running to the Polish frontier and tried to cross into Poland. The Polish border guards asked what was happening. 'Well,' replied the rabbits, 'the Soviet government has issued a decree ordering the death of all camels in Russia.' 'Yes,' said the guards, 'but you are not camels, you are rabbits.' 'That's right,' answered the rabbits, 'but does the NKVD know that?'" As told by Alexander Pokrovsky in Fischer, *Thirteen Who Fled*, p. 190.

324. Scott, *Behind*, pp. 292–93. Selivanov temporarily returned as editor on 17 October 1937 but soon was removed form the masthead again. Perhaps he was rearrested.

325. Rumors of all kinds were also pervasive in Smolensk, according to Fainsod, *Smolensk*, p. 157.

326. Scott, *Behind*, pp. 190–93.

327. Magnitogorsk procuracy: Archival file "Nariad 33/. Postanovleniia na prodlenie sroka po NKVD 1938–1939 gg.," l. 35.

328. When the terror was wound down in late 1938, Moscow sent instructions that wives were to be arrested only "if the women (wives of convicts) actually committed some kind of counterrevolutionary crime. . . . If they have been arrested only because they are the wives of convicts and no concrete crimes on their part have been established by the investigation, it is necessary to close their cases, free them, and return their passports." The order, dated 10 December 1938, was signed by A. Gurzman, deputy director of the procuracy's department for special cases. Magnitogorsk procuracy: Archival file "Nariad 32/C. Perepiska s vysshestoiash-chimi organizatsiiami 1938 g.," l. 90.

329. After moving in with her sister, who worked at the steel plant, Kozhev-nikova was herself arrested. She recounted how

one night we heard a knock at the door. The NKVD came in, said I was arrested, and brought in witnesses to observe the arrest. . . . They asked me whose boy that was . . . They told me if I took him with me I couldn't take my things. If I left my son behind I could take some stuff. . . . I fell into the hands of the investigator V. V. Ia-roslavtsev. He interrogated me ten hours straight. Then he left me, and was replaced by Fedorov. They insulted me any way they could. They wanted me to sign a document against my husband to the effect that he was a spy, that he went around and met with Germans. Iaroslavtsev stuck tobacco butts in my mouth. I was not allowed to go to the toilet. I was soaked in milk, I was nursing a baby boy. They gave me five years suspended under article 58-11 and -12, the same article they gave all wives of arrested husbands.

MR, 9 February 1989.

330. In writing of the people who did his family a good turn, Pisarenko *fils* added that the Stalinists were "mostly functionaries-careerists" for whom "our cause [*cosa nostra*!], 'the interests of the cause' (no matter which, 'socialism' or some other 'ism'), were higher than humanity, goodness, honor, and truth." *MR*, 30 November 1988.

331. *MR*, 6 January 1938.

332. Scott, *Behind*, pp. 195–96.

333. The poet Mikhail Liugarin [Zabolotnyi] recalled that in the fall of 1937, "they tried to make me confess that Ruchev, Makarov, and I plotted to destroy the blast furnaces and that we wanted to go to Moscow to kill Stalin." Liugarin was sentenced to three years and sent to Ivdel, near the Arctic, to cut timber, but given the length of his pretrial detention (two and a half years), his sentence was up in just half a year. Upon returning to Magnitogorsk, however, he was told to leave the city within twenty-four hours. So he went to a nearby village to live with relatives. He was rearrested on 9 May 1947 and sent to Norilsk, where he stayed until being released in 1954. *MR*, 2 July 1988. According to Klavdiia Makarova, her husband Vasilii Makarov was picked up late at night, in late fall 1937, at their apartment. The next day she was evicted and herself soon arrested. In 1942 she received a note indicating that her husband was dead. No date, place, or cause of death was given. In fact, Makarov was executed on 10 January 1938. *MR*, 13 August 1988 and 24 October 1990. The poet Boris Ruchev [Krivoshchekov] was also arrested in 1937, sentenced to ten years, and sent to work on the construction of a Magadan-Yakutsk railroad. He survived by getting a job as a nurse in the medical station. After his sentence expired in 1947, he was not permitted to leave the Khabarovsk region. Later he was allowed to resettle in Kirghizia, where he worked as a bookkeeper. In February 1957 Ruchev was rehabilitated and allowed to return to Magnitogorsk. During his long imprisonment and exile he sent many letters and poems to Stalin, never once receiving a reply. *MR*, 15 June 1988. One of the few persons from the city's literary collective not arrested was Valentin Serzhantov, who later became Magnitogorsk's leading historian (defending a candidate's dissertation in 1959). In 1931 Serzhantov, not yet twenty years old, worked as a common laborer on the coke plant foundation, took qualification courses, and also did volunteer "cultural work" in the barracks at night. In July of that year he was promoted to the editorial staff of *Magnitogorskii komsomolets*, writing stories on heroes of labor and the birth of the new man. In 1933 he was accused of using his position as deputy editor to criticize people he did not like and in general of conducting himself like a sergeant (a pun on his name). In 1989 Serzhantov, then living in Cheliabinsk, refused repeated requests for an interview. *Buksir*, December 1932, nos. 9–10; *MR*, 12 March 1933.

334. This was the opinion of John Scott, who himself felt this way. Scott, *Behind*, p. 205

335. A large outdoor demonstration took place in April 1938 to mark the up-

coming elections to the Supreme Soviet of the RSFSR scheduled for June. After the meeting was opened by the secretary of the Stalin raikom Smurov (Griaznov had been demoted to second secretary), Nosilevskii, a steel smelter and Stakhanovite, supposedly remarked, "We'll raise vigilance, and to the end destroy all enemies who hinder us as we move to new victories." *CR*, 24 April 1938. The plebiscitary nature of Soviet elections was not concealed by the regime. *V pomoshch izbirateliu* (Moscow, 1937), p. 4 (a pamphlet of information that originally appeared in *Pravda*).

336. Fedor Merkulov, people's commissar for ferrous metallurgy, issued a number of awards throughout the entire branch on 26 March 1939, including several to people in Magnitogorsk. Moshkovtsev, "Magnitka (1743–1941)," pp. 182–83. As of 1939, twenty-three people in Magnitogorsk had received state awards, including two Orders of Lenin, eighteen Orders of the Red Banner, and three awards of the "Badge of Honor." *MR*, 12 March 1939; reprinted in Eliseeva, *Iz istorii*, pp. 199–200.

337. *MR*, 1 February 1938.

338. As Djilas wrote, "Despite oppression, despotism, unconcealed confiscations, and the privileges of the ruling echelons, some of the people—and especially the Communists—retain the illusions contained in their slogans." Djilas, *The New Class*, p. 30.

339. From memoir accounts written by defectors from cities other than Magnitogorsk we know that in NKVD prisons the main issue of discussion was, Why? Some victims accepted the regime's contentions that there really were such spies and enemies, preferring to believe that they had been arrested mistakenly, perhaps by enemies within NKVD. Others recognized the arbitrariness of the arrests and offered various theories. Some people embraced mystical explanations; others surmised that the terror was functional, a form of social prophylaxis to preempt potential crime; or an unavoidable way to satisfy the country's need for a labor force in far-off places. Still others subscribed to the notion that the terror was unintended, having snowballed because of the mutual denunciations, or because the NKVD operatives had proposed a "counterplan" to their assigned obligations. There were even some people who attributed it all to sunspots. Such deduced explanations are less important for the light they shed on the inner workings of the regime than the sense they convey of the terror's reception by those arrested, especially the bewilderment experienced by people who considered themselves loyal. Knowing their own innocence, few loyalists wanted to accept that an apparently capricious terror could have grown out of the sacred cause of the revolution. But that the terror spoke the language of the socialist revolution was indisputable, and one of the reasons it was so difficult to fathom by its victims. Beck and Godin, *Russian Purge*, pp. 213–77.

340. *CR*, 10 August 1938.

341. Scott, *Behind*, p. 83.

342. In June 1936, during the exchange of party cards, someone evidently overheard Vasilii Vlasov, who led a circle for the discussion of party history, remark that Lominadze "fell victim to the Stalinist regime" and "took his life because he did not wish to endure the servitude Stalin created." Vlasov was expelled from the party.

Later, on 28 August 1937, he was arrested, accused of having ties to the "Lominadze group" and of having been an "active Trotskyite" during his Moscow student days in the 1920s. Vlasov had been under interrogation for more than eight months when, in a memo to the Magnitogorsk NKVD dated 5 May 1937, City Procurator Sorokin wrote that he needed more evidence and asked the NKVD to locate arrested members of the Lominadze gang so they could be interrogated. Magnitogorsk procuracy: Archival file "Nariad 34/C. Perepiska c NKVD i RKM 1936–1937 gg.," ll. 81–83.

343. Konstantin Bazilevskii, a nonparty white-collar employee of the construction trust, "at a number of meetings of workers and engineers . . . passed anonymous notes to the presidium with anti-Soviet content." Bazilevskii was at first released for improper investigation procedure. Among the questions he allegedly sent to Khitarov at a 16 December 1936 meeting following the return of the Magnitogorsk delegates from the Supreme Soviet were:

> "Why didn't you speak about the repeal of the death penalty?"
> "How and where are we going to vote in a new way?"
> "How were you elected bosses received, what did they serve you, were there any drinking bouts and what kind?"
> "Why was the 28 June 1936 issue of *Magnitogorskii rabochii* removed from circulation? Where is Selivanov [the editor]?"
> "Where is Piatakov?"
> "Will the labor-settlers [dekulakized], having received the right to vote, get citizenship, passports to travel around without guard?"

These questions were deemed counterrevolutionary at the meeting. In addition, at a lecture on Mayakovski in the Central Library, Bazilevskii allegedly asked if the lecturer knew the poet's verses criticizing Soviet reality and the verses not published because of censorship. Under interrogation, Bazilevskii allegedly admitted writing the anonymous notes, but he denied that they were counterrevolutionary. A psychiatrist examined him and what was called a "strange" diary of his. On 24 December 1936, he was arrested. Sorokin reported that he thought Bazilevskii was not a counterrevolutionary, but vacillated politically because of unspecified psychiatric reasons. Magnitogorsk procuracy: Archival file "Nariad 34/C. Perepiska c NKVD i RKM 1936–1937 gg.," ll. 47 (dated 10 April 1937), 94.

344. The writer A. Pismennyi argued that there were four possible reactions to the situation that took shape in the 1930s: (1) active opposition to the party and, since the two were indivisible, to Soviet power—a course to which few people were inclined, as much out of a genuine sympathy for Soviet power (rather than the party) as an instinct for self-preservation; (2) indifference to and avoidance of public and political events, both good and bad; (3) calculated hypocrisy—a widespread but by no means easy form of behavior, involving the constant display of false enthusiasm; and (4) the easiest course of all, faith—belief in the class struggle and the fact that Stalin was defending the general interest by leading the crusade against oppositionists and enemies. *Knizhnoe obozrenie*, 6 October 1989, p. 10.

AFTERWORD: STALINISM AS A CIVILIZATION

1. *The New Class* (New York: Praeger, 1957), p. 30.

2. Timasheff, *The Great Retreat*. Virtually all English-language textbooks on the history of the USSR adopt Timasheff's line.

3. Veniamin Kaverin, *Epilog: Memuary* (Moscow, 1989), pp. 96–99. The date of the Magnitogorsk cemetery's founding remains mysterious, for initially the city had no cemetery. The first doctor on the site in 1929, desperately fighting an outbreak of scarlet fever, claimed he had wanted to establish one, but that a decision was instead taken to build a crematorium. GARF, f. 7952, op. 5, d. 308, l. 80.

4. The Soviet émigré Lev Kopelev, a young enthusiast sent to facilitate the brutal collectivization process in the Ukraine, put it eloquently: "I convinced myself and others that the main thing had remained unchanged, that all our ills, malefactions and falsehoods were inevitable but temporary afflictions in our overall healthy society. In freeing ourselves from barbarity, we were forced to resort to barbaric methods, and in repulsing cruel and crafty foes, we could not do without cruelty and craftiness. . . . Insight came later: it grew slowly and irregularly." *The Education of a True Believer* (New York: Harper and Row, 1980; originally published in Russian, 1978), pp. 122–23.

5. B. N. Bulatov and G. P. Gekker, *Magnitogorsk* (Moscow-Leningrad, 1931), p. 158.

6. *MR*, 11 October 1937. The Pedagogical Institute was initially organized as a night school, which opened in 1936. In 1938, it switched to daytime and took over the premises of a converted elementary school. *MR*, 9 May 1938.

7. The Mining and Metallurgical Institute, for example, was located in a decayed barracks on the Ezhovka section of the Fifth Sector (initially it had been located in building no. 25 of Kirov district). In 1939 the institute had 680 students (including those studying at the *rabfak*), for whom there were thirty teachers, one professor, and five docents. Poor as its facilities were, the institute was far better off than the industrial trade high school. The latter had changed location four times in three years, and in 1936 was still without a permanent site. Founded in 1931, the trade high school graduated 420 students by 1938, at which time it had 260 students, 145 of whom attended at night. *MR*, 9 January and 15 October 1936, 24 September and 28 December 1938, and 20 June 1939.

8. *MR*, 23 July 1936.

9. *MR*, 5 August and 20 October 1936. In 1937 the city decided to accredit its elementary-school teachers. Of the almost 600 teachers in the city, 283 passed the test; another 231 retained the right to teach under the condition that they attend courses; 45 were to be reexamined, and 16 had lost the right to teach. The newspaper complained that only 97 teachers were enrolled in any courses. *MR*, 28 March 1937. By 1941 the number of elementary-school pupils had declined to 21,801, by which time there were still approximately 600 teachers, or less than one for every 350 pupils. This ratio was actually a marked improvement over the situation of four years earlier, when the ratio was closer to one teacher for 500 pupils. *Materialy o rabote*, p. 12. Teachers also functioned as social workers. See the comments by John Scott on his wife, Mariia Scott, who was among the first

class of twenty-odd graduates from the city's fledgling Pedagogical Institute and worked as a teacher in a school for the children of the dekulakized. Scott, *Behind*, p. 132.

10. The newspaper added that this was less the students' fault than the result of improper training, insisting that the country needed not just technical specialists but "socialist technical specialists." *MR*, 16 May 1936.

11. The newspaper lamented the fact that of the 13,000 to 15,000 pupils of pioneer age living in the city, only 6,200 belonged to the organization, but this was still a sizable number and in subsequent years it would grow. *MR*, 28 December 1936.

12. V. Bulgakov, *Za obraztsovoe*, pp. 48–49.

13. Gary's schools became famous under the direction of William Wirt, a pupil and disciple of John Dewey. Quillen, "Industrial City," pp. 170–71 (one of the first school teachers was R. R. Quillen, evidently a relative of the author); See also Randolph Bourne, *The Gary Schools* (Boston: Houghton Mifflin, 1916), based on a visit in 1915. Gary schools were, of course, segregated. Neil Betten and Raymond Mottl, "The Evolution of Racism in an Industrial City, 1906–1940: Case Study of Gary, Indiana," *Journal of Negro History* 59, no. 1 (1974): 51–64. See also Arthur Shumway, "Gary, Shrine of the Steel God: The City that Has Everything, and at the Same Time Has Nothing," *The American Parade* 3, no. 2 (1929): 23; and [Howard Harries], *The Story of Gary, Indiana: An Illustrated Study of the Building of the Most Marvellous City on the American Continent* (Gary: 1908).

14. The eyewitness René Fülöp-Miller, writing that "for the Bolsheviks, industrialized America became the Promised Land," offered several examples. Fülöp-Miller, *The Mind and Face of Bolshevism*, pp. 29–33. In his 1924 codification of Leninism, Stalin alluded to the combination of "Russian revolutionary sweep" and "American efficiency." *Sochineniia*, vol. 6, pp. 186–87. This talk, according to Mariia Scott, reached the countryside. Buck, *Talk About Russia*, pp. 13–14. See also Jeffrey Brooks, "The Press and Its Message: Images of America in the 1920s and 1930s," in Sheila Fitzpatrick et al., eds., *Russia in the Era of Nep: Explorations in Soviet Society and Culture* (Bloomington: Indiana University Press, 1991), pp. 231–52.

15. Tommaso Campanella, *The City of the Sun: A Poetical Dialogue*, trans. by Daniel J. Donno (Berkeley: University of California, 1981). Written in Italian in 1602, the dialogue circulated in manuscript until its publication in Latin in 1623.

16. Foma Kampanella, *Gorod solntsa: Perevod s latinskogo i kommentarii F. A. Petrovskogo. S predisloviem V. P. Volgina* (Moscow: Akademiia Nauk, 1934; 1947). Campanella's life and thought would have been known to a Russian-language audience through a handful of scholarly works of the late nineteenth and early twentieth centuries. See, for example, B. I. Gorev, *Ot Tomasa Mora do Lenina, 1516–1917: Populiarnye ocherki po istorii sotsializma v biografiiakh i kharakteristikakh*, 4th ed. (Moscow, 1923).

NOTE ON SOURCES

1. For further examples, see the helpful *A Researcher's Guide to Sources on Soviet Social History in the 1930s*, ed. Sheila Fitzpatrick and Lynne Viola (Armonk, N.Y.: M. E. Sharpe, 1990).

2. Other local newspapers included the *Magnitogorskii pioner, Magnitogorskii komsomolets* (moved out of Magnitogorsk in 1936, when it became an oblast-level paper), *Magnitogorskii metall* (factory paper), *Magnitostroi* (construction), *Gorniak* (mine), *Magnitogorskii gudok* (railroad workers' party committee), *Izvestiia Magnitogorska* (dekulakized peasants), and *Borba za metall* (the labor colony). A full list of locally published newspapers appeared in *Magnitogorskii rabochii*, 5 May 1936 (officially celebrated as press day). As of 1 January 1933 the main city daily employed 182 people. By July 1933, this was down to 109, a result of mandatory staff reductions. MFGAChO, f. 16, op. 1, d. 14, l. 100.

3. The position of editor was held by prominent members of the city party committee, and appointments to the editorship were confirmed at city party conferences. Accordingly, the fate of the editors followed the fortunes of the local party secretary, who seems to have exercised ultimate control over editorial matters. According to the recollections of one insider, for example, "all the more or less critical material appeared within a few hours on Lominadze's desk and made it into the newspaper only with his approval." *MR*, 2 September 1936. Between 1934 and 1939 there were at least seven editors (listed with the years of their removal): Malyshev (1934), Bezbabichev (1935), Umanskii (1935), Kariaev (1937), Selivanov (1937), Lianov (1937), Selivanov (1937), Prokhorchik (1938), Dolgikh (1939). For two periods in 1938 the masthead carried the designation "editorial collegium."

4. *MR*, 18 March 1934; GARF, f. 7952, op. 5, d. 284, ll. 9–10.

5. *CR*, 5 May 1936.

6. *MR*, 18 April and 11 May 1936, 6 May 1937.

7. *MR*, 11 July 1936.

8. Perhaps the most interesting party archive documents are the assessments of the prevailing mood within the ranks that each organization was required to prepare regularly. In addition to the reports made by the party secretaries, each party organization had among its members a secret informant (*osvedomitel*) charged with compiling separate reports.

9. Even in 1991, I was not able to see the documents of the so-called first department (*pervyi otdel*) of the steel plant. Concerned with security, this department's files contain detailed information about such subjects as the foreigners employed at the plant, industrial accidents, and the condition and operation of the machinery. All these matters, however, received at least some treatment in the press and other published sources.

10. The original publication plans, dated 16 October 1931, contained a list of twenty-six factories. Several dozen more were later added, sometimes through the efforts of local enthusiasts. Only about a dozen volumes were published. GARF, f. 7952, op. 1, d. 3, l. 3; op. 1, d. 28, l. 2; op. 8, d. 243, ll. 1–2. In 1938, before they were turned over to GARF—which initially refused the offer citing a lack of space—the documents were sifted, with some removed. It is likely, although impossible to establish beyond doubt, that the documents on Magnitogorsk were also

purged. If they were, it is unclear what effect, if any, such an operation might have had on them. Ibid., op. 1, d. 11, ll. 1–14.

11. The 7952 collection is divided according to region. Opis 5 treats the Urals and Siberia. Of the 794 total files contained therein, 289 are on Magnitogorsk (by contrast, there are just 23 for Novokuznetsk). Opis 6 covers the Ukraine (just 152 total files), opis 4 Leningrad (240 files), and opis 3 Moscow (the largest number of files on a Moscow enterprise is the 175 for Serp i molot). Only opis 7 (the Moscow metro construction), with 405 files, and opis 9 (the Moscow-Kazan Railway), with 300 files, top the number on Magnitogorsk. In addition to the opisi themselves, see the published guide, A. M. Gorkii i sozdanie istorii fabrik i zavodov (Moscow, 1959), which contains a bibliography.

12. GARF, f. 7952, op. 5, d. 139, ll. 1–2, 5–6.

13. Ibid., ll. 3–15.

14. Ibid., d. 203, ll. 69 ff.

15. Ibid., d. 301, l. 79.

16. One of the first completed chapters dealt with the coke plant construction and the "heroic pouring of concrete" (GARF, f. 7952, op. 5, d. 372, ll. 1–32). This was also the subject material chosen by Valentin Kataev for his novel, Vremia, Vpered! Another early chapter, dated April 1933 and written by Valentin Serzhantov, one of the original three members of the local editorial board, treated the role of the Komsomol (ibid., d. 200, ll. 41–54). After the war Serzhantov turned it into a dissertation for the candidate of science degree.

17. The two-volume document collection, covering the years 1929–34, can be found in GARF, f. 7952, op. 5, d. 384.

18. Ibid., d. 301, l. 97.

19. V. N. Eliseeva, "Istoriografiia voprosa o soiuze rabochego klassa i krestianstva v khode stroitelstva MMK," Istoriografiia istorii sozdaniia i razvitiia soiuza rabochego klassa i krestianstva na Urale (Sverdlovsk, 1982), pp. 132–43; Istoriia zavodov: Sbornik, 1932, no. 1, pp. 52–56, no. 3, p. 7; 1934, nos. 3–4, pp. 11–12; GARF, f. 7952, op. 5, d. 412, l. 3; and d. 382, ll. 2–12. See also Buksir (Magnitogorsk), 1933, no. 1; and L. P. Galtseva, "My byli romantikami i mechtateliami," in Poety litbrigady (Cheliabinsk, 1969), pp. 5–30.

20. According to some sources, locals had insisted on a visit to Magnitogorsk by the Moscow brigade in 1933. GARF, f. 7952, op. 5, d. 382, l. 1.

21. Valentin Serzhantov, one of the locals with the greatest stake in the efforts, wrote a sharp piece that was published in the city newspaper in late 1936 on the status of the forlorn project. He asserted that the Muscovites sent in had done nothing but acquaint themselves with materials already collected. The newspaper also printed a response to Serzhantov by the history project's senior and deputy editors, who admitted that there had been a delay, which they blamed in part on the Magnitogorsk editorial collective formed in 1932 and in part on the magnitude of the project. "The work turned out to be extremely vast and complicated," they wrote. "It was necessary to catalogue a huge mass of material, transcribe the memoirs of hundreds of people, and above all to study this material and give a true appraisal to all events, the entire path of construction, evaluate people and facts, that is, to write a thoroughly Bolshevik history of the Magnitogorsk factory." The editors of the Magnitogorsk newspaper claimed to be satisfied with this response to Serzhantov

yet congratulated themselves for publishing his original article, an act they called a tribute to "openness" (*shirokaia glasnost*). Around Magnitogorsk shops, a majority of people involved were said to have agreed with Serzhantov's criticisms, which he evidently presented in a series of public lectures. *MR*, 23 and 27 December 1936, 16 January 1937.

22. In an effort to explain the delays, I. Rakhtanov, a Moscow writer assigned to write the history of Magnitogorsk, wrote after a visit to the site in 1934 that "the history of Magnitogorsk is not just some routine essay. It is a great scientific, artistic, monumental book. And from this arises all the difficulties. How to combine the scientificity with the artistic quality? How to portray people in such a book? What is a fact? Where are the limits of artistic truth? . . . These are truly colossal tasks. The word *Magnitostroi* carries the significance of an entire epoch, and that epoch is now taking place. We don't have the advantage of hindsight, the freedom to look back calmly. . . . It is difficult to write the history of Magnitostroi, difficult but necessary and very honorable." GARF, f. 7952, op. 5, d. 400, l. 3.

23. GARF, f. 7952, op. 5, d. 323, passim; d. 401, l. 6; and d. 462, ll. 10–13.

24. *MR*, 22 January 1937.

25. Fedor Galiguzov and Mikhail Churillin, *Flagman otechestvennoi industrii: Istoriia Magnitogorskogo metallurgicheskogo kombinata im. Lenina* (Moscow, 1978).

26. This work was supervised by the enthusiastic visiting correspondent for *Komsomolskaia pravda*, Semen Nariniani. GARF, f. 7952, op. 5, d. 231, l. 24. Instructions received from Moscow dated 28 November 1931 listed the purposes of such efforts as informing the outside world, educating new workers politically, battling against Trotskyism and other falsifications, and demonstrating the superiority of socialism over capitalism. Ibid., d. 320, ll. 1–8.

27. Viz. GARF, f. 7952, op. 5, d. 190 and d. 214, passim.

28. Petrazhitskii received a salary from the steel plant for this work and even employed a paid assistant. *MR*, 20 and 26 March 1936.

29. John Scott, *Behind the Urals: An American Worker in Russia's City of Steel*, enlarged edition prepared by Stephen Kotkin (Bloomington: Indiana University Press, 1989).

Select Bibliography

The following bibliography contains sources specifically on Magnitogorsk. Reference to other materials used in this monograph can be found in the endnotes.

ARCHIVAL MATERIALS

Gosudarstvennyi arkhiv Cheliabinskoi oblasti (GAChO)
    Fond 804 (Cheliabinskaia oblastnaia planovaia komissiia)
Gosudarstvennyi arkhiv Rossiiskii federatsii (GARF). (Formerly Tsentralnyi
    gosudarstvennyi arkhiv Oktiabrskoi revoliutsii, or TsGAOR.)
    Fonds 7952 (Istoriia fabrik i zavodov), 5451 (VTsSPS)
Gosudarstvennyi arkhiv Sverdlovskoi oblsati (GASO)
    Fonds 225 (Uralgipromez), 241 (Uralplan), 1150 (Vostokostal)
Haven, William A. (1888–1973). Papers, 1916–1972. Case Western Reserve
    Historical Society, Cleveland, Ohio.
Hoover Institution Archives, Stanford, California. Russian Subject Collection,
    boxes 17–20, American Engineers in Russia, 1927–1933; Nicolaevsky
    Collection; Jay K. Zawodny Collection, "Twenty-six Interviews."
Magnitogorsk procuracy. Archival files (thirteen in all, variously numbered).
Magnitogorskii filial gosudarstvennogo arkhiva Cheliabinskoi oblasti
    (MFGAChO)
    Fonds 10 (Magnitogorskii gorodskoi sovet), 99 (MMK), 118 (zavkom)
Magnitogorskii kraevedcheskii muzei
Rossiiskii gosudarstvennyi arkhiv ekonomiki (RGAE). (Formerly Tsentralnyi
    gosudarstvennyi arkhiv Narodnogo Khoziastva, or TsGANKh.)
    Fonds 3429 (Vesenkha), 4086 (GUMP), 7297 (NKTP)
Rossiiskii tsentr khraneniia i izucheniia dokumentov noveishei istorii
    (RTsKhIDNI). (Formerly Tsentralnyi partiinyi arkhiv, institut Marksizma-
    Leninzma, or TsPA IML.)
    Fonds 17 (Urals obkom), 85 (Ordzhonikidze), 558 (Stalin)
Scott, John (1912–1976). Papers. State Historical Society, Madison, Wisconsin.
Tsentralnyi arkhiv kinofotodokumentvo (TsGAKFD)

U.S. National Archives, Washington, D. C. Embassy (Moscow) reports, decimal file 861, Living Conditions [in the USSR].

UNPUBLISHED SOURCES

Baryshev, A. A. "Zdravookhranenie Magnitogorska: Istoriia stanovleniia i razvitiia, s 1929 g. po 1975 g.," Magnitogorsk, 1976.
Brion, Ida. "Partiia bolshevikov v borbe za sozdanie Magnitogorskogo metallurgicheskogo kombinata, 1929–1931 gg.," candidate's dissertation, Sverdlovsk, 1949.
Korolkov, V. K. "Borba KPSS za sozdanie i osvoenie Magnitogorskogo metallurgicheskogo kombinata, 1929–1933 gg.," candidate's dissertation, Leningrad, 1955.
Scott, John. "Heavy Industry in the Soviet Union East of the Volga; A report prepared for the Board of Economic Warfare," Washington, D.C., 1943, typescript 815 pp., declassified, Library of Congress.
Serzhantov, Valentin. "KPSS—Vdokhnovitel i organizator stroitelstva i osvoeniia Magnitogorskogo kombinata im. tov. Stalina—Moshchnoi metallurgicheskoi bazy strany, 1929–1937 gg.," candidate's dissertation, Moscow, 1959.
Zuikov, Valentin. "Komsomol na stroitelstve i osvoenii Magnitogorskogo metallurgicheskogo kombinata imeni Stalina 1929–1933 gg.," candidate's dissertation, Sverdlovsk, 1950.

LOCAL NEWSPAPERS

Borba za metall
Cheliabinskii rabochii
Gorniak
Izvestiia Magnitogorska
Magnitogorskii gudok
Magnitogorskii komsomolets
Magnitogorskii metall
Magnitogorskii pioner
Magnitogorskii rabochii
Magnitostroi
Uralskii rabochii

LOCAL JOURNALS

Magnitostroi (Magnitogorsk)
Partiinyi rabotnik (Cheliabinsk)
Za magnitostroi literatury (previously *Buksir*) (Magnitogorsk)
Za tekhnicheskoe vooruzhenie (Magnitogorsk)
Uralskii kommunist (Sverdlovsk)
V pomoshch partaktivu (Sverdlovsk)

BIBLIOGRAPHIES OF PUBLISHED SOURCES

A. M. Gorkii i sozdanie istorii fabrik i zavodov. Moscow, 1959.
Bannikova, A. A., comp., *Flagman Metallurgii: Magnitogorskii metallurgicheskii kombinat im. Lenina. K 110-letiiu so dnia rozhdeniia V. I. Lenina. Rekomendirovanii bibliograficheskii ukazatel.* Cheliabinsk, 1980, 11 pp.
Bibliograficheskii ukazatel knig i broshiur po istorii fabrik i zavodov. Moscow, 1932.
Demidova, S. E.; Matveeva, T. F.; and Rakhmatullin, A. R., comps., *Magnitogorsk 1929–1979: Rekomendirovannyi ukazatel literatury.* Magnitogorsk, 1979.
Literatura o Magnitogorske: Bibliograficheskii ukazatel. Magnitogorsk, quarterly 1979–1984.

PUBLISHED SOURCES

Alkatsev, D. K. and Troshev, Zh. P. *Avraamii Pavlovich Zaveniagin: Ocherki zhizni i deiatelnosti.* Krasnoiarsk, 1975.
Ankudinov, Leonid G. "Trudovoi podvig stroitelei Magnitki." In *Cheliabinskaia oblast za 40 let sovetskoi vlasti.* Cheliabinsk, 1957, pp. 435–50.
———. *Magnitostroi.* Cheliabinsk, 1979.
Antipova, I. V. and Shkolnik, M. I. "Iz istorii sozdaniia Magnitogorskogo metallurgicheskogo kombinata (1929–1931 gg.)." *Istoriia SSSR*, 1958, no. 5: 25–50.
Avdeenko, Aleksandr. *Ia liubliu.* Moscow, 1933.
Baikov, Alexander A. *Magnitogorsk.* Moscow, 1939, in English.
Baranov, A. *Magnitogorskaia plotina.* Sverdlovsk, 1931.
Barshch, M.; Vladimirov, V.; Okhitovich M.; and Sokolov, N. "Magnitogore." *S.A. Sovremennaia arkhitektura* 5, nos. 1–2 (1930): 38–57.
Bogdanov, N. *Gigant piatiletki.* Sverdlovsk-Moscow, 1931.
Bondarev, A. and Alkatsev, D. "V etom—Ves Sergo: Magnitogorskie stranitsy zhizni G. K. Ordzhonikidze." *Ural*, 1969, no. 11: 128–33.
Buck, Pearl. *Talk About Russia (with Masha Scott).* New York: John Day, 1945.
Bükschmitt, Justus. *Ernst May.* Stuttgart, 1963.
Bulatov, B. N. and Gekker, G. P. *Magnitogorsk.* Moscow-Leningrad, 1931.
Bulgakov, V. *Za obraztsovoe kultobsluzhivanie novostroek: Ocherki po kultrabote v Magnitogorske.* Moscow, 1932.
Bumazhnyi, Lev and Morozov, Mikhail. *Magnitogorsk.* Moscow, 1958.
Chagan, Z. *U podnozhia Magnitnoi gory.* Moscow-Leningrad, 1930.
Chaplygin, Iurii. "Lager pressy u gory Magnitnoi." *Sovetskaia pechat*, 1957, no. 10: 46–48.
Davies, Robert W. "A Note on the Defence Aspects of the Ural-Kuznetsk Combine." *Soviet Studies* 26, no. 2 (April 1974): 272–73.
Dela i liudi: Sbornik. Magnitogorsk, 1931.
Dmitrevskii, V. "Rafael Khitarov." In *Vozhaki Komsomola: Sbornik.* Moscow, 1978, pp. 46–132.

Dzhaparidze, E. "Magnitka." In *Revoliutsionnyi derzhite shag*. Moscow, 1970, vyp. 2, pp. 183–90.

Egorov, Pavel Ivanovich. *The Magnitogorsky (Magnetic Mountain) Metallurgical Works*. Moscow, 1929.

Elfimov, Iu. N. *Marshall industrii: Biograficheskii ocherk A. P. Zaveniagina*. Cheliabinsk, 1982.

Eliseeva, V. N. "Borba za kadry na stroitelstve Magnitogorskogo metallurgicheskogo kombinata v gody pervoi piatiletki." In *Uchenye zapiski Cheliabinskogo pedagogicheskogo instituta*. Cheliabinsk, 1956, tom 1, vyp. 1.

———. "Iz istorii proektirovanii i stroitelstva Magnitogorskogo metallurgicheskogo kombinata." In *Iz istorii revoliutsionnogo i sotsialisticheskogo stroitelstva na iuzhnom Urale*. Cheliabinsk, 1957.

———. "Predislovie." In *Iz istorii MMK i goroda Magnitogorska, 1929–1941 gg.* Cheliabinsk, 1965, pp. 3–46.

———. "Istoriografiia voprosa o soiuze rabochego klassa i krestianstva v khode stroitelstva MMK." In *Istoriografiia istorii sozdaniia i razvitiia soiuza rabochego klassa i krestianstva na Urale*. Sverdlovsk, 1982, pp. 132–43.

Emelianov, V. S. *O vremeni, o tovarishchakh, o sebe*. Moscow, 1968.

Ernst, Louis. "Inside a Soviet Industry," *Fortune*, October 1949, 116–19, 172, 174, 177–78.

Fedorov, Evgenii Aleksandrovich. *U gory Magnitnoi: Povest*. Leningrad, 1947.

Galiguzov, Ivan Fedorovich and Chirillin, M. E. *Flagman otechestvennoi industrii: Istoriia Magnitogorskogo metallurgicheskogo kombinata im. Lenina*. Moscow, 1978.

Galtseva, L. P. "My byli romantikami i mechtateliami." In *Poety litbrigady*. Cheliabinsk, 1969, pp. 5–30.

Garri, A. "Serdtse giganta: Magnitstroi letom 1931 goda." In *Reportazh s mesta sobytii*. Moscow, 1967, pp. 108–14.

Gekhman, Ia. A. and Gurevich, M. E. *Potochnoe stroitelstvo zhilykh domov v g. Magnitogorske*. Moscow, 1957.

Gerasimov, P. M. "Gora Magnitka." In *Byli industrialnye*. Moscow, 1973, pp. 291–310.

"Gigant i stroitel." *SSSR na stroike*, 1932, no. 1.

Grishchenko, Petr and Kokonini, Vladimir. *Trudovye prazdniki i traditsii*. Moscow, 1974.

Gugel, Iakov. "Vospominaniia o Magnitke." In *God vosemnadtsatyi: Almanakh shestoi*. Moscow, 1935, pp. 318–49.

Haven, William, "The Magnitogorsk Mines and Metallurgical Plant." *Blast Furnace and Steel Plant* (January 1931): 121–24, 144.

———. "Magnetegorsk [*sic*]. Some Comments on the Design and Construction of a Mining and Metallurgical Plant for the USSR." *Mechanical Engineering* 54 (July 1932): 461–66, 497.

Hays, Fred N. "Five Great Power Plants Rise at Magnitogorsk." *Power* 76, no. 2 (August 1932): 79–81.

Hindus, Maurice. "Pinch-Hitter for the Soviets." *American Magazine* 113 (April 1932): 21–33, 134–36.

Holzman, Franklyn D. "The Soviet Ural-Kuznetsk Combine: A Study in

Investment Criteria and Industrialization Policies." *Quarterly Journal of Economics* 71 (1957): 368–405.

Iakovlev, Iu. V.; Zubets, V. M.; and Arkhipov, V. M. *Flagman Sovetskoi metallurgii v rekonstruktsii*. Cheliabinsk, 1979.

Iakovlev, Surat. *Za khozraschet*. Magnitogorsk, 1931.

Itogi raboty zavoda za vosem mesiatsev pervogo stakhanovskogo 1936 goda. Moscow, 1936.

Itogi raboty zavoda za chetyri mesiatsa 1937 goda. Moscow, 1937.

Iunost Magnitki: Dokumentalno-khudozhestvennaia kompozitsiia. Moscow, 1981.

Ivanov, Fedor. *Magnitogorskii kombinat—Pervenets sotsialisticheskoi industrializatsii SSSR*. Cheliabinsk, 1958.

Ivanov, N. "Magnitka—Legendarnii podvig Sovetskogo naroda." *Planovoe khoziaistvo*, 1979, no. 4: 41–45.

Iz istorii Magnitogorskogo metallurgicheskogo kombinata i goroda Magnitogorska (1929–1941 gg.): Sbornik dokumentov i materialov. Cheliabinsk, 1965.

"K 50-letiiu Magnitogorska." *Arkhitektura SSSR*, 1979, no. 7: 4–35.

Kak pisat o svoem metode raboty. Magnitogorsk, 1936.

Kak predupredit gripp. Magnitogorsk, 1940.

Kartashov, N. [Shneiveis, R.]. *Tovarisch direktor*. Moscow, 1974.

Kataev, Valentin. *Vremia, Vpered!* Moscow, 1933. Translated as *Time, Forward!* Bloomington: Indiana University Press, 1961.

Kazarinova, Valentina I. and Pavlichenkov, V. I. *Magnitogorsk: Opyt Sovetskoi arkhitektury*. Moscow, 1961.

Khailov, A. I. "Pereferiinye zhurnaly." In *Ocherki istorii Russkoi Sovetskoi zhurnalistki 1917–1932*. Moscow, 1960, pp. 463–567.

Kirstein, Tatjana. *Sowjetische Industrialisierung—geplanter oder spontaner Prozess? Eine Strukturanalyse des wirtschaftspolitischen Entscheidungs-Prozesses beim Aufbau des Ural-Kuzneck Kombinats 1918–1930*. Baden-Baden, 1979.

———. *Die Bedeutung von Durchführungsentscheidungen in dem zentralistisch verfassten Entscheidungssystem der Sowjetunion*. Wiesbaden, 1984.

Kolotilii, A. G. "Inostrannye trudiashchiesia na Magnitostroe." In *Tvorcheskaia deiatelnost rabochego klassa Magnitki*. Magnitogorsk, 1967.

Komsomol na lesakh novostroek: Sbornik. Moscow, 1931.

Kondakov, A. *Sila pechati (Iz opyta "Magnitogorskogo Rabochego")*. Cheliabinsk, 1959.

———. *Stalnoe serdtse rodiny*. Moscow, 1961.

———. "Prodolzhenie epopei." In *Zhurnalisty rasskazyvaiut: Ocherki*. Moscow, 1974, pp. 82–91.

Koordinaty podviga: Iz istorii Cheliabinskoi oblastnoi komsomolskoi organizatsii 1918–1968. Cheliabinsk, 1968.

Korin, E. *Na novykh putiakh*. Sverdlovsk-Moscow, 1931.

Leonidov, I. I. "O proekte novogo Magnitogorska." In *Russkii gorod: Istoriko-metodlogicheskii sbornik*. Moscow, 1971, pp. 224–29.

Liudi Stalinskoi Magnitki. Cheliabinsk, 1952.

Luzin, V. Ia. "Iz istorii razvitia stakhanovskogo dvizheniia na Magnitogorskom
    metallurgicheskom kombinate (1935–1937 gg.)." In *Voprosy istorii KPSS*.
    Cheliabinsk, 1970, vyp. 5, pp. 85–101.
Magnitka, 50 Let. 4 vols. Cheliabinsk, 1979.
Magnitka: Kratkii istoricheskii ocherk. Cheliabinsk, 1971.
Magnitka: Polveka v stroiu. Moscow, 1982.
Magnitka—Stal i liudi: Fotoalbom. Moscow, 1979.
Magnitka—Stal i liudi: Rasskazy ob opyte MMK. Moscow, 1976.
"Magnitogorsk." In *Kratkaia Geograficheskaia Entsiklopedia*. Vol. 2. Moscow,
    1961, pp. 511–12.
Magnitogorsk: Materialy v pomoshch propogandistu, lektoru i agitatoru.
    Magnitogorsk, 1960–.
Magnitogorsk v tsifrakh: K 60-letiiu Sovetskoi vlasti. Statisticheskii sbornik.
    Magnitogorsk, 1977.
"Magnitogorskii Metallurgicheskii Kombinat" In *Bolshaia Sovetskaia
    Entsiklopedia*. 2d ed. Moscow, 1938.
*Magnitogorskii metallurgicheskii zavod: Materialy k piatiletnemu planu
    khoziaistva Urala*. Sverdlovsk, 1928.
Magnitogorskii metallurgicheskii zavod: Proekt. Leningrad, 1929.
Magnitogorskii teatr imeni Pushkina (Cheliabinsk, 1940).
Magnitostroi v tsifrakh: Statisticheskii otchet za 1931 g. Magnitogorsk, 1932.
Malenkii, Aleksei Georgevich. *Magnitogorsk: The Magnitogorsk Metallurgical
    Combine of the Future*. Moscow, 1932.
Malyshkin, Aleksander. *Liudi iz zakholustia*. Leningrad, 1977.
Mariasin, A. M. *Vtoroi gigant gory Magnitnoi*. Sverdlovsk, 1933.
Markevich, Nikolai. *Rozhdenie giganta*. Moscow, 1931.
*Materialy o rabote Magnitogorskogo soveta deputatov trudiashchikhsia za 1940
    god*. Magnitogorsk, 1941.
May, Ernst. "K proektu generalnogo plana Magnitogorska." *Sovietskaia
    arkhitektura*, May–June 1933, no. 3: 17–25.
———. "Cities of the Future." In Walter Laqueur and Leopold Labedz, eds., *The
    Future of Communist Society*. New York: Praeger, 1962, pp. 179–85.
Melnikov, N. V. "Gornii inzhener Nikolai Nikolaevich Partrikeev." In *Gornye
    inzhenery—Vydaiushchiesia deiateli gornoi nauki i tekhniki*. 2d ed. Moscow,
    1974, pp. 190–95.
Mindlin, Emilii. *Nachalo Magnitogorska*. Moscow, 1931.
———. "Pervii den tvoreniia: Magnitostroi v nachale 1930 goda." *Nauka i
    zhizn*, 1977, no. 5: 102–7.
Mishkevich, G. "Delo ob Atach-gore: Istoriia gory Magnitnoi." *Ural*, 1963, no.
    11, pp. 149–59.
Mislavskii, N. P. *Magnitogorsk*. Moscow, 1931.
Moia Magnitka: Sbornik. Cheliabinsk, 1979.
Mullin, John R. "City Planning in Frankfurt Germany, 1925–1932: A Study in
    Political Utopianism." *Journal of Urban History* 4, no. 1 (November 1977):
    3–28.
*My aktivno uchastvuem v sotsialisticheskom stroitelstve: Zheny ITR MMK im.
    Stalina o svoei rabote*. Magnitogorsk, 1936.

Nariniani, Semen D. *Na lesakh Magnitostroia.* Magnitogorsk, 1930.
———. *Magnitogorskii metallurgicheskii kombinat.* Moscow, 1931.
———. *Na stroike mirovogo giganta: Opyt komsomola Magnitogorska.* Moscow, 1931.
———. *Doroga v sovershennoletie.* Moscow, 1934.
———. *Ty pomnish, tovarishch. . . . Ocherki o komsomoltsakh pervoi piatiletki.* Moscow, 1957.
———. "Kak eto bylo." In *Slavnye traditsii: Sbornik dokumentov, ocherkov, vospominanii.* 2d ed. Moscow, 1960, pp. 136–42.
———. *Zvonok iz 1930 goda: Povest v semi voprosakh i otvetakh.* Moscow, 1970.
———. "Schastlivii den." In *Zhurnalisty rasskazyvaiut: Ocherki.* Moscow, 1974, pp. 66–81.
———. "Romantiki Magnitogorska." In *Pervye piatdesiat: Izbrannye stranitsy.* Moscow, 1975, pp. 108–15.
Neilandt, K. *Martenovskoe proizvodstvo na Magnitogorskom metallurgicheskom zavode.* Sverdlovsk-Moscow, 1932.
Nesterova, Z. N. *Magnitogorsk.* Moscow, 1951.
Nikiforova, T. A. *Magnitogorsk vchera, segodnia, zaftra.* Cheliabinsk, 1978.
Nikolaev, I. I. *Zdravookhranenie na Magnitostroe.* Moscow-Leningrad, 1931.
Nosov, G. I. "Stalinskaia Magnitka." *Oktiabr,* December 1949, no. 19: 142–59.
Obzor raboty zavoda za ianvar 1937 goda. Magnitogorsk, 1937.
Obzor raboty zavoda za pervoe polugodie 1936 goda. Magnitogorsk, 1936.
Orlova, A. P. "Vsesoiuznaia komsomolskaia stroika na Magnitostroe." In *Rabochii klass—Vedushchaia sila v stroitelstve kommunizma.* Magnitogorsk, 1970, pp. 10–418.
———. "Rol komsomola v organizatsii i razvitii massogo sorevnovaniia na stroitelstve Magnitogorskogo metallurgicheskogo kombinata (1929–1933 gg.)." In *Iz istorii KPSS za pobedu sotsialisticheskoi revoliutsii i postroenie kommunisticheskogo obshchestva.* Moscow, 1971, vyp. 2, pp. 123–200.
Ostrovskii, Zinovii. *Magnitostroi.* Moscow, 1932.
Otchet o rabote zavodskogo komiteta MMK im. tov. Stalina. Magnitogorsk, 1937.
Otchet rabochego komiteta soiuza stroitelnykh rabochikh k obshchepostroechnoi konferentsii za vremia sen.-iiun. Magnitogorsk, 1930.
Paramonov, I. V. *Puti proidennye.* Moscow, 1970.
Pervoe mezhraevoe soveshchanie organov KK-RKI Urala, Sibiri, Bashkiri, i Kazakhstana po Uralo-Kuzbassu: Stenograficheskii otchet. Sverdlovsk-Magnitogorsk, 1931.
Pervye itogi obshchestvennogo smotra oborudovaniia i agregatov. Magnitogorsk, 1939.
Pesnia ob Uralo-Kuzbasse (dlia dvux-golosnogo khora). Moscow, 1932.
Petrov, Iurii. *Magnitka.* Moscow, 1971.
———. *Gordost moia, Magnitka.* Moscow, 1979.
———. "Molodostroi Magnitki." *Molodoi kommunist,* 1979, no. 5: 50–54.
Piat let Magnitogorskogo metallurgicheskogo kombinata im. Stalina 1932–1937 gg. Moscow, 1937.

Polonskii, Lev. *Magnitka zovet: Stranitsy istorii velikoi stroiki i zhizni Chingiza Ildryma.* Baku, 1971.
Polonskii, Viacheslav Pavlovich. *Magnitostroi.* Moscow, 1931.
Polozhenie o rabote tovarishcheskikh sudov. Magnitogorsk, 1939.
Popriadukhin, Iu. *Magnitostroiu vne ocheredi.* Sverdlovsk-Moscow, 1931.
Printsmutil, G. *Magnitogorskie bolsheviki v boiakh za tekhniku.* Moscow, 1932.
Puzis, G. *Magnitogorsk: Voprosy stroitelstva novogo sotsgoroda.* Moscow, 1930.
Reshetko, T. N. "*Komsomolskaia pravda* na Magnitostroe: Iz istorii komsomola strany na stroitelstve Magnitogorskogo metallurgicheskogo kombinata." In *Deiatelnost KPSS po sozdaniiu materialno-tekhnicheskoi bazy kommunizma (po materialam Urala).* Cheliabinsk, 1976, vyp. 10, pp. 127–36.
Rezoliutsiia pervoi Magnitogorskoi partkonferentsii po kultstroitelstvu na 1932 g. (Magnitogorsk, 1932).
Roman, R. *Krokodil v Magnitogorske: Nedostatki v stroitelstve.* Sverdlovsk, 1931.
Romanov, V. F. "Magnitogorskii metallurgicheskii. . . . " *Voprosy istorii* 50, no. 9, (1975): 102–14.
Rosenberg, Michael. *Die Schwerindustrie in Russisch-Asien: Eine Studie über das Ural-Kusnezker Kombinat.* Berlin, 1938.
Rudin, M. *Geroicheskie dni Magnitogorska.* Sverdlovsk-Moscow, 1931.
Sbornik instruktsii po tekhnike bezopasnosti. Magnitogorsk, annually 1937–1942.
Schmidt, H. "Die Tätigkeiten deutscher Architekten und Spezialisten des Bauwesens in der Sowjetunion in den Jahren 1930 bis 1937." *Wissenschaftliche Zeitschrift der Humboldt-Universität zu Berlin. Gesellschafts- und Sprachwissenschaftliche Reihe* 16, no. 3 (1967).
Scott, John, "Magnetic City: Core of Russia's Industrial Might." *National Geographic,* May 1943, pp. 525–56.
————. *Behind the Urals; An American Worker in Russia's City of Steel.* Bloomington: Indiana University Press, 1989; originally published in 1942.
Seminog, A. "Poslednii beton." In *Po leninskii zhit, rabotat, uchitsia: O rabote Cheliabinskoi oblastnoi komsomolskoi organizatsii VLKSM.* Cheliabinsk, 1974, pp. 244–50.
————. "Ulybka romantiki." *Uralskii sledopyt,* 1977, no. 9: 3–6.
Seredkina, Aleksandra. *Borba Magnitogorskoi partorganizatsii za sozdanie giganta chernoi metallurgii—MMK: V pomoshch lektoru.* Magnitogorsk, 1958.
————. "Rozhdenie Magnitki," *Magnitka: Kratkii istoricheskii ocherk* (Cheliabinsk, 1971).
Serekin, A. I.; Luzin, V. Ia.; and Seredkina, A. V. "Avangardnaia rol kommunistov v stroitelstve i osvoenii Magnitogorskogo metallurgichgeskogo kombinata (1929–1941 gg.)." In *Pobeda oktiabrskoi revoliutsii na Urale i uspekhi sotsialisticheskogo stroitelstva za 50 let Sovetskoi vlasti.* Sverdlovsk, 1968, pp. 129–34.
Serzhantov, Valentin. *Magnitogorsk: Kratkii istoricheskii ocherk.* Cheliabinsk, 1947.
————. *Magnitogorsk (K 25-letiiu. 1930–1955 gg.).* Cheliabinsk, 1955.

————. "KPSS—Vdokhnovitel i organizator sozdaniia Magnitogorskogo kombinata—Moshchnoi metallurgicheskoi bazy strany (Iz istorii stroitelstva Magnitogorskogo zavoda v 1929–1930 gg.)." In *Uchenye zapiski Cheliabinskogo pedagogicheskogo instituta.* Cheliabinsk, 1956, tom 1, vyp. 1.

————. "Metallurgi Magnitki v borbe za osvoenie novoi tekhniki v gody vtoroi piatiletki." In *Iz istorii revoliutsionnogo dvizheniia i sotsialisticheskogo stroitelstva na iuzhnom Urale.* Cheliabinsk, 1959.

————. *Kommunisticheskaia Partiia Sovetskogo Soiuza—Vdokhnovitel i organizator stroitelstva i osvoeniia Magnitogorskogo kombinata im. I. V. Stalina—Moshchnoi metallurgicheskoi bazy strany (1929–1937 gg.).* Moscow, 1960.

————. "Magnitostroi—Vsenarodnaia stroika pervoi piatiletki." *Iz istorii sotsialisticheskogo stroitelstva na iuzhnom Urale.* Cheliabinsk, 1969, pp. 99–148.

Set partiinogo prosveshcheniia v partorganizatsii: Magnitogorskogo metallurgicheskogo zavoda. Magnitogorsk, 1936.

Shatilin, Aleksei Leontevich. *Na domnakh Magnitki.* Moscow, 1953.

Sherover, Miles. "Magnitogorsk: Epic of Soviet Labor." *Current History* 36 (July 1932): 405–10.

Shibaev, D. E. "Za sotsialisticheskii gorod Magnitogorsk." *Sovetskaia arkhitektura,* May–June 1933, no. 3: 25–30.

Skazinskii, V. *Magnitogorskii gigant im. tov. Stalina.* Sverdlovsk-Moscow, 1930.

Slovo o Magnitke. Moscow, 1979.

"Smolianinov, Vadim Aleksandrovich." In *Bolshaia Sovetskaia Entsiklopedia.* 3d ed. Moscow, 1976.

Sorevnovaniie gigantov: Magnitostroi-Kuznetskstroi. Magnitogorsk, 1931.

Sotsialisticheskii zakaz izobrateliam ekspluatatsii MMK im. Stalina. Sverdlovsk-Magnitogorsk, 1934.

Stakhanovskii opyt Magnitogorskogo rudnika: Sbornik statei. Magnitogorsk, 1936.

Stakhanovskaia praktika: Sbornik statei stakhanovtsev prokatnykh tsekhov. Magnitogorsk, 1938.

Stakhanovskaia praktika: Sbornik statei stakhanovtsev remontno-mekhanicheskikh tsekhov. Magnitogorsk, 1938.

Stalinskaia stroika. Magnitogorsk, 1939.

Stanovlenie i razvitie goroda Magnitogorska. Magnitogorsk, 1967.

Stroitelstvo i ekspluatatsiia Magnitogorskogo metallurgicheskogo zavoda im. tov. Stalina. Sverdlovsk-Magnitogorsk, 1934.

Stuck, Robert W. "First-Hand Impressions of Soviet Russia." *Case Alumnus* 12, no. 2 (November 1932): 7–9.

Tekhnicheskaia instruktsiia po vedeniiu zimnikh betonnykh rabot i kamennoi. . . . Magnitogorsk, 1931.

Tekhniko-ekonomicheskie pokazateli raboty zavoda za desiat mesiatsev 1936 goda. Magnitogorsk, 1936.

Tekhpromplan domennogo tsekha 1934 goda. Sverdlovsk, 1934.

Tishchenko, F. V. *Novye metody proizvodstva stroitelnykh rabot: Odno-etazhnye karkasnye stroeniia, opyt Magnitostroia.* Magnitogorsk, 1932.

Titova, V. N. "K voprosu ob istorii internatsionalnykh sviazei Uralskikh i nemetskikh rabochikh." In *Rodnoi krai i shkola*. Cheliabinsk, 1974, vyp. 2, pp. 87–93.

"Tovarishch Magnitka." *Komsomolka v stroiu*. Moscow, 1977, pp. 35–47.

Tretia gorodskaia partiinaia konferentsiia. Magnitogorsk, 1931.

Tsekhanskii, Ian. *Parol "Magnitostroi."* Moscow, 1931.

Vasilev, Georgii and Ivanov, Anatolii. *Bolshaia Magnitka*. Cheliabinsk, 1964.

Vneocherednaia partiinaia konferentsiia: Rezoliutsii. . . . c 25 po 28 iiulia 1930 g. Magnitogorsk, 1930.

Vovk, I. G. "Daesh Magnitku." *Voprosy istorii* 42, no. 4 (1972): 207–10.

Zapletin, N. P. "Magnitostroi arkhitektury." *Stroitelstvo Moskvy*, 1933, nos. 5–6, pp. 10–32.

Zaveniagin, Avraamii. "Magnitogorskii zavod im. Stalina." In *Otvet metallurgov tovarishchu Stalinu*. Moscow, 1936, pp. 72–91.

"Zaveniagin, Avraamii Pavlovich." In *Bolshaia Sovetskaia Entsiklopedia*. 3d ed. Moscow, 1972.

Zhigunov, P. *Udarnyi eshelon—Magnitostroiu*. Leningrad-Moscow, 1932.

Zhirkin, Vasilii. *Magnigortsy v borbe za tekhnicheskii progress*. Moscow, 1956.

Zverev, A. *Na stroike giganta*. Sverdlovsk, 1931.

Photograph Credits

Hopfner, Rosemarie, and Volker Fischer, eds., *Ernst May und das neue Frankfurt, 1925–1930* (Berlin: Ernst und Sohn, 1986): figs. 13 and 16.

Magnitogorsk City Museum: figs. 3 and 19.

Magnitogorskii rabochii: figs. 31–32, 37, 39–41, 43–44, 46–52, 54–58, 60, 64.

Magnitogorsk Metallurgical Complex, photograph archive: figs. 1–2, 4–12, 14–15, 17–18, 20–30, 33–36, 38, 42, 45, 53, 61–63, 65–66.

Magnitogorsk procuracy archives: fig. 59.

Index

Shevchenko, Vasilii (coke plant chief), 318, 319, 325, 497n61
Shevchuk, Vladimir (Stakhanovite), 210, 499n83
Shilov (convict), 512n185
Shmidt, Iakov, 44, 46, 48, 405nn58, 59, 409nn77, 80, 414n111, 546n54
Shock work, 203, 492n24; artels and, 89, 493n31; brigades, satire on, 494n32; Kataev on, 493n25; socialist competition, 204, 205
Shock workers, 90–93
Shoddy workmanship, 60, 451n53, 453n67; on dam, 92; on mine plumbing, 464n168; on railroad, 45; in superblocks, 122
Shortages, 45, 430n23; of food, 97, 244; of labor, 94–95, 223; of supplies, 58, 62, 404n54; of water, 92. *See also* Supplies
Shurov, Vladislav (obkom second secretary), 321, 322, 328
Siberia, 38, 67, 81
Siegelbaum, Lewis: on shock work, 492n24; on Stakhanovism, 495n44, 500n86
Siemens-Bauunion, 43, 402n35
Sikharulidze (deputy), 257
Siniavskii, Andrei: on USSR as civilization, 375n3
Sixteenth Party Congress (1929), 40
Sixth Sector, 137
Slag dump, 476n60
Smagin, Mikhail: expulsion of from party, 559n124, 560n130
Smarin (bookkeeper), 558n118
Smirnov (Menshevik), 548n291
Smolianinov, Vadim, 44, 403n44
Smurov (secretary of Stalin raikom), 591n335
Snopov, Dmitrii (city soviet chairman), 314, 562n153
Sobolev, M. P. (third obkom secretary), 573n225
Social identity, terms of, 224, 236–37, 505n137
Socialism, Soviet, 151–52, 356, 363;

appeal of, 358; belief and disbelief in the regime, 227–30, 358, 508nn151, 152; conspiracies against, 281–82; loyalty to the regime, 230, 508n152; national identity, 230, 509n156; as noncapitalism, 30, 32, 356, 360; politically correct behavior under the regime, 508n152; revolutionary mission of, 227; scarcity as leverage, 246
Socialist abundance, 267, 532n159, 533n169; Stalin on, 532n161
Socialist city, the, 33–34, 116; as device for building socialism, 34–35; failure of, 142–44; nature of, 142, 150–51, 466n7; 1929 symposium, 396n24
Socialist City. *See* Kirov District
Socialist competition, 204
Socialist culture, 180–81, 186, 187–89, 191–92, 355. *See also* Cultural transformation
Socialist market, 59
Socialist realism, 180, 191–92, 482n120
Socialist Revolutionary party, alternative to Bolshevism, 386n57
Societal property, need to protect, 254, 526n93
Soiuzkoks, 46
Sokolov, Aleksei (NKVD operative), 584n290
Sokolov, I. M. (new acting procurator), 339–40, 583n284
Soldatikov (procuracy employee), 340
Soria y Mata, Arturo: linear city, 110
Sorokin, Ivan (city procurator), 325, 331, 333, 334, 352, 565n171, 566n178, 572n218, 577n243, 578n256, 583n287; after arrest, 584n289; arrest and expulsion, 339–40; attack on Zaveniagin, 587n307; on Bazilevskii, 592n343; biography, 578n254; and blooming mill case, 337–39, 582n278; charges against, 583n285; and jurisdiction, 583n284; and NKVD, 339, 592n342; report to